Praise for *Last Call*

Named "One of the Year's 10 Best"
by *The Wall Street Journal*

"This is a great book: witty and graceful, balanced and deep. It is captivating social history told in a narrative that races along like a Bimini rumrunner angling into a south Florida bay."

—*Minneapolis Star Tribune*

"A remarkably original account of the Prohibition era, a fourteen-year orgy of lawbreaking that permanently transformed American social life . . . A narrative delight."

—*The New York Times Book Review*

"Okrent's dazzling history leaves us with one whiskey-sharp insight above all others: The War on Alcohol and the War on Drugs failed because they were, beneath all the blather, a war on human nature."

—*Slate*

"As Daniel Okrent shows in *Last Call*, his superb history of the Prohibition era, obtaining a drink with a lot more kick than a bottle of pop wasn't at all difficult. . . . Fortunes were made by taking advantage of exemptions for 'medicinal' alcohol, for hard cider made by farmers from fermented fruit, and for sacramental wine used in religious services. And that was just the legal stuff."

—*The Wall Street Journal*

"*Last Call* is a potentially, um, dry story, but Okrent is a born storyteller. In his hands, the prodigiously researched narrative, rife with tales of corruption, adventure, and backstabbing, flies like fiction."

—*Entertainment Weekly*

"This book is an extraordinary accomplishment, both scholarly and readable."

—*Barron's*

"Okrent fills a vast canvas with captivating characters, from the hatchet-wielding saloon buster Carry Nation ('six feet tall, with the biceps of a stevedore, the face of a prison warden, and the persistence of a toothache') to Canadian bootlegger Sam Bronfman, whose audacious smuggling laid the foundations of a billion-dollar family fortune."

—*Time*

"The movement to repeal Prohibition was a vexed and convoluted affair itself, well explained here; but before taking it up, Okrent brings us through the wild years of Prohibition. He describes in entertaining detail the ingenious casuistry and lucrative operations that arose out of the law."

—*The Boston Globe*

"It's a stunningly thorough, well-researched, and often unforgiving glimpse into one of the most bizarre social experiments ever conducted . . . an illuminating tour de force, and a great addition to the bookshelves of both casual readers and historical enthusiasts alike."

—*San Francisco Book Review*

"*Last Call* is the most persuasive and best-documented explanation as to why and how America decided to ban alcohol. . . . This is sure to be one of the year's best American history books."

—*BusinessWeek*

"Daniel Okrent's remarkable new history of Prohibition . . . explains with clarity and gusto how 'a mighty alliance of moralists and progressives, suffragists and xenophobes' led to the ratification of the Eighteenth Amendment."

—*The Christian Science Monitor*

"Brilliantly researched . . . *Last Call* is fun, fascinating, and as effervescent as champagne."

—*People*

"Okrent makes this complex and detailed story into a page-turning read. . . . He has fashioned a work of popular history at its best, the kind that teaches us something new on every page while keeping us thoroughly entertained."

—*The Courier-Journal*

"Okrent, a journalist-scholar with a novelistic sense of narrative, goes through Prohibition's influence on language, literature, the media, the judiciary system."

—*The Miami Herald*

"We all know how the story ends, but the historical play-by-play, with all its sensational headlines and criminal ingenuity, is something to be savored."

—*Oxford American*

"If you are interested in American history, and especially if you enjoy expressing your liberty with a drink now and then, *Last Call* is top-shelf reading."

—*Wine Spectator*

"As Daniel Okrent demonstrates in *Last Call,* his witty and exhaustive new history of Prohibition, the so-called Noble Experiment created nothing like a virtuous teetotaler's paradise. 'The drys had their law,' as Okrent observes, 'and the wets would have their liquor.'"

—*The Washington Post*

"Okrent draws the reader in with creative storytelling and something new (and actually useful) on every page."

—*Newsweek*

"A remarkable exploration of the era and the movements that led to one of the nation's biggest mistakes . . . *Last Call* does what great history should: acts as a window to the past that opens to a greater understanding of our present."

—*Forbes.com*

"*Last Call* makes for rowdy, riveting reading about the characters who got us into Prohibition, and those who dragged us out."

—*The Plain Dealer*

"An assiduously researched, well-written, and continually eye-opening work on what has actually been a neglected subject."

—*Publishers Weekly* (starred review)

"Okrent's style is bracing and wry, his research is vast and impressive, and his insight is penetrating."

—*Kirkus Reviews* (starred review)

"This sprightly written and thoroughly annotated work is recommended for both the general reader, to whom it is directed, and the scholar."

—*Library Journal*

"Okrent asks and answers some important questions in this fascinating exploration of a failed social experiment."

—*Booklist*

"Belongs on the shelves of every serious student of the U.S. in the twentieth century."

—*Foreign Affairs*

LAST CALL

The Rise and Fall of Prohibition

DANIEL OKRENT

SCRIBNER

New York London Toronto Sydney

SCRIBNER
A Division of Simon & Schuster, Inc.
1230 Avenue of the Americas
New York, NY 10020

Book design by Ellen R. Sasahara

Manufactured in the United States of America

11   13   15   17   19   20   18   16   14   12

Library of Congress Control Number: 2009051127

ISBN 978-0-7432-7702-0
ISBN 978-0-7432-7704-4 (pbk)
ISBN 978-1-4391-7169-1 (ebook)

For my sister, Judith Simon,
and in memory of absent friends:

Robert N. Nylen (1944–2008)

Richard Seaver (1926–2009)

Henry Z. Steinway (1915–2008)

Contents

THE EIGHTEENTH AMENDMENT TO THE
CONSTITUTION OF THE UNITED STATES

Ratified January 16, 1919

Section 1.

After one year from the ratification of this article the manufacture, sale, or transportation of intoxicating liquors within, the importation thereof into, or the exportation thereof from the United States and all territory subject to the jurisdiction thereof for beverage purposes is hereby prohibited.

Section 2.

The Congress and the several States shall have concurrent power to enforce this article by appropriate legislation.

Section 3.

This article shall be inoperative unless it shall have been ratified as an amendment to the Constitution by the legislatures of the several States, as provided in the Constitution, within seven years from the date of the submission hereof to the States by the Congress.

Prologue

January 16, 1920

THE STREETS OF San Francisco were jammed. A frenzy of cars, trucks, wagons, and every other imaginable form of conveyance crisscrossed the town and battled its steepest hills. Porches, staircase landings, and sidewalks were piled high with boxes and crates delivered on the last possible day before transporting their contents would become illegal. The next morning, the *Chronicle* reported that people whose beer, liquor, and wine had not arrived by midnight were left to stand in their doorways "with haggard faces and glittering eyes." Just two weeks earlier, on the last New Year's Eve before Prohibition, frantic celebrations had convulsed the city's hotels and private clubs, its neighborhood taverns and wharfside saloons. It was a spasm of desperate joy fueled, said the *Chronicle*, by great quantities of "bottled sunshine" liberated from "cellars, club lockers, bank vaults, safety deposit boxes and other hiding places." Now, on January 16, the sunshine was surrendering to darkness.

San Franciscans could hardly have been surprised. Like the rest of the nation, they'd had a year's warning that the moment the calendar flipped to January 17, Americans would only be able to own whatever alcoholic beverages had been in their homes the day before. In fact, Americans had had several decades' warning, decades during which a popular movement like none the nation had ever seen—a mighty alliance of moralists and progressives, suffragists and xenophobes—had legally seized the Constitution, bending it to a new purpose.

Up in the Napa Valley to the north of San Francisco, where grape growers had been ripping out their vines and planting fruit trees, an editor wrote, "What was a few years ago deemed the impossible has happened." To the

1

south, Ken Lilly—president of the Stanford University student body, star of its baseball team, candidate for the U.S. Olympic track team—was driving with two classmates through the late-night streets of San Jose when his car crashed into a telephone pole. Lilly and one of his buddies were badly hurt, but they would recover. The forty-gallon barrel of wine they'd been transporting would not. Its disgorged contents turned the street red.

Across the country on that last day before the taps ran dry, Gold's Liquor Store placed wicker baskets filled with its remaining inventory on a New York City sidewalk; a sign read "Every bottle, $1." Down the street, Bat Masterson, a sixty-six-year-old relic of the Wild West now playing out the string as a sportswriter in New York, observed the first night of constitutional Prohibition sitting alone in his favorite bar, glumly contemplating a cup of tea. Under the headline GOODBYE, OLD PAL!, the American Chicle Company ran newspaper ads featuring an illustration of a martini glass and suggesting the consolation of a Chiclet, with its "exhilarating flavor that tingles the taste."

In Detroit that same night, federal officers shut down two illegal stills (an act that would become common in the years ahead) and reported that their operators had offered bribes (which would become even more common). In northern Maine, a paper in New Brunswick reported, "Canadian liquor in quantities from one gallon to a truckload is being hidden in the northern woods and distributed by automobile, sled and iceboat, on snowshoes and on skis." At the Metropolitan Club in Washington, Assistant Secretary of the Navy Franklin D. Roosevelt spent the evening drinking champagne with other members of the Harvard class of 1904.

There were of course those who welcomed the day. The crusaders who had struggled for decades to place Prohibition in the Constitution celebrated with rallies and prayer sessions and ritual interments of effigies representing John Barleycorn, the symbolic proxy for alcohol's evils. No one marked the day as fervently as evangelist Billy Sunday, who conducted a revival meeting in Norfolk, Virginia. Ten thousand grateful people jammed Sunday's enormous tabernacle to hear him announce the death of liquor and reveal the advent of an earthly paradise. "The reign of tears is over," Sunday proclaimed. "The slums will soon be only a memory. We will turn our prisons into factories and our jails into storehouses and corncribs. Men will walk upright now, women will smile, and the children will laugh. Hell will be forever for rent."

A similarly grandiose note was sounded by the Anti-Saloon League, the mightiest pressure group in the nation's history. No other organization had ever changed the Constitution through a sustained political campaign;

now, on the day of its final triumph, the ASL declared that "at one minute past midnight . . . a new nation will be born." In a way, editorialists at the militantly anti-Prohibition *New York World* perceived the advent of a new nation, too. "After 12 o'clock tonight," the *World* said, "the Government of the United States as established by the Constitution and maintained for nearly 131 years will cease to exist." Secretary of the Interior Franklin K. Lane may have provided the most accurate view of the United States of America on the edge of this new epoch. "The whole world is skew-jee, awry, distorted and altogether perverse," Lane wrote in his diary on January 19. ". . . Einstein has declared the law of gravitation outgrown and decadent. Drink, consoling friend of a Perturbed World, is shut off; and all goes merry as a dance in hell!"

HOW DID IT HAPPEN? How did a freedom-loving people decide to give up a private right that had been freely exercised by millions upon millions since the first European colonists arrived in the New World? How did they condemn to extinction what was, at the very moment of its death, the fifth-largest industry in the nation? How did they append to their most sacred document 112 words that knew only one precedent in American history? With that single previous exception, the original Constitution and its first seventeen amendments limited the activities of government, not of citizens. Now there were two exceptions: you couldn't own slaves, and you couldn't buy alcohol.

Few realized that Prohibition's birth and development were much more complicated than that. In truth, January 16, 1920, signified a series of innovations and alterations revolutionary in their impact. The alcoholic miasma enveloping much of the nation in the nineteenth century had inspired a movement of men and women who created a template for political activism that was still being followed a century later. To accomplish their ends they had also abetted the creation of a radical new system of federal taxation, lashed their domestic goals to the conduct of a foreign war, and carried universal suffrage to the brink of passage. In the years ahead, their accomplishments would take the nation through a sequence of curves and switchbacks that would force the rewriting of the fundamental contract between citizen and government, accelerate a recalibration of the social relationship between men and women, and initiate a historic realignment of political parties.

In 1920 could anyone have believed that the Eighteenth Amendment, ostensibly addressing the single subject of intoxicating beverages, would set off an avalanche of change in areas as diverse as international trade, speedboat design, tourism practices, soft-drink marketing, and the English language itself? Or that it would provoke the establishment of the first nationwide criminal syndicate, the idea of home dinner parties, the deep engagement of women in political issues other than suffrage, and the creation of Las Vegas? As interpreted by the Supreme Court and as understood by Congress, Prohibition would also lead indirectly to the eventual guarantee of the American woman's right to abortion and simultaneously dash that same woman's hope for an Equal Rights Amendment to the Constitution.

Prohibition changed the way we live, and it fundamentally redefined the role of the federal government. *How the hell did it happen?*

PART I

THE
STRUGGLE

———◆•●•◆———

If a family or a nation is sober, nature in its normal course will cause them to rise to a higher civilization. If a family or a nation, on the other hand, is debauched by liquor, it must decline and ultimately perish.

—Richmond P. Hobson, in the U.S. House
of Representatives, December 22, 1914

Chapter 1

Thunderous Drums and
Protestant Nuns

AMERICA HAD BEEN AWASH in drink almost from the start—wading hip-deep in it, swimming in it, at various times in its history nearly drowning in it. In 1839 an English traveler marveled at the role liquor played in American life: "I am sure the Americans can fix nothing without a drink," wrote Frederick Marryat in *A Diary in America*. "If you meet, you drink; if you part, you drink; if you make acquaintance, you drink; if you close a bargain you drink; they quarrel in their drink, and they make it up with a drink. They drink because it is hot; they drink because it is cold. If successful in elections, they drink and rejoice; if not, they drink and swear; they begin to drink early in the morning, they leave off late at night; they commence it early in life, and they continue it, until they soon drop into the grave."

To Americans reading Captain Marryat's book, this would not have been news. The national taste for alcohol (or—a safer bet—for the effects of alcohol) dated back to the Puritans, whose various modes of purity did not include abstinence. The ship that brought John Winthrop to the Massachusetts Bay Colony in 1630 had more than ten thousand gallons of wine in its hold and carried three times as much beer as water. When the sixteen-year-old Benjamin Franklin first compiled a list of terms for "drunk," in 1722, he came up with 19 examples; fifteen years later, in the *Pennsylvania Gazette*, he could cite 228 (including "juicy," "thawed," and "had a thump over the head with Sampson's jawbone"). By 1763 rum was pouring out of 159 commercial distilleries in New England alone, and by the 1820s liquor was so plentiful and so freely available, it was less expensive than tea.

In the early days of the Republic drinking was as intimately woven into the social fabric as family or church. In the apt phrase of historian W. J. Rorabaugh, "Americans drank from the crack of dawn to the crack of dawn." Out in the countryside most farmers kept a barrel of hard cider by the door for family and anyone who might drop by. In rural Ohio and Indiana the seed scattered by John Chapman—"Johnny Appleseed"—produced apples that were inedible but, when fermented, very drinkable. "Virtually every homestead in America had an orchard from which literally thousands of gallons of cider were made every year," wrote food historian Michael Pollan. In the cities it was widely understood that common workers would fail to come to work on Mondays, staying home to wrestle with the echoes and aftershocks of a weekend binge. By 1830 the tolling of a town bell at 11 a.m. and again at 4 p.m. marked "grog-time." Soldiers in the U.S. Army had been receiving four ounces of whiskey as part of their daily ration since 1782; George Washington himself said "the benefits arising from moderate use of strong Liquor have been experienced in all Armies, and are not to be disputed."

Drink seeped through the lives of the propertied classes as well. George Clinton, governor of New York from 1777 to 1795, once honored the French ambassador with a dinner for 120 guests who together drank "135 bottles of Madeira, 36 bottles of port, 60 bottles of English beer, and 30 large cups of rum punch." Washington kept a still on his farm, John Adams began each day with a tankard of hard cider, and Thomas Jefferson's fondness for drink extended beyond his renowned collection of wines to encompass rye whiskey made from his own crops. James Madison consumed a pint of whiskey daily.

By 1810 the number of distilleries in the young nation had increased fivefold, to more than fourteen thousand, in less than two decades. By 1830 American adults were guzzling, per capita, a staggering seven gallons of pure alcohol a year. "Staggering" is the appropriate word for the consequences of this sort of drinking. In modern terms those seven gallons are the equivalent of 1.7 bottles of a standard 80-proof liquor* per person, per week—nearly 90 bottles a year for every adult in the nation, even with abstainers (and there were millions of them) factored in. Once again figuring per capita, multiply the amount Americans drink today by three and you'll have an idea of what much of the nineteenth century was like.

Another way: listen to thirty-three-year-old Abraham Lincoln summa-

---

*Historians, demographers, and economists derive liquor consumption statistics from various data, including manufacturing records, tax receipts, and, provocatively, deaths by cirrhosis.

rizing domestic life in Sangamon County, Illinois. "We found intoxicating liquor used by everybody, repudiated by nobody," he told a temperance meeting in 1842. "It commonly entered into the first draught of an infant, and the last thought of the dying man." It was, he said, "the devastator."

"TEMPERANCE": WHEN LINCOLN SPOKE, the word's meaning was very different from what it would soon become. For decades it had meant moderation, both in quantity and in variety. The first prominent American temperance advocate, the Philadelphia physician Benjamin Rush, encouraged the whiskey-riddled to consider a transitional beverage: wine mixed with opium or laudanum. This was the same Rush—respected scientist, signer of the Declaration of Independence, friend to Jefferson and Adams—who insisted he knew of a drunk who had made the mistake of belching near an open flame and was "suddenly destroyed."

By 1830 those seven gallons of pure alcohol per capita had confirmed the earlier fears of Harvard literature professor George Ticknor, who in 1821 had told Thomas Jefferson that if the consumption of liquor continued at its current rate, "we should be hardly better than a nation of sots." Moderation itself was called into question. Just before he took up the cause of abolitionism, William Lloyd Garrison—whose alcoholic father had abandoned his family when William was thirteen—published a journal that bore the slogan "Moderate Drinking Is the Downhill Road to Intemperance and Drunkenness." General Lewis Cass, appointed secretary of war by Andrew Jackson, eliminated the soldiers' entire whiskey ration and forbade the consumption of alcoholic beverages at all army forts and bases. Cass was able to do this only because of the improvement in water quality, for among the reasons the whiskey ration had persisted was the foul water supply at many military installations.

At roughly the same time, the nation's first large-scale expression of antialcohol sentiment had begun to take shape. The Washingtonian Movement, as it became known, arose out of a Baltimore barroom in 1840, when six habitual drinkers pledged their commitment to total abstinence. In some ways they couldn't have been more dissimilar from the prohibitionists who would follow them. They advocated no changes in the law; they refused to pin blame for their circumstances on tavern operators or distillers; they asked habitual drinkers only to sign a pledge of abstinence. In the same speech in which he condemned the ubiquity of alcoholic beverages, Abraham Lincoln (who thought mandatory prohibition a very bad idea) praised the Washingtonian reliance on "persuasion, kind, unassuming persuasion. . . . Those whom they desire to convince and persuade are their old friends and companions. They know they are not demons."

The movement's tactics may not have included any elements of compulsion, but the Washingtonian methodology was not entirely as unassuming as Lincoln might have believed. In the grand American tradition, Washingtonian evangelists poured out a lot of sulfurous rhetoric to lure something between three hundred thousand and six hundred thousand men out of the dungeon of inebriety. "Snap your burning chains, ye denizens of the pit," John Bartholomew Gough urged his listeners, "and come up sheeted in the fire, dripping with the flames of hell, and with your trumpet tongues testify against the damnation of drink!" Certainly the most successful of Washingtonian platform speakers, Gough was a reformed drinker (and, conveniently, a reformed stage actor as well) who in 1843 alone addressed 383 different audiences and the next year achieved national prominence when he drew twenty thousand potential converts to a single event on Boston Common to bear witness to his zeal.

The year after that, Gough took part in another grand American tradition when he backslid so spectacularly it became a minor national scandal. He was found in a brothel near Broadway and Canal streets in lower Manhattan, in relative repose following a six-day bender. Gough later claimed he had been drugged, that the drugging had led him to a round of drinking, and that at one point "I saw a woman dressed in black [and] I either accosted her, or she accosted me." By all accounts he remained totally abstinent thereafter, and by the time he stopped lecturing thirty-four years later Gough had delivered more than ten thousand speeches to audiences estimated at more than nine million people. Among his listeners was a San Francisco surveyor who named one of the city's main thoroughfares in his honor—out of either a sense of gratitude or, possibly, irony.

RECALLING THE NASCENT temperance movement in the 1840s, one of its most devoted adherents would salute the work of the Washingtonians. They had changed many lives, he said, through "their mission of peace and love." But, he added, "we also saw that large numbers who were saved by these means, fell back again to a lower position than ever, because the tempter was permitted to live and throw out his seductive toils. Our watchword now was, Prohibition!"

The exclamation point was entirely characteristic of Phineas Taylor Barnum; the taut, one-word epithet that preceded it, bearing its declaratory capital *P*, represented something new. Prohibition—the legislated imposition of teetotalism on the unwilling—was an idea that had been lurking beneath the earnest pieties of the temperance movement and was transformed in the late 1840s into a rallying cry. Barnum may have been the nation's best-known convert to the cause, a relentless proselytizer who used his protean promotional skills to persuade men to take the same pledge he had. At his American Museum in New York City, Barnum drew in crowds eager to gawk at his collection of "gipsies, albinoes, fat boys, giants, dwarfs [and] caricatures of phrenology," but that was only the beginning of the show: he also did all he could to direct them to the museum's theater, for presentations of "moral plays in a moral manner." One of these, *The Drunkard; or, The Fallen Saved*, was an overripe melodrama that drew as many as three thousand people to a single performance.* The lead character's extravagant case of the DTs in the fourth act was an especially popular scene.

Barnum was among hundreds of thousands of Americans who turned toward prohibitionism because, he wrote, "Neal Dow (may God bless him!) had opened our eyes." A prosperous businessman from Portland, Maine, Dow had first made his mark on the public life of his hometown in 1827 when, at the age of twenty-four, he somehow persuaded the volunteer fire department to ban alcohol at its musters. Perhaps the firemen had become chagrined at their "most disgraceful exhibitions of drunkenness" at these "burlesque occasions" (even as they enjoyed them enormously). Just as likely, they were moved (or intimidated, or flabbergasted) by the cauterizing fire of Neal Dow's passion.

Dow came by his reformist ardor naturally and lived by it wholly. His father was a prominent abolitionist; his great-grandfather on his mother's side was a man "of great physical and mental vigor" memorably (and prophetically) named Hate-Evil Hall. In his thirties, by now head of his family's successful tannery, Dow led a group of Portland employers who chose to deny their workers their daily "eleveners"—grog time. Elected mayor in 1851, he immediately persuaded the Maine legislature to enact the nation's first statewide prohibitory law, mandating fines for those convicted of selling liquor and imprisonment for those engaged in its manufacture.

The Maine Law, as it came to be known, enabled the antiliquor forces who had been stirred by the Washingtonians to use this template to pass

---

*Some sources assert that *The Drunkard* was the most commercially successful American play until *Uncle Tom's Cabin* surpassed it a few years later. It remained a staple of the temperance movement through much of the nineteenth century, eventually disappearing from view until 1964, when it was transformed into an unlikely (and short-lived) musical by the twenty-one-year-old Barry Manilow.

similar laws in a dozen other states. Just as his cause became a national movement, so Dow became a national celebrity, admired not just by Barnum but by many other prominent men. Some embraced him with almost unseemly fervor. The education reformer Horace Mann called Dow "the moral Columbus" and apparently did not blush when he equated the significance of the Maine Law with "the invention of printing." This was no longer a movement; it had become a fever.

Which meant, of course, that it could not last. Republican politicians, fearing that prohibitionism was divisive and might weaken the unity that had formed in the young party around the slavery issue, began to tiptoe around it. In Portland, unrest broke out in 1855 among Irish immigrants who despised Dow and his law; after an angry crowd of three thousand had gathered on the night of June 2, one man was killed and seven wounded by militiamen who had been ordered to quell the riot. By the end of the decade states that had enacted versions of the Maine Law had repealed them—Maine included.

THE OPPOSITION OF Portland's Irish community could have been seen as an augury. For the next three-quarters of a century, immigrant hostility to the temperance movement and prohibitory laws was unabating and unbounded by nationality. The patterns of European immigration were represented in the ranks of those most vehemently opposed to legal strictures on alcohol: first the Irish, then the Germans, and, closer to the end of the century, the Italians, the Greeks, the southern European Slavs, and the eastern European Jews. But the word "ranks" suggests a level of organization that did not exist among the immigrant populations in whose lives wine or beer were so thoroughly embedded. Only the German-American brewers showed an interest in concentrated action, when they united in response to the imposition of a beer tax during the Civil War.

But even a group as powerful, wealthy, and self-interested as the United States Brewers' Association met its match in the foe who would engage it for nearly half a century: women. Specifically, women of Protestant, Anglo-Saxon stock, most of them living in the small cities and towns of the Northeast and Midwest. They were led into battle by a middle-aged housewife whose first assault took place in her hometown of Hillsboro, Ohio, in 1873, inspired by a man famous for his advocacy of abstinence, chastity, gymnastics, health food, loose clothing, and the rights of women.

When Dr. Dioclesian Lewis showed up in town, he could usually count on drawing an audience. Dio, as he was called (except when he was called "beautiful bran-eating Dio"), was no doctor—his MD was an honorary one granted by a college of homeopathy—but he was many other things: educator, physical culturist, health food advocate, bestselling author, and one of the more compelling platform speakers of the day, a large, robust man "profoundly confident in the omnipotence of his own ideas and the uselessness of all others." He was also the inventor of the beanbag.

On December 22, 1873, Lewis's lecture caravan stopped in Hillsboro, a town of five thousand about fifty miles east of Cincinnati. That evening he spoke about "Our Girls" (the title of one of his recent books); the next, he gave a free lecture on the subject of alcohol. In it he urged the women of Hillsboro to use the power of prayer to rid the town of its saloons—not by calling down the wrath of God, but by praying for the liquor sellers, and if possible praying *with* them.

The next morning seventy-five Hillsboro women emerged in an orderly two-by-two column from a meeting at the Presbyterian church, taller ones in the rear, shorter in front, and at their head Eliza Jane Trimble Thompson. She was the daughter of an Ohio governor, the wife of a well-known judge, a mother of eight. She had never spoken in public before, much less led a demonstration of any kind. Inside the church, chosen by the others as their leader, she had been so strangled by nerves that she had been unable to speak until the men, temperance advocates though they were, had left the room. She was fifty-seven, a devout Methodist. As she left the sanctuary of the church and emerged into the bitter, windy cold, she led the women in singing the sixteenth-century German hymn "Give to the Wind Thy Fears," translated by John Wesley himself.

On that Christmas Eve and for ten days after, Thompson led her band to Hillsboro's saloons, its hotels, and its drugstores (many of which sold liquor by the glass). At each one they would fall to their knees and pray for the soul of the owner. The women worked in six-hour shifts, running relays from their homes to the next establishment on the list, praying, singing, reading from the Bible, and generally creating the largest stir in the town, said a Cincinnati newspaper, since news of the attack on Fort Sumter twelve years before. If they were allowed inside, they would kneel on a sawdust floor that had been befouled by years of spilled drinks and the expectorations of men who had missed, or never tried for, the spittoon; if not, they would remain outside, hunched for hours against the winter cold. At William Smith's drugstore, the proprietor joined them in prayer and vowed never to sell liquor again. Outside another saloon, they knelt in reproachful humility while the customers leaned against the building, hands in their pockets, unmoved by the devout spectacle before them.

The events in Hillsboro launched the Crusade, a squall that would sweep across the Midwest, into New York State, and on to New England with the force of a tropical storm. In eleven days Thompson and her sisters persuaded the proprietors of nine of the town's thirteen drinking places to close their doors. Down the road in Washington Court House, the gutters ran with liquor decanted by repentant saloonkeepers. As the Crusade spread from Ohio into Indiana in January and February 1874, federal liquor tax collections were off by more than $300,000 in just two revenue districts. In more than 110 cities and towns, every establishment selling liquor yielded to the hurricane set loose by Eliza Thompson.

But hurricanes don't last, and within a few months this one was spent. Some saloons remained closed; many did not. This is not to say that the sacred ardor of the women had been spent in vain. If nothing else, in many towns the saloon operator was ever after marked as an outcast, a pariah. Andrew Sinclair, in *Era of Excess*, cites the playwright Sherwood Anderson recalling how the saloonkeeper in the northern Ohio town where Anderson was raised "walked silently with bent head. His wife and children were seldom seen. They lived an isolated life."

ELIZA THOMPSON WAS blessed with devoted successors who, flushed with reverence, would always refer to her as Mother Thompson. But she herself had been fortunate in her predecessors—a group of women in upstate New York who had begun to agitate against alcohol at about the time of the Washingtonians and would provide a direct link to the women who eventually carried Thompson's crusade forward. One of these women was a schoolteacher named Susan B. Anthony. Another, Elizabeth Cady Stanton, was a journalist's wife. Within a very few years they were joined by Lucy Stone and Amelia Bloomer, two more women whose names, like Anthony's and Stanton's, still resonate today for reasons seemingly far removed from the purported evils of booze.

In fact the rise of the suffrage movement was a direct consequence of the widespread Prohibition sentiment. Before she began to campaign for women's rights, Amelia Bloomer found her voice as an agitator in a temperance publication called *The Water Bucket*. Lucy Stone began publishing *The Lily*, which would become an early and important outlet for suffragists, because, she wrote, "Intemperance is the great foe to [woman's] peace and happiness. . . . Surely she has a right to wield the pen for its suppression." And Susan B. Anthony, who as a teenager feared for the future of the Republic because its leader, Martin Van Buren, had a taste for "all-debasing wine," was virtually shoved into the suffrage movement by men who believed the temperance battle was theirs to lead.

Anthony had given her first public speech in 1849, to a group called the Daughters of Temperance. The Sons were less accommodating. In 1852 she was not allowed to address an Albany meeting of the Sons of Temperance specifically because she was a woman. "The sisters," said the group's chairman, were there not to speak but "to listen and learn." The same year, at a New York State Temperance Society meeting in Syracuse, the same result. In 1853 it happened again, at a World Temperance Society convention in New York City (where Amelia Bloomer was given the boot as well). Finally Anthony cast her lot with Stanton (who had declared alcohol "The Unclean Thing") and proceeded to give half a century's labors to the cause of suffrage.

One could make the argument that without the "liquor evil," as it was commonly known to those who most despised it, the suffrage movement would not have drawn the talents and energies of these gifted women. "Had there been a Prohibition amendment in America in 1800," wrote the critic Gilbert Seldes in 1928, when the actual Prohibition amendment was very much on the national mind, "the suffragists might have remained for another century a scattered group of intellectual cranks." Seldes arrived at this provocative conclusion because he believed that the most urgent reasons for women to want to vote in the mid-1800s were alcohol related: They wanted the saloons closed down, or at least regulated. They wanted the right to own property, and to shield their families' financial security from the profligacy of drunken husbands. They wanted the right to divorce those men, and to have them arrested for wife beating, and to protect their children from being terrorized by them. To do all these things they needed to change the laws that consigned married women to the status of chattel. And to change the laws, they needed the vote.

But the changed laws, and the universal vote, were decades away. Not even the efforts of the women who banded together in the 1840s to threaten sexual abstinence if their husbands could not achieve alcohol abstinence could keep liquor from continuing to permeate the national fabric. More and more, roadside taverns that had provided the traveler with dining table and bedroom as well as the companionship (and the cruelty) of the bottle found their clientele in nearby towns and farms. These were men seeking release from the drudgery of their lives, but in too many instances they found as well a means of escape, even if temporary, from the responsibilities of home and family. The quantity of liquor served in these places was as great as the quality was not, unless the quality you sought was the one that put you on the shortest route to oblivion.

A drunken husband and father was sufficient cause for pain, but many rural and small-town women also had to endure the associated ravages born of the early saloon: the wallet emptied into a bottle; the job lost or the farmwork left undone; and, most pitilessly, a scourge that would later in the century be identified by physicians as "syphilis of the innocent"— venereal disease contracted by the wives of drink-sodden husbands who had found something more than liquor lurking in saloons. Saloons were dark and nasty places, and to the wives of the men inside, they were satanic.

TWENTY YEARS AFTER Mother Thompson's Crusade had subsided, her most important follower was generous with credit. Thompson, said Frances Willard, "caught the universal ear and set the key of that mighty orchestra, organized with so much toil and hardship, in which the tender and exalted strain of the Crusade violin still soared aloft, but upborne now by the clanging cornets of science, the deep trombones of legislation, and the thunderous drums of politics and parties."

That was one way of putting it. Another would have been "Mother Thompson's Crusade launched the Woman's Christian Temperance Union." But Frances Willard was no more likely to utter so declarative a sentence than she was to walk into a saloon and chug a double rye. At thirty-five Willard was among the small group of women who in 1874 founded the WCTU; at forty she took control of the organization, and for the rest of her eventful life she was field general, propagandist, chief theoretician, and nearly a deity to a 250,000-member army—undoubtedly, the nation's most effective political action group in the last decades of the nineteenth century. Willard's rhapsodic prose style apparently inspired others as well. To one of her most ardent admirers, Hannah Whitall Smith, Willard (who was always known to her family and friends as "Frank") was "the embodiment of all that is lovely, and good, and womanly, and strong, and noble, and tender in human nature." To another, the historian and U.S. senator Albert J. Beveridge, Willard managed to be both "the Bismarck of the forces of righteousness in modern society" and "the greatest organizer of sweetness and light that ever blessed mankind."

The woman who educed such adoration was raised on a farm in Janes-ville, Wisconsin. At sixteen, she asked her parents to sign a pledge she had pasted in the family Bible. Fashioned as a series of rhyming couplets, the oath began, "A pledge we make, no wine to take / Nor brandy red that turns the head." Several couplets later it concluded with "So here we pledge perpetual hate / To all that can intoxicate." When Willard moved to Evanston, Illinois, with her parents a few years later, she found herself in what she would call a "Methodist heaven." The new college that dominated the town (the predecessor of Northwestern University) had been established, its founders said, in "the interests of sanctified learning." This mission was abetted by a legal proscription against the sale of alcoholic beverages within four miles of its campus and buttressed by the creation of a similarly liquor-loathing women's school that soon opened nearby. Willard graduated from North Western Female College as valedictorian, became president a decade later, and assumed the position of dean of women at the university when the two schools merged in 1873.

But 1874 was the year of the Crusade, and on a trip east Willard found herself on her knees in Sheffner's Saloon, on Market Street in Pittsburgh, singing "Rock of Ages." Taking measure of the "crowd of unwashed, unkempt, hard-looking drinking men" arrayed behind her, "filling every corner and extending out into the street," Willard wrote, "I was conscious that perhaps never in my life, save beside my sister Mary's dying bed, had I prayed as truly as I did then." A week later she was back in Chicago, about to walk away from her academic career so she could give her life to the temperance cause.

Forging a new alloy out of the moral commitment of Eliza Thompson and the feminist fire of Susan B. Anthony, Willard very explicitly made temperance a woman's issue—and women's issues, she argued, could not be resolved if authority was left solely in the hands of men. She had further come to believe that encouraging temperance was no longer enough. Only some form of legal prohibition could crush the liquor demon, and no such prohibition would ever be enacted without the votes of women. In 1876 she stunned a WCTU audience into silence when she made the case that women should have the right to vote on matters relating to liquor. Only three years later, her commitment to suffrage enabled her to unseat the WCTU's founding president, the antisuffragist Annie Wittenmyer. Susan B. Anthony would soon begin to appear at WCTU conventions, and Willard installed Lucy Anthony, Susan's niece, as head of the WCTU lecture bureau. The merging of Anthony's campaign and Willard's brought a critical realignment among the era's feminist activists: the WCTU had acquired a very specific goal, and the suffrage movement had acquired an army.

"I have cared very little about food, indeed, very little about anything,"

Willard once said, "except the matter in hand." This dedication to her cause was magnified by her astonishing productivity. She began each day with a devotional reading, and then immediately after breakfast, whether at home in Evanston or on one of her cross-country speaking tours, she would charge into eight hours of dictation to her stenographer. She traveled constantly, in one year addressing audiences in every state and territorial capital except Boise and Phoenix. In 1881, accompanied by her secretary and lifelong companion, Anna Gordon, she went south to organize WCTU chapters in states where women's political activity was even less welcome than it was in much of the north. She also traveled abroad (having founded the World WCTU in 1883), particularly to England, and numbered among her friends and supporters such fellow enemies of alcohol as Leo Tolstoy and the British philanthropist Lady Henry Somerset. Books poured out of her: polemics, memoirs, political manuals. She did step away from the temperance campaign long enough to publish *A Wheel Within a Wheel: How I Learned to Ride the Bicycle* ("As nearly as I can make out, reducing the problem to actual figures, it took me about three months, with an average of fifteen minutes' practice daily, to learn, first, to pedal; second, to turn; third, to dismount; and fourth, to mount independently this most mysterious animal"). But even in her homeliest concerns, Willard rarely wandered far from the cause. She called her pet dog Hibbie, a diminutive for the name she had originally bestowed on him: Prohibition.

Willard's army marched behind two concepts. The first, "Home Protection," seemed perfectly anodyne. But beneath its surface blandness lay a subtle variation on the themes of the Crusade, repackaged for a more urgent purpose: by insisting that the elimination of alcoholic beverages was necessary for the health, welfare, and safety of the American family, the women of the WCTU were now praying not for the sinner, but for those sinned against. The images Home Protection evoked (and that its propagandists used shamelessly) were the weeping mother, the children in threadbare clothes, the banker at the door with repossession papers. The moral crusade was now a practical one as well.

Willard's second principle, which blossomed as her fame and influence grew, was "Do Everything." Perceiving that the energies of the WCTU could be harnessed for broader purposes, Willard urged her followers to agitate for a set of goals that stretched far beyond the liquor issue but harmonized with the effort to improve the lives of others. Her "Protestant nuns" (as Willard sometimes called her followers) campaigned for suffrage, of course, but also for prison reform, free kindergartens, and vocational schools. After reading Edward Bellamy's *Looking Backward* in 1889, Willard declared herself a "Christian socialist" and broadened the WCTU's agenda once again, agitating for the eight-hour day, workers' rights, and government ownership of utilities, railroads, factories, and (she was nothing if not eclectic) theaters. Along the way she also took up the causes of vegetarianism, cremation, less restrictive women's clothing, and something she called "the White Life for Two"—a program "cloaked in euphemism," wrote Catherine Gilbert Murdock in *Domesticating Drink*, that "endorsed alcohol-free, tobacco-free, lust-free marriages."

As exceptional as Willard was, her determination to connect Prohibition to other reforms was neither original with her nor uncommon. In its first national campaign, in 1872, the Prohibition Party endorsed universal suffrage, public education, and the elimination of the electoral college, and would soon take up a range of issues reaching from federal control of interstate commerce to forest conservation. Dio Lewis was a harvesting machine of causes and campaigns. At the moment he took the abstinence pledge in 1845, Frederick Douglass had said, "if we could but make the world sober, we would have no slavery," partly because "all great reforms go together." The great abolitionist Wendell Phillips—who said he was also "a temperance man of nearly 40 years' standing"—may have been speaking for Douglass, William Lloyd Garrison, Neal Dow, and all the others who had labored for both temperance and abolition when he argued that the defeat of slavery proved that government action was an appropriate weapon in the battle against moral wrongs.

In fact, Phillips may have been speaking for anyone who had managed to cross the gulf between persuasion and compulsion, between the traditional meaning of temperance and the new meaning of prohibition. Or, decked out in its permanent capital *P*, Prohibition—not just a word but a declaration, an apotheosis.

COMMEMORATING THE CENTENNIAL of American independence in 1876, the Manhattan lithography shop of Nathaniel Currier and James Merritt Ives reissued a popular item Currier had first published in 1848, *Washington's Farewell to the Officers of His Army*. The great general stands in the exact center of the print, his associates arrayed around him, his tricorne hat on a stout table by his side. Washington is in full dress uniform; his right hand, fingers curled into a fist, rests on his breastbone. He looks to be making an emphatic gesture, but the officers in the picture seem lost in thought. It doesn't make a lot of sense.

It did, however, when Currier first published a version of the image twenty-eight years earlier. In that version there's no hat on the table; a decanter and some wineglasses occupy that spot. Nor is Washington making that peculiar fist. His fingers are extended, the better to grip the glass of wine he's holding. He's apparently delivering a heartfelt toast to the officers, whose considered expressions convey both their sadness and their humility.

The original image makes historical sense. Washington's fondness for Madeira found expression in the postprandial bottle (and accompanying bowl of hickory nuts) he shared with his guests almost nightly. At the event depicted—his valedictory at Fraunces' Tavern, in 1783—he had opened the emotional proceedings by pouring himself a glass of wine and inviting his officers to join him. Currier and Ives were businessmen, however, and business required them to oblige the temperance agitators who objected so vociferously to the original image. It was easy enough to obliterate the decanter and glasses by drawing in the hat; chopping off Washington's own goblet, as well as the top two joints of his fingers, may have required a little more skill, but presumably it was worth the effort. That this self-censorship occurred as early as 1876, when the WCTU and its allies were only beginning to develop their strength and their strategy, suggests the degree to which aggressive actions would soon replace the prayerful entreaties of Mother Thompson—not least because they worked.

This became clear in the dazzling career of a former chemistry teacher from Massachusetts named Mary Hanchett Hunt, who became one of the most influential women in the country through her religiously inspired temperance work, even if her tactics proved to be not so holy. In her late forties, stirred by what she described as "a great hunger to do more for the Master," she left behind her position as the leader of the Hyde Park Ladies Sewing Society to become as influential an agitator as the Prohibition movement would ever know. According to William Jennings Bryan, the campaign she led "did more than any other one thing" to bring the Eighteenth Amendment into being. In Hunt, the coercion Wendell Phillips had celebrated found its agent.

Hunt believed it her mission to reach the nation's children, to saturate them in facts—as she perceived them—that would make young people despise alcohol as much as she did. Invited by Frances Willard to speak at the WCTU convention in 1879, she enlisted the union's battalions in an assault on the nation's school boards, which she intended to put in a "state of siege." Through them, she said, a program of "Scientific Temperance Instruction" could be introduced into every American classroom. But Hunt was not prepared to entrust school boards alone with this grave responsibility. "It is our duty not to take the word of some school official," she declared, "but to visit the school and carefully and wisely ascertain for ourselves if the study is faithfully pursued by all pupils." With Willard's support, at least in the early stages, Hunt sought to have two or more monitors from every single WCTU chapter lay siege to their own local boards. Lest anyone underestimate the audacity of what she was trying to accomplish, she borrowed from the educational taxonomy and called these local enforcers "superintendents."

In 1881 she began to aim higher. Having persuaded the WCTU to commit itself to legally mandated temperance instruction, Hunt targeted the state legislatures. She took control of as many of these campaigns as possible, in some instances moving to the capital of a particular state to direct petition drives and demonstrations, while simultaneously handling legislators with such skill—and such effect—that she acquired the epithet "Queen of the Lobby." Vermont, in 1882, was the first state to pass a compulsory temperance education law; the crucial New York legislature capitulated in 1884; the next year Pennsylvania went a step further, tying state funding to local compliance with the statute's provisions, among them mandatory temperance examinations for all new teachers. Hunt had a falling-out with Willard around this time, but her juggernaut no longer required Willard's personal sanction. In 1886 Hunt took her caravan to Congress, which promptly passed a law requiring Scientific Temperance Instruction in the public schools of all federal territories and in the military academies as well. By 1901, when the population of the entire nation was still less than eighty million, compulsory temperance education was on the books of every state in the nation, and thereby in the thrice-weekly lessons of twenty-two million American children and teenagers.

What many of these millions received in the name of "Scientific Temperance Instruction" was somewhat different from what the three words implied. The second one was arguably accurate, but what Hunt called "scientific" was purely propaganda, and what she considered "instruction" was in fact intimidation. Students were force-fed a stew of mythology ("the majority of beer drinkers die of dropsy"), remonstration ("persons should not take a stimulant before bathing"), and terror ("when alcohol passes down the throat it burns off the skin, leaving it bare and burning"). These specific "insights," as embarrassing as they were even to the WCTU leadership, were not spontaneously generated; they entered the curricula of an estimated 50 percent of all American public schools in textbooks bearing the one imprimatur most valuable to any publisher: the approval of Mary Hunt.

The textbook endorsement program was an arm of the prodigious operation Hunt had assembled in her home on Trull Street in Boston. In one room Hunt created the Scientific Temperance Museum (among its prized artifacts: pens governors had used to sign temperance education bills into law). In the Correspondence Room as many as five secretaries handled her mail and managed her punishing schedule. But only Hunt could attach her signed endorsement to a textbook's copyright page, and publishers and authors who sought it had to survive her grueling interrogations. Professor Charles H. Stowell of the University of Michigan Medical School, the author of a series of health and anatomy books, spent more than a year negotiating word-by-word changes with Hunt before she agreed to sign off on *A Healthy Body*, a volume Stowell and his publisher, Silver, Burdett & Company, intended for students in the intermediate grades. Unlike those authors of "unscientific and unpedagogical" books who did not seek her seal of approval, Stowell generally had no issue with Hunt's authority; he was a stalwart antiliquor man himself, and in his textbook for high school students he described alcohol as "a narcotic poison [with] the power to deaden or paralyze the brain." He drew the line only when Hunt insisted on inserting in one of his books the claim that a single drink of liquor seriously affected one's vision.

Stowell thereby showed more steel than the scholar who told a committee investigating Hunt's work that "I have studied physiology and I do not wish you to suppose that I have fallen so low as to *believe* all those things I have put into those books." But it was Hunt's way of doing business, not her editorial standards, that led Stowell's publishers to fall out with her. In 1891 she informed the firm, which was ready to publish one of Stowell's books, of the "utter impossibility" of meeting their schedule. She couldn't possibly provide an endorsement for at least six weeks, she said—unless, that is, the publisher picked up the tab for Emma L. Benedict, "my Literary Assistant," whom Hunt was taking to Atlantic City "for a couple of days rest between engagements."

The record doesn't reveal the reaction inside the offices of Silver, Burdett to this mild ransom demand. But a few days by the seaside weren't so costly, and soon the firm ponied up the money. The company's compliant posture stiffened, though, when Hunt presented its officers with what could only be called a shakedown. When Stowell's next volume was completed late that same year, Hunt once again stalled, and this time she wasn't coy about her intentions: she wanted to be paid for her endorsement. "Did you think I was doing this work for nothing?" she asked. O. S. Cook, Stowell's editor, told Hunt that his firm had come to "plainly understand that you demand a definite arrangement as to compensation, before you will indorse the books." When she requested a meeting to discuss the matter, the firm made its final response: "Our position is clearly known to you. Any further discussion would undoubtedly prove fruitless."

It was true that Hunt never accepted a salary from the WCTU in the twenty-seven years that she patrolled America's classrooms, and it was also true that she and her supporters repeatedly denied that she received or expected payment from publishers. The chairman of her advisory board, the Reverend A. H. Plumb, condemned these "unjust charges" before a New York state senate committee in 1895 and two years later insisted that the rumor that Hunt demanded a 3 percent royalty on textbooks she endorsed was a calumny spread by Silver, Burdett.

But in 1906, a few months after her death—around the same time the WCTU, with genuine relief, converted the remnants of her operation into a rather benign "clearinghouse for alcohol information"—associates learned something distressing about Mary Hunt. For years she had maintained a bank account in the name of something she called the Scientific Temperance Association (her WCTU work had been conducted through her Department of Scientific Instruction). Into this account she had deposited royalties on endorsed books published by A. S. Barnes & Company and Ginn & Company—money intended "in whole or in part for the maintenance of the work at 23 Trull St."

But those words shouldn't serve as an epitaph for Mary Hunt. Something she had said in a congressional hearing back in 1886, before twenty-two million schoolchildren in a given year were administered their three-times-a-week serving of temperance education, is more appropriate: "The day is surely coming," she had told the congressmen, "when from the schoolhouses all over the land will come trained haters of alcohol to pour a whole Niagara of ballots upon the saloon." And would they ever.

Chapter 2

The Rising of Liquid Bread

ARRY AMELIA MOORE GLOYD NATION was six feet tall, with the biceps of a stevedore, the face of a prison warden, and the persistence of a toothache. Her mother believed herself to be Queen Victoria. Her first husband was a rotten drunk. Her religious passions led her to sit on her organ bench and talk to Christ, "my constant companion," playing a musical accompaniment as the conversation proceeded. She once described herself as "a bulldog running along at the feet of Jesus, barking at what He doesn't like," and she applauded the assassination of William O. McKinley, "a whey-faced tool of Republican thieves, rummies, and devils." She said she published her newspaper, *The Smasher's Mail*, so "the public could see by my editorials that I was not insane."

Well, maybe. But of all the liquor haters stationed along the steep and twisting path from temperance to Prohibition, none quite hated it with Carry Nation's vigor or attacked it with her rapturous glee. In her autobiography, a document about as lucid as a swamp, Nation nevertheless approaches coherence when she describes the methodology that made her famous in her campaign against the "jointists"—that is, the saloon operators. In early 1901, the same year her put-upon second husband divorced her on grounds of desertion, she picked up the weapon that would become her Excalibur: a hatchet.

This is how the Senate Bar, a Topeka saloon favored by state officials, fell to a Nation attack (or, using another of her neologisms, a "hatchetation"): "I ran behind the bar," she wrote,

> smashed the mirror and all the bottles under it; picked up the cash register, threw it down; then broke the faucets of the refrigerator, opened the door and cut the rubber tubes that conducted the beer. Of course it began to fly all over the house.

I threw over the slot machine, breaking it up and I got from it a sharp piece of iron with which I opened the bungs of the beer kegs, and opened the faucets of the barrels, and then the beer flew in every direction and I was completely saturated. A policeman came in and very good-naturedly arrested me.

She concluded, "Mr. Cook was sheriff and I was treated very nicely by him and Mrs. Cook."

Nation had been wielding a prosaic armamentarium of rocks, hammers, bricks, lead canes, and iron rods before the hatchet made her famous. The hatchet soon transformed itself from weapon to symbol to calling card for her new career as a platform speaker (she sold miniature replicas everywhere she went). Though the Prohibition lectures she delivered on the vaudeville circuit sometimes found surprisingly attentive audiences ("They need me," she explained), Nation was as likely to be the object of sport, especially when she spoke to college students. At Yale a group of undergraduates tricked her into posing with a tankard of beer in her hand while they puddled into laughter behind her. She wasn't openly ridiculed at Harvard, but was nonetheless appalled by what she encountered there and urged parents to rise up against such "slaughter, bloody anarchy, and treason." This dithyramb had a specific provocation: "While I was at Harvard," she wrote with grave alarm, "I saw Professors smoking cigarettes."

It may have been easy to dismiss Nation as a sideshow, but like her nonviolent predecessors, she must have had something to do with the undeniable fact that the children and grandchildren of the Washingtonians' generation were drinking much less hard liquor than had their forebears. All the prayer, the agitation, the indoctrination, and the political activity had to some degree worked. By the end of the nineteenth century, production and consumption of whiskey and other distilled spirits had declined substantially, to a per capita figure not radically dissimilar from what it would be a full hundred years later.

But this change in habit disguised the cold fact that something had come along to replace the rotgut, moonshine, grain alcohol, and all those other cheap elixirs, as potent as battery acid, that had been the basic stock of the down-at-heels saloon. Picture Carry Nation in that Topeka bar, hatchet in hand, her black dress saturated in the liquid bursting from the faucets she had opened and from the rubber tubing she had slashed: just as Nation was drenched in beer, so was the entire country. In 1850 Americans drank 36 million gallons of the stuff; by 1890 annual consumption had exploded to 855 million gallons. During that four-decade span, while the population tripled, that population's capacity for beer had increased twenty-four-fold.

There was nothing mysterious about this change. Immigration was responsible, of course, at first from Ireland and Germany. The Germans brought not only beer itself but a generation of men who knew how to make it, how to market it, and how to pretend it was something it was not. The four-year-old United States Brewers' Association declared in 1866 that hard liquor caused "domestic misery, pauperism, disease and crime." On the other hand, the brewers maintained, beer was "liquid bread."*

It also was the substance that composed the ocean upon which a vast new armada of saloons was launched. As the cities filled with immigrants; as a similar settlement of the West accelerated, particularly in the predominantly male lumber camps and mining towns (the states in the Northwest, wrote historian John Higham, "were competing with each other for Europeans to people their vacant lands and develop their economies"); and as a clever and worldly young brewer named Adolphus Busch figured out that pasteurization kept beer fresh enough to ship across the country on the newly completed transcontinental railroad, it became the national beverage.

That the proliferation of saloons was abetted *by* immigrants (usually German or Bohemian), largely *for* immigrants (members of those nationalities, but also Irish, Slavs, Scandinavians, and many, many others), was not lost on the moralists of the WCTU and other temperance organizations. As early as 1876 Frances Willard had referred in a speech to "the infidel foreign population of our country." Near the end of her career, Willard called on Congress to pass immigration restrictions to keep out "the scum of the Old World." In the Mesabi and Vermilion ranges of northern Minnesota, congressional investigators counted 256 saloons in fifteen mining towns, their owners representing eighteen distinct immigrant nationalities. "If a new colony of foreigners appears" in Chicago, the muckraker George Kibbe Turner wrote in 1909, "some compatriot is set at once to selling them liquor. Italians, Greeks, Lithuanians, Poles—all the rough and hairy tribes which have been drawn to Chicago—have their trade exploited to the utmost." U.S. census figures indicated that 80 percent of licensed saloons were owned by first-generation Americans. Among the

---

*Some temperance activists did acknowledge that beer was not as dangerous as the hard stuff. Rev. Lyman Beecher (father of Henry Ward Beecher and Harriet Beecher Stowe) said that beer "enables the victim to come down to his grave . . . with more of the good-natured stupidity of the idiot, and less of the demonic frenzy of the madman."

rapidly proliferating unlicensed operations, the percentage could only have been higher.

There was no typical saloon. In Portland, Oregon, for instance, you could take your beer at August Erickson's polished mahogany bar, a wonder of marketing and craftsmanship wrapping around all four sides of a grand room nearly the size of a city block. But farther down Burnside Street, you were likely to find a dark, fetid place whose most notable feature was the metal trough that ran below the bar on the patrons' side, stinking of spilled beer and, according to historian Madelon Powers, the urine of customers whose bladders were temporary holding tanks for the beer they gulped by the gallon.* Lucy Adams, a schoolteacher who arrived in Portland in 1902, described a scene that could have existed outside both Erickson's and the rougher places: "The stench of stale beer and whiskey often mixed with the nauseating smell of vomit on the sidewalks, and drunken staggering men blocking my way almost turned my stomach." From some saloons, she added, "I saw men and women and even children emerging onto the sidewalk carrying pails of beer to take to their homes." Jacob Riis noted the same phenomenon in New York: "I doubt if one child in a thousand, who brings his growler to be filled at the average New York bar, is sent away empty-handed." A growler was a metal pail, its inside often smeared with lard. This may have corrupted the flavor, but it had an economic benefit: it kept down the foam, leaving room for more beer.

In all, the best estimates indicate that the number of saloons in the United States increased from 100,000 in 1870 to nearly 300,000 by 1900. In Leadville, South Dakota, population 20,000, there was one saloon for every 100 inhabitants—women, children, and abstainers included. San Francisco in 1890 might have seemed barely more saloon-sodden than that, reporting one for every 96 residents—but this was a measure only of the city's 3,000 licensed establishments, while less restrictive estimates threw in an additional 2,000 unlicensed places. Visiting Cincinnati at the peak of her renown, Carry Nation was asked why she had not taken to the local streets with her hatchet. Her answer would have been just as apt in dozens of American cities: "I would have dropped from exhaustion before I had gone a block."

Jacob Riis had more energy than Nation did, perhaps because his weapons—a camera and a notebook—were less taxing to use than her hatchet.

---

*Although these gutters were likely designed strictly to drain away spillage, Powers reports that in her research for *Faces Along the Bar: Lore and Order in the Workingman's Saloon, 1870–1920*, she learned that they were commonly called "pissing troughs."

Conducting research in 1889 and 1890 for what would become his epoch-shaping exposé *How the Other Half Lives*, Riis set out to count Manhattan's saloons south of Fourteenth Street. When he wrote up his findings he decided to make his point about "the saloon's colossal shadow" over the lives of the immigrant poor by juxtaposing the number with a count of churches in the same area. Saloons won in a landslide, of course, 4,065–111. More to the point, though, was Riis's observation that in the saloons "the congregations are larger by a good deal [than in the churches]; certainly the attendance is steadier and the contributions more liberal the week round, Sunday included."

It may have been a rueful acknowledgment, but Riis knew the intensity with which the huddled masses yearned to drink freely. If you considered the nasty living conditions that Riis and others chronicled, it was difficult not to see that the saloon offered something very valuable: in the best cases companionship and comfort, in the worst an escape into oblivion. After a visit to some of the city's tenements, Henry Codman Potter, Episcopal bishop of New York, expressed wonder "not that the poor creatures who live in them drink so much, but they drink so little." In *The Jungle*, Upton Sinclair—an antialcohol campaigner for decades—described why his brutalized Lithuanian immigrant, Jurgis Rudkus, habitually followed a day's labor in the "steaming pit of hell" that was the meatpacking plant with a trip to the saloon: he was seeking "a respite, a deliverance—he could drink! He could forget the pain, he could slip off the burden, he could see clearly again, he would be master of his brain, of his thoughts, of his will." In a word, "His dead self would stir in him." Jack London, who knew whereof he spoke, gave saloon culture a more exalted coloration: in the saloon, he wrote, "life was different. Men talked with great voices, laughed great laughs, and there was an atmosphere of greatness."

The typical saloon featured offerings besides drink and companionship, particularly in urban immigrant districts and in the similarly polyglot mining and lumber settlements. In these places, where a customer's ties to a neighborhood might be new and tenuous, saloonkeepers cashed paychecks, extended credit, supplied a mailing address or a message drop for men who had not yet found a permanent home, and in some instances provided sleeping space at five cents a night. In port cities on the East Coast and the Great Lakes, the saloonkeeper was often the labor contractor for dock work. Many saloons had the only public toilets or washing facilities in the neighborhood, and by the 1890s most saloonkeepers had realized there was indeed such a thing as a free lunch—the complimentary spread they'd use to lure customers and promote the sale of beer. Jon M. Kingsdale, a historian of saloon life, described the free lunch offered by a typical working-class saloon in Chicago's Seventeenth Ward: "a choice of frankfurters, clams, egg sandwiches, potatoes, vegetables, cheeses, bread and several varieties of hot and cold meats." Other places may not have been quite so openhanded, but even a humble assortment of sardines, pickles, pretzels, and crackers guaranteed the one thing a hungry saloongoer could count on: the food would be so salty that only another schooner of suds could quell his thirst. The sardines "were more than fish," wrote George Ade in *The Old-Time Saloon*. "They were silent partners."

A naïf wandering into a saloon in, say, 1905 would have been struck not only by the generous buffet but also by the decorations that surrounded it. One ornament on many saloon walls was a cast-iron hatchet with a die-cut profile of Carry Nation's face adorning the blade and the slogan "All Nations Welcome But Carrie" in bas-relief on the handle. (Although christened "Carry," Nation used both spellings.) Even the dingiest of dives was almost certain to have on the wall above the back bar a large chromolithograph of Cassily Adams's famous *Custer's Last Fight* or some comparable heroic scene. Another standard adornment was a painted mirror, usually depicting a female nude, ample of flesh and suggestive of pose. Someone unfamiliar with saloon economics might understandably wonder how it was that a saloonkeeper could buy such relatively lush appurtenances while peddling something as cheap as beer.

In fact, the saloonkeepers didn't buy the paintings or the mirrors, or in many cases the furniture, the brass footrails, the iron or porcelain spittoons, even the cutlery in the drawers and the glassware shelved beneath the bar. They didn't have to pick up the tab for the food, either. By the end of the first decade of the twentieth century, saloonkeepers had become subsidized servants of the institutions that paid for everything: the breweries themselves.

It was an obvious evolutionary step. As pasteurization, refrigeration, and an efficient network of rail lines developed, so did national brewing companies. The consequent competition was played for higher stakes than before, and the surest way a brewer could secure his piece of the local action was through the "tied house." If a saloon operator would agree to serve only one brand of beer, the brewer would provide cash, loans, and whatever other emoluments were necessary to furnish the place, stock the lunch table, meet the license fee (which in some cities ran as high as $1,500), and when necessary line the pockets of a politician or three.

A modest personal investment could thus be leveraged into a going business. Wrote George Kibbe Turner, "No man with two hundred dollars, who was not subject to arrest on sight, need go without a saloon in Chicago." At one point half the city's population patronized a saloon on an average day, a flood accommodated by the competition among the breweries: if Gustave Pabst's agents bankrolled a place on one corner, you could count on Adolphus Busch's men showing up to finance another one across the street. By 1909 some 70 percent of American saloons—in New York and Chicago, more than 80 percent—were owned by, in debt to, or otherwise indentured to the breweries.

This was a fortress worth defending. Escalating competition within the industry did not keep the brewers from lining up shoulder to shoulder when confronted with a common enemy. When they first came together to oppose the excise tax on alcohol that had been levied to finance the Civil War, they expressed their solidarity by conducting their convention proceedings entirely in German. At the end of the war, although they couldn't get rid of the tax, they did lobby successfully to have it reduced from a dollar a barrel to sixty cents per. Only slowly did it dawn on them that the more their industry was intertwined with the needs of the federal government, the likelier they were to acquire allies in the fight against the temperance movement. By 1875 onward, fully one-quarter of federal revenues came from the beer keg and the whiskey bottle, a proportion that in 1913 would lead a prominent temperance leader to describe this generous source of funds, not inaccurately, as "a bribe on the public conscience."

But even with a bribe securely in place, the brewers could not ignore the growing antialcohol sentiment challenging their very existence. In 1867 the United States Brewers' Association by formal resolution characterized the temperance movement as "fanatical" and vowed to oppose any candidate "of whatever party, in any election, who is in any way disposed toward the total abstinence cause." Soon the brewers began to create and support a string of propaganda and lobbying organizations whose names never quite said what they really were: the first was the National Protective Organization, which became the Personal Liberty League, which in time was supplanted by the National Association of Commerce and Labor. It would have been just as accurate to call any one of them Euphemists for Legal Beer.*

As the stakes increased and as the WCTU and its allies gained adherents, so did the brewers' tactics sharpen. By 1890 the terms "wet" and "dry," as both adjectives and nouns (the latter spawning a plural form,

---

*Distillers played this game, too. For fifty-two years, Chicago liquor dealers published a trade journal called *The Champion of Fair Play*.

"drys," that could not have survived the Age of Spell-Check), had come into general use, an indication that the country at large had begun to divide itself over the Prohibition issue. The brewers took their campaign to the public, but not always *in* public; by surreptitiously paying news-paper editors to run anti-prohibitionist articles, they remained to a large degree offstage. When the purchase of editorial backing was insufficient, they set their sights on politicians. In 1900 a family friend wrote to Gus-tave Pabst about an Idaho alfalfa rancher and former U.S. senator named Fred T. DuBois who was trying to return to Washington: "I think it could be for the interest of the brewers to secure his cooperation—he is aggres-sive and able—if you think well of it—send me $1000–$5000. I think it will be the best investment you ever made." As this took place in the era when U.S. senators were chosen by state legislators and not by popular vote, one can be confident that the money wasn't meant to underwrite the purchase of bumper stickers. DuBois was returned to the Senate for another term, and the leading historian of the Pabst company suggests he did so with some of the family's money tucked into his wallet.

THE MOST FORCEFUL advocate of the brewers' anti-Prohibition campaign was the most accomplished man in the industry, Adolphus Busch. The youngest of twenty-one children of a prosperous Rhineland merchant, Busch immigrated to the United States in 1857, went into the brewery supply business, and in 1861, at twenty-two, married Lilly Anheuser, the daughter of one of his customers. (The familial bond did not lack for fur-ther adhesive, as Adolphus's brother Ulrich married Lilly's sister Anna.) Adolphus soon took over the management of his father-in-law's company and in time appended his surname to it.

Busch was a genuine visionary. Where others saw brewing as a fairly straightforward enterprise, he saw it as the core of a vertically integrated series of businesses. He built glass factories and ice plants. He acquired railway companies to ferry coal from mines he owned in Illinois to the vast Anheuser-Busch factory complex sprawled across seventy acres of St. Louis riverfront. (A local joke: St. Louis was "a large city on the [banks of the] Mississippi, located near the Anheuser-Busch plant.") Busch got into the business of manufacturing refrigerated rail cars and truck bod-ies that could be used not just by breweries but also by such substantial customers as the Armour meatpacking company. He paid one million dol-lars for exclusive U.S. rights to a novel engine technology developed by his countryman Rudolf Diesel, and for $30,000 purchased the painting of

Custer's Last Stand that, with the Anheuser-Busch logotype prominently appended, would soon grace the walls of thousands upon thousands of saloons. In 1875 Busch produced thirty-five thousand barrels of beer; by 1901, his annual output—primarily of a light lager named for the Bohemian town of Budweis—surpassed a million barrels. His brewery became so well known that it even inspired a popular song, the deathless "Under the Anheuser Bush," by the authors of "Wait 'Til the Sun Shines, Nellie." (From the chorus: "Come, come, come and make eyes with me, / Under the Anheuser Bush.")

Adolphus had a potent personal aura. He spoke five languages, built palaces for himself and his wife in St. Louis, Pasadena, Cooperstown, and Wiesbaden, and traveled in a style appropriate for the monarch he was. Whenever Adolphus and Lilly returned from a trip to their home at Number One Busch Place (situated right on company property in St. Louis), brewery employees fired a cannon. Coupled with his company's preeminence in the industry, his grand manner enabled him to dominate industry councils. This became especially clear in 1903, when he helped craft an agreement, eventually signed by nine breweries, to fund a committee "promoting anti-prohibition matters in Texas," one of Anheuser-Busch's largest markets. When some brewers expressed an unwillingness to continue underwriting the committee's activities, Busch argued, "It may cost us millions and even more," he wrote, "but what of it if thereby we elevate our position?" He concluded his appeal by offering another $100,000 of Anheuser-Busch support for the Texas campaign, money that would help fund such "anti-prohibition matters" as paying the poll taxes of blacks and Mexican-Americans who were expected to vote for legal beer, purchasing the editorial support of newspapers (according to an internal report, "We have sent checks in advance, and the average country editor, struggling to make a living, hates to return checks"), and engaging in some rather more mysterious activities. In 1910, after the brewers' political agent in east-central Texas was able to undo a dry victory in Robertson County, he explained that he had engineered the reversal through means that "are best not written about."

Busch's motives went beyond the merely pecuniary: "Besides losing our business by state-wide prohibition," he wrote during the Texas battle, "we would lose our honor and standing of ourselves and our families, and rather than lose that, we should risk the majority of our fortunes." It was the sort of call to arms that inspired both employees and competitors, and that led to something of a national festival in 1911, when Adolphus and Lilly's golden anniversary was marked by celebrations in thirty-five cities. A similar nationwide outpouring of respect and love from the brewing industry occurred two years later, when Adolphus Busch died, at the age of seventy-four, from cirrhosis of the liver.

IN 1915, when the formal effort to put the prohibition of alcoholic beverages into the Constitution was just beginning to accelerate, the members of the USBA found a catalog of the sins of the saloon nailed to their figurative door. As summarized by Hugh Fox, an English vicar's son whom the brewers had hired to be their chief strategist, it sounded like an index to the most fevered of WCTU dreams: "selling in prohibited hours, gambling, selling to intoxicated men, rear rooms, unclean places, invading residential districts, the country saloon, the social evil, selling to minors, keeping open at night, brewers financing ignorant foreigners who are not citizens, the American bar, brewery-controlled saloons, cabarets, Sunday selling, treating, free lunch, sales to speakeasies, bucket trade, signs, screens, character of the men, too many saloons."

It's unlikely that anyone had produced so succinct a summary of the transgressions of the saloon business in the four decades since Mother Thompson had fallen to her knees in a Hillsboro joint. But this particular compilation did not come directly from the prohibitionist camp. It was assembled by William Piel, a Brooklyn brewer, to indicate the extent of the mess in which the brewers now found themselves. Despite the millions they had expended to combat the temperance forces, despite the tens of millions who enjoyed (or depended upon or were enslaved by) their product, the brewers had a serious problem.

You could tell how serious it was just from the circumstances of Hugh Fox's presentation: he spoke at a meeting of the "joint harmony committee" of brewers and distillers. For these two to harmonize was as likely as a group of alley cats howling a major chord. Although the beer men and the liquor men had occasionally attempted to come together over the preceding decades to fight the temperance troops, each side was convinced that association with the other would be more like infection. In 1871, when both groups were still trying to reduce the federal alcohol tax that had survived the Civil War, a trade magazine called the *American Brewers' Gazette and Distillers' Journal* lopped off the second half of its title when the brewers declared that their interests and the distillers' were "not only not identical, but, on the contrary, decidedly inimical." In the ensuing years, even as the distillers organized themselves into a powerful trust consisting of eighty-one companies spread from Maine to California, the brewers regarded them as lepers. The distillers produced "the worst and cheapest kind of concoctions," Adolphus Busch told a friend, while the brewers made "light, wholesome drinks."

The distillers were equally narrow in their perceived self-interest. When they adopted a program of saloon reform under the rubric of the Model License League, whereby the number of saloon licenses would be limited by law, and bad conduct (selling to minors, ignoring closing hours, and so on) could lead to revocation of a license, they effectively put themselves in permanent opposition to the brewers—who happened to own most of the saloons the Model License League would limit. "You cannot prevent prohibition by maintaining that beer is less harmful than whiskey. The strength of the [Prohibition] movement is due to the prejudice against the saloon," the Cincinnati distiller Morris F. Westheimer told one of the meetings ostensibly called to bring the two camps together. Westheimer pointed out that the distillers, much of whose business had largely moved from dependence on sale by the drink to sale "in the original package," would "prosper without the saloon." And he told the brewers that if they chose to go it alone and continue to assault the distillers in their effort to save their own necks, the distillers would agitate to close the saloons altogether. He concluded, "Your separation would force us to cooperate with the enemy."

Westheimer delivered his speech in 1914, but for all its mighty rhetoric and persuasive logic, he might as well have been talking to a classroom of kindergartners. For by then, the enemy didn't particularly need the cooperation of anyone who wasn't part of the broad and highly unlikely alliance now spearheaded by a potent organization called the Anti-Saloon League. The league had been founded in 1893 by the Reverend Howard Hyde Russell, but it was not Russell's way to claim parentage. "The Anti-Saloon League movement," he said many years later, "was begun by Almighty God."

Chapter 3

The Most Remarkable Movement

THE TOWN OF Oberlin, Ohio, named for an Alsatian cleric who ministered to the poor, was founded in 1833 by two Presbyterian clergymen who chose "to plant a colony somewhere in this region whose chief aim will be to glorify God & do good to men." From its very beginning the colony and the eponymous school at its heart attracted men and women desperate to change the world. Oberlin College was the nation's first coeducational institution of higher learning and among the first to admit black students. Frances Willard's parents gave up their prosperous farm in upstate New York to study at Oberlin; pioneer feminist Lucy Stone was an early graduate. The Oberlin community possessed deep conviction (it was a central cog in the Underground Railroad), and its own style of passionate intensity: at one point, dietary restrictions at the college were so severe that in addition to alcohol, tea, coffee, and meat, the list of proscribed foods included pepper, gravy, and butter.

Before Howard Hyde Russell found his way to this moral Eden, he had been a prosperous lawyer in Iowa. But at twenty-eight, urged on by what a sympathetic biographer called "the prayerful influence of his wife," Russell was gripped by a conversion that pulled him to Oberlin. Ordained at thirty-one, he occupied a series of ever-larger pulpits over the next five years and then returned to northeastern Ohio to create the founding cell of what would become an organization with dues-paying adherents numbering in the millions. The Anti-Saloon League may not have been the first broad-based American pressure group, but it certainly was the first to develop the tactics and the muscle necessary to rewrite the Constitution. It owed its success to two ideas, one core constituency, and an Oberlin undergraduate who sat in the front row of the balcony of the First Congregational Church on a June Sunday in 1893 and heard Russell outline his plan to deliver the nation from the death grip of alcohol.

35

The two ideas that drove the ASL were focus and intimidation. The decision to declare war on alcohol and only on alcohol—to choose one target at which all the organization's weapons could be fired—was a direct rebuke to the unfocused efforts of both the WCTU and the Prohibition Party. Frances Willard's "Do Everything" policy had been distracting (how could members concentrate on the Prohibition effort if they were also supporting the Armenians against the Turks, as they did in 1895?) and divisive (it was a rare antialcohol industrialist who would cooperate with an organization led by a socialist, even if a Christian one). The Prohibition Party was no better; among the many reasons for its dismal electoral record—it had never garnered more than 2.2 percent of the vote in a presidential election—was its earnest devotion to a list of diffuse (and sometimes nutty) causes ranging from government ownership of public utilities to judicial review of post office decisions. The ASL would abide no such diversions. "The Anti-Saloon League is not in politics as a party, nor are we trying to abolish vice, gambling, horse-racing, murder, theft or arson," one of its early leaders said. "The gold standard, the unlimited coinage of silver, protection, free trade and currency reform, do not concern us in the least." They cared only about alcohol, and about freeing the nation from its grip.

Strategically focused, the ASL could more effectively apply its intimidating tactics. "Intimidation" might seem too tough a word for the forthright application of democratic techniques, but as practiced by the ASL, democracy was a form of coercion. Russell was direct about this: "The Anti-Saloon League," he said, "is formed for the purpose of administering political retribution." The ASL did not seek to win majorities; it played on the margins, aware that if it could control, say, one-tenth of the voters in any close race, it could determine the outcome. Russell liked to cite rail baron Jay Gould's credo—that he was a Republican when he was in Republican districts, a Democrat when he was in Democratic districts, but that he was always for the Erie Railroad. The ASL had no problem supporting a Republican today and a Democrat tomorrow, so long as the candidates were faithful on the only issue the league cared about. As an ASL official in Pennsylvania put it, there was "one big question mark before the name of every candidate for public office. Is he right on this question?"

To gather the support needed to fund the group's efforts and to line up those 10 percent of the voters who could tip the balance on election day, Russell and his colleagues mobilized the nation's literalist Protestant churches and their congregations. Any pressure group would be fortunate to be blessed with a constituency like this one. It was scattered across the American landscape, yet easily reached when there was a message to deliver or an action to initiate. By its self-definition, it wore the mantle of moral authority. In its religious ardency, it was prepared for apocalyptic battle. The Anti-Saloon League was, its own slogan affirmed, "the Church in Action Against the Saloon."

The leadership, the staff, and the directorates of the ASL and its affiliate organizations were overwhelmingly Methodist and Baptist. Clergymen occupied a minimum of 75 percent of the board seats of any state branch. "The real secret of the League's success," wrote the generally unsympathetic Frank Kent of the *Baltimore Sun*, "is its unrivaled opportunity to reach the hundreds of thousands of churchgoers while they are in church and through their pastors." An annual "Field Day" brought ASL representatives to more than thirty thousand congregations nationwide, there to present the league's program and to fill the collection plate with the pledges that funded its activities. Pastors in country, town, and city stood at the ready should they be asked to deliver a particular message on a particular Sunday. "I can dictate twenty letters to twenty men in twenty parts of the city and thereby set 50,000 men in action," said an ASL spokesman in Philadelphia. "I can name 100 churches that can marshal 20,000 men in Bible classes alone."

Once the ASL had established its capillary network of churches, it did not take long for it to replace the WCTU at the head of the Prohibitionist column. This was assured to some degree by Frances Willard's death in 1898, but even more so by the deflected attention of WCTU leaders, who preferred to devote their energy and their accumulated political capital to the beatification of their beloved leader. In one day twenty thousand people made the pilgrimage to WCTU headquarters in Chicago to view her casket. Not long after, headquarters was relocated to her Evanston home, a tidy piece of Methodist gingerbread she called Rest Cottage. Several rooms were turned into a Frances Willard museum, the whole presided over by Anna Gordon, Willard's secretary, companion, and heir. In the Capitol Building in Washington, hers was the first likeness of a woman to be represented in Statuary Hall, alongside Samuel Adams, George Washington, and Robert E. Lee. Her birthday became an official school holiday in South Carolina, Pennsylvania, Wisconsin, and Kansas.

The WCTU continued to grow after Willard's death, but the cult of personality devoted to the woman who, almost two decades later, was still being called "our lamented leader" placed her successors in permanent shadow. The organization remained a powerful army, but command and control of the Prohibition movement passed into the hands of the ASL.

✦ ✦ ✦

IN 1908 the Reverend Purley A. Baker, a fearsome Methodist preacher from Columbus who had succeeded Howard Russell as the ASL's national superintendent, engaged in a little boasting: "In no instance has the League ever nominated a candidate for public office," Baker said. "Nevertheless, we are the most skillfully and completely organized political force in the country." And that was before Wayne Bidwell Wheeler put his hand on the wheel.

How does one begin to describe the impact of Wayne Wheeler? You could do worse than begin at the end, with the obituaries that followed his death, at fifty-seven, in 1927—obituaries, in the case of those quoted here, from newspapers that by and large disagreed with everything he stood for. The *New York Herald Tribune*: "Without Wayne B. Wheeler's generalship it is more than likely we should never have had the Eighteenth Amendment." The *Milwaukee Journal*: "Wayne Wheeler's conquest is the most notable thing in our times." The editorial eulogists of the *Baltimore Sun* had it absolutely right, while at the same time completely wrong: ". . . nothing is more certain than that when the next history of this age is examined by dispassionate men, Wheeler will be considered one of its most extraordinary figures." No one remembers, but he was.

Need it be said that after her only son's death, Wheeler's aged mother told reporters, "Wayne always was a good boy"? Certainly not to anyone who knew him when he was an undergraduate at Oberlin. Penniless when he arrived there in 1890, Wheeler supported himself by waiting on tables, serving as his dormitory's janitor, teaching school every summer vacation, and selling a range of goods that began with books and programs for sporting events and ran to furniture, classroom supplies, and rug-making machines. He was a small man, maybe five feet six or five-seven, and even at the peak of his power in the 1920s he looked more like a clerk in an insurance office than a man who, in the description of the militantly wet *Cincinnati Enquirer*, "made great men his puppets." Wire-rimmed glasses, a tidy mustache, eyes that crinkled at the corners when he ventured one of the tight little smiles that were his usual reaction to the obloquy of his opponents—imagine Ned Flanders of *The Simpsons*, but older and shorter, and carrying on his slight frame a suit, a waistcoat, and, his followers believed, the fate of the Republic.

When Howard Russell recruited Wheeler to become one of the ASL's first full-time employees, he was seeking "a loving, spirited self-sacrificing soul who yearns to help the other fellow." In the janitor's room in Oberlin's

Peters Hall, where they first discussed the job, the two men concluded their meeting by praying together for divine guidance. Years later Wheeler said he joined the ASL staff because he was inspired by the organization's altruism and idealism. But despite all the tender virtues Wheeler may have possessed, none would prove as essential as a rather different quality, best summarized by a classmate's description: Wayne Wheeler was a "locomotive in trousers."

In fact, "power plant" was more like it. While clerking for a Cleveland lawyer and attending classes at Western Reserve Law School, Wheeler nonetheless worked full time for the league, riding his bicycle from town to town so he could speak to more churches, recruit more supporters. After he earned his law degree in 1898 and took over the Ohio ASL's legal office, his productivity accelerated with the additional responsibility. He initiated so many legal cases in the league's behalf, delivered so many speeches, launched so many telegram campaigns, organized so many demonstrations ("petitions in boots," he called them) and remained in such demand by Ohio congregations that Howard Russell was led to moan that "there was not enough Mr. Wheeler to go around." If he had the time and the inclination to court a fellow Oberlin graduate with the euphonious name of Ella Belle Candy, it was partly because Ella's businessman father, who believed in the cause, promised to provide the financial security that a league salary could not. They married in 1901.

By then the ASL was well along in remaking Ohio politics. It had thirty-one full-time, paid staff members coordinating a legion of zealous pastors standing by on permanent alert. John D. Rockefeller, who was a lifelong teetotaler as well as America's wealthiest Baptist, favored the organization with his financial support, matching 10 percent of whatever the league was able to raise from other sources. The objective articulated by Russell—to call to account politicians who committed "high crimes and misdemeanors against the home, the church and the state"—was no longer just an audacious threat; for scores of officeholders it had become chilling reality. By 1903, the year Wheeler became the ASL's Ohio superintendent, the league had targeted seventy sitting legislators of both parties (nearly half the entire legislative membership) and had defeated every one of them.

The newly elected Ohio legislature installed that year was custom-built by the ASL—Wayne B. Wheeler, general contractor. Now it could enact a law that had long been the league's primary goal: a local-option bill placing power over the saloon directly in the hands of voters. If Cincinnatians voted wet, Cincinnati would be wet, and if Daytonians voted dry, their town would be dry. Once different versions of the measure had passed both houses of the legislature, Governor Myron T. Herrick persuaded members of the conference committee to adopt some modifications he deemed necessary to make the law workable and equitable. "Conference committees are dangerous," Wheeler believed, partly because they made it possible for governors to step in and preempt the ASL's legislative agenda. Playing for stakes greater than those the league had ever risked before, Wheeler decided to take on Herrick.

He was not an easy target. A successful lawyer and banker in Cleveland, Herrick was the political creation of Senator Mark Hanna, the Republican Boss of Bosses who had also invented William O. McKinley.* Herrick had been elected governor with the largest plurality in Ohio history, had substantial campaign funds of his own, and had gladdened many a church-minded heart when he vetoed a bill that would have legalized racetrack betting. Additionally, Ohio Republicans had lost only one gubernatorial election in two decades.

Wheeler and the ASL crushed him. They sponsored more than three hundred anti-Herrick rallies throughout the state, mobilizing their supporters in the churches by invoking Herrick's role in modifying the local-option bill and by suggesting that the governor—"the champion of the murder mills"—was a conscious pawn of the liquor interests. When the Brewers' Association sent out a confidential letter urging its members to lend quiet but material support to Herrick (his Democratic opponent was a vocal temperance advocate), Wheeler said he "got [a copy of the letter] on Thursday before election, photographed it and sent out thousands of them to churches on Sunday." In what was at the time the largest turnout ever for an Ohio gubernatorial election, every other Republican on the statewide ticket was elected, but Myron T. Herrick's political career was over.

Money sometimes being thicker than alcohol, Wheeler's opposition to so prominent a member of the business establishment temporarily led John D. Rockefeller to reduce his financial support for the ASL. But Wheeler was unfazed. "Never again," he said, "will any political party ignore the protests of the church and the moral forces of the state." Or, more accurately, never again would they ignore Wayne B. Wheeler, who

---

*Another of Hanna's protégés, even if from the distance of a century, was Karl Rove, the political mind behind George W. Bush. "Some kids want to grow up to be president. Karl wanted to grow up to be Mark Hanna," a friend told *Esquire* magazine in January 2003. "We'd talk about it all the time. We'd say, 'Jesus, Karl, what kind of kid wants to grow up to be Mark Hanna?'" In many ways, though, Rove's feel for hardball politics suggested that the historical figure he most resembled was Wayne B. Wheeler.

was now launched on a national career that would eventually make him, in the words of an ASL associate, the figure who "controlled six Congresses, dictated to two Presidents . . . , directed legislation for the most important elective state and federal offices, held the balance of power in both Republican and Democratic parties, distributed more patronage than any dozen other men, supervised a federal bureau from the outside without official authority, and was recognized by friend and foe alike as the most masterful and powerful single individual in the United States."

IN JANUARY 1909 Hugh Fox of the United States Brewers' Association sent his membership a letter that bordered on the apoplectic. He asked the brewers to consider "what we have to reckon with—That the League has over 800 business offices, and at least 500 men and women on its regular salary list, in these offices alone? That besides this, that it employs large numbers of speakers on contract, from the governor of Indiana down to the local pastor of the Methodist Church? Do you realize," he continued, "that the men who are managing these movements have capitalized the temperance sentiment which has been evolved in a century of preaching and agitation?"

Thomas Gilmore, Fox's counterpart over at the liquor distillers' office, told his employers at their 1908 convention in Louisville that the ASL was "the most remarkable movement that this country has ever known." But in Gilmore's lexicon "remarkable" could encompass his belief that the league was also "the most autocratic, the most dictatorial, as well as the most dangerous power ever known in the politics of this country." The brewers' man and the distillers' man seemed to be on the same page, but in fact their organizations still refused to come together. Christian Feigenspan, a powerful New Jersey brewer, declared that "many of the brewers see their salvation" in separating themselves from the distillers. Pittsburgh distiller A. J. Sunstein saw his industry's deliverance in "reducing the number of licenses"—that is, closing down a lot of brewery owned saloons. Seemingly disinterested parties like Arthur Brisbane, the influential Hearst editor and columnist, campaigned aggressively for what he called "suppression of whiskey traffic and the encouragement of light wine and beer."

The alcohol industry would have been fortunate had their opponents been similarly divided. In fact, the various factions of the growing anti-alcohol alliance could be encompassed by no imaginable organization: Billy Sunday, meet Jane Addams: you may never realize it, but you'll be working together now. Industrial Workers of the World, shake hands with the Ku Klux Klan: you're on the same team. But what had become known as the "Ohio Idea"—the ASL's determination to isolate antialcohol sentiment from all other causes and ideologies—enabled the league to regard all the disparate drys as allies. In the two decades leading up to Prohibition's enactment, five distinct, if occasionally overlapping, components made up this unspoken coalition: racists, progressives, suffragists, populists (whose ranks also included a small socialist auxiliary), and nativists. Adherents of each group may have been opposed to alcohol for its own sake, but each used the Prohibition impulse to advance ideologies and causes that had little to do with it.

This is probably most clearly the case among the racists—specifically, those arrayed across the southern states in the resentful formation that had arisen from the ruins of the Civil War and the reforms of Reconstruction. Before the Civil War the South had been slow to enlist in the temperance movement, in part because of its connection to abolitionism. Once white southerners reclaimed their dominance after the end of Reconstruction, alliance became much easier. Still, although the North and the South had similar attitudes toward liquor, wrote the Washington correspondent of the *Atlanta Constitution* in 1907, "the South has the negro problem." Lest his readers misunderstand him, he elaborated by recalling the Reconstruction era and the "terrible condition of affairs that prevailed when swarms of negroes, many of them drunk with whisky . . . roamed the country at large." It was a familiar characterization, and its reach extended beyond the boundaries of the old Confederacy. Frances Willard herself had adopted the imagery, asserting that "the grogshop is the Negro's center of power. Better whiskey and more of it is the rallying cry of great dark faced mobs."

Even those who affected concern for black southerners indulged in similarly toxic rhetoric, often salted with a patronizing helping of pseudoscience. "Under slavery the Negroes were protected from alcohol," proclaimed an official publication of the Methodist Church, and "consequently they developed no high degree of ability to resist its evil effects." An editorialist in *Collier's* assured his readers that "white men are beginning to see that moral responsibility for the negro rests on them, and that it is a betrayal of responsibility to permit illicit sales of dangerous liquors and drugs." In Congress a boldly disingenuous Representative John Newton Tillman of Arkansas tried to make the case that Prohibition would bring an end to southern lynchings, for fewer black men would commit horrible crimes if liquor were unavailable.

But in that same speech, delivered on the floor of the House of Representatives in 1917 (and encompassing in its ample length references to

Martin Luther, Pope Urban II, four former senators from Maine, Lord Chesterfield, Robert Bruce, and "the Prince of Peace Himself"), the quotable Congressman Tillman also said liquor "increases the menace of [the black man's] presence." In Thomas Dixon Jr.'s widely read novels from the first decade of the twentieth century, *The Leopard's Spots* and *The Clansman*—the source material for D. W. Griffith's *Birth of a Nation*—black men with "eyes bloodshot with whisky" wander the streets and invade the homes of whites, their extravagant drunkenness intensifying the constant threat of plunder and rape. In Dixon's cosmos, the black man was "half child, half animal . . . whose passions, once aroused, are as the fury of the tiger." Carnality wasn't a necessary element of the white southerner's blind fear; to some, the risk to their perceived dignity was nearly as frightful. Civil War hero General Robert F. Hoke's daughter Lily was convinced that the men of North Carolina would vote dry in an imminent 1908 Prohibition referendum "because the people do not wish drunken Negroes to push white ladies off the sidewalks."

What these same people also did not wish was the continued presence, granted by the loathed Fifteenth Amendment to the Constitution, of the black man in the voting booth. Despite the antiliquor position taken by Booker T. Washington and some other southern black leaders, white prohibitionists in many states had stopped trying to convince black men to support their cause after black votes defeated a no-liquor amendment to the Tennessee constitution in 1887. Failing to persuade, the drys chose instead to demonize. They conjured not an argument but an image: the waking nightmare of a black man with a bottle of whiskey in one hand and a ballot in the other. It was this perceived threat that had set off what C. Vann Woodward would call "the third national prohibition wave," which crashed ashore in 1906 in a Democratic primary campaign in Georgia (the first two waves, Woodward said, were set in motion by the Washingtonian Movement of the 1840s and the rise of the WCTU in the 1880s). Gubernatorial candidate Hoke Smith—General Hoke's nephew, as it happened—set out to persuade white Georgians that the black vote was controlled by the liquor interests, an argument that assured his election and enabled him to push through in his first year as governor a one-two combination of laws that took both ballot and bottle away from the state's black citizens. First Smith signed a measure summarily disenfranchising Georgia's black voters by means of a viciously effective grandfather clause; once that was done—once the ballot was ripped from the hands of black men who might have voted wet—the passage of harsh local-option laws was a snap.

In the ensuing months, additional Prohibition laws, often congenitally linked to Jim Crow voting laws, were enacted not only in North Carolina (Lily Hoke had been right), but in Oklahoma and Mississippi as well. Discriminatory voting laws in Alabama enabled a local Baptist publication to predict a coming dry victory in that state with great glee: "The stronghold of the whiskey power in the state has been eliminated by the disfranchisement of the Negro, and others like him."

The sentiment was grotesque but the analysis was sublime. The brewers' extensive efforts to secure the support of blacks had marked them as the enemy of southern whites and as nakedly cynical, too. No one believed that their persistent opposition to poll taxes, for instance, arose from any nobler instinct than their deep affection for profits. In Texas, Adolphus Busch's staff of field agents included four black men "competent to handle the colored voters," in the words of one indiscreet manager. Their competence was amplified by a kit each one carried, consisting of the powers of attorney and the cash necessary to pay an individual's poll tax, a few pieces of wet propaganda, and a poster of Abraham Lincoln.

The distillers, supported by the wholesalers who distributed their products, didn't need to meddle in the feudal southern political system to incite the region's rage. For all the high-minded rhetoric they offered in opposition to the saloon, they were doomed to ignominy because of who they were and how they went about marketing their products. It certainly didn't help that the distilling business had become a largely Jewish industry—perhaps not as uniformly as the beer industry was German, but close enough to inspire the mistrust and loose the venom of nativist bigots. When John Tillman explained to his congressional colleagues how he wished to save the Negro from lynching by denying him his liquor, he made it clear who was guilty of debauching the black man. Reading from a list of liquor industry figures, Tillman asserted that their names—Steinberg, Schaumberg, and Hirschbaum, for example—demonstrated that "I am not attacking an American institution. I am attacking mainly a foreign enterprise." This perception was not limited to the South. Even *McClure's* magazine, that paragon of muckraking probity, referred in 1909 to the "acute and unscrupulous Jewish type of mind which has taken charge of the wholesale liquor trade of this country."

In one spectacularly combustible instance, a St. Louis distiller fed the stereotype with a marketing effort that dry forces turned into a national scandal. Lee Levy had been in the liquor business in Texas for nearly twenty years when he arrived in St. Louis in 1902, at the age of forty-six, and set up a distillery on the north side of town near the Mississippi River.

Within four years he had succeeded well enough to earn himself a listing in *The Book of St. Louisans*, a directory of the city's "leading living men." Two years after that he was described in *Collier's* by Will Irwin as "A gentleman of St. Louis taking his fat, after-dinner ease, sitting on plush, decked with diamonds, lulled by a black cigar, and planning how he shall advance his business." This was not meant as a compliment.

Levy's appearance (if you can call it that—there's no reason to think Irwin had ever met him) in one of America's largest and most influential magazines was prompted by an incident in Shreveport, Louisiana, in which a black man named Charles Coleman was charged with the rape and murder of a white fourteen-year-old named Margaret Lear. Coleman's trial took four hours, the jury presented a guilty verdict after three minutes of deliberation, and he was hanged in the Shreveport jail one week later. (Coleman was spared a less punctilious lynching only by the array of state militia circling the courthouse.) The terrible story made it into the pages of *Collier's* because Coleman had been drunk, and because Irwin had been traveling the South looking into how liquor was sold to the region's blacks. He had no idea exactly what Coleman had been drinking, but he took a leap and suggested it might have resembled the item that had been found in the pocket of a black man charged with rape in Birmingham: a half-empty bottle of gin bearing a brand name, an illustration, and the words "Bottled by Lee Levy & Co., St. Louis." The brand name did not appear in *Collier's* because, Irwin wrote, "If I should give its name here . . . this publication could not go through the mails." The illustration did not appear because, as a U.S. attorney would later assert in court papers, "said picture is wholly unfit to be further described in this instrument, and a further description thereof would be an insult to this honorable court." The brand name of Levy's product was Black Cock Vigor Gin. The figure portrayed in the illustration was a white woman, mostly nude.

According to the custom of the day, Irwin had been no more direct when referring to Margaret Lear's rape, which he called "the nameless crime." He had less scruple about identifying the concoction he believed Coleman had been drinking as "nigger gin," a catchall term for the cheap stuff marketed to impoverished southern blacks at fifty cents a pint (wholesale price for Levy's: twenty-seven cents).* Irwin mentioned other distillers in the "nigger gin" business, among them men with such suspicious names as

---

*A magazine description of nigger gin: "There was a brief wave of heat as from a match, then a flash of sweetish, pungent, bitter vapor which seemed to leave all the membranes of the throat covered with a lingering, nauseating mustiness."

Weil, Dreyfuss, and Blutenthal. The dry Nashville *Tennessean*, which leapt onto the story as if it were a chariot sent from heaven, listed the local joints owned by whites who sold Levy's gin to blacks. It asked its readers to "set aside all other reasons for the crusade against the saloon and consider this one—the Negro problem." The front-page editorial, bordered in black, continued, "The Negro, fairly docile and industrious, becomes, when filled with liquor, turbulent and dangerous and a menace to life, property, and the repose of the community." A white clergyman warned Nashvillians, "This gin, with its label, has made more black rape fiends, and has procured the outrage of more white women in the south than all other agencies combined. It is sold with the promise that it will bring white virtue into the black brute's power." The *Memphis Commercial Appeal*, a wet paper, demurred; it was "an insult to the South and all the good women of this section," editors wrote, to blame the crime on the distiller and absolve "the poor black beast" who committed it.

Beyond the national readership *Collier's* enjoyed, newspaper readers in cities from Atlanta to Los Angeles learned about Lee Levy and his gin, even if its name was suppressed. Although Levy remained in the liquor industry, he and his business partner were convicted of sending "improper matter through the mails" and expelled from the distillers' Model License League. The federal judge who sentenced them said he went light on the penalty—$900 in fines—because a postal inspector claiming to be an Arkansas liquor dealer had entrapped them: "I am opening a place in Argenta Ark," the inspector had written on his order for twenty-four quarts, "and I can use Your Black Cock Gin to advantage."

AT FIRST GLANCE, a form of race hatred could have been seen as the motivation of the second component of the dry coalition, the *bien-pensant* northeasterners who would come to be known as progressives. When the twenty-three-year-old Theodore Roosevelt arrived in Albany early in 1882 to begin his first term in the New York legislature, he was horrified by the twenty-five Democratic members of Irish extraction who sat across the aisle. "They are a stupid, sodden, vicious lot, most of them being equally deficient in brains and virtue," he wrote in his diary. The typical Irish member of the Assembly, he added, "is a low, venal, corrupt and unintelligent brute." Among them were some who could not "string three intelligible sentences together." Roosevelt characterized one particularly loathsome assemblyman, "Big John" McManus, as "unutterably coarse and low." Chief among Big John's sins: he owned a saloon. Roosevelt disliked McManus to such a degree that he once chased off the much larger man by threatening to "kick you in the balls."

But even more than their personal distaste for the Irish Democrats, Roosevelt and his allies detested the political culture they represented. Just as the urban saloon served as mail drop, hiring hall, and social center for the immigrant masses, so too was it birthplace, incubator, and academy for the potent political machines that captured control of the big cities of the East and Midwest in the last quarter of the nineteenth century. In New York in 1884, twelve of the twenty-four members of the board of aldermen owned saloons, and four others owed their posts to saloon backing. In Detroit, where the saloonkeepers' political arm—the Keep Your Mouth Shut Organization—controlled only one-third of the city's legislative seats, their fraternal order attempted to compensate for this minority status by endorsing a "Saloon Slate" of municipal officials who swore not to enforce closing hours. For more than three decades Chicago's First Ward remained in the absolute control of Michael "Hinky Dink" Kenna and "Bathhouse John" Coughlin, proprietors of a saloon called the Workingmen's Exchange, and in Boston, where a settlement house worker said "the affiliation between the saloon and politics was so close that for all practical purposes the two might have been under one and the same control," a ward politician named Patrick J. Kennedy launched a political dynasty from his tavern in Haymarket Square.

The connection between liquor and politics was not a new one. When twenty-four-year-old George Washington first ran for a seat in the Virginia House of Burgesses, he attributed his defeat to his failure to provide enough alcohol for the voters. When he tried again two years later, Washington floated into office partly on the 144 gallons of rum, punch, hard cider, and beer his election agent had handed out—roughly half a gallon for every vote he received. In the city slums of the late nineteenth and early twentieth centuries, the various comforts and services offered by the neighborhood saloon put its proprietor in an ideal position to dispense, along with beer and liquor, the coin of political patronage: credit, favors, jobs. In the poorest neighborhoods, where a harder currency—the cash to buy another drink—was scarce, selling one's vote for the price of a bar tab was a common transaction. Consequently, when the brewers looked at the saloon, they saw more than a source of profit. They saw as well the guarantor of the political power they needed if they were to hold off the growing armies of temperance.

Roosevelt and the other Protestant aristocrats who championed urban reform saw the very same thing and did not find it pleasing. The corrupt culture of the political machines (the saloon-controlled New York board of aldermen was known as the "Boodle Board") was violently offensive to reformist sensibilities; the immigrant composition of the machines' support was an affront to the native Protestant's sense of his own prerogatives. Elizabeth Cady Stanton was carrying the torch for female suffrage when she described the horrifying prospect of "Patrick and Sambo and Hans and Yung Tung, who do not know the difference between a Monarchy and a Republic, who never read the Declaration of Independence . . . making laws for Lydia Maria Child, Lucretia Mott, or Fanny Kemble." Substitute Tom, Dick, and Harry for Lydia, Lucretia, and Fanny, and if their last names remained unmistakably pure, the prevailing progressive sentiment would have been identical to Stanton's.

At the same time, many progressives who despised the immigrants' way of life sought to improve it. Through charity, activism, and government action, the progressives believed they could make the lives of immigrants better, more stable, more conventional—in a word, more American. Not for a minute did they see the assimilation of the great wave of immigrants as an easy task; David Starr Jordan, the first president of Stanford University, who was a dedicated dry and a political ally of Roosevelt, wrote that "most of them . . . are very different from the Anglo-Saxon—very much less capable of self-government, and on the whole morally and socially less desirable." But if the saloon could be abolished through the sort of aggressive government intervention the progressives favored, there was a chance, said H. D. W. English, president of the Pittsburgh Civic Commission, that the "polyglot class" could be lifted up from "his dirt and beer."*

To the immigrant workingman, of course, elimination of the saloon would be an act of repression. As Arthur S. Link wrote about the men and women of the progressive movement, "The fact that they were potentially or actively repressive does not mean that they were not progressive." They were dry not because they hated alcohol, but because they hated what alcohol did to those who did not encounter it in crystal goblets arrayed on white tablecloths. "When the laboring man works eight hours and spends none of his time at the saloon, he will save up more money and better his economic status," wrote the influential editor William Allen White in

---

*Historian James H. Timberlake noted that the progressives' cousins in the social Darwinist camp saw the same degradation in the saloons but regarded it as a virtue: they believed that "alcohol, by killing off generation after generation of the unfit, was acting as a progressive factor in natural selection and improving the race."

what sounded like progressive sentiment at its noblest. "When the workingman spends his evenings at home or at the library, and has good books and a gramophone and an automobile, society will be better off." But three decades later in his autobiography, White employed some unfortunate imagery that, however rueful it might have been, reflected a chillingly suggestive attitude toward the immigrant's plight. The reformers of the first decade of the twentieth century, he wrote, "believed faithfully that if we could only change the environment of the under dog, give him a decent kennel, wholesome food, regular baths, properly directed exercise, cure his mange and abolish his fleas . . . all would be well."

Other prominent figures of the progressive movement, such as the settlement house pioneers Jane Addams and Lillian Wald, supported Prohibition not out of an antipathy to the mores of the urban immigrants but because of a genuine empathy. Their commitment to the dry cause arose from the same instinct that had led the best of the abolitionists—those who not only objected to slavery but believed the black man to be the white man's equal—into the temperance movement. Neither were they unsympathetic to the impulses that led men to saloons. Though Addams never wavered in her support for Prohibition, she believed that "if alcohol was associated intensively with these gross evils, it was also associated with homely and wholesome things," notably the conviviality that drink could bring to the dull grayness of the urban slums. Unlike Addams, her fellow Chicago reformer Episcopal priest Samuel R. Fellows did not understand what it was about the saloon that gave its clientele their homely pleasures. In 1895 he opened a place on Washington Street that had a bar, barmaids, spittoons—all the trappings of the saloon but two: the second *o* (he called it the Home *Salon*) and the booze. It did not last.

The progressives also exalted the methodology of science, under the meticulous supervision of a self-selected elite. The archtypical progressive agency for scientific inquiry was launched by the president of Columbia, the president of Harvard, the Episcopal bishop of Pennsylvania, and forty-seven other men whose good fortune could in most cases be attributed either to blue chips or silver spoons. The Committee of Fifty for the Investigation of the Liquor Problem bore a name as imposing as its membership and a mission worthy of both: countering the hegemony of misinformation and propaganda fostered by Mary Hunt's Scientific Temperance campaign—not in behalf of the wet cause, but with loyalty only to the facts.

The Committee of Fifty left two enduring legacies. First, it produced several academically sound studies of the physiological effects and the social consequences of alcohol. These were of course uncorrupted by Huntian mythology, but they were also free of liquor industry eyewash and aristocratic contempt for the dry point of view; in fact, after considering the findings of the committee's investigators, Charles W. Eliot, the Harvard president, forswore the moderate drinking in which he had long indulged and became a teetotaler.

The Fifty's other bequest was the blue-ribbon committee approach, which in its careful incrementalism confirmed literary critic Van Wyck Brooks's assertion that the progressives were "born middle-aged." Like the Fifty, these committees invariably were composed of a self-selected elite who investigated facts, discussed solutions, emerged into the public square with a lengthy report, and then attempted to institutionalize the solutions through legislative action.

Among these proliferating committees, two assumed the challenge of unpacking one of the most prominent, and most profoundly flawed, alcohol-related reforms of the era. New York State's comprehensive effort to regulate its saloons had been pushed through the legislature by John Raines, a formidable politician (one colleague called him "eagle-faced") from the Finger Lakes region. Among the provisions of the Raines Law, as it became known, was a Sunday closing rule aimed at the saloons—a particularly potent measure because Sunday, when workers controlled their own time, had always been the saloonkeeper's best day. Conveniently, the law exempted many of its advocates from its strictures: because the preferred weekend dining and drinking places of the well-to-do were hotel restaurants, Raines crafted the measure to exclude any establishment that served meals and had at least ten bedrooms. As in the south, it was prohibition for the other guy, not for me.

But Raines failed to anticipate the resourcefulness of his law's targets. Instead of being weakened, the measure strengthened the saloon business immeasurably. In Brooklyn alone, where there had been thirteen hotels before the Raines Law, there were soon more than two thousand—virtually all of them saloons whose back rooms or upstairs spaces had been subdivided by the addition of flimsy walls, made accommodating by the provision of threadbare cots, and turned profitable by the new business they immediately and inevitably attracted: prostitution. The requirement that these "hotels" offer food was solved with the invention of the "Raines sandwich," described by Jacob Riis as "consisting of two pieces of bread with a brick between . . . set out on the counter, in derision of the state law which forbids the serving of drinks without 'meals.'"

This did not sit well with the reformers. Soon the eradication of the saloon/hotels became the primary goal of a new body, the Committee of Fourteen.* This time, though, the Episcopal rectors, settlement house officials, Columbia professors, and other progressive notables on the committee (including the future secretary of war and secretary of state, Henry L. Stimson) welcomed three new allies to the committee. The newcomers hated the saloon just as much as the reformers, but in some ways they came from a different planet: all three were members of the Anti-Saloon League, including Howard Hyde Russell, its founder.

It was the beginning of a beautiful friendship. Progressive support for Prohibition was further cemented by prohibitionist support for the progressives' favorite causes. In 1906 the ASL endorsed the initiative and referendum movement, which would grant citizens the right to enact (or revoke) state laws by popular vote. When the progressive stalwart Hiram Johnson was elected governor of California in 1910, his running mate was A. J. Wallace, a Methodist minister who was president of the state branch of the ASL. Worker's compensation statutes made for especially tidy progressive/prohibitionist co-ventures, for once these most progressive of labor laws were enacted, large employers took a sudden interest in workplace safety and their employees' drinking habits. Hugh Fox of the United States Brewers' Association sent a bulletin to his members: "The passage in many states of Worker's Compensation laws, which placed the burden of proof on the employer instead of the employee," was a catastrophe for the beer industry. U.S. Steel, Pittsburgh Steel, and other industrial giants "have all declared against the saloon," Fox wrote, and some, like the Diamond Watch Company, announced they would fire any worker known to drink "intoxicating liquors."

These corporations were profoundly unprogressive institutions, of course, and they had other reasons to want to take drink away from their employees. (As Dr. Thomas Darlington, a former New York City health commissioner who had gone to work for the steel industry's trade association, explained in 1914, "the use of liquor has a direct bearing upon wages; if a man is addicted to alcohol he wants more money for the family.") But the politics of Prohibition had become so knotted with unlikely alliances, conflicting motives, and disingenuous arguments that a three-cushion shot (progressives to ASL to industrialists) around an issue like worker's com-

---

*This numerical trope did not die easily. Several years later, a dry-only Committee of Nineteen got to work, its labors in turn promoted by the Committee of Sixty, which had picked up the torch lit by that numerical whopper, the Committee of One Thousand—the group that would gather on the steps of the Capitol in 1913 and demand a constitutional amendment to remove alcoholic beverages from American life.

pensation didn't seem odd at all. Summarizing the Anti-Saloon League's single-issue focus, Wayne Wheeler said, "This one thing we do." But if the "one thing"—Prohibition—could only be achieved by making common cause with other groups whose goals could be made to line up with its own, the ASL could be very accommodating. Soon its march to victory was propelled forward by the three remaining groups in the dry coalition of convenience—the populists, the suffragists, and the nativists, who would push Prohibition into the Constitution with peculiar implements: a tax, a social revolution, and a war.

Chapter 4

"Open Fire on the Enemy"

H E DIDN'T DRINK IT to excess, but Alexander Hamilton cared enough for liquor that he considered it an all-but-essential component of a democracy. "There appears to be no article . . . which is an object of more equal consumption throughout the United States," he wrote in 1792. For a man trying to raise the money necessary to run a government, that made it the very model of a taxable item. If some people drank more than others, Hamilton argued, it was a matter of personal choice and had nothing to do with what part of the country they lived in—or, by extension, what social class they arose from, the number of people in their families, the phases of the moon, or anything, really, other than a taste for liquor. Hamilton even found social value in taxing alcohol: it might discourage people from drinking the stuff.

This was not the last time a government official considered using a liquor tax as a weapon. Richmond Hobson, the Alabama congressman who introduced what would become the Eighteenth Amendment in the House of Representatives in 1913, hinted at (or maybe threatened) a much less complicated alternative when he told the House that "Congress could make every State in the country dry" by simple majority. All it had to do was enact a law imposing such enormous taxes on alcohol that the trade would collapse under the weight of unbearably high prices. There were some in the Anti-Saloon League who approvingly called this "prohibition by indirection," and they might have been tempted to turn to Hamilton's example to justify the approach. But as Hamilton's real interest was revenue and the encouragement of abstinence only a peripheral virtue, the precedent he and Congress set with the Excise Act of 1791 did not put the ASL's "indirectionists" on the side of history.

Hamilton's Excise Act instead triggered two different reactions, one temporary and one that would be embedded in the fabric of the Republic:

53

the rye farmers of western Pennsylvania launched the Whiskey Rebellion of 1794, and generations of federal officials became transfixed by the prospect of tax revenue corked inside every bottle of alcohol. The rebellion was to some degree the inevitable reaction to an alcohol tax, for whiskey was not simply a commercial product to Pennsylvanians. It also served as a medium of exchange and as a delivery system, just as it later would for the corn farmers of Kentucky and Tennessee. A man had a choice: he could transport a wagonload of grain across the Alleghenies, or he could reduce the wagonload to a few convenient, compact, rot-resistant, and highly profitable jugs of whiskey. To the rye farmers of the Monongahela Valley, liquor was a portable cash crop.

George Washington was initially reluctant to send the militia to suppress the Pennsylvania rebels. He worried that critics would say, "We now see for what purpose an army was raised." In fact the opposite was true—without a tax on alcohol, it would have been all but impossible for the United States to maintain an army. After lapsing in 1802, the alcohol excise was reimposed under James Madison to pay for the War of 1812, suspended in 1817, and then brought back by Abraham Lincoln in 1862 to finance the Civil War.

This time the tax did not fade away when the war ended, for it had become addictive. (It had also spawned an underground, tax-free trade in an illegal substance that would forever be known as moonshine, and a collection apparatus staffed by men from the Bureau of Internal Revenue who would forever be known as revenuers.) For most of the next thirty years the impost on alcohol annually provided at least 20 percent of all federal revenue, and in some years more than 40 percent. By the time the excise was doubled to cover the cost of the Spanish-American War, the brewers had finally realized that the tax they had once so strongly opposed might be their salvation, and they patriotically (and shamelessly) declared that they had financed 40 percent of the war's cost. A decade later they even rewrote their own history, claiming that the United States Brewers' Association had been founded in 1862 to "assist the government" in devising an alcohol tax that would "ensur[e] safe and easy collection and the prevention of fraud." But the only fraud was the brewers' own: they had in fact formed the USBA specifically to *oppose* the excise tax.

By 1910 the federal government was drawing more than $200 million a year from the bottle and the keg—71 percent of all internal revenue, and more than 30 percent of federal revenue overall. Only external revenue—the tariff—provided a larger share of the federal budget, and by the end of the first decade of the twentieth century the tariff's continuation was the most intensely debated issue in American public life. It would be hard enough to fund the cost of government without the tariff and impossible without a liquor tax. Given that you wouldn't collect much revenue from a liquor tax in a nation where there was no liquor, this might have seemed an insurmountable problem for the Prohibition movement. Unless, that is, you could weld the drive for Prohibition to the campaign for another reform, the creation of a tax on incomes.

No one was better equipped to yoke these two causes together than William Jennings Bryan, the dominant leader of the Democratic Party from 1896 until the election of Woodrow Wilson in 1912. Bryan was a devoutly religious man, a passionately engaged crusader for whatever issue he championed. By his own description he was "clad in the armor of a righteous cause." His prominent jaw might have been the prow of a ship steaming toward glory; his large bald dome shone like a beacon when, glistening with sweat, he reached his oratorical heights. His lifelong avoidance of alcohol may have been the only expression of moderation in his very large life. A reporter who traveled with him during the 1900 presidential campaign claimed Bryan ate six meals a day and that he once saw him consume in one breakfast a whole cantaloupe, two quail, a helping of Virginia ham, six eggs, two plates of pancakes in butter, and "many cups of coffee, fried potatoes, and side dishes of various kinds before he left the table 'quite refreshed' and ready to begin a day's campaigning."

Were it not for his deplorable views on race, Bryan was what a later generation might have called a Faith-Based Liberal. But he did not want for capitalized epithets in his own time. When he first entered Nebraska politics, supporters called him the Boy Orator of the Platte. To the devoted admirers who backed him in his three failed presidential campaigns he was the Peerless Leader, and after that (and most famously) the Great Commoner. Biographers who understood the importance of religion in Bryan's life called their books *Defender of the Faith* and *A Godly Hero*. Opponents who understood this just as well coined less complimentary nicknames. To H. L. Mencken, Bryan was the Fundamentalist Pope, and to Clarence Darrow, his opponent in the Scopes Monkey Trial of 1925, he was the Idol of All Morondom.

Bryan was easy to lampoon, especially in the 1920s, after most of his other political battles had ended and he had poured his public energy into the promotion of biblical inerrancy (his favored admonition to the Darwinians: "It is better to trust in the Rock of Ages than to know the age of rocks"). But between 1913 and 1919, in the greatest burst of constitutional activity since the Bill of Rights, amendments establishing the income tax, direct election of senators, Prohibition, and woman suffrage were engraved into the nation's organic law. Bryan was in the forefront of the campaign for each.

After Bryan called on Edward VII in 1906, the king said that his visitor was "agreeable and intelligent but a little gaseous, you know." Yet it was precisely this spacious eloquence that had propelled Bryan to the forefront of public consciousness. The rhetorical flourish that established his historical reputation was his famous "Cross of Gold" speech at the 1896 Democratic convention, an oration so stirring it won the thirty-six-year-old ex-congressman his party's presidential nomination. But Bryan had first come to national attention three years earlier. In his second (and last) term in the House as a little-known member from Nebraska, he had dedicated his oratorical power to the successful effort to insert a provision for a tax on incomes into a pending tariff bill. He could not have found a more effective way of capturing the energy of the boiling populist movement of the 1890s had he seized the bankers and industrialists of the Northeast by the throat and proceeded to strangle them. Across the South and the West, the outrage at "the money power" focused on the tariff. The despised impost on imported goods and materials kept the price of necessities artificially high while simultaneously elevating the profits of eastern industrialists and financiers. An income tax would exact several pounds of flesh from the plutocrats—in Bryan's plan, only the very wealthy would be subjected to it—and simultaneously sabotage one of the strongest arguments for maintaining the tariff.

But in 1895 the Supreme Court declared the income tax unconstitutional. Economist E. R. A. Seligman called it "the Dred Scott decision of government revenue." Like any unpopular Supreme Court decision on an issue of intense debate, this one led the losing side to turn controversy into crusade. For the next decade and a half the income tax became the longed-for sword that Bryan's supporters and other advocates of income redistribution hoped would slay the money power. So consuming was the passion among its supporters from the South and West that for some it took on the color of monomania. Biographer Harold B. Hinton wrote that Representative Cordell Hull of Tennessee, who was known as the "father of the income tax" two decades before he became Franklin Roosevelt's long-serving secretary of state, felt about the tax "as Sir Galahad had felt about the holy grail." When the income tax was finally legalized, it was the industrialized East that yielded before it: 44 percent of the revenue collected came from New York State alone. It was not a coincidence that eight of the first nine legislatures to have ratified the amendment (starting with Alabama, where the vote was unanimous in both houses) were in southern or border states.

For at least two elements of the Prohibition army the struggle for an income tax was an appealing cause, irrespective of the alcohol question. For the progressives, it was an obvious way to enhance the power and effectiveness of government. For many of the racially motivated prohibitionists of the South, whose populist anger was monochromatic but nonetheless real, it was a way to avenge Reconstruction by striking back at the economic and political imperialists of the North.

And to those in the dry movement who understood political and governmental reality, imposition of an income tax was also an absolutely necessary step if they were going to break the federal addiction to the alcohol excise tax. This had been obvious to the leadership of the WCTU as early as 1883, when the editors of the organization's official organ, *The Union Signal,* coyly asked their readers, "How, then, will [we] support the government" if the sale of liquor is prohibited? The editors had a ready answer for their own question: an income tax, they wrote, was "the most just and equable arrangement ever made for the equalization of governmental burdens." In 1895 the Prohibition Party recognized that "the [excise] tax receipt . . . is a pledge on the part of the State to defend and foster the thing taxed." Wanting to neither defend nor foster, the party soon nailed an income tax plank to its platform. Leaders of the Anti-Saloon League were well aware of what one called the "alleged 'loss of revenue' argument." By the time Congress voted to approve a constitutional amendment authorizing income tax, the antiliquor caucus and the protax caucus were remarkably congruent. Among the most ardent congressional supporters of the tax were the House and Senate sponsors of the Eighteenth Amendment, Richmond Hobson of Alabama and Morris Sheppard of Texas; Senator Wesley L. Jones of Washington, who would later take credit for the most punitive enforcement code enacted during the entire reign of constitutional Prohibition; and, from Yellow Medicine County, Minnesota, a lugubrious small-town lawyer named Andrew J. Volstead.

The fortunate intersection of the dry forces and the tax forces also enabled leaders of the tax campaign, foremost among them Cordell Hull, to develop a reciprocal fondness for the ASL's goals. Hull was the son of a farmer who also operated a whiskey still. In 1908 he stayed away from Tennessee during the explosive debate over state Prohibition that had been detonated by the Levy's gin affair. Although he never spoke publicly on the liquor issue, Hull consistently voted dry in Congress, and as late as 1932, when the remaining national support for Prohibition could have been measured in millimeters, he was among the leaders of a plainly hopeless effort to keep a Repeal plank out of the Democratic Party platform. The ASL backed him throughout his career.

THE ANTI-SALOON LEAGUE couldn't have asked for a better year than the one it enjoyed in 1913. The fact that a liquor control law failed miserably in the New York State senate in January was of so little consequence that two months later the league's official publication, *The American Issue*, could nonetheless proudly honor the bill's thwarted sponsor, thirty-one-year-old Franklin Delano Roosevelt, for his loyalty to their cause. Roosevelt was about to join the Wilson administration as assistant secretary of the navy; presumably Secretary Josephus Daniels, who would soon decree the U.S. Navy, all its bases, and all its ships alcohol-free, was pleased to have at his side this promising young man whom the ASL hailed as "an advocate of Christian patriotism." A moderate dryness was not the young Roosevelt's only qualification for the mantle of Christian rectitude; he also supported a ban on Sunday baseball.

Of far greater moment to the ASL were two events that revolutionized its strategy, which for years had focused on state-by-state passage of Prohibition laws. The congressional override of William Howard Taft's veto of the Webb-Kenyon Act demonstrated that the league's reach had become national. Webb-Kenyon was a measure outlawing the importation of alcoholic beverages into a dry state. The stunning 246–95 override vote in the House of Representatives showed not just the power of the anti-liquor forces, but also how broadly representative they had become.

Webb-Kenyon was followed by enactment of the income tax that the Sixteenth Amendment had authorized. As Congress prepared to take up the matter, the Anti-Saloon League could at last consider moving past its piecemeal approach. On April 22 the ASL executive committee revealed a new and vastly more ambitious policy. "The chief cry against national prohibition," the statement said, "has been that the government must have the revenue." Now, though, "The adoption of the Income Tax Amendment to the Federal Constitution furnishes an answer to the revenue problem." The time had come for all foes of alcohol to focus on the ASL's new goal. "National prohibition," the committee said, "can be secured through the adoption of a Constitutional Amendment."

To the varied forces of the dry movement this was a bolt of lightning both shocking and illuminating. Ahead of them the ASL and its allies saw a future uncluttered by tax issues or other traps; behind them they felt a supporting wind that had been gaining strength for years. At the printing plant the league had opened in 1909 on land donated by the town of Westerville, twelve miles from Columbus, eight presses ran constantly, disgorging more than forty tons of prohibitionist propaganda each month. (Ever mindful of electoral arithmetic, Wayne Wheeler made sure the plant was a union shop.) A new cadre of leaders, most of them trained in the Ohio branch of the league—thirty-four of forty-eight state superintendents began their ASL careers there—had spread across the country, armed for battle with the weapons they had been trained to use in their home state.

The policy statement announcing the ASL's commitment to the amendment strategy was entitled "The Next and Final Step." But it was a step that could not succeed without extracting Wheeler from his state superintendency in Ohio and sending him to Washington. Although this didn't happen formally until 1916, Wheeler's influence in the highest councils of the ASL began with the decision to push for a Prohibition amendment. Shuttling between Columbus and the ASL's Washington office, where the league's lobbyists were poised like raptors on the third floor of the Bliss Building, directly across the street from the Capitol, Wheeler displayed the strategic savvy and the unstoppable drive that would soon see him replace the ASL's legislative superintendent, Edwin Dinwiddie. John W. Davis, who was Wilson's solicitor general (and in 1924 would be the Democrats' presidential candidate), called Dinwiddie a "goggle-eyed, weasel-faced lobbyist." More appropriate (and undeniably accurate) epithets would eventually accrue to Wayne Wheeler—for vivid instance, when the editors of the *New York World* proclaimed him "the legislative bully before whom the Senate of the United States sits up and begs."

By the time Wheeler stepped out onto the national stage he had already mastered his legislative parlor tricks. When Lincoln Steffens had visited Columbus several years earlier, Wheeler had explained his tactics to the great muckraker. "I do it the way the bosses do it, with minorities," Wheeler said. By delivering his voters to one candidate or another in a close race, he could control an election: "We'll vote against all the men in office who won't support our bills. We'll vote for candidates who will promise to." Wheeler, who had greeted Steffens amiably—as "a fellow reformer," Steffens recalled—now "hissed his shrewd, mad answer" to those politicians who would betray ASL voters. "They'll break their promise. Sure. Next time, we'll break them. . . . We are teaching these crooks that breaking promises to us is surer punishment than going back on their bosses, and some day they will learn that all over the United States—and we'll have national prohibition."

With the ASL's decision to embark on the "next and final step," Wheeler's skill at manipulating majorities through the power of a minority became yet more crucial. The referendum and initiative movement, which drys had supported before they had fully grasped how to control legislatures, turned out to be potentially ruinous to the ASL. When two candidates opposing each other in a popular election could be differentiated by isolating one issue out of many, Wheeler's minority could carry the day; a candidate with, say, the support of 45 percent of the electorate could win with the added votes of the ASL bloc. But when voters were offered a simple yes-or-no, dry-or-wet choice on a ballot measure, a minority was only a minority. In a statewide popular vote on a dry law, wrote historian Jack S. Blocker Jr., the ASL "wielded no power greater than its actual numbers"; in legislative elections, the power of Wheeler's minority could be measured in multiples. A constitutional amendment required legislative majorities in thirty-six states, as well as the two-thirds majorities required in both houses of Congress. Achieving these numbers required the talents of Wayne Wheeler.

At the league's annual convention in Columbus in November 1913, the public campaign for the amendment was launched with a decision to petition Congress formally the following month. Addressing the delegates, Wheeler sounded more like the clergymen who ran the ASL than the political operative who would turn their faith into law. "As Moses said to the children of Israel that they should go forward," he told the zealous assembly, "just so the time has come for the moral forces of this great nation to march on against the last bulwarks of the enemy.

"I do not know how you may feel about this," he concluded, "but I would rather die than run from such a conflict."

LIFTED BY LAW, by numbers, and by the buoyant tide of history, the amassed forces of the Anti-Saloon League descended on Washington on December 10, 1913. In the preceding ten months the state legislatures, in ratifying the income tax amendment, had liberated the Prohibition movement from the burden of the revenue problem. Congress, with the Webb-Kenyon override, had demonstrated its willingness to accept—or perhaps its fear of disobeying—the ASL's commands. The league had even been granted an entirely fortuitous gift to its publicity efforts when a useful, if risible, document fell into its hands: a letter on the stationery of the Kentucky Distillers' & Distributing Company addressed to the Keeley Institute in Dwight, Illinois. Keeley's was the leading drying-out sanatorium of its age, where alcoholics were given four injections of gold chloride daily to suppress "the irresistible craving of nerve cells for alcohol." The distilling company's letter proclaimed, "Our customers are your prospective patients," and offered Keeley's the chance to buy 40,000 names for $400. The only revelation that might have been worse for the wets was the statement made by a liquor dealer at an industry meeting the year before: "We must create the appetite for liquor in the growing boys. . . . Nickels expended in treats to boys now will return in dollars to your tills after the appetite has been formed."

Wet newspapers would later contest the genuineness of the distillers' letter, and the authenticity of the liquor dealer's grotesque argument would not be confirmed until many years later. But no one could challenge the impact of the spectacle that unfolded in Washington when the ASL presented its petition. Washington in the late autumn of 1913 was filled with mendicants seeking the charity of Congress. Two weeks after a national meeting of suffragists was convened in the capital (the *Washington Post* had headlined its front-page story "Fair Cohorts Meet"), and just two days after the International Antivivisection and Animal Protection Congress was gaveled to order (featured speaker: William Jennings Bryan), Washington was occupied by the dry armies. From one mustering point fifty young girls dressed in white led a long column of women from the WCTU; from another marched the men of the ASL, representing all forty-eight states. After the two parades merged on the steps of the Capitol they presented a petition demanding a constitutional amendment to the men who would introduce it in their respective chambers: in the House the flamboyant Richmond Hobson of Alabama, and in the upper chamber Morris Sheppard of Texas, a Shakespearean scholar who was one of the Senate's leading progressives. Thousands of bystanders had left the city's sidewalks to follow the two parades to the Capitol. Apart from presidential inaugurations, Capitol guards told reporters, it was the largest crowd ever to gather on the building's steps. It may have been the only one to break out into a full-throated "Onward, Christian Soldiers." Afterward, the ASL leadership gathered across the street in the Bliss Building in "a council of war" to establish the order of battle. As Wheeler would remember it years later, their mission was simple: "Open fire on the enemy."

◆　　◆　　◆

THE MERGED CHORUS of male and female Christian soldiers singing on the steps of the Capitol that December day was an expression of the drys' most valuable alliance. The adoption of the income tax amendment and subsequent passage of the Revenue Act of 1913 may have confirmed the virtue of tacit collaboration with other interest groups, but the ASL's partnership with women who backed a suffrage amendment proved the value of a far more active embrace. The social revolution that was the suffrage movement would bring the Prohibition movement to the brink of success.

A congressional resolution calling for a Prohibition amendment to the Constitution had been introduced in every Congress since 1876, but none had ever emerged from committee. No version of the universal suffrage amendment had gotten as far as floor debate since 1890. Back then, the two measures had occasionally been linked in the holy advocacy of politicians who perceived both as expressions of moral virtue—for instance, thirty-year-old William Jennings Bryan, running in his first campaign for public office. But in the twenty-four years leading up to the congressional session of 1914, when both measures were reported out of committee on the same day, they had become welded to each other, not because of any moral congruence, but because of an expedient relativism that might have made a purist like Bryan wince.

Among the more forthright exponents of this relativistic connection was one of America's least likely advocates of Prohibition, the novelist Jack London, who once said that the fact he had lived to be twenty-one was a miracle. An early life of crime had something to do with London's self-appraisal, but so did the dangerous charms of liquor. "Alcohol was an acquired taste," he wrote in 1913, looking back. "It had been painfully acquired." H. L. Mencken saw virtue in this. "London, sober, would have written nothing worth reading," Mencken told Upton Sinclair eight years after London's death. "Alcohol made him."

That was Mencken being Mencken; in truth, it's hard to imagine that one man, even one as protean as London, could both drink to excess and write to excess (twenty-one novels, three story collections, three memoirs, one play, and uncounted essays and occasional pieces—all in the space of barely fifteen years). You also have to consider the dramatis personae in the Sinclair-Mencken exchange: the former was so dry he was Saharan, while the latter, who liked to call himself "ombibulous," was the single most effusive publicist for booze the Republic has ever seen. (Mencken once bragged that "I drink every known alcoholic drink and enjoy them all.") But there's no question that London, who had a friendly Oakland bartender ship premixed cocktails in bulk to his Sonoma County ranch, drank enough to qualify him to write a book about booze.

John Barleycorn: Alcoholic Memoirs opens with a description of London's horseback trip into town from his ranch to cast his vote on a California woman suffrage proposition in 1911. "Because of the warmth of the day I had had several drinks before casting my ballot, and divers drinks after casting it," London wrote. "Then I had ridden up through the vine-clad hills and rolling pastures of the ranch, and arrived at the farm-house in time for another drink and supper." London had opposed women's right to vote years earlier, and though he had lately acknowledged that its coming was inevitable, he had shown no enthusiasm for it. But now, he told his wife, he had found an excellent reason to cast his ballot for suffrage. London believed that "the moment women get the vote in any community, the first thing they proceed to do is close the saloons"—and, therefore, "when no one else drinks and when no drink is obtainable," he would finally be able to stop drinking. London wanted the suffragists to vote him into sobriety.

London's insight into the dry campaign's dependence on the suffrage movement was incontrovertible. Not only had the suffrage movement found its most effective generals among women who had first developed their political skills in the temperance ranks; additionally, thousands of women in the WCTU had come to realize that no antialcohol weapon could be as potent as the franchise. What had changed by the time London cast his wishfully opportunistic suffrage vote was the nature of the connection between the drys and the suffragists: comfortable affinity had been transformed into absolute interdependence.

This was not a relationship easily arrived at. Like the leaders of the Anti-Saloon League, most prominent suffragists perceived that their movement's power resided in undiluted devotion to one cause. "My personal belief as to prohibition, pro or con, is nobody's business but my own," Susan B. Anthony wrote to the Oregon suffragist Abigail Scott Duniway in 1896. She was "glad to see women awakened from their apathy" by the liquor wars, but she had chosen by this point in her career to stick to the position she had adopted on all political issues except the one to which she had dedicated herself. Until she was granted the vote, Anthony said, she would not offer her opinion on any other public question.

But it wasn't hard to guess Anthony's position—after all, she had entered political life as a temperance worker, and her link to the Prohibition cause was periodically reinforced by fruitful collaboration with the WCTU. Anthony boldly introduced Frances Willard to a congressional committee in 1888 as "the commander-in-chief of an army of 250,000 women," and "Do Everything" Willard, whose thirst for suffrage was almost as strong as her loathing for alcohol, provided Anthony a forum at the WCTU's national conventions. But Anthony was seventy-six when she sent her steely letter to Abigail Duniway, and a constitutional amendment granting women the vote remained some distance beyond the horizon. She had chosen to expend her remaining energies on suffrage alone.

Yet even a commitment like Anthony's could yield to urgent opportunism. By 1899, as the ASL prepared for its annual convention in Des Moines, her resolve had weakened. "I wish to ask a great favor," she wrote to the ASL's secretary, James L. Erwin. Would the league consider adopting a resolution "declaring for the enfranchisement of women"? Noting that drys were still a minority in the body politic, she made the point that Jack London would later offer as common wisdom. "It must be evident to every logical mind that what is needed is an additional balance of power . . . sure to throw itself into the scale against the saloon," Anthony told Erwin. This led to her obvious conclusion: "The only hope of the Anti-Saloon League's success lies in putting the ballot into the hands of women."

The brewers certainly knew the connection. The great suffragist's thoughts, even her language, echoed a resolution the United States Brewers' Association had adopted several years earlier. The resolution declared, "When woman has the ballot, she will vote solid for prohibition." Consequently, the USBA made it official policy to oppose woman suffrage "everywhere and always," a matter of conviction so deeply rooted it could only have been motivated by financial self-interest. It was no different for the distillers. In 1912, at a convention of the National Retail Liquor Dealers' Association, the industry's position was made clear when the organization's president issued this call to arms: "Gentlemen, we need fear the Woman's Christian Temperance Union and the ballot in the hands of women; therefore, gentlemen, fight woman suffrage!"

The brewers' antisuffrage position was fortified by their millions of dollars. Their reach into the streets and alleyways of many cities was further lengthened by a previously unexampled instance of labor-management amity, as self-interest placed tens of thousands of brewery employees (not to mention barrel makers and wagon drivers and ice haulers and scores of other working legions) at the ready for the next antisuffrage rally or referendum. But, even more, the cravenness of the brewers' campaign was betrayed by their wish to hide it from public view. In 1906 a state suffrage amendment in Oregon was defeated when the brewers secretly enlisted Oregon's saloonkeepers and hoteliers in an elaborate get-out-the-vote operation. Secrecy also prevailed when the USBA paid the nationally known suffragist Phoebe Couzins to repudiate her previous position and mount an ostensibly independent campaign as an antisuffrage speaker and writer. (Couzins explained her shocking switch with bland opacity: "Observations made during my struggle to get the privilege of the ballot for my sex convinced me I was wrong.") Adolphus Busch, who had personally promised Couzins a lifetime annuity on top of her monthly stipend from the USBA, told a colleague, "if ever should it become known that she is in the pay of the brewers . . . all of her work would be in vain."

Of all the brewers' secret efforts against suffrage, a campaign that began in Texas and then went national may have been the most brazen. Distributing scores of free articles to hundreds of rural newspapers through a false front called the Farmers' Educational and Cooperative Union, the brewers' publicists-in-disguise promised country editors that the articles would provide a "discussion of both sides of important questions confronting the farmers of this nation." What they actually supplied, without rebuttal, was the bogus testimony of bogus farmers, who offered such sentiments as "God pity our country when the handshake of the politician is more gratifying to woman's heart than the patter of children's feet." Another favored form was the rhetorical puzzler that required no answer: "Is it not sufficient political achievement for woman that future rulers nurse at her breast, laugh in her arms and kneel at her feet?"

Apparently not. With a common enemy as bellicose, as deceitful, and as powerful as the brewers, the hardening of the prohibition-suffrage alliance was inevitable. Did it matter that the success of the Prohibition movement was not foremost in Susan B. Anthony's constellation of desire? No more than the fact that voting rights for women was not the passionate ideal of ASL superintendent Purley A. Baker, who sidestepped the league's single-issue policy in 1911 to declare himself in favor of suffrage, which he called "the antidote" to the efforts of the beer and liquor interests. (It was this sort of elasticity that won for Baker the nickname the wets hung on him: Purely A. Faker.) When the brewers' Texas campaign was uncovered, it was the ASL's formidable propaganda machine that brought it wide public attention. Eventually, in 1916, the Anti-Saloon League would formally endorse woman suffrage—the only time in its history it violated its single-issue pledge.

The brewers' tactics had been self-defeating almost to the point of idiocy. The more they fought female suffrage, the more they guaranteed the antipathy of millions of American women, a large segment of whom might otherwise have been opposed to, or at least neutral on, Prohibition. And when the tide finally began to race in the direction of suffrage, women who had endured decades of unabated and frequently dishonest assault from the brewers, the distillers, and their allies in the hotel, restaurant, and tobacco industries carried Prohibition along with them.

"The fanatical and misinformed women," as Adolphus Busch called them, would rout the brewers and their allies with stunning efficiency. In one three-year stretch in the 1910s, seven western states adopted Prohibition—all of them states where women had achieved the vote. Michigan's entrance into the Prohibition column was helped along by the revelation that the Macomb County Liquor Dealers' Association had been financing the state's antisuffrage forces. Jeannette Rankin of Montana, the first woman member of Congress, felt compelled to endorse the Prohibition cause in her state because of "political exigency." In 1918, when Texas women were granted the right to vote in the state's Democratic primary, they supported the dry candidate over the wet ex-governor James E. "Pa" Ferguson by a ten-to-one margin.

As clueless about what had happened as the brewers who had supported him, the defeated Ferguson called the women's votes "illegal." But those votes were indeed legal, they were growing, and by the end of the decade both suffrage and Prohibition would enter the Constitution virtually as brothers. Or, it might have been said, sisters.

Chapter 5

Triumphant Failure

ANY YEARS AFTER the most glorious day in her husband's political career, Grizelda Hull Hobson received a letter from one of his old friends from the U.S. Naval Academy Class of 1889. The friend, a retired admiral, recalled something that Richmond Hobson had said as a freshman at Annapolis, a sentence that "became almost a classic at the Academy." Unwilling to abide the verbal hazing hurled at every plebe, Hobson confronted a midshipman who had been tormenting him. "Sir," he declared, "I do not desire nor will I tolerate your scurrilous contumely."

Coming from most sixteen-year-olds, Hobson's baroque rhetoric would have been as preposterous as it was precocious. Coming from Hobson, it was both those things, but it was also an augury of the man he would become—bold, eloquent, offended by impropriety, and a bit mad. The first three, at least, were qualities that would enhance his huge importance to the Prohibition movement. So were the calluses he developed to repel the censure of others. Not long after the encounter with his contumacious tormentor, Hobson's meticulous observance of regulations prompted him to report his classmates' slightest violations to academy authorities. His fellow midshipmen responded by applying a less official but equally rigorous code of conduct—the young Alabaman was placed "in Coventry," and with the single exception of one classmate, no one spoke to him for two years. Hobson barely flinched. As an admirer put it, he "got along without their society so well that he saw no reason for resuming it."

Hobson would later celebrate his ostracism in his bestselling gosh-and-gee-whiz novel for boys, *Buck Jones at Annapolis*. Its hero just happened to be an upright and courageous son of the South who not only suffers his own term in Coventry ("the most terrible punishment possible on this earth") but, like Hobson, graduates first in his class. Of course it was a bestseller: by the time *Buck* was published, in 1907, Hobson had been a national figure for nearly a decade. He had won his renown as a Spanish-American War hero, for his bravery while commanding a failed mission aboard the USS *Merrimac* in Cuba; on emerging from a Spanish prison, he then advanced it with a spasm of self-promotion that anticipated the publicity rituals of a latter age.

Hobson began his postrelease lecture tour in front of a sold-out audience at the Metropolitan Opera. He wrote a four-part series about his war experience in *Century* magazine. He allowed a Boston sheet-music publisher to issue "Hobson of the Merrimac: Waltzes for Piano"; its cover featured a photograph of the handsome hero in three-quarter profile—serious of mien, erect of posture, the "smouldering fierceness of his eyes" (if only the printer had been able to replicate their steely blue!) focused slightly to his left, fixed on . . . well, perhaps on the very near future. As he traveled across the country to San Francisco, where he would embark for his next naval posting in the Far East, a newspaper report noted that he had kissed a young woman at one of his appearances. Within days the nation's hero-hungry press had decided that Hobson's osculatory skill matched his military prowess, and sold thousands of newspapers in celebration of it. Flocks of women lined up on depot platforms to kiss him—163 in Chicago, 419 in Kansas City, 350 more in Topeka. By the time he got to Denver, he had had enough. "When the kissing is fast and furious it sometimes gets just a little tiresome," he told a reporter. "It sometimes happens that when some ancient lips are presented I would fain pass them by unkissed, but when I start in I have to take it as it comes. There is no selecting; everything goes."

"Fain pass them by"? This was of a piece with "contumely" and various other Hobsonisms that even in the early 1900s veered toward the archaic. But the particularity of his language, the righteous fire of his delivery, and preparation that would have done credit to a surgeon—he timed his speeches precisely to the second—made him an irresistible orator. After returning from the Far East (where he endured another round of Coventry, this one administered by officers resentful of his celebrity), he went home to Alabama and Magnolia Grove, the magnificent family plantation ninety miles southwest of Birmingham, and began a life in politics.

Hobson entered the House of Representatives in 1906 and, like so many other drys, almost immediately lined up with the progressives. He opposed the tariff, sought to break up industrial trusts, introduced a resolution calling for the abolition of the Electoral College, and supported both the income tax and woman suffrage.* He was also the House's leading advocate of a strong navy, and with uncanny foresight predicted in 1911 that Japan would one day attack the Pacific fleet. His defining issue, the one that made him one of the most popular platform speakers of the day, was the elimination of the trade in alcoholic beverages. But the one that would eventually determine the arc of his political career was, for a southern politician in the early twentieth century, a fairly enlightened position on race.

Hobson's racial attitudes intersected with his military allegiance. He introduced one bill that would have made it illegal in the District of Columbia to discriminate against any uniformed member of the armed forces, white or black, and another to open Annapolis and West Point to students from the Philippines and Puerto Rico, after both had become U.S. colonies. These positions were surprising to many of his southern colleagues, but not nearly as much as Hobson's public criticism of the dishonorable discharges Theodore Roosevelt meted out to the members of an all-black regiment that had been implicated on spurious charges in the Brownsville Affair of 1906.** Rising on the floor of the House despite the warnings of friends, Hobson addressed the plight of the 167 black soldiers, forever barred from military or civil service. "I saw black men carry our flag on Santiago Hill," he declared. "I have seen them at Manila. A black man took my father, wounded, from the field of Chancellorsville." Invoking a paternalism that is discomfiting to modern sensibilities, he spoke of the former slaves who had stayed at Magnolia Grove to care for his mother and grandmother. He also said that because "the white man is supreme in this country," it was the white man's responsibility to "give absolute justice to the black man." Then Hobson concluded with words that, for an Alabama Democrat in 1909, would have been no less remarkable had they advocated immediate and complete integration. "We are

---

*Not that he was particularly enlightened about women in general: Hobson thought that any woman who experienced carnal desire was a "sex pervert," and attributed promiscuity to the effects of alcohol. He wasn't crazy about sexual urges in men, either, but accepted their evolutionary necessity.

**On August 13, 1906, two white men were shot, one fatally, in Brownsville, Texas. Soldiers in the all-black 25th U.S. infantry regiment, billeted in nearby Fort Brown, were held responsible, despite the lack of reliable incriminating evidence and the existence of much that was exculpatory. The soldiers, unable to tell investigators who might have been responsible for the shootings, were ordered dishonorably discharged by President Roosevelt, without trial, for their putative failure to cooperate. In 1972 Richard M. Nixon ordered honorable discharges entered into the military records of all of the accused men.

standing here on the field of eternal justice," he said, "where all men are the same."

He would pay for it. Five years later, in an effort to move up to a vacant Senate seat, Hobson faced off in the Democratic primary against his House colleague Oscar W. Underwood, who opposed Prohibition on the grounds that it was an infringement of states' rights. Underwood won the backing of the state's liquor dealers and didn't bother to hide his wetness from the voters. This wasn't because he believed Alabama had suddenly gone moist, but because he had a more effective weapon. As much as white Alabamans cared about the liquor question, they cared more about the race issue.

Hobson was hardly a race liberal. In his celebrated and endlessly repeated platform oration, "Alcohol, the Great Destroyer," which he delivered on the floor of the House for the first time in 1911, he had even warned that liquor could turn black men into cannibals. But Underwood and his supporters used Hobson's advocacy for the Brownsville soldiers, and his other slightly moderate views on blacks in the military, like a bludgeon. They attacked Hobson as "the only Southerner in Congress to stab his people on the great issue" and insisted that his positions would lead inexorably to "the national enfranchisement of the negro." Underwood's campaign literature reached its rhetorical pinnacle, or nadir, on the service academy issue. Admitting Filipinos—whom campaign literature characterized as "negroes, negritos, and negorillas"—to West Point or Annapolis would mean "exact social equality! In the same room! At the same table with our boys!"

On primary day, race trumped booze: Underwood overwhelmed Hobson, taking 62 percent of the vote. This was just four months after Hobson had greeted the marching members of the ASL and the WCTU on the Capitol steps on the day he formally introduced his constitutional amendment. After his defeat the Hobson Amendment, as it became known, lay untouched in the Judiciary Committee, a grenade that might explode on contact with any politician whose district was not overwhelmingly wet or dry—in other words, the sort of district for which the tactics of the ASL had been devised. And by all conventional measurements, the legislative potency of the amendment's lame-duck sponsor was approaching zero.

IN THE HOUSE of Representatives on December 22, 1914, the day Hobson would lead the debate on his resolution for a constitutional amendment, Speaker Champ Clark of Missouri gaveled the House to order with an unusual admonition: "There are going to be ten mortal hours of speech making here today, and maybe more," Clark announced. "And some of it, perhaps, will be rather lively, and the chair asks members to help keep order, and the people in the galleries, too." This was understandable: the galleries were jammed with battalions of pilgrims, most of them women, who occupied every seat and crowded every aisle. What appeared to be a large banner suspended from the railing of the south gallery was in fact a petition, and if any of the men slowly filing into the House chamber had been able to get close to it, they would have seen that the twelve thousand signatures on the enormous document were not those of individuals, but of organizations.

This should not suggest that getting the measure to this point—an actual floor debate, with an actual vote to follow—had been anything but a murderously difficult task. The months it had taken to extract the Prohibition resolution from the fearful members of the Judiciary Committee were an indication of Hobson's weakened position. His legislative hopes to a large degree rested in the hands of the majority leader, who shared with the Speaker responsibility for scheduling floor debates and votes. The leader happened to be the wet Oscar Underwood, the man who had sent Hobson tumbling toward retirement.

But Hobson was not without resources. He knew that less than three weeks earlier, Speaker Clark had been delivering a speech to the Detroit Board of Commerce when his hosts had felt it necessary to turn off the lights and cut him short. Clark was so drunk he had lapsed into incoherence, his words slurred, his gestures unsteady. The *New York Times* described the event with a respectful delicacy: "Mr. Clark began his address but faltered and was plainly seen to be indisposed." Hobson was similarly respectful, but for different reasons. When news of Clark's indiscretion reached him, Hobson immediately sent out a flight of telegrams to his dry allies. He asked them to "omit all references to Speaker Clark's experience in Detroit" in their speechmaking and other publicity efforts. He said this was "in accord with Christian principles," but he added that discretion "may have an important bearing upon the Speaker's future relations with our cause. I regard this as very important." Blackmail usually is.

The "ten mortal hours of speech making" that Clark decreed on December 22 accommodated the remarks of more than fifty members of the House. They were not temperate in their comments. W. W. Rucker of Missouri shouted in behalf of Hobson's resolution that it was time to "quit this degeneration of mankind!" Minority leader James Mann of Illinois, speaking against, warned that Prohibition would bring about "an army of government spies, with every township in the country under surveillance."

Martin A. Morrison of Indiana, who was somewhere in between, said the day should be called "the Slaughter of the Innocents," for how they voted would end the political careers, he estimated, of more than a hundred of his colleagues.

All day long members came and went, to get dinner or to leaf grimly through the stacks of cards, letters, and telegrams piling in drifts in their offices. On the House floor, pages raced back and forth. Some brought more telegrams; some delivered fistfuls of the pink postcards that had been distributed in the hundreds of thousands by Prohibition activists, each bearing the picture of an innocent (and presumably vulnerable) child. Always Hobson remained at his desk. He accepted flowers sent by some of the women in the galleries. He ate a sandwich.

As the measure's floor manager, Hobson had addressed the House early in the day. Six feet tall, his sandy hair thinning on top, his eyes drawn into their characteristic squint, he leaned forward on the balls of his feet as he spoke to his colleagues. It was the posture he had perfected on the lecture stage while declaiming "Alcohol, the Great Destroyer." On this December Tuesday, his colleagues knew it was likely the last time they would hear the Hero of the *Merrimac* call down the heavens with his famous speech.

"What is the object of this resolution?" he began, his deep baritone ringing with purpose. "It is to destroy the agency that debauches the youth of the land and thereby perpetuates its hold on the nation." He argued that because his amendment forbade only the use, manufacture, and transportation of alcohol "for sale"—critical words—it was not coercive; it would not prevent men and women from making and drinking their own. Less ingenuously, he picked up a refrain that had become increasingly popular among congressional drys, saying he wasn't even asking members to vote for or against liquor, only to allow the state legislatures the opportunity to pass judgment on the amendment. Therefore, he insisted, any congressman who voted against the resolution would be voting "to deny the States and the people their right of referendum."

But most of the speech was a replay of "The Great Destroyer." He proceeded through many of the tropes that had thrilled and horrified his audiences for years. He explained that alcohol is "a loathsome excretion of a living organism"; that it will make a civilized young man successively "become semicivilized, semisavage, savage, and, at last, below the brute"; that "nearly two-thirds of all the money in circulation in America in the course of a year" passed through the grasping hands of the liquor trust. He described how alcohol corrupted family life, deformed the economy, and befouled politics and government. He claimed that "there are nearly twice as many slaves, largely white men, today than there were black men slaves in America at any one time"—slaves, of course, to the alcohol demon.

Finally Hobson concluded, not with his customary invocation of the Lord of Hosts, but with a challenge to the men whose ranks he would soon be leaving. "In the name of your manhood," he told his colleagues, "in the name of your patriotism, in the name of all that is held dear by good men, in the name of your fireside, in the name of our institutions, in the name of our country, and in the name of humanity and humanity's God, I call on you to join hands with me and each one to do his full duty."

On the rostrum, Speaker Clark did not gavel the galleries into silence. He may have been thinking how he had compromised himself in Detroit. But he also might have been recalling what he had said to reporters on that unfortunate day. Hobson, he had told them, was "a knight errant," Clark said. "Had he lived in the days of chivalry he would have been one of those who went in search of the Holy Grail. In our day, confronting our problems, he is a political lunatic."

Clark had especially wanted to make sure that his listeners understood what he thought of Hobson's prediction that nationwide Prohibition was just ten years away. After a pause, he pressed his point. "Have you got that?" Clark asked the reporters. "Hobson is a lunatic."

THE MORNING OF the debate, the *Chicago Tribune*'s Washington correspondent had predicted that some members would claim illness to avoid having to show up at the Capitol Building and others would find it "imperative to leave Washington a day earlier than they had contemplated in order to keep their Christmas engagements." But it turned out that 90 percent of the House was well enough to come to work, apparently prepared for what the man from the *Tribune* called "political judgment day for the 433 members of the House—at least for such of them as expect to be candidates again for public office." The final vote on the Hobson Amendment was 197 for, 190 against—not the two-thirds majority the Constitution required, but an astonishing result nonetheless. Because the measure failed in the House, it did not come to a vote in the Senate during that congressional session. But if there were an antonym for Pyrrhic victory, headline writers would have plundered it hungrily. In losing this first real test of a Prohibition amendment, the dry forces had won. Dry votes came from both parties and from every part of the country. Nearly two-thirds of the affirmative voters lived in towns with fewer than ten thousand people, but that shouldn't suggest the dominance of rural conservatives; among members of the Progressive Party in the House, seventeen of the eighteen who voted went dry.

The editors of the *Nation*, who admired Hobson's passion (and his principled valor during the Brownsville controversy), said he "fought not for results but for causes," and on this day his cause was triumphant. He had experienced an equally glorious defeat once before, when he was imprisoned by the Spanish navy. He called the feeling that gripped him then "the ecstasy of martyrdom."

Hobson's last major speech in his final weeks in the House was a veinpopper in behalf of woman suffrage. In his first notable oration after he returned to private life, he again invoked the suffrage cause, but this time in the service of a greater passion. "Seek the enfranchisement of women everywhere," Hobson shouted from the podium at the 1915 ASL convention in Atlantic City, unreeling an inventory of urgent imperatives. "Make general use of the government frank in sending out dry speeches and other documents. Request all papers and periodicals to decline liquor advertisements. . . . Call the Salvation Army into action. . . . Develop local fights so as to produce the best effect on the national field."

Then: "Take the offensive everywhere," Hobson cried as he brought his philippic to its close and his audience to its feet. "Attack! Attack! Attack!"

THAT 1915 ASL CONVENTION was like none that had preceded it. The fire stoked by the symbolic triumph of the Hobson Amendment warmed old campaigners and drew new ones to its brightening glow. The former heavyweight champion (and former heavyweight drunk) John L. Sullivan, whose framed likeness was once almost as common in American saloons as *Custer's Last Fight*, spoke in behalf of the cause. Delegates accepted a resolution of solidarity from a new organization called the Catholic Prohibition League of America, which unconvincingly claimed a membership of thirty thousand. Dr. J. H. Kellogg, the famous physician from Battle Creek who had placed cornflakes on the American breakfast table, came to speak; Booker T. Washington, who believed liquor a particular scourge among blacks, sent felicitations. An especially fervent chorus of cheers rang out when a speaker quoted British prime minister David Lloyd George, whose country had been at war for a year: "We are fighting the Germans, the Austrians, and drink," Lloyd George had declared, "and the deadliest of these is drink."

The spread of temperance sentiment in other countries—especially while World War I raged across Europe—was, for the ASL, evidence that its members were marching in step with a worldwide army of the righteous. Lloyd George never tried to institute actual Prohibition in Britain, but he did employ wartime pleas to patriotism in what the *Atlantic Monthly* called a "heroic onslaught" against booze, evidenced by a series of trade regulations and sumptuary laws that restricted alcohol consumption. These included a sevenfold increase in excise taxes and the imposition of the peculiar schedule of pub closing hours—not revoked until 2005—that added a phrase to the repertoire of every British bartender: "Time, gentlemen, please." Other countries (all of them northern, none of them Catholic) were gripped by what a French economist described as *"le delirium anti-alcoolique."* The new temperance laws included the issuance of individual "drinking licenses" in Sweden, the suspension of liquor sales in German industrial areas, and the suspension of *all* liquor sales in Iceland (a ruling revoked, at least insofar as Spanish wine was concerned, when the Spaniards retaliated by tripling import duties on Icelandic fish). Norway and Finland would both have a form of Prohibition in place before the decade was over, and provincial Prohibition laws would sweep across all of Canada save for Catholic Quebec.

The most surprising foreign expression of the prohibitory impulse came in a decree issued by Czar Nicholas II in October 1914: from that point forward, it declared, the sale of vodka was forever banned throughout the Russian Empire. He may as well have ordered fish to leave the ocean. Within a year of the decree, a Petrograd newspaper reported that "tens of thousands of illicit distilleries" had opened for business. In the United States, however, Nicholas's action was exalted by a spectrum of drys that ranged from the Woman's Christian Temperance Union to radical elements of the labor movement. In 1919 the Central Labor Council in Tacoma would even attribute the success of the Russian Revolution to an unexpected by-product of the czar's ruling: a clearheaded proletariat, no longer befogged by alcohol, was at last able to rise and throw off its chains. This was not entirely fanciful; Lenin himself said that "to permit the sale of vodka would mean one step back to capitalism." It wasn't until 1923, six years after the fall of the Czar, that spirits containing more than 20 percent alcohol were again made legal in the Soviet Union.

The Tacoma unionists were not alone on the left flank of the dry movement. The socialist leader John Spargo, biographer of Karl Marx and Eugene V. Debs, attacked the liquor trade as an exemplar of capitalism and liquor itself as a corrupter of human potential. The great black union organizer and pamphleteer A. Philip Randolph argued that Prohibition would bring lower crime rates, higher wages, less corrupt politics, and other benefits of particular value to the black community. No less radical a group than the Industrial Workers of the World believed liquor was the enemy of the working classes, a poison poured into their lives by capitalist exploiters intent on weakening them. In Oregon the IWW distributed leaflets cautioning workers that they "can't fight booze and the boss at the same time."

The Baptist and Methodist clergy; the Progressive Party and its allies; the women of the suffrage movement; the western populists; most southern Democrats; the Industrial Workers of the World; official sentiment in other Anglo-Saxon and Nordic nations—was it any wonder that the Anti-Saloon League believed constitutional Prohibition was not only possible, but imminent? During the amendment debate Richmond Hobson had set the target: "I here announce to you the determination of the great moral, the great spiritual, the great temperance and prohibition forces of this whole Nation to make this question the paramount issue in 1916." And then, he said, "We will have a President and a Congress that will give us what we want."

JUST FIVE DAYS before the Hobson Amendment's triumphant failure, Congress had enacted a much more modest measure called the Harrison Narcotics Tax Act. The law empowered the Internal Revenue Service to tax, and thus to regulate, opiates, coca derivatives, and other drugs. On its face a tax measure, the Harrison Act in fact conferred on the federal government conventional police powers regarding a matter of personal behavior. The administration of Woodrow Wilson, true to its belief in a strong central government, supported its passage and could have seen it as the logical precedent for federal regulation of the liquor traffic.

Wilson was enough of a progressive to appreciate the argument, but he was enough of a realist to understand that his party's growing strength owed much to Irish-American, Italian-American, and other ethnic Democrats in the big cities of the north. His closest aide, Joseph Patrick Tumulty, was a proud son of Jersey City's Fifth Ward and a product of its redoubtable political machine. He was also former counsel to that city's liquor dealers' association and Wilson's emissary to northeastern Democrats, whose clubhouse style was rather different from the president's (Wilson's handshake was once likened to "a ten-cent pickled mackerel in brown paper"). To this part of the Democratic coalition, Prohibition was as welcome as a rash.

But the two other bulwarks of the party were for the most part as dry as powder. With the unreconstructed southerners, whose racial views he shared, Wilson had a natural affinity; in the populist economic views of the westerners, he saw a mirror of his antitariff, pro–income tax position. Wilson enjoyed the occasional highball (usually Scotch), and he believed that moderation was an acceptable form of temperance. But though he was generally dubious about prohibitory laws, he had little to gain from fighting the ASL. He risked nothing by dodging confrontation with the league. The northern ethnic voters who were the ASL's natural enemy weren't likely to seek refuge in the high-tariff, overwhelmingly Protestant, anti-immigration Republican Party. Wayne Wheeler observed that the Prohibition movement may not have had Wilson's support, but "we did not have his open opposition."

This was obvious in two of Wilson's most important appointments. The ascension to cabinet rank of Secretary of the Navy Josephus Daniels and Secretary of State William Jennings Bryan brought Prohibition sentiment into the highest reaches of the executive branch. Daniels's General Order 99 eliminated the traditional "wine mess" (it was in fact more likely to be stocked with bourbon or rye than wine) from all U.S. naval installations. This was an expression of his own dry views, but it was also a form of populist leveling: alcohol had long been denied to sailors, and Daniels's order was a conscious effort to apply the same rules to their officers. The *New York Herald* dubbed Daniels "Sir Josephus, Admiral of the USS Grapejuice Pinafore," but he was unmoved.

For his part, Bryan, who was loyally mindful of Wilson's noncombatant stance in the liquor wars, generally soft-pedaled his antialcohol position once he joined the administration; in 1914 he even opposed the Hobson Amendment, considering it a futile distraction from more pressing issues. But when Bryan's official duties ran up against his personal dedication to abstinence, a lifetime of teetotalism could not be suppressed. This became apparent barely six weeks into his tenure as secretary of state. The occasion was Bryan's first formal diplomatic function, a luncheon in the Presidential Suite of the Willard Hotel honoring James Bryce, who was about to return to London after six years as British ambassador to the United States. The guests, largely other ambassadors and their wives, had just taken their seats at the brightly decorated tables when Bryan rose to speak. His welcome contained a message that would have been no less surprising at a diplomatic event had he delivered it in pig latin: there would be no wine served at the luncheon. The deep ruby liquid in the glasses was grape juice.

Not since he'd strapped the Cross of Gold to his back in 1896 had Bryan given such ripe material to his detractors. His guests were politely accepting; the Russian ambassador, who told his luncheon companion that he "had not tasted water for years," managed to survive the meal because he had been forewarned by Bryan and "had taken his claret before he came." But the press shredded Bryan, and some northeastern Republicans began to disparage the Wilson-Bryan foreign policy as "grape juice diplomacy." Although Bryan did get some support, it was likely to invite derision—for instance, George Bernard Shaw offered his approval of the alcohol-free policy and earnestly suggested that the Bryans introduce vegetarianism to the diplomatic circuit as well.

The Prohibition forces, especially in Washington, had long been accustomed to the ridicule of the well-born, the well-connected, and the self-contented—the people Congressman Andrew J. Volstead of Minnesota called "sporty" and the WCTU characterized as "so-called respectable." As far back as the 1870s, when "Lemonade Lucy" Hayes was First Lady and presided over a dry White House, the bemused secretary of state, William M. Evarts, said that at state dinners "the water flowed like champagne." But by the time Bryan resigned as secretary of state in 1915 to express his disagreement with Wilson's increasingly belligerent policy toward Germany, ridicule and mockery bore a puny sting. The dry movement was cresting, and Bryan—three times defeated for the presidency, more than twenty years removed from Congress, now exiled from the cabinet—threw himself into it.

The campaign he joined was by this point firmly under the control of the Anti-Saloon League. The ASL's assiduous attention to Congress had made wet politicians wobble, uncertain politicians sprint for dry shelter, and dry politicians flex their biceps. Heading toward the 1916 elections, the league's grassroots activities suggested that each of these tendencies would soon be amplified. The forty tons a month of printed matter that had poured from the league's Westerville printing plant in 1912 had grown to ten tons a day. Threatened by dry boycotts, the *New York Tribune*, the *Chicago Herald*, and the *Boston Record*, among other papers, had ceased accepting liquor ads. In some states, polling lists were dissected and scrutinized by "Captains of Ten," each captain charged with determining the wetness or dryness of all ten voters on his or her list. In Illinois ASL leaders claimed that the system enabled them to acquire data on every voter in the state. Nationwide, league expenditures approached the 2009 equivalent of $50 million annually. ASL founder Howard Hyde Russell, long removed from daily management of the organization, was, he said, "engaged almost continuously in holding luncheon-meetings for manufacturers, business and professional men," and in 1916 alone raised money for the amendment campaign in more than a hundred cities. That was probably more productive, if less entertaining, than the "water wagon tour" he led the year before, a cross-country automotive caravan on the Lincoln Highway, complete with male vocal quartet.

The core unit of both the political effort and the fund-raising apparatus was the league's massive speakers' operation, which by the late stages of the amendment campaign had more than twenty thousand trained lecturers ready to deliver the ASL gospel and to reap the ASL tithe (by policy, the ASL would not provide organizations with a speaker to explain the former if he was not allowed to solicit the latter). Promotional materials enumerated the qualities of each speaker: Ira Landrith, an Ohio leaflet indicated, was "the peer of any man on the American platform," whereas L. J. Taber "appeals especially to farmers, although capable of addressing Opera House Audiences." As different as they might have been, both the peerless Landrith and the capable Taber, like all the league's envoys, were urged to follow the ASL's formal "Suggestions to Speakers," which explained in minutest detail when to arrive, where to stand, where to position ushers with the collection trays, how long to talk, and when to make the financial pitch. "Do not beg," speakers were admonished. Instead, make the audience "feel that it is a privilege to have a part in the great fight."

Presumably these directives were not imposed on the league's stars, its so-called honorarium men—the highly paid speakers who drew the largest audiences and could raise the largest sums. The honorarium speakers were generally the driest of the congressional drys, men like Senator Wesley L. Jones of Washington and Representative Alben Barkley of Kentucky (who would become Harry Truman's vice president in 1949). The biggest draws, however, were two men no longer in public office, Bryan and Hobson. Untethered from the Wilson administration, Bryan used the ASL circuit both to serve the cause and to maintain his presence in the national arena. In a single week in 1915, delivering an average of ten speeches a day, he addressed more than a quarter million Ohioans. In Ann Arbor five thousand students turned out to see him; in Philadelphia he demonstrated a new piece of histrionic business before an audience of twenty thousand when he fell to his knees and begged the assembled to pledge total abstinence. "It is a little easy to laugh at Mr. Bryan for doing things like this in times like these," the *New Republic* said. "It is even a little hard not to." But more than twelve thousand Philadelphians took up his pledge.

Bryan's lecture agent for the Chautauqua circuit, Charles F. Horner, advised his client to continue to devote "a great deal of attention to the prohibition proposition"; this was what audiences wanted. In one year the ASL alone paid Bryan $11,000 to take his righteous thunder to the dry masses—in 2009 terms, roughly $135,000. But this was easily topped by Hobson, who averaged $19,000 (more than $200,000 in 2009 dollars) during the eleven years he spent on the road for the ASL. His early fame and his years declaiming his "Great Destroyer" speech (and distributing it, too—he estimated he had handed out more than two million copies) had made him a proven draw; the prominence he had acquired through his eponymous amendment magnified his appeal. Hobson was negotiating fees with the ASL and the WCTU barely two weeks after the 1914 vote on his amendment, during his last weeks in Congress, and soon he was back on the sawdust trail with an updated version of "The Great Destroyer." He gave eighty-three speeches for the ASL in a single summer and continued at such a pace that his wife complained to league management. "His strength and health mean nothing to you but they mean <u>everything</u> to me," she wrote. She also thought it was dangerous for "a man of his national reputation" to give speeches "on street corners after dark."

It was no doubt a relief to Mrs. Hobson when her husband was unable to come to terms with the WCTU. Anna Gordon—the political, spiritual, and legal heir to Frances Willard—saw proof of her once-powerful organization's waning influence in the behavior of her own members, who now gave their cash and their pledges to the ASL. "[We] lack the funds to push work we call on them to do," she told Hobson, and therefore the WTCU had to decline his offer of services. You could hear Gordon's sigh in the ensuing sentence: "The Anti-Saloon League has money."

DRY HISTORIANS AND PUBLICISTS generally tiptoe around Richmond Hobson. There are plenty of reasons: the sometimes absurd theatricality; the righteousness worn not just as a cloak but as a banner; the speeches saturated in the melodramatic nonsense typical of Mary Hunt's Scientific Temperance Instruction, which he had been fed while at the Naval Academy ("If both parents are alcoholics, one child out of every seven will be born deformed and will be incurable"). One ASL officer told Peter Odegard, the first serious scholar to write about the league, that "on Hobson's first visit [to a particular town] he was worth more than they paid him as a subscription getter; that on his second he was probably worth his salary, but that if he spoke a third time in the same place, he positively did damage to the temperance cause."

His skills as a political strategist, however, were keen. This was demonstrated most vividly in the letter he sent in March 1915 to Ernest H. Cherrington, the man who ran the ASL's vast publishing efforts. "We must not let liquor [interests] fight off submission beyond the reapportionment of 1920," Hobson wrote. "We must put over submission of the amendment next year." Hobson had recognized the tremors of a vast demographic shift that would transform the nation. In 1910, 46 percent of Americans lived in cities. Continuing immigration, the prolific birthrates of the largest immigrant groups, and the accelerating flight from the farms to the cities meant that by 1920 the urban population was almost certain to be a majority. After the constitutionally mandated decennial census, congressional districts would be redrawn, with results that could be catastrophic for the drys.

Cherrington was the worldliest and the most emotionally moderate member of the ASL's leadership. He genuinely believed that the solution to the nation's drinking problems lay not in coercion but in education. But he also believed that "when the great cities of America actually come to dominate the state and dictate the policies of the nation, the process of decay in our boasted American civilization will have begun." Less than two weeks after hearing from Hobson, Cherrington sent a letter to James Cannon Jr., chairman of the ASL's committee on constitutional revision. If the Eighteenth Amendment didn't pass the House of Representatives by 1920, Cherrington explained, "it will then be possible to re-district the states so as to absolutely insure for the liquor forces more than one-third" of the House. In any subsequent reapportionment, the rural/urban balance and the native-born/foreign-born balance would only tilt further toward the wets. "One thing is sure," Cherrington continued. "If we are to save the situation so far as the Congress to be elected in 1916 is concerned, the work must be done at once or it will be too late."

By election day that year, the ASL's leadership, its publicists, and its fifty thousand lecturers and fund-raisers and vote counters on the front lines had completed their work. Two years earlier, terrified members of the House Judiciary Committee had been unwilling even to take a vote on the Hobson Amendment. Now the ASL had responded to what Wheeler considered the primary lesson he'd learned during his early battles with Mark Hanna: the need to "make it safe for a candidate to be dry." While the rest of the nation remained in suspense as the votes in the 1916 presidential balloting were counted in California—the state's thirteen electoral votes would reelect Wilson—the managers of the Anti-Saloon League slept comfortably.

"We knew late election night that we had won," Wheeler would recall a decade later. The league, he wrote, had "laid down such a barrage as candidates for Congress had never seen before and such as they will, in all likelihood, not see again for years to come." Every wet measure on every statewide ballot was defeated. Four more states had voted themselves dry, including Michigan, the first northern industrial state to make the leap. Some form of dry law was now on the books in twenty-three states. And Wheeler wrote, "We knew that the Prohibition amendment would be submitted to the States by the Congress just elected."

Chapter 6

Dry-Drys, Wet-Drys, and Hyphens

I T'S A TRUISM of political dynamics that the party of change will always be more motivated than the party of the status quo. The latter may have inertia on its side, but inertia will not hold against the press of passion. Once the ASL, the WCTU, and the other antialcohol zealots acquired the support of other political movements that used the Prohibition campaign for their own transforming purposes, the results were catalytic. With so many allies, the drys could even welcome those whose interests were patently commercial and not worry about the evident cupidity. Among the new recruits to Prohibitionism were allies as disparate as Asa Candler, founder of the Coca-Cola Company (he was a teetotaler who also happened to see opportunity on the other side of the dry rainbow) and theater owner Lee Shubert (who was not known to be a teetotaler, but longed to see Broadway's bars empty, their occupants relocated into his theaters). At last the drys seemed to be on the side of history.

Meanwhile, the Candlers and the Shuberts on the other side—that is, the distillers, the brewers, and those others whose wet passions were pecuniary—achieved little traction with their larger constituency: a nation of drinkers long accustomed to believe that the whiskey on the sideboard or the beer on the saloon bar were no more a matter of government concern than the butter in the icebox. George Ade carved an appropriate epitaph for the anti-Prohibitionists in his 1931 elegy, *The Old-Time Saloon*: "The Non-Drinkers had been organizing for fifty years and the Drinkers had no organization whatever. They had been too busy drinking."

If there were such a thing as an archetypal American in the 1910s, he or she lived in a middle-sized town, attended a Protestant church, and had a few generations of native-born ancestors interred in a nearby cemetery. Even if one ignored the predatory brewers and distillers, it would have been difficult for this average American to find someone to identify with on the wet side of the political ledger. The most numerous of the wet activists were cogs in political machines that were both urban and ethnic. The most powerful wets were the "Standpat" Republicans in Congress, who generally opposed the income tax, the vote for women, child labor legislation, and anything else that transferred an ounce of power to the federal government or subtracted it from the plutocrats whose interests they tended to serve. Congressional opponents of Prohibition like Henry Cabot Lodge of Massachusetts, Elihu Root of New York, and Henry Algernon du Pont of Delaware were not men whose interests resonated on Main Street or in Middletown.

With few respectable allies, the brewers, distillers, wholesalers, and dealers for a time attempted to recast their own sorry image. The brewers tried to represent themselves as honorable providers of nourishing beverages for the working classes, and the distillers loudly opposed the saloon and its accompanying evils. As Michigan prepared to vote on a statewide dry law, Detroit brewer George H. Gies distributed a series of advertising cards that attempted to assign to beer the virtues of mother's milk. One depicted a handsome woman cradling a baby in her left arm and gripping a brimming stein in her right hand; the sunny couplet beneath the illustration read "Lager's amber fluid mild, / Gives health and strength to wife and child." In 1914 the National Retail Liquor Dealers' Association endorsed the noble work of the Anti-Profanity League of America, whose founder, one Arthur Samuel Colborne, prowled the Manhattan saloons warning their habitués that "you start with 'hell,' 'devil take it,' 'Dad Burn it,' 'Gee whizz' . . . and by and by you won't be able to open your trap without letting loose an awful, awful blasphemous oath."

The brewers' flight to virtue was only a side trip; the low road was where they were comfortable. They organized boycotts against companies that allied themselves in any way with the dry cause, even going so far as to put the Blackstone Hotel in Chicago on their do-not-patronize list because the Blackstone supported and conscientiously observed the state's Sunday closing laws. Among other firms similarly blacklisted were B. F. Goodrich, because two of its officers had contributed to the ASL; H. J. Heinz, because its president belonged to a dry Sunday school association; and such other potent enemies as Cadillac, Procter & Gamble, and Western Union. After a Packard Motor Car executive publicly blamed the brewing interests for encouraging "the drunken darkies' orgies and white slavery," he was ordered by Henry B. Joy, Packard's nervous president, to

The march to Prohibition began in December 1873, when a group of prayerful women stationed themselves outside the saloons and barrooms of Hillsboro, Ohio. Within weeks, "Mother Thompson's Crusade," as it was called, had spread across the Northeast and Midwest.

Frances Willard, the dominant figure in the Woman's Christian Temperance Union, considered herself a "Christian socialist" and called her supporters "Protestant nuns." A U.S. senator said Willard was "the Bismarck of the forces of righteousness."

Mary Hanchett Hunt led the campaign that made her grossly inaccurate "Scientific Temperance Instruction" compulsory in every state. Among STI's "facts": "when alcohol passes down the throat it burns off the skin," and "the majority of beer drinkers die of dropsy."

In the original 1848 Currier and Ives engraving of Washington's farewell to his officers (4), the general offered a toast. Reissued in 1876 as the WCTU was gaining strength, the wineglass had been removed from his hand, and a hat replaced the decanter and goblets on the table (5).

THE FAMOUS AND ORIGINAL

BAR ROOM SMASHER

CARRIE NATION
MANAGEMENT JAMES E. FURLONG

CARRIE NATION

MANAGEMENT
JAS. E. FURLONG

7

My Boys may go
to ruin
through
the
legalized
saloon
by YOUR
consent
but your boys never
will by my consent.

6

8

Much of the campaign for Prohibition revolved around gentle, family-related themes (6). But Carry Nation (she wasn't particular about the spelling of her first name) was singularly audacious. Once she started destroying saloons with her hatchet, she found the vaudeville circuit as comfortable as the church pew. She also published a newspaper, she said, so "the public could see by my editorials that I was not insane."

The Anti-Saloon League convention, 1915, in Atlantic City. Speakers included former heavyweight champion John L. Sullivan and Dr. J. H. Kellogg, the man who gave America cornflakes.

Richmond P. Hobson, who introduced the Prohibition amendment in Congress, exhorted his colleagues to pass it "in the name of your manhood." The Speaker of the House considered Hobson "a political lunatic."

Andrew Volstead never joined the ASL or delivered an antiliquor speech. But the enforcement law he wrote led to the word "volsteadism"—according to *Webster's Third*, "the doctrine of or adherence to prohibition."

"The liquor interests hate Billy Sunday as they hate no man," said an ASL publication. Said Sunday, "I will fight them till hell freezes over, then I'll buy a pair of skates and fight 'em on the ice."

Wayne B. Wheeler, the brilliant tactician who dominated the ASL, was considered—by a critic—"the most masterful and powerful single individual in the United States," who "controlled six Congresses, dictated to two Presidents [and] held the balance of power in both Republican and Democratic parties."

As secretary of state in 1914, William Jennings Bryan served grape juice at state dinners. The following year, as a stump speaker for the ASL, he was delivering as many as ten speeches a day.

COMPLIMENTS OF
GEORGE H. GIES,
16 Monroe Avenue,
DETROIT MICH.

AGAINST PROHIBITION NO. 2.

Lager's amber Fluid mild,
Gives health and strength to wife and child.

15

COMPLIMENTS OF
GEORGE H. GIES,
16 Monroe Avenue,
DETROIT MICH.

AGAINST PROHIBITION NO. 3.

The youngster, ruddy with good cheer,
Serenely sips his Lager Beer.

16

Trying to distinguish "healthful" beer from dangerous liquor, brewers
liked to refer to it as "liquid bread." Detroit brewer George H. Gies
took the healthfulness argument several steps further.

Adolphus Busch said brewers should be willing to "risk the majority of our fortunes" to fight Prohibition; he used quite a lot of his own money to bribe newspaper editors, buy votes, and pay operatives to influence elections through means, said one of his agents, that "are best not written about." But the brewers—almost all of them of German extraction—were rendered helpless after the United States entered World War I and the ASL turned the nation's anti-German feeling against them.

19

On January 16, 1920, this Detroit liquor store had no trouble depleting its stock. Within hours, a vast and unstoppable illegal trade was born, giving rise in turn to the creation of multistate criminal syndicates. Much of the public that had once responded to songs like this 1866 number (20) would, by 1920, be hearing a very different tune.

20

21

write a letter to the United States Brewers' Association apologizing for his action, which he characterized as "a great injustice to the Packard Co."

The brewers also invested in or purchased outright newspapers in Chicago, Newark, Montgomery, Washington, and other cities. Hearst editor Arthur Brisbane, who had long attacked liquor and campaigned for beer, turned out to be not as disinterested as he had once seemed: in 1917 he bought the *Washington Times* with cash supplied by a group of fifteen beer barons. Among the backers who provided their man Brisbane with the cash to build a platform ("We looked upon him as our agent in this matter," said the general manager of the Miller Brewing Company) were gentlemen whose names were wreathed in the scent of malt and hops: Schmidt, Ruppert, Hamm, Pabst, and of course, Busch.

They also bore the unmistakable whiff of something else: the beer industry's indelible Germanness. The Busches were especially attached to their ancestral home—so attached, in fact, that "ancestral" is a misnomer. Adolphus had been decorated by the Kaiser (who had visited Villa Lilly, the Busch family estate in Langenschwalbach); two of Adolphus and Lilly's daughters were married to German military officers; and son August— head of the family after Adolphus's death—threw annual parties at his Missouri farm in honor of the Kaiser's birthday. Vacationing in Langenschwalbach in the summer of 1914, Adolphus's widow had even chosen to remain there when World War I broke out.

The ethnic coloration of the brewing industry had been a bugbear of the temperance movement as far back as 1876, when Frances Willard referred to "the infidel foreign population." To the brewers, of course, this population was their most reliable constituency; according to the United States Brewers' Association's chief political strategist, Percy Andreae, "the staunchest friends our industry possesses in this country" were "the millions and millions of falsely described foreign citizens." Andreae, whose value was such that the brewers paid him $40,000 a year—the 2009 equivalent of $860,000—earned at least part of his salary by also serving as vice president and official spokesman of the American Association of Foreign-Language Newspapers, writing (and underwriting the translation of) pro-beer editorials for these papers—signed by others, of course. The brewers also bankrolled the entire cost of the Washington lobbying office of the German-American Alliance, a national civic group that the brewers transformed into a virtual subsidiary.

To the drys, foreignness was not an endearing quality. Many of the same progressives who battled the big-city political organizations, campaigned against the saloon, and supported labor unions also embraced the cause of immigration restriction. The partnership forged by the German-American Alliance and the Ancient Order of Hibernians "to oppose the enactment . . . of any sumptuary laws or laws abridging the personal liberties of citizens" was exactly the sort of political treaty that could make progressive blood run cold. Italian-Americans, who worked in conjunction with the GAA to oppose the Prohibition amendment, were tarred as well; Stanford chancellor David Starr Jordan darkly noted that although San Mateo County was "9/10 Anglo-Saxon," he had determined that "about one-half the arrests for speeding, hit-and-run driving, or worse, are all men with Italian names, mostly from Naples and Sicily."

Xenophobia was yet more intense in the South, even though—or perhaps because—in some southern states the population was as much as 99 percent native stock. When foreigners showed up on their turf, many southerners recoiled. In *Look Homeward, Angel*, Thomas Wolfe described the small claque of wets that young Eugene Gant encountered when he accompanied his father to the polls. Outcasts in a dry-dominated town, "they had never been told they stood for liberty," wrote Wolfe. "They stood rubily, stubbornly, with the strong brown smell of shame in their nostrils, for the bloodshot, malt-mouthed, red-nosed, loose-pursed Demon Rum." In Atlanta, a bourbon-swilling thirty-five-year-old knockabout named William Joseph Simmons created the modern Ku Klux Klan just weeks after the lynching of Jewish factory manager Leo Frank, whose wife was the daughter of a former saloonkeeper and granddaughter of a liquor wholesaler. It was a later edition of the KKK that focused its venomous loathing on black people; this version had a special hatred for Jewish and Catholic immigrants.* The Klan, which supported woman suffrage in behalf of Prohibition, in turn supported Prohibition as a weapon against the immigrants.

This was obviously very fertile soil for the Anti-Saloon League. But Woodrow Wilson made it even more fruitful. He may have been indifferent to the ASL cause, but his own war-making propaganda was built around anti-European, particularly anti-German, feeling. When he went before Congress in 1917 to request authority to enter the war that had

---

*The populist-demagogue-turned-racist-demagogue Tom Watson of Georgia, who was a patron of the KKK, expressed the intensity and paranoia of anti-Catholic feeling in a scary document called "What Goes on in Nunneries." In convents, he said, "bachelor priests keep unmarried women under lock and key" and kill their children. He also said that in the confessional, priests gave married women information on "sexual practices and techniques with [their] husband[s], extra-marital activities, masturbation, homosexuality, and unnatural fornication."

been burning its way across Europe for nearly three years, he had said, "We have no quarrel with the German people. We have no feeling towards them but one of sympathy and friendship. It was not upon their impulse that their Government acted in entering this war." But a combination of temperament, upbringing, and political strategy had led Wilson to take a less charitable attitude toward some of his own country's people. While preparing the nation for the war he wanted it to enter, Wilson had already launched his campaign of "anti-hyphenism." Specifically, he set out to demonize some of those Americans who were "born under other flags but welcomed under our generous naturalization laws to the full freedom and opportunity of America." Employing a provocative metaphor to characterize these enemies of the Republic, Wilson charged that some had "poured the poison of disloyalty into the very arteries of our national life."

BACK IN 1912, when the formal push for the Prohibition amendment was launched, before the ratification of the Sixteenth (income tax) and Seventeenth (direct election of senators) amendments, the Anti-Saloon League's leaders were setting themselves a historically daunting task. Except for the three amendments enacted during the aftershocks of the Civil War, the Constitution had been amended exactly twice in the preceding 118 years.

It was one of those Civil War amendments that posed the last roadblock to congressional approval of constitutional Prohibition. The South (with the exception of Catholic Louisiana) may have been the part of the country with the most intense antiliquor sentiment and the widest range of state liquor laws. In Alabama, for instance, liquor advertisements of any kind were forbidden, even in out-of-state newspapers that circulated within the state, an ordinance enforced with particular vigor by the bone-dry Jefferson County district attorney (and future U.S. Supreme Court justice) Hugo L. Black, who actually won a case against an out-of-state shipper by positing that the address labels on his boxes constituted advertising. But despite the white South's general sympathy for the dry cause, its distinctive politics—particularly its regionwide attachment to the concept of states' rights—compelled the ASL to devise a distinctive lobbying approach. It also required a distinctive lobbyist to carry it out. Enter the Reverend James Cannon, "the Dry Messiah."

James Cannon Jr. was nasty, brutish, and short. He was also a frighteningly hard worker, as shrewd as a serpent, and untouched by Hobsonian vainglory. Shod in high-buckle shoes, his slight frame clad summer and winter in long woolen underwear, for twenty-five years he wore a beard, said a biographer, "for the sole reason that he had no time to shave." William Randolph Hearst, who disagreed with Cannon on most matters, said he had "the best brain in America, no one excepted." In time, H. L. Mencken would say that Cannon's "merest wink [could] make a President of the United States leap like a bullfrog."

Utterly convinced of the righteousness of his cause, Cannon could have been a Puritan in the age of Cromwell; instead he was a warrior in the age of Wheeler. He came from a well-off Maryland family, but his father's loyalties to the South led the Cannons to move to Virginia during the Civil War. As a young man, Cannon traveled a few hundred miles north to earn two degrees from Princeton, then returned to Virginia to enter the Methodist ministry. By his early forties he had become one of the most dominant individuals in the public life of his state. Modest, too, after a fashion: "I do not remember that I ever attempted to use my influence with the Legislature," he told the *Richmond Times-Dispatch*, recalling the years before he became a national figure, "except on measures pertaining to education . . . prohibition, gambling, vice, Sabbath observance, moving pictures, and child labor."

Cannon's authority couldn't have emanated from a less likely seat. The Blackstone Female Institute, which he served as principal, was a two-year college in the south-central part of the state. He offered this advice to candidates for admission: "No young ladies are wanted as students at the institute who are not willing to accept the guidance of the principal as that of an older friend, who is planning to give them such training as will develop them into helpful and attractive women." He never held public office or played an official role in Virginia's dominant Democratic Party, but a Democrat he was, and a dry, and he could deliver. In 1914, after Cannon had risen to the forefront of the temperance forces in the commonwealth, he engineered a stunningly successful statewide dry vote. Soon the Anti-Saloon League came calling.

The ASL's literature declared the organization "Interdenominational and Omni-Partisan." But though it was barely the former (almost all of its managers were stationed along the abbreviated gamut that ran from Baptist to Methodist), it was not even remotely the latter, despite the situational endorsements it had bestowed on dry Democrats, especially in the South. The league's leadership was ineradicably rooted in the Republican soil of small-town Ohio. This made Cannon necessary; even if Hobson had stayed in Washington, his distance from his southern colleagues on racial matters, as well as the prissy rectitude that had alienated his classmates at

Annapolis, would have guaranteed his failure as a lobbyist. Wheeler and his predecessor, Edwin Dinwiddie, could make deals with Democrats, but neither could be fully admitted into the party's innermost councils. "So I was put in to deal with them," Cannon said, "as a Democrat with Democrats."

Specifically, southern Democrats. Cannon was more likely to part the Potomac than to be invited to sit at the same table as the northern Democrats from Tammany Hall and the other big-city machines. His manner—not only the outlandish clothing, but also a sense of humor that a Virginia acquaintance believed "could be lightly balanced on the back of a gnat"—didn't help. Neither did his incivil attitude toward those who disagreed with him. One friend said, "Like most humorless men, he had to make life into a crusade to make sense of it." Unlike Wheeler, who extended his personal cordiality even to the wets he publicly lacerated, Cannon, wrote Herbert Asbury in *The Great Illusion*, was "violent, abusive, . . . and given to wholesale denunciation" of his enemies. Among those was an institution fairly important to many of the machine Democrats. The Roman Catholic Church, Cannon said, was the "mother of ignorance, superstition, intolerance, and sin."

But among his own, he could be eminently practical. When he started a dry newspaper in Richmond, Cannon promised not to "promote any form or species of gambling"; three weeks later, when he realized readers wanted their horse racing news, he relented. A prominent Virginia dry said that "many of Cannon's most ardent supporters in the General Assembly were drunk when they were enacting dry legislation," yet Cannon abided their intemperance. That was a healthy attitude for anyone assigned to keep tabs on dry southern politicians. Cannon didn't need to worry about the "dry-drys"—anyone who "voted with the Anti-Saloon League and was yet dry personally," as Mencken archly described them in *The American Language*. The "wet-drys," though, were far more numerous and much less reliable. In fact, the dedicated abstinence of Senator Morris Sheppard, who had replaced Richmond Hobson as the primary congressional sponsor of the Prohibition amendment, was so singular that almost ten years after his resolution was adopted, he was saluted by Senator William Cabell Bruce, one of the leading congressional wets. Among all the dry members of the Senate, Bruce observed, Sheppard was one of only three he could name who actually didn't drink.

The "wet-drys" were especially abundant in southern Democratic politics. Throughout his public life as governor and senator, the viciously racist Cole Blease of South Carolina never hid his fondness for moonshine. At the other end of the dignity spectrum, the learned and judicious

Senator John Sharp Williams of Mississippi openly declared on the Senate floor that he was certain his "splendid" supply of liquor would last him the rest of his life. Wayne Wheeler explained away the attitudes of the "wet-drys" by asserting that "men vote as they pray rather than as they drink." It would have been less disingenuous to have said, "Men vote as their instinct for political survival would have them vote."

More difficult for Cannon and the other ASL operatives charged with minding the southern Democrats was a subset of the "wet-drys." These politicians supported dry legislation in their own states and were prepared to vote dry in Congress, but only if they could get past a particular logical (and ideological) impediment. A Prohibition amendment would supersede state laws, and however dry their sympathies might have been, these southerners swore a higher loyalty to states' rights. Most of them also feared that a Constitution that could be amended to allow the imposition of federal liquor laws could also be amended to grant women a federal right to vote. This was the argument they used if they wanted to sound respectable. If they wanted to sound honest, they acknowledged that accepting the validity of the pending Prohibition amendment would logically require them to accept the validity of an amendment already in the Constitution—the Fifteenth, affirming the voting rights of all men, black and white.

For many southern politicians the stand they took on constitutional Prohibition was tactical—in effect, they had to decide which position was likeliest to preserve the iron segregation that had set in with the enactment of state Jim Crow laws. In his maiden House speech in 1914, thirty-one-year-old Carl Vinson of Georgia grandly declared, "The principles of State rights are as sacred [as] the virtue of the vestal virgins." Former senator Joseph Bailey of Texas put it more crudely but also more frankly: handing the federal government authority over liquor control, he said, would establish a precedent that would in time guarantee that "there will not be a square foot of territory in the United States where it will be unlawful for negroes and white people to intermarry." Alabama's flamboyant "Cotton Tom" Heflin, who once shot a black man on a Washington streetcar (and considered it one of his major professional accomplishments, along with the role he played in establishing Mother's Day), used the same image that southern drys had been brandishing for decades to explain his reluctance to vote dry: it was the state and not the federal government, Heflin said, that "protected our women from the lust and carnality of the brutes in our midst." Every county in Heflin's district was dry. His state was largely dry. But Heflin and others like him were consistent: they valued genuine racism more than false temperance.

In the end, though, when the Eighteenth Amendment was brought to a vote in the House of Representatives in December 1917, James Cannon and his colleagues were able to pry from the wet column nine southern and border state House Democrats who had voted against the Hobson Amendment in 1914, and they lost none going the other direction. Although the final vote of 282–128 seemed a landslide, in requiring a two-thirds majority the Constitution *demanded* a landslide; without the nine who had migrated from wet to dry, the resolution, which had passed the Senate with ease, would have died in the House. The promising young Sam Rayburn of Texas was among those who made the switch, and even Carl Vinson, despite his poignant regard for southern virtue and vestal virgins, jumped to the dry side. There proved to be little political peril in testing the elasticity of the states' rights argument: Vinson would remain in Congress for another forty-seven years, and Rayburn would serve another forty-four, for seventeen of them as Speaker of the House.

AS IT TRAVELED its path from the Hobson Amendment of 1914 to the Sheppard Amendment of 1917, Prohibition leapt ahead of universal suffrage in the reform queue. It also underwent substantial legislative tinkering but little discussion of its core substance. Some dry leaders continued to lean on the coy argument that the entire matter was merely procedural. The debate wasn't about Prohibition, these Drys tried to say, it was only about "submission" of the amendment to the states—that is, attaining two-thirds majorities in both houses of Congress so the states would have a chance to decide for themselves in the ratification process. This was like a prosecutor in a death penalty state charging someone with murder but disclaiming any responsibility for the consequences of a conviction. The Senate judiciary committee hadn't even bothered with hearings; neither had its House counterpart. Floor debate in the Senate was largely given over to an argument over timing. The House crammed its discussion of the resolution into a single afternoon. Who could object? The real debate had been taking place for more than sixty years.

But there had indeed been negotiations that took the form of debate, largely within the councils of the Anti-Saloon League and its allies. Five issues had arisen after Hobson had crafted his resolution, and four were resolved through changes in the language of the proposed amendment. By decree of Wayne Wheeler, the fifth went unresolved and remained live ammunition for both wets and drys for as long as the Eighteenth Amendment lived.

The most significant of the changes was the deletion of four iterations of the words "for sale." The Hobson Amendment had proscribed not just the sale of intoxicating beverages but also their "manufacture for sale, transportation for sale, importation for sale, and exportation for sale." "We do not say that a man shall not drink," Hobson had told the House in his dramatic floor speech of December 1914. "We ask for no sumptuary action. We do not say that a man shall not have or make liquor in his own home for his own use." He said that in the phrasing of his resolution, "The liberties and sanctity of the home are protected." The Hobson Amendment was aimed solely at the saloon, the distillers, the brewers—in a word, the liquor traffic. To Hobson of the *Merrimac*, any amendment that appeared to infringe on personal liberty would grant "the choice of battleground to the enemy."

In 1914 Wayne Wheeler agreed with him; in fact, Wheeler and Purley Baker were among the acknowledged coauthors of the Hobson Amendment. But so much had changed by the time the Sixty-fifth Congress convened in March 1917 that Wheeler was emboldened. Before the end of the month word had gone out by telegram from ASL headquarters: the moderating "for sale" was being junked. *Any* manufacture, transportation, importation, and exportation of intoxicating beverages, for any purpose and from any source, would be covered by the amendment.

The second linguistic adjustment, added as a separate section of the amendment, was the grant of "concurrent" powers of enforcement to the states. Hobson proposed this change himself at the ASL's convention in 1915, and it mollified some of the states' rights advocates. He argued that allowing the states to share enforcement responsibility would maintain "the balance of power between the Federal government and the states."

The last two tweaks of the Sheppard Amendment were connected to each other. In addition to the congressional wets, a few moderate drys whose votes were still somewhat in question wanted to provide compensation to the distillers and brewers, much of whose property was about to become worthless. At the time the Sheppard Amendment was pending, thirteen million gallons of bourbon were aging in Kentucky warehouses alone. Nationwide, the liquor and beer industries represented nearly $1 billion in invested capital, by that measure making the combination the nation's fifth largest industry. The *New Republic* said any dry who argued against compensation was "exactly as mindful of property interests . . . as the Russian Bolsheviki."

But hard-line drys countered with an argument that was more theological than political or economic. According to officials of the Methodist

Church, the alcohol interests' "day of grace has been sinned away." Less holy was the breathtakingly disingenuous no-compensation argument Representative Daniel E. Garrett of Texas had offered when Congress first debated the Hobson Amendment. After the Thirteenth Amendment abolished slavery, he said, four billion dollars' worth of "property" had been rendered valueless. "I doubt if any man deplores more than myself that the institution of slavery ever existed in this country," Garrett claimed, and "as it has been with human slavery, so shall it be with alcoholic liquors." Therefore, he argued, the liquor and beer interests "must pocket their loss just as our fathers had to pocket theirs when you took their niggers away from them. That is all there is to it." The *Congressional Record* noted the response from at least part of the House: "[Applause and laughter.]"

One of the conciliatory drys who had supported the idea of compensation was Warren G. Harding, the junior senator from Ohio. Harding was about as moist as a dry could get, both in his attitude (he said he preferred to think of temperance not as a moral issue but as a political one) and in his personal life (he favored Scotch and soda, and owned stock in a brewery). The most authoritative student of his prepresidential career, historian Randolph C. Downes, captured Harding's posture on the issue perfectly: "Let there be no mistaking the fact that Senator Harding was both opposed to national prohibition and in favor of it, depending on whom he was dealing with." In the summer of 1917 he was dealing with Wayne Wheeler.

To a large degree Harding owed his election in 1914 to the support of Wheeler and the ASL, who had backed the malleable and affable Republican over a Democrat who was a confirmed wet. As the Sheppard Amendment came up for Senate debate, Wheeler was in his usual seat in the gallery, which had become a sort of second headquarters for the ASL. Harding requested a meeting, and what eventually emerged from their conversation in the Capitol lobby was both a compromise and a ruse. Harding not only believed that the liquor interests deserved compensation, but also felt there should be a cap on how much time the states were allowed for ratification, a constraint that had never been applied to previous amendments. Harding suggested five years. Wheeler stretched it to seven, in exchange giving Harding and other moderates a new opening clause to the amendment, stipulating that its provisions would not take effect until one year after its ratification. This gave twelve months' grace for the brewers, the distillers, the wholesalers, the saloon owners, the bartenders, the barrel makers, the bottlers, the teamsters, the ice dealers, and all the other people dependent on the American taste for alcoholic beverages—twelve months to find another use for their facilities and another line of work. This was not compensation; it was the facsimile of compensation. Four years later, Herbert Hoover would call Congress's failure to seriously consider compensation "an insult to private property."

All told, the linguistic tinkering that shaped the Eighteenth Amendment during its journey through the Sixty-fifth Congress had turned a morally inspired measure into a punitive one (the excision of the limiting "for sale"); provided some balm for the states' rights caucus ("concurrent" enforcement); closed off the compensation debate (the one-year delay); and, in the case of the seven-year ratification limit, accomplished nothing meaningful relating to Prohibition, but did establish a new precedent. Three of the next four amendments to the Constitution were freighted with Warren Harding's seven-year-limit innovation, and one—the Equal Rights Amendment of 1972—expired just three states short of ratification when the clock ticked its final mandated second in 1979.

More important than any of these emendations, though, was the word change that didn't happen. Some very dry-drys wanted the Eighteenth Amendment to proscribe the manufacture, sale, transportation, importation, and exportation of "alcoholic beverages." Wheeler, however, was determined to stick with "intoxicating liquors," a vaguer term whose meaning Congress would have to define in later legislation, in the process turning that definition into the subject of political warfare, public debate, learned analysis, and high comedy for the next sixteen years.

AS 1917 DREW to a close, submission had been accomplished. Ratification seemed a more daunting prospect. Though by this time twenty-three states had dry laws of one form or another, very few were as "bone dry" as the Eighteenth Amendment. Looming ahead was the trench warfare of the state-by-state ratification campaign, in which the drys would need to win a minimum of thirty-six separate battles to reach the three-quarters requirement.

In the end, however, ratification sped along with astonishing velocity, fueled by an assault on the German-American Alliance conducted by the U.S. Senate in the form of an inquiry, but organized by Wayne B. Wheeler in the form of an inquisition. "We are not willing it be known at present that we started the investigation," Wheeler told Purley Baker. Nonetheless, he pointed out, "You have doubtless seen the way the newspapers have taken up the German-American Alliance. They are giving it almost as much attention as the Acts of Congress itself. We could not have bought for $50,000 what we have gotten on this investigation."

The income tax had made a Prohibition amendment fiscally feasible. The social revolution wrought by the suffragists had made it politically plausible. Now the drys had found the final tool they needed to wedge the amendment into the Constitution: a war.

Chapter 7

From Magna Carta to Volstead

WILLIAM ASHLEY SUNDAY of the Philadelphia Phillies, who became world famous for loving Christ and hating alcohol, put away his glove, his bat, and his spikes in 1890. He had just completed a season in which he had stolen eighty-four bases and earned $3,500, roughly nine times the wages of the average American industrial worker. But at last he had decided to turn away from the sporting life and toward Jesus, an inclination that had already set him apart from many of his teammates. Like Sunday, most ballplayers of the day were largely itinerant and marginally educated; unlike Sunday, who indulged in an occasional glass of beer or wine, many drank like champions. Countless careers were ended by booze, and numerous lives lost (notable among these was the great Philadelphia outfielder Ed Delahanty, who attempted a drunken walk one night across a railroad bridge over Niagara Falls). An alcoholic aroma wafted over the stands as well. The original American Association, half of whose founding owners were brewers, was so drink sodden it became known as the "Beer and Whiskey League." The top row of the grandstand in Sportsman's Park in St. Louis was an open bar, and in San Francisco's Recreation Park, where the Seals of the Pacific Coast League played, eight rows of seats stretching from first base, behind home plate, and over to third base comprised the "Booze Cage." This was where a seventy-five-cent ticket got the fan a choice of two beers or a shot of whiskey, with a ham sandwich and a ballgame thrown in.

Billy Sunday had always been religious. But in 1888, while he sat on a Chicago curbstone with some other players, hymns from a nearby mission caught his ear and his heart. Turning to his teammates, he said he really didn't want another drink and then went across the street and found shelter in the stainless calm of the mission. Two years later, when he gave up baseball for the life of an evangelist, his verbal facility, italicized by his hyperphysical platform style, put him on his way to becoming the most successful American preacher of his era, perhaps the most successful one ever. The essay on Sunday in the authoritative *American National Biography* does not equivocate: "Incredible as it may seem, reliable statistics indicate that Sunday preached to more than 100 million people" in his forty years in the pulpit. By his own account, early in his career he had used "sentences so long they'd make a Greek professor's jaw squeak." Only after he "loaded my Gospel gun with rough-on-rats, ipecac, dynamite, and barbed wire" did he achieve his extraordinary success. "What do I care if some puff-eyed little dibbly-dibbly preacher goes tibbly-tibbling around because I use plain Anglo-Saxon words?" Sunday asked. "I want people to know what I mean and that's why I try to get down where they live."

Sunday's speeches were devoted first to his fundamentalist view of Jesus (a contemporary observer said he "flings out the name of Christ as if he were sending a spitball right into your teeth"). His fanatic opposition to the beer and liquor interests came a close second. To Sunday liquor was "God's worst enemy" and "hell's best friend," and he considered those who profited from the alcohol trade earthly Satans. "I will fight them till hell freezes over," he told a rally at the University of Michigan, where he persuaded a thousand students to join the campaign for a statewide Prohibition law. "Then I'll buy a pair of skates and fight 'em on the ice."

"The liquor interests hate Billy Sunday as they hate no other man," an Anti-Saloon League publication said in 1913. This wasn't strictly because of the size of his following (which was enormous), or its intense devotion (in 1914 a magazine poll attempting to determine who was "the greatest man in the United States" placed Sunday eighth, tied with Andrew Carnegie). In as many as 250 speeches a year, addressing the enormous audiences he could command in the late 1910s, Sunday gave shape to the new attitude—increasingly ferocious, even vengeful—that characterized the Prohibition forces as they stood at the edge of victory. No more tibbly-tibbling, said Billy Sunday: "I have no interest in a God who does not smite."

Cue Kaiser Wilhelm, World War I, and Wayne B. Wheeler.

AFTER THE EIGHTEENTH AMENDMENT was ratified, resentful wets frequently expressed the belief that the Great War that exploded in Europe in 1914 and that America entered in 1917 was especially great for the Anti-Saloon League and its allies. In one of the favored mythologies they would clutch to their bosoms throughout the fourteen years of Prohibition, the wets attributed the amendment's adoption to the absence of two million soldiers from American shores and voting booths. This argument mistakenly presumed that all of these men were beer loving and devoted to personal liberty. In truth, the missing men and boys—many of them below voting age, in aggregate likely as divided on the issue as the rest of the country—weren't a factor. Further, the series of War Revenue Acts that Congress passed at Woodrow Wilson's request, which increased liquor taxes to help finance the war effort, in effect made the purchase of alcoholic beverages in the early days of World War I a patriotic act.

Still, the prohibitionists did find a number of ways to tie their cause to the nation's defense. Not six months after the first doughboys landed in Europe in June 1917, the ASL officially denounced America's French allies for their failure to supply pure drinking water to American soldiers, putting them at risk of developing a taste for wine. The populist, antibusiness, Bryan-led wing of the dry coalition, capitalizing on the looming disappearance of liquor tax revenues, used the war crisis to usher in sharply progressive income tax rates (by the time Prohibition took effect, the highest bracket had been jacked up past 70 percent, or more than six times the prewar level). Bryan accused the distillers of harboring a "passion for dollars" that might "make drunkards of the entire army and leave us defenseless before a foreign foe." This was not simply Bryanesque minstrelsy; Thomas Gilmore, president of the distillers' Model License League, in fact attempted to persuade Congress to give liquor to the soldiers to "insure the steadiness of nerve that wins battles." After all, Gilmore explained, "the man who rushes a rapid fire gun should be given the relief from terror that alcohol imparts."

The notion of national emergency also handed the drys the keys to an arsenal of practical arguments easily draped in patriotic rhetoric. The month the United States entered the war, the distinguished (and passionately dry) Yale economist Irving Fisher assembled a group of famous Americans, few of them previously associated with the movement, to endorse the need for national Prohibition; the lineup included novelists Upton Sinclair and Booth Tarkington, aviation pioneer Orville Wright, and E. H. Gary, chairman of U.S. Steel. Then Fisher parlayed his (and their) renown by issuing an analysis of the damage being done to the war effort by the wanton waste of food resources. The same amount of barley used in American breweries could instead yield eleven million loaves of bread a day, Fisher said. Distinguished though he might have been (Fisher's *Theory of Interest* is still considered a milestone in economic thought nearly eighty years after it was published), his numbers didn't always parse; in Fisher's writings, the eleven million figure sometimes denoted a wildly inflated count of American soldiers at the front, and his associates some-times said the daily loaves of bread left unbaked by the brewers' disloyalty numbered five million, not eleven. Whatever the precise figure, it was cer-tainly sufficient to nourish the army and to feed the starving Belgians as well. "How can we justify the making of any part of our breadstuffs into intoxicating liquor," Bryan asked, "when men are crying out for bread?" Anticipating the end of the war, the advent of Prohibition, and an inevita-ble grain surplus, Billy Sunday took a more cheerful approach. "The prob-lem of what to do with the farm surplus will be solved in a jiffy," Sunday said. "The children of drunkards will consume this surplus in the form of flap-jacks for breakfast."

The brewers tried to counter with statistics, asserting at one point that the entire industry used less than three-quarters of 1 percent of the nation's grain production. Even if accurate, it was a futile defense. The dry assault included attacks on the alcohol industry's use of railroad stock, fuel oil, and other war necessities. "The people have been requested to have heat-less days, meatless days, wheatless days," Wayne Wheeler said in a letter to President Wilson. But, he continued, "the breweries and saloons of the country continue to waste foodstuffs, fuel and manpower and to impair the efficiency of labour in the mines, factories and even in munitions plants near which saloons are located." In a full-page ad in the *New York Times*, Dr. Kellogg of Battle Creek said that the liquor interests, who "use more fuel than all schools and churches combined," were "conspirators against the public welfare."

Their political power catalyzed by these appeals to patriotism, congres-sional prohibitionists used the emergency to enact measures that didn't require constitutional sanction. Wilson, who needed the drys' support on a variety of his war initiatives, by and large stayed out of the way. Between April 1917 and November 1918—the length of the U.S. involvement in World War I—a series of "for the duration" laws, proclamations, and exec-utive orders first outlawed the sale of alcohol to soldiers, then proscribed the importation of distilled spirits, and, in the landmark Lever Food and Fuel Control Act of 1917, forbade their manufacture as well. Dry zones were established around naval bases (sale of liquor was forbidden within five miles) and around coal mines, shipyards, and munitions plants. In the name of the war effort, Food Administrator Herbert Hoover (who at this point in his career opposed Prohibition) ordered the amount of grain available to the brewing industry reduced by 30 percent. Legal beer was limited to 2.75 percent alcohol by weight. Even Theodore Roosevelt, who had long dismissed prohibitionists as "extremists" and believed that they suffered "a particularly annoying form of egoistic lunacy," sounded the dry trumpet: "When we must feed our army and help the armies of our allies," Roosevelt wrote to the head of the Methodist Church's Board of Temperance, Prohibition, and Public Morals, "not a bushel of grain should be permitted to be made into intoxicating liquor."

All this was concurrent with another product of war that served dry interests: the radical reshaping of the powers and perceptions of the federal government, a process that would further diminish the shock of constitutional Prohibition. Distrust of federal power had, of course, made even some dedicated drys oppose the idea of a constitutional amendment. But Wilson's expression and exaltation of national purpose, which provided a noble soundtrack for the federal government's sudden leap into countless aspects of American life, would make the idea of federal enforcement of Prohibition no more alien than, say, the military draft. The war emergency handed proponents of government activism a hunting license. As Charles Merz put it in *The Dry Decade*, the wartime emergency enabled Wilson, with scant public opposition, to "seize railways, requisition factories, take over mines, fix prices, put an embargo on all exports, commandeer all ships, standardize all loaves of bread, punish all careless use of fuel, draft men for an army, and send that army to a war in France." Compared to all that, closing down distilleries and breweries didn't seem so radical at all.

THE WAR'S CLINCHING contribution to the dry cause arrived in February 1918, as the Eighteenth Amendment was beginning its journey through the state legislatures. "We have German enemies across the water," a dry politician named John Strange told the *Milwaukee Journal* that month. "We have German enemies in this country too. And the worst of all our German enemies, the most treacherous, the most menacing, are Pabst, Schlitz, Blatz, and Miller."

Strange's call to arms was the preface to the Senate investigation of the German-American Alliance conceived, directed, and brilliantly exploited by Wayne B. Wheeler, an extravaganza that played out as the perfect accompaniment to the ratification campaign. Wheeler arranged for the appointment of the subcommittee that conducted the inquiry. He recruited the witnesses and bankrolled their expenses. But the stage for this final act of dry dramaturgy had been prepared by journalist George Creel, whom Wilson had placed at the head of a malignant propaganda body officially called the Committee of Public Information but known to critics as the "House of Truth." Employing a tactic it may have borrowed from the ASL, Creel's organization spread seventy-five thousand "Four Minute Men" throughout the country to advance the war cause in brief and usually inflammatory orations before every conceivable audience. Said Creel, "People do not live by bread alone; they live mostly by slogans." He also told his men that fear was "an important element to be bred in the civilian population." When the fear was attached to all things German, it proceeded to breed like an out-of-control virus.

Soon Red Cross leaders were claiming that German-Americans had penetrated their organization and were putting ground glass in bandages meant for U.S. troops. Addressing the members of the Union League Club in New York, Elihu Root—former secretary of state, former secretary of war, Nobel Peace Prize winner, recently retired U.S. senator—said, "There are men walking about the streets of this city who ought to be taken out at sunrise and shot for treason." In his infamous "Babel Proclamation," Governor William L. Harding of Iowa declared speaking German in public or on the telephone unlawful. German books were burned in Wisconsin, playing Beethoven in public was banned in Boston, and throughout the country foodstuffs and street names of German origin were denatured by benign Anglo-Saxonisms. Nearly ninety years before french fries became freedom fries during the Iraq War, sauerkraut became liberty cabbage and, in an odd homage to the president, Cincinnati's Berlin Street became Woodrow Street. "Cotton Tom" Heflin of Alabama, who could always be counted on to transcend the limits of ordinary, everyday bias, said, "We must execute the Huns within our gates. The firing squad is the only solution for these perverts and renegades."

The most horrifying single example of anti-German hysteria was described by historian David M. Kennedy in *Over Here*, his history of the home front during World War I:

> Near St. Louis in April 1918, a mob seized Robert Prager, a young man whose only discernible offense was to have been born in Germany. He had, in fact, tried to enlist in the American Navy but had been rejected for medical reasons. Stripped, bound with an American flag, dragged barefoot and stumbling through the streets, Prager was eventually lynched to the lusty cheers of five hundred patriots. A trial of the mob's leaders followed, in which the defendants wore red, white, and blue ribbons to court, and the defense counsel called their deed "patriotic murder." The jury took twenty-five minutes to return a verdict of not guilty.

As anti-German passions raged, Wheeler married them to his own cause. The German-American Alliance made it an easy coupling. Founded in 1901 to promote unity among Americans of German birth or extraction, it had been transformed by the Prohibition issue into the brewers' most prominent and powerful ally. The GAA held the line on suffrage as well: "Our German women do not want the right to vote," the Nebraska chapter asserted in 1914, "and since our opponents desire the right of suffrage mainly for the purpose of saddling the yoke of prohibition on our necks, we should oppose it with all our might." By 1914, GAA membership approached two million, and its political clout in some places, especially the large cities of the Midwest, was commensurate with its size. But then the guns of August rang out, and by 1917 the GAA had been identified by Wheeler as an organization whose "leaders urge its members to vote only for those who stand for Germanism and oppose Prohibition." "Germanism" meant anti-Americanism, and by Wheeler's conflation, it also meant "wet."

Wheeler knew he had scored a kill from the moment the Senate hearings opened with his star witness, Gustavus Ohlinger. A Toledo lawyer of Swedish and German extraction, in 1915 Ohlinger had published *Their True Faith and Allegiance*, a tract that had identified first- and second-generation German-Americans as "prophets of disunion." (His own family, Ohlinger boasted, had "been in this country for 250 years.") "Before he had testified 20 minutes the committee was on fire," Wheeler told Purley Baker. Baker must have been thrilled. He believed Germans were "a race of people . . . who eat like gluttons and drink like swine."

From that moment forward a steady sequence of congressional reports and administrative rulings initiated and then publicized by Wheeler and the ASL consigned the brewers to their final defeat. The first set of hearings alone produced more than seven hundred pages of subpoenaed documents. It was conclusively established that the United States Brewers' Association had funded the Washington office of the German-American Alliance and that annual support for the GAA was the third largest item in the USBA's annual budget, after salaries and publications. When the brewers captured control of the American Association of Foreign-Language Newspapers, they provided prepackaged editorials attacking Prohibition and implicitly supported a 1915 editorial campaign against war-preparedness spending. When the names of the brewers who had staked Arthur Brisbane to the *Washington Times* and had funded other wet papers were revealed, the list read like a page from the Munich telephone book. During the war, it turned out, the Anheuser-Busch Company had cabled nearly $300,000 in cash to Adolphus Busch's widow, who remained at Villa Lilly with her daughter Wilhelmina, caring for wounded German soldiers. News that the Busch family held a million dollars in German war bonds was not mitigated by the fact that they had been purchased before the United States entered the war. The blacklist of American corporations the brewers had boycotted was duly subpoenaed, leaked, and then published, along with reams of other documents from the USBA's files that had nothing to do with Germany and the war, but everything to do with the chronic depravity of the beer kings.

The brewers had not been unaware of the war's threat to their welfare. As early as 1914 the Anheuser-Busch executive committee had considered removing German names from their labels (they did remove them from bottles sold in Australia and Canada). August A. Busch, Adolphus's son and heir, took to wearing a small American flag button in his lapel and ordered the removal of portraits of German heroes that decorated the walls of the company's plants. More substantively, Gustave Pabst's son Henry, among many other members of brewery families, enlisted in the marines; the Busch family contributed half a million dollars to the U.S. war effort; and a group of Milwaukee brewers purchased $2 million in Liberty Bonds.

But none of this mattered. The hearings had branded the brewers' underhanded tactics as outright disloyalty. When the Newark brewer Christian Feigenspan was called before the Senate committee, he could offer only a faint, weary explanation of how it had all gone wrong. A long-serving president of the USBA, Feigenspan was cultured and capable, among the best the brewing industry had to offer. But the ASL's onslaught against all things German had brought him to his knees. Trying to explain what had led the brewers to engage in their various subterfuges and misdeeds, Feigenspan offered a preposterous, even shameless, explanation. He said Percy Andreae, the brewers' chief publicist, had "hypnotized our convention one year"—a convention of some of America's most powerful businessmen—and thereby won the authorization to conduct his covert campaign.

This sounded more like an acknowledgment of defeat than the roar of the powerful enemy Purley A. Baker evoked that fall. "Does anyone doubt," Baker asked an ASL conference in Columbus, "in the light of the immediate past, that if there had not been a strong, virile Prohibition movement to combat the propaganda of this disloyal but well-financed organization, that America would have been sufficiently Germanized to have kept her out of the war?"

+ + +

ON JANUARY 8, 1918, the thirty-three members of the Mississippi state senate and the ninety-six members of the state house gathered in Jackson to vote on the Eighteenth Amendment to the Constitution of the United States. The vote, which proceeded without debate, took exactly fifteen minutes, passing 28–5 in the upper house and 93–3 in the lower one. Mississippi was much more agreeable to this second constitutional amendment ever to place limits on individual behavior than it was to the first one. It didn't get around to ratifying that one—the Thirteenth, abolishing slavery—until 1995.

As the accumulating ratification votes would soon establish, the rapidly expanding (and usually wet) urban populations were rendered irrelevant by the anti-German hysteria and also by geography and demography. Richmond Hobson had asserted in a strategy brief four years earlier that because the major cities were concentrated in relatively few states, the seemingly daunting challenge of winning approval in thirty-six separate state legislatures would be much easier than winning two-thirds margins in Congress. You could conceivably write off the twelve most urbanized states—the Connecticuts, the New Jerseys, the Pennsylvanias—and still achieve ratification.

But even Hobson could not have imagined how smoothly ratification would proceed—"as if a sailing-ship on a windless ocean were speeding ahead, propelled by some invisible force," said the *New York Tribune*. Had the *Tribune* editors looked more closely, they would have realized that the "invisible force" was actually an obvious one: the universal malapportionment of state legislatures. Forty-four years later, in what Chief Justice Earl Warren called "the most important case of my tenure," the Supreme Court would decide that legislative seats had to be apportioned according to the principle of one man, one vote. But in 1918 the legislatures, and thus the ratification process, were rigged. The ASL's demonization of the brewers as disloyal servants of the Kaiser had softened the remaining opposition; the makeup of the state legislatures buried it.

You could find many reasons for legislative malapportionment: the inherent peculiarities of many state constitutions; the intrastate conflict arising from the shrinking population of the countryside and the booming growth of the cities; the eternal unwillingness of those in power to yield it. But in terms of Prohibition, there was only one consequence: this distortion of democracy was a blessing for the dry cause. In New York, for example, the legislature was configured in such a fashion that an urban assemblyman might represent seven times as many people as the rural representative at the next desk. Put another way, in choosing members of the state assembly, the vote of a farmer from upstate Preston Hollow—more than likely native born, Republican, and dry—was equivalent to the vote of seven Democratic, Irish-American wets from Hell's Kitchen in Manhattan. In New Jersey, where each member of the state senate represented a single county irrespective of population, the man from Cape May County served just 19,640 constituents, while his colleague from Essex County represented 652,089.* The farmers and fishermen who controlled Maryland's legislature had conspired to avoid any redistricting since 1867; in the intervening decades, while the population of urban, ethnic Baltimore had jumped 175 percent, the population in the rest of the state had increased only 46 percent. By 1918 democracy in Maryland had been imprisoned for half a century.

That these were not necessarily anomalies became clear as the race to ratification accelerated through 1918 and into early 1919. Statewide wet majorities were rendered irrelevant by the rotten-borough legislatures. The very same day the citizens of Missouri rejected a dry amendment to the state constitution by a margin of 47 percent dry to 53 percent wet, they elected a legislature that just two months later would ratify the Eighteenth Amendment by a 75 percent to 25 percent margin. In Ohio, the sacred cradle of the ASL, legislative districting and assiduous politicking put ratification over by a combined legislative vote of 105–42; however, when left to their own devices, Ohio voters rejected the very same measure in a referendum.

Not that it did them any good: as Hobson had written, "once ratified, always ratified." Under Article V of the Constitution the legislatures, however misshapen by rural domination, had the authority to enact constitutional Prohibition, and they did so with the speed of an epidemic, immune from referenda or gubernatorial vetoes. Setting aside Connecticut (population 67 percent Catholic) and Rhode Island (76 percent Catholic), both of which held out and refused to ratify, more than 80 percent of the nation's state legislators voted dry. Generally speaking the more rural the state, the more arid the vote: among the six states whose legislatures were

---

*Because the lower house of the legislature was apportioned by population, New Jersey found itself in the odd position of having its senate voting to ratify, its lower house against. This wasn't resolved until the latter body came around in 1922, ratifying the Eighteenth Amendment two years after it had been put into effect.

unanimous for ratification were Idaho, Kansas, South Dakota, Utah, and Wyoming. The only one of the six with any substantial urban presence was Washington, hardly an urban stronghold.

On January 16, 1919, when Nebraska's lower house went 98–0 for Prohibition (three days earlier one lone state senator out of the chamber's thirty-two had demurred), the Eighteenth Amendment was embedded in the United States Constitution. From the moment of submission it had taken 394 days to meet the approval of thirty-six state legislatures— less than half as long as it had taken eleven of the first fourteen states to approve the Bill of Rights.

THE OPENING CLAUSE of the Eighteenth Amendment—"After one year from the ratification of this article . . ."—meant that life in the United States was no different on January 17, 1919, from what it had been on January 15. This didn't stop people from airing their reactions. H. L. Mencken sold his 1915 Studebaker and told his friend Ernest Boyd that he "invested the proceeds in alcohol." William Jennings Bryan passed the time reading congratulatory telegrams. A woman in Missouri received a letter from her fiancé, a captain in the 129th Field Artillery, still with the U.S. Army near Verdun in northeastern France. "It looks to me like the moonshine business is going to be pretty good in the land of the Liberty Loans and Green Trading Stamps," thirty-four-year-old Harry S. Truman wrote to Bess Wallace, "and some of us want to get in on the ground floor. At least we want to get there in time to lay in a supply for future consumption."

Truman couldn't have been serious—at least not terribly serious—but his perception was on target. The experience of states that had already gone dry suggested there was a large and liquid gulf between how people voted and how they drank. Washington banned the in-state sale of liquor in 1916 but allowed individuals with permits to import it from other states; 34,000 permits were issued in Spokane County, where there were only 44,000 registered voters. Kansas had been officially dry since 1880, but enough saloons were operating under the protection of corrupt or lenient politicians for Carry Nation to have fashioned a career from their presence.

The most vivid example of thirsty behavior in a Prohibition desert played out in the month immediately after ratification, as Congress prepared to enact the legislation that would engrave into law the procedures, penalties, appropriations, exceptions, and hundreds of other necessary details that the 112 words of the Eighteenth Amendment didn't begin to address. After Michigan went bone dry in 1918 (the referendum that passed in 1916 didn't go into effect until then), you couldn't buy liquor in the state legally. But U.S. Highway 25, running from Dry Detroit to Wet Toledo, was so convenient for smugglers that it became known as the "Avenue de Booze." When a court decision made the liquor traffic along its sixty miles temporarily legal in February 1919, the *Detroit News* described "two almost continuous streams" of cars pouring along its length. "Those bound Detroitward and loaded to capacity with Toledo liquor" had their "rear fenders almost scraping the tires"; those going south were empty, ready to load up. "Wrecked automobiles dotted the length of the highway after the mad rush of Wednesday night," the paper noted.

Detroiters who were parched but carless "stormed" Toledo-bound interurban streetcars in the "thousands," the *News* reported, carrying "cheap, dirty suitcases, paper parcels, oil cans, bags and boxes" to fill up in Ohio and then tote back home. On the return trip, the Toledo train station was so crowded that would-be passengers "shouldered their heavy burdens and trudged three miles along the tracks to the city limits, only to find the incoming cars were jammed with new arrivals." After the governor of Michigan obtained a court injunction and heavily armed state police and federal agents were stationed on the highway (in the appropriately named border town of Temperance, Michigan), it was finally "safe for an innocent motorist to venture out on the highway . . . without being crowded into the ditch or trampled down by liquor runners."*

The Michigan experience suggested that only the hopelessly naïve believed that the moonshine business, the smuggling business, and any other form of illegal trade in alcohol would evaporate in the glorious sunlight of Prohibition. Men planning to get in on what Truman called "the ground floor" tended not to record their thoughts in letters that would be preserved in scholarly archives, but certainly they realized the opportunity that lay ahead of them. Back in the original debate over the Hob-

---

*The most prominent of the early Detroit smugglers were the Billingsley brothers of Oklahoma, a family of criminal operators who had set up operations in Michigan shortly after statewide Prohibition was established. The youngest of the Billingsleys, Sherman, opened one of the plushest New York speakeasies, the Stork Club, a few years after his release from a fifteen-month sentence in the federal prison in Leavenworth, Kansas.

Among the suspected smugglers arrested during the Toledo frenzy was a young Detroit delicatessen owner, Sam Boesky. Sam's son Ivan, who would become the most notorious stock market operator convicted in the insider-trading scandals of the 1980s, called one of the firms he set up to handle his market activity Farnsworth & Hastings Ltd.—a name he took from the location of the deli Sam ran (and from which the police believed he sold contraband liquor) at the corner of Farnsworth and Hastings streets in Detroit's East Side Jewish ghetto.

son Amendment, wet representative J. Campbell Cantrill of Kentucky had said the measure was effectively "a resolution legalizing the manufacture of intoxicating liquor without taxation," a privilege the legal distillers and brewers had never enjoyed. For those willing to risk the perils of unlawful activity, selling liquor without having to pay state or federal taxes was a business model of considerable appeal. Vastly enhanced profit margins could underwrite a lot of the overhead associated with lawbreaking—for instance, the cost of corrupting police, judges, politicians, and anyone else remotely involved in enforcement. William Howard Taft, serving as a professor of law at Yale during the interval between his presidency and his eventual appointment as Chief Justice of the Supreme Court, said, "The business of manufacturing alcohol, liquor and beer will go out of the hands of law-abiding members of the community, and will be transferred to the quasi criminal class." The only ill-chosen word in that sentence was "quasi."

THE MAN WHOSE legislative skills were called upon to prevent the realization of Taft's prediction was Andrew John Volstead, whose name would forever be attached to Prohibition as if it were an especially cheerless leitmotif in a Wagnerian opera. In Webster's unabridged *Third New International Dictionary*, "volsteadism" was still defined in the 1996 printing as "the doctrine of or adherence to prohibition." The word is much better remembered than the man.

He might not have minded, for Volstead did not seek attention; his sponsorship of the legislation required to enforce the Eighteenth Amendment thrust attention upon him. Born Andreas Joseph Vraalstad in 1859, the son of Norwegian immigrants, he was about as colorful as the snow that each winter blanketed his hometown of Granite Falls, Minnesota, and no more eager for the spotlight than a cloistered monk. "He had few inferiors when it came to dealing with the newspaper correspondents," one of them wrote, and Volstead would not have argued the point. He found press attention so disagreeable he once ran across the White House lawn to avoid being photographed. Volstead chewed cut-plug tobacco and indulged in the occasional glass of homemade chokecherry wine, but that was about as far from the straight and narrow as he would wander. He even wore a tie while tending the peonies in the garden of his wood-frame home in Granite Falls.

After serving fourteen years as the Yellow Medicine County prosecuting attorney, Volstead entered Congress in 1903 and generally aligned himself with the progressive, prosuffrage, pro–income tax wing of the Republican Party. He had been in the House sixteen years before assuming the chairmanship of the Judiciary Committee and, therefore, responsibility for the National Prohibition Act, which was the formal name of the legislation that would turn the Eighteenth Amendment's stark declarations into a code of enforcement. Volstead's one distinguishing physical characteristic was a broom of a mustache so luxuriant it reached his lower lip and made his face one of the most recognizable in the Capitol. But because of the duty that fell to him, both history and his wet colleagues in Washington saw something else when they looked at him. James A. Reed of Missouri—the most eloquent, most aggressive, most vituperative, and wettest wet in the Senate—said, "I have gazed upon pictures of the celebrated conspirators of the past," the leaders of "fanatical crusades, the burners of witches, the executioners who applied the torch of persecution, and I saw them all again when I looked at" the congressman from Granite Falls. Of course, Reed also said that Volstead was foreign-born and "speaks a very broken English," so it's somewhat understandable that he got everything else about him wrong, too.

Volstead was indeed a dry, but not a terribly vociferous one. He'd never delivered a speech on the subject and never joined the ASL. The Prohibition Party twice put up candidates to run against him. But he recognized "the vast movement that has gone on in this country in the last few years," and he believed in the rule of law. The Constitution had turned against liquor, and after the Sixty-sixth Congress opened for business in March 1919, Volstead did his best to implement the sacred document's intentions.

The legislative process that turned the Volstead Act into law encompassed all the elements that had come to characterize Prohibition's progress in Washington: the unshirted zealotry of the dry-drys, the winking compromises of the wet-drys, the general irrelevance of wets of every degree of dampness, and the canny tactical decisions of Wayne Wheeler. It incorporated the semantic tap dancing that could imbue a single, uninflected word with a meaning that would affect the lives of millions, and it accommodated political dissimulations even Wheeler would come to regret.

The sixty-seven separate sections of the Volstead Act indicated the breadth of its concerns and at the same time suggested how many different parties had a stake in it. The final bill covered everything from the definition of "intoxicating" (its single most crucial sentence) to whether de-alcoholized beer could still be called beer or "near beer" (it could not) to whether a foreign ship would be allowed to pass through the Panama

Canal if it carried a few bottles of rum for its crew (it would, but only if it was in transit from one foreign country to another and wouldn't be visiting a U.S. port along the way). Parties of interest weighing in on the law ranged from rabbinical associations fearful of a ban on sacramental wine to the Farm Bureau to the nation's manufacturers of hair tonic, flavor extracts, industrial dyes, and men's hats. And, most crucially, the Anti-Saloon League.

Popular accounts have long attributed the bill's authorship to Wheeler, partly because his eulogists wanted to credit him with it and partly because it was unimaginable that he wouldn't have commandeered the process. In fact Wheeler did fashion a version of a Prohibition enforcement law out of a number of existing state laws and presented it to Volstead and to the measure's Senate sponsors. But Volstead, who found Wheeler's draft "too loosely drawn" and possibly vulnerable to court challenges, spent several months crafting a measure so tight that not one of its provisions was ever deemed unconstitutional. Even though Wheeler may have spent nearly as much time in the committee room as many of its members, he never claimed sole authorship of the act. Grilled by hostile wets during a Senate hearing several years later, he was asked if he had dictated the various amendments to the bill as it passed through Congress. Wheeler replied, "Only in part."

The parts he seemed to care about most were the section enumerating the acts deemed criminal and the one that defined "intoxicating liquors." What was carefully kept out of the criminal code was any specific proscription against drinking or buying alcohol; savvy drys knew that without this enormous carve-out no user would ever testify against his supplier. Wheeler also got what he wanted in the definition of "intoxicating liquors," the vague formulation he and his allies had inserted (instead of "alcoholic beverages") in the amendment itself. This conscious dodge had enabled fence-sitters, conflict avoiders, and wishful thinkers to support the amendment in the hope that the eventual definition would leave room for some of the milder forms of liquid stimulation. Herbert Hoover, virtually a national hero because of his leadership of the wartime Food Administration, said he didn't think it was possible for a man to get drunk on beer that was 2.75 percent alcohol.

But now the drys had a much smaller mountain to climb. To pass the Volstead Act they needed only a majority in each house of Congress, rather than two-thirds of each house plus three-quarters of the state legislatures. The prudence that had replaced "alcoholic beverages" with "intoxicating liquors" in the text of the Eighteenth Amendment could now be cast aside.

"Alcoholic" was not something that could have been argued; anything containing alcohol was alcoholic, and Wheeler believed that if the word had been included in the text of the Eighteenth Amendment, the amendment would have died in Congress. Now, though, Wheeler's hammer came down on a stunningly severe definition of "intoxicating"—anything ingestible that contained more than 0.5 percent alcohol. This proscribed the lightest of wines, the most diluted forms of beer, and, if you really wanted to get serious about it, the naturally occurring fermentation that takes place in some recipes for sauerkraut (up to 0.8 percent alcohol) and German chocolate cake (0.62 percent). After this definition of "intoxicating" was established, a House Judiciary Committee report said, "No one who supported this amendment had in mind that there could be any question as to the meaning of the term." On the contrary: its appeal to Wheeler and his allies when they inserted the term into the amendment had been its exquisite vagueness. Less vague was the meaning of "beverage," at least to Representative Nicholas Longworth of Ohio, a future Speaker of the House with little patience for Prohibition. He said a beverage was "anything you can eat with a sponge."

Apart from his insistence on the strict definition of the word that was the Eighteenth Amendment's fulcrum, Wheeler displayed a surprising willingness to compromise on other aspects of the Volstead Act and to accommodate exceptions that would render it less than absolute. Having won the larger war, taking prisoners wasn't at the top of his agenda. Wheeler wasn't going to win meaningful support for the bill by accommodating the religious practices of the nation's Jews and Catholics; they had been nearly unanimous in their opposition to Prohibition. But the delegation of Orthodox rabbis who called on Volstead (much to the later dismay of the Reform rabbinate) nonetheless came away with continued access to sacramental wine for their congregants, as did the Catholic Church. Many hard-line drys wanted to deny physicians the right to prescribe alcohol, but this, too, wasn't worth the fight. No one questioned the need for the continued production of industrial alcohol for its many critical and/or popular uses, and if the enabling regulations were too loose, they could be tightened later. In a nod to those who had invested in their personal cellars (including various dry senators and representatives), Wheeler agreed to a clause that allowed individuals to continue to own, and to drink in their own homes, alcohol purchased before the Eighteenth Amendment's effective date.

Wheeler was so obliging he even allowed a single exception to the definition of "intoxicating"—in this case not because of a sudden fit of permissiveness, but because he had little choice. America's rural population and its elected representatives had nourished and sustained so much of the Prohibition crusade that ignoring their interests might have made passage of an effective enforcement act impossible. As a result, Section 29 of the Volstead Act specifically exempted cider and other "fruit juices" that just might happen to acquire an alcoholic tinge through the natural processes of fermentation. They were not subject to the 0.5 ceiling but to a determination of whether they were "intoxicating in fact"—a condition, said the very dry and very rural Senator Thomas Sterling of South Dakota, "for the jury to determine in any given case." As intended by Wheeler and Volstead, and as later interpreted by the courts, the law made home manufacture of hard cider perfectly acceptable. No husbandman would be denied the barrel by the homestead door, the jug stashed in a corner of the field, the comforting warmth on cold country nights. One dry honest enough to object to this dodge, Alben Barkley of Kentucky, noted that if it was legal to transform the juice of the apple into something stronger, then "Why not corn juice?"

Several years later, alighting on a justification for his departure from dry orthodoxy, Wheeler explained—apparently with a straight face—that the exception was meant to "enable the farmers and housewives of the country to conserve their fruits."

DID IT MATTER that the Volstead Act failed to provide a judicial procedure other than jury trial for anyone accused of any violation, dooming the federal court system to an unremitting fourteen-year flood of petty cases? Did it matter that the army of federal agents hired to enforce the act would not be part of the civil service because Andrew Volstead, among others, feared that civil service protection would guarantee "the offices would be filled with Wets that we could not get rid of"? Did it matter that the total initial appropriation for federal enforcement of this radical and far-reaching new law amounted to $2.1 million, or slightly less than the amount paid in one day a few months later for muskrat pelts at the St. Louis fur auction?

Not really. By the time the Volstead Act became law, the drys had become giddy in their political dominance and confident they would retain power sufficient to correct any errors or omissions. They believed that their cause had been sanctified by the long, long march to ratification, that it had truly been a people's movement every bit as glorious as any other in the nation's history. They were not alone in this belief, and they found strong defenders when their enemies attributed the movement's success to manipulation or deceit. "Prohibition was written into the Constitution with as much deliberation as attended the enactment of any amendment to the Constitution," wrote Felix Frankfurter of Harvard Law School. It was, he added, "the culmination of fifty years of continuous effort." Those who had organized to oppose it—the brewers, chiefly—had in fact been far more deceitful than the worst of the drys. "Pressure groups are our oldest political inheritance," said Wayne Wheeler, whose expertise on the nature of pressure groups was underscored by the fact that it was he who had coined the term. "They are lineal descendants of the group of barons who met King John at Runnymede" and crafted the Magna Carta.

Disorganized, dysfunctional, and disbelieving, the wets had watched the approach of Prohibition, said the *San Francisco Wholesalers' and Retailers' Review*, "in a dumb stupor." Now they had to adjust. Industrialist Henry Clay Frick, who did not employ men who drank but who had long owned an interest in the Old Overholt rye distillery, thoughtfully began to distribute his own reserves of Overholt to his pals while it was still legal; Senator Philander C. Knox of Pennsylvania, who had voted in favor of the Eighteenth Amendment, took receipt of twenty cases. In St. Louis, the Busch family stepped up production of a nonalcoholic "cereal beverage" called Bevo; by 1919 state laws and the various wartime codes had already cut sales of their intoxicating brands by 80 percent. In New York, Assistant Secretary of the Navy Franklin Delano Roosevelt had four cases of Old Reserve delivered to his townhouse on East Sixty-fifth Street—which, he told a friend, "is for the time being at least on the 'wet' list."

But perhaps more important than the celebrations of the drys or the adjustments of the wets was the stirring of activity in some quarters that had remained untouched by the decades of debate. Consider, for instance, the bustle in the Canadian prairie town of Yorkton, Saskatchewan, where Harry Bronfman, the thirty-three-year-old operator of the local railroad hotel, opened something called the Canada Pure Drug Company in a ramshackle warehouse building next door at 29 Front Street. Now, on Christmas Day 1919, only twenty-two days before the Great Dry Future was to begin 160 miles to the south, Harry and his younger brother Sam prepared to stock the shelves of the "drug company." Across Front Street, in the Canadian Pacific Railway freight shed, five carloads of Scotch whiskey were waiting to be unloaded.

In 1921 Andrew J. Volstead, who was a realistic man, told his House colleague John Nance Garner that although "we will gradually work out the machinery that will, with the cooperation of the states, make the country dry, we cannot hope that this law can be enforced so as not to be violated. All laws will be violated."

If he had only known. Over the next decade, the product of eighty years of marching, praying, arm-twisting, vote trading, and law drafting would be subjected to a plague of trials, among them hypocrisy, greed, murderous criminality, official corruption, and the unreformable impulses of human desire. Another way of saying it (and it was said often in the 1920s): the drys had their law, and the wets would have their liquor.

PART II

THE
FLOOD

The prohibitionists say that the liquor issue is as dead as slavery. The wet people say that liquor can be obtained anywhere. You'd think they'd both be satisfied.

—Marjory Stoneman Douglas, in the *Miami Herald*,
    October 7, 1920

Chapter 8

Starting Line

O N FRIDAY, JANUARY 16, 1920, at the First Congregational Church in Washington, the luminaries gathered in front of the buzzing crowd didn't look like they'd command the sort of frenzy that had greeted Billy Sunday that day at his tabernacle in Norfolk, Virginia, when he declared that "Hell will forever be for rent." Andrew Volstead's drooping mustache, James Cannon's antediluvian high-buckle shoes, and Wayne Wheeler's resemblance to a small-town clerk were material for a caricaturist, not for a victory party. Josephus Daniels, the navy secretary who had dried up the American fleet, was at the First Congregational, too, and so were Howard Hyde Russell, the sixty-five-year-old founder of the Anti-Saloon League, and Anna A. Gordon of the Woman's Christian Temperance Union. The WCTU would soon be launching a campaign "to help protect the woman worker." One of the slogans Gordon and her colleagues cooked up for the effort, "Equal Pay for Equal Work," would be unveiled in a week and would resonate for decades.

The WCTU could look ahead to its next campaign because its last one was now completely, irrevocably over. Secretary Daniels told the crowd, "No man living" would ever see the Volstead Act modified. Other notables offered similar declarations. Then, around 11:15 in the evening, after several hours of speechifying, the warm-up speakers receded into the immense shadow of the man now moving toward the lectern. William Jennings Bryan would have no victory in his long public life greater than this one. Freeing the nation from the death grip of alcohol even obliterated some of the remnant pain from his three failed presidential candidacies. He had spent the early part of the week delivering speeches in Nebraska, four on Monday alone, but still had the energy to make the twelve-hundred-mile trip to Washington. Nothing could have kept Bryan from participating in this event, in this city, in this church where Frederick Douglass had once been a congregant, and where the end of a different form of slavery would be memorialized at midnight.

The crowd had waited three hours for Bryan's speech. Some, it could have been said, had been waiting for decades. If the long service had made anyone's attention waver or diluted anyone's passion, Bryan restored them with the rolling rhythms of his oratory. For forty minutes he spoke, the great bald dome of his head gleaming with sweat, the trumpetlike sonorities of his broad vowels filling the room. At midnight he paused so that the congregants could rise and sing the doxology. Then, as they took their seats, Bryan gathered himself for a fiery conclusion. Drawing from the gospel of Saint Matthew, he yoked the liquor trade to those who would have killed the infant Jesus. "They are dead that sought the young child's life!" he boomed. Then again, even louder: "They are dead!" And once more, his arms raised, his eyes aglow, a saint in the grip of ecstasy: "They are dead!"

THE LIQUOR INDUSTRY wasn't dead, of course; a new version, this one illegal, underground, and nearly ubiquitous, would emerge with the birth of the dry utopia. Not two hours after rapture swept the First Congregational Church, halfway across the country agents from the Bureau of Internal Revenue apprehended two truckloads of whiskey departing a warehouse in Peoria, Illinois—"stolen," it appeared, by officials of the distillery that had produced it. It was the first recorded arrest made under the Prohibition laws—the first of hundreds of thousands to come.

Still, many Americans greeted Prohibition with due respect: they began to drink less. A significant portion of the population either felt duty-bound to take the constitutional strictures seriously or found the procedural roadblocks erected by the Volstead Act too daunting. Alcohol-related deaths fell in 1920, as did arrests for public drunkenness. Generally speaking, the closer one lived to the middle of the country, especially in towns and cities inhabited by Protestants of northern European extraction, the more likely it was that drinking was down. Helen and Robert Lynd reported that in Muncie, Indiana—the real *Middletown*—where there had once been a saloon for every 140 adults, drinking declined because civic and social leaders chose to go dry, thereby setting an example for their neighbors. Still, the big cities of the coasts were not unscathed, as hotels and restaurants dependent on bar business shut their doors. One of the first to give up the fight was Holland House, on Fifth Avenue in New York. It closed during Prohibition's very first month, its celebrated Bamboo Cocktails (sherry, dry vermouth, orange bitters) gone forever.

Evidence of the drying-up came from many sources. Welch's Grape Juice began to set new sales records. Diminished criminal behavior led Grand Rapids, Michigan, to abandon its work farm. Chicago closed one of its jails. "We were all elated by the marked decrease in so-called disorderly conduct," Jane Addams would recall. "Our neighborhood registered a general lack of street disorders and also of family quarrels, which had so often put a mother and little children into the streets, turned out by a drunken father, sometimes in the middle of the night." Songwriter Albert Von Tilzer, who had taken America out to the ballgame in 1908, was cashing royalties from a new song called "I Never Knew I Had a Wonderful Wife Until the Town Went Dry."

But the front-page headline in the January 17 edition of the ASL's *American Issue*—CONSTITUTIONAL PROHIBITION IS IN EFFECT / ALL LIQUOR STAINS WIPED FROM THE STARS AND STRIPES—would prove a gross overstatement. In fact the best estimates by authoritative scholars indicate that in the decade after the arrival of the Eighteenth Amendment, alcohol consumption dropped only 30 percent.

After the house of Prohibition had begun to crumble in the late 1920s, Deets Pickett, a publicist for the Methodist Board of Temperance, Prohibition and Public Morals, paused in fond recollection of those early, slightly dry days. "We learned to drink milk as never before," he sighed, "and our tables were loaded with fresh vegetables and fruits . . . and the young people became taller and healthier and more vigorous."

AMONG THOSE WHO had feared the arrival of Prohibition, the legendary oenologist A. R. Morrow was hardly characteristic, except insofar as he considered the new regime both unpleasant and disruptive of a way of life. Morrow, who knew the wines of California better than any other living being, had a palate so refined and a nose so sophisticated that he spurned all highly seasoned foods in order to protect his sensory acuity. Needless to say, he never smoked. He also never swallowed the wines he tasted, fearing that even a hint of inebriation could dull his edge. But the onset of Prohibition brought to Morrow's life what he thought would be a radical change. Convinced that his career was over, he discarded all caution and, for the first time, swallowed a mouthful of wine.

What shocked Morrow was not the effect, but the absence of effect: his taste buds remained as keen as ever. He was one of those millions who believed in the miracle of the grape, the wonders of the hop, or the marvels embedded in a bushel of corn or rye, and then discovered that the arrival of the dreaded day changed their lives much less than they had feared. However much the population at large cut back on their alcohol consumption, from the very beginning those who really wanted to drink inevitably found a way. Take Baron M. Goldwater of Phoenix, who arranged to have the bar, back bar, and brass rail of his favorite saloon installed in the basement of his house, where his son Barry, ten years old at the advent of Prohibition, would soon be making beer. Or consider the father of another future U.S. senator. Joseph P. Kennedy sold off much of the stock from his father's East Boston liquor business to grateful friends and associates, and cellared several thousands of dollars' worth of wine in his Brookline house.

The wine in Joe Kennedy's basement was there legally, courtesy of the clause in the Volstead Act that legitimized alcoholic beverages already stored in an individual's residence as of midnight on January 16. Like Kennedy, most beneficiaries of this provision were wealthy. They had money to invest in an inventory they might not consume for years, and they owned residences large enough to store it. The propertied (and bibulous) classes, who were not shy about exploiting their advantage, had won an exception that was nearly as broad, and nearly as focused on a single constituency, as the gift of cider that Congress had bestowed on the nation's farmers. The wealthy took advantage of both the exception and the lead time to buy and store as much as they wished, even after liquor and wine dealers began shutting their doors in late 1919. By January 16, 80 percent of the merchandise stored in the cellars of the Union Club at Fifth Avenue and Fifty-first Street in Manhattan had been transferred to the members' homes. In New Orleans civic leader Walter Parker, a member of the Stratford Club, built two new wine cellars in his house, purchased a stock of more than five thousand bottles, and proceeded to dip into it daily for the next fourteen years. In Los Angeles, Charlotte Hennessy, mother of actress Mary Pickford, simply bought the entire inventory of a liquor store and had it relocated to her basement.

Despite the ease with which they could satisfy their thirsts, many of the well-off chose to devote considerable energy to disputing the legitimacy of the Eighteenth Amendment. It would not be inaccurate to say that the eventual repeal of Prohibition was born in 1920 in the clubs and salons and dining rooms of the American aristocracy, who considered constitutional Prohibition an affront to republican (and Republican) principles. The first public manifestation of this phenomenon was a legal challenge orchestrated by that most distinguished of American lawyers, Elihu Root.

Root was the beau ideal of the governing class, a brilliant and wealthy man who despised the very idea of Prohibition, both as an intrusion on the rights of the individual and as an assault on the rights of the states. He was broad enough in his thinking to believe that individual rights extended to working people, but in this instance he was sufficiently narrow to frame the workingman's exercise of those rights as the inevitable by-product of desperation. Prohibition, Root told his friend Everett P. Wheeler, "takes away the chief pleasure in life for millions of men who have never been trained to get their pleasure from art, or literature, or sports, or reform movements." One imagines that most American workers, confronted with the choice, would opt for their beer even if the infinite joys of reform movements had been available to them. The selfless patriots who financed Root's legal challenge—the brewers, of course—likely imagined that, too.

The Elihu Root who had gotten so hot under the collar with his anti-German rhetoric during the war ("there are men . . . who should be shot for treason") was barely less ardent when he took his case to the Supreme Court in March 1920, accompanied by the eminent constitutional lawyer William D. Guthrie. To a degree, this was advocacy suited for a surrealist: Root and Guthrie were trying to persuade the justices to declare a constitutional amendment . . . unconstitutional. Their case was built on three legs and one crutch: the Fifth Amendment; the Tenth Amendment; a belief that the Constitution was an inappropriate vessel for what was essentially a criminal statute; and blind hope. The effort failed, but not without a blaze of rhetorical glory. Root and Guthrie's friend Nicholas Murray Butler, the wet president of Columbia University, described the closing moments of the argument: "Mr. Root put his glasses in his pocket, and, drawing himself up to his full height, pointing his finger at the Chief Justice, with the whole nine Justices fixing their eyes upon him, he concluded his argument with these memorable words . . . : 'If Your Honors . . . shall find a way to uphold the validity of this amendment, the government of the United States, as we have known it, will have ceased to exist.'"

The justices were unconvinced, and somehow the government managed to survive. Root and Guthrie, as well as Butler, would remain opposed to Prohibition. But one month after the Supreme Court defeat, Guthrie was peripherally involved in a lawsuit that concluded much more happily for all involved. His daughter Ella wanted a divorce from Eugene S. Willard, and there remained a final, contentious issue impeding a settlement. It was finally resolved when the parties agreed to divide their supply of legal liquor equally—half to his house in Locust Valley on Long Island, and half to hers on Park Avenue.

✦ ✦ ✦

THOSE WITH NEITHER means nor storage space resorted to strategies homelier than those available to the wealthy. Within days of the onset of the dry era, portable stills, some with a distilling capacity as little as a single gallon, were on sale in cities across the country. That same week illegal liquor began leaking through the border from Canada, much of it into the poor and working-class neighborhoods of eastern and midwestern cities. The long-anticipated arrival of Prohibition—the world had known its starting date for a year—had accommodated establishment of elaborate distribution networks; as the *Daily Mail* of Fredericton, New Brunswick, reported, even before January 16, "Enough smuggled Canadian stock is said to be hidden in the woods [over the Maine border] to keep authorities busy for over a year." Before January was out the head of the U.S. Customs Service told Congress that the quantities pouring in from Canada now constituted a flood, and his forces had been able to intercept only "an infinitesimal quantity." Then a sequence of events in the remote upper Michigan mining town of Iron River established that slaking the thirst of the American working class was not exclusively contingent on Canadian ingenuity.

Of the innumerable headlines that focused the nation's attention on Iron River in the last week of February 1920, the most dramatic may have been the one in the *St. Louis Globe-Democrat*. Stretching across the top of the front page, in two lines of the declarative black capitals generally reserved for wars, presidential elections, and horrible natural disasters, it read ARMED INVASION IS BEGUN TO CRUSH PROHIBITION REBELLION IN MICHIGAN. The unembarrassed use of "rebellion" also featured prominently in the *New York Times* version, and in Chicago the *Tribune* took the next and obvious step in its eight-column screamer: WHISKY REBELLION, the paper called the events in Iron River, and added, ARMED FORCE TO DESCEND ON MINING COUNTRY.

In fact, the armed invasion force included fewer than two dozen federal Prohibition agents. The rebellion largely consisted of the maneuvers (either impudent or bold, depending on your perspective) of a young district attorney. And there was no whiskey involved at all—the drink in question was a homemade zinfandel pressed from grapes shipped in from California and known in upper Michigan as "Dago Red." But the events in Iron River would demonstrate that insofar as alcoholic beverages were concerned, the interests of the working poor and the well-to-do coincided—in this instance, because the former wanted their wine, and because the latter very much wanted them to have it.

The story broke on February 23, when a federal agent named Leo J. Grove seized three barrels of homemade wine from the basement of a grocery store belonging to the Scalcucci brothers, provisioners to the Italians, Austrians, Hungarians, Poles, Croatians, Serbs, and other immigrants who had been drawn to the area by the lure of jobs in the iron mines. District Attorney Martin S. McDonough asserted that the wine had been illegally expropriated; because one of the Scalcuccis lived above the grocery store, he said, Grove had improperly invaded his "home" without a warrant. McDonough thereupon seized the wine, returned it to the Scalcuccis—and arrested Agent Grove for the illegal transport of liquor. In his Chicago office, Alfred V. Dalrymple, chief Prohibition officer for the midwestern states, was displeased. He declared that Iron County "is in open revolt." Telling the press he would take "as many men as are necessary" to subdue the rebellion, Dalrymple said, "I do not want bloodshed, but if the state authorities stand in the way, and they are backed by their political cohorts, I am going to shoot."

Dalrymple arrived in town at midnight on February 24 with sixteen of his own men and what was variously described as "a host" or "an army" of reporters, photographers, and newsreel cameramen. One of the first tableaux they encountered was a rural, winterized version of the panic that had gripped many American cities five weeks earlier. The *Tribune* reporter described "bobsleds drawn by oxen and horses" and hand sleds pulled along the snowy roads by men, women, and children, all laden with bottles and casks destined for "the hills, mine shafts, tunnels, and underbrush," there to be hidden from Dalrymple's invaders.

Mostly, though, the press contingent got indoor pictures of Dalrymple staring down the thirty-four-year-old McDonough in the lobby of the Iron Inn or exterior shots of him out in the frigid February weather, sledgehammer in hand, smashing open the barrels of wine his men had managed to intercept. As vivid gouts of Dago Red saturated a nearby snowbank, turning it a deep, grapy purple, a cameraman from Pathé News gave a local man called "Necktie" Sensiba fifty cents to drop to his knees and eat the snow. The high school kids who joined him didn't have to be paid.

That was about it; by 4 p.m. on the twenty-fifth, sixteen hours after Dalrymple's arrival, he suddenly announced that he had important business in Washington, would be leaving within the hour, and would issue no more statements. The business, it turned out, was an investigation of the entire silly affair, ordered up by Dalrymple's boss, Prohibition commissioner John F. Kramer. As Dalrymple and his men boarded the train for Chicago, Iron River residents got out their sleds again and toted their bottles and barrels back to their homes. McDonough, the young prosecutor, was hailed as a hero in the iron country of northern Michigan and beyond. The *New York Times* reported that telegraph wires into Iron County were jammed with congratulatory messages from sixteen states. One, from New York district attorney Edward Swann, saluted McDonough for his "courageous stand against Dalrymple's theatrical attempt to gain notoriety for himself."

At least some of McDonough's courage emanated from a motivation little noted at the time. "These foreigners"—the mine workers of Iron County—"always have had their grape presses and their homemade wine," McDonough said during the rebellion. "They drink this in preference to water. They carry it to their work in their dinner pails and they won't work without it."

McDonough, whose father-in-law had founded Iron River four decades earlier when he opened some of the county's first iron mines, also said, "We have a large number of foreign workers here, and we wish to keep them."

IN THE FIRST seven months of that first dry-but-wet year, 900,000 cases of liquor found their way from Canadian distilleries to the border city of Windsor, Ontario. This worked out to roughly 215 bottles of booze for every man, woman, and child in the area. This sounds like a lot only if you don't believe the court testimony of the Windsor woman who had personally acquired nine barrels of that whiskey, plus another forty cases of it in bottles. During the late war, she told a magistrate, she had turned to the bottle to soothe her anguish about the Canadian boys at the front, in the process developing a taste for the stuff that she had not been able to shake after the armistice. Poor dear—simple math suggested she'd been drinking roughly ten bottles a day. Or perhaps she, and all the other Windsorites on the receiving end of the whiskey flood, just might have been sending it across the mile-wide Detroit River to Michigan. It was as if the whole eastern end of Ontario, and much of the north as well, had been lifted up and tilted so that every drop of liquid in the province could run downhill to Windsor.

Another conduit through Ontario—the Michigan Central tracks connecting Niagara Falls to Windsor, and thus the northeastern United States to Detroit and beyond—carried its own cargo of liquor in the summer of 1920. On June 6, an honest customs inspector boarded a train that had originated in Boston, crossed into Canada at the falls, and was now in Windsor, poised to enter the international rail tunnel to Detroit. He entered the first car and asked the occupants to hand over any liquor they were carrying. This produced twelve bottles, which the inspector placed on the floor as he entered the second car to continue his rounds. When he turned around a moment later, all twelve bottles had disappeared. Undeterred, he moved along the train, tapping the coat and pants pockets of the next car's occupants and reaping another harvest of flasks and bottles.

Inspector Graham probably didn't know that the pockets he patted belonged to two hundred Massachusetts Republicans on their way to the party's national convention in Chicago. Though the *Boston Evening Transcript* reported the misadventure, the tone of its report was conspicuously lighthearted (Graham had been "in pursuit of suspicious gurgles"), even blasé: it characterized the delegates' train trip as "politically uneventful." Beyond that, little mention of the event appeared in the newspapers. Already, at this early moment in the evolution of Prohibition, the personal habits of the men who had placed the Eighteenth Amendment in the Constitution, or who presided over its enforcement, weren't a matter of public concern.

Not even to Wayne B. Wheeler, who asked American politicians for public loyalty, not private virtue. Wheeler knew that the victories of 1919 could be undone if Congress failed to appropriate funds for enforcement, so he devoted most of 1920 to building a barrier against such an eventuality. Without continued support from both major parties, Wheeler believed, the Eighteenth Amendment could be undermined as quickly and as thoroughly as the Fifteenth. Yet as the two political parties gathered for their conventions that summer, Wheeler wanted nothing but inaction.

He was pleased that the Republicans picked the privately soaking but publicly parched (and always pliable) senator Warren G. Harding as their candidate. He was displeased that the Democrats chose Harding's fellow Ohioan, the sometimes-wet-sometimes-dry governor James M. Cox, as theirs. But Wheeler cared less about the parties' candidates than about their platforms. In that prebroadcasting era, when the only information American voters could get about national candidates came in printed form, the endlessly debated, widely circulated platforms were essential documents—and Wheeler didn't want a word about Prohibition in either one of them. "Fearing that either or both party conventions would reject" a strong dry proposal, wrote his research assistant, Justin Steuart, Wheeler chose not to risk any inference that the ASL's power and influence had waned.

The Republicans obliged; not even an allusive mention of Prohibition or the Volstead Act appeared anywhere in the 102 paragraphs of their platform, not even in the section devoted to recent GOP legislative successes. There, the party confined its self-congratulation to its efforts regarding such concerns as telegraph reform, postal pay rates, vocational education, and the future of the shipping industry. The party's controlling document boasted of its support for the pending Nineteenth Amendment—woman suffrage—but whispered not a word about what it had done for the Eighteenth.

The Democrats approached their convention a few weeks later knowing two very important things: that the other party had remained silent on Prohibition and that members of their own party wouldn't have to suffer the confiscation of hip flasks en route to San Francisco. That was because they didn't have to take any along. San Francisco had officially declared its distaste for Prohibition even before it had started. Back in 1919, the city's considerate board of supervisors, mindful of the hardship about to be visited upon its citizens, had unanimously repealed the city ordinance banning unlicensed saloons. A judge—a *federal* judge, in fact—had declined to give a jail sentence to Louis Cordano of Mission Street, who had been convicted of a prohibition violation; among Italians, the judge said, wine "is as necessary as coffee to the average American and tea to the average Englishman." A few months before the Democratic convention got under way on June 28, an examination of a panel of fifty prospective criminal trial jurors revealed that exactly two of them identified themselves as dry.

As a result, the Democrats' sojourn by the Bay was eagerly anticipated by delegates who were, in the disapproving words of a dry delegate from Minnesota, "in communion with the spirit of John Barleycorn." Republican Mayor James Rolph Jr., who believed in accommodating his guests even if they were Democrats and even if they voted dry, provided delegates and the press corps with what a grateful H. L. Mencken characterized as "Bourbon of the very first chop, Bourbon aged in contented barrels of the finest white oak, Bourbon of really ultra and super quality." Delivered by "small committees of refined and well-dressed ladies," Mayor Rolph's bourbon was also free of charge. If you stood in a San Francisco hotel lobby and looked thirsty, wrote another journalist at the convention, "all sorts of unknown Samaritans will charitably ask you up to their room."

The Democrats who managed to drag themselves to the Cow Palace to adopt a platform and nominate a candidate seemed no more eager to address Prohibition than the Republicans had been. This was definitely true of the dry leaders who had come to the convention to loom over the proceedings like armed prison guards on a catwalk. Dry Democrats were James Cannon's responsibility, and Cannon (along with William Jennings

Bryan, platform committee chairman Senator Carter Glass of Virginia, and any other dry in an influential party position) was Wayne Wheeler's responsibility. President Wilson asked his supporters to introduce a plank modifying the Volstead Act to allow the sale of beer and light wines, but Glass refused even to allow a debate on its merits. Scanning the horizon in the other direction, the ASL had to contend with a runaway train when Bryan, who did not appreciate subtlety, introduced a militantly dry floor resolution. To Cannon fell the counterintuitive task of persuading dry delegates to vote down the Bryan resolution. His private reasoning: if the Democrats had such a plank while the Republicans did not, the ASL's meticulously balanced posture of nonpartisanship would be endangered. His public position, as described by Senator Glass: Cannon nobly "shrank from the idea of having [Prohibition] made a political issue."

An ailing Bryan was devastated. The Boy Orator of the Platte was now a very old sixty, plagued by diabetes and crippled by his evident irrelevance; some called him the party's "Beerless Leader." A wisecrack published as the convention opened was not far off the mark: "There are several hundred men in this convention who would like to nail William Jennings Bryan to his cross of gold and leave him there to die of thirst." As the Democrats prepared to vote on the resolution, Wheeler encountered Bryan at the rear of the hall, prostrate on a makeshift bed fashioned from a cast-off door and two wooden supports. "I put an old coat under his head for a pillow," Wheeler would remember. "He seemed dead tired, and the expression on his face indicated that he was suffering greatly. He took me by the hand and with tears coursing down his cheeks told me he was ready to die if he could make his party take the right action as to prohibition and adopt his resolution."

Abhorred by the wets, abandoned by the drys, Bryan and his resolution were overwhelmed, losing by a vote of 929.5–155.5. Not even half a year had passed since his apotheosis in the First Congregational Church in Washington; now, he said, "My heart is in the grave." For much of the rest of the convention wet delegates, the fortunate beneficiaries of Sunny Jim Rolph's largess and Wayne Wheeler's political calculations, crooned chorus after cheerfully cynical chorus of that tuneful old favorite, "How Dry I Am."

Chapter 9

A Fabulous Sweepstakes

P ROHIBITION WAS BETTER than no liquor at all," the saying went, and it didn't take much effort to convince the thirsty. The evidence was everywhere. In New England the liquor came from ships anchored beyond the three-mile limit and ferried to shore by an enormous fleet of sailboats, skiffs, dinghies, rowboats, and even a few seaplanes. In Philadelphia the primary source was the chemical industry of the Delaware Valley, where denatured alcohol produced under government permit for industrial uses could be diverted, renatured, diluted, flavored with a little juniper oil, and made available on Market Street within days. Chicagoans depended on the resourceful (if murderous) Genna brothers, who oversaw hundreds of home stills situated in apartments all over the Near West Side, a network so large the entire neighborhood reeked of alcohol fumes. The $15 a month the Gennas paid to each mom or pop distiller for their output added up to very little, really, if you considered that the brothers' operation grossed $350,000 a month.

Denver drinkers could look to cunning moonshiners who placed animal carcasses near their distilleries, thus disguising the telltale scent of sour mash with the more potent aroma of rotting flesh. Across the South, moonshine technology developed along local lines, Georgia contributing the Double-Stacked Mash Barrel Still, Virginia the Blackpot Still, and Alabama the Barrel-Capped Box Still, which in turn spawned a North Carolina variant fueled by propane instead of wood (no telltale plume of smoke to tip off hijackers, competitors, or lawmen).

The liquor available in Kansas—dry by state law since 1880—was largely a concoction called Deep Shaft, named for the mines in the southeast part of the state where it originated. In Detroit, so near to the bounteous output of its Canadian neighbors, subterfuge was generally unnecessary. Wrote newspaperman Malcolm Bingay, "It was absolutely impossible to get a drink in Detroit unless you walked at least ten feet and told the busy bartender what you wanted in a voice loud enough for him to hear you above the uproar."

In Washington, Warren G. Harding could get his drinks from Taylor, his manservant at the house he kept near the golf course at the Chevy Chase Club, who kept it stocked with bourbon and Scotch; from his attorney general, Harry Daugherty, who had large quantities of seized liquor delivered by Justice Department employees to his infamous den of iniquity, the Little Green House on K Street; or from his friend Representative Nicholas Longworth of Ohio, Teddy Roosevelt's son-in-law, "who did not have the slightest intention of complying with the Eighteenth Amendment and never pretended to." That was the verdict of his wife, Alice, who believed that the family's butler made "a passable gin." The Longworth cellars also produced a homemade beer that won compliments from Arthur Balfour when the British diplomat visited Washington for the 1921 Disarmament Conference.

It was of course no surprise that Harding's Washington was awash in alcohol from the moment of his inauguration. In the Senate he'd been a dry only as a matter of convenience, doing what he felt necessary to stay on the right side of the Anti-Saloon League, which was so powerful in Ohio. Harding never really thought Prohibition would work, and his attitude toward liquor was probably best demonstrated in a sociable nature that made him, said one of his contemporaries, "not at all averse to putting a foot on the brass rail."

This was a common posture among those who frequented the private rooms at Harding's White House. The president set the tone when he arranged to have $1,800 worth of liquor that he'd purchased before January 16, 1920, transferred to the presidential living quarters from his home on Wyoming Avenue. (Going in the other direction, Woodrow Wilson had his personal supply relocated from the White House to his home on S Street.) Harding provided liquid hospitality to guests ranging from Adolph S. Ochs, publisher of the *New York Times*, to the floating cast of characters who took part in his regular poker games. Those were among the most freely lubricated nights at the White House, when Florence Harding graciously took on the responsibility of filling and refilling the glasses of her husband's Ohio cronies (including Attorney General Daugherty) and his higher-toned Washington pals. Thus could the First Lady find herself from time to time accommodating not only the nation's chief legal officer, but a future Speaker of the House (Longworth), two U.S. senators (Frank Brandegee of Connecticut and Joseph Frelinghuysen of New Jersey), the chairman of the U.S. Shipping Board (advertising pioneer Albert Lasker), and occasionally even the daunting secretary of the treasury, Andrew W. Mellon, the vastly wealthy man whose department was responsible for enforcing the Eighteenth Amendment. Florence Harding's friend Alice Longworth, who said "no rumor [about the Harding White House] could have exceeded the truth," recalled "air heavy with tobacco smoke, trays with bottles containing every imaginable brand of whisky . . . cards and poker chips ready at hand—a general atmosphere of the waistcoat unbuttoned, feet on the desk, and the spittoon alongside."

Because of the Teapot Dome scandal and various other outrages that brought dishonor to his administration and that for the most part became known only after what Samuel Hopkins Adams called Harding's "timely death," there's much about this least respected of presidents that has been sifted out of his historical image. He began his administration by throwing open the gates of the White House, allowing average citizens to roam the grounds of this highly symbolic piece of public property. He brought black citizens back into federal positions (Woodrow Wilson had all but purged them during his administration), implored Congress to pass an antilynching bill, and forthrightly denounced the Ku Klux Klan. On October 26, 1921, in one of the boldest speeches ever delivered by an American president, he traveled into the heart of the South to tell an enormous crowd in Birmingham, "I would say let the black man vote when he is fit to vote; prohibit the white man voting when he is unfit to vote." Wilson had refused to pardon Eugene V. Debs, who had been imprisoned on a preposterous espionage charge arising from the domestic hysteria that accompanied World War I; Harding pardoned him on Christmas Day of the first year of his presidency, with the probably unprecedented proviso that the recipient of the pardon had to come visit him in the White House.

But there was this persistent thing about Warren Harding, however enlightened (if ineffectual) some of his statements might have been: his inability to make a decision. He told one of his speechwriters, "I listen to one side and they seem right, and then—God!—I talk to the other side, and they seem just as right." He both smoked and chewed tobacco, and at times would grow so desperate to calm his raging anxiety that he'd grab a cigarette, rip it open, and stuff its contents straight into his mouth.

The *New Republic* said Harding had none of "those moral or intellectual qualities which would qualify him even under ordinary circumstances for statesmanlike leadership." That was accurate but not really the point. What Harding lacked was the courage of his convictions—which, practically speaking, meant he had no convictions at all.

WAYNE WHEELER HAD two primary responsibilities once the Eighteenth Amendment was ratified: keeping Congress and the president in line. This took vigilance but little heavy lifting. Congress was no problem at all; the ASL had effectively seized control of both House and Senate in the 1916 elections and had only tightened it since. The feckless Harding would have required more attention had he not been so inherently complaisant. Wheeler's grip on the short leash he allowed Harding was so firm that when he wanted something from the president, Harding would respond with the eagerness of a puppy. When Wheeler objected to the pending Supreme Court appointment of Senator John K. Shields of Tennessee, who had voted for the Eighteenth Amendment but against the Volstead Act, Harding capitulated instantly. On one occasion, hoping "to see you briefly concerning some matters of mutual interest," Wheeler heard back from Harding by return mail: "I need not tell you," the president wrote, "that I will always try to make it possible to see you when you find occasion to call." Not that it was always a pleasant prospect for Harding. When Treasury Secretary Andrew Mellon announced his permissive interpretation of a particular Volstead Act provision, Harding parried Wheeler's speedy complaint with a doleful response: "Somehow," Harding wrote, "I had rather expected your letter."

But Wheeler never complained publicly about anything Harding did; to do so, wrote his ASL colleague Justin Steuart, "might be construed as evidence that he lacked influence with the administration." If so, that would have been virtually the only such evidence extant. When the president was about to appoint a chief Prohibition enforcement officer, the Harding administration took pains to assure Wheeler that "no one would be appointed for this position who was unacceptable" to the ASL. This was how the nation won the services of Roy A. Haynes of Ohio.

If you can judge a man by his friends, then Haynes could be convicted on the basis of the wild enthusiasm in his behalf displayed by Representative W. D. Upshaw of Georgia, the driest dry in the House. Upshaw had given himself the nickname "Earnest Willie." Having lost the use of his legs in an accident, he was also billed from time to time as "the orator on crutches" or "the Rolling Chair Evangelist." Sometimes he was called "the Georgia Cyclone."* He signed his mail "Yours very dry." A religious fundamentalist and political naïf, Upshaw was an object of perpetual mirth to wets, who loved to bait him, and of substantial consternation to the ASL, which couldn't control him. Said one league official, "No one questions Mr. Upshaw's sincerity, but he is ranting and intemperate." Indiscriminate, too: Upshaw's single-minded devotion to the Prohibition cause led him to support both the Ku Klux Klan and woman suffrage, believing that both abetted the dry movement. Even more avidly, he endorsed Roy Haynes's appointment as Prohibition commissioner. Upshaw applauded Haynes's "unsullied integrity" and "amazing genius and energy," and said "the story of [his] victories reads like a revised edition of the Acts of the Apostles, with *Scottish Chiefs* and the *Arabian Nights* thrown in."

Ranting, intemperate, indiscriminate—and, judging by his appraisal of Haynes, Upshaw was also either profoundly disingenuous or just plain stupid. Roy Haynes had three characteristics ("qualifications" would be a gross overstatement) that might have led Wheeler to choose him for the job of supervising a national force of federal agents. He had been editor of a daily newspaper in Hillsboro, Ohio, where Mother Thompson had launched her Crusade back in 1873. He was a Harding crony. And, crucially, he was willing to be the ASL's hand puppet—or, as the head of the New York State branch of the ASL called him, "Wheeler's special pet."

A large, doughy man whose sunny nature was as expansive as his waist and as predictable as the bow tie he wore every day, Haynes was convinced that leading the federal enforcement effort was a swell assignment. He seemed equally convinced that he was good at it. The evidence? In the first full year of Prohibition, he said, church membership in the United States had grown by 1.2 million, and if that wasn't a sign of the nation's turn in a moral direction, what was? And how about the wonderful "fact" he cited the following year—that 85 percent of the nation's drinkers had sworn off the stuff since the dry regime began? This was an assertion so patently at odds with reality that critics found it as humorous as the admonitory fables Haynes liked to cite. Once, warning against the perils of bootleg liquor, he told the story of "a young woman on a Hoboken ferry-boat who took a drink from a flask carried in the pocket of her escort. Almost immediately,

---

*For a man who had been severely crippled at eighteen, this particular nickname was less counterintuitive than it might have appeared. According to one contemporary account, Upshaw possessed an uncanny ability to "move about without assistance when carried away while speaking by bursts of strong emotion and temper."

she staggered to the stern, plunged into the Hudson and was drowned." The lesson was clear, Haynes concluded: "Who drinks bootleg drinks with Death."

This sort of thing gave Haynes a second constituency beyond Wheeler, Upshaw, and other dry consuls—namely, vaudeville comedians who could get a laugh virtually by mentioning his name. These same satirists considered Haynes's boss, Secretary of the Treasury Andrew W. Mellon, less useful, which surely disappointed any dry with a sense of humor. The drys considered Mellon their most influential enemy, the one ranking member of the Harding administration least in sympathy with the ASL's goals, its methods, and its membership.

Mellon's Treasury Department housed Haynes's Prohibition Bureau and his field agents, just as it had always been home to the federal agents in the Bureau of Internal Revenue. Frequently described as the second- or third-richest man in the United States after John D. Rockefeller and perhaps Henry Ford, except when he was described as richer than either of them, Mellon was a man of refinement (his collection would become the foundation of the National Gallery of Art) and an austere, even forbidding manner. In addition to the powerful Mellon Bank of Pittsburgh, he controlled Gulf Oil, Alcoa Aluminum, a hefty chunk of U.S. Steel, and the Republican Party of Pennsylvania. He affected no interest in how he was perceived by the public—Mellon once asked a journalist "just why should the secretary be expected to talk to the reporters?"—except when he had something to hide. About to sue his wife for divorce in 1911, he first arranged to have the tame Pennsylvania legislature pass a law allowing the trial to proceed in private, before only a judge—no public, no reporters, not even a jury.

His son referred to Mellon's "ice-water smile," but even that chilly facsimile of gaiety rarely appeared in public. Taut and contained, his 145 pounds stretched over a nearly six-foot frame, his white hair and gray mustache offsetting a sharply angular, even cadaverous face, Mellon looked as if he had been carved from chalky stone. And if the personal connection with his flabby, backslapping Prohibition commissioner was hard to discern, the philosophical bond between Mellon and Haynes was nonexistent. In fact, that Andrew W. Mellon was secretary of the treasury to some extent revealed how little Harding and his inner circle must have cared about enforcing the Volstead Act. Mellon drank and didn't apologize for it. He made no apparent effort to hide his disapproval of the law and the amendment that had spawned it. He loathed the income tax and believed that the best means of supporting what he believed should be very limited government were the sharply regressive excise taxes of the sort that had once been levied on liquor, beer, and wine. He even owned, with his brother Richard, a company that was the pride of Westmoreland County, Pennsylvania, where the Whiskey Rebellion had begun in 1794: the Old Overholt rye distillery.

Mellon had purchased his original one-third interest in Old Overholt from his friend Henry Clay Frick in 1887 (Frick's maternal grandfather Abraham Overholt, né Overholtzer, had founded the distillery in 1810). The transaction could only have been an act of sport or love; the $25,000 that Mellon had paid Frick for his shares was small change for the Mellon family. To the drys, though, it was palpable evidence of Mellon's unfitness for running the federal department responsible for implementing the Volstead Act. When Mellon's impending appointment first became known, William H. Anderson, the ASL's New York state superintendent, sent out alarmed notice of his involvement in Old Overholt to hundreds of daily newspapers. Senator Matthew M. Neely of West Virginia said that "a thief will never enforce the law against larceny; a pyromaniac will never enforce the law against arson; a distiller will never enforce the Volstead Act." But for once even Wheeler was unable to persuade Harding to cleave to the ASL catechism.

ANDREW MELLON CERTAINLY didn't set out with great enthusiasm to apply the law. Even apart from his personal distaste for Prohibition, he considered the Volstead Act extreme, impractical, and essentially unenforceable. The odd thing was that Roy Haynes, his unlikely lieutenant, didn't entirely disagree. Yes, the hymns he sang about increased churchgoing and other examples of post-Volstead moral uplift may have been filled with assertions about the decline of drink. But how could he justify keeping a force of twenty-five hundred men in the field if there was no booze to chase down? Nobody may have been drinking it, Haynes seemed to say, but for some reason there was plenty of stuff out there.

The force Haynes commanded was inept and venal. Dry politicians had all but guaranteed this when they exempted enforcement agents from the job protections provided members of the civil service, asserting that it would be all too easy for a wet applicant to pass a civil service examination and then, once hired, subvert the law. Unflinching sympathy with the Volstead Act, drys insisted, was the most important qualification, both for getting an agent's job and for keeping it. The real sine qua non for any aspiring agent was endorsement by the ASL, which had added to its other assets the ripe fruits of political patronage. In most of the country hiring power effectively belonged to the ASL, in league with its congressional allies. The more upstanding national officers and state superintendents of the ASL may have earnestly desired a skilled national police force that would enforce the law, but earnestness (compounded by naïveté) was easily snuffed out by expedience. The league used enforcement jobs to reward their faithful troops; dry politicians went along to ensure their own incumbency; and together they guaranteed the bureau's corruption and incompetence.

Some prohibitionists did keep their hands clean. Senator George Norris of Nebraska, whose dryness was a direct extension of his righteously progressive principles, recognized the perils of a politicized appointment process and refused to have anything to do with selecting agents. Andrew Volstead claimed a similar position. But when Attorney General Daugherty (who also happened to be the president's chief political operative) declared that the civil service was a "hindrance to the government," as he told Congress in 1922, the signal was unmistakable. In the increasingly corrupt Harding administration, where political exigency was holy writ, the Prohibition Bureau became, as one historian of the civil service would describe it, "a chaos of spoils."

George Norris's Senate colleague John W. Harreld of Oklahoma was typical of congressional drys. Harreld openly admitted that his reelection prospects were directly tied to his ability to appoint the enforcement agents in his state, and he acted accordingly. But this was not a moral defect that afflicted only the drys. Many wet members of Congress were just as craven, as they took their all-you-can-eat turns at what the despairing Norris called "the political pie counter." Drys charged that the very wet representative Fiorello La Guardia of New York presided over appointments in his city, and the all-wet senatorial delegations from saturated New Jersey and soaking Maryland handed out enforcement jobs to the like-minded. An officer of the National Civil Service League suggested that, at least on this issue, wet and dry could come together not as enemies but as coconspirators: "The plain fact is that the congressmen wanted this plunder," he said.

ASK CONSUMERS OF popular culture who came of age in the middle of the twentieth century what the term "Prohibition agent" connotes, and most will conjure up an image of actor Robert Stack as Special Agent Eliot

Ness, from the 118 episodes of *The Untouchables* that ran on ABC Television between 1959 and 1963.* The real Eliot Ness was named after the novelist George Eliot, had almost nothing to do with the conviction and imprisonment of Al Capone, once ran for mayor of Cleveland (losing by a two-to-one margin), and died a semidrunk in 1957.

Asked the same question, the parents of those who grew up watching *The Untouchables* would likely recall the real-world New York duo of Isidore Einstein and Moe Smith. As early as 1922 this picaresque pair was so well known that headlines in the *Times* could refer to the corpulent Einstein and the lumbering Smith solely by their nicknames ("Izzy and Moe Raid Thespian Retreat"; "Izzy and Moe Pour Whisky Into Sewer"; "Sees Izzy and Moe, Bartender Faints"). That Izzy and Moe spent only four years in the Prohibition Bureau before they were fired in 1925 did not obscure their accomplishments or lessen their renown.

Ness, Einstein, and Smith were not the only agents who achieved fame through the popular media. During the 1920s and early '30s tabloid newspapers in particular amplified the mythmaking by coining dramatic epithets for publicity-friendly members of the Prohibition service. M. T. Gonzaulles became celebrated as "the Lone Wolf of Texas," William R. Hervey was "the Kokomo Schoolmaster," and Samuel Kurtzman, working the Canadian border, was "the Plague of the North." Al "Wallpaper" Wolff, in Chicago, got his nickname from the thoroughness of his raids: "We'd get a warrant, go in and arrest them, call the trucks and move 'em out. We'd move everything but the wallpaper." Female agents made especially good copy. "Tall and slender" Daisy Simpson was "the Woman with a Hundred Disguises," who feigned illness outside illegal establishments and busted proprietors when they offered her a restorative sip of brandy.

Less well known, at least until they began showing up in court on the wrong side of the witness dock, were the agents, officers, regional directors, and all the other functionaries low and high who joined the service out of loyalty to something more negotiable than Volsteadian orthodoxy. Some, like "Stewart McMullin"—the name turned out to be as fraudulent as his stated credentials—were simply goons. The first agent to kill a suspected

---

*Stack was the star of the show, but over its four-year run *The Untouchables* featured a collection of actors that could have stocked two decades of Emmy broadcasts. At various times the cast included Peter Falk, Martin Landau, Lee Marvin, Carroll O'Connor, Jack Klugman, Harry Dean Stanton, Rip Torn, Ed Asner, Telly Savalas, Darryl Hickman, Jack Warden, Martin Balsam, and Harry Guardino. As there were few roles for women in a show about Chicago mob wars, the high point for actresses was undoubtedly Barbara Stanwyck's two appearances as Lieutenant Aggie Stewart.

bootlegger in the line of duty, McMullin turned out to have killed another man when he was fourteen, had served one prison term for altering checks and another for armed robbery, and at the time he was given his badge was still incarcerated at Dannemora State Prison in upstate New York. S. Glenn Young, who as a marauding vigilante in southern Illinois eventually wrote his way onto the front pages with a submachine gun, was a wife beater, a hireling of the Ku Klux Klan, and an uncontrollable bully. In Norfolk, Virginia, agent Layton H. Blood tried to open what he called "a pool room in the nigger part of town," funded by the ASL and designed to entrap black bootleggers. "By the way," Blood asked his supervisor in Washington, "does the Treasury Department have any appropriation for fumigating their representatives? You know our colored brethren have a smell all their own [and] I'll need delousing more than any bird you ever saw."

But one didn't need to explore McMullin's murderous mind, Young's deep thuggishness, or Blood's loathsome racism to locate the rotten core of the Prohibition Bureau in its early days. That could be found, as the hallowed phrase would later have it, where the money was. Emory Buckner, the U.S. attorney for the Southern District of New York, said the $1,800 a year paid to Prohibition agents was not a living wage in his jurisdiction, yet "men clamor for the jobs." It was as if the willingness to accept a meager salary (equivalent to slightly more than $20,000 in 2009) guaranteed you the lucky number in a fabulous sweepstakes. The universal prize: a piece of the millions upon millions of dollars in bribes and blackmail that even a moderately adept agent could extract from the lawbreakers operating within his jurisdiction. New York editor Stanley Walker said most Prohibition agents "were fairly decent fellows, and their demands . . . were never extortionate." They didn't need to be; there was enough dirty money for everybody.

So evident was the corruption that saturated the Prohibition force from the very beginning that President Harding was moved to say, "There are conditions relating to [the Volstead Act's] enforcement which savor of nation-wide scandal. It is the most demoralizing factor in our public life." Coming from Warren G. Harding, this was saying quite a lot.

IT'S UNCLEAR WHETHER Mabel Willebrandt, assistant attorney general of the United States from 1921 to 1929, began the practice of starting her day with an ice-cold bath before or after she left her husband. That happened in 1916, around the time she determined that unhappy marriages resulted from "letting the whole relationship just drop to a dead level of bodily contact." Though she was not without suitors, including one wealthy man known as "the Alaskan Reindeer King" and another who built Hollywood's glamorous Chateau Marmont, Willebrandt never married again. But after she became, without question, the most powerful woman in the nation, Willebrandt did adopt a two-year-old girl. The child learned to endure the daily ritual in the icy bathtub in Willebrandt's home in the Columbia Heights section of Washington, D.C., just as she learned to sleep outdoors, protected only by a tent, even in the Washington wintertime. "Life has few petted darlings," Willebrandt said, and as her biographer, Dorothy M. Brown, wrote, her daughter "would not be one of them."

Of course not. Mabel Willebrandt, aka "the Prohibition Portia," possessor (said the *New York Times)* of "one of the keenest legal minds in the United States," did not achieve her eminence by being soft. Born in a sod hut on the lonely plains of southwestern Kansas, she eventually found her way in the early part of the twentieth century to Southern California. When she applied for a position as a schoolteacher in South Pasadena, she reported that she'd studied "trigonometry, physics, chemistry, Greek, rhetoric, elocution, public speaking, European history, ethics, sociology, political science, physical science, physical culture, commercial law, commercial geography, freehand drawing, domestic science, household economy, clay modeling, and gymnastics." The courses she was qualified to teach included "English language, grammar, American history, modern history, civics, geography, arithmetic, and nature study." If needed, she indicated, she also stood ready to teach "algebra, geometry, botany, zoology, biology, physiology, physiography, Latin, English literature, English composition, pedagogy, penmanship, and public school music." And baseball.

Is it a surprise that barely ten years later, this protean individual attained the highest position any woman had yet reached in the federal government, and that she did it before her thirty-third birthday? Not to anyone who would watch Willebrandt inscribe her name across the history of the 1920s. "Who is the outstanding woman in American political life today, among those holding appointive positions?" *Better Homes and Gardens* wondered in 1928. "I have asked dozens of women all over the country," the writer said. "Dozens of men, too, for that matter! And the answer in every case has been the same . . . Mabel Walker Willebrandt."

Mabel Walker Willebrandt? Eight decades later it's a name that's utterly obscure. But Willebrandt was as well known in her time as Wayne Wheeler, and if she was just as quickly forgotten, it wasn't because she hadn't left her mark. Had the *Better Homes and Gardens* question used "most important" or "most influential" instead of "outstanding," the dozens who offered Willebrandt's name could as easily have been thousands. For eight years under Warren G. Harding and his two immediate successors, Willebrandt served as the assistant attorney general responsible for Prohibition enforcement policy, for the prosecution of Volstead Act violations, and for the defense of the act before the Supreme Court. If the government's battle on booze had a face, it was Mabel Willebrandt's—"the delightful luncheon companion," said the *Atlanta Constitution*, "who neither paints, powders, nor uses lipstick."

Willebrandt said she hated "that girly-girly stuff"—the strongly scented garlands of prose inevitably draped on the few women in public office during the 1920s. The *Constitution* commented on her blue eyes, while the *New York Times* described them as "wide, earnest, truthful [and] brown." Frances Parkinson Keyes, on the brink of her long career as a popular novelist, said Willebrandt's "invariable costume during the day is a strictly tailored suit, worn with a simple and immaculate blouse." But Keyes hastened to point out that at home, Willebrandt favored "dainty and exquisite dresses . . . with a flower at waist or shoulder." For readers of the era's women's magazines, that was a much more appealing image than any strictly tailored suit.

Unlike Wheeler, who devoted his life to a single issue and spent what little leisure time he allowed himself among a tightly circumscribed set of associates, Mabel Willebrandt got around. Her closest female friend may have been Andrew Volstead's daughter Laura, but she had unlikelier pals as well, among them the record-breaking aviator Jackie Cochran, and the man who "will do most anything for me," motion picture baron Louis B. Mayer. But her tilt toward Hollywood shouldn't suggest that Willebrandt had turned frivolous. She especially enjoyed dinner parties at the home of Supreme Court Justice Louis D. Brandeis, she wrote, because at the Brandeis table, "the conversation is guided into stimulating excursions of research. The guest partakes of the eager enjoyment of pursuing truth at intellectual frontiers." Willebrandt was instrumental in launching the career of a young lawyer named John J. Sirica, who would confirm her faith in him half a century later as the presiding judge in the Watergate trials. Her most notable friend might have been the fellow she urged Attorney General Harlan Fiske Stone to name as director of the Justice Department's Bureau of Investigation in 1924—Laura Volstead's old law school classmate, twenty-nine-year-old J. Edgar Hoover.*

---

*Willebrandt told Stone that her friend Edgar was "honest and informed" and "operated like an electric wire, with almost trigger response."

Mabel Willebrandt did not win her position in the Harding subcabinet through passionate commitment to the Eighteenth Amendment. In fact she hadn't particularly supported its passage. She openly acknowledged she'd been a social drinker before 1920, when she was still working as a public defender representing women dragged into Los Angeles police court. (She had indeed won that teaching job in South Pasadena, but all those academic skills were deployed only to keep her afloat financially while she completed night law school at the University of Southern California.) Her police court clients were a collection of prostitutes and drunks who might have offended Willebrandt's lingering Victorian sensibilities had they not excited her blossoming progressive impulses. Senator Hiram Johnson, the shining knight of California's dry progressives, heard about Willebrandt from one of her law school professors. This was around the time that the new Harding administration, nodding in the direction of recently enfranchised women, began casting about for a symbolic appointee. Johnson, who especially liked the fact that Los Angeles conservatives deprecated Willebrandt's progressive fervor, sponsored her ascension.

When Willebrandt took her oath of office in 1921, one might have gauged the depth of the Harding administration's commitment to the Eighteenth Amendment by examining the bona fides of the men alongside whom she was expected to lead the war on liquor: a secretary of the treasury (Andrew Mellon) who loathed Prohibition, an attorney general (Harry Daugherty) who flouted it regularly, and a Prohibition commissioner (Roy Haynes) who was a punch line. For chief prosecutor of Volstead violators, a thirty-two-year-old woman only five years out of law school probably seemed just right.

What happened next, of course, was something devotees of dime novels, fairy tales, or other ritualized clichés could have predicted: she became a terror. The division of authority spelled out in the Volstead Act was based on longstanding protocols arising from the enforcement of the tax code. The treasury secretary, through the director of Prohibition, was responsible for a field force of agents who uncovered violations of the law; they, in turn, handed the offenders over to the Justice Department—to Willebrandt and the U.S. attorneys in every federal judicial district—for trial. The nicest thing she had to say about the risible Haynes was that he was "a politician in sheep's clothing." She felt those Harding appointees who actually believed in the idea of a dry America were no better. They comprised "a regime of preachers," she said. "Many of them are well-meaning, sentimental and dry, but they can't catch crooks."

Then there were the Prohibition department's own home-grown

crooks, the grafters, extortionists, and thieves in the agent force who would lead Willebrandt to say, "I refuse to believe that out of our one hundred and twenty million population . . . it is impossible to find four thousand men in the United States who can not be bought." And she said that after eight years of trying.

THE BATTALION OF moralizers and malefactors that Roy Haynes led and Mabel Willebrandt suffered did not bear the burden of policing Prohibition violations alone. The peculiar second clause of the Eighteenth Amendment, assigning "concurrent" enforcement power to the federal government and to the states, mandated (or at least encouraged) armies of cops across the nation to stand shoulder to shoulder in the booze wars. The relative strength of the Anti-Saloon League in various parts of the country could be measured by the proliferation of state laws designed to be "concurrent" with the federal strictures. Anyone arrested for insobriety in Vermont was subject to a mandatory jail sentence if he failed to name the person from whom he acquired his liquor. At one point Indiana vested train conductors and bus drivers with the authority to arrest passengers carrying alcohol and made it illegal for retailers to put flasks or cocktail shakers in their shop windows. Mississippi decreed debts related to the acquisition of intoxicating beverages uncollectible. Iowa banned the sale of Sterno, from which alcohol could be extracted by filtering it through a rag or, among drunks with better table manners, through a loaf of bread.

Yet some local police departments that wanted to make meaningful attempts to enforce Prohibition found temptation too tasty to resist. In Indiana this did not take long: in a series of missives that became known as the "Dear Jerry Letters" after they were leaked to a newspaper in 1921, the newly installed federal Prohibition director for the region instructed Indianapolis police chief Jeremiah Kinney to distribute any confiscated liquor to the director's associates. In Chicago a brief spasm of serious enforcement efforts collapsed shortly after the revelation—by the city's mayor, no less—that an estimated 60 percent of the city's police force was in the liquor business.

When Mabel Willebrandt charged that these nonfederal policing efforts were beset by "sleeping sickness," she may have been referring to the states' stuporous response to funding requirements. Only eighteen states bothered to appropriate as much as a dollar for enforcement. In some jurisdictions this reflected a distaste for the whole business; New York repealed its state enforcement code in 1923, and Maryland never

142 / LAST CALL

even bothered to enact one. An ASL publication solemnly declared, "Any state that fails to . . . pass enforcement legislation [should] become a ward of the nation, and be considered one of the backward states in loyalty to the Union." New Yorkers and Marylanders seemed to bear the obloquy without much pain.

Some of the demurring legislatures that chose not to support the enforcement effort were not necessarily motivated by wet sentiment. Even where ASL-backed officials were in the majority, dry passions were usually not as intense as the tightfistedness that shaped the era's fiscal policies. In a decade that witnessed the overnight evaporation of alcohol-derived excise taxes; suffered a drastic plummeting of income tax rates following the end of World War I; and endured the prevailing government parsimony that hovered like a scowl over the administrations of Warren G. Harding, Calvin Coolidge, and Herbert Hoover—in such a time, legislatures did not appropriate public funds eagerly.

In some states, notably Pennsylvania, the disconnect between the laws and the means to enforce them approached the surreal. The state's dominant Republican Party was divided into an archconservative (and hence largely wet) faction controlled by the wellborn, wealthy, and imperious senator Boies Penrose, and a progressive (and thus mainly dry) bloc led by the wellborn, wealthy, and crusading Gifford Pinchot. Penrose, in state politics a confederate of Andrew Mellon, led a powerful political machine built on a dazzling use of patronage and a belief that government was a weapon to be wielded in the interests of the moneyed classes. (He once said, "I'd rather dictate to damned fools than serve them.") Pinchot, a member of Theodore Roosevelt's inner circle who had first attained prominence as the conservation-minded director of the U.S. Forest Service, was a progressive who believed government was an implement designed to improve the lot of the people, whether or not they wanted their lot improved.

When Penrose died in 1922, Pinchot took advantage of disarray within the state party to win the Republican gubernatorial nomination. Elected in November, he pledged to bar liquor from the governor's mansion (itself a startling proposal), to appoint only those judges who swore fealty to the Eighteenth Amendment, and to lead "the first honest-to-God attempt made in this state" to bring Pennsylvania into line with the Volstead Act. Pinchot detested Andrew Mellon and, according to one Mellon family biographer, gave credence to preposterous rumors that the Mellon-controlled Gulf Oil Company had been importing liquor in oil drums and parceling it out from roadside gas stations.

Pennsylvania's first federal Prohibition director, a former state senator named William C. McConnell, was a soldier in the Penrose army who after less than a year in office was implicated along with forty-six associates, including sixteen enforcement agents on his staff, in a four-million-dollar corruption scheme. Pinchot could not have been pleased when the assistant U.S. attorney prosecuting McConnell was fired, or when all the evidence in the case miraculously disappeared. He may not have been surprised, either. "Politics first, law enforcement second, has been the order," Pinchot said of the Penrose hegemony. McConnell had done what was "expected and intended by the power to which his appointment was due."

Pinchot expected and intended something altogether different. Confident, efficient, blessed with the mien and manner of a noble warrior—historian Patricia O'Toole wrote that his face "had features so fine he could have modeled for coinage"—Pinchot did not pause before beginning his "honest-to-God" effort to dry up Pennsylvania. In his first month in office he turned the state police into a commando army. A single week saw raids on illegal liquor operations in eighteen counties. Reminding Republican legislators that he was now head of the party, that he had led them to victory at the top of the ticket in November, and that they had pledged their support to his legislative program, Pinchot got all the laws he wanted. Swollen with the pride of a triumphalist, gleaming with the righteousness of a reformer, Pinchot announced that he had achieved his legislative success without making a single promise in exchange for a vote. "This is an unbought victory," he proclaimed, "and ten times as valuable on that account."

Unbought, perhaps, but unfunded as well. After Pinchot's glorious moment had passed, the legislators who had gone along with his program stiffened. It was one thing for the Pennsylvania legislature—any legislature, really—to give militant drys the laws they wanted, but quite another to provide the funds necessary for their enforcement. As a result, the legislators decided that the total appropriation for Pinchot's ambitious program should amount to precisely . . . zero.

FOR THE DRYS, it never got that bad on the federal level. But Wayne Wheeler, familiar as he was with every hillock and valley on the political landscape, had early on recognized the prevailing resistance to government spending. In 1920 Wheeler told Morris Sheppard that five million dollars would be a sufficient appropriation for all federal enforcement of Prohibition (by way of comparison, the sum wouldn't even have covered the payroll of Columbia University that year). It is difficult to believe that

Wheeler truly thought you could patrol a nation so vast, with its borders so porous and its angry wets so thirsty, on such a minuscule budget. It is not difficult to believe that he knew it was a fool's errand to risk defeat by demanding sizable appropriations from a Congress dominated by cheese-parers. A Republican Congress in the 1920s was more likely to sing a few choruses of the "Internationale" than issue large checks for government activities. Roy Haynes tried to pry some money loose by boasting that the sum of fines, assessments, and taxes collected from Volstead violators was substantially greater than the government's enforcement expenditures, but Congress ignored the hint and chose not to invest any further even in so profitable a venture.

Consequently, in the first several years of Prohibition, the drys got only as much enforcement as they were willing to pay for. The staff of Roy Haynes's Prohibition Department initially consisted of only 1,500 ill-trained field agents and 1,500 office personnel tucked into the Bureau of Internal Revenue. The other main component of the federal enforcement effort was the Coast Guard. If Haynes's 1,500 field agents seemed a thin detachment to spread across the entire country, consider the armada charged with patrolling the nation's 4,993 miles of coastline: in 1920 the entire Coast Guard fleet consisted of twenty-six inshore vessels, some converted tugboats, and twenty-nine cruising cutters, one of which was based in Evansville, Indiana. Congress did not hand any meaningful additional appropriations to the Coast Guard from the time the Eighteenth Amendment was ratified until 1925, five years into its teetering reign.

Underfunded, ill-staffed, overseen by the indifferent Mellon and the incompetent Haynes, the federal enforcement effort was orphaned by the Harding administration. Dauntless Mabel Willebrandt—the only high-ranking government official who seemed to believe that federal laws were meant to be enforced—did her best. Federal district judges frustrated by overcrowded courts and underenthusiastic prosecutors were adopted as her pen pals and pelted with pep talks. U.S. attorneys who did not commit wholeheartedly to pursuing lawbreakers found themselves threatened with dismissal. She also decided to use other parts of the federal code—tax laws, tariff laws—to broaden her authority beyond the limits of the Volstead Act, which she dismissed as "puny" and "toothless."

Willebrandt's was one method of overcoming administrative inertia or legislative inaction. Gifford Pinchot, in Pennsylvania, devised a different one. After the fair-weather drys of the Pennsylvania legislature refused to fund his enforcement program, Pinchot turned toward the WCTU. State Chapter President Ella George of Beaver Falls accepted the governor's challenge and persuaded the Pennsylvania WCTU to donate to his enforcement effort 60 percent of the money the legislature had denied him.

The virtuous governor Pinchot did not let this generosity go unremarked. He may have been an idealist, but he was not an ingrate. Apparently having learned a thing or two from his adversaries in the Penrose machine, or perhaps from the ASL, he thanked Mrs. George by granting her the right to pass on all political appointments in Beaver County.

Chapter 10

Leaks in the Dotted Line

A S SAM BRONFMAN would remember it, the 120-mile trip by dogsled from Kenora to Lake of the Woods wasn't a lot of fun. It was the winter of 1916 in the flat, lonely expanse of northwestern Ontario, long before the Trans-Canada Highway was built, and the twenty-seven-year-old Bronfman needed to get to his destination as quickly as possible. Even if the highway had existed then, he probably would not have driven. Bronfman hated to drive, and for the last forty-nine years of his life, after his marriage to the worshipful woman who would always refer to him as "My Sam," he never once took the wheel of a car. Sam Bronfman paid people to do the driving for him.

In Bronfman's telling, the epic journey from Kenora (six days out, six days back, nothing to eat along the way but the venison bagged by his guide) became the foundation myth of one of North America's great fortunes. Under the peculiar division of federal and provincial powers in the Canadian constitution, a broken-backed form of Prohibition had settled over the Dominion four years before the bone-dry version reached the United States. Individual provinces could not stop the manufacture or the interprovincial shipment of alcoholic beverages—those were federal matters—but they could ban sales within their boundaries. By 1919 every English-speaking, Protestant-dominated province had voted itself dry (Quebec, of course, remained true to its cultural origins). This provided a loophole for savvy entrepreneurs: if you could ship the stuff from a wet place to a dry place and find a way to distribute it once it arrived, you could make some meaningful money.

That's how young Sam Bronfman found himself on that dogsled in 1916, on his way to a distant lumber camp where he hoped to find the owner of a small Kenora hotel who had put up the place for sale. At least one other buyer was waiting for the hotel man to return to Kenora, and

Bronfman didn't wish to give another bidder a chance. Under local law, the hotel maintained a license allowing it to store liquor. Under federal law, Bronfman saw opportunity. Kenora's greatest distinction up to that point in its history was its renaming. One gets a sense of the sort of place it had been from the town's original name: until 1905 Kenora was known as Rat Portage. But now, in this westernmost town of any size in Ontario, whose prohibition laws were not yet as severe as Manitoba's or Saskatchewan's, Bronfman could establish a depot for liquor, ship it in from an operation he had purchased in Montreal, and then forward the goods into the prairie provinces. The hardship of the voyage to Lake of the Woods, aggravated by the limitations of his guide, demonstrated Bronfman's commitment to his vision. "I could hardly face the return trip," he said in the late 1960s. "All that son-of-a-bitch could shoot was deer. He never even found a rabbit, a bird, or even a bear."

That was how Bronfman spoke all his life: directly, coarsely, and with his own interests trumping everyone else's.* The third son of Yechiel and Mindel Bronfman—in chronology if not in affect—he became the dominant Bronfman of his generation, he said many years later, for the same reason "a horse win[s] a race. I just did." He was two years old in 1891, when Yechiel and Mindel brought their family from Soroca, a small farming town in what is now Moldova, to the not dissimilar landscape of eastern Saskatchewan. Farming led to horse-trading, which led to other commercial ventures, and soon the Bronfmans had accumulated enough capital to start buying small hotels in small towns. "Hotel" was an overly grand term for most of them. In places like Emerson and Yorkton and Kenora and the other dusty communities that captured the Bronfman family's interest, the hotel, close by the railroad station, offered minimal accommodations to the prairie travelers of those days. It had beds, it served meals, it probably had a pool table, and it definitely sold liquor.

The Kenora opportunity didn't last long; in 1918 interprovincial alcohol sales were banned by Parliament. But even though Canadian law allowed the shipment of liquor only if its intended use was medicinal, you hardly needed to be at death's door to merit a legal shot of brandy. The Bronfmans built up a very nice business with the cooperation of local physicians, who were rewarded with a two-dollar bonus for each liquor prescription fulfilled by a Bronfman-controlled outlet. Sam and his three

---

*The coarseness increased commensurately with his fortune. Biographer Nicholas Faith said a characteristic Bronfman insult would have him calling someone "a cocksucking son of a cocksucking cocksucker."

brothers continued to do fine, even after the doctors upped their demands to three dollars per. The scale of the family business changed radically, however, when the status of liquor changed south of the border. That was why Sam and his older brother Harry would come to spend Christmas Day 1919 by the railroad siding in Yorkton, Saskatchewan, unloading five freight cars packed to their roofs with Scotch. Twenty-seven more cars followed soon thereafter, and for several days the brothers worked twenty-hour shifts as they filled their warehouse, and any other building they could get their hands on, with this new currency.

Years later, recounting the details to a would-be biographer, Sam quoted Tennyson, saying the family had seized "the skirts of happy chance." That sounded a lot better than saying the Bronfmans had embarked on a fifteen-year period of cupidity and criminality, which they would eventually whitewash from memory through decades of audacious public relations and phenomenal business success.

IT WAS ALMOST fated that the Bronfman family would make its fortune from alcoholic beverages; in Yiddish, which was their mother tongue, *bronfen* is the word for "liquor." The illegal trade in booze also happened to be a business that did not operate under the discriminatory codes of the day. As the Canadian journalist and historian James H. Gray pointed out in *The Roar of the Twenties*, at the time Sam, Harry, and their brothers Abe and Allan were getting into the liquor business, there had never been a Jewish CPA in all of Canada; there were no Jews in the nation's insurance industry; strict quotas kept doors barely ajar in the medical schools; and throughout the western provinces, from Winnipeg all the way to Vancouver, the number of Jews working in the banking business was precisely one.

The same ethnic distinctions that divided the American public over the Prohibition issue—native-born Protestants against everybody else—played out in Canada as well. In the east, Anglophone Canada's chronic suspicion of French-speaking Catholics was intensified by Quebec's unwillingness to join the dry parade. In the west, Manitoba's chief police official guessed that 95 percent of the province's bootleggers were Jewish. Archdeacon G. E. Lloyd, soon to become the Anglican bishop of Saskatchewan, held the Jews of the illegal liquor industry at arm's length, warning them that because Canada had chosen to grant them "rights enjoyed by other white men, they must not defile the country by engaging in disreputable pursuits." A Manitoba cleric named R. H. Glover went a giant step further, charging that "a group of American Jews, assisted and abetted by certain prostitute gentiles whose God is the dollar, have succeeded in debauching Canada from ocean to ocean."

What was odd about Glover's dark accusation was that he believed the debauching Jews were Americans. If there was any basis for this, it had to be the seismic shift, after January 16, 1920, from the tolerated wink-wink-nudge-nudge of Canada's so-called medicinal liquor business, to the large-scale, cross-border smuggling trade the Bronfmans would soon dominate. Canadian prohibitionists, every bit as sunny as their American counter-parts about domestic dryness, simply didn't want to believe their country-men would engage in forbidden behavior. Back when Ontario closed down its taverns and liquor stores, a Toronto dry activist cheerfully reported that the St. Charles Bar on Bay Street, where he had once counted 128 men in various stages of inebriation, had turned into a soft-drink parlor where men could spend their idle hours "sipping near beer and buttermilk." But even the rosiest glasses could not misapprehend the scene developing on the prairie, where Sam Bronfman and his brothers had discovered liquid gold.

Soon the alchemy of desire led them to start manufacturing their own stock. In the very beginning of the Bronfmans' cross-border business, the liquor flowed upstream, as American distillers disposed of much of their presumably valueless inventory by sending it to Canada. In the first year of U.S. Prohibition the Bronfmans imported some 300,000 gallons of whis-key from American distilleries, mixed it with raw alcohol and water, and began shipping a much larger quantity of seriously degraded product back across the border. When their supply of Old Crow and Sunny Brook and other American brands ran out, the Bronfmans began importing enor-mous quantities of pure neutral spirits from Scotland, diluting it, and add-ing appropriate coloring. (Caramel was a favorite; some other blenders used prune juice for color and creosote to add a smoky flavor.) Before the end of the year they were sending 26,600 cases—almost 64,000 gallons—of their goods back to the United States each month.

The Bronfman product was mixed, bottled, and stored in a series of export houses—in the local idiom, "boozoriums"—strung along Saskatch-ewan's border with North Dakota, in towns like Gainsborough and Car-ievale and Bienfait. The Bulman Brothers printing company of Winnipeg provided labels. "Anybody could walk in and buy 1000 or 5000 labels any time they wanted to," Sam would remember, and soon case upon case of bottles bearing either counterfeit brands or invented ones would emerge from the boozoriums, all dressed up for, say, the eighteen-mile trip from Estevan, Saskatchewan, to Noonan, North Dakota. Among the Bronf-

mans' faux Scotches were unimaginative but likely brands such as Old
Highland and Prince of Wales, as well as inventive, if improbable, ones like
Glen Levitt.*

In the farming communities that housed the boozoriums, liquor export
was a valued industry. Under provincial and federal statutes, the Bronfmans, their distributors, and their customers broke no laws as long as they
paid appropriate taxes on their profits and appropriate customs duties on
anything crossing the border. The difference in scale between their old
"pure drug" business and the liquor business was easily measured. Settling
a dispute with Canadian tax authorities in 1921, Sam and Harry agreed
to pay $550 in income tax for 1918, $7,644 for 1919—and $113,694 for
1920. Even that last figure fails to give a sense of the size of the Bronfman
enterprise. When Harry Bronfman said in 1922 that "the liquor business
in Saskatchewan is controlled by me," it was quite a business: based on
Harry's testimony in a trial that same year, the *Winnipeg Tribune* calculated
the family's profits at $391,000 each month.

For all the businesslike nature of the prairie smuggling racket, it was a
racket nonetheless. The boozoriums were adorned with stout locks, iron
bars, and assorted weaponry. The vehicles used to move the goods south
were largely of a variety known in border towns as the "Whiskey 6," six-
cylinder Buicks or Studebakers, their backseats removed, their suspen-
sions reinforced by heavy-duty springs. Many carried thick chains that
could be attached to the rear bumper and dragged along the dirt roads,
raising enough dust to allow escape—from honest cops doing their duty,
from dishonest cops looking for an extortion opportunity, or from energetic hijackers. At the border Canadian officials required the southbound
runners to present itemized manifests in order to compute the amount
of export duty owed the Dominion government. The customs receipts
handed back to the runners were invaluable to American border agents as
well; they used them to determine the size of the bribes they were owed.

In 1969 Sam Bronfman's son Edgar, who had succeeded his father as
head of the family's giant Seagram's empire, wrote that during U.S. Prohi-
bition, the company "sold its products only in the Dominion" of Canada.
Two decades later, Edgar was no longer quite so sure. In his memoir, *Good
Spirits: The Making of a Businessman*, he continued to insist that everything
Sam had done during Prohibition was "perfectly legal," but he did add a

---

*In Saul Bellow's *Herzog*, the protagonist remembers his father, a small-time Montreal bootlegger, at the kitchen table in their dingy flat, labels and paste pot at the ready: "Well, children, what shall it be—White Horse, Johnnie Walker?" Then, Herzog recalls, "We'd all call
out our favorites" and get to work.

qualifier: it was "never clear," he said, how much his father and uncles had had to do with bootleggers.

Nevertheless, the Bronfman liquor didn't make it across the border by accident, and it didn't find its way from North Dakota to the cities of the upper Midwest through transubstantiation. The Bronfmans were playing a game rough enough to have led to the murder, never solved, of Sam and Harry's brother-in-law, Paul Matoff, who was killed by a blast from a 12-gauge shotgun as he sat in the family's boozorium in Bienfait counting the money he had just collected from an American bootlegger. The North Dakota police did not arm themselves with heavy-duty machine guns in order to apprehend a few wheat farmers hoping to make an extra buck. The Bronfmans had representatives in the United States, at least one of whom—the salesman responsible for Chicago and Minneapolis— was bold enough to carry business cards declaring that he was an agent for the wholesale liquor operation of the Bronfman-controlled Yorkton Distributing Company, and advertising its six outlets "near [the] international boundary in Saskatchewan." By 1923 the bootlegging business had enabled Sam to build such valuable connections in the United States that he was able to get prized tickets to the Dempsey-Firpo championship fight in New York. His benefactor was a bright young entrepreneur named Meyer Lansky.

ARTHUR J. TUTTLE was as straight as a judge could be. He'd been a prosecutor in Ingham County, Michigan, then U.S. attorney for Michigan's Eastern District, before William Howard Taft appointed him to the federal bench. He made his judicial reputation handing down severe sentences to traffickers in prostitutes—"white slavers," in the argot of the day—who were brought into his court for violating the Mann Act. He was devoted to his apple farm in the central Michigan town of Leslie, his hunting cabin in the state's Upper Peninsula, his college fraternity, and the Republican Party.

Judge Tuttle was also devoted to the idea of Prohibition and believed deeply in its enforcement. Whether his court had either the authority or the means to play an effective role in enforcement was another matter. At the time the Eighteenth Amendment was ratified, Tuttle was the lone federal judge in a district that encompassed Detroit and every other large city in the state except Grand Rapids. That was fine until the advent of the Volstead Act exploded the orderly calm of his marble-and-mahogany courtroom. In Prohibition's first eighteen months, Tuttle's caseload jumped more than threefold, the increase coming chiefly from proceedings initiated under the Volstead Act or customs laws—codes violated minute by minute on the Detroit River, just four blocks away from the judge's chambers.

But August 1921, the nineteenth month of Prohibition, made the tripling of that first year and a half seem almost inconsequential, and Tuttle himself was partly responsible for it. The judge's decisions generally were true both to the intent of the Volstead Act and to the body of laws that preceded it, but he came down against the former when the latter compelled him to do so. In that second Prohibition August, Tuttle enjoined the Collector of Customs and the Bureau of Internal Revenue from trying to stop bonded rail shipments originating at the Hiram Walker Distillery in Windsor from passing through the United States on their way to Mexico. That would have been a violation of an 1871 U.S.-Canada treaty, Tuttle determined, even if the federal actions were intended to address "the evils sought to be remedied" by the Volstead Act. For Canadian customs officials, a journalist soon wrote, it became "kind of a grand gesture to issue a bill of lading for Mexico and watch a two-seated boat rowed into the river." By 1925 Hiram Walker was claiming annual shipment of one hundred thousand cases of Canadian whiskey to "Cuba."

Of even greater moment than Tuttle's ruling in the Hiram Walker case was a decision handed down that same month by an obscure Windsor police magistrate named W. E. Gundy. An Ontario brewery had sought to establish that even though shipping its product across the river to Detroit was a violation of U.S. law, U.S. law was not a matter of concern to Canadians. The court agreed, and the *New York Herald* marked this moment in international jurisprudence succinctly: "Magistrate Gundy expressed the opinion that the United States was big enough to take care of its own laws."

The immediate result was a volcanic spasm of activity on the docks on the Canadian side of the river. The freelance transshipment of goods by enterprising Canadians (like that Windsor woman who had claimed to have been sipping her way through ten bottles a day) was now overtaken by industrial-scale operations. Just one day after Gundy's decision was announced, the contents of seven hundred trucks were transferred to a fleet of small boats that immediately set out for the constitutionally dry shores of Michigan. Canadian authorities looked on impassively as what was soon dubbed the "Mosquito Fleet" scattered across the mile-wide river, an armada of skiffs and dinghies and motor launches "so heavily laden with beer and whiskey that their gunwales were washed by water." The *Detroit News* noted that although federal prohibition agents in Michigan did not have a single boat of their own, at times in the preceding months they had made use of a vessel belonging to the Detroit police department. But "the police boat . . . had not been employed by them recently," the *News* added, "as it had been hoped that the liquor traffic would die out naturally with the enforcement of prohibition in Ontario."

That was as naïve as counting on enforcement of Prohibition in Saskatchewan and Manitoba. There, the Bronfman interests kept Canadian officials happy by paying export taxes and keeping a large number of people productively employed. When the Saskatchewan government considered confining the export houses to the province's large cities, citizens of the farm town of Carnduff, population six hundred, petitioned legislators to let them keep their boozorium, which they deemed essential to the local economy. For Windsor, which now seemed welded to Detroit by the same river that had previously been a dividing line, Prohibition was the equivalent of a land rush. One glance at the bustling export docks could help a government official sense the weight of the money flowing into the local, provincial, and federal treasuries ("Rum running has provided a tidy bit toward Canada's favorable balance of trade," said the *Financial Post*). The same prospect provided an even more thrilling sensation for those who had mastered the distribution of Canadian liquor to U.S. customers. Imagine the math: if you could ring up nearly $400,000 a month in profits out on the prairies, what could you do if you set up operations in the heavily populated East?

IN 1923, explaining how growing quantities of liquor were being smuggled into the United States from Canada, Roy Haynes said, "You cannot keep liquor from dripping through a dotted line." By then, the Canada-U.S. border from one end to the other was so wet it's a wonder it didn't bleed off the maps. In the West, the British Columbia government cashed in by charging each of the export houses a hefty annual license fee. Large, whiskey-laden freighters originating in the United Kingdom began to dock at the piers in Victoria, even though the cargo would never alight on Canadian land. At the eastern end, fishermen who had long extracted their earnings from the Bay of Fundy and the Gulf of Maine turned to a vastly more lucrative trade. All along the 3,987-mile land border in between, this new, bottled crop enriched people on both sides of the line. A few years after Prohibition ended, a young man from Norwich, Vermont, gave an interviewer from the Federal Writers' Project a succinct explanation of why he had abandoned the stonecutting trade for the bootlegging life: "Work?" he asked. "Me work? Only suckers work."

Only suckers and those who harbored dreams quite a bit larger than escape from the granite quarries. For instance, Sam Bronfman. In 1922 he was thirty-three years old, less than five feet six inches tall, with a receding chin, thinning hair, and a fortune among the largest in all of western Canada. He'd already had a liveried chauffeur for ten years, a Cadillac that turned heads as it cruised the streets of Winnipeg, and a temper that could peel paint. He believed that "you were somebody if you had money," his son Edgar said years later, "and if you had a lot of money you were more of a somebody." This would have explained his answer when he was asked what he believed was the greatest invention in the history of the world: "interest."

Bronfman's decision to transfer his base of operations from Winnipeg to Montreal, and his market from the upper Midwest to the rich, thick belt that ran from New York to Chicago, was inevitable. He would later acknowledge that he was slow to exploit the bejeweled cornucopia that was Detroit and the rich opportunities strung along the Eastern Seaboard, from Boston south. In time the delivery of liquor by rail into Windsor and by ship to Boston, New York, and other East Coast cities would make the Bronfmans wealthy beyond even Sam's dreams. But first he had to develop a source of supply more reliable than the thousand-gallon redwood vats of his Saskatchewan boozoriums.

"MY HUSBAND WAS the most wonderful man in the whole world." Those were the opening words of a privately published memoir that Saidye Rosner Bronfman wrote several years after Sam's death in 1971. She truly believed it. The memoir, titled *My Sam*, recalls her long marriage to a man who loved to serenade her ("Baby Face" was his favorite song), surrounded her with servants ("If you want another maid," he told her, "get another maid"), and forbade her to make gefilte fish (all that chopping, he said, reminded him of how hard his "dear little mother" had labored). They had married in 1922, when he was thirty-three and she was twenty-six, and though the wedding had been nice enough, there wasn't really a honeymoon, unless you consider nearly two years lived on the road a honeymoon. Back and forth across Canada and the United States they traveled, visiting "Winnipeg, Vancouver, Calgary, Regina, Chicago, Buffalo, Detroit," Saidye wrote, "packing and unpacking, always living out of a suitcase." And her version of a stationmaster's call didn't even include Ottawa and Los Angeles and Louisville, all of them stops on the same ceaseless tour. The Bronfmans went to Ottawa for a family wedding; to

Los Angeles to visit Sam's widowed sister Jean, who was living there with her two young children (Jean's husband was the Bronfman brother-in-law who had been blown away by the shotgun blast in Bienfait); and finally to Louisville, ostensibly to attend the Kentucky Derby.

It was a convenient reason, but a false one. The visit to Kentucky, like the couple's expeditions to so many other places, was a business trip. In this specific case, the business was the Greenbrier Distillery, about fifty miles from Louisville. This was what Sam had been looking for all those months he had been scouring the continent: a permanently idled distillery he could purchase cheaply, then dismantle, ship north, and reassemble on Canadian soil. The Bronfmans found the perfect spot for it in the Montreal suburb of Ville LaSalle, on the banks of the St. Lawrence. Every day for two years, Sam, Harry, and Allan would visit the site to watch their future take form in the rising bulk of the reborn distillery.

Sam called this daily ritual his "hour of devotion." But in 1926 he and Allan made a trip that qualified as a pilgrimage. They sailed that year to Great Britain to meet with the men who controlled the Scotch whiskey industry. The Bronfmans had been buying from the Scots since 1920, importing thousands upon thousands of barrels, blending it with their own production, and marketing it as "highland whiskey." Now they had a bigger idea: they wanted to create a partnership on the western side of the Atlantic, with both parties sharing in the profits bottled up in the famous brand names the Bronfmans wanted to import.

In London the dour, careful men on the other side of the table had reason to listen. The year before, the Distillers Company Limited, a combination of several family firms that had been in existence since 1877, had finally brought into its fold the five leading brands in the British whiskey industry: Johnnie Walker, Dewar's, White Horse, Haig & Haig, and Black & White. Upon completing what became known as the "Big Amalgamation," the DCL, by this point the world's largest liquor company, controlled virtually all of Scotland's distilling facilities, the most prominent brands, and several of the UK's leading gin producers as well, including Tanqueray and Gordon's. Operating the way any healthy cartel would, it had quickly established a schedule of protocols—price fixing, brand allocation, quality control—governing sale to the illicit American market. In their internal documents, the Scots referred to the United States only as "the scheduled area," while otherwise maintaining the pretense that the whiskey they were shipping across the Atlantic was intended for Canada, Bermuda, or the British islands of the Caribbean.

The top officers of Distillers Company Limited had known the

Bronfmans to be reliable trading partners who were quick with payment for the malt they'd been importing for their simulated "highland whiskey." They approved of the quality of the Bronfman product (from their suite at the Savoy, Sam and Allan had sent over samples for the Scots to taste), and they had chosen either to be complimented or to remain indifferent when Sam had made the audacious decision, in 1924, to call the Bronfman family business Distillers *Corporation* Limited. Sam was not the only audacious Bronfman: "There was no special reason for the name," Allan blandly told an interviewer four decades later.

The original DCL tempered its eagerness to enter into a Bronfman partnership with Scottish prudence. After further meetings in Edinburgh, the Scots sent Sam and Allan home with an equivocal response. Less than a month later the firm's chairman, William Henry Ross, arrived in Montreal with his deputy Thomas Herd to do some research. Although the DCL was nearly as old as the sixty-four-year-old Ross, it was he who had turned it into a formidable trust. Six feet five, full-bearded, and blade thin (*Fortune* said he looked like George Bernard Shaw as painted by El Greco), Ross was austere in manner but exceptionally adroit in extracting agreement from the disagreeable. "No man but William Ross could have made a Dewar and a Walker sit down at the same table together," said one of the whiskey barons.

The report Ross and Herd later delivered to their fellow DCL directors—"an investigation as to the position of the Scotch Whisky trade in Canada"—was a monument to the compelling force of self-interest. They found the Bronfmans' Ville LaSalle distillery more than adequate, its location near railroad facilities auspicious, the records of the business in excellent order, and "the statements made by the Brothers Bronfman when in London and Scotland to be strictly accurate." But because part of their mission was "to enquire into the general character and respectability" of their potential partners, the Scotsmen expanded their investigative efforts in Montreal. "We had to set about our enquiries very judiciously," they wrote, "but were met at the outset with the fact that the Jews to which the Bronfmans belong are not generally regarded with favour in Canada." Their informants "admitted that the Brothers Bronfman were honest hard-working men who could be relied upon to fulfil any financial obligations undertaken by them, but notwithstanding this fact they advised us to have no dealings with any of the Jews." Ross and Herd cited two reasons for not going into a direct partnership with the Bronfmans: one they summarized as "race," and the other they characterized as "the class of business with which they were associated"—namely, bootlegging.

Funny thing, though: all the other Canadian distillers, the two wrote, also happened to be "doing their utmost to develop this particular outlet." Because that made it impossible for DCL to take a position in the Canadian market with clean hands in any case, maybe it made sense to work out something with the Bronfmans, but . . . not with the Bronfmans. The solution Ross and Herd proposed was a separate DCL-controlled holding company formed specifically to enter into a partnership with Sam and his brothers, "thus removing all direct touch with the Bronfmans." The summary was brilliant: "The Bronfmans would expect to be represented on the board of the Holding Company," wrote Ross and Herd, "but as this would be a private company and not a Trading concern their connection with same, even if known, should not affect the business prejudicially."

Besides, the Scots added, the Bronfmans "possess considerable political influence and have a good outlet for their distillery products." In 1926 a liquor cartel couldn't ask for more in a North American partner. For the next five years, while the British market for whiskey and gin dropped more than 6 percent annually, and even as a worldwide depression bared its teeth, the directors of DCL paid their shareholders of its common stock a dividend yielding 20 percent annually.

NEARLY FORTY YEARS after Sam Bronfman's deal with the Scots and his subsequent purchase of the old Canadian firm of Joseph E. Seagram & Sons,* he sat down with two reporters working on a profile for *Fortune*. He had long been one of the wealthiest men in North America, a celebrated industrialist, philanthropist, and civic leader. He had been named a Companion of the Order of Canada, counted the prime minister of Israel among his friends, had met the queen of England. Discussing the rise of the Bronfmans, he said, "This operation from the beginning was one man. You've probably gathered that."

Certainly the vast global operation that the House of Seagram would become was the creation of the brilliant, driven, and explosive "Mr. Sam," as he was known to employees and other sycophants. But during the *Fortune* interview, he had chosen to forget how, at least in the early days, he had depended on his brothers. Each had played a critical role in Sam's rise. The brothers who were most visible were Harry, with whom Sam prob-

---

*In 1992, when Sam's son Edgar was asked why anyone would have sold a Canadian distillery in 1928, he replied, "*Goyim.*"

ably had the most in common, and Allan, a lawyer whose negotiating skills put him at the center of much of Sam's deal making.

Yet in the Prohibition years the eldest Bronfman, Abe, might have been the irreplaceable one. While Harry ran the operation at the Montreal distillery and Allan traveled with Sam to London, Edinburgh, and New York, Abe toiled in less worldly places. Early on this put him in St. John, New Brunswick, presiding over the cars and trucks ferrying liquor across the border to Vermont. Soon, first from St. John and later from Halifax, and then the North Atlantic island of St. Pierre, Abe would direct a complex logistical operation: loading Bronfman product into the holds of schooners bound for points south or onto trains headed for Detroit; filing bills of lading with Canadian customs officials indicating that the cargo was on its way to Cuba; submitting to those same officials stacks of falsified landing certificates that had been procured by a Bronfman agent in Havana and mailed back to Canada; and collecting great stacks of money. Some of that money would find its way to the Bank of Montreal, which was willing to accept it for deposit because, an internal document said, the unnamed depositor in question—"a liquor exporting concern whose product finds a market in the U.S.A."—had managed to "prevent their name or the name of this bank being connected with remittances from United States sources." Abe was good at this sort of thing: no fingerprints, no foul.

It was never clear exactly how much cash the Bronfman-owned Canadian Distributing Company and Atlantic Import Company brought in during those early years. Testifying before a Royal Commission examining the liquor export business in 1927, Abe said he could not produce the companies' ledgers. "They were in the way," Abe told the inquiry in sworn testimony. "I had no further use for them, and I burnt them up." Abe's associate in Nova Scotia, a Bronfman brother-in-law named Barney Aaron, was less forthright with the commission member who was curious about some outgoing shipments that had been cleared for Lima, Peru. How, the commissioner wondered, would a boat get to Lima, which is inland from the port city of Callao? Aaron demurred at first, pointing out, "I am not a navigator." Then he became more helpful. "Lima," he explained, "may have been built before the ocean was near the shore there."

Sam Bronfman was more careful than Abe or Barney during those hearings. He saved his candor for the *Fortune* interview, nearly four decades later. Even though "I have no proof," he said, he couldn't help but suspect that a certain quantity of the liquor the family had put on those boats had somehow ended up in the United States.

Chapter 11

The Great Whiskey Way

ON THE FIRST dry day of the era that would not be so dry after all, Baltimoreans could watch the 4,125-ton cargo ship *Lake Ellerslie* depart the city's harbor on a liquor-laden voyage down the Atlantic coast. They probably paid little attention to its destination. No one knew that within a few years, if not months, it would be easy enough to get a drink in Baltimore. But back on that January Saturday in 1920, onlookers watching the big freighter steam out of the harbor could only contemplate the irrevocable void the ship was leaving behind—a void precisely the size of the 34,667 cases and 1,860 barrels in its capacious hold. Observers quick with a pencil could have calculated that this ran to something in the area of 438,000 bottles' worth of whiskey and wine, now drained from Baltimore forever.

The parade of ships sailing into Nassau harbor on the island of New Providence in the Bahamas had begun several months before the *Lake Ellerslie* arrived in the new dawn of Prohibition. Along Bay Street, boys rolled heavy barrels from the docks, dodging wooden-wheeled horse carts burdened with precarious stacks of liquor cases. The motley collection of stables, houses, chandleries, and shanties near the waterfront had been drafted into service as warehouses. It was not long before the steamships and the sailing vessels began arriving all day and all night, leaving mountainous accumulations of off-loaded goods on the rickety pier, hundreds upon countless hundreds of cases from each boat. Because there weren't enough able-bodied men to serve as stevedores, the Bahamian policemen who tried to keep order on the increasingly unruly waterfront soon had to contend with a new form of traffic: the startling spectacle of island women walking from the harbor quays toward the warehouses with graceful purpose, wooden cases poised on their heads.

Bahamian drinking habits had not changed. The liquor that was pouring in from everywhere—Scotch from Glasgow, gin from Liverpool, rum from Jamaica, 60,000 bottles of Hill & Hill Kentucky Straight Bourbon directly from the distillery in Owensboro—was going out just as fast. Up to this point Nassau had been the somnolent terminal for a desultory trade in sponges, sisal, and turtles; now it became a boomtown, the ideal way station and staging area for a vast traffic in liquor. In 1918 Scotch exporters had sent 914 gallons of their product to the Bahamas; two years into Prohibition the Bahama-bound export had soared to 386,000 gallons. Outbound traffic leapt proportionally. Accounting for all sources, a U.S. Coast Guard historian estimated that at the peak of the trade ten million quarts of liquor passed through the Bahamas in a single year. The liquor shipped out of Nassau, an alarmed federal prosecutor in New York said in 1921, was "spreading like a fan up the Atlantic Coast," as thousands of cases filled the holds and crowded the decks of hundreds of northbound ships, often as not serving as sleeping pallets for their crews.

A *New York Herald* reporter, trying to convey to his readers a sense of what had happened in the Bahamas, explained that outbound ships "were loaded after nightfall by negroes to whom a shilling a day once was affluence" but who now consider the "night lost [if it] does not enrich them by $10, $20 and even $50." The latter figure seems unlikely, but the sudden riches were evident everywhere. According to a dispatch in the *Times* of London in March 1920, just two months into the Prohibition era, the liquor business had already "transformed the Bahama Government's financial condition as if by magic from a deficit to a comparatively huge surplus." A government economic development brochure attributed this to "the conditions supervening in the United States early in 1920." Translation: the colony's revenue from its export tax—the small price bootleggers were asked to pay for their use of the Bahamas as a depot—brought Nassauvians into the twentieth century. After the completion of a sewage system, a 2,300-volt diesel generator, a modern wharf some two hundred yards long, a newly dredged harbor, and miles of resurfaced roads and streets, the colony's British governor, Sir Bede Clifford, said it would be appropriate to erect near the statues of Christopher Columbus and Queen Victoria a third one: a monument to Andrew J. Volstead.

The stone likenesses of the Admiral of the Ocean Sea and the Grandmother of Europe stood a few blocks apart, in front of confectionery-pink government buildings in downtown Nassau. As for the Patron Saint of the Bahamian Economy, his monument could have been situated roughly halfway between them, in front of the Lucerne Hotel, a white wooden structure set behind an eight-foot wall on Frederick Street. The stolid Volstead would not have felt very comfortable at the Lucerne, but its habitués would have been happy to salute his statue daily. The royal palms in the hotel's courtyard, its three stories of broad verandas, and the bougainvillea and hibiscus in its gardens (home to a tame pelican named Nebuchadnezzar) provided a congenial marketplace for the principals of the Bahamian bootlegging industry and their clients.

"The men who made the greatest fortunes in Nassau never sailed a ship nor sold to any person in the United States a pint of booze," a local historian wrote in 1934. These entrepreneurs were largely the agents, importers, and freight forwarders who turned the wheels of the business, abetted by representatives of the Royal Bank of Canada and other respectable financiers. The bankers were ready to extend loans secured by collateral as safe as a U.S. Treasury bond: the next shipment of booze coming into the port. By 1923 Roland Symonette, an ordinary seaman from the island of Eleuthera who had become a Bronfman family partner, had already earned $1 million U.S. from the Bahamian liquor trade.*

The Lucerne was where the financiers and middlemen convened for both business and pleasure, dining and drinking with the men who actually put their hands on the liquor. They were a spicy mix of sea captains, adventurers, and freelance opportunists. The best known among them was Bill McCoy, skipper of a series of twin-masted schooners that conducted an illegal liquor trade for much of the 1920s. According to the American consul in Kingston, Jamaica, McCoy was "the chief liquor smuggler operating from Nassau." Contrary to the legend fostered by the teetotaling McCoy, the quality of the goods he delivered up and down the Atlantic coast did not give birth to the phrase "the real McCoy," which dates back to the nineteenth century. However, the quantity he moved—175,000 cases by some estimates—went a long way toward confirming his place in the popular mythology of the time. McCoy possessed many other attributes that lent themselves to mythmaking: he was tall, he was good looking, he was a fine seaman, and he had an excellent ghostwriter.

Although Frederick F. Van de Water published *The Real McCoy* under his own name, he wrote it in McCoy's first-person voice, and there's every reason to believe the book's description of the people who hung out at

---

*Like the Bronfmans, Symonette later learned how to erase the stain of bootlegging from his fortune. After four decades spent channeling his earnings into real estate, shipbuilding, construction, and other more conventional industries, Symonette's success was memorialized by two distinct honors. First, in 1964 he became the premier of the newly self-governing Bahamas. But he won yet more appropriate recognition in 2001, when his country put Symonette's face on its fifty-dollar bill.

the Lucerne: "slit-eyed, hunch-shouldered strangers, with the bluster of Manhattan in their voices and a wary truculence of manner." The publisher of the *Nassau Tribune* referred to the bootlegging crowd and the business they conducted as "the orgy of the Lucerne." But apart from the notorious Bootleggers' Ball that rocked the hotel for more than thirty-six champagne-spilling, chair-busting, knife-brandishing hours in late July 1921, this was an orgy driven not by carnality but by greed.

Any skipper hanging around the Lucerne and wanting to run liquor up the eastern seaboard had no problem acquiring the goods. The easiest way was to make arrangements with the owners of a vessel like the *Dreamland*. "Vessel" may not be the right word; a child's bathtub toy traveled greater distances than the *Dreamland*. It was a hundred-foot-long barge permanently anchored near North Cat Cay, a dot on the map near Bimini, westernmost of the Bahama Islands, only fifty miles off the Florida coast. The *Dreamland* had no sails, no engine, no means of propulsion at all, but it did have lights, refrigeration, and extensive storage facilities. In Nassau, finding someone prepared to sell you smuggling-worthy liquor—which is to say, any liquor at all—was no more difficult than finding your way to, say, the Market Street establishment of Gertrude Lythgoe, "Queen of the Bootleggers." A thirty-five-year-old former stenographer from Bowling Green, Ohio, Lythgoe happened to find bootlegging more rewarding than office work, and life at the Lucerne more stimulating than life in Bowling Green. "She says she is no smuggler," a *Wall Street Journal* correspondent told his readers, and consequently she "is not responsible for what happens to the liquor after she sells it."

The nature of the financial responsibility taken on by the men like McCoy who ran the merchandise up the coast was suggested by two procedural maneuvers they all had to execute. The first required a change in a ship's legal status. Because any vessel flying the American flag was subject to American law anywhere in the world, a prudent captain sailed under foreign colors. Nassau being British, that meant figuring out a way to sail under the Union Jack. Nassau being Nassau, it wasn't hard for an American buccaneer to find someone who would buy his vessel, obtain British registry, and then sell it right back to him for the same price, minus a suitable commission for his trouble. Between 1921 and 1922 the net tonnage of vessels registered in the Bahamas increased tenfold.

Changing registry was something you had to do only once; that's how the swift, twin-masted, 114-foot American fishing schooner *Arethusa*, which Bill McCoy acquired in Gloucester, Massachusetts, became the swift, twin-masted, 114-foot British rumrunner *Tomoka*. The other procedural maneuver had to be repeated on each voyage out of Nassau: payment of the export tax that would dredge Nassau harbor, build a water system, and bestow upon the town all those other municipal goodies. The $6 per case export duty, said McCoy, meant that "each time [I] took 5,000 cases of Scotch [out of the harbor], I left $30,000 in the hands of the customs authorities." Then he'd sail up the Great Whiskey Way to Montauk or Block Island or Nantucket, where he'd earn back the cost of the goods, the duty, the wages and provisions for his crew—and twice as much again.

Until they were beset first by modern pirates and then, in mid-decade, by a greatly enhanced Coast Guard effort, life for the smugglers was remarkably congenial. In August 1921, the *Standard-Times* of New Bedford, Massachusetts, reported that a schooner lying off the uninhabited island of Nomans Land, about twenty miles away, was "dispensing refreshment in a truly hospitable manner to all drought-ridden individuals who can sail, row or swim out to the trim-looking fisherman." The "genial captain"—Bill McCoy, making one of his first press appearances—told the paper to advise its readers, "Come out any time you want to; the law can't touch us here, and we'll be very glad to see you." Near Miami small boats dropped anchor and hung poster-sized price lists over the gunwales no more self-consciously than if they'd been selling potatoes.

Early on, the buyers coming out to the ships were retail customers, people with access to a boat able to traverse the three miles separating the mainland from international waters. Along the south shore of Long Island, in an area known to bootleggers as "the Rendezvous," a cruise near, say, Fire Island Light was a waterborne version of big-city shopping. An officer on the *Cask*, a four-masted schooner that had been diverted from its prior duty in the timber trade, described how people in motor launches would pull up alongside, inquire after the prices the captain had placed on the ship's offerings, and then scoot away to do some comparison shopping at the next ship bobbing on the coastal swells. Customers less sensitive to price and more inclined to build a relationship with a single, reliable supplier were every captain's ideal. "It was like going to a supermarket," said an officer on a schooner that worked northern waters. "We had a good reputation and lots of customers. They would carry your mail ashore and bring you anything you wanted." Cruising the New Jersey coast on his own yacht, Robert Wood Johnson II, of the pharmaceutical Johnson & Johnsons, got into the habit of pulling up alongside a rumrunner, buying a bottle or two, and enjoying his evening cocktails at sea.

There were annoyances, of course—like, for instance, extortion. In *The Diary of a Rum-Runner*, the pseudonymous "Alastair Moray" of the *Cask* reported that a tariff amounting to a dollar a case had to be paid to "state police, coast guards, etc." buzzing around the ship's anchorage off Long Island. The three-mile limit protected bootleggers from American law but did not shield them from the annoying attentions of dishonest American enforcement personnel. Since all the *Cask*'s customers would have to make it back to shore through well-patrolled American waters, the ship's crew was compelled either to buy off the authorities or provide them with other rewards. In his log for July 18, 1923, Moray described an encounter with an army lieutenant, a naval commander, and a Coast Guard captain aboard a patrol boat. "The Coast Guard captain was on duty, but the other two were only joy-riding," he wrote. Moray welcomed them aboard, took them belowdecks, and offered them whiskey. "We all partook, and waxed merry thereon," he continued. "They stayed about one and a half hours. When they went, I gave them a small souvenir to remind them of their visit. They have elected themselves the ship's godfathers, and might prove very useful."

OF PROHIBITION'S MANIFOLD gifts to American posterity, few were of greater value than its enrichment of the language. The *Dictionary of American Slang*, published in 1960, listed more colloquial synonyms for "drunk" than for any other word; most of them originated in the 1920s. "He was taken for a ride" was the Chicago-bred euphemism for what mobsters did when they dumped the body of a troublesome competitor or an errant confederate in a distant suburb. The "Maryland Free State" was an epithet that arose not from the liberty-loving ardor of colonial forebears, nor from Maryland's loyalty to the Union during the Civil War, but from the typewriter of Hamilton Owens, editor of the *Baltimore Sun*, in a salute to the legislature when it declined to pass a state enforcement act in 1923. "Powder room" was coined to denote the minimal bathroom facilities for women hastily installed in formerly all-male saloons once they had become universally accommodating speakeasies. A dry Massachusetts banker named Delcevere King wanted to find an opprobrious word to describe imbibers who openly violated the Eighteenth Amendment. Publicized in the pages of the *Boston Herald*, the contest King sponsored drew more than twenty-five thousand entries. Thus did the English language acquire "scofflaw," winner of first prize and two hundred dollars.

Oddly, the most ubiquitous term to materialize from the long decades of temperance agitation and the subsequent reign of the Volstead Act is one that fell into disuse, at least in its most popular sense, virtually the minute Prohibition came to an end: rum. "Used generically as a hostile name for intoxicating liquors," says the *Oxford English Dictionary*, it first popped up in Canada in 1800 and migrated south by the 1850s. By the time it had been captured by the stump speakers and pulpit pounders of the early twentieth century, it had become a common signifier for the loathed item itself, and an all-purpose modifier for everything associated with it: the "rum demon" sold by "rum barons" who ruled a "rum traffic" conducted by "rumrunners." The *OED* misses the term's ironic capture by drinkers, who had no problem calling an illegal drinking place a "rum hole" and a nose reddened by overindulgence a "rum blossom."

"Rum Row," though, belonged to everyone—brief, alliterative, and perfectly descriptive of the remarkable phenomenon that evolved out of those early, sunny days of coastal bootlegging. Inevitably, demand grew so great and prices so high that the freelancers were elbowed aside by industrial-scale operators. By 1923, from the Gulf of Maine to the tip of Florida, an enormous fleet of old freighters, tramp steamers, converted submarine chasers, and ships of various other descriptions—"anything with a bottom that could float and a hold that could be filled with booze," McCoy said—lay at permanent anchor just outside the three-mile limit. No more loitering off New Bedford for McCoy and his competition; the rumrunners now sailed up the coast from Nassau, off-loaded their goods onto the Rum Row ships, and raced back south to pick up another shipment. The vessels on the Row remained immobile for months at a time, functioning as floating warehouses for a second network of seafarers operating locally.

The liquor from these "mother ships," as the Rum Row depositories were called, found its way to shore much as Canadian liquor made it across the Detroit River from Windsor. Small boats of every imaginable description would dash out to the Row, usually under cover of night, load up, then hurry back to shore. On foggy evenings the smugglers would get their bearings by transmitting international code to a U.S. Navy radio direction-finder station, whose operators had no way of knowing who was doing the signaling. On nights they weren't taking advantage of services provided by the government's nautical representatives, the rumrunners sought to abuse them: when a Coast Guard vessel was in the vicinity, the miscreants would send out a distress call to draw the Guard boat to a false alarm miles away.

A telltale dark patch on its port side indicated that a boat had probably spent some time bobbing up against a rum ship, but there was no shame in this. For a coastal fisherman in the Northeast, whiskey was a more valuable catch than cod. "You knew right away when a man stopped fishing and started running rum," a Massachusetts woman recalled many years later. "In the first place, his family began to eat proper." In Florida, boatyard operators loyal to the fishermen/bootleggers on whom they depended refused to make wharfside space available to the Coast Guard and declined to repair their vessels. At the northern end of the Row in Maine, Canadian fishermen got into the game as well. A New Brunswick newspaper did not disguise the trade's appeal: "It beats carrying sardines."

Local boatmen who knew every cove and bay had no trouble finding places to land their bounty; the names of the most popular drop-off spots in the area of Brunswick, Maine—Halfway Rock, Gun Point—suggest the furtiveness of their activity. In resort areas from fall through spring, smugglers would commandeer the docks of summer houses shuttered for the season. If an inshore runner happened to encounter law enforcement officials waiting for him to pull ashore, he'd toss his cargo overboard in a relatively shallow inlet. This was a nuisance, not a loss. Having first packed the liquor in "hams"—six-bottle burlap bags weighted down with salt for instances like this—the smuggler could return a few days later, after the salt had dissolved, to find his investment bobbing safely on the surface.

With minor local variations this routine was repeated the entire length of the Atlantic coast, as men and women in seaside communities boosted their earning power and the economic health of their communities by collaborating with the large-scale entrepreneurs of Rum Row. "Hundreds of such men" were operating out of every one of the "liquor ports," noted the *New York Times*. This was especially true near the enormous New York market, where the greatest concentration of mother ships took up positions in a line running westward from Montauk to the Rockaways and south to Cape May. This traffic, said William E. Reynolds, commandant of the Coast Guard, "was entirely unprecedented in the history of the country." Just before Christmas in 1924, the *Times* reported, a flotilla of eighteen steamers stood at anchor southeast of Asbury Park, New Jersey, "loaded deep with cargoes worth millions." Other substantial fleets established permanent residence on the seas near Boston, Norfolk, and Savannah. Vancouver-based bootleggers set up similar operations offshore from major West Coast ports, and a tendril of the original Rum Row reached from the Keys along the Gulf Coast, with thicker nodes near Tampa, Mobile, Galveston, and New Orleans. In many places nightfall unveiled a constellation of ship's lights so dense, recalled a captain who serviced vessels anchored off Highland Light on Cape Cod, "you would think it was a city out there."

In daylight an innocent beachgoer might have perceived it differently: the long line of hulking ships and the smaller boats flitting among them looked like a fleet preparing to launch an invasion. The less innocent (which is to say virtually anyone who lived within a day's drive of the coast) knew better. This wasn't an invasion, but a sort of inverse blockade, an unsiege: the boats were there not to deny Americans something they needed but to provide them with something they wanted.

IN 1922 BILL McCOY put a northern exclamation mark on his claim that he'd invented Rum Row when he sailed into port on the North Atlantic island of St. Pierre. McCoy knew at least two things about this unlikely place: its harbor remained ice-free in winter, and its business was conducted under the flag of France. For a rumrunner, these were auspicious qualities. For the rest of the world, Damon Runyon provided a more measured appraisal. "Now if you are never in St. Pierre," he wrote in the unmistakable syntax of the guys, dolls, and other suspects who sidle through his stories, "I wish to say you miss nothing much, because what is it but a little squirt of a burg sort of huddled up alongside some big rocks off Newfoundland, and very hard to get to, any way you go."

The French were the first Europeans to get there, stumbling across St. Pierre and the adjacent island of Miquelon in 1536. The British booted them out in 1713, and for the next century control of these scraggy, barren outposts bounced back and forth between Paris and London. After the French took permanent possession in 1815, St. Pierre became a depot for the French fishing fleet and eventual home to six thousand souls trying to pull their livelihoods out of the cold ocean fifteen miles south of Newfoundland. The larger Miquelon was more thickly populated, but only if you were counting the purple sandpipers, snowy egrets, and Atlantic puffins that were its primary residents.

But then the Eighteenth Amendment came along and the eastern seaboard developed a thirst. When the Bahamian government raised its import duties, Bill McCoy led a stream of rumrunners who shifted at least part of their business north from the Caribbean. On July 8, 1922, just months after McCoy's first visit, the *Sable Island* sailed into the harbor, 12,000 cases of whiskey in its hold. Within weeks the St. Pierrais economy was transformed. In mild weather teams of oxen dragged the bounteous cargo away from the docks to be stored in basements and toolsheds; when the snows arrived horse-drawn sleighs did the toting. "The modest docks of St. Pierre's toy harbour were buried in an avalanche of freight, pungent with the smell of superior liquor," wrote the Canadian journalist Peter C.

Newman. "The odor grew so strong that at times the fog that rolled up St. Pierre's steeply inclined streets with the nightly tides would carry a distinct Scotch flavour."

Bill McCoy always considered his opening of the St. Pierre rum-running business a gift to the local population, who could now sustain themselves on a commodity more valuable than fish (and easier to land, too). As the growth of the business accelerated, the island's fishermen abandoned their nets and became longshoremen, except for those who climbed aboard the whiskey fleet. More than a thousand vessels departed the tiny port for Rum Row in 1923 alone. Every basement, barn, and shed was turned into a stockroom. The six million bottles that passed through that year worked out to a thousand bottles for every man, woman, and child on the island. Although the island's four-cents-per-bottle tax was less than one-tenth of the Bahamian levy, customs income ran to three times St. Pierre's annual operating budget.

The *bon temps* rolled during what became known in later years as *le temps de la fraude*. New offices for importers and *négociants* replaced the fish processing operations on the street facing the dock. To make room for the vast quantity of bottles and cases overflowing from every roofed structure on the island, fish were evicted from St. Pierre's refrigeration plant, which was converted into a liquor warehouse. The grand—for St. Pierre—L'Hotel Robert opened for business, its guest rooms occupied by English-speaking men sporting double-breasted overcoats, broad-brimmed fedoras, and fat billfolds. The Robert's three-story facade was topped by an ornate wooden cornice, which was itself an exciting phenomenon on treeless St. Pierre. But wood soon became a common building material, as residents ripped up shipping cases to make shingles for their roofs, sills for their windows, and walls for their sheds. One especially resourceful islander built a brand-new home out of a matched suite of Scotch cases. The stenciled logo of a ship, repeated on each of the panels that lined the house's walls, gave the place its name: Villa Cutty Sark.

In addition to the Scotch coming in from Glasgow, there was Irish whiskey ferried across the ocean by Norwegian steamers and so much bubbly sailing in from Le Havre that newspaper poets began to link St. Pierre with Nassau: the "Isle of Champagne" and the "Isle of Rum." But the most valuable of the goods—or, better, the goods that made St. Pierre so valuable—was the variety represented in the hold of the *Sable Island*: all 12,000 of those cases were Canadian Club. To the Canadian distilling industry, St. Pierre might as well have been known as the Isle of Gold.

For all the factors that made St. Pierre so attractive—the ice-free harbor, the low import duties, the willing Catholic population—none was as important to the Canadians as its status as part of metropolitan France. Under Canadian law no duty was owed on liquor manufactured for export; shippers were required to post a tax bond as their goods left Canada, but would have the bond redeemed on the presentation of landing certificates from a foreign port. St. Pierre lay just fifteen miles off British Newfoundland, but for duty purposes it was as foreign as the Congo. No longer did Canadian distillers have to supply their agents in Havana and other distant ports with the wads of cash required by local officials before they would stamp fake landing certificates. No longer did they have to use middlemen to transfer their goods to the rumrunners sailing toward Boston and New York. Vessels hailing from Halifax and other Canadian ports could chug into St. Pierre's harbor and get legal stamps on the landing certificates required to release their tax deposits from bond. Soon a gilt-lettered sign reading "Northern Export Co." went up on the stone facade of a building across from the St. Pierre dock—the local branch of the growing Bronfman empire. In any given week the Bronfman inventory stashed on St. Pierre was valued at more than $1 million. One of the rum-running ships working the waters between Halifax and St. Pierre might have been named in honor of the Bronfman success: the *Mazel Tov*.

In time, warehousing the goods became unnecessary. The St. Pierrais government decided to certify landing upon a ship's arrival in port; duty paid, it could turn around and steam straight for Rum Row, neither crew nor cargo ever touching St. Pierre soil. The sea lanes stretching from St. Pierre to Cape Cod to Long Island became so thick with shippers, hijackers, and Coast Guard patrols that the rumrunners had to devise secure communications systems. Some depended on verbal codes ("chien oiseau" meant "200 cases arrived and landed"), some were numerical ("02716–22699" denoted "boat in trouble"). Many issued lead-covered codebooks that could be tossed safely—that is, irretrievably—into the sea if the ship was boarded by hostile parties. The Bronfman operatives, as always more sophisticated than the competition, relied on codes broadcast over a private radio station they had established expressly for this purpose.

Sometimes, though, the business required very little artifice. One could always proceed in the fashion favored by National Distilleries Limited of Montreal, which sent the following letter to a St. Pierre–based agent: "Dear Sir," it began, "The bearer, Captain Tremblay, is going to go on the *Columbia* acting as Pilot and Navigator." If Rum Row had had a chamber of commerce, it might have used the letter's concluding sentence as its motto: "His duties are to bring the vessel to a position known to him."

✦   ✦   ✦

"RUM RUNNING IS DOOMED," Roy Haynes declared in the summer of 1923, "and, unless I mistake the clear indications, the day of its doom is near." Assuming that they did not know that Haynes was wrong about virtually everything, the editors of the *Glasgow Evening News* would have been surprised by his comment. Just weeks before, the *News* had described the parade of liquor ships departing the mouth of the Clyde, bound west by southwest across the North Atlantic to the coast of the United States and a rendezvous at the Rendezvous.

Of course, the Scotch whiskey industry was not entirely responsible for the rapid industrialization of Rum Row. The French had a hand in it, and so did the Hamburg-based distillery that conflated two famous brands in a counterfeit Scotch they marketed as "Black & White Horse Whisky." American mobsters had also taken a substantial position in the business. "To cut costs and increase efficiency, we chartered our own ships to bring the Scotch across the Atlantic," Meyer Lansky told an interviewer half a century later. ". . . By the middle twenties we were running the most efficient international shipping business in the world." But Lansky also noted that the mob's interest in greater efficiency had not been unprovoked: "Those fine upright men in Britain kept squeezing us for higher prices."

The "fine upright men" were the lords of the Scotch whiskey industry, operating their "scheduled area" racket. In 1919, when the United States was turning dry, British distillers were turning peckish. World War I had been rough on them, not only restricting foreign trade but pinching their domestic markets as well. During the war the prime minister—David Lloyd George, who'd famously said that drink was a greater enemy to the United Kingdom than the Germans—hit the industry with new excise levies, redoubling taxes he had already doubled during the war. British temperance advocates, inspired by the American example, appeared to be gaining ground.

One of the whiskey lords who turned his attention to the growing threat was Lord Dewar of Homestall. Tommy Dewar had made his family's White Label brand an international success, for three decades traveling the world to promote Scotch generally, Dewar's specifically, and with particular delight a philosophy of living that became known as "Dewarism." This was a fundamentally hedonist code expressed in upward of 150 aphorisms tinted by Dewar's sybaritic enthusiasms ("Of two evils, choose the more interesting") and his Conservative politics ("If we are here to help others, I often wonder what the others are here for").

But Dewar also invoked more solemn principles of modern business. "Yesterday's success belongs to yesterday" was a famous example, and never had it applied more than in 1920, as Dewar and his colleagues faced what the Scotch Whisky Association in its annual report called "the prohibition virus." Dewar railed against the threat posed by British drys, and William H. Ross of the powerful Distillers Company Limited was alarmed as well. "The fact that America has, through a cleverly contrived plot, suddenly voted herself 'dry,'" said Ross, "has been hailed by the extremists of this country as an indication that people here will follow suit." In a word, the distillers were on the brink of panic.

As it developed, Prohibition wasn't much of a problem for the Scotch lords. British temperance activists won little public sympathy. Additionally, the nation's crushing war debt obliged Lloyd George's government to promote exports, and few British products were as promotable as the millions of gallons of whiskey aging in casks from Speyside to Islay. Nor was there a potential market larger than the millions of Americans, pining for liquor, who were conveniently situated between those tariff-free outposts of empire, Canada and the Bahamas. The American thirst was so great, said the London *Evening Standard*, that all the decent liquor was "lodged (not too securely) in the cellars of millionaires," who were compelled to defend their stock "by force of arms." This wasn't remotely accurate, but for a Scotch distiller looking to the export trade, it couldn't help but warm the blood.

If ever there was a seller's market, this was it. Any faint resistance to exploiting American Prohibition was swept away when the cupidity of the distillers was catalyzed by a combination of imperial pride and the British commitment to freedom of the seas. Sir Auckland Geddes, ambassador to Washington, employed diplomatic understatement when he informed George Curzon, the foreign secretary, that "the enactment of Prohibition has inflicted hardship on the Trade." British sensitivities were not mollified when William Jennings Bryan threatened invasion of Bimini if the UK continued to tolerate its use as "the base of a conspiracy against the Prohibition law." As an increasingly marginalized figure in a minority party, Bryan had no authority to act on his threats, but he was a former secretary of state, and his words were widely reported in the London press.

To the British foreign office eventually fell the responsibility of conducting an arduous negotiation with the American State Department regarding the three-mile limit, which had been universally recognized as the demarcation line between national and international waters since the eighteenth century. The Americans wanted to push the line outward, hoping to strain the resources of inshore smugglers who would have to traverse many more than six miles of open seas on a round-trip. To another branch of the British government, the Colonial Office, fell the responsibility of fielding American demands that the British crack down on the bootlegging business that was growing exponentially in the Caribbean colonies. The U.S. consul in Nassau sent his superiors in the State Department a local newspaper's summary of the Colonial Office response to American pleadings: "We are doing our best for you but cannot be expected to infringe on the prerogatives of our own people to help you enforce one of your fool laws."

At the same time, U.S. secretary of state Charles Evans Hughes had been under great pressure to forbid all foreign ships, even passenger liners, from carrying liquor inside American coastal waters. The primary advocate of this position was the Justice Department, in the formidable person of Mabel Walker Willebrandt, who seemed to relish a fight like this one. Having sharpened her saber during her assaults on Andrew Mellon's inconstant devotion to the Volstead Act, she now turned her attention to Hughes, accusing the State Department of failing to enforce the Constitution and electing instead "to 'give aid and comfort' to the British Embassy."

The possibility that champagne and whiskey might be stripped from the pantries of their liners brought the British to the negotiating table, and Lord Curzon eventually acceded to an extension of the three-mile limit. The new treaty established that a nation's coastal waters began at "an hour's steaming distance" from the shore—as later interpreted by American authorities, twelve nautical miles. Curzon wasn't happy about the compromise but considered this change in long-established international law a necessary acknowledgment of the prevailing political reality in the United States—a reality that he described as "Puritanism run mad."

Curzon's counterpart in the Colonial Office made no concessions at all. Winston Churchill believed that "a State is only responsible for the enforcement of its own laws," and had no obligation to implement the laws of another nation. He flatly refused to use British influence, authority, or power to interfere in any way with the liquor trade of the Bahamas or any other British colony in the Caribbean. Several years later, summing up his view of the Eighteenth Amendment, Churchill landed on a phrase that went beyond Curzon's sputtering invocation of Puritanism. Prohibition, Churchill said, was "an affront to the whole history of mankind."

✦   ✦   ✦

THE BRITISH ROLE in the Prohibition era did not end with the signing of the twelve-mile-limit treaty. The final chapter wouldn't be written until after the lords of the Scotch industry had established a schedule of price controls, credit requirements, and other rules regulating access to Rum Row; after they had successfully opened an alternative depot on St. Pierre, nearer the population centers of the Northeast; and after they had forged their phenomenally profitable joint venture with Sam Bronfman.

After all that, the enduring epitaph for the British role in the bootlegging business was uttered by Sir Alexander Walker, heir to the firm that had been founded in Ayrshire a century before by his grandfather Johnnie. Summoned before a Royal Commission on Licensing in 1930, Walker was asked if the distillery industry could have stopped the export of liquor to the United States.

"Certainly not," Walker replied.

The examiner pressed. "You could not?"

Said Walker, "We would not if we could."

Chapter 12

Blessed Be the Fruit of the Vine

B Y ANY OBVIOUS STANDARD, Horatio F. Stoll chose an unpropitious time to start a magazine for the California wine industry. Long before launching *California Grape Grower* in December 1919, Stoll had been an indefatigable publicist for the growers and winemakers, starting out before the dark cloud of the Eighteenth Amendment had even begun to form on the horizon. He worked in a Napa County vineyard, he wrote about wine for the *Los Angeles Times* and the *San Francisco Argonaut*, and he helped popularize the raffia-wrapped chianti of California's first large-scale winery, Italian Swiss Colony. In 1910 he turned his attention from trying to promote the industry to trying to save it. As chief propagandist for the California Grape Protective Association, Stoll spent the decade leading up to the Eighteenth Amendment—and the seemingly perverse start-up of his magazine—as the voice of the growers and vintners.

That voice was a blend of hand-wringing and hucksterism. The signs he posted along wine country roadways were characteristic: "This vineyard gone after Prohibition." So was a brochure entitled "How Prohibition Would Affect California," an unmistakable example of Stoll's high-stepping jauntiness. There wasn't a single teetotaler "among the world's really great men," Stoll wrote; on the contrary, he said, the roster of wine-loving giants ran from Alexander the Great and Julius Caesar to Columbus, Dickens, Lincoln, and Bismarck, not to mention Verdi, Wagner, and Admiral Dewey. How he knew what he claimed to know about the drinking habits of his Hall of Fame was unclear, but it set up the punch line: "What names can the prohibitionists show to compare with those above?" the brochure asked. "Has there ever been a prohibitionist who was a really great man . . . unless it be Mohammed, the first prohibitionist?"

For all his ebullient flackery, Horatio Stoll could not claim sole credit for the California wine industry's notable victories. The successive defeat of four separate ballot initiatives that would have established statewide Prohibition could also be credited to the heavily Italian and Irish population of San Francisco, until 1920 the state's largest city. The industry's place in California's culture was no small factor, either. Winemaking may not have been fully appreciated elsewhere in the United States in the early part of the twentieth century (broadly speaking, only immigrants and the wealthy drank wine), but some ninety thousand acres of California soil planted in wine grapes, and an annual crop valued at seventy-five million dollars, made it central to the state's economy.

This posture of strength blinded the winemakers to what was coming across the Sierras from Washington. Even as late as the winter of 1918, with ratification of the Eighteenth Amendment well under way and rolling downhill, the prominent Sonoma County winemaker Sam Sebastiani could remain convinced that national Prohibition was a dead letter. Returning from a trip to New York, Sebastiani confidently told the *Sonoma Index-Tribune* about a "consensus of opinion" that had formed in the East: "After the war, the future of wine will be even more wonderful." The cause for this jolly consensus, Sebastiani said, was the anticipated return to American shores of more than a million wine lovers. At that moment these potential customers were enduring the trenches of the Western Front, but Sebastiani was convinced that a few months in France would also lead them to discover the wonders of wine—"by observation," the *Index-Tribune* hastened to add.

When Horatio Stoll published the first issue of *California Grape Grower* in December 1919, just one month before the Eighteenth Amendment and the Volstead Act were scheduled to bring California's wine trade to its knees, he was betting his future on an industry that did not appear to have one. On a fact-finding tour of the state's wine regions four months earlier, Stoll had found the growers every bit as clueless as Sebastiani. Everywhere he traveled the vines were heavy with fruit and the disposition of the growers was as sunny as the California skies. He had been "amazed" to find the industry "making absolutely no preparations for the disposal of their crop," Stoll wrote in his premier issue. "Lulled into a sense of false security . . . ," Stoll explained, "the grape growers announced they were going to make wine, because the ban would surely be lifted before the crop was ready to be harvested." They somehow believed that sixty years of agitation, culminating in the capitulation of both Congress and the state legislatures, would magically unravel in less than two months.

That was about as likely as Sam Sebastiani's addled vision. But not too many years later a grape grower writing in a popular magazine suggested

that if they had only known, his associates in the California wine industry would have spent those fifty years "donat[ing] large sums to the Anti-
Saloon League and the Woman's Christian Temperance Union." Growers
who had ripped out their vines and replaced them with prunes or apricots
or apples soon regretted following what had appeared to be a prudent path.
It turned out that the last pre-Prohibition harvest, in 1919, was accompanied, wrote Stoll, by "the unexpected demand for fresh wine grapes from
Eastern cities and buyers . . . offering from $25 to $30 per ton. Before the
season was over, $65 per ton was gladly paid."

"Unexpected" was understatement. Over the previous decade California wine grapes had brought as little as $9.50 per ton, and never more than
$30. But after that glorious fall of 1919, the unexpected became the norm.
In 1921 the price reached $82, then $105, and at one giddy moment in
1924 it spiked to a shocking $375. Defying the laws of economic gravity,
volume increased as well. At the same time that the California growers
were filling boxcars with their harvest, grape imports from Argentina and
Chile jumped from 18,000 pounds in all of 1921 to nearly half a million
in just the first four months of 1922. And all those buyers weren't paying
those startling new prices because they intended to make grape juice.

THE ENGINE THAT drove the California Grape Rush of the 1920s was
the fruit juice clause of the Volstead Act. This was the language Wayne
Wheeler inserted into the act ostensibly to allow farmers' wives to "conserve their fruit," but really to mollify rural voters who wanted their hard
cider. The clause gave small-scale apple growers a tiny bonanza of their
own: "On pleasant autumn days," a University of Kansas official wrote,
"the highroads in the apple districts are dotted every mile or two with little
'stands' where home-made cider is offered for sale to the thirsty wayfarer."

But if it was wine you were after, you didn't need to do any wayfaring,
at least not if you lived anywhere with a large population of southern or
eastern European immigrants. Though it hadn't been spelled out in the
Volstead Act, regulations soon established that the head of a household
was allowed to produce two hundred gallons a year of fermented fruit juice
for his family's use. As this worked out to nearly three bottles a day, only
a very large family—or an exceedingly bibulous small one—was likely to
consume this much on its own. For any self-respecting bootlegger, there
wasn't enough money to be made peddling wine; a quart of industrial gin
at 50 proof packed as much of an alcoholic punch as six bottles of the typical homemade wine, and it was a lot easier to transport. But to the home

vintner in Boston or Baltimore, in Helena or Hibbing, red wine took on the color of money.

"Grapes are so valuable this year that they are being stolen," the *St. Helena Star* told its readers during the Napa Valley's first Prohibition harvest, in 1920. The next year a state agriculture official announced that the acreage in grapes was "increasing by leaps and bounds since the enactment of the Federal Prohibition Law." The year after that, vineyard land that had sold for $100 an acre in 1919 was bringing more than $500. As expensive as this was, if you wanted to buy land in the California wine country, all you had to do was pledge next year's crop as collateral. For someone like Conrad Viano, an Italian immigrant who fell in love with a forty-year-old vineyard in Contra Costa County that reminded him of his native Piemonte, there was nothing to it: he took out a mortgage to buy the land and had it virtually paid off with the proceeds from his first harvest.

Those growers who had ripped out their vines and planted fruit trees rushed to get back into grapes—after a fashion. Where Semillon and zinfandel and other respectable varietals had once reigned, the new king was a ragamuffin called alicante bouschet. In the town of Escalon, ten miles north of Modesto, Joseph Gallo jump-started his grape-growing business by planting ten of his twenty acres in alicante; his teenaged sons Ernest and Julio stenciled the family symbol, a rooster, onto the shipping crates. In the Livermore Valley, where everyone but the Wente brothers seemed to have uprooted their grapes in favor of prunes and apricots and apples, old vineyards burst into new life, their vines thick with alicante. From Sonoma to Fresno, established vineyardists grafted their cabernets and Rieslings onto this unappealing subspecies—"a grape so deplorable," wrote the epicurean journalist/novelist Idwal Jones, "it ranks somewhat below the gooseberry."

Alicante made truly lousy wine, but the alchemy of Prohibition turned its deficiencies into money. Its large clusters produced a bountiful crop. Its thick, tough skin enabled it to survive the indignities of shipping. Better still, alicante's uncommonly dark red flesh produced something that not only looked like decent wine but managed to maintain that deception after two or three pressings, or god knows how many dilutions. During the 1921 harvest, Horatio Stoll reported, "buyers by the hundreds are wiring for Alicantes, for everywhere the Italian is willing to pay from 50¢ to $1.00 more" for a box of this outcast grape than for any other varietal. After his magazine had been blessed with ten alicante-endowed years of prosperity, Stoll explained the phenomenon in 1929 with one telling set of numbers: on the standard scale used to measure color in grapes, anything that scored over 150 had "more than three times the color usually necessary for wine or juice." Zinfandel scored a pale 38, cabernet sauvignon a respectable 86. Alicante weighed in at a bruising 204.

For the home winemaker wishing to supplement his income by selling some of his two hundred allotted gallons (or an additional several hundred unallotted gallons) to his neighbors, alicante was more than worth its outlandishly inflated price. In 1926 an American Federation of Labor official told a Senate committee that not only did 90 percent of working-men make some sort of alcoholic beverage at home, "they even make wine out of parsnips." Relative to parsnips (or dandelions, elderberries, choke-cherries, or other unprepossessing candidates), alicante was a *premier cru*. Add some sugar to it during the fermentation process, and a ton of alicante could produce five or six hundred gallons of something that may not have tasted much like wine but at least looked like it, and definitely acted like it. For the Slovenian coal miners of Bearcreek, Montana, this fecundity meant that the annual boxcar of grapes that arrived from California would yield nearly ten thousand gallons of wine (if you could call it that), "second wine" (made from the sugar-supplemented dregs), and distilled moonshine (made from the dregs of the dregs). Thirsty people will believe almost any-thing; the Bearcreek miners thought they were getting zinfandel.*

By the time the growers had retooled their operations to meet the clamorous demand, a robust, elaborate, and entirely legal distribution sys-tem had developed. You could find the command center—the San Fran-cisco railyards at Front Street and Broadway—by following what *Sunset* magazine described as "the sour fumes of wine" enveloping the place. No wonder. Over here, several odd-looking trucks with crushing machines and eight-hundred-gallon tanks mounted on their beds are pulled up next to freight cars; they're in competition with the operators in the abandoned warehouses nearby, where signs read "Grapes Crushed While You Wait." Over there, a man explains his business: he mashes to order, and once the grapes have been turned into juice it's out of his hands. "What happens to it after you take it away ain't our business," he tells an interviewer from *Sunset*. Some of the crushers deliver. Wine industry historian Leon Adams, who was a newspaper reporter in San Francisco in the 1920s, said, "One would select his grapes from trucks or from freight cars and then have the truck with the crusher go alongside, pour the grapes into the crusher,

---

* The iron miners who belonged to the Italian Club in the town of Virginia, Minnesota, took pains to procure more suitable grapes, dispatching a grocer named Cesare Mondavi to the San Joaquin Valley late each summer to acquire their supply. Inspired to get into the grape business himself, Mondavi soon moved his family to California, where his precocious son Robert would make his own name in the winemaking world.

and the crusher truck would then go to the individual's home address and through the pipe send the [juice] down into the cellar or wherever the wine was going to be fermented. This was quite a San Francisco institution."

But all that was strictly for the local market. The big-time operators could be found elsewhere in the freight yard, bidding against each other for the contents of single carloads, or a whole train's worth, bound for points east. In a matter of minutes a shipment could be sold and resold and sold once again before it left the yard, its destination changing with each transaction. In 1919 some 9,300 carloads of grapes left California for New York alone; by 1928 the number had more than tripled. Another 40,000 carloads headed for other eastern markets. In one frustrating season, Napa growers were unable to ship much of their crop because the railroads were already running at capacity; the county horticultural commissioner said "it would have taken three times the number of refrigerated cars available" to get their grapes to market. Looking, as newspapers will, for a vivid way to illustrate the deluge, the *Fresno Republican* did some musing, some measuring, and some multiplication, and calculated that the 1,265 stacked-to-the-brim freight cars that left California on a single glorious day during the 1925 harvest carried 8,635,365,375 grapes—more or less. During the harvest, wrote a reporter for *Business Week* describing the rail traffic, "all minor commodities must stand aside"—the grapes were too valuable.

On the other side of the country, the Pennsylvania Railroad expanded its Jersey City freight terminal strictly to accommodate the thousands upon thousands of grape-laden boxcars. Here another round of trackside auctions ensued, local distributors taking the handoff from the shippers and in turn selling their goods to the next link in this vast supply chain: to the retailers in city produce markets, like the seven-block-long Paddy's Market on Manhattan's Ninth Avenue, whose stalls were a wall of purple every October; to those described by *California Grape Grower* as "the army of pushcart vendors who cover every part of the metropolis when grapes are arriving in great quantities"; or to the "block buyers," designated purchasers who negotiated directly on behalf of the residents of their particular city block. Versions of the same system existed in Boston and Philadelphia, in Syracuse and Erie, in Paterson and Altoona and Canton—in the hundreds of cities and towns where immigrant populations were large and sympathy for Volsteadism small. In 1926 the chief investigator for the Prohibition Bureau described what he called the "twilight zone" of Prohibition: in tenement neighborhoods, he wrote, "you will see grapes everywhere—on pushcarts, in groceries, in fruit and produce stores, on carts and wagons and trucks . . . Wine grapes in crates, by the truckload, and by the carload." Like the spent ammunition left behind on a deserted battlefield, telltale evidence would linger long after the grapes had disappeared. You could tell you were in a wine-consuming neighborhood, a California grower said, "by the large quantities of grape pomace or waste in the streets."

How large? In 1917, when wine was legal, Americans consumed 70 million gallons—imported, domestic, and homemade. By 1925 Americans were drinking 150 million gallons of just the homemade stuff, all of it also legal in its own peculiar way. Back when Congress was debating Richmond Hobson's constitutional amendment in 1913, Representative Richard Bartholdt of St. Louis, a leading wet, said the measure would turn "every house in the country . . . into a distillery." A more appropriate word would have been "winery," but he was on the right track.

THE ALICANTE BOOM could not last. Easy money got too easy, and before long overplanting outstripped even the ravening demand. Growers tried the usual tactics employed by cartels. By 1926 members of the California Vineyardists' Association had agreed to let half their grapes die on the vine. The next year the association urged its members to cut back on shipping. Some growers attempted to fix prices. But even as prices dropped to forty dollars a ton, the growers had little to complain about. Some even argued against any liberalization of the Volstead Act that would have allowed the manufacture and sale of light wines. The growers had learned to love the grape-shipping business too well. In Fresno, a member of a winemaking family remembered, you could tell who the growers were by their silk shirts and Cadillacs.

It was different for the growers' former customers, the California vintners. As rewarding as alicante was for the growers, it was worse than an insult to the vintners. If you were in the wine business, you could only look on sourly as the craft you had mastered was ceded to unschooled immigrants adding sugar to grape residue in basement washtubs. Long-established winemakers went into the canning business. The University of California's celebrated department of viticulture and enology closed its doors. Someone had a harebrained notion to build a "floating winery" aboard a ship that would load up with grapes on the San Francisco docks, then take to the sea. The winemaking would begin at the three-mile limit, the product aging nicely as the ship chugged across the Pacific toward the Japanese market. ("What is there to stop a fleet of wineries, staining with purple most all the seven seas?" asked a wishful writer for the *San Francisco Examiner.*) Boat-borne winemaking was only slightly less likely than the notion pushed by the *California Grape Grower,* which made the case for production of such items as grape butter, grape catsup, and that perennial favorite, grape fudge.

In one notable instance, though, a grower and a winemaker, working in concert, found a way not merely to make it across the dry river of Prohibition but, with the protection of the law, to turn it into a fountain of cash. The Wente brothers, in the Livermore Valley, never ripped out their vines; they never had to negotiate with brokers or shippers; and alicante grafts never threatened their fine Semillon grapes or the famous "Wente clone" that became parent to 80 percent of all California chardonnays. The Wentes were blessed by an arrangement they had made to sell their entire output to Georges de Latour, a winemaker in Rutherford, eighty miles to the north. Once, when he was late with some money he owed them, de Latour put one of the brothers at ease. "I will tell you something, Mr. Wente," de Latour said. "My business is with the church. They are slow paying—but they are good."

Judging by the wealth he would accumulate, "good" was an understatement. Georges Marie Joseph de Latour had arrived in California from his native Périgord in the early 1890s. Trained as a chemist, he first made his living not in wine but in one of its lowlier by-products, tartaric acid, a scummy substance derived from grape skins that could be refined into cream of tartar, which was the active element in baking powder and a useful substance in various other culinary endeavors; you could even clean pots with it. He soon married, and with his wife bought four acres of Napa Valley wheat fields and orchards in 1900. For a time he continued to drive around the Northern California wine country in a horse-drawn wagon, collecting discarded grape skins from growers who were happy to be rid of them.

Thirty years later the wagon was long in his past; de Latour now traveled in a Cadillac Custom Imperial touring car. He owned two fine houses, one atop Pacific Heights in San Francisco and the other deep in the four-hundred-plus acres of vines he owned in and around Rutherford. He had a debutante daughter and a box at the opera, and was acknowledged in the newspapers as the head of "one of the best known families in San Francisco." The de Latours dressed for dinner every night, the urbane Georges in a tuxedo, his regal wife Fernande always putting an acute accent on her elegant wardrobe with one of her famously stylish hats. They supported themselves not on inherited wealth but on the dividends they extracted from the family business, Beaulieu Vineyards. By the early 1930s, after more than a decade of Prohibition, these dividends exceeded a hundred thousand dollars a year, or more than a million dollars at 2009 values. Yet the de Latours still were able to invest the equivalent of many additional millions in land, in buildings, and in the grapes he bought from the Wentes and other growers. These were grapes that he, almost alone among Napa Valley winemakers, could turn into legal, salable, and eminently respectable wine.

In a 1959 motion picture called *This Earth Is Mine*, Claude Rains plays a character loosely based on de Latour—or, more accurately, Rains plays a character loosely based on Claude Rains playing Georges de Latour; he's at best a facsimile of a facsimile. The Rains character bears no trace of the impenetrable French accent that de Latour never lost (so thick, said journalist Ernie Pyle, that "a stranger can hardly follow him"), and he spends most of Prohibition growing grapes and then regularly, determinedly, and inexplicably plowing them back into the ground. But in many other respects Rains is perfect: he's debonair, generous, utterly devoted to making good wine, and respected by the grandest landowners and the lowliest grape pickers. No one in the Napa Valley ever had anything bad to say about Georges de Latour. He was "a very good man, capable, honest, ethical, a gentleman in every way," rival winemaker Louis M. Martini recalled. "An elegant, patrician man, like all his family." And, said Martini, "he knew wine."

With such qualities, de Latour might have been a successful vintner in any circumstances, but his rise during Prohibition was a breathtaking ascent abetted by a sentence and clinched by a clause. The sentence, dating from 1912, read, "This letter will introduce Mr. George [*sic*] de Latour, an estimable Catholic of this Diocese, who is about to visit the Eastern States for the purpose of introducing altar wines, which he makes in Napa Valley, California." It was addressed, companionably, "To the Reverend Clergy" and signed, persuasively, "P. W. Riordan, Archbishop of San Francisco." And when a clause in the Volstead Act authorized the manufacture and sale of sacramental wine under the Eighteenth Amendment, it became the key to a fortune.

A devout Catholic as well as an estimable one, de Latour had not stumbled into Archbishop Riordan's good graces by accident. Those four original acres of wheat fields and orchards were soon planted in grapes, and in 1904 de Latour incorporated as Beaulieu Vineyards. Among his first board members were two Catholic priests; one, Father D. O. Crowley, would remain by his side for two decades, guaranteeing the purity of the sacramental wines Beaulieu began producing in 1908 and maintaining a direct connection to the archbishop's office. Soon de Latour opened a marketing office in New York. It did a decent enough business, but nothing compared to what was to come. By the time he made his deal with the Wente brothers in 1918, Prohibition's moment had arrived, and so had Georges de Latour's.

De Latour wasn't the only California winemaker whose business was tied to the church. Other Catholic vineyard families—the Beringers and the Martinis in Napa, the Concannons down in Livermore—were also able to win "ecclesiastical approbation," the formal nod from a bishop indicating to parish priests that a vintner's wines were acceptable for Communion. But de Latour already had other assets: his New York sales office, which had a decade's worth of satisfied accounts by the time Prohibition began; an intimate friendship with Riordan's successor, Archbishop Edward J. Hanna (who would officiate at the wedding of de Latour's daughter Hélène to a French nobleman); and a certain sense that altar wines might have a market far from the altar.

When he made his deal with the Wentes—he would end up purchasing the family's entire production for the full fourteen years of Prohibition—de Latour was placing a bet on the sacramental wine business. It did not take long to start cashing in. Just before Prohibition began he hired Charles W. Fay, a political operative who had been San Francisco postmaster throughout the Wilson administration and had continued to play a prominent role in California politics during the 1920s. Soon de Latour was granted, in March 1920, the Prohibition Bureau's permit number Cal-A-1, allowing him to make, ship, and sell sacramental wines. That same month Archbishop Hanna congratulated him on the rapid growth of his business. By 1922 de Latour had distributors in seven eastern and midwestern cities, in addition to his headquarters in San Francisco; the next year he began buying up large tracts of vineyard land and all the grapes that came with them (including a large piece acquired directly from the Diocese of Northern California). By the middle of the decade he was storing 900,000 gallons of wine in a vast new building that covered more than an acre, and shipping prodigious quantities via a rail spur running up the Napa Valley that the Southern Pacific had opened expressly to handle his business.

To many this seemed like an awful lot of Communion wine. Prohibition Bureau records indicate that occasionally wine warehoused by one of Beaulieu's wholesalers would go missing, and although Ernest Wente was certain that de Latour played by the rules, he also believed he chose to look the other way when Beaulieu's production fell into what Wente called "illegal channels." It didn't have to fall very far, for de Latour's church business lay not only with the priests whose signatures were required by law on order forms, but implicitly with their congregations as well. When a priest took receipt of an order for, say, 120 gallons of Beaulieu (a not uncommon amount), he suddenly had an inventory of 46,000 communion sips, more or less—or, perhaps, 10,000 communion sips, with nearly a hundred gallons set aside for members of the congregation. Sometimes the wine didn't even leave the rectory. In 1932, six cases of Beaulieu's best were shipped to Chicago expressly for the use of Cardinal George Mundelein. "I advise priests to buy a large quantity at a time—for instance a half barrel or a barrel," de Latour told E. C. Yellowley, the second-ranking man in the Prohibition Bureau who, over the years of their professional relationship, would become a close and valued friend. De Latour explained that bulky shipments made in-transit theft more difficult. He did not explain that they also made postdelivery allocation quite a bit easier.*

Beaulieu's wines were put into circulation beyond the altar by the irresistible physics of the era, that form of gravity that deposited potable alcohol in the cupboards of people whose need was not particularly spiritual. But one historian who praised de Latour's ability "to move a lot of wine without the trouble and expense of actually having to market it" wasn't looking very closely. In the promotional materials he sent out to priests across the country, the message of the Eucharist—"Who so eateth my flesh, and drinketh my blood, hath eternal life"—seemed less central than the message of the market. "I have had many favorable comments on your wine and, personally, consider it to be of the very best produced in California," read a testimonial from Archbishop Hanna reprinted in one of the Beaulieu brochures. Photographs of the vineyards and descriptions of the winery—"sheltered by the foothills of the Coast Range mountains"—lent sales materials an aroma more commercial than ecclesiastical. So did the product offering, which suggested a connoisseurship one doesn't necessarily associate with the Communion rail. In 1921 de Latour was offering sauterne, Chablis, Riesling, cabernet sauvignon, Tokay, sherry, Angelica,

---

*When the friars of the Christian Brothers were beginning to develop their own wine business at their property on Napa's Mont La Salle, they guarded against theft by shipping half barrels of wine packed inside flour barrels labeled "Mr. La Salle Products."

burgundy, port, and muscatel. Before Prohibition was over he had added Madeira, Malaga, and Moselle, as well as a blend he called "Beaulieu Special."*

But de Latour's most brilliant marketing gesture was the construction of a guest cottage for visiting clerics and a standing invitation to any who wished to visit Beaulieu and test the wines on the spot. Other de Latour guests included political figures and Hollywood celebrities, but as pleasing as those visitors might have been, they were mere signifiers of the de Latour family's stature; the priests who came to Rutherford materially contributed to it. The guest cottage was built deep into the vineyard, next to the family's summer residence, a sprawling, six-bedroom wooden structure decorated inside with Louis XVI furniture and outside with verandas, gardens (one Italian, another French), a rooftop bell imported from Florence, and one of the first swimming pools in northern California. Invited to join the de Latours for dinner, how could Father Meyer of Milwaukee, or Monsignor Brody of New York, or Bishop Cantwell of Los Angeles, or any of the hundreds of other churchly guests who made the pilgrimage to Rutherford consider any other Communion wine?

If any clinching was needed, de Latour had provided the perfect environment for closing the sale: there on the veranda, shaded by a grove of sycamores, the lush rows of vines gleaming in the distance, he had built an altar, where the visiting priests could commune with the blood of Christ under circumstances that could place even an atheist in the grip of ecstasy.

"WE STARTED OUT about 10 a.m. and after about 100 miles arrived at a Frenchman's house," an eighteen-year-old Englishman traveling through California in 1929 wrote in his journal. "I can't recall his name, but he makes the wine which is used for sacramental purposes."

Randolph Churchill had come to Beaulieu as his father's traveling companion. During a lengthy tour of North America, Winston Churchill, who considered Prohibition "at once comic and pathetic," had entered the constitutionally dry United States with some trepidation. But before the party crossed to Seattle from Victoria, British Columbia, Randolph had filled flasks and medicine bottles with whiskey, demonstrating the initiative that led his father to write to Randolph's mother with button-popping pride.

---

*De Latour distributed some of these same wines under the medicinal exception in the Volstead Act, with one definitional difference: in his contract with agents handling the drug store business, they were described as "medicinal preparations . . . unfit for beverage purposes."

Invoking Zeus's cherished cupbearer, Churchill told his wife, "Randolph acts as an unfailing Ganymede. Up to the present I have never been without what was necessary."

Not that there was any reason to worry on the day they were luncheon guests at Beaulieu. "A moment's halt, a momentary taste," Churchill wrote in the de Latour guestbook. Their host, Churchill told Clementine, "had over a million gallons stored in his factory which was a goodly sight to see in this dry land." Randolph, in his diary, was more allusive: "Christ has come to the aid of Bacchus in a most wonderful way."

Christ was not alone on his aid mission, for de Latour produced kosher wine as well. The quantity was only a fraction of what he made for the Catholic Communion (not to mention the Lutheran, Russian Orthodox, and other denominations whose clergy also traded with Beaulieu), but it was a business worth pursuing. In 1923 de Latour had concluded an agency agreement with two Chicago men who had "a wide acquaintance among the Jewish rabbis and congregations throughout the State of Illinois," granting them exclusive distribution rights within the state. Beaulieu wines were certified as kosher by a San Francisco rabbi whose imprimatur cost de Latour ten cents a gallon. By all the available evidence, Beaulieu's kosher wines were truly kosher. This could not be said about the wines of Louis M. Martini, up the road in St. Helena. Martini liked to sneak into his winery on Saturdays, when his own koshering rabbi was off the premises observing the Sabbath. Then, recalled his son, Martini would secretly spike the wine with "the ingredients that made the wine palatable."

With the exception of social worker Lillian Wald, Utah governor Simon Bamberger, Rabbi Stephen M. Wise, and those other progressives who saw Prohibition as a lever to lift the downtrodden, American Jews had opposed the Eighteenth Amendment with the near unanimity and absolute vehemence that seized American Catholics. For both groups, it wasn't simply a matter of protecting the free practice of their respective religions. Like the Catholics, the Jews peered behind the Prohibition banner and saw the white-hooded hatred of the Ku Klux Klan and the foaming xenophobia of the nativist pastors who dominated the Methodist and Baptist churches. It was a view summarized by a speaker at the annual meeting of the Central Conference of American Rabbis in 1914: the effort to place Prohibition in the Constitution, the rabbi declared, could be attributed to "the ambition of ecclesiastic tyrants."

The CCAR, as the umbrella organization for America's Reform rabbis, represented the most liberal, the most assimilated, and the most economically privileged branch of American Jewry, and it decided against taking a position on Prohibition during the run-up to ratification because the subject itself was "beneath the dignity of the conference." Their Orthodox brethren, less inclined to stay on the sidelines, lobbied Andrew Volstead directly while his bill was under consideration, which helped cement the sacramental exception into the final legislation. The regulations that the Prohibition Bureau subsequently put in place covering the distribution of wine for the Jewish sacraments were in one respect narrower than they were for Catholic rites, limiting individual families to ten gallons a year. But whereas the hierarchical structure of the Catholic Church provided an organized, supervised distribution process—the archbishop approved a vendor, and the priests in his diocese purchased Communion wine under his authority—the amorphous structure of American Judaism did not accommodate a formalized system. Consequently, any individual rabbi presenting a list of congregants could legally obtain the prescribed quantity and assume responsibility for distributing it.

But there were rabbis and there were rabbis, and then there were rabbis who weren't really rabbis. Insofar as wine was concerned, men bearing this ancient and honored title occupied three distinct categories: rabbis who believed wine to be a necessary part of the sacrament, properly distributed under prevailing rules; rabbis who believed that unfermented grape juice was not only an acceptable substitute, but a politically necessary one; and rabbis (and faux rabbis) who saw the distribution of wine as an unalienable and profitable right. Particularly among the Orthodox, disapproval of the intrusions of civic authority into sacred matters was offset by the opportunity to improve their financial circumstances. Unlike their Reform counterparts, the Orthodox rabbis in the United States in the 1920s were to a large extent unassimilated, impoverished immigrants from eastern Europe. The scholar Hannah Sprecher, in her authoritative and sympathetic monograph on the Prohibition era's wine-selling Orthodox rabbis, concludes, "The temptation to profit from wine transactions was great." When Congregation Talmud Torah of Los Angeles made its jump from 180 members to 1,000 in the first months of Prohibition, its rabbi, Benjamin Gardner, bemoaned his membership's clamor for "wine, wine, and more wine." But he was being somewhat disingenuous. A Talmud Torah trustee charged Gardner not only with peddling wine to outsiders as well as members, but with running a sort of concession business on the side: apparently Gardner was doing so well he had offered cash to another synagogue for the rights to sell wine to *its* members.

Gardner's story was resonant because the political climate in heavily Protestant, proudly dry Los Angeles—it was the only constituency in the

country that ever elected a Prohibition Party candidate to Congress*—
was notably unsympathetic to wets and wet sympathizers. The *Los Angeles
Times* delighted in patrolling rabbinical abuses. Rabbi Gardner became
"Rabbi" Gardner after his third appearance in the paper. When another
"purported rabbi" named Harry Margolis was arrested for a third Volstead
violation and bond was set at $5,000, the *Times* closed its report by inform-
ing readers that "Margolis went down into his jeans and produced $5000
cash." The biggest splash was made by the case of the Groves brothers—a
federal Prohibition agent, a former secretary of the state Democratic Party,
and a third, uncredentialed brother—who, the *Times* said, "disposed" of
half a million gallons "through 'paper' Jewish congregations represented
by men professing to be rabbis but who in reality were bootleggers."

In hundreds of instances, though, they were rabbis *and* bootleggers. A
particularly credible account of the racket, "Stamping Out Wine Congregations," appeared in the national social-work magazine *Survey*, written by
Rabbi Rudolph I. Coffee of Oakland. There were seven Jewish families in
the East Bay town of San Leandro who managed, Coffee wrote, to conduct
religious services only on the high holy days. But once the town's "poor but
respected Hebrew teacher" was named the tiny congregation's rabbi and
made a commission arrangement with his suppliers—he would be paid
for every gallon he moved—things changed. Soon membership swelled
to 250, among them a worshiper who lived in Red Bluff, California, nearly
two hundred miles to the north. Next door to San Leandro, in Alameda,
same story: in this case, the rabbi of a small congregation withdrew five
thousand gallons of wine in one nine-month period, thanks in large part to
a membership roster lengthened with the names of the dead. It was a common practice; an investigation in 1924 by the state's Prohibition director
Samuel R. Rutter indicated that the names on some lists of "wine congregations" were "promiscuously selected from obsolete city directories."

This practice was hardly confined to California. The leading Orthodox
rabbi in Omaha, Zvi Grodzinski, complained to colleagues that other local
rabbis were "conducting a free-for-all and selling their sacramental wine
to Jews and Gentiles alike." The celebrated Prohibition agent Izzy Einstein busted New York rabbis operating out of tiny tenement rooms who
claimed congregations in the hundreds. In Providence, Rhode Island, the
Reform rabbi Samuel Gup complained that "our local Orthodox rabbis
have broken the law continuously; they sell wine for profit, they sell it to

---

*Charles H. Randall served three terms, from 1915 to 1921, and was later elected president
of the Los Angeles City Council.

anyone, Jew or non-Jew, who is willing to pay for it." His colleague, Rabbi Joseph Krauskopf of Philadelphia, said the illegal wine selling of some of his Orthodox counterparts was "a public scandal."

There were rabbis who pocketed the revenue collected from their customers and also took commissions from the wineries that supplied them. There were even rabbis who opened what Major Chester P. Mills, the chief federal enforcement officer in New York, forthrightly called "wine stores." A typical one had a sign in the window reading "Kosher Wine for Sacramental Purposes" and a rabbi behind the counter signing up customers to "join" a synagogue at the same time they picked up the goods. Schapiro's, the long-established kosher winery on New York's Lower East Side, did a large sacramental business (and a decent under-the-table business as well) in its famously viscous and alcoholically potent "wine so thick you can cut it with a knife." But those seeking an even greater alcoholic kick (not to mention a more appetizing experience) had plenty of other choices. There were rabbis who dealt in sacramental champagne, sacramental crème de menthe, sacramental brandy, and various other liquors utterly unconnected to any aspect of Jewish religious practice. All of them, however, were deemed legal by a federal judge in the District of Columbia who ruled "it is not the content of the beverage, but the purpose for which it will be used that determines whether or not it is a sacramental wine." The *New York Herald* suggested that under such an interpretation, 100-proof rye would be perfectly acceptable at the Sabbath table.

It was quite a time to be a rabbi looking for a supplement to his income—or to be someone who merely claimed to be a rabbi. "To the Prohibition bureau," wrote Herbert Asbury in *The Great Illusion*, "any man who dressed in solemn black, possessed a Jewish cast of countenance, and wore a beard was automatically a rabbi." But Asbury's mention of the Jewish cast of countenance was gratuitous, for Izzy Einstein encountered rabbis named Patrick Houlihan and James Maguire, and Major Mills said he "found two Harlem Negroes posing as rabbis, claiming to have 'got religion' in the Hebraic persuasion." Mills said he suspected that their conversion dated from some time after the arrival of the Eighteenth Amendment.

IN THE AGE-OLD PHRASE, this was not good for the Jews. The fact that some of the malefactors weren't Jewish was no comfort. The regular tom-tom beat of newspaper stories was a daily agony, each one attributing widespread lawbreaking to regulations specifically crafted for the benefit of Jews. It was a situation that summoned another long-established idiom, this one in Yiddish: it was "a *shande* for the *goyim*"—a communal embarrassment, suffered in full view of gentile America. A Hebrew phrase was invoked as well, this one directly from the Talmud: the sacramental wine scandals, wrote Rabbi Leo M. Franklin of Detroit, president of the CCAR, were becoming a *hillul ha-shem*, a desecration of the name of God.

For Franklin and the Reform rabbis, the illicit fountains of sacramental wine turned Prohibition—once "beneath the dignity of this conference"—into an obsessive concern. The problem had become especially acute when Henry Ford found in the Jewish use of sacramental wine a fortuitous merger of two of his most loathed enemies: Jews and alcohol. In his notoriously anti-Semitic *Dearborn Independent*, the ultra-dry Ford seized on the rabbinical wine scandals as evidence of Jewish perfidy. The advent of Prohibition was "Jewish luck," the *Independent* said. Conflating the sacramental wine business with the undeniable Jewish presence in the bootlegging industry, the paper proceeded to enumerate "certain illegitimate commercial advantages" bestowed by Prohibition: "The Jew is the possessor of the wholesale stocks; he is the director of the underground railways that convey the stuff surreptitiously to the public. . . . The bulk of the liquor permits—a guess at 95% would not be too high—are in the hands of Jews, [for] if you can sign a Jewish name to it, you can get it." The rant continued: "'Rabbinical wine' is a euphemism for whiskey, gin, Scotch, champagne, vermouth, Absinthe, or any other kind of hard liquor." What was most horrid about Ford's diatribe was how much of it was accurate.*

But in some ways the worst part of it was the portion of the *Independent* article that was not in Ford's voice or in the words of the hate-mongering hirelings who wrote his screeds. This was a direct quotation from someone who said he had been in contact with "not less than 150 men in all parts of the country" who called themselves rabbis and were in the business of distributing wine for the Jewish sacraments. "They were men without the slightest pretense at rabbinical training or position who, for the purpose of getting into the wholesale liquor business, if you will, organized congregations." Their technique was straightforward: "They simply gathered around them little companies of men; they called them congregations; and then, under the law as it now exists, they were privileged to purchase and distribute wine." The man the *Independent* chose to quote was Rabbi Franklin himself.

---

*Ford also reached into the past in his frenzied assault, reminding readers that Lee Levy's gin had been responsible for the rape and murder of fourteen-year-old Margaret Lear.

For a man of Franklin's prominence and probity, this was a double agony. The spiritual leader of Detroit's aristocratic Temple Beth El, Franklin happened to be a friend and neighbor of Ford. Starting in 1912 the automaker had given the distinguished rabbi a new car to drive every year. Though Franklin declined the gift once Ford began his anti-Semitic campaign in the *Independent* in 1920, the two men had maintained cordial relations. At the same time Franklin was convinced that even uninflected reports about the wine-dealing rabbis—the kind appearing daily in the newspapers—could only foment more anti-Semitism. "We must . . . do what we can to clean our own skirts of the scandal that will come and I am therefore urging you to take rather drastic measures," he wrote to Rabbi Edward N. Calisch, his successor as CCAR president. Franklin's solution: petition Congress to rescind the sacramental exception.

This triggered a sectarian war. Reform rabbis offered learned disquisitions arguing that Talmudic law allowed the ceremonial use of unfermented grape juice instead of wine "in the case of necessity." It was as if they had picked up the tune the WCTU's Department of Unfermented Wine had been trying to insinuate into Christian liturgy. The WCTU's solution to the Communion issue was an unfermented, pasteurized product first bottled in 1869 by Dr. Thomas Bramwell Welch, a Methodist minister/ dentist from Vineland, New Jersey, and initially marketed as "Dr. Welch's Unfermented Wine." It achieved its first great success after Welch's son, Charles, was appointed to the Methodist committee that formally authorized Communion use of what was by then called "Welch's Grape Juice." The Reform rabbis seemed to be suggesting something similar.

The Orthodox rabbis soon responded theologically with their own treatises and emotionally with cries of pain. The Reform rabbis and their supporters, according to an article in an Orthodox publication, had ignored "the sentiments of Jews who for two thousand years attached a sanctity to the use of wine in connection with festive celebrations." A respected Conservative Talmudic scholar who endorsed the Reform interpretation received threatening letters. It did not help when the use of sacramental wine was conflated with other aspects of Orthodox practice that did not meet the approval of assimilated Reform Jews. "Ask Jews to Drop Yiddish and Wine," read a *New York Times* headline over a report on a 1923 convention of Reform laymen. To the Orthodox, this was like asking them to deny who they were.

In the end the petition to Congress failed, and the sacramental wine privilege enjoyed by American Jews stayed in place. But the relentless headlines ("Jewish Rabbis Reap Fabulous Sums by Flouting Dry Laws") and the Orthodox-Reform tensions continued until civil authority intervened. In 1926 the Prohibition Bureau tightened regulations by closing down the wine stores, revoking hundreds of rabbinical permits, and slicing the maximum family allotment from ten gallons a year to five. Total legal withdrawals of wine for Jewish religious rites plummeted in some cities by as much as 90 percent.

But the real effect of the Volstead Act's sacramental wine exception on the American Jewish community could be calibrated by measuring the difference between statements made by two rabbis, one before the controversy began and one after it concluded.

Rabbi Gotthard Deutsch of Cincinnati in 1914, quoting the 104th Psalm: "'Wine is made to gladden the hearts of men,' and in rabbinical teachings it is a sin to reject the gifts of God."

Rabbi Louis Wolsey of Philadelphia in 1926: "Prohibition is an Anglo-Saxon–Protestant issue that we Jews ought to keep out of."

Chapter 13

The Alcohol That Got Away

H E OWNED SOME DRUG-STORES, a lot of drug-stores," Daisy
Buchanan said. "He built them up himself." To Daisy this was a
perfectly reasonable explanation of her new neighbor's wealth.
To her husband, more knowing about the world beyond the boundaries of East Egg, it was evidence that Jay Gatsby had made his money as a
bootlegger. Modern readers in the grip of F. Scott Fitzgerald's prose may
not recognize the meaning of Tom Buchanan's explanation, but Fitzgerald knew his contemporaries would understand. In 1925, when *The Great
Gatsby* was published, the meaning of "drug-stores" was as clear as gin.

Tom did have it wrong when he identified the millions of gallons of
liquor that moved across pharmacy counters during the 1920s as mere
"grain alcohol." Price lists for "medicinal whiskies" told a fuller story. The
brochure distributed by the Frankfort Distillery of Louisville—"for physician permittees only"—informed pharmacists that, for sums ranging
from $19.50 to $30, they could acquire twelve pints of Paul Jones Rye,
Old Pirate Rum, Red Star Gin, White Star Brandy, or top-of-the-line
Broad Ripple bourbon. Of course, the fortunate pharmacist wasn't meant
to drink any of this (although who was to say he didn't?); he was to make
it available to customers bearing prescriptions from licensed physicians,
who had suddenly discovered a new and unexpected income stream.

The legal distribution of alcoholic beverages for medicinal purposes
was the third of the main exceptions enumerated in the Volstead Act. But
unlike the stipulation allowing sacramental uses and the farmer-friendly
waiver exonerating cider and homemade wine, it was the one exception
that authorized the legal distribution of hard liquor. Fifteen thousand physicians had lined up for permits before Prohibition was six months old.
For most of the 1920s a patient could fill a prescription for one pint every
ten days, and a doctor could write a hundred prescriptions a month on

numbered, government-issued forms that resembled stock certificates and were as dearly cherished. Although there were many regional differences, the tab was generally $3 to purchase the prescription from a physician and another $3 to $4 to have it filled. Dentists were similarly licensed, as were veterinarians who believed their patients could use a belt of Four Roses. Congress had been very obliging to the healing professions.

American doctors knew that pharmacists (and grocers and mail-order merchants and carnival shills) had been selling alcohol for decades. The outstanding figure in the alcohol-as-curative industry was Lydia Estes Pinkham, a housewife from Lynn, Massachusetts. The daughter of prominent abolitionists and herself an active campaigner for women's rights, Pinkham suddenly needed to earn a living after her husband's real estate investments evaporated in the Panic of 1873. Cooking up a hash of roots and herbs in her kitchen, she packaged the result as a catchall remedy for "female complaints." Soon Lydia E. Pinkham's Vegetable Compound achieved one of the great marketing triumphs of the late nineteenth century. Some attributed this to her innovative use of national newspaper advertising or the way she turned her name into a brand by placing it on a range of products, among them sewing kits, recipe collections, and a "Private Text-Book for Ailments Peculiar to Women." Others thought the secret to Pinkham's success was the 20.6 percent of each bottle that was pure alcohol.

This was odd, for Pinkham was not only an abolitionist and a feminist but also a devoted temperance worker. She maintained that the alcohol in her elixir was necessary to keep its unicorn root, fenugreek seed, and other ingredients soluble, and this may in fact have been the case. But in the late nineteenth and early twentieth century, when saloons were closed to women and social drinking was rare, a bottle of Pinkham's tonic was a welcome presence in many homes and socially respectable as well.

Not everyone—maybe no one—was fooled by this. It did not take an advanced degree in mathematics to determine that a single 14.5-ounce bottle of Pinkham's contained the equivalent of 7.5 ounces of 80-proof whiskey. Nor did it take a physiology class to realize that this was more than enough to make a large person pleasingly high, and a small one—a typical American woman, say—flat-out drunk. Among nineteenth-century wets, Pinkham's was so prominent a signifier of dry hypocrisy that it spawned a popular drinking song set to the tune of "I Sing of My Redeemer." A sample verse: "Mrs. Jones she had no children / And she loved them very dear. / So she took three bottles of Pinkham's / Now she has twins every year."

More convincing evidence that the power of Pinkham's did not ema-
nate from the miraculous properties of unicorn root could be found in
the flood of products that tried to compete by incorporating even more
alcohol in their formulas (not to mention the occasional dash of cocaine or
opium). In 1902 testing by the Massachusetts board of health determined
that Whiskol, "a non-intoxicating stimulant," contained 28.2% alcohol.
Hoofiand's German Tonic registered at 29.8 percent, Warner's Safe Tonic
Bitters at 35.7 percent. At least the makers of Richardson's Concentrated
Sherry Wine Bitters—the champ, weighing in at a nuclear 47.5 percent, or
95 proof—used the word "wine." The people behind Kaufman's Sulphur
Bitters were rather less ingenuous, proclaiming on the label that their
product "contains no alcohol," when in fact it contained 20.5 percent alcohol (and, as it happened, no sulphur). But the nerviest of the peddlers of
all this crypto-booze were the people behind Colden's Liquid Beef Tonic,
who didn't say that it contained 26.5 percent alcohol, but did say it was
"recommended for treatment of the alcohol habit."

BY 1917, long after Pinkham's tonic and all the others had been dismissed as
quack remedies, the House of Delegates of the American Medical Association had permanently ousted alcohol from the approved pharmacopoeia,
passing a unanimous resolution asserting that its "use in therapeutics ... has
no scientific value." But in 1922 the AMA demonstrated how open minds
can be changed—or, perhaps, how capitalism abhors a missed opportunity.
It took only two years of Prohibition for the AMA to revisit the question
it had settled just five years before. The results of a national survey of its
members, a "Referendum on the Use of Alcohol in the Medical Profession," revealed an extraordinary coincidence: the booming prescription
trade had been accompanied by a dawning realization among America's
physicians that alcoholic beverages were in fact useful in treating twenty-
seven separate conditions, including diabetes, cancer, asthma, dyspepsia,
snakebite, lactation problems, and old age. Consequently, the association
declared, any regulation of the medicinal use of liquor was "a serious interference with the practice of medicine." Thus the assertion that medicinal
alcohol had "no scientific value," from the AMA's unanimous resolution of
1917, no longer had any scientific value.

Doctors did extraordinarily well by Prohibition, but the Volstead Act
did little to the actual substance of their practice, other than making the
average office visit shorter: it did not take long to write "Whiskey—Table-

spoon three times a day," which was the standard phrase inscribed on the government forms by Dr. Harry P. Taylor of Covington, Kentucky, or "Spiritus Frumenti," a more dignified Latin term meaning "spirit of grain" that was preferred by Dr. C. O. Gutierrez of Cannonsville, New York. A Detroit physician came up with instructions that were more to the point: "Take three ounces every hour for stimulant until stimulated." Prohibition had a much greater impact on druggists, some of whom did phenomenally well, some of whom were squeezed out of business, and all of whom saw their industry turned upside down.

"I do not believe there will be many drug stores, so called, of the saloon type," a Fifth Avenue pharmacist had told the *New York Times* a week before the Volstead Act went into effect. "The druggist is too jealous of his reputation and too proud of his work to be willing to give up either of them for doubtful monetary gain." In fact, the cash flow from few enterprises gushed with quite the velocity that Prohibition brought to the drugstore business. Almost from the start individual pharmacists devised practices appropriate to their clientele. Those with high-end customers, mindful of the power (and profit) in brand names, dispensed the prescribed "medicine" in the distillers' own bottles, which looked exactly as they had before 1920 except for a sober, qualifying phrase on their revised labels: a 100-proof pint of Old Grand-Dad, for instance, still announced that it was "Bottled in Bond," but just beneath that familiar legend appeared the improbable "Unexcelled for Medicinal Purposes." Most pharmacists bought the goods in bulk containers, increasing their profits by diluting the liquor before decanting it into one-pint medicinal vials. At the bottom end of the retail ladder were operations like Markin's, a drugstore on the North Side of Chicago. After police officers apprehended a drunk emerging from the store with bottle in hand, an assistant city attorney informed Mayor William E. Dever in 1923, "The officers testified that [the liquor] burned their tongues and that when they touched their matches to it, immediately there was a flame."

Some establishments assumed the name "drugstore," but never bothered with drugs and by no stretch of the imagination could be considered stores. At the corner of Sixth Avenue and West Fourth Street in Manhattan, the Golden Swan had been operating as a saloon for years and, as its unofficial name—the Hell Hole—indicated, none too glamorously. The site of some of Eugene O'Neill's most prodigious drinking bouts, the Hell Hole was one of the models for Harry Hope's hopeless bar in *The Iceman Cometh*. ("It's the No Chance Saloon . . . , the End of the Line Café . . . ," one of O'Neill's characters says. "No one here has to worry about where they're going next, because there is no farther they can go.") When Prohibition arrived, the Hell Hole's proprietor closed up briefly, claimed on its reopening that it was now a drugstore, and then, having bought off the local cops, continued to operate just as he had before.

A legitimate pharmacist around the corner or down the street could deal with that; people who still needed their Sal Hepatica, their Carter's Little Liver Pills, or their Ivory soap weren't going to get their orders filled at the Hell Hole. Much more problematic from a competitive standpoint were the legitimate drugstores that operated by illusion. They sold the same conventional remedies and toilet items they'd always sold and kept a licensed pharmacist stationed behind an elevated counter, but those were mostly for show. These stores made so much money selling liquor that they could keep prices on their other products low enough "to seriously injure the legitimate drug business," according to a Senate inquiry. Sherman Billingsley, later the operator of the celebrated speakeasy the Stork Club, got his start in the New York booze business by buying up majority interests in drugstores in the Bronx, Brooklyn, and Harlem; moving into midtown Manhattan, wrote Ralph Blumenthal in *The Stork Club*, Billingsley later "opened new drugstores around the homes and apartments of showgirls he courted, flamboyantly naming the businesses after them."

Hoping to block the opening of faux pharmacies that were really just liquor retailers, Ambrose Hunsberger, president of the Philadelphia Organization of Retail Druggists, proposed that the Prohibition Bureau withhold a medicinal liquor license from any new drugstore until after its first full year of operation. Of course, critics could reasonably point out that such a regulation might provide a very comfortable advantage to a liquor-dispensing druggist who had already been around for a while.

Take, for instance, Charles Walgreen, who had built his Chicago-based chain from nine locations in 1916 to twenty just four years later. In 1922 Walgreens introduced the malted milk shake, which family historians have credited with the chain's next growth spurt. But it's doubtful that milk shakes alone were responsible for Walgreens' rocketing expansion from 20 stores to an astonishing 525 during the 1920s. Something Charles Walgreen Jr. told an interviewer many years later suggests another possibility. The elder Walgreen worried about fire breaking out in his stores, his son recalled, but this apprehension transcended concern for his employees: he "wanted the fire department to get in as fast as possible and get out as fast as possible," Charles Jr. remembered, "because whenever they came in we'd always lose a case of liquor from the back."

◆　◆　◆

OPPORTUNITY BRED INGENUITY. The most successful entrepreneur in the early stages of the medicinal liquor business, a clever Chicago lawyer named George Remus, looked at Prohibition and, he said, "saw a chance to make a clean-up." Few had a better view of the possibilities than Remus: he'd been a pharmacist before attending law school, and his work as a criminal defense lawyer enabled him to study the levers and gears of illegal enterprise. Like rumrunner Bill McCoy he was a teetotaler, his perspective on liquor unaffected by personal tastes or unclouded by personal habit. He cared only about the money, and his care was rewarded. In one year Remus deposited $2.8 million into one of his many bank accounts—the equivalent, in 2009, of more than $32 million.

The Chicago lawyer had found his way to Cincinnati like a dowser searching for water, the stick twitching violently when Remus realized that 80 percent of America's bonded whiskey was stored in distillery warehouses within three hundred miles of Fountain Square. Each of these bonded facilities was regularly patrolled by a government "gauger" charged with monitoring the wholesale trade in medicinal liquor. (Monitoring the wholesale trade in withdrawal permits—you could buy counterfeits at $6 to $8—was someone else's responsibility.) The gauger would take an inventory of how much was on hand, add to that the amount withdrawn since his last count by totting up the accumulated permits, and determine whether the sum of the two numbers matched the previous month's inventory figure. This measurement system also determined the amount of taxes owed on the released medicinal liquor.

When Remus bought a distillery, what he was really acquiring was all the bonded inventory that had accumulated before January 16, 1920. The fourteen distilleries (and millions of gallons) he purchased included small brands like Rugby, such established names as Fleischmann's, and his greatest prize, Jack Daniel's, whose distillery had been relocated to St. Louis after Tennessee went dry in the wake of the Levy's gin scandal of 1908. All that whiskey was perfectly legal so long as it lay dormant in those bonded warehouses. It was also perfectly legal when Remus, the former druggist, purchased a pharmacy in Covington, Kentucky, renamed it the Kentucky Drug Company, and began withdrawing the whiskey he owned, in thousand-case lots, for distribution in the medicinal market. But it was not at all legal when the drug company's trucks were hijacked by Remus's own employees, a brilliant stratagem that diverted all that liquid medicine into the bootleg market—a bootleg market that differed from the drugstore market in two financially appealing ways: fewer middlemen, no taxes.

From Death Valley, his farm northwest of Cincinnati—so named because of the hired gunmen who patrolled the road that led to it—Remus ran a business so vast that it grossed as much as $25 million in a single year and so complex that it employed hundreds of drivers, guards, salesmen, office personnel, and warehouse workers. Plus, of course, the lawyers, politicians, Prohibition agents, police officers, and other confederates necessary to any self-respecting criminal operation. In St. Louis, in addition to the cash he handed out to sheriff's deputies, tax collectors, court clerks, and the like, he had been careful to enrich members of both the Republican and Democratic city committees. This was of great help to him when, no longer content with removing measured quantities of medicinal liquor, Remus began to have his men tap the barrels in the Jack Daniel's distillery, draining the contents through a web of hoses and pipes directly into waiting tanker trucks. Gaugers he had not paid off did not notice that the liquor in the missing barrels had been replaced by booze-scented water. Gaugers he did pay off noticed nothing at all. Eventually, though, even Remus's profligate bribery failed him. "A few men have tried to corner the wheat market, only to find there is too much wheat in the world," Remus told an interviewer in 1925. "I tried to corner the graft market, but I learned there isn't enough money in the world to buy up all the public officials who demand a share."*

CRIMINAL BEHAVIOR was not always a necessary element in the creation of medicinal alcohol fortunes. As Prohibition began, twenty-nine million gallons of liquor reposed inside bonded warehouses, aging impatiently in both cask and bottle. Bourbon distillers who had done very well in the days when liquor was legal now saw an opportunity to do even better without ever coming into direct contact with the illegal trade. The Wathen brothers of Louisville, makers of Old Grand-Dad, reorganized as the American Medicinal Spirits Company and eventually gathered fifty-eight additional brands under that name. Employees of the Brown-Forman Company witnessed a particularly momentous day in 1926, as a train bearing a dozen armed guards and 6,750 legal gallons of Old Forester departed the distill-

---

*Remus eventually did a few years' time in the federal penitentiary in Atlanta, first in a cushy part of the prison that a frustrated Mabel Willebrandt called "Millionaires' Row," and later in his own apartment in the prison's hospital building; he ate dinner each evening with two other well-connected bootleggers in the peaceful hush of the prison's Catholic chapel. After his release he shot and killed his wife, who had been having an affair with the federal agent who had put him in prison. For that act, Remus served no prison time at all.

ery on Howard Street in Louisville. It was bound for the warehouse of a Boston druggist confident he could resell 54,000 pints of fine bourbon in the local medicinal market.

The size of the Brown-Forman shipment headed for Boston, noted the *Louisville Herald-Post* with the hand-wringing concern of a local booster, was evidence that "because of the heavy demand for medicinal whiskey the . . . warehouses in Kentucky were fast being emptied," and it was therefore "necessary to renew the manufacture of the Kentucky product to supply the legitimate demand." Not really; by this point Brown-Forman had addressed its shrinking supply by purchasing the entire stock of one of its competitors, Early Times.

Early Times had inventory; Brown-Forman had a sales apparatus. David Schulte of New York had neither. Schulte had begun his working life picking strawberries on eastern Long Island, soon became a clerk in a Manhattan tobacco store, and with remarkable speed established a chain of cigar stores and a booming wholesale grocery business. Once Prohibition began he demonstrated that one needn't be a distiller or a druggist to make a killing in medicinal liquor. In 1925 Schulte bought the Old Overholt rye distillery in western Pennsylvania, once the semihobby of Andrew Mellon and Henry Clay Frick, from the Mellon-controlled Union Trust Company for $4.5 million, inventory included—then turned around and sold it all to a marketer of medicinal spirits for $7.7 million. *Time* once said Schulte's name was "a symbol of hard-earned wealth," but in the 1920s, wealth that came from medicinal liquor came very, very easily.

NOT EVERY STATE countenanced the medicinal use of alcohol. Twelve forbade it entirely, and nine more allowed doctors to prescribe only pure, tasteless, undiluted alcohol—no medicinal Old Grand-Dad, no therapeutic Jack Daniel's, no curative "Rare Old Jamaica Rum / Imported in Wood / Exceptionally Fine." (This fairly unscientific description appeared in a price list "for physicians and dentists . . . for Medicinal Purposes Only" issued by the wholesale drug division of the S. S. Pierce Company of Boston.) When both the governor and the attorney general of Indiana publicly acknowledged that they had "secretly" obtained whiskey for severely ill members of their families, in contravention of state law, the fundamentalist Reverend John Roach Straton of New York's Calvary Baptist Church weighed in. Said Straton, "They should have permitted members of their families to have died and have died themselves rather than violate their oaths of office."

But no state regulated such alcohol-laden substances as perfume and toilet water, paint and varnish, antifreeze and smokeless gunpowder. Even drys as extreme as Straton had to tolerate the production and distribution of felt hats, photographic film, smelling salts, and pencils, all of which required alcohol in the manufacturing process. The Volstead Act had not carved out an exception for nonpotable alcohol so much as it had made the alcohol that people drank the exception. Of the "hundreds of uses" for alcohol, said Prohibition Commissioner Roy Haynes, "only one is outlawed" by the Volstead Act. Unsurprisingly, that one illicit use deformed the entire legal trade in industrial alcohol. Between 1920 and 1925 American production of legally manufactured industrial alcohol nearly tripled; by 1930 it had doubled once more. Impartial authorities placed the quantity diverted to the bootleg trade at 60 million gallons in a single year. Diluted to 80 proof, that was the equivalent of 150 million gallons, or 750 million fifths, of drinkable liquor. If that seemed like a lot for a nation of 115 million—including infants, children, and abstainers—there was a ready explanation: in a bizarre role reversal, some of it was actually being exported to Canada, where it could be sold at lower prices than that country's legal, taxed liquor. As a consequence, Treasury Department officials found themselves participating in an international conference addressing a problem defined succinctly in the *New York Herald Tribune*: "how to keep America from forcing its illegal liquor on a friendly neighbor."

In the United States, a gallon of alcohol flowed into the bootleg trade through a process that was only superficially complicated. The law required it to be denatured before it could leave the distilling plant—that is, made undrinkable by the addition of a noxious substance. Some of the seventy-six government-approved denaturants were unpleasant but fairly mild, like soap, menthol crystals, or various emetics; others, including formaldehyde, sulphuric acid, and iodine, were out-and-out poisonous. But removing the odious additives by redistillation or other procedures was a process any self-respecting chemist could engineer. One of the noted practitioners of this alchemy was Anastassoff Sreben, a Bulgarian-born chemist who worked his magic behind the false fronts of the Southern Disinfectant Company, the Chicago Essential Oil and Chemical Company, and various other enterprises based in a single building on the North Side of Chicago. Other firms named in the same indictment included Vidor Perfumeries, Temson Spice, Puritan Cosmetics, and the Sheik Toilet Preparations Company.

The names were fraudulent. These were "cover houses," whose ostensible businesses required large quantities of industrial alcohol. "Ostensible" is the operative word. A permit was required to withdraw alcohol from a distilling plant for, say, delivery to a manufacturer of aftershave lotion. The permit holder's only further obligation was to present to federal authorities a receipt establishing that the goods had indeed been delivered to the aftershave company. Whether the company in fact made aftershave was beyond the jurisdiction of the Prohibition Bureau. Enforcement agents would have to deal with the withdrawn alcohol only after it had been diluted, flavored, colored, placed in bottles bearing counterfeit labels, and shipped out to a thirsty public.

Roy Haynes tried to explain away the preposterous system that made this all so easy. "It seems better to take the risk" of industrial alcohol being diverted for beverage use, he said, "than to make the regulations so onerous that honest people cannot secure the alcohol they need" for their manufacturing businesses. Emory Buckner, U.S. attorney for the Southern District of New York, saw it differently: the industrial alcohol business, he said, was "a perfect carnival of corruption."

In this carnival, Philadelphia was the big top. New York area "cutting plants," as they were called, may have pumped out more product (by one informed estimate, almost a million gallons a month). Many other cities produced so much they had to throw some away; in Paducah, Kentucky, the superintendent of city construction warned that "this stuff they have been pouring into the sewers is eating the life out of the sewer lining." But nowhere else in the country did the industrial alcohol racket capture its market as quickly and run as smoothly as it did in Philadelphia. This was partly due to the city's proximity to the enormous complex of small-to medium-sized chemical factories that had been drawn to the Delaware Valley by the magnetic force of the DuPont Corporation. It was also due to an extraordinarily efficient criminal operation known as the Seventh Street Gang, under the direction of a gambler and fight promoter named Max "Boo Boo" Hoff. Operating as the Quaker Industrial Alcohol Company, the Glenwood Industrial Alcohol Company, and the Consolidated Ethyl Products Company, Hoff and his associates ran a vertical enterprise, beginning with the manufacture of alcohol, then managing its diversion to cover houses, its reformulation and repackaging as liquor in a cutting plant, and its wholesale distribution. Hoff and his confederates produced almost 1.5 million gallons of undiluted alcohol in a single year—diluted to 80 proof, 3.375 million gallons of regular-strength booze. Philadelphia alone couldn't absorb this output; in one two-week stretch in 1925 Hoff and company sent forty loaded freight cars to St. Louis, Chicago, and St. Paul.

The man Mayor W. Freeland Kendrick hired to deal with this geyser of illegal liquor and all the other rampant violations of the Prohibition laws was Marine General Smedley P. Butler. A two-time winner of the Medal of Honor, Butler was appointed Philadelphia's director of public safety in late 1923. Known as "Old Gimlet Eye" or "the Fighting Quaker," he was a sinewy five-foot-four package of intense ambition, zealous determination, and considerable tactical brilliance. He had lied his way into the U.S. Marine Corps when he was only sixteen and gone on to command American troops in China during the Boxer Rebellion; in various expeditionary incursions into Nicaragua, Honduras, Panama, Mexico, and the Philippines; in putting down an insurrection in Haiti; and in the enormous American military encampment at Brest, France, during World War I. Butler was granted a leave from the Marine Corps by Calvin Coolidge, over the objection of the navy secretary, so he could clean up Philadelphia. On taking the job he announced that he would not only confront the bootleggers, the saloon owners, and the corrupt cops, but also those members of the city elite who thought themselves above the law. "The day has passed in Philadelphia when societies and organizations can hold banquets in big hotels and serve liquor," he said. He also said he would succeed in Philadelphia or be "torn apart in the attempt."

This story could end no other way: Butler failed miserably. Hoff's operation was so lucrative it could afford to buy off the head of the police department's Detective Bureau, hundreds of street cops, and the necessary complement of federal agents. A grand jury estimated the annual graft collected by members of the police department alone at $2 million. The bounty was so rich it led to cops bribing other cops, most notoriously by paying for the privilege of assignment to the department's elite enforcement squad, where the opportunities for payoffs were almost limitless. The political world was covered by Hoff's choice of a lawyer: Congressman Benjamin Golder, a vital gear in the Republican machine that dominated Philadelphia politics.

Hoff's reach extended into the city's commercial establishment as well. His productive relationship with the Reading Railroad was built on a shipping agreement covering a territory stretching west to Minnesota and north to the Canadian border. He financed the expansion of his business through the otherwise respectable Union National Bank, which laundered his cash flow by lending him money on no other collateral than the $10 million he kept under pseudonymous names in fourteen separate accounts. Boo Boo Hoff, said a district attorney who tried (and failed) to put him in jail, was "like a giant spider in the middle of a great web with eyes in front and behind." He was "a man who sees everything, knows everything and controls everything in the underworld."

The revelation of Union National's complicity in Hoff's racket led to the resignation of its president, Joseph S. McCulloch, and the sale of Union National to another bank. Newspapers began referring to Philadelphia as "the Wall Street of the Rum Ring." Butler returned to active duty in the Marine Corps, leading an expeditionary force into China in 1927. "Trying to enforce the law in Philadelphia," he said when he had reached the end of the line as director of public safety, "was worse than any battle I was ever in." He also said, "Sherman was right about war, but he was never head of police in Philadelphia."

Oddly, though, it wasn't Boo Boo Hoff or other criminals who brought down Old Gimlet Eye. His career crashed because of a more influential group—the bootleggers' customers, especially those who might have been among Hoff's business associates at the Reading Railroad or Union National. He had had it, Butler said, when Mayor Kendrick refused to allow him to raid the Ritz-Carlton and Bellevue-Stratford hotels. The Philadelphia elite that held its functions at the Ritz and the Bellevue may have had more respectable suppliers than Boo Boo Hoff. But Butler knew that even the finest of smuggled goods had one very important characteristic in common with the booze bubbling out of Hoff's toilet water factories, the booze cooking in tenement stills and backwoods moonshine plants, the booze leaking from synagogues and churches, or the booze flowing south from Canada, north and east from the Caribbean, and across thousands of drugstore counters from East Coast to West: it was going wherever there was a thirst for it.

Chapter 14

The Way We Drank

A SAMPLE OF THE coming literature of Prohibition, as predicted by the humor magazine *Life* in 1919: "She sipped her buttermilk slowly and calmly noticed the effect. After the second bottle, she was a woman emancipated. She reached across the table and untied her handsome admirer's cravat." The magazine predicted this was the style that would inevitably characterize American literature under Prohibition. "The Hero may still flick the ashes from his cigarette," *Life* explained, "but when the time comes for him to take a drink, he must order a chocolate soda."

In fact the hero of the 1920s did nothing of the sort, except perhaps in the work of Upton Sinclair, the one prominent American novelist who began the Prohibition era as a dry and ended it drier. (Sinclair even wrote a novel about "a conscientious Prohibition agent"—evidence, said *Time*, of the author's enduring habit of picking "preposterous prigs" for his heroes.) It was F. Scott Fitzgerald, of course, who cued the downbeat for the literary bacchanal of the 1920s. Three years before *The Great Gatsby*, in *The Beautiful and the Damned*, Fitzgerald introduced Gloria Patch, who "drinks excessively, drives recklessly" and "declares brazenly, 'I detest reformers, especially the sort who try to reform me.'" Gowan Stevens, in William Faulkner's *Sanctuary*, discovers how "to drink like a gentleman" at the University of Virginia but develops a new skill when he returns home to Prohibition Mississippi: learning to add enough lemon, sugar, and water to a glass jar of moonshine to neutralize at least some of its explosive toxicity. Ernest Hemingway managed to have alcoholic drinks of one kind or another show up on more than half the pages of *The Sun Also Rises*.* And

---

*Hemingway's expatriate characters do not hide their distaste for Prohibition or for those responsible for it. When Jake Barnes and Bill Gorton take their extended, wine-soaked

why not? Hemingway said in 1923 that "a man does not exist until he is drunk."

That was the same year that H. L. Mencken experienced the rapid depletion of his well-stocked cellar, wrote William Manchester, during "a devastating visit" from Sinclair Lewis. For a drunk of such prodigious appetites, Lewis was nonetheless able to maintain a sharp focus on the drinking around him—in his description of the women of *Main Street* outside the Sauk Prairie saloons, "waiting for their husbands to become drunk and ready to start home"; in George Babbitt's leering suggestion to his guests, "Well, folks, do you think you could stand breaking the law a little?"; and in the very first words of Lewis's celebrated portrayal of a moralistic hypocrite: "Elmer Gantry was drunk."

That drinking became a sine qua non of American fiction in the 1920s is inarguable; that it was a reflection of what was going on in much of American life was a safe bet as well. What remains dubious is the suggestion that it was the prohibition of liquor that led the young, the stylish, or the Babbitts to ingest it so avidly. No one who has read the early novels of Evelyn Waugh, soaked as they are in the fizzy frolics of England's Bright Young Things, could possibly attribute short skirts, hot music, and hip flasks to Prohibition, nor could anyone who paid attention to the frantic pursuit of the new and the daring in Weimar Germany. By 1927 Edmund Wilson was able to enumerate ninety-seven different colloquial terms for drunkenness, ranging from "squiffy" and "zozzled" through "corned" and "scorching," and finally culminating in "ossified," "embalmed," and "buried." Some of the more extreme terms, Wilson noted, had become less common because "this kind of fierce protracted drinking has now become universal, an accepted feature of social life instead of a disreputable escapade." It was World War I that ripped western civilization from the lingering embrace of the nineteenth century—that had, said the dry progressive Senator George Norris of Nebraska, brought about the "almost universal change which had overtaken civilization." Prohibition was an accelerant, not a cause.

"We find many things to which the prohibition of them constitutes the only temptation," wrote William Hazlitt in 1823. A century later, drinking was not one of them. No extrinsic impulse or appeal was needed to get people interested in liquor. In fact, that was the whole point.

---

fishing trip, they fall into a sardonic colloquy, each claiming acquaintanceship with Wayne Wheeler. When Jake finally says, "The saloon must go," Bill replies, "The saloon must go, and I will take it with me."

✦ ✦ ✦

OF THOSE FEW NOVELISTS of the 1920s who did not seem particularly interested in drinking, either as a subject or as a pastime, Willa Cather was among the most prominent. Liquor was not absent from her work, even in the books set in earlier decades; in *A Lost Lady* the presentation of "a glittering tray" of cocktails was "the signal for general conversation" in the prairie town of Sweet Water. Although she was not an abstainer, Cather tended to avoid the liquor-saturated world of the other writers who lived near her in Greenwich Village. (When novelist Dawn Powell gave parties at her apartment on East Ninth Street, she would fill her aquarium with gin.) Still, she could not help but notice the dizzying rearrangements of daily life spinning around her. "The world broke in two in 1922 or thereabouts," Cather wrote many years later in an essay looking back at the decade. Generations of historians have used the phrase as an epigraph for the era, suggesting as it does the disjunction between the proprieties of a more settled time and the lubricious behavior that characterized urban life in the twenties. But something Cather said in an interview in 1924 defined the era with more precision: "Nobody stays at home anymore."

To critic Malcolm Cowley, this was evident in the invention of "the 'party,' conceived as a gathering of men and women to drink gin cocktails, flirt, dance to the phonograph or radio and gossip about their absent friends." For the first time, men and women were drinking together outside the home, at events where dinner wasn't served. *Vanity Fair* published an instructive article explaining "how to bait your social hook in these trying days of drought"—in other words, how to write an invitation that suggested that lawbreaking would be abided but did not say so outright. One suggestion: add a note telling your guests "Bring your corkscrew."

Even more than at the house parties that became commonplace, Americans learned to drink in new ways at a new/old institution. The speakeasy was a substitute for the saloon that would prove to be much more than a saloon. Mencken traced the word's origin to "speak softly shop," a nineteenth-century Irish phrase used to define any illegal drinking place—where, presumably, voices were kept lowered to avoid attracting attention.* As a catchall term in Prohibition America, it came to denote any publicly accessible place where one could buy a drink. By 1930 the U.S. speakeasy was so ubiquitous, so indelibly part of American culture,

---

*The idiom continued to evolve in Ireland, courtesy of James Joyce. From *Ulysses*, published in 1922: "'Tis, sure. What say? In the speakeasy. Tight. I shee you, shir."

that H. I. Phillips, a columnist for the *New York Sun*, was led to declare that "the history of the United States could be told in 11 words: Columbus, Washington, Lincoln, Volstead, two flights up and ask for Gus."

It didn't take much more than a bottle and two chairs to make a speakeasy, but once those requisites were in place the permutations were endless. In black neighborhoods like Harlem, many private apartments—called "hooch joints," "buffet flats," or "beer flats"—took on a semipublic aspect, open to virtually anyone who happened to be black; whites were suspect, as they might be from the Prohibition Bureau, which was a virtually all-white force. Italian rooming house proprietors on Federal Hill in Providence invited nonresidents into their parlors, where they could purchase platefuls of pasta accompanied by the bottles of homemade wine and grappa that adorned the red-checkered tablecloths; culinary historians attribute the American fondness for southern Italian cuisine to the exposure it received in similar places from Boston to San Francisco. In downtown Detroit, a block from City Hall, customers of the Bucket of Blood were offered decent food, ample drink, and, for the newspapermen who used the Bucket as an auxiliary press room, a series of telephone lines, including one connected directly to the phone of Mayor Frank Murphy's secretary. In Boston, where Mayor James Michael Curley's car horn played the opening notes of "How Dry I Am," four speakeasies were located on the same block as police headquarters. Of the 113 establishments licensed to sell soft drinks in Sheboygan, Wisconsin, the two that actually confined themselves to nonalcoholic beverages went out of business.

New York, which according to its police commissioner accommodated thirty-two thousand illegal drinking spots by the end of the 1920s, of course offered the greatest variety. The most famous of the New York speakeasies was the "21" Club, which opened its doors on West Fifty-second Street in Manhattan on New Year's Day 1930. But "21" was really just the latest in a series of places operated by its founders, Jack Kriendler and Charlie Berns, beginning in 1922. First the partners operated an illegal establishment in Greenwich Village called the Redhead, which was followed by an illicit operation called the Fronton, which was in turn succeeded by a lawbreaker at 42 West Forty-ninth Street, the Puncheon Club—also known as the Grotto, the Iron Gate, "42," and Jack & Charlie's. Short-term leases were generally the only kind available in the speakeasy business, as few landlords were willing to become dependent on their tenants' ability to manage their bribe portfolios; so were name changes, to confuse tax authorities. It was at the Puncheon that Berns and Kriendler suffered their only arrests for what would be a decade of nightly Volstead violations. At "21," at last settled in a building they owned with a name they would keep, they decided to stop paying bribes and invested instead in an elaborate system that made them effectively raidproof. On an alert from the doorkeeper, the bartender could press a button that sent the entire contents of the back bar tumbling down a shaft, past a series of bottle-breaking metal grates, and finally onto a pile of rocks in the basement. Any remaining liquid drained into a sump. All that was left behind were shards of glass and a lingering aroma, but an odor was not admissible evidence.

Apart from "21," which was sui generis, Manhattan speakeasy style ran from O'Leary's on the Bowery ("Not for the squeamish," according to a contemporary description, ". . . for the sight and smell of a dozen sodden derelicts is none too pleasant") to the Bath Club on East Fifty-third Street (its decor, wrote the same commentator, was "all marble and gold. Flunkies in droves. Hat boys who won't touch a coat, and coat boys beneath whose station it is to handle a Borsalino"). At the Bath, an orchestra played chamber music in the dining room; at O'Leary's, "A bum in the back room howls like a wolf in the night." The Stork Club and the Country Club, the Hyena and the Ha! Ha!, the Beaux Arts and the Club Pansy and the Cave of Fallen Angels—the names alone suggested that New Yorkers had options for every taste.

The speakeasies witnessed drinking habits and practices notably different from the rituals of the old saloons. However caustic some of the liquor handed across the bar in pre-Volstead days had been, most of it was distilled by professionals, was unlikely to be poisonous, and usually bore a label that honestly reflected its origin. Speakeasy liquor could have been anything from single-malt Scotch smuggled by way of Nassau to diluted embalming fluid. Most of the good stuff entered a tightly circumscribed market dominated by well-connected bootleggers, like the polo-playing LaMontagne brothers of New York, purveyors to their own social circle. The LaMontagne business crumbled after the brothers were convicted of supplying champagne for a bachelor party at the Racquet & Tennis Club, but an even more precipitous collapse befell Sir Broderick Hartwell, "the rum-running Baronet," who had promised British investors in his bootlegging operation a 20 percent return every sixty days but lost fifty-six thousand cases of liquor in a mutiny aboard one of his ships. Mutinies, hijackings, even shifts in the weather were likely to affect the prices reported in periodicals read by LaMontagne or Hartwell customers. From *The New Yorker*, January 16, 1926, under the standing head "The Liquor Market": Gin is selling for $36 a case, and Scotch is "up slightly (after a post-holiday drop" at $59). From another notice several weeks later: "Chianti market practically cornered by restaurant trade, but small quantities, high grade, offered @ $4.50 per bottle." *Variety* also published running reports on bootleggers' price lists. The daily papers generally stayed away from this sort of service to readers, although the *New York World* occasionally hinted at market conditions, as in the December 24, 1923, headline over a story describing how delivery boats from Rum Row had made it ashore despite a thick fog the night before: "Rum Kings Assure Wet Christmas."

But in most speakeasies, the shortage of quality goods intensified demand and multiplied deceit. In the saloon era, calling for liquor by brand name was almost unheard of; in the speakeasy era, it became a habit, first as a means of protecting oneself from alcohol of questionable origin, and secondarily as a way of expressing one's level of taste. Berry Brothers, liquor purveyors to the British royal family, created Cutty Sark in 1923 specifically for the export market, which was largely the American market; Haig & Haig was repositioned as a brand aimed directly at the bootleg trade. Broderick Hartwell's business, as long as it lasted, was devoted to the proprietary brands his wealthy customers insisted upon. When he was building his own brand, Tommy Dewar publicized the perilous alternative—the liquor of unknown provenance he once characterized as "squirrel whiskey," so called because, he said, "it will make men talk nutty and climb trees. It will send the average Sunday School teacher walking ten miles through three feet of snow to shoot his own parson." Naturally, there was an alternative: Drink Dewar's! Decades later, many of the liquor industry's best-known brand names owed their prominence to the ubiquity of Prohibition-era rotgut.

Of course, in so robust and so unregulated a market—no state liquor authorities, no tax stamps, no legitimate retail stores—cheating was as inevitable as a morning-after headache. "Overboard stuff" was the generic term used in the trade for blended industrial liquor in counterfeit bottles that were then "soaked in sea water to give [them] an overseas appearance," according to one practitioner. Joseph P. Kennedy, who was responsible for the liquor served at his Harvard tenth reunion in 1922, told a friend who wanted to buy some that the blended whiskey he had provided—whipped up from 190-proof alcohol—"was perfectly satisfactory to all the fellows in the class who are, of course, used to the best—and the worst." The federal enforcement director for the New York district reported that "dollar-a-drink clubs with polished brass bar rails and elite customers served

precisely the same poison as the dime-a-shot dumps of the wharf sides."
There were exceptions, of course, but in too many places, if you ordered
Brand X, you got Brand X; if you ordered Dewar's or Gordon's, you paid
twice as much—and got Brand X.

AT THE PARTIES and in the speakeasies, in suburban country clubs and
inner-city social clubs and the blind pigs, blind tigers, and blind you-
name-its stretched across the continent,* Prohibition changed not only
where Americans drank, but *who* drank as well.

Recalling the era, the songwriter Alec Wilder once said, "A pretty girl in
a speakeasy was the most beautiful girl in the world." A pretty girl—truth
be told, virtually any kind of girl—in a drinking establishment was one
of the astonishments of Prohibition, a shock both severe and enduring.
Social life in America was changed forever. "Prohibition would do more
than close the saloon," wrote historian Catherine Gilbert Murdock. "It
would also let domestic drinking out of the closet." One didn't have to
agree with Wilder to believe it was more pleasing to see Mother having a
drink in a speakeasy than to imagine her furtively sipping from her husband's supply, or—much worse—to picture her alone in the upstairs bathroom, chugging from the bottle of Mrs. Pinkham's.

But women didn't have to be secret tipplers to be attracted to speakeasy culture. Many speaks were set up as restaurants specifically to attract
women, just as many restaurants became speaks to avoid losing business
to the newcomers. Table service made it unnecessary for women to perch
on a barstool or poise a foot on a brass rail. New styles of entertainment—
jazz bands, torch singers, dances like the Charleston and the shimmy—
emerged to accompany coeducational drinking. As mild as they might
have seemed individually, together these innovations "set up conditions
peculiarly attractive to women," a dry publicist acknowledged. The instal-
lation of "powder rooms" sealed the deal.

The sexual integration of the drinking culture began as a localized phenomenon in the big cities. In New York, for instance, arrests of women for
public drunkenness spiked immediately after the Volstead Act went into
effect and remained at elevated levels through much of the decade. Leon &

---

*Literary scholar Kathleen Drowne writes that the term "blind pig" and its regional variants
were rooted in Maine, where a nineteenth-century tavern owner "sold his patrons tickets to
view a blind pig he kept in the back room. Along with admission, every viewing customer was
treated to a free glass of rum."

Eddie's, on speakeasy-jammed West Fifty-second Street, declared the new era with a sign over its entrance: "Through These Portals the Most Beautiful Girls in the World Pass OUT." Wrote Heywood Broun, "Sex barriers have been burned away. In New York there are not a dozen places run for the patronage of men alone." Like Alec Wilder, Broun found this generally delightful: "The light laughter of soprano voices rings now where once sodden male wretches stood and sang *Mother Machree*." At times, though, the feminization of the drinking experience made Broun long for the pre-Prohibition days, when it was possible, he said, to get a drink without elbowing his way to the bar "through a crowd of schoolgirls."

Another barrier fell with the arrival of the "black and tans," integrated cabarets and nightclubs, usually in black neighborhoods and usually featuring leading African-American jazz musicians. Some night spots, like the Cotton Club in Harlem (partially owned by the bootlegger Owney Madden), practiced an especially bizarre form of segregation: all-black neighborhood, all-black entertainment, all-white clientele. But blacks and whites mingled comfortably at places like the Catagonia Club and the Club Ebony, and the predawn "breakfast dances" at Small's Paradise (they started when other nightspots closed) were completely biracial. Detroit saw its first stirrings of racial integration in the Harlem Cave and the Cozy Corner, two nightspots in the all-black neighborhood known as Paradise Valley. In the African-American magazine *The Messenger*, coeditor Chandler Owen called the black-and-tan "America's most democratic institution," where "we see white and colored people mix freely. They dance together not only in the sense of both races being on the floor at the same time, but in the still more poignant and significant sense of white and colored people dancing as respective partners." In New York's black daily, the *Amsterdam News*, a columnist argued that "the night clubs have done more to improve race relations in ten years than the churches, white and black, have done in ten decades."

This being the age of ballyhoo, the ways of Sodom-on-the-Hudson were broadcast through the rest of the country by radio, by the tabloid press, and most of all by the glowing beacon of Hollywood. Many in the entertainment business had welcomed Prohibition, believing people who once filled the saloons would gravitate to the movie houses. But glamour, illicit or not, was the motion picture industry's most reliable product, and few settings were more glamorous than the uptown New York speakeasy. The advent of talking pictures put the sound—and the attitudes—of New York on display for the entire country. Ravenous demand for material for the talkies, wrote Raymond Moley, led to "the frenzied filming of Broad-

Representative W. D. Upshaw of Georgia took any opportunity he could find
to demonstrate that he was the "driest of the drys." Wets treated him as a living
parody of dry priggishness, and Upshaw usually rose to their expectations—
both in writing (he signed his mail "Yours very dry")
and in front of the cameras.

23

As the "Prohibition Portia," Assistant Attorney General Mabel Willebrandt was the most visible—and powerful—woman in American public life through the 1920s. Still, newspapers described her in the familiar vocabulary of the women's pages: the *Atlanta Constitution* said she was a "delightful luncheon companion who neither paints, powders, nor uses lipstick."

24

25

Willebrandt's efforts in the Justice Department were frequently undermined by the icy indifference of Andrew Mellon (25) and the buffoonish Roy Haynes (24). Mellon, it was said, was the "only Treasury Secretary under whom three president served." A crony of Attorney General Harry Daugherty, Haynes was primarily responsible for dispensing patronage on behalf of Wayne B. Wheeler of the ASL.

26

Almost from the beginning, enforcement was a practical failure. But even sporadic effort produced good visuals. This barrel-smashing assault took place in the first months of Prohibition; the raid on the contents of a Detroit warehouse (27) occurred a few years later.

27

The honeymoon trip that Sam and Saidye Bronfman took in 1922 included a sidetrip to Kentucky, where Sam bought the Greenbrier Distillery. Dismantled, shipped to Canada, and reassembled, it was quickly put to use as the foundation of Bronfman's enormous bootlegging business.

In any given week, Bronfman had a million dollars' worth of inventory stashed on the North Atlantic island of St. Pierre. Virtually every man, woman, and horse on the island was engaged in unloading, storing, and reloading liquor destined for the United States; many houses were shingled with used packing crates.

After Congress appropriated money for a vastly enlarged Coast Guard, bootleggers on Rum Row were much more likely to be apprehended. Seizures of ships like this one increased, but so did bribery and violence.

32

Georges de Latour built Beaulieu
Vineyards on the lucrative (and legal)
business of providing communion
wines for the Catholic Church. Many
California grape growers shipped
their crop to New York, where Paddy's
Market, which stretched along seven
blocks of Ninth Avenue, became
a bazaar for home winemakers.
Because the Volstead Act allowed
rabbis to distribute sacramental
wines to synagogue members, "wine
congregations" exploded in size, and
wine stores like this one opened in
Jewish neighborhoods.

33

34

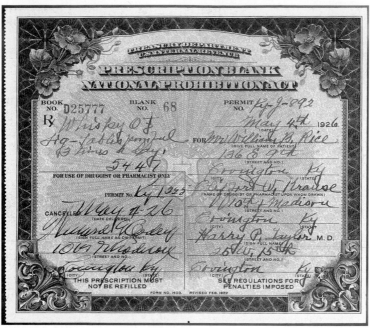

35

36

The going price paid to physicians for a legal liquor prescription was two dollars. "Spiritus Frumenti"—abbreviated by this Kentucky pharmacist as "spir. fru." (36)—is the Latin term for such elixirs; in most cases, it was straight rye.

Physicians and pharmacists supplying medicinal liquor were required to submit records to the Prohibition Bureau. This ledger, maintained by a doctor in Providence, Rhode Island, suggests that almost everyone seemed to suffer from the same ailment.

S. S. Pierce of Boston was one of the leading distributors of "medicinal liquor," which they offered to pharmacists in a number of tasty varieties.

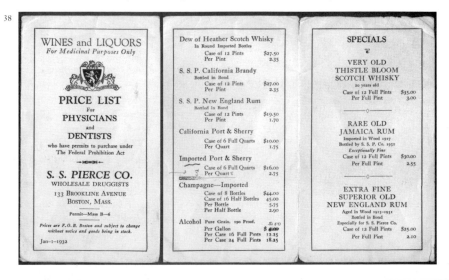

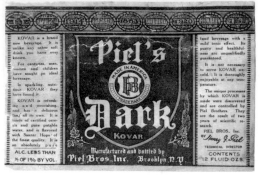

39

40

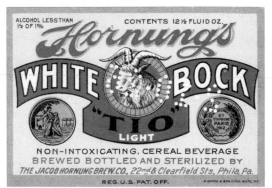

41

42

43

Near beer was available everywhere, but under the law, the word "beer" itself could not be used in describing it. Brewers tried to claim it was as good as the real thing—but, some asked, if that were true, why had they bothered to make the real thing in the first place? Malt syrup (44), for home brewing, was a more successful product.

44

way plays," which in turn "brought the clink of highball glasses, the squeal of bedsprings, the crackle of fast conversation to a thousand Main Streets."

For a while Hollywood production codes dictated that actual drinking could not be shown on screen, so there was a lot of bottle pouring, glass holding, and back-to-the-camera chugging. Still, the ladies of the WCTU created a Motion Picture Department to agitate for "the production of clean films." A self-described "Christian lobbyist" named Wilbur Fiske Crafts declared his intention to "rescue the motion pictures from the hands of the Devil and 500 un-Christian Jews" who were corrupting the nation. But the box office was voting for the speakeasy and its liberated women. A scholarly survey of 115 films released in 1929 established that drinking—virtually all of it illegal, of course—was depicted in 66 percent of them, more often than not favorably. In *After Midnight*, a shy and virginal Norma Shearer takes her very first drink and bursts into bloom. Joan Crawford became a star by hoofing on a speakeasy tabletop in *Our Dancing Daughters*. It was a self-sustaining cycle: Hollywood showed stylish characters drinking, moviegoers (a hundred million of them were attending pictures every week by 1930) mimicked the characters, and Hollywood thereby justified providing more of the same.

"We took the position that motion pictures should depict and reflect American life," said director Clarence Brown. "And cocktail parties and speakeasies were definitely a part of that life."

"TO THE HIGH SCHOOL INTELLECT," the *Detroit News* editorialized in 1924, "it is chic and charming to have an intrigue with a bootlegger, to carry a flask on the hip, to produce it where its possession may enhance a reputation for derring-do, and to imbibe from it in the presence of lovely and impressionable femininity." This pursuit of chic, the paper surmised, was what had motivated the young men at a high school dance at the Hotel Statler, a dance that made headlines when it was shut down because of excessive drinking.

Had one of those accused of misbehaving not been Howard C. Kresge, son of the retailing titan S. S. Kresge—believed to be the single largest financial backer of the Anti-Saloon League—it's doubtful the event would have attracted press attention. Similar spotlights would illuminate the alcohol-related arrests of Carroll Hepburn, son of the ASL's Virginia superintendent, and Thomas Heflin Jr., namesake, heir, and embarrassment to the ranting Alabama senator. ("It's like this," young Tom told New York reporters. "If one state wants booze, no other state should have the right to prevent it from getting it.") But as much as they liked to leer at the transgressions of fallen drys, it was difficult for most newspapers to get excited about the drinking habits of Prohibition-era youth. In Sonny Kresge's case, the *News*'s dudgeon climbed no higher than a tut-tutted warning: more refined people might be inclined to "keep him out of the best society." He might be labeled a "bounder."

American youth's turn toward drink was inevitable. When F. Scott Fitzgerald said the 1920s were "a children's party taken over by the elders" who had "discovered that young liquor will take the place of old blood," he had it backward. "This is not a case of the revolt of the youth," said W. H. P. Faunce, president of Brown University, "but a case in which youth is led by the revolt of middle age." The day before the *Detroit News* called out Sonny Kresge for getting too frisky at the Hotel Statler, it reported on "a veritable Babylonian revel" of older citizens taking place not three miles away. From Moriarity's on East Fifty-eighth Street in Manhattan ("almost a Yale-Harvard-Princeton club," wrote one of the regulars, the Treasury secretary's son, Paul Mellon) to the roadhouses of Meaderville, Montana (which served the "best gin fizzes in the world," recalled Josephine Weiss Casey of Butte), drinking among American young people was exactly as ubiquitous as it was among their elders. That was part of the appeal; one of the things Josephine Casey liked about the roadhouses was that they weren't just for "kids like us." In the absence of laws governing age limits (or closing hours, or distance from schools, or any of the other stipulations that button down a regulated liquor trade), drinking was not simply a way to imitate adults but an entry pass into their world. Stanley Coulter, dean of Purdue University's School of Science, attributed the excessive drinking on his campus to the example of "idiotic alumni."

Although some of the enterprising young indulged in beer (at Bowdoin College, in Brunswick, Maine, students brewed their own in the college's science labs), like their parents they mostly drank gin. It was so easy to flavor industrial alcohol with oil of juniper and a dash of glycerin, dilute it with tap water, and slap a fake Gordon's label onto the bottle that it became the favorite product of industrial-scale bootleggers and backroom hustlers alike. According to one expert on the homemade variety, "The gin is aged about the length of time it takes to get from the bathroom where it is made to the front porch where the cocktail is in progress."

Ready availability being the most precious of Prohibition virtues, gin was lifted above the historical pedigree that led Willa Cather to call it "the consolation of sailors and inebriate scrub-women." *Fortune*, which helpfully (and repellently) explained, "before prohibition, Gin went into

Martinis and Negros [*sic*]," said that Prohibition made it an acceptable drink for the presumably better bred. Not that these new gin connoisseurs knew much about it: the Philadelphia banker Gardner Cassatt (nephew of painter Mary Cassatt) patronized Walnut Street bootlegger Joel D. Kerper for five years and swore by the quality of Kerper's gin in testimony before a grand jury. In fact, Kerper was a major client of Philadelphia's industrial-alcohol distillers and a beneficiary of their counterfeiting. When he shipped liquor to the Maine summer homes of Philadelphia's elite in boxes labeled "varnish" or "floor paint," he was being more honest than his customers knew.

"The beverage known in Prohibition times as gin," as Herbert Asbury called the fake variety, begat another innovation in American drinking habits: the mixer. Whiskey cocktails of various types had existed for decades, and so had the martini, but the dubious quality of Prohibition liquor compelled further innovation, usually in a highball glass. Quinine water, or tonic, originally developed in India as an antimalaria nostrum, became a masking agent for gin of dubious origin. Ginger ale replaced soda water as the standard mixer for whiskey because its flavor could smother the laboratory odors of fake rye. William Grimes, in his history of the cocktail, *Straight Up or On the Rocks*, pointed out how the triumph of ginger ale was complete when Greta Garbo uttered her first on-screen lines, in *Anna Christie*: "Gimme a viskey, ginger ale on the side, and don't be stingy, baby."

Of course, the soft-drink industry enjoyed a further boon from the patronage of those who chose to obey the laws, an outcome predicted at the start of the decade by enemies of "the soft-drink trust." This was a term wet propagandists had found convenient in their effort to stamp the mark of greed on Prohibition supporters like Asa Candler of Coca-Cola. It turned out to be a misnomer: companies trying to cash in on the rapidly expanding market included such unlikely coconspirators as the shell-shocked Anheuser-Busch, which introduced coffee-flavored Caffo and something called Buschtee. (Another soft drink, called Kicko, apparently never made it out of the Busch test labs.) But even though the brewers who moved into soft drinks or de-alcoholized "near beer" sold enough to keep their doors open, none benefited nearly as much as Coca-Cola, which saw its sales triple during Prohibition. Astute marketing enabled Coke to position itself, as one of its advertising slogans had it, as "The Drink That Cheers But Does Not Inebriate."

The men who ran the soda-pop business couldn't lose. Americans who violated the Prohibition laws required the bottlers' product to make liquor palatable, and those who obeyed the laws needed it to quench their thirst.

As a result, said Louis Steinberger, president of a New Jersey soft-drink trade association, his industry found business "so good under Prohibition that [we] are determined to offend neither the Wets nor the Drys, and let the fight go merrily on."

IT'S SOMETHING OF a surprise that with all the illegal liquor sloshing around the United States, there apparently still wasn't enough to satisfy demand. But sometimes illegal behavior can be no fun if it doesn't have an element of excitement attached to it, and it did not take long for Americans in search of spirits to add some adventure to the hunt.

The *Montreal Gazette* suggested one of the possibilities. By 1925, the paper reported, the city's tourism business had grown exponentially—numbering "hundreds of thousands of tourists a year . . . due in considerable part" to Prohibition. Seventy miles to the southeast in Quebec's Eastern Townships, a collection of roadhouses and dives known as "line houses" sprouted along the U.S. border. The tiny town of Abercorn, population three hundred, soon had five hotels catering to Americans arriving after a seventy-five-cent taxi ride from the train station in Richford, Vermont. The line houses branched into bootlegging as well. At Labounty's, a line house east of Abercorn in a hamlet called Highwater, young men from Vermont searching for legal booze also found lucrative work. Bootleggers hired the Vermonters to drive cars loaded with liquor seventy-five miles south to Barre. All were instructed to leave the cars in a designated garage, go for a walk, and return an hour later, when they'd find $125 waiting on the seat. The drivers never touched the goods or met anyone involved at the American end of the trip.

More than 3,100 miles across the continent in Victoria, British Columbia, a columnist described the American "refugees from Volstead" pouring into the city. These masses were neither tired, nor poor, nor huddled. "Their appearance does not at all suggest privation . . . ," C. D. Smith wrote in the *Daily Colonist*. "They are mostly clothed in plus-fours and their one look is of assured triumph and anticipation." After addressing a hostile American Bar Association convention in Seattle, Mabel Willebrandt acknowledged that it had been a difficult assignment talking to the lawyers "when a great many of them had spent that day over the Canadian line." Even Windsor, Ontario, so close to the twenty-four-hour party that was Detroit, benefited from the cross-border larking. New hotels went up to accommodate the rush; so did a warehouse on the Windsor riverfront, built at government expense expressly for the storage of the hotels' liquor stocks.

It took a little more effort for Volstead refugees to find fun in the sun, but the adventure only added to the sense of sport that characterized liquor tourism. Within three months of Prohibition's onset, a travel agent in Coconut Grove, Florida, had established a private seaplane service direct from a Miami-based barge to the Bimini Rod and Gun Club. Reaching for the irony that characterized much reporting about Prohibition, Samuel Hopkins Adams, in *Collier's*, noted that one Bimini-bound operation even managed to make the return flight with a full load of liquor aboard: "This was quite without prejudice to the law," Adams wrote, "since there is no restriction upon the importation of alcohol when the human stomach is the container." A steward on the Hamburg-American passenger liner *Reliance* said his U.S. patrons "learned about Daiquiri cocktails at Havana, rum swizzles at Trinidad, and punch at Kingston."

The spectacularly named Inglis Moore Uppercu, a New York–based Cadillac dealer, made his mark in the world of liquor tourism when he founded Aeromarine Airways, the first regularly scheduled, U.S.-based international air service. Aeromarine shuttled Americans from Miami to some of the brighter spots in the Caribbean on three wooden-hulled flying boats named the *Niña*, the *Pinta*, and the *Santa Maria*, each of them tricked out with wicker armchairs and mahogany veneers. "The Limousines That Fly to Bimini," as Uppercu's early ads called them, were also flying to Cuba by November 1920, where their passengers planted the seeds for the stylish, all-night Havana of the coming decades and where the bootleggers who followed them laid the foundation of the mobster-dominated gambling mecca that was soon to blossom. A Newark bartender named Donovan took apart his bar plank by plank and reconstructed it in the lobby of Havana's Telégrafo Hotel, a home away from home for New Jerseyites who could afford the trip. An advertising campaign offered jointly by the Bacardi rum-making family and the fledgling Pan American Airways featured the slogan "Fly with us to Havana and you can bathe in Bacardi rum two hours from now." To welcome those arriving by sea, Facundo Bacardi thoughtfully sent wireless greetings to U.S.-based ships as they chugged into Havana's harbor, inviting passengers to visit his distillery. Bacardi told *The New Yorker* that business had never been so good.

For William Jennings Bryan, the spectacle of Prohibition-induced tourism was all too vivid. After his humiliation at the 1920 Democratic convention in San Francisco, he had started his withdrawal from political life, moving to Miami and settling in a Spanish-style waterfront mansion he called the Villa Serena. Bryan spent some of his time in Florida holding weekly Bible classes for audiences numbering in the thousands and some of it making a living. In *The Perils of Prosperity*, William E. Leuchtenberg describes how, during the great Florida land boom, a Coral Gables real estate operator hired Bryan "to sit on a raft under a beach umbrella and lecture on the beauties of the Florida climate."

But Bryan was less rhapsodic about the view from the lawn of the Villa Serena, where he could watch ships from the Bahamas hook up with the rumrunners of Biscayne Bay. His 1921 call for an invasion of Bimini had gone unheard, so the following year he turned his attention to the perfidy of those American citizens chasing the bottle on foreign soil and in some cases trying to bring it back home. For thus "conspiring" against the Constitution, Bryan told Representative W. A. Oldfield of Arkansas, such malefactors should be stripped of their citizenship.

"AS YOU SAIL AWAY, far beyond the range of amendments and thou-shalt-nots, those dear little iced things begin to appear, sparkling aloft on their crystal stems." This effusion was not the sort of come-on a drinker was likely to encounter in advertisements for places like Sloppy Joe's Bar on Zulueta Street in Havana (Joe's slogan was more concise: "Where the Wet Begins"). Those "dear little iced things" were at the center of a sales pitch for the elegant oceangoing ships of the French Line, which competed with Cunard not just for supremacy in the transatlantic passenger trade but also, in effect, for designation as World's Biggest, Fanciest, and Fastest Bar.

The British grabbed the lead early in the decade, perhaps on that day in February 1920, four weeks after Prohibition's birth, when the *Daily Express* of London informed its readers that Cunard's *Mauretania* "has docked at Southampton with empty bins. A record stock of wines and spirits has been utterly consumed by American passengers." Many years later E. B. White would recall how the lure of Prohibition-free seafaring tantalized New Yorkers. From their docks on the Hudson, wrote White, "the transatlantic liners sounded their horns of departure, and the citizens listened uneasily to this midnight invitation to revelry, debauchery, and escape." Aboard ship, smoking rooms doubled as drinking rooms and stewards doubled as bouncers. According to maritime historian John Maxtone-Graham, the ocean passage from the United States to the United Kingdom spawned "a new transatlantic stereotype, the drunk American."

At first the stereotype careened around the decks and parlors of British and French ships, for American liners, operating under the American flag and American law, went dry when the rest of the country did. Unlike the rest of the country, though, U.S.-registered ships were dry in fact as well as in name. The drop-off in business was so precipitous they might as well have slammed into a field of icebergs. A correspondent for the *New York Tribune*, describing a voyage on the *President Harding*, wrote, "It hurt [the crew] to think Americans deserted them to go on foreign lines merely because they could not, as one officer remarked, 'wait seven days for a drink.'"

It hurt the shipping industry even more, an insistent pain that led to a government agency's willful defiance of the Eighteenth Amendment. For a brief period American ships relaxed the rules, at the direction of Albert Lasker, the Chicago advertising executive (and majority owner of the Chicago Cubs) who headed the U.S. Shipping Board. A federal agency established to subsidize the American shipping industry, which had not recovered from the world war, the board seemed to believe that ignoring the Volstead Act was a more promising course of action than seeking additional appropriations from a chronically parsimonious Congress. Ads in the Paris edition of the *New York Herald* for the liners *George Washington* and *America* soon proclaimed "Excellent Cuisine—Choice Wines and Liquor." Menus distributed on board offered a choice of six different clarets, four champagnes, five liqueurs, and nine varieties of hard liquor, including an anonymous "American rye" priced 20 percent higher than Haig & Haig, Jameson, Johnnie Walker, or any of the other imported brands.

Lasker's policy was soon torpedoed by August A. Busch, son of Adolphus. Any Busch without power—Prohibition had rendered the family politically irrelevant—was a very unhappy Busch indeed. This one channeled his peevishness into mischief making. After a trip on the *George Washington*, he said he had "never seen so great a consumption of liquor as during this particular voyage"—proving, he asserted, that the U.S. government was "incomparably the biggest bootlegger in the world." Busch made this declaration in a letter sent to Warren G. Harding, then distributed it nearly as widely as he had once distributed beer.

Busch was no more concerned about booze on ships than he would have been had passengers been caught playing shuffleboard for nickels. His goals were more complex: he wanted to embarrass the Harding administration, discredit the Eighteenth Amendment, and, while he was at it, stick a knife into his old enemies, the distilling interests. But in the process he provoked the interest of Wayne B. Wheeler, who perceived an opportunity. Waving a series of ancient Supreme Court decisions involving maritime law in front of Congress and the White House, Wheeler showed that his political muscles had not atrophied. In October 1922 Harding declared American ships permanently dry and simultaneously announced that foreign ships coming into U.S. ports also had to be free of liquor.

At first the British were dismissive. "If the measure came into operation," a shipping executive said two days after Harding's announcement, ". . . our British ships would be governed by the United States—and such a state of affairs could not be tolerated." Then the British turned angry, and Parliament considered legislation that would have made it mandatory for American ships to have liquor aboard if they wished to use British ports. But the final phase of the British response was acceptance, and for a time westbound Cunard and White Star liners, when they approached the three-mile limit off Long Island, would pause to dump into the sea any alcoholic beverages that hadn't been downed by passengers and crew. When Lord Curzon finally agreed to stretch the three-mile limit, the American *quid* for the British *quo* granted British ships the right to bring liquor into American ports, so long as it was secured under seal. "Is it possible that any civilized country could continue to occupy the position now occupied by the United States?" asked Thomas Royden, chairman of the Cunard Line. He quickly found his own answer: transatlantic Volsteadism, he said, "renders [the United States] ridiculous in the eyes of the world." Senator James W. Wadsworth, an aristocratic wet from upstate New York, was even harsher: "How the world must despise us for making such asses of ourselves."

Things worked out fine for the British and other foreign ships. Although they had to put stoppers in their bottles and locks on their storerooms when they came within twelve miles of the United States, they otherwise remained free to host the floating revels for 99.6 percent of the journey across the ocean. The dehydrated American liners, for their part, were compelled to promote other virtues. Thus did Albert Lasker attempt to win the attention of transatlantic travelers by setting up driving ranges on the aft decks of American ships, by showing first-run movies, by bringing aboard name-brand orchestras, and by offering unlimited caviar to first-class passengers.

All these innovations survived the end of Prohibition. One other did not. The Coca-Cola company, seeing a possible opening, had designed a handsome new bottle, its neck wrapped in foil to resemble champagne.

Coke's foreign department hoped it would replace the genuine article at bon voyage parties and shipboard banquets. But American travelers, by then wise to the ways of secreting bottles in their luggage, were never again without access to the truly real Real Thing. They just took it aboard with them.

EIGHT DECADES OF MOVIES, television shows, retro fashion trends, piquant musical quotations, and thickly clouded memories have left us with a crowded vision of Prohibition drinking: a montage of raccoon coats, rolled-up stockings, bobbed hair, and cloche hats, the entire tableau surmounted by a totemic hip flask in shimmering silver. Two elements are missing from this picture: pain and desperation.

These were ushered in by a jolt of greed. Derelicts were poisoning themselves before Prohibition with alcohol of less than vintage quality—Sterno filtered through a sock, for instance, or diluted antifreeze solution ("addicts claimed that a little rust improved the flavor and gave their bodies needed iron," wrote Herbert Asbury). But Prohibition stimulated the avarice of low-grade bootleggers, who extended their inventory of repurposed industrial alcohol with the addition of wood alcohol, isopropyl alcohol, and other toxic compounds, turning reports of paralysis and death into a newspaper staple (from the *New York World*, January 1, 1927: FOUR NEW RUM DEATHS; 20 MORE TO BELLEVUE; 760 DIE HERE IN YEAR). An operation based in Buffalo distributed its goods twice weekly in one-gallon cans—the delivery truck "called like a milkman," a customer said—and what might normally cause a headache if properly diluted would almost certainly produce blindness if not; tests found that the stuff in the cans was 38 percent wood alcohol.* A two-ounce bottle of "Jamaican Ginger," aka "Jake," could be had for as little as thirty-five cents. Up to 80 percent pure alcohol, it was enough to create a little buzz at first—but in one horrifying instance, a contaminated batch permanently crippled five hundred people in Wichita alone. The poison Jake, which came from a distilling operation that had carelessly added a potent neurotoxin called tri-ortho-cresyl phosphate, attacked the nerves in the hands and feet, giving victims an odd, shuffling gait that became known as "Jake Walk" or "Jake Leg." One of the several blues songs spawned by the Jake Leg epidemic explained a further complication:

---

*The phrase "blind drunk" derives from the capacity of wood alcohol to attack the optic nerve and destroy retinal cells.

It's the doggonest disease
Ever heard of since I been born
You get numb in front of your body,
You can't carry any lovin' on.

Just like the cinematic cocktail parties and speakeasies that Clarence Brown invoked to "reflect American life," poisonous alcohol made it into the movies, too. In one of Brown's films, 1925's *The Goose Woman*, Louise Dresser plays a fallen opera star who satisfies her alcoholism with hair tonic. But the songs and films and other cultural expressions of the poison epidemic didn't necessarily make people pay heed. It was as if the perils of poisonous liquor made the less toxic, more conventional stuff seem positively healthful. Once the first few years of Prohibition had passed and tipplers and tasters realized the earth had not stopped in its orbit, arrests for public intoxication and drunk driving soared. So did cirrhosis deaths and hospitalizations for alcoholic psychosis. After one factored in the unquestionably large numbers of nondrinkers—either sworn teetotalers or obliging law-abiders—it was clear that the rate of per capita consumption among those who did drink resembled a fever chart.

Strikingly, this seemed particularly true among the well off and the well educated. The student council of Marymount College, a Catholic women's school in New York, declared that "over-indulgence is to be found among the wealthy rather than the poorer classes." British visitors expressed shock at the amount of drinking they encountered among their hosts; one, newspaper publisher Sir Charles Igglesden, described seeing "men swallow four or five cocktails" before dinner, "drinking against time, as it were." In a genial letter to her ex-husband, the former Mrs. Andrew Mellon wrote, "I find that people expect more [liquor] at a dinner party than before Prohibition." (She also sought advice on how to move a case of bootleg Scotch from Newport to her winter home—if the secretary of the treasury didn't know how to do that, who would?) A *Vanity Fair* story by Clare Boothe Brokaw secured the catchphrase "Have a little drinkie" in the argot of the rich. To Brokaw drinking was "the greatest anodyne for that most intense of all social and human agonies—boredom."

Such stylish insouciance guaranteed that excess was the mode, especially (and unsurprisingly) among the young, who were following the example of their elders. "The girls simply won't go out with the boys who haven't got flasks to offer," said the police chief of Topeka, Kansas. His counterpart in Boise, Idaho, commenting on the behavior of young people in his jurisdiction, said, "Drinking is done almost everywhere, by almost everybody." Jean Hamilton, dean of women at the University of Michigan, filled her out-box with letters to parents whose daughters overindulged. "For a girl to place herself as completely at a man's mercy as to be helplessly intoxicated is very serious," Hamilton wrote to the parents of a sophomore named Pauline Izor. Izor had been so drunk "that she fell twice and was unable to get up by herself."

The case of Pauline Izor was neither especially extreme nor especially rare. What gives it enduring relevance is the unexceptional remainder of her story. She married a physician, raised a family, and eventually returned to Ann Arbor four decades later as housemother at a Michigan sorority. Looking at her picture in an old yearbook, one sees a handsome woman of sixty or so in a light-colored dress with a scalloped neckline, pearl earrings decorously accenting her coiffed hair. She's sitting in the center of four rows of smiling young women in identical white blouses; as housemother, she is effectively their full-time chaperone. It may be automatic to read the word "speakeasy" and picture in the mind's eye a generic nineteen-year-old flapper, cloche on her head, flask in her hand, kicking up her happy heels in a buoyant Charleston. But to look at Pauline Izor at sixty—or at a photograph of one's own mother or grandmother—and to try to imagine her as a falling-down drunk is unfathomable. From the distance of eight decades, the mind's eye easily projects the image of gaiety we've been bequeathed by the tribunes of popular culture. But we can no sooner conjure the image of our grandmothers teetering on the edge of alcohol poisoning than we can imagine them robbing banks; it won't compute.

Consequently, a three-dimensional sense of the excesses of Prohibition-era drinking, especially among the young, can be found only in darker corners. At Dartmouth College, a junior named Robert T. Meads was sentenced to twenty years' hard labor in the state penitentiary for having shot and killed senior Henry E. Maroney in a dispute over payment for bootlegged liquor. Summer resorts in Pennsylvania saw the rise of "Fatty Arbuckle parties," which aspired to emulate the notorious San Francisco bacchanal that had led to the death of showgirl Virginia Rappe.* And although criminal behavior or tragic consequences were not ubiquitous components of the alcoholic excess of the period, desperation definitely was. Nowhere was this more clearly memorialized than in a simple

---

*After three trials, motion picture comedian Roscoe "Fatty" Arbuckle was eventually acquitted of any responsibility in Rappe's death, but his acting career was destroyed.

declarative sentence in John O'Hara's *Appointment in Samarra*, where he describes a typical evening among the young married couples at the Lantenengo Country Club of Gibbsville, Pennsylvania: "There were innumerable vomitings, more or less disastrous."

IT WAS HER HORROR at excessive among the young that would eventually shape the life of Pauline Morton Sabin. It was some life: Sabin was the daughter of Theodore Roosevelt's secretary of the navy; heiress to the Morton Salt fortune; wife of a J. P. Morgan partner; first woman member of the Republican National Committee; and chatelaine of Bayberry Land, a twenty-eight-room home on 298 acres in Southampton, New York, and The Oaks, a 1,961-acre plantation in Goose Creek, South Carolina. She had supported Prohibition from the beginning, believing "a world without liquor would be a beautiful thing" and fondly imagining that her two boys would grow up in a dryer, safer, and generally better country. But Sabin saw the beautiful thing turn ugly.

"Girls of a generation ago would not have ventured into a saloon," she would write. "Girls did not drink; it was not considered 'nice.' But today girls and boys drink, at parties and everywhere, then stop casually at a speakeasy on the way home." This fretful comment appeared in a widely distributed pamphlet entitled "Why American Mothers Demand Repeal." To Sabin and the other women who would eventually join her crusade to end Prohibition—an effort that would make her the Wayne Wheeler of Repeal—the revolution that had brought the Eighteenth Amendment and the Volstead Act into being had not put an end to excessive drinking but had fostered it.

The law said one thing; the young people Sabin knew ignored it. Prohibition, she believed, had become "an attempt to enthrone hypocrisy as the dominant force in this country." Nothing, it appeared, could stanch the flood of alcohol that washed the country from coast to coast—or the political dishonesty, cultural dislocations, and contagion of crime that rode in its wake.

PART III

THE WAR OF
THE WET AND
THE DRY

"The thing that sticks out clearly now is that for years our politics promises to be thoroughly saturated with this wet and dry stuff. It will warp the whole political fabric, prevent clear thinking—even by those who are capable of thinking clearly—and hide the merits of the men who run for office in a fog of feeling."

—Frank Kent, *Baltimore Sun*, quoted in an Anti-Saloon League reprint, circa 1922

Chapter 15

Open Wounds

AULINE SABIN WAS in Paris when Warren Harding died. The president's long-planned trip to the American West in the summer of 1923 had first made headlines in Denver in late June, when he delivered an uncharacteristically strong appeal for aggressive Prohibition enforcement. Even more surprising, it was on this same trip that he finally decided to stop drinking, a determination induced by the importunate pleadings of his wife, Florence, and his hovering conscience, namely Wayne Wheeler. When Harding suffered his fatal stroke in San Francisco on August 2, details of the Teapot Dome conspiracy and the other scandals that would forever soil Harding's reputation had not yet become fully known. In her suite at the Crillon—the same suite, overlooking the Place de la Concorde, where David Lloyd George had lived during the Paris Peace Talks—Sabin wrote in her diary, "In his simple way Harding had many qualities which almost made him a great man." Her friend Alice Roosevelt Longworth was more temperate in her appraisal. "Harding was not a bad man," she said. "He was just a slob."

No one could mistake Calvin Coolidge for a slob—or for a great man. Longworth said the Coolidge White House and the Harding White House were as different "as a New England front parlor is from the backroom of a speakeasy." Coolidge was unlike his predecessor in nearly every way, skeptical where Harding was credulous, cautious where Harding was impetuous, circumspect where Harding was loquacious. Only in one key respect were the two presidents similar: even considering Harding's belated conversion in Denver, neither man was particularly interested in enforcing Prohibition. In Coolidge's case this was consistent with his general position on the role of government. "If the federal government should go out of existence," he said, "the common run of people would not detect the difference in the affairs of their daily life for a considerable length of time."

It was as if he viewed government as a vestigial organ of the body politic. The president's inclination toward inactivity, wrote Walter Lippmann, "is far from being indolent inactivity. It is a grim, determined, alert inactivity."

Coolidge's reluctance to strengthen Prohibition enforcement was sharpened by other impulses besides his devotion to stasis. He believed that government should keep its nose out of the lives of citizens. He so hated to spend federal money that in 1926, with the economy in the midst of a spectacular boom, he whacked the Prohibition Bureau's budget by 3.5 percent. And though there's every reason to believe he remained personally dry during his years in the White House, he was not a stranger to beer or wine in the years before and after. (In 1930, on finishing his second glass of a fine Tokay that William Randolph Hearst had offered him, a delighted Coolidge declared, "I must remember this!") Apart from his support for an expanded Coast Guard, Coolidge's most visible effort in behalf of Prohibition occurred at a state dinner in Havana, when he toasted Cuban president Gerardo Machado with a glass of water. His solution to all the vexing problems brought on by the Volstead Act and its profligate violation was either foolishly naïve or a conscious evasion: if people would only stop buying from bootleggers, he told a governors' conference in 1923, "the rest would be easy."

In at least one instance, though, Coolidge felt compelled to act. During the summer of 1924 he mobilized the full might of the federal government to crack down on a bootlegging operation that had provoked his concern. The investigation, initiated by the president himself, was conducted under the personal supervision of his closest friend in Washington, Attorney General Harlan Fiske Stone, who had been his classmate at Amherst College. It was advanced through the efforts of the newly appointed director of the Bureau of Investigation,* J. Edgar Hoover; at least four members of Hoover's staff; the agent in charge of the bureau's New York office; and Stone's brother-in-law, John D. Willard, a western Massachusetts clergyman. Convictions, the attorney general told Willard, "would be personally gratifying to the president." Stone issued a series of personal directives. To avoid exposing details of the delicate inquiry to telegraph operators, alternative means of communication were employed. Stepping across a commonly recognized ethical line, Willard solicited privileged information about a criminal defendant from the defendant's own attorney. Finally, four months after the operation was launched, indictments were issued. The defendants: four men in Holyoke, Massachusetts, who were

---

*The "Federal" prefix was not added to its name until 1935.

found in possession of thirteen bottles of liquor and thirty-seven cases of beer—barely enough alcohol to keep a self-respecting speakeasy stocked for a weekend. But the Holyoke men had been selling liquor to students at nearby Amherst, specifically to the young men of Phi Gamma Delta. As Stone had told his man on the ground in Amherst, Coolidge had been "concerned about reports of bootlegging in his fraternity."

AMBIVALENT ABOUT PROHIBITION, but absolutely devoted to the Republican Party, Pauline Sabin quickly lined up behind Coolidge to support his election in 1924. On the other hand, Gifford Pinchot's absolute devotion to Prohibition stimulated his growing ambivalence toward the Republican Party. His roots in the progressive movement and his labors for the dry cause shaped the Pennsylvania governor's lopsided public persona, sort of a cross between Teddy Roosevelt and Savonarola. Pinchot was among a large number of drys who considered Coolidge a wimp and a closet wet, and in 1924 he flirted with challenging the president as the candidate of the Prohibition Party.

Would that it were so clear for Wayne B. Wheeler. He could neither give his unqualified support to the inconstant Coolidge, nor could his familiar array of electoral threats intimidate a very popular president. But Wheeler was not so constrained in his dealings with Congress. Influence on Capitol Hill was calibrated regularly in roll calls, and he owned those no less than he owned his own name. He bragged that he could unseat any senator or representative who was an "enemy of the Constitution," and joked that he would have them "shot at sunrise on the next election day." In the congressional elections of 1920, 1922, and 1924, the Anti-Saloon League continued to dominate by controlling the margins, handing its 10 or 20 percent of the electorate to candidates willing to lash themselves to the dry mast. Senatorial wets like Atlee Pomerene of Ohio and Augustus Owsley Stanley of Kentucky fell to ASL-sponsored candidates who had little in common other than an enduring obligation to the angels of their electoral deliverance—Wheeler and the league.* Pomerene lost to Simeon D. Fess, "the Driest of the Drys," who considered anyone who would violate the Volstead Act "an anarchist and . . . an enemy of the government"; Stanley fell to Frederic M. Sackett, an aristocratic Republican

---

*Stanley's grandson and namesake, Augustus Owsley Stanley III, made his own contribution to the free exchange of banned substances as the first large-scale distributor of LSD, in the 1960s. He later became the soundman for the Grateful Dead.

from Louisville who was known to brag about his richly stocked cellar but who promised not to drink a drop so long as Prohibition lasted. Some people may have believed him.

To Wheeler, who dispatched his top assistant to Kentucky to guarantee Stanley's defeat, Sackett's personal habits were of no consequence. "Prohibition was not voted into existence by total abstainers," Wheeler said, nor was the abstinence of elected officials essential to its maintenance. What mattered was Sackett's vote on the Senate floor, and had he (or any other dry) been inclined to wander during the nose counting, it would not have been for lack of discipline. Wheeler's baleful presence in the Capitol Building was a visible manifestation of his muscle. Morris Markey, in *The New Yorker*, called him "the frowning Nero in charge of local destinies [who] sits heavily in the gallery," offering a definitive thumbs-up or thumbs-down during Prohibition-related debates. Representative John Philip Hill of Maryland, a leader of the wet forces in the House, called Wheeler the "generalissimo" whose every order could muster an instant majority.

Because Wheeler was their ticket to reelection, compliant drys had a more benevolent view. Representative Elmer Thomas of Oklahoma spoke for many of his colleagues when he wrote Wheeler to say, "[I] beg to advise you that I shall be pleased to support any bill which you recommend." Without Wheeler as both enforcer and lodestar, the dry caucus on Capitol Hill might have degenerated into riot—progressives at war with reactionaries, Republicans battling Democrats, country populists assaulting representatives of the mercantile elite. It's difficult to imagine a coalition that could accommodate, say, both Morris Sheppard of Texas, the passionately earnest, liquor-hating author of the Eighteenth Amendment, and Cole Blease of South Carolina, who openly reveled in the pleasures of drink. Sheppard and Blease were opposites in ideology, in manner, in their very essences. The courtly, Yale-educated Sheppard, whose support for progressive legislation prefigured the New Deal, rose each year on January 16 to commemorate the anniversary of the amendment's ratification with speeches layered in Shakespearean eloquence and brightened by his sunny optimism. The reactionary, hate-filled Blease, who opposed schools for black people because education could "ruin a good field hand and make a bad convict," drew on an oratorical armory of insult and attack, among its frequently used weapons such epithets as "pap-sucker," "belly-crawler," and, of course, "nigger lover." Yet Wheeler's coalition was as ample as his discipline was firm, and the dry caucus on Capitol Hill could accommodate both men.

It was the same outside Congress: the house of Prohibition had many rooms. A sample of the dry rolls circa 1924 would have included the Methodist evangelist Bob Jones, whose catalog of evils extended beyond liquor to dancing and the movies, and the indicted (for bribery) lawyer Thomas B. Felder, a chronic alcoholic who had written Georgia's Prohibition law—and then acquired a small fortune representing wholesale liquor dealers and rumrunner Bill McCoy. Prohibition made allies of the earnest reformer Dr. Clarence True Wilson of the Methodist Board of Temperance, Prohibition and Public Morals, whose other favored cause was Simplified Spelling, and "the bootleggers' terror," Federal District Judge John F. McGee of Minnesota, who so delighted in locking up Volstead Act violators that he once issued 112 sentences in 130 minutes, an orgy of retribution that required the impressment of a fleet of sightseeing buses to ferry the miscreants to jail. The profoundly pragmatic Wall Street financier Bernard Baruch was a dry ("I believed you could legislate against the abuses of liquor," he wrote years later in his memoirs, disbelievingly), as was the chronically spacey Henry Ford, who expected Prohibition, in its final triumph, to "have made prosperity universal and . . . [have] abolished poverty." There may be no clearer demonstration of the drys' pragmatic acceptance of every variety of ally than a comment made by Mabel Willebrandt—a federal official, a feminist, a progressive—when she was asked about the faithfully dry Ku Klux Klan: "I have no objection to people dressing up in sheets, if they enjoy that sort of thing."

THE UN-DRY HAD a cobbled-together alliance of their own. By 1924, a vocal wet caucus had formed in Congress. Its numbers were small but the personalities who dominated it were enormous. The untamable leader of Senate wets was James A. Reed, a Democrat who had emerged from Kansas City's notorious Pendergast machine. When Reed likened Andrew Volstead to "burners of witches" and "executioners," he was drawing on the milder entries in his vocabulary of abuse. A Senate colleague said that when Reed spoke of an opponent, "it was as if he had thrown acid upon him"—for instance, when he charged that Prohibition was enacted by "half-drunk legislators" suffering from "the leprosy of hypocrisy." Reed called suffragists "Amazonian furies" who chanted "in rhythmic harmony with the barbaric war dance of the Sioux." Supporters of the League of Nations, he said, were evidently prepared to submit to the rulings of "black men from Liberia and voodoo worshipping Haitians . . . wearing rings in their noses as well as ears." To his friend (and drinking buddy) H. L. Mencken, Jim Reed was "for our time, the supreme artist in assault." Given

Mencken's own skills, this was like Babe Ruth praising someone for his hitting ability.

Reed's counterparts in the House hadn't quite his aptitude for vituperation but they were not without verbal resources. In addition to John Philip Hill, who once said the Anti-Saloon League was in business "to protect the American Bootleggers' Union," House wets were led by Fiorello La Guardia of New York and, toward the end of the decade, James Montgomery Beck of Pennsylvania. Knowing that legislative success on Prohibition issues was probably unattainable, Hill and La Guardia chose to conduct their campaign against the drys in the press. ("He lives by headlines," *Time* said about Hill. "If newspapers were abolished, he would curl up and die.") La Guardia, like Hill, tried to get himself arrested for making illegal booze (he failed because the New York cops ignored him; Hill succeeded, but was acquitted by a genially wet Baltimore jury). La Guardia would do whatever he could to goad, frustrate, and mortify his dry colleagues, most notably when he proposed a hundred-million-dollar increase in the Prohibition Bureau's budget, which at that point had not yet topped three million dollars. This legislative gambit forced tightfisted drys to vote against beefed-up enforcement, and at the same time underscored the hopelessness of the government's underfunded efforts. La Guardia also loved to publicize the bureau's chronic corruption, at one point suggesting that 150,000 Prohibition agents would not be enough to enforce the law—for "you will have to have 150,000 agents to watch the first 150,000." La Guardia was fond of this trope. A few years earlier, as president of the New York City board of aldermen, he had said that it would take 250,000 policemen to enforce Prohibition in the city, and 250,000 more to police the police.

Although a Republican like Hill and La Guardia, Beck was a different species of public figure. The first two men were raucous, demonstrative characters, and La Guardia in particular veered leftward on most issues. The formal and forbidding Beck was virtually a Royalist, archconservative in politics and style. Looking grimly at the world through his pince-nez, he saw "incredible frivolity and selfishness" everywhere, except when he found himself "in a dark and sombre wood." The Dante quote was out of character for Beck. He usually relied on Shakespeare, his speech filled, wrote biographer Morton Keller, with "quotations which came cascading forth to edify—or plague—dinner audiences, courtrooms, and readers of his books."

Keller called his Beck biography *In Defense of Yesterday*, and "yesterday" covered a lot of ground. Beck was an eighteenth-century man adrift in the twentieth century, a self-invented aristocrat loose among the rabble.

Before entering Congress he had resigned as solicitor general because he found even the laissez-faire Harding administration too willing to expand the role of government. Two years later Philadelphia's corrupt Republican machine handed him a dismal congressional district in South Philadelphia, overwhelmingly comprised of blacks and immigrants. That did not mean he represented their perceived interests. Beck disdained any legislation that was even remotely progressive. He opposed woman suffrage, child labor legislation, the League of Nations, the Sherman Anti-Trust Act, the income tax, even Morris Sheppard's bill to reduce infant mortality.

The eastern Protestant elites who controlled so much of the nation's wealth in the 1920s divided themselves on wet/dry issues along the same lines that divided them on most political issues. Improve-the-masses progressives like John D. Rockefeller Jr. and Gifford Pinchot, who saw Prohibition as a logical undertaking for activist government, were arrayed against wet conservatives like Beck, who believed government existed only to preserve order and protect private property. Pinchot's wife, Cornelia, an outspoken progressive who had devoted most of her energies to suffrage and improved conditions for factory workers, joined the Woman's Christian Temperance Union only after "I found out that the wet lobby was against everything in which I was interested," including child labor laws and woman suffrage. When she said "the reactionary movement as a whole is 95% wet," she was not far wrong.

Prohibition stirred conservative members of the privileged classes as had no issue since they had been steamrollered by the populist-powered income tax amendment. For all of Fiorello La Guardia's antic showmanship and parliamentary razzle-dazzle, it was Beck and other men of wealth and stature who had first begun to mobilize an organized political opposition to the Anti-Saloon League. The Association Against the Prohibition Amendment announced its birth late in the ratification process in 1918, when an admiralty lawyer named William H. Stayton sent a solicitation letter to the six hundred men in his address book. Among the AAPA's earliest members were men whose very names conjured up money and social position, including Stuyvesant Fish, Kermit Roosevelt, Marshall Field, and Vincent Astor (not to mention John Philip Sousa). One of its earliest fund-raising efforts took place at the New York Yacht Club. But the AAPA failed to establish meaningful traction until it won the attention, in 1926, of Pierre S. du Pont—chairman of his family's chemical colossus; chairman of the du Pont–controlled General Motors Corporation; and soon the dominant figure in an invigorated AAPA.

Before that happened, though, the AAPA's fumbling efforts in electoral politics would demonstrate to many of the wet Tories that effective opposition to the dry regime would not come from the voting public. Following the Anti-Saloon League model, in 1922 the association endorsed a roster of wet candidates for Congress, whereupon everyone on the endorsement list received a letter from Wayne Wheeler freighted with warning. It was a measure of Wheeler's might that year, and again in 1924, that many of these candidates ran the other way, rejecting the AAPA's blessing for fear it would guarantee their defeat.

This would not have troubled Pierre du Pont, who believed he and his friends might foster good government if only they would "refuse to contribute to any party that tries to promote indiscriminate voting." As he told a Republican colleague, "It is futile for people to dictate government by committing representatives to certain policies, or to know the qualifications of candidates." Voters, he explained, "must learn to leave these matters to those who do know, trusting them to carry out their work." In the context, "them" really meant "us." By the end of the decade du Pont would put his money, his friends, his friends' money, and their collective reputation where his euphemism was.

OF THE TWO structural elements that shaped the dry regime, only the Volstead Act was flexible. By general acknowledgment, the Eighteenth Amendment was both inelastic and indestructible. Any amendment to modify or revoke the Eighteenth would require ratification by three-quarters of the forty-eight state legislatures, just like the original. "Thirteen dry states with a population of less than that of New York State alone can prevent repeal until Halley's Comet returns," Clarence Darrow said. (As of the 1920 census, the total population of the thirteen smallest states was 5.1 million; of New York, 10.4 million.) The great defense lawyer, who was as wet as the Flood, believed "one might as well talk about taking his summer vacation on Mars." But every provision of the Volstead Act was vulnerable to the whim of congressional majorities—and, to some degree, to the mood swings of voters in specific districts. This became clear in 1922 when Andrew J. Volstead, seeking his eleventh term in Minnesota's Seventh Congressional District, was defeated for reelection.

Volstead once imagined the perfect epitaph: "He naturally made many enemies, but we love him for the enemies he made." Some of those were the southerners he attacked in his righteous, unyielding, and futile campaign for an antilynching law. Many more, though, reviled Volstead for his eponymous connection to Prohibition enforcement: for instance, the

Milwaukee man who blamed him for the spread of poisonous liquor and believed he should be "convicted of murder in the first degree and punished by death"; or the Philadelphian who said "You made a Bolshevik out of me"; or the New York cop who suggested that "a perfectly good bullet" would be wasted on Volstead. "You are not worth it," he wrote on New York Police Department stationery. "Even the nit that preys on a cootie's testicles has a greater sense of shame, of honor and of self-respect than has Andrew J. Volstead!"

Yet the politician who vanquished the author of the Prohibition enforcement laws was himself a dry—dryer, he claimed, than Volstead himself. O. J. Kvale was a Lutheran minister who in a contested Republican primary in 1920 had accused Volstead of atheism. (The evidence: one Sunday morning, while the God-fearing residents of Granite Falls gathered in church, Volstead was seen tending his garden.) Running as an Independent the next time around, the desert-dry Kvale won with the support of Prohibitionists more wrathful than the cautious Volstead. But he had another group in his corner as well: wets eager to display the symbolic scalp of Prohibition's symbolic enforcer—and to see the next-ranking member of the Judiciary Committee, a Republican wet from Pennsylvania named George S. Graham, assume supervisory responsibility for any modification of the Volstead Act.

To the ASL, this was no small matter. Alterations in the act could be sown by the sympathetic Graham, conceivably to blossom in the benign inattention of the complacent Coolidge. Following Graham's ascension, Wheeler and his allies were obliged to turn their efforts toward the construction of a fortress around the Volstead Act and the sacred words inscribed at its center: the quantification of "intoxicating" at one-half-of-one-percent alcohol. Dry strategists were wise enough to understand that the American political system did not accommodate the idea of a permanent majority in Congress, which was what they would need to protect the Volstead Act. They consequently chose to change both the qualifications for voting and the way the votes were counted. Just as the pre-1920 drys had strengthened their hand by encouraging the woman suffrage movement, the post-1920 drys enlisted in a new crusade designed to change the composition of the American electorate. Suffrage had expanded the franchise, but this time the drys and their allies sought to constrict it. Their apparent weapon was ethnic bigotry, their subtler one an unprecedented—and successful—effort to subvert the first article of the Constitution.

◆　◆　◆

LONG BEFORE Kenneth L. Roberts became a celebrity with the publication of his blockbuster historical novels (*Northwest Passage*, *Rabble in Arms*), he tried his hand at journalism. In his fiction Roberts treated Benedict Arnold as a hero and painted British loyalists as victims of the Revolutionary War. As a journalist he had been no less provocative. Traveling through Europe on assignment for the *Saturday Evening Post*, he rendered his postwar surveys of the political landscape in a froth of racial invective. He described "streams of undersized, peculiar, alien people moving perpetually through consulates and steamship offices and delousing plants, on their way from the slums of Europe to the slums of America." He said the immigrants heading to the United States "are the defeated, incompetent and unsuccessful—the very lowest layer of European society." Polish Jews, he said, were usurers and liquor dealers; Slavs "have been brought up to break the laws of the people who govern them." Immigrants from the eastern reaches of Austria-Hungary "wear clothing that seems to have ripened on them for years, and they sleep in wretched hovels with sheep and cows and pigs and poultry scattered among them." His occasional efforts to dilute this flood of acid provided opportunity for yet further insult: "Even the most backward, illiterate, dirty, thick-headed peasants of Southeastern Europe have their good points."

Roberts's articles were influential less for their putative revelations than for their vivid articulation of what was already on the American mind. Between 1900 and 1915 more than 6.2 million people from southern and eastern Europe had arrived on U.S. shores. The 1915 publication of *The Passing of the Great Race*, by the Manhattan patrician Madison Grant, had given an academic gloss to the theory of what its proponents called "racial hygiene" (and what later came to be known to more temperate scholars as "scientific racism").* World War I had aggravated the chronic American xenophobia, and by the early 1920s it had become acute, as nativists seized on a new reason to hate the immigrants: their apparent refusal to obey the law. Roy Haynes, the Prohibition commissioner, attributed 80 percent of the liquor law violations in New York City to aliens. Imogen B. Oakley of the General Federation of Women's Clubs wrote that "those who ought to know" said 75 percent of bootleggers were aliens, and most of those were Italians or Russian Jews. A Prohibition Bureau official testifying before Congress invoked a similar figure, this time citing his source as

---

*Grant's theory held that northern Europeans—he called them "Nordics"—were "a race of soldiers, sailors, adventurers, and explorers" whose very existence was threatened by intermarriage with the lowly "Alpines" and "Mediterraneans." And even these lower castes could be corrupted, as "the cross between any of the three European races and a Jew is a Jew."

"general information," which was either more or less reliable tha
who ought to know."

There was anti-immigrant prejudice in this game of bobbing for n
bers, but the results were not wildly inaccurate. Although the figuɪ
weren't authoritatively quantified for several years,* it had been clear from
the stroke of midnight on January 16, 1920, that the bootlegging racket
was an industry custom-made for immigrants. It was a quick-turnover
business that had no entrenched establishment, required little capital,
demanded no particular training, and could exploit ready markets within
the various ethnic communities before branching out into society at large.
The outstanding (and sympathetic) historian of early-twentieth-century
immigration, John Higham, said Prohibition created "dazzling opportunities" for the children of the immigrant slums.

For drys, demonizing the immigrant had been part of their playbook
since Frances Willard asked Congress to keep out "the scum of the old
world." Now, with Prohibition in place, they leapt at the opportunity to
further their cause by throwing gasoline on the anti-immigrant bonfire.
They were not content to rely on the phenomenon reported in the *New
York Times*—a reverse diaspora that had immigrants returning voluntarily
to their European homelands "because, they declare, America has gone
dry, which they consider tyranny." Instead, the ASL's agents in Congress
tried to push unwilling immigrants back across the Atlantic with a measure
mandating immediate deportation of any alien found in violation of the
Volstead Act. "In many places," Wheeler wrote in a letter to House drys,
"most of the offenders against the liquor and narcotics laws are aliens."
The members responded with a resounding 222–73 vote to launch the
deportation program.

A distracted Senate never got around to voting on the alien deportation law, but it was a sideshow in any case. The expulsion of even several thousand bootleggers would have done nothing to further the much
more important dry goal, which was the preservation of dry congressional
majorities. One tack pursued by southern and western drys would have
excluded aliens from the census figures used to determine representation
in the House. Under the Constitution, House districts are based on total
population, noncitizens included—a situation, Representative Homer
Hoch of Kansas once said, that "gives aliens an influence upon legisla-

---

* A study in the late 1920s established that roughly half of the professional bootleggers were
eastern European Jews, another 25 percent Italian, and the remainder a mix of ethnicities,
including Polish and Irish.

tion to which they are not entitled." His fellow Kansas dry, Representative Edward C. Little, was less delicate: "It is not best for America that her councils be dominated by semicivilized foreign colonies in Boston, New York, Chicago." Cotton Tom Heflin, always unwilling to be topped, said "lawless, criminal aliens" were "gnawing at the vitals of this American Government," and failure to act would "increase the political power of the Pope of Rome in the United States." Hoch, in particular, beat this drum for years, at one point complaining, "It is not fair that New York should cast four extra votes on important issues affecting the whole country, because 1,600,000 aliens happen to congregate there."

But this line of reasoning was doomed. Using the same logic, northern wets argued that disenfranchised blacks should not be included in computing the number of House members allotted to each southern state. Dry southerners and their allies, trapped by their own logic, found their way out of the corner by bolting the doors to the country itself. Their vehicle was the Immigration Restriction Act of 1924, which established annual quotas based on the national origin of people already in the United States. The ceiling was set at 2 percent. Thus, if there were, say, 100,000 Americans of Spanish origin, then 2,000 more Spaniards would be allowed in each year. A similar, temporary measure had been enacted in 1921, using 1910 census figures to determine the baseline. This time out, Congress did not disguise its bigoted intent; instead of using four-year-old numbers from the 1920 census, it elected to turn the clock back to 1890 and use a thirty-four-year-old census as the measuring stick. This eliminated from the equation 4 million Italians, 2 million eastern European Jews, 1.5 million Polish Catholics, and millions of other Slavs, Greeks, Hungarians, Romanians, and other non-"Nordics" whose forebears hadn't had the foresight to reach American shores by 1890. More than three decades later, under the new law, 34,007 immigrants from Great Britain would be allowed through the golden door of liberty each year—joined by fewer than 4,000 Italians, barely 2,000 Russians, and not even 500 Hungarians. It was a result that seemed to have been traced from a stencil provided by Kenneth Roberts in his very first anti-immigrant article in the *Post*: of southern and eastern Europeans, he wrote, "It is no more possible to make Americans out of a great many of them than it is possible to make a race horse out of a pug dog."

From the Prohibitionists' point of view, the Immigration Restriction Act was particularly endearing because they didn't have to expend any political capital to get it passed—it had the support of a coalition so broad you would think Congress was voting to endorse motherhood. House sponsor Albert Johnson of Washington was dry enough. But his Senate cosponsor, David A. Reed of Pennsylvania, was a thoroughgoing wet who said he wanted "to preserve the racial composition of America." The Ku Klux Klan—at this point in its history more concerned about the rising economic and political clout of Catholics and Jews than with any threat from powerless blacks—was of course a strong backer of the act, its leaders ranting about "inferior races" and "European riff-raff." Detroit Klansmen set up an auxiliary organization called the Symwa Club, its ungainly name an acronym for Spend Your Money With Americans. But the American Federation of Labor, led by its wet (and immigrant) president, Samuel Gompers, backed the law as well, in an effort to block the competitive threat of new workers pouring into the American labor market. So did most progressives, both dry and wet ("a great many," wrote historian Arthur S. Link, motivated by their chronic anti-Semitism). In fact, only six senators voted against the Immigration Restriction Act. Such broad support for national quotas enabled Wayne Wheeler and the ASL, who left no legible fingerprints on the legislation, to stay true to their pledge: they were interested only in the single issue of Prohibition. (The ASL had been able to justify its support of the futile alien deportation effort because Prohibition was overtly at its center—violation of the Volstead Act, after all, was the trigger for the measure's penalties.)

But in another legislative struggle that would last the entire decade of the 1920s, involving a clause in the Constitution that had been drafted 130 years before the Eighteenth Amendment, the ASL could not pretend to be above the fray. It was well enough that the Immigration Restriction Act would pay off in the years ahead, as the waning of southern and eastern European immigration would eventually change the complexion of the House of Representatives. A new campaign to block congressional reapportionment after the 1920 census was more urgent: it was designed to protect the dry fortress at that very moment.

THE DRY REFUSAL to allow Congress to recalculate state-by-state representation in the House during the 1920s is one of those political maneuvers in American history so audacious it's hard to believe it happened. In its disregard for constitutional principle and its blatant political intent, it would almost rank with Franklin Roosevelt's Supreme Court–packing plan of 1937—that is, if anyone remembered that it even happened. The episode is all the more remarkable for never having established itself in the national consciousness.

The roots of the drys' reapportionment strategy were embedded in the warnings sounded by Ernest Cherrington and Richmond Hobson as far back as 1915, when they had recognized the need to enact a Prohibition amendment before the 1920 redistricting, which would inevitably favor the cities. Since the Cherrington-Hobson strategy was not an example of democracy at its best—let's change the Constitution before Congress becomes more representative—it's no wonder that both men had kept their communications on the subject private. But in 1917, just days before Congress prepared to vote on the Eighteenth Amendment, Wayne Wheeler went public. "We have got to win it now," he told twenty-five hundred delegates to the ASL's annual convention, "because when 1920 comes and reapportionment is here, forty new wet Congressmen will come from the great wet centers with their rapidly increased population."

Never in American history, not even during the tumult of Civil War, had Congress disregarded the constitutional mandate, enunciated in Article 1, Section 2, to reapportion itself following completion of the decennial census. In each of the three most recent opportunities—1890, 1900, and 1910—the process consumed less than nine months. As late as January 1921, Wheeler himself believed that reapportionment was imminent and warned the ASL faithful to "be on guard." But a threatened majority, like a threatened animal, will do what it can to preserve itself. Between 1921 and 1928, forty-two separate reapportionment bills were introduced in the House. Not one became law.

The principle that bound the foot-draggers together was the obvious one: members from the underrepresented states wanted reapportionment, and those from the overrepresented did not. This of course lined up very neatly with the dry-wet divide in the House, which continued to reflect a rural-urban split. (The same held true in the Senate, where by the chamber's very definition rural states had disproportionate power, Nevada's representation no different from New York's.) The dry congressmen who blocked reapportionment offered arguments dressed in varying degrees of candor. The 1920 census was flawed, said Oscar Bland of Indiana, because men from the farms had been drawn to the big cities during World War I and had not yet returned. James G. Strong of Kansas said he didn't want to "transfer a representative of our form of Government from an American state like Iowa to one where so many do not speak the English language." In 1927 Democratic minority leader Finis Garrett of Tennessee dismissed a nearly successful reapportionment bill as "silly." But it was Representative Ira G. Hersey of Maine who provided a forthright summary of all the prohibitionist objections: he said the failure to pass a reapportionment bill was "simply a silent consent of Congress that they are satisfied with the present apportionment."

"Satisfied with the present apportionment"! It was the equivalent of a jewel thief who'd been sentenced to jail saying he was satisfied with his room at the Ritz. The dissatisfied were those who represented urban America, where, thanks to immigration and increased birth rates, cities were growing even faster than the farm population was shrinking. Detroit provided an outstanding example of the inequities. Its population had doubled between the 1910 census and the unacknowledged 1920 census, but its congressional representation had remained constant; as a result, its two House members represented 497,000 people each, while in the House as a whole the average congressman stood for 212,000. As the decade stretched on, the imbalance only grew worse. By 1929 one of those Detroit districts was home to more than 1.3 million people, while at the same moment ten separate districts in Missouri contained fewer than 180,000 people each. "The situation grows more and more menacing," said Representative Emanuel Celler of Brooklyn, and though this did not trouble the drys, they could not disagree with Celler's conclusion: "It is the city versus the country." That is, the wet versus the dry.

Throughout the decade these egregious imbalances distorted the shape of a legislative body charged with determining the definitions in the Volstead Act, shaping the structure of the federal court system, appropriating funds for a wide range of enforcement agencies, setting penalties for Volstead violators, and otherwise governing the way the Eighteenth Amendment brushed against the life of every American. Shortly before reapportionment was finally enacted in June 1929, effective with the 1932 elections, the editors of the *Washington Post* defined the issue with unimpeachable clarity. "The Constitution can not be violated in this fundamental matter of equal representation," their editorial read, "even at the behest of the Antisaloon League." But it had been, for an entire decade.

IN 1904, when Alfred Emanuel Smith arrived in Albany from the streets of Manhattan's Lower East Side as a newly elected state assemblyman, he was thirty-one years old. His formal education had stopped when he completed the eighth grade, and his working career had largely consisted of the sort of patronage jobs that New York City's Tammany Hall Democratic organization handed out as generously as modern political organizations hand out bumper stickers. Smith did not win his appointment to the committee responsible for banking legislation or to the one charged with writing laws relating to the state's forests because of his experience. "He had been in a bank only once in his life, to serve a jury notice," wrote historian Oscar Handlin, "and he had never seen a forest."

Smith never left the Lower East Side very far behind him. He couldn't lose the accent, which marked his origins as effectively as a neon sign around his neck, and he wouldn't lose his affinity for the slap-on-the-back clubhouse bonhomie that he wore as comfortably as his trademark brown derby. Even when he had to go to one of the black-tie events he was expected to attend after he was elected governor, the famous hat went with him. "Sure, it's my brown derby," Smith told a surprised constituent at a glittery Manhattan theater opening. "Why not?"

But Al Smith rose to the governorship of the nation's largest state on winds more substantial than his easy manner. He was whip smart and leather tough, and though he was steadfast in his support for progressive social legislation and muscular, effective government, Smith also believed those muscles weren't meant to break the bounds of privacy. He did not consider it "the function of law to jack up the moral tone of any community." That, he said, was "the function of the home and the church." In 1923, four months into his second term as governor, he acted on his convictions by signing a bill repealing New York State's "little Volstead" law, the Mullan-Gage Act, which had turned the federal violations spelled out in the original into state crimes as well.

In New York City, at least, Mullan-Gage had been an utter failure. Violations were so rampant, wrote Samuel Hopkins Adams in *Collier's*, "that jurymen would have to be drawn at the rate of 18,000 per day to keep up with the rate of arrests." For the judicial system the strain was unbearable; for the police the distraction from more pressing responsibilities was deplorable. The repeal of Mullan-Gage did not legalize alcoholic beverages in New York, for the Volstead Act remained in force. Repeal only meant that New York police and New York courts, no longer bound by the state to enforce federal antibooze laws, could hand full responsibility over to Washington—"where," said Smith, "it rightfully belongs." If speakeasies kept the racket down and didn't disrupt the peace of the neighborhood, city police left them alone. A sign went up over the bar at Leon & Eddie's, on West Fifty-second Street: "The bar closes at three o'clock. *Please help us obey the law.*"

Other states had already told the feds they would have to go it alone. Massachusetts voters had rejected its state enforcement law. Symbolically, at least, the Maryland Free State remained forever free, its legislators never once approving an enforcement law, its police and courts thumbing their noses at the feds. But New York was different—not just because it was the nation's largest state, but because the repeal of Mullan-Gage was the first time a legislature and a governor eliminated enforcement laws already in place. For all the virtue inherent in the rule of law, Smith had seen plainly that this law, by this time, did not in fact rule, except on paper. "Al is really a very stupid man," an admirer once said. "All he can see is the point."

AS THEIR QUADRENNIAL national convention was about to begin in New York in June 1924, the Democratic Party called upon its faded knight, William Jennings Bryan, to draft a formal tribute to the Republican president who had died the previous summer. "Our party stands uncovered beside the bier of Warren G. Harding," Bryan's memorial statement began—until he realized how that would sound when read aloud. In Bryan's next draft, "bier" became "grave."

Bryan had been brought into discussions of the impending convention by his party's 1920 vice presidential candidate, Franklin D. Roosevelt. In 1923 Roosevelt wrote Bryan about the "hopeful idiots who think the Democratic platform will advocate repeal of the 18th amendment" and wanted to hold the convention in soaking-wet New York. The hopeful idiots won on the geography but hadn't a chance with the platform. Nor did Bryan, who wanted a ringing endorsement of Prohibition nailed into place. Four years into the reign of constitutional Prohibition, the Democrats were so evenly, ferociously, and irretrievably divided over the subject that it turned the convention into a nightmare, the party's presidential chances into dust, and, for the first time since ratification, the debate over Prohibition itself into live political ammunition.

New York, awash in booze, was the perfect place for the story to play out. In his memoirs Izzy Einstein said he and Wheeler discussed plans to keep the convention dry, but such an outcome was hardly likely. The city's taps had been opened wide, warned the federal Prohibition director for New York and Northern New Jersey, "in anticipation of the convention and the expectation of resulting appetitive demands." The director, Palmer Canfield, added another decorative element to his baroque phrasing when he said the increased "liquoral humidity" was inevitable. Canfield also said, "It will be no better and no worse, no wetter and no dryer."

That was certainly true. Official "reception committees" could direct the visiting delegate to Manhattan's five thousand speakeasies; unofficial hosts—hotel bellmen, cabbies, prostitutes—knew where to get a bottle a delegate could enjoy in his room. "Good rye is hardly obtainable," *Variety* had said in one of its regular market reports, so Democrats made do with lesser merchandise. Wet operatives kept dry leaders entertained at endless social events, almost as if trying to seduce them with the wonders of Sodom. The favored presidential candidate of the drys, former Treasury secretary William G. McAdoo, complained to a friend, "Some of my best men have been hopelessly drunk since they landed in New York."

But none of this got in the way of the speedy resolution of the Prohibition plank in the Democratic platform. True to his pattern, Wayne Wheeler opposed Bryan's wish for a strong dry statement and enlisted the support of his emissary to the Democrats, Bishop Cannon. Neither man was willing to risk the possibility of losing in a direct confrontation with the wets. The platform committee quickly agreed on an anodyne promise to "respect and enforce the constitution and all laws." What some feared would blow up the party had turned out to be a hiccup. The heavy artillery was instead expended on another platform issue and on the presidential nomination—two inevitable battles between wet and dry that had led one journalist to say that the Democrats could avert disaster only if they could keep the convention from starting. "Old wounds will be torn open and new ones will be inflicted," Stanley Frost wrote in *Outlook*. "The battle will have a violence and deadliness which may lead to almost any result the most active imagination can conceive."

The volatile platform issue, at least nominally, was the Ku Klux Klan. After the founder of the modern Klan, William J. Simmons, had been expelled from the secret order for chronic drunkenness (he spent his later years in an Atlanta movie house, smelling of bourbon and cloves, as he watched *Birth of a Nation* over and over), the next Imperial Wizard, a Dallas dentist named Hiram M. Evans, ushered in a new emphasis on the anti-Catholic and anti-Jewish parts of its program. This enabled the Klan to break out of the race-obsessed South and spread its influence across the map. The Klan of the 1920s "enrolled more members in Connecticut than in Mississippi, more in Oregon than in Louisiana, and more in New Jersey than in Alabama," wrote historian Stanley Coben. Over half a million Klansmen lived in Illinois, Indiana, and Ohio. Klan-backed candidates, all running on platforms both dry and xenophobic, were elected governor in Oregon, Colorado, and Kansas. In Detroit a Klan candidate whose name wasn't even on the ballot was nearly elected mayor in an avalanche of write-in votes.

Nativism could find no better running mate than Prohibition. In many towns there was little distinction between membership in the Klan and in an ASL-affiliated church. At the national level the Anti-Saloon League did not overtly incite religious prejudice; Wheeler in fact worked to develop alliances with dry Catholics and Jews, and Ernest Cherrington made a conscious effort to keep the ASL's public communications ecumenical. But to men like Roy Haynes, the Wheeler acolyte who headed the Prohibition Bureau, the Klan's vigilant dryness was an exploitable asset.

This became tragically clear in 1923 and 1924 when Williamson County, in southern Illinois, saw its law enforcement apparatus taken over by a vigilante army of between twelve and thirteen hundred Klansmen. Through the intervention of dry congressman Edward E. Denison, the Klansmen had been deputized by Haynes to clean up the county, which had been in the grip of bootleggers. The vigilantes were led by S. Glenn Young, who had earlier been drummed out of his position in the Prohibition Bureau as "a distinct and glaring disgrace . . . unfit to be in government service." After midnight on February 1, 1924, Young's marauders raided the homes of immigrant Italian mineworkers, terrorizing women and children, and, if they found wine in the house, hauling their husbands and fathers off to jail. Rev. A. M. Stickney of the Marion Methodist Church provided ideological support, declaring that Catholics and Jews controlled America's newspapers and insisting that only the Klan could protect America from disaster. Stickney also took pains to note that the assassins of Lincoln, Garfield, and McKinley had all been born Catholic. Marching behind Young, who carried a submachine gun, Klansmen briefly seized control of the local government. Riots punctuated the ensuing war between Klan vigilantes and bootlegger-supported local officials; by its end, twenty people were dead.

As wets at the Democratic convention in June 1924 prepared to introduce a platform resolution condemning the Ku Klux Klan, they did not have to cite the events in "Bloody Williamson." Although the religious, ethnic, and racial prejudices of the Klan were enumerated in the condemnation resolution, there wasn't a soul on the hot and crowded convention floor in Madison Square Garden who didn't know that the fight over the resolution was really a struggle between wet and dry. Southern wets supporting the presidential candidacy of Oscar W. Underwood—the race-baiter who had vanquished Richmond Hobson in the Alabama senatorial primary ten years earlier—voted to condemn the Klan; western drys backing the progressive McAdoo lined up in its support. There were no anomalies, however, in the anti-Klan position of the large cadre of delegates—urban, heavily ethnic, utterly soaked—supporting the third major candidate, Al Smith. But there were not enough Smith and Underwood delegates to carry the day, and the resolution failed by one lone vote, out of

1,085 cast. Asked to explain how the Klan had survived the censure resolution, Imperial Wizard Evans, who had spent the convention monitoring the proceedings from a heavily guarded suite in the McAlpin Hotel, was triumphantly smug: "They were afraid of what we might do."

Al Smith had come to the convention in his hometown as McAdoo's main opponent for the presidential nomination. His repeal of the Mullan-Gage law had made him, as it was expressed in the heaven-rattling testimony of the Reverend Bob Jones, "the worst-hated man in America"—except insofar as the same action had made him, among the wet half of the Democratic Party (and among not a few wet Republicans as well), one of the best loved. The same knife edge on which the Democratic Party was balanced during the vote on the Klan resolution split it asunder during the presidential balloting. A two-thirds majority was required to win the nomination, and neither side would, or could, give in to the other. For sixteen sweltering, contentious days, while wet delegates rose to sing "The Sidewalks of New York" whenever Smith's name was mentioned, and dry delegates wired home for more cash to pay for their hotel rooms, and exhausted newspaper reporters sought relief and distraction in Manhattan's speakeasies and cabarets—during these murderous two-plus weeks, the Democrats went through 103 excruciating ballots before settling on corporate lawyer John W. Davis, a former solicitor general. This was the same man who had once called Wayne Wheeler's predecessor in the ASL's Washington office "a goggle-eyed, weasel-faced lobbyist," but who had also vowed to Wheeler that the Eighteenth Amendment was "a fixed fact" that "has passed beyond the reach of profitable discussion." John W. Davis was neither dry nor wet, nor remotely capable of defeating Calvin Coolidge in November.

From the perspective of a conservative Republican like James Montgomery Beck, the disorganized and disorderly proceedings had proved that the Democrats were "more of a mob than a party." The convention led the genial Will Rogers to famously declare, "I'm not a member of any organized political party, I'm a Democrat." But it was a prophetic and oddly poetic phrase uttered a year earlier by William H. Anderson, an outspoken New York ASL leader, that summarized the lesson of the 1924 convention and simultaneously suggested the future of both the Democratic Party and the Eighteenth Amendment.

"Governor Smith," said Anderson, "is just the kind of man wanted by those who want that kind of man."

Chapter 16

"Escaped on Payment of Money"

I N AN ATTEMPT to memorize poetry," Irving Fisher wrote in 1926, "Professor Vogt of the University of Christiania found that on days when he drank one and one-half to three glasses of beer it took him 18 per cent longer to learn the lines." To an extreme dry like Fisher—which is to say, to an extreme dry who also happened to be one of America's foremost economists—this was a "fact" to fall in love with. Fisher wasn't going to miss the chance to attribute the strength of the U.S. economy to computations made by Professor Vogt during his attempt to master the *Odyssey*, in Norwegian, while a little bit in the tank. He had made a similar calculation in 1919, when he extrapolated from a study showing, he said, that "two to four glasses of beer will reduce the output of typesetters by 8 per cent." From this he determined that withholding those beers from those typesetters, and from everyone else in the American labor force, "will add to the national output of the U.S. between 7½ to 15 billion dollars' worth of product, every year."

Fisher loved to express complexities with numbers, but computation wasn't his only work for the dry cause. He was the drys' leading expert on virtually any subject, before virtually any audience.* He declared himself dedicated to "the abolition of war, disease, degeneracy, and instability of money," and considered alcoholic beverages a contributor to each of these plagues. He gave speeches, testified before Congress, and wrote advertisements, pamphlets, and books about the virtues of the dry laws; in 1928

---

*Expertise, in general, was his stock in trade. Fisher was coauthor of a bestselling hygiene textbook, inventor of a precursor of the Rolodex, founder (with the support of Alexander Graham Bell) of the Life Extension Institute, and a noted eugenicist. He was also considered an expert on the English language. Asked whether "Yes, We Have No Bananas" could be considered grammatically correct, Fisher replied, "Yes, it would be correct, if the statement was preceded by the question 'Have you no bananas?'"

one of the latter, *Prohibition at Its Worst*, was turned into a movie with the counterintuitive title (for modern viewers) *Deliverance*. In the years after ratification, Fisher seemed to find evidence for the wonders of Prohibition behind every statistic he encountered—for instance, the discovery, in 1924, that arrests in New York City for the use of "foul language" had dropped 20 percent since pre-Volstead levels. He was not inclined to consider other causes—like, possibly, a wider acceptance of profanity in the Jazz Age city—when he could grab a number and pronounce it evidence. When Fisher determined that a single drink reduced efficiency by 2 percent, he said that this translated to more than a billion dollars of GNP. Dartmouth professor Herman Feldman, bemused by the unlikely exactitude of Fisher's calculations, said a 2 percent loss in efficiency could instead be the result of "a mere depressing thought."

Fisher was not alone in his attempts to measure the effects of Prohibition with numbers of dubious precision and indeterminate relevance. From Washington came the pronouncements of Prohibition Commissioner Roy Haynes, as jolly as ever: five times as many new houses were built in 1922 as in the last entirely wet year; three thousand people were joining churches every day; in some cities drunkenness among women was down 80 percent. Other dry boosters credited Prohibition for empty prison cells, longer life expectancy, and increased savings rates, not to mention the growing popularity of bowling, which "undoubtedly absorbs not only some of the time but some of the money that was formerly spent on drink." Even an increase in gambling reflected well on Prohibition: criminologist Winthrop D. Lane attributed the gambling spike to "the higher wages earned by boys and young men" after the country went dry.

Dry numerologists might have learned their tricks from the wets. Before the Eighteenth Amendment was enacted, the United States Brewers' Association had been twisting statistics for years. The brewers had smugly noted that per capita savings were lower in states with dry laws, a finding that ignored the obvious disparity in wealth between the wet states of the Northeast and the dry ones of the South and West. The USBA went so far as to argue that the low birth rates in dry states "show conclusively how prohibition lowers the standard of virility." Roy Haynes, observing from the other end of the telescope, claimed Prohibition was responsible for a sharp decline in "arrests for offenses against chastity."

The numbers became a jump ball, each side trying to tip them toward its own goal. Arrest rates for drunkenness? If they were up, wets attributed them to increased drinking, drys to more effective enforcement. Frequency of alcoholism? When Dow Jones president Clarence W. Barron, a wet, told his friend J. H. Kellogg that Bellevue Hospital in New York was treating more alcoholics than it had before Prohibition, the dry Dr. Kellogg divined the reason: "because practically all the other alcoholic wards in New York have been closed and so [Bellevue] gets them all."

Wolcott Gibbs would have had a different take on Barron's news. The satirist invented the "president of the American Institute for the Dissemination of Trivia" to pass judgment on such data: "These figures can be interpreted in only two ways," Gibbs's man said. "Either people are drinking a lot more, or else they don't hold it too good." In fact, one can examine every uninflected statistic that emerged from the 1920s—cirrhosis rates, alcohol-related deaths, incidence of alcoholic psychosis—and it's inescapably clear that Americans *as a whole* consumed less alcohol during Prohibition than before. The outstanding work of economists Jeffrey A. Miron and Jeffrey Zwiebel in the 1980s and 1990s established that "alcohol consumption fell sharply at the beginning of Prohibition, to approximately 30 percent of its pre-Prohibition level," and by the time of Repeal had risen "to about 60–70 percent of its pre-Prohibition level." Tax data collected immediately before and after Prohibition—a precise measurement of alcohol legally purchased—confirms this appraisal.

But national numbers obscure individual behavior. Though many millions clearly lived by the law, those who did not drank more than their share. What Irving Fisher, Morris Sheppard, Ernest H. Cherrington, and other intellectually capable and intellectually honest drys didn't understand was how much those who drank *wanted* to drink, either out of biological necessity, psychological weakness, or free choice. Had they paid attention to the post-ratification experience of the brewing industry, the drys might have recognized the limits of law's ability to defeat appetite.

As in most brewery-related enterprises, Anheuser-Busch had led the way. The technique of removing the alcohol from beer at the conclusion of the brewing process was put to profitable use in 1916 when August A. Busch introduced a "cereal beverage" called Bevo (the name was derived from *pivo*, the Bohemian word for "beer"). Bevo never made much of an impact in the Deep South, where several states banned its distribution. Alabama's statute, for example, prohibited the sale of anything that "tastes like, foams like, smells like or looks like beer," and even proscribed containers that looked like beer bottles, irrespective of what was inside or on the label. But as state Prohibition laws spread through the rest of the country, so did the sales of near beer. By 1918 Anheuser-Busch was producing five million cases a year, and the company built the world's largest bottling facility, at a cost of $10 million, just for Bevo.

By the time national Prohibition arrived, other brewers were jumping into the business. Stroh's Temperance Beer showed up in Detroit. In Brooklyn, Piel's offered three new de-alcoholized beers (Pilsner Light, Dortmünder Golden, and Münchener Dark), advertising them as "new brews with the real pre-war taste." Other brewers aped Bevo in their branding: Pabst created Pablo, Miller weighed in with Vivo, and Schlitz called its entry Famo. The Frankenmuth Brewery in Michigan tried Franko. None could use the vernacular term "near beer," for the Volstead Act expressly forbade the use of the word "beer" on labels or in advertising. The Dick Brothers brewery, in Quincy, Illinois, hurdled this roadblock by naming their offering Nearo. No one thought the Dicks were honoring a Roman emperor.

But none of these companies was prepared for the shock that came after barely six months of constitutional Prohibition, when the market for near beer suddenly flattened, then nose-dived. In the beer-loving cities of the East and Midwest, demand for punchless brews evaporated. By 1923, wrote Ronald J. Plavchan in his authoritative history of Anheuser-Busch, "Bevo sales were almost negligible." The same year, a New Jersey dry named George S. Hobart stumbled across the reason for the collapse. Hobart's local brand, Feigenspan's, was insisting in its advertising that its near beer was "as mellow and tasty as ever," and Anheuser-Busch was claiming, "Same old process. Same old flavor. Same old value." If near beer is just as good as the real thing, Hobart asked ingenuously, then why had the brewers ever bothered to make the real thing in the first place?

It was a question only a nondrinker could have raised. George Hobart meant to demonstrate that the brewers hadn't needed alcohol in their beers after all. Considering the advertising rather than what was actually in the bottle or the barrel, he of course established precisely the opposite. A nation that had consumed an annual twenty gallons of beer *per person* as late as 1914 was indifferent to near beer because "mellow and tasty" were incidental virtues. Beer drinkers wanted alcohol.

Not that this ended up bothering the brewers who had been engaged in the expensive process of de-alcoholizing their Bevos and Famos and Nearos. In no time they turned to a new item that kept the doors of hundreds of breweries open during Prohibition. The wondrous product that put the alcohol back in the beer and the brewers back in the chips was malt syrup, also known as malt extract. A more accurate name would have been "beer starter." With the addition of water, yeast, and time, the syrup blossomed into real, foamy, alcohol-rich beer. And, purchased in its packaged form, pre-fermentation, it was every bit as legal as the grapes that went into homemade wine. For the brewers it was in one respect even better than selling beer, since it enabled them, like the grape growers, to move their merchandise without having to go through the trouble of fermenting and bottling it. "A product that will employ our 1,000,000 bushels of grain tanks is not to be lightly ignored," said August A. "Gussie" Busch Jr., the general superintendent of his father's brewery.

Until they found salvation in malt syrup, brewers had been struggling to reconfigure their facilities for the manufacture of apple butter, cider vinegar, processed livestock feed, or ice cream. For a business that had always been dependent on refrigeration, ice cream made a lot of sense, and Stroh's, among others, stayed in that business for decades after Repeal.* But to the profit-minded former brewer, malt syrup could make ice cream seem about as appealing as turnips. Grocery stores stacked the syrup cans high on their shelves, and thousands of "malt shops" offered filters, bottles, bottle stoppers, yeast, and the syrup itself. Pabst tweaked its famous Blue Ribbon trademark for the new business, offering Pabst Blue Label syrup as well as a premium brand called Pabst Black Label. Anheuser-Busch was more direct, slapping the Budweiser name and logo on its syrup products and on Budweiser Yeast to boot. Soon there were two malt syrup trade associations, a malt syrup trade magazine, and that surest sign of success, an agitated Wayne B. Wheeler, who in 1925 asked one of his friends in Congress if "the time is ripe to prohibit the sale and distribution of these malt sirups and malt supplies."

It wasn't, nor would it ever be. Like the great California Grape Rush, the malt syrup boom could not be quelled. In 1926, five years after the reliably oblivious Roy Haynes had declared that "the home brew fad is taking its final gasp," Anheuser-Busch was selling more than six million pounds of malt syrup annually, a level the company would maintain until Prohibition's end despite the explosive growth of large-scale, mob-controlled brewery operations in some cities in the mid- to late twenties. "If you really want to know," Gussie Busch told an interviewer decades later, "we ended up as the biggest bootlegging supply house in the United States."

DRYS DIDN'T UNDERSTAND DRINKERS, in scores of different ways. Bootleggers and speakeasy operators understood them in the one truly impor-

---

*August A. Busch, whose vast facilities produced glucose, corn oil, infant formula, soft drinks, and a broad variety of other products during Prohibition, entered the ice cream market with a chocolate-coated bar he named Smack.

tant way: drinkers were customers, and had to be treated as such. Whether you were Captain John Simms of Yarmouth, Nova Scotia, who delivered directly to private clients in Greenwich, Connecticut, or the "small pint men" of Athens, Georgia, who banded together to defend their contribution to the community in the pages of the local paper, you recognized that this was a service industry. "A bootlegger is making his money as honest as some of these nice honest-to-goodness people," the Athens group wrote in a letter provoked by threats from the city's mayor. The most accurate summary of this dynamic—"I make my money by supplying a public demand"—was attributed to a young Chicago go-getter named Alphonse Capone.

Had the drys comprehended the fundamental desires of the drinking public, they might have taken a different approach to their presumptive stewardship of the era they had created. Both Richmond Hobson, the highest-paid speaker on the ASL roster, and Ernest H. Cherrington, the league's chief publicist, tried to argue that education was more important than enforcement in the drive to rid America of alcohol—"not by the next general election," Cherrington said, "but by the next generation." But inside the ASL, Hobson was considered a crank and Cherrington could be dismissed as a man of words, not action. The dry movement continued to be dominated by those who demanded action and were able to provoke it.

It was as if the ASL zealots and their sympathizers elsewhere in the movement had come to believe that enforcement of the dry laws was more important than their effectiveness. They were like generals in later, bloodier wars who thought success or failure could be calibrated by body counts. In this war, they believed arrest totals were the paramount goal—both for the aggregated numbers that could be used to excite the faithful and for the discomfort and inconvenience (it was rarely more than that) suffered by the booze purveyors and their customers. As long as bartenders and bootleggers were harassed and punished, it almost didn't matter if they stopped their bartending and their bootlegging. The mania for impressive statistics—numbers of arrests made, for instance—encouraged the Prohibition Bureau to spend its energy pursuing two hundred people with a pint each rather than chasing down a single big-time mobster who was selling his goods to two hundred speakeasies.

In much of the nation harassment, which was easy, triumphed over punishment, which was difficult. One of the nobler aspects of the Volstead Act was its guarantee of the right to a jury trial for anyone charged with a violation. It was a requirement, it soon turned out, that the legal system was incapable of handling. In New York the first four thousand arrests under the Mullan-Gage law (the state version of the Volstead Act that Al Smith soon torpedoed) resulted in fewer than five hundred indictments, which led in turn to only six convictions and not even one jail sentence. Mabel Willebrandt acknowledged that "juries will not convict if the punishment does not fit the crime," and she was proven right in city after city, as juries effectively nullified the law because they didn't think any punishment at all was appropriate for breaking the liquor laws. After Smedley Butler was fired as director of public safety in Philadelphia, he offered a statistic that was simultaneously a boast and an admission of defeat: in two years, his police force had made 227,000 liquor violation arrests. To Old Gimlet Eye, this indicated that his men had nabbed 15 percent of the city's population; to anyone else, it indicated that they had arrested the same people over and over and over again. And again.

No one better understood the causes and consequences of this phenomenon, or did more to expose it, than Emory Buckner, who was appointed U.S. attorney for the Southern District of New York in 1925. Few career paths were less likely than Buckner's. Born the son of an impoverished Methodist minister in Pottawattamie County, Iowa, as a youth he studied shorthand, eventually putting in three years as a court stenographer in the Oklahoma Territory. But at twenty-three Buckner decided to enroll at the University of Nebraska, where his academic brilliance and engaging manner won the attention of Roscoe Pound, dean of Nebraska's law school. Convinced that Buckner deserved exposure to a wider world, he wrote some letters, raised some money, and dispatched his twenty-seven-year-old protégé to Harvard Law School, tuition and some expenses paid.* Pound's instincts were correct: even though Buckner had to work part time as a stenographer to support his young family, in Cambridge his life was broadened by the sort of people he never would have met in Nebraska. Among his closest friends at Harvard, and after, were Elihu Root Jr., who would become Buckner's law partner, and Felix Frankfurter, who would become a Supreme Court justice. Among the clients of his stenography service was Henry James.

Graduating third in a class of 190, Buckner moved to New York. He was as successful there as he had been in Cambridge, and by the early 1920s had become one of the city's most admired and most prosperous lawyers. In March 1925, Harlan Fiske Stone, running a Justice Department that was both tainted by the lingering reek of the Harding administration and

---

*Pound followed him six years later, joining the Harvard Law faculty in 1910 and becoming dean in 1916.

embarrassed by New York's epic lawlessness, asked Buckner to clean things up. "If I am licked," Buckner wrote to his law partners upon accepting the appointment, ". . . I will have the satisfaction of knowing that I was licked by things from the outside and by nothing inside of myself."

Wet in his life and his politics, Buckner swore off his nightly brandy and soda for the duration of his tenure. Yet it would have been understandable if he had been driven back to drink by the corruption, inefficiency, squalor, and rampant injustice he encountered when he took office. "I found that the great United States Court in the Southern District of New York had degenerated," he said. "Not into a police court . . . but into whatever is in the subcellar under a police court." Proceedings were conducted without court stenographers or clerks. Six judges and one magistrate were expected to dispose of fifty thousand cases annually. Even if each had worked full time on nothing but Volstead cases, together they would have been able to handle fewer than four thousand a year—and had they done that, no other federal matter would have been adjudicated anywhere in the district, which stretched all the way to Albany. When in frustration Buckner suggested that prosecutions proceed under police court rules—that is, without juries—he was told this was unconstitutional. Buckner's response was swift: "Apparently it has become easy to amend the Constitution for other purposes."

Even worse than the strain imposed on the courts was the atmosphere surrounding them. The fifth floor of Manhattan's Federal Building, Buckner said, was home to "a seething mob of bartenders, peddlers, waiters, bond runners, and fixers." The fixers, he said, were found even in the men's rooms, attempting to bribe jurors hearing those few cases that made it to trial. In the courtrooms crooked lawyers encouraged perjury. The Justice Department was asking Buckner's office for ten thousand convictions a year—the body count—and the only way to even approach the number was to settle, fast, on reduced charges, a guilty plea, and a modest fine. To the bootleggers, speakeasy operators, crooked druggists, fake rabbis, fallen priests, alky cookers, and various other violators dragged into court, the fines were simply fractional additions to their overhead. "To call such proceedings 'law enforcement' is a farce," Buckner said. "To call such fines 'convictions' is grotesque." He suggested that the notation on a defendant's record should read "Escaped on payment of money."*

---

*An especially vivid demonstration of this phenomenon was revealed in congressional testimony presented in 1926. A man who apparently made his living as a defendant, standing in for actual lawbreakers, was shocked to learn that a zealous prosecutor had arranged to have him sentenced to three days in jail. "Now, my contract was to appear in court, answer the

The court situation in New York was possibly more sordid than it was elsewhere in the country, but it was far from unique. Beyond the nickels devoted to the Prohibition Bureau, the resolutely dry Congress, in league with the falsely dry Harding and the hypothetically dry Coolidge, had appropriated virtually nothing to support the legal apparatus that such a radical change in the criminal law required. When Mabel Willebrandt took over her "division" of the Department of Justice, a full nineteen months after the Volstead Act had gone into effect, the staff consisted of four people, Willebrandt included. Congress created no new judgeships, authorized no new positions for U.S. attorneys' offices, and appropriated no money for new federal prisons—of which there were, as late as 1925, exactly three.

By one accounting, U.S. attorneys across the country spent, at minimum, 44 percent of their time and resources on Prohibition prosecutions—if that was the word for the pallid efforts they were able to sustain on such limited resources. In North Carolina and West Virginia, the federal prosecutors devoted 70 percent of their time to Prohibition violations; in Minnesota, 60 percent; in southern Alabama—where Mabel Willebrandt would directly supervise one of the most aggressive enforcement efforts in the nation—Volstead prosecutions consumed a staggering 90 percent of the federal docket. In wet New Jersey, prosecutors addressed the overload with a modus vivendi that made Willebrandt despair: they would "please the Drys by filing cases," she recalled years later, "and take care of the Wets by never bringing the cases to trial."

In state courts the prosecution of local ordinances and statutes took on one of two humors—either a vigor that outshone federal efforts or something close to torpor. The first condition did not necessarily arise from earnest devotion to the law. In many states Prohibition was a profitable venture even for those local law enforcement officials who didn't accept bribes. Under Indiana's "Wright Bone Dry Law," lawyers accustomed to a five-dollar-a-day fee for prosecuting capital cases were rewarded with a bounty of twenty-five dollars for every Prohibition conviction. In Seattle, where the docks teemed with bootleggers unloading their boats into waiting trucks in the middle of the day, King County sheriff Claude G. Bannick, whose office split fines fifty-fifty with local justices of the peace, worked out a mutually beneficial arrangement: violators were always fined, never jailed, so they could be set free to violate once again—to the profit

---

calendar, and pay a $100 fine," he told the judge, "but not to go to jail. I was not the man at all. I was never arrested in my life.'"

of Bannick and the JP's. Ohio, so often the trailblazer in novel applications of dry theory and practice, attained a dubious pinnacle in its pursuit of lawbreakers. Small towns and villages were authorized by law to operate "liquor courts" run by local officials, few of them judges. The law also directed that more than half the revenue from fines was paid out to the presiding official and the town. But what gave the Ohio system its special piquancy was a provision in the statute granting each liquor court jurisdiction not just within its own village limits, but anywhere in its county. This brought out the entrepreneurial gene in many local officials, like those presiding over the tiny community of North College Hill, whose 1,104 residents happened to share Hamilton County with the heavily German, thoroughly wet, and very large city of Cincinnati. Like a land-bound privateer, Mayor A. R. Pugh personally led North College Hill's raids into neighboring jurisdictions, netting more than $20,000 in revenue for his village (and himself) in one period of less than eight months. The mayor knew he could count on the cooperation of the town prosecutor and the town judge, because he held both of those jobs, too.

By 1927 the dwindling number of states still spending any money on Prohibition enforcement together appropriated less than 15 percent of what they allocated for the enforcement of fish and game laws. In the resolutely wet cities and states, where targeted spending was nonexistent, local enforcement ran the gamut from ineffectual to ridiculous. It was almost as if much of the country was returning to the pre-1920 days of local option, when a particular locality could decide at the ballot box whether to be dry or wet. The Eighteenth Amendment had taken away the voters' legal right to make such a choice, but the Constitution could not compel either citizens or officials to see what they chose not to see. "Under the old local-option plan a community decided whether or not it would have liquor," Samuel Hopkins Adams wrote in 1921. "Under the new it decides whether or not it will have the law."

Various cities and states declared their options publicly. In 1927 a report prepared for the Connecticut Department of Labor contained the sort of boast one wouldn't really expect from a government office: "Connecticut industries rank high, have world renown, and even its bootlegging industry is credited with greater reliability and more reasonable prices than that of other states." The following year the Detroit Board of Commerce released survey data indicating that the city's illicit alcohol trade employed fifty thousand people and racked up $215 million in annual sales, making it the city's second largest industry (and this didn't include the estimated $2 million paid annually into a "graft trust" that was shared by a group of roughly one hundred Prohibition agents). The auto industry, of course, was Detroit's largest by a huge margin. But relative to the rest of the competition alcohol did quite nicely—the chemical industry, which ranked third in its contribution to the local economy, was responsible for just 40 percent of the economic activity generated by the booze business.

No survey could determine the wettest city in the country, but there were several contenders for the title. New York was an obvious claimant, but Emory Buckner would develop a few new law enforcement strategies that actually paid off from time to time. After Chicago's wet, corrupt, and mob-backed Big Bill Thompson was returned to the mayor's office in 1927 ("When I'm elected," he promised, "we will not only reopen places these people have closed, but we'll open 10,000 new ones"), the nation's second-largest city might well have become its wettest. But during the four-year tenure of mayor William E. Dever and police chief Morgan A. Collins— "these people," in Thompson's phrase—the mob's base of operations had been pushed into suburban Cicero, periodic sweeps had temporarily put a stopper in parts of the booze trade, and Collins could receive a letter like this one, from an officer of the Mid-City Trust & Savings Bank: "This has been the cleanest, soberest day (Monday) that we have enjoyed in this Bank for four years. Every Monday we have from 50 to 100 drunks after their money. To-day we had only two partially drunk customers. Now spike the rest of the Bungholes for keeps. Yours for a clean city, C. L. Sayler."

Like Emory Buckner, Dever thought Prohibition a bad idea but felt duty-bound to enforce it. Politicians and prosecutors of similar inclination held office in most American cities at one time or another during Prohibition, forcing long stretches of uncontrolled wetness to yield periodically to recurring bouts of at least nominal dryness. Usually the outcome resembled what had happened in New Jersey, where Colonel Ira L. Reeves had been responsible for a burst of intensified Volstead enforcement. Reeves's bitter self-evaluation was concise. He hadn't gotten rid of liquor at all. Instead, he wrote, "I had raised the price of alcoholic beverages and reduced the quality." But in at least four major cities—Baltimore, San Francisco, New Orleans, and Detroit—not once was there a lull in the wet storm that blew in on the heels of the Eighteenth Amendment.

Baltimore had all the ingredients. It was a port city, with a large Catholic population, no state enforcement law, a semiofficial bootlegger operating inside the State House in Annapolis, and a famously corrupt police department that also happened to be a model of collective efficiency: speakeasy operators who made regular payments to a "fund for disabled policemen" were excused from any court proceedings. Baltimore also had

H. L. Mencken leading the wet cheers in his column in the *Sun* and spreading the word to his prominent friends. To F. Scott Fitzgerald, who was living in Paris at the time, Mencken wrote, "Baltimore is now knee-deep in excellent beer. I begin to believe in prayer." To Bishop James Cannon, with whom he had struck up an unlikely friendship, Mencken explained that no, it wasn't true that a stranger could walk off the street into a bar anywhere in Baltimore and be served instantly. "You would have to be introduced," Mencken said, "by a judge, a policeman, or some other reputable person."

San Francisco was a contender for many of the same reasons: working port, large Italian and Irish populations, corruption that reached into the highest echelons of the federal enforcement effort, and a you've-gotta-be-kidding-me disdain in the local version. Colonel Ned M. Green, federal Prohibition administrator for northern California, was a self-professed drinker eventually indicted for diversion of seized liquor. (Although he was known for the whiskey- and champagne-laced dinners he hosted at his suite in the Whitcomb Hotel, Green insisted that the incriminating evidence had actually been provided him by "friends with a mistaken idea of kindness.") Judge Sylvain J. Lazarus was known to order police to return confiscated bottles to their original owners, and the San Francisco County district attorney did double duty as an officer of the local branch of the Association Against the Prohibition Amendment. The city's proximity to the nation's most fecund grape-growing regions added to the moisture. According to Sonoma County winemaker Antonio Perelli-Minetti, San Francisco was "the only place in the United States where the distribution of wine was practiced without guns," because trash collectors had taken on responsibility for delivering demijohns brimming with California red and picking up the empties. No less an expert than General Smedley Butler, visiting San Francisco on New Year's Eve 1926, observed the partying crowds tumbling out of the city's big hotels and said he had "never before witnessed such an orgy."

Sociologist Martha Bensley Bruere, who collected data from ninety-two cities for her 1927 book, *Does Prohibition Work?* (conclusion: sort of), placed the crown for wettest city on another heavily Catholic port, New Orleans. "There is general disregard of the law and scorn for it," Bruere wrote. "Most of the men drink something every day." Izzy Einstein, who always measured how long it took him to procure liquor in any city he visited, would have agreed; the cabbie who picked him up at the New Orleans train station offered to sell him a bottle just thirty-five seconds after pulling away from the curb. When Georges de Latour divided up the market for sacramental wines and hired agents to represent Beaulieu in various parts of the country, he made sure to keep the lucrative Louisiana market for himself. Much of the hard stuff in New Orleans came from neighboring St. Bernard Parish, where Sheriff L. A. Mereaux—a graduate of Tulane Medical School who lived in an 1808 mansion with its own private racetrack—collected a toll on all the bootleg booze passing through his jurisdiction. Visiting New Orleans in 1927, Michigan lawyer Lloyd T. Crane sent a postcard of the landmark Old Absinthe House to his friend Judge Arthur J. Tuttle: "From appearances," he wrote on the back, "it is the only place where liquor is not sold here."

But the champion had to be the heavyweight in Tuttle's own jurisdiction, Detroit. By the time the Board of Commerce designated bootlegging the city's second largest industry, Detroit had already lived through ten years of experience as the "City on a Still," as historian Larry Engelmann called it. The two years of state Prohibition that had preceded the federal variety had accelerated a process that would become familiar in most other American cities: a brief period of law observance followed by a spasm of illegal importing, a futile tremor of enforcement, and finally a sustained deluge inundating the entire city. From across the river in Windsor came as many as half a million cases of liquor a month, most of it either dispatched by the Bronfman brothers in sealed railroad cars bearing forged documents, or ferried over in the hundreds of small boats that made up the so-called Mosquito Fleet. The Mosquitoes were more dangerous than the name might suggest. The boatmen were often armed and willing to shoot it out with the understaffed and underequipped Detroit branch of the U.S. Customs Service, which for a time had responsibility for patrolling a hundred miles of waterway, from Lake Erie to Lake Huron, with just three boats and twenty men. There were reports of a pipeline leading directly from the Hiram Walker Distillery on the Canadian side to some unknown spot in Detroit (probably untrue), and of a motorized cable pulling a pair of sled-mounted containers from an uninhabited Canadian island at the northern end of the river to a waterside house in Grosse Pointe Park (almost certainly true). The Ambassador Bridge, spanning the Detroit River, and the automobile tunnel beneath it opened in 1929 and 1930, respectively, both of them privately financed creations of Prohibition. "In less than three years," wrote Malcolm Bingay of the *Detroit News*, "around $50,000,000 was spent so that people could get back and forth—quickly—between Detroit and our ever-kind liquor-supplied neighbors of Windsor."

For a lot of the booze flowing across the river, Detroit was only a way station. An estimated 1,500 to 2,000 cases of liquor went on to Chicago daily, mostly under the auspices of an intercity criminal alliance forged between Al Capone and Detroit's infamous Purple Gang. What stayed behind, plus what emerged from the hundreds of illicit distilleries and breweries scattered around southeastern Michigan, was sufficient to stock the back bars of the speakeasies, blind pigs, and beer flats that multiplied like mushrooms—Detroit had 7,000 of them by 1923, three times as many by 1928 (one journalist counted 150 on a single, soaking block). On New Year's Day 1924, the front page of the *Detroit News* reported that 100,000 drinkers had clogged the city's downtown business district in a "carnival of drunkenness" the night before, their "ribald cries and profanity" a sure sign that "it was drink, drink, drink everywhere." Soon Detroit's legitimate restaurant business began to collapse in the face of the untaxed, unregulated competition. In time, so many waiters, waitresses, cooks, and other restaurant workers fled for jobs in the prospering speaks and pigs that the AFL-affiliated Hotel and Restaurant Employees union had to shift their organizing efforts to places that, under the law, did not exist.

Local judges yawned at the liquor laws. In the summer of 1923 a prosecuting attorney showed up in a Detroit courtroom to tell Judge Edward J. Jeffries that the evidence in a bootlegging case—a large quantity of seized liquor—had mysteriously disappeared from police headquarters. "That's a poor place to bring liquor," Judge Jeffries told the prosecutor as he dismissed the case. Clarence Darrow, in Detroit two years later to defend a black man in a controversial murder trial, spent his lunch hours drinking with judges and other officials at Cohen's speakeasy near the courthouse. Unwilling to leave the building on the day the case went to the jury, Darrow and his colleagues waited for the verdict while sharing a supply of Scotch in an adjacent courtroom that had been unlocked by an obliging court officer.

Enforcement did take place in Detroit; it just didn't have anything to do with drinking. A succession of mayors and police chiefs would occasionally crack down on places that were disorderly, or fostered criminal activity, or belonged to an ugly category known as "school pigs," sleazy operations set up near high schools. But any establishment that obeyed the rest of the criminal code—all the laws that had nothing to do with Prohibition—was left alone. Mayor John W. Smith was a progressive, good-government Republican who came to believe Prohibition was "a tragic joke." Running for reelection in 1927, he openly declared he would not enforce any wet laws, yet he won the support of some of the city's most notable citizens, among them architect Albert Kahn, auto magnates Fred J. and Charles T. Fisher, and the city's greatest athletic hero, Ty Cobb. Smith ended up losing to a dry, John C. Lodge—but in Detroit "dry" was a relative term,

which Lodge made clear when he said he intended to be "practical" in his enforcement policy. Which meant Detroit stayed wet.

To Judge Tuttle, trying to keep up with an exploding docket in federal court, the situation in southeastern Michigan was an outrage made worse by the indifference of local officials. The federal presence in Michigan was limited to just three federal judges, two U.S. attorneys, two federal marshals, and a local office of the Prohibition Bureau that was underfunded and wracked by corruption. A note from a woman complaining about bootlegging in her neighborhood provoked Tuttle to spill out his frustrations in a lengthy letter. There were hundreds of state judges, hundreds of state prosecutors, and thousands of local cops, he told her, yet everyone seemed to expect him to enforce the law on his own. "The people seem to be turning to the Federal Government and expecting Uncle Sam to do everything," he wrote. Why didn't she ask her local police to do their jobs? To Michigan's attorney general, he bitterly complained that Volstead cases had been "crowding all other classes of business out of my court."

At least Arthur J. Tuttle's frustrations never approached those that afflicted his Minnesota colleague, federal district judge John F. McGee—the "bootleggers' terror" who had commandeered sightseeing buses to ship Volstead violators off to jail. "The fact is that the United States District Court has become a Police Court," McGee wrote from his chambers in 1925. Eighty percent of the cases brought before him were Prohibition related, he added, "with the end not in sight. I started, in March 1923, to rush that branch of the litigation and thought I would end it, but it ended me." Then McGee put down his pen and blew his brains out.

THE TENSION BETWEEN federal and state enforcement programs could not be resolved. Nor could the burden on the federal courts be relieved. Emory Buckner's friend Felix Frankfurter proposed that the federal system confine its efforts to interstate violations and illegal imports, "leaving to the states all intra-state violations of the law." This sort of federal focus might have imperiled, or at least diminished, the cross-border smuggling business. But the medicinal alcohol market, the sacramental wine scam, the booming wine grape business, the malt syrup bonanza, and large portions of the enormous industrial liquor·racket would have enabled New York, Baltimore, San Francisco, et al., to remain exactly as they were: open cities with open taps. Yet even if a plan like Frankfurter's could have been effective, it could never have pleased the drys, who remained as committed to notional enforcement as they were to the authentic variety.

The disharmony created by federal effort at its most earnest and local resistance at its most craven resounded most strikingly in Mobile, Alabama. Its status as a port with a majority Catholic voting population had long made Mobile an exotic presence in Alabama. During the push toward state Prohibition in the first decade of the century, Mobilians made what a contemporary journalist called "a spectacular but ineffectual threat" to secede from the state rather than submit to a dry law. They really needn't have bothered; until 1923 state and federal Prohibition disturbed the liquor trade in Mobile about as much as it disrupted the caribou business in the Yukon. A version of Rum Row operated offshore in the Gulf, moonshine from stills scattered across the southern Alabama countryside flowed straight downhill to the black part of town, and members of the city's political and commercial establishment profited from a protection racket that would have been impressive in Detroit or Chicago. Dry resistance, such as it was, was centered in the St. Francis Street Methodist Church, where in 1924 members of the Men's Club heard a visiting politician chastise them for their inaction against corruption and liquor. "Wrong cannot exist when men and women take up the banner of Christ," the visitor said. He challenged them not to "sit supinely" while depredation ravaged their city.

The speaker was thirty-eight-year-old Hugo Lafayette Black, brought to town as a special prosecutor by Mabel Willebrandt. He had not yet begun his passage from loyal member of the Ku Klux Klan to champion of individual rights on the U.S. Supreme Court. Dry both personally and politically, he had been the scourge of Birmingham at the onset of statewide Prohibition nine years earlier, when as the chief prosecutor of Jefferson County he had subdued bootleggers and saloon operators by summoning moralistic passion and exceptional legal skills. As a local judge, he handed out maximum sentences as if they were business cards. Like Gifford Pinchot's enforcement agents in Pennsylvania, who were paid by the WCTU, on this new assignment Black had to get his first few paychecks from the Mobile Citizens' League until the Justice Department figured out how to compensate him.

Black arrived in Mobile on the heels of another unlikely character dispatched by the attentive Willebrandt: Izzy Einstein. During his extended stay in the city, "the Sherlock Holmes of the prohibition enforcement officers," as the *Mobile Register* called him, penetrated every aspect of the city's liquor business. He rolled out his usual set of disguises—in his career he'd posed as a farmer, a streetcar conductor, a gravedigger, an opera singer, and countless other types—but the Mobile assignment didn't require his usual subterfuge. "Izzy believes that his Hebraic personality and his for-

eign accent are invaluable assets in his work," the *Register* reported. "In nine cases out of ten," Einstein told the newspaper, "I am taken for granted as a traveling salesman. I just happen to be that type." The worst part of his stay in Mobile was gathering the evidence. "This is just my first experience with southern shinny," he said. "Just tasting it made me violently ill." But he never had the opportunity while in Mobile to utter the famous words he always used when revealing his identity to an unsuspecting bartender or beer peddler: "There's sad news here. You're under arrest." Given the length of the investigation and the size and influence of the quarry, Einstein had to stay under cover until the task was complete.

That happened on November 13, 1923, when a regiment of federal agents armed with eighty-five search warrants swept across Mobile. A month later, U.S. attorney Aubrey Boyles obtained indictments against 117 people, among them a bank president, a prominent shipbuilding executive, the Mobile County sheriff, five deputy sheriffs, one state legislator, several lawyers, at least one physician, a member of the county revenue board, and Mobile police chief P. J. O'Shaughnessy, who on the day the indictments were handed down tried to escape to friendlier environs. O'Shaughnessy said he'd decided to take a train to New Orleans because he wanted a drink.

Bringing in a prosecutor with Hugo Black's talent, experience, and dedication to the dry cause was a smart move on Willebrandt's part, but she didn't do it because she was dissatisfied with Boyles, the sitting U.S. attorney. She had no choice but to import legal talent after the Mobile political establishment came up with a clever way to derail the federal prosecution: they arranged for local officials to arrest Boyles for attempted bribery.

Following nine months' effort on the part of Attorney General Harlan Fiske Stone, the ludicrous charges brought against Boyles were vacated. But so was the conviction of one of the Mobile ringleaders, Frank W. Boykin, a businessman and political fixer who would later serve fourteen terms representing Mobile in the U.S. House of Representatives. When a telegram that Black sought as evidence turned up missing, the future congressman told the court, "I ate it." After two trials, a jury heavy with Klansmen finally gave Black sustainable convictions of several key figures in the Mobile case—a feat that led directly to his election to the U.S. Senate and in turn to his eventual elevation to the Supreme Court.

TO EMORY BUCKNER, New York City's police department could be less cordial or cooperative than some of the bootleggers he tried to shut down (one of those he convicted, a large-scale operator named "Big Bill" Dwyer, told Buckner while the jury was out, "You know, while you were speaking, I thought to myself, I really *should* be convicted"). Mabel Willebrandt, who was sympathetic to Buckner, figured that each of the thirty-two thousand speakeasies in New York probably paid a beat cop five dollars a day to keep the taps and the cash register open. Her estimate was wildly low for speaks located in midtown Manhattan, where protection money could run to $150 a week, leading the operators of the Bath Club and other upmarket spots to form a sort of bribery collective, paying off the authorities from a common pool of money. But even so, Willebrandt's calculations were eye-popping. "It is clear," she said, "that if the police of New York City, and some of the politicians who control their appointments, are not collecting at least one hundred and sixty thousand dollars a day or sixty million dollars a year from the speakeasies alone, they are either very honest or very stupid. Take your choice!"

Roy Haynes's force of federal agents may have been just as corrupt, but unlike the city cops they at least had to go through the motions to keep their jobs. The thousands of Volstead violators left unmolested by the NYPD were instead rounded up by Haynes's men, who delivered them by the wagonful to the badly degraded Federal Court in downtown Manhattan. This led an exasperated Buckner to concoct an opportunity that quickly became known as "Bargain Day." Publicly promising to request light fines in exchange for guilty pleas, he invited defendants to the Old Post Office Building south of City Hall, where his staff, working with two cooperative federal judges, could process five hundred cases at a time and clear up the backlog. This early example of plea bargaining was cemented into American legal practice when the Supreme Court affirmed its constitutionality in 1930—in the words of legal scholar Jason Mazzone, writing in 2009, a "momentous development" in American criminal law.

Buckner also perfected a widely used procedure that enabled him to avoid the criminal court process entirely. Under the federal civil code, any structure identified as a "common nuisance" could, upon issuance of an injunction, be seized under the legal doctrine of civil forfeiture and closed for an entire year. Buckner reached into his pocket for $1,500 of his own money, handed it to four young lawyers on his staff (including John Marshall Harlan, who would be appointed to the Supreme Court thirty years later), and sent them out to collect evidence at the city's speakeasies. After buying a few drinks, they needed only swear to a judge they had done so, and they'd instantly have an injunction in hand. Within hours court officers would visit the offending establishment and clamp a padlock on the door. Although Buckner's "Four Horsemen," as they were inevitably called, succeeded in closing down such high-end establishments as the Colony Club and the Club Deauville, they were shut out when Judge John C. Knox told Buckner he didn't much like the idea of padlocking the Hotel Astor. Buckner obligingly withdrew that request, but the procedure soon became so familiar that Billy Rose produced a Broadway revue called *Padlocks of 1927*, with a cast that included a young hoofer named George Raft and the raucous speakeasy hostess Texas Guinan. Guinan, who famously greeted her customers with a loud "Hello, suckers!," took to wearing a necklace of padlocks from time to time.

Emory Buckner knew that padlock raids were never going to dry up New York. According to historian Michael Lerner, they just changed the nature of speakeasies: when Buckner's men were on the prowl, speakeasy operators stopped investing in fancy interiors and fixtures, opting instead, as *The New Yorker* put it, for "the informal conjunction of a back parlor and a bucket of paint." But even if padlock cases didn't stop the flow of liquor, they consumed very little time or effort. When coupled with the efficiencies achieved on Bargain Day, they enabled Buckner's men to turn their attention away from petty cases and toward the big-time bootleggers who were exercising increasing control over the New York market.

This was what concerned Buckner most. Reluctant dry he may have been, but he could not disguise his alarm at the growing muscle being wielded by large-scale criminal enterprises that were fueled by liquor money. To go after them, he believed, it was necessary for law enforcement officials to forget about the raw numbers of arrests and convictions that were longed for by the dry establishment. "It seems an impossible thing to persuade those who want law enforcement that what is required here in this district is less enforcement," he told friends. His goal, Buckner said, was to "make an effort to stop 49 arrests out of 50, and yet mak[e] the fiftieth more effective than all combined."

Buckner's plan made sense. It was endorsed by Mabel Willebrandt, who had long thought the Prohibition Bureau would be far more effective if it aimed its efforts at the generals instead of the foot soldiers, mess cooks, and camp followers clattering along behind the big bootlegging syndicates. But when Buckner gave an interview to an inconsequential new magazine—it was the nine-month-old *New Yorker*—he made the mistake of saying, "The man who buys liquor when he is thirsty for it is not a criminal in the sense that a check forger or thief is a criminal." He was further reported to have said, "I have no particular quarrel with him."

As a result, Buckner got into a quarrel with a more potent adversary.

Two days after the magazine appeared on newsstands, Wayne Wheeler was in the White House. Buckner's apostasy had led Wheeler to complain formally to President Coolidge and to make sure his displeasure was known to the press. "He is becoming a regular visitor," the *Times* reported, oddly surprised, "and today he was the first on the list of White House callers." Wheeler's widely publicized visit compelled Coolidge to let it be known that the White House could not possibly countenance a policy that suggested possession of illegal liquor was not a crime. Wheeler gloated. Buckner, whose regard for Coolidge was slight, nonetheless disclaimed his "no particular quarrel" comment, and in the following week's issue *The New Yorker* chastised him for allowing Wheeler "to stampede him into half-hearted retreat."

Not that it made any difference. In that same issue, the magazine's regular feature, "The Liquor Market," reported that a case of Scotch could be obtained for something between $50 and $70, imported gin was holding at $65, and champagne was up to $80 to $120, "depending on reliability and brand." Overall, prices remained "steady, but subject to inflating by individuals." The price gouging resulted not from shortages brought on by padlock raids or by the crackdown on the syndicates. The higher prices showing up here and there, the magazine concluded, were simply "due to pre-holiday and football demand."

Chapter 17

Crime Pays

W AYNE WHEELER RARELY had much trouble with congressional committees. When he wanted a change in
the law—the banning of medicinal beer, say, or tougher
penalties—he could count on one of his Capitol Hill allies to serve up a
hearing custom made for a Wheeler star turn. When those hearings were
momentarily seized by a wet representative or senator trying to pillory
Wheeler and the ASL, he still managed to perform with poise. By nature a
polite and cordial man, at times even jovial, he was as cool under pressure
as he was hot when applying it. He didn't even complain in 1922 when
Representative George Tinkham, a big-game hunter from Massachusetts,
tried to mount Wheeler's head on his wall.

The superwet Tinkham, who once said he considered Wheeler's "very
presence in the Capitol an offense against decency," compelled him during
a committee hearing to read aloud a lengthy list of wet political committees, by way of demonstrating the alleged breadth of opposition to Prohibition. Wheeler could have been reciting a school honor roll as he tripped
amiably through the list: "The American Liberties League . . . the Constitutional Liberty League . . . the Light Wine and Beer League of America . . . the National Order of Camels . . ."—no explanation asked, none
given—"the Self Determination League of Liberties . . . the Sanity League
of America . . . the Auxiliary of Caravans for Women, Order of Camels . . ."
It was likely that some of these groups had fewer members than syllables
in their names. When the hearing concluded, Wheeler noted that portions
of the proceedings were hardly germane. But, he said, he had wanted to
demonstrate his willingness to cooperate.

Wheeler's adroit manipulation of congressional opponents finally
failed him in April 1926. A subcommittee of the Senate Judiciary Committee convened that month ostensibly to consider various amendments

to the Volstead Act. No one believed that was its actual mission. For one thing, the likelihood of any moderating amendment getting through the still-dry Senate was nil. For another, one of the five members of the subcommittee was H. L. Mencken's "supreme artist of assault," the ungovernable James A. Reed of Missouri, who treated his political enemies as if they were fish he had landed. He'd inflict as much pain as he could as he yanked out the hook.

Back when Reed compared Andrew Volstead to "the burners of witches," he had won the unprecedented censure of the House of Representatives (by a vote of 181–3). Reed loathed the League of Nations, despised woman suffrage, and detested the "snooping spinsters" who supported federal aid to state maternity programs. Oswald Garrison Villard, editor of the *Nation*, said, "No other public man has such a mastery of bitter sarcasm, or is a better hater" than Jim Reed. If there was anyone in public life Reed hated more than Wayne Wheeler, he managed to keep it a secret.

In the 1926 hearings the "truculent Senior Senator from Missouri," said the *New Republic*, "assumed with his usual lordly manner the real leadership of the wet cause in Washington." As a member of the Senate's Democratic minority, Reed did not control the subcommittee's gavel, but he nonetheless dominated the hearings, which the *New York Times* called "a war of words as bitter as any Washington has known in a generation." Over three long weeks of testimony he elbowed aside the other subcommittee members, all of them drys. At times Reed demonstrated why he was called "the Bellowing Bull of Missouri"; at other moments he filleted dry witnesses with a stiletto; and when friendly wets stepped up to testify, he displayed the manners of a maitre d', presented with the charm of your favorite uncle.

The wet witnesses and their sympathizers took the stage first. The opening lines of this tightly scripted drama were delivered by Senator William Cabell Bruce of Maryland, who would soon celebrate the marriage of his son David to Andrew Mellon's daughter Ailsa at a lavish and evidently dry reception. (This might have been why Bruce called Prohibition "a blight upon the entire joyous side of human existence.") But he had more practical reasons for opposing it as well: most of the $443,839,544.98 in liquor tax revenues the federal government had collected in the last fully wet year, he said, was now going into "the pockets of foreign and domestic lawbreakers." Reed gave a great deal of time to the testimony of Emory Buckner, whose criticism of the underfunded and ill-designed federal enforcement effort was both informed and eloquent, and he welcomed twenty congressmen from New York City, Albany, and Buffalo who dropped by en masse from the opposite wing of the Capitol Building to condemn the ASL and make the case for the legalization of light wines and beer.

The wide berth Reed gave wet witnesses turned claustrophobic when it came time to hear the parade of drys summoned by his colleagues. When Patrick H. Callahan, a varnish manufacturer from Louisville, stepped forward in behalf of the Association of Catholics Favoring Prohibition, Reed made certain to find out how many members the organization had (320) and how that compared to the number of Catholics in the United States (an abashed Callahan was forced to admit there were something between eighteen and twenty million). The unprepossessing Fred T. Smith, chairman of something called the Citizens' Committee of 1000 for Law Enforcement, hardly fared better. Pressed by Reed to state his occupation, Smith said, "I preach law enforcement and patriotism and religion up and down the country, and sell asbestos when I have a little extra time."

Reed pushed dry witnesses as if they were playthings and pulled them as if they were taffy, taking so much time with his questions, his badgering interjections, and his own speechifying that the briefly rebellious majority members of the committee voted to grant the drys extra time because Reed had consumed so much of it. Bishop Cannon, Ella Boole of the WCTU, a black woman named Marie Madre-Marshall "representing," said another dry witness, "the 15 million colored people who have suffered from lack of enforcement"—for seven long days the drys took their places at the witness table to offer their fervid testimony, to endure Reed's unrelenting inquisition, and, happily or not, to adorn the front pages of newspapers across the nation. Each morning crowds lined up hours before the hearing room opened; the small portion that managed to squeeze in—maybe a third of those waiting—were treated to the Jim Reed Show, which they watched either in strangled horror or with unchecked awe. The only light moment came when Reed, his blue-gray eyes wide with theatrical innocence, asserted that he himself was impartial and only trying to find out the facts. The anxious and tired crowd exploded in tension-relieving laughter. Reed immediately reached for the acid; their outburst, he said, was "the laughter of fanatics and fools."

The hearings, said the *Times*, were "the all-absorbing topic of comment and debate" throughout Washington. By the time the third week began, the coming confrontation between Jim Reed and Wayne Wheeler was anticipated in drawing rooms and on street corners, a heavyweight contest with more explosive potential than any battle the Prohibition debate had produced. Wheeler had been taking his place in the front row of the audience every day, to provide support for his fellow drys and also because Reed refused to let him know on what day he might be asked to testify. Wheeler was not well in the spring of 1926; doctors had diagnosed chronic heart trouble, he told a colleague, caused by "long years of overdraft on my reserve force." When the committee was not in session, he remained in bed at his apartment near the National Zoo. He "looked like a corpse," a colleague would recall, "haggard, weary, and spent."

Finally, on a Saturday that the *Times* expected to culminate in "a spectacular war of words between Mr. Wheeler and Sen. Reed," the last half of the last scheduled day of hearings arrived. By then the committee had spent fifteen days taking more than 1,400 pages of testimony from 133 witnesses. It was shortly after the lunchtime recess when Wheeler finally settled in his chair at the witness table and began to read his prepared remarks. He took most of an hour to present his rebuttal of the wet witnesses. He attacked the unfaithful Emory Buckner, he challenged the licentious pro-beer congressmen, and he defended a federal police apparatus that had been assaulted by several witnesses who were part of that apparatus. Crime may have been rampant, and illegal liquor may have been everywhere—Wheeler could hardly deny it. But that did not mean he lacked an explanation. In one sentence near the end of his speech he alit upon a formulation on which one could have balanced the entire war between the wets and the drys. "The very fact that the law is difficult to enforce," said Wayne B. Wheeler, "is the clearest proof of the need of its existence."

At least he didn't have to endure much in the way of questions. Jim Reed had not bothered to come back after lunch.

REFLECTING ON THE two years he had spent teaching school back in the 1880s, Wayne Wheeler once said, "No one can hold the confidence of his pupils or associates who cannot keep a smiling exterior, no matter how disturbed he is inside." Reed had scratched Wheeler's smiling exterior and disturbed his insides so severely that he traveled to Battle Creek for a three-week rest cure as soon as the hearings ended. His friend Dr. Kellogg prescribed green vegetables, fig bran, and three or four enemas a week at bedtime. Wheeler was wary when he returned to Washington and told Scott McBride it had proved impossible to "overdraw on [my] health account for twenty years and get it back in [just] twenty days."

Jim Reed, of course, couldn't have felt better. Writing in 1943, the dry publicist Ernest Gordon described the critical impact of the hearings: they "gave the impression that Prohibition," for the first time since its enactment, "was not a settled question." That may not have been Reed's primary intention—he doubtless would have been gratified simply for having inflicted punishment and provoked humiliation—but there was no question that he had turned Prohibition, six years into its dominion, from a fact into a debate. It was a change of circumstance so delightful he immediately hopped aboard another Senate committee, this one investigating campaign spending, and zeroed in on the finances of the ASL and other dry groups.

Reed's most gleeful moment in these proceedings may have come when he forced one of Gifford Pinchot's advisors, whose salary was paid by the Pennsylvania WCTU, to admit that the governor's WCTU-funded field agents were each spending eight to ten dollars a day on drinks while gathering evidence—all the more impressive when you consider that a shot of rye in a Philadelphia speakeasy went for just fifty cents. But that was sideshow. The earlier hearings had altered the rules of engagement between wet and dry. Where the discussion had previously concerned the evils of alcohol, the Reed Committee forced a change of subject. At issue was not the law itself, or the reasons for the law, but what the drys insisted was the *enforcement* of the law. Ten years earlier, "submission"—as in, submission to the states for ratification—had been the euphemism congressional drys had used in place of the scarier "Prohibition." Now "enforcement," or in formal usage "law enforcement," became the stand-in for the real issue that propelled the Prohibition wars: who would control the country, the wets or the drys?

From the dry perspective, the power of the enforcement trope lay in its incontrovertibility: who could be against law enforcement? This was especially the case as the criminal activity that had blossomed at Prohibition's dawn—largely local, infrequently violent—multiplied in scale and in carnage. It wasn't as if the police sirens and the tommy guns hadn't sounded before 1926; the *New York Times* wrote about the new-style gangster as early as 1923 ("He shoots from ambush, and preferably at backs"), and in 1924 Senator Frank L. Greene of Vermont was severely wounded in a crossfire between Prohibition agents and bootleggers just blocks from the Capitol Building. But by mid-decade the trials of George Remus and, later, "Big Bill" Dwyer—the New York bootlegger who claimed Emory Buckner had almost convinced him of his guilt—revealed criminal operations of a size and sophistication Americans had never known.* And as often as the drys used the rise of organized crime to underscore the need for Prohibition, the wets used it to demonstrate Prohibition's failure.

It was true that criminal activity had been "organized" before Prohibition; in 1919 Henry B. Chamberlin, director of the Chicago Crime Commission, noted that "modern crime, like modern business, is tending toward centralization, organization, and commercialization." But Prohibition offered a graduate course for training in the crime industry. John Torrio, originally from Brooklyn, began to bring Chicago mobsters into the illegal liquor business on a large scale (with the assistance of another Brooklyn import, twenty-year-old Al Capone). Until then the Torrio operation had largely devoted its organizational skills to running gambling operations and brothels, many of whose managerial requirements—servicing a wide range of locations, handling large sums of money, seeing to the safety of one's allies and the discomfort of one's foes—were identical to those required by the booze trade.

But those earlier businesses had not required the transportation and distribution networks that would make crime not only organized but interregional. First, Torrio, Capone, and similar entrepreneurs across the country needed vehicles. In New York, Meyer Lansky launched his bootlegging business from the car and truck rental operation he ran from a garage underneath the Williamsburg Bridge. Once the mobsters had wheels, they still had to build alliances with confederates in distant cities. Chicago's supply of Canadian whiskey arrived courtesy of the efficient forwarding services of Detroit's Purple Gang. Boo Boo Hoff needed western associates to unload and distribute the goods he shipped by rail from Philadelphia to St. Louis and St. Paul. Moe Dalitz's operation in Cleveland, using planes as well as boats, ferried Bronfman liquor across Lake Erie—"the Jewish lake," bootleggers called it—and distributed it through a network that included various Ohio and Pennsylvania affiliates, as well as Lansky's New York operation. After internecine warfare and a more effective Coast Guard crippled Rum Row, Massachusetts had to get its liquor via an eight-hundred-mile overland corridor from Detroit. During his

---

*The Dwyer trial involved sixty defendants, including thirteen Coast Guardsmen and a rising young hood named Francesco Castiglia, who were charged with a conspiracy that reached as far as the Gulf and the Pacific Coast, and was alleged to have been responsible for millions of dollars in smuggled liquor, official corruption on a grand scale, and twelve deaths. Dwyer served barely a year in prison; Castiglia, who would soon become known as Frank Costello, was the beneficiary of a hung jury.

Mobile investigations, Hugo Black established that the city's bootleggers had business relationships with mobsters in Detroit and Chicago.

These alliances were the first manifestations of a crime syndicate operating on a national scale. In time they became the foundation of multilateral "peace conferences," such as the 1929 meeting in the Hotel President in Atlantic City, when mobsters from Chicago, Cleveland, Philadelphia, Newark, and New York granted each other territorial exclusivity, enabling them to operate unencumbered in their respective cities. Eventually this sort of arrangement would harden into formal partnerships, such as the cartel established by Lansky and his fellow New Yorker Lucky Luciano, Abner "Longy" Zwillman of Newark, Charles "King" Solomon of Boston, Daniel Walsh of Providence, and a few others who together would control the entire bootleg business from Boston to Philadelphia. They fixed prices throughout their territory, struck an exclusive distribution deal with their Canadian suppliers, and rewarded John Torrio for brokering the arrangement by granting him a fungible inventory of five thousand cases of liquor a month.

Most of the actors on this lucrative stage were young men who had seen opportunity and grabbed it. By 1926 Lansky, already running his "most efficient international shipping business in the world," was only twenty-four years old. The elegant Longy Zwillman, who eventually would sell his legal post-Repeal distribution business to his pre-Repeal trading partner Sam Bronfman for $7.5 million, was either twenty-two, twenty-three, or twenty-seven, depending on which of his birth certificates you consulted. Luciano was twenty-seven, and so was Capone. The image of Capone refracted through decades of popular culture gets jarred somewhat when his age is factored in: he was only twenty-five when he took over Chicago from his mentor Torrio, was fundamentally gone from the city before he turned thirty, and when he emerged from his eventual prison sentence a syphilitic wreck, he was only forty.

Despite their youth, their ghetto origins, and the fact that they were by any measure engaged in criminal activities, an odd respectability accrued to many of these mobsters. In some places their ethnic loyalties and their hatred of dry vigilantes led them to take part in anti–Ku Klux Klan campaigns. They also acquired a certain glamour from their involvement in the entertainment industry; Longy Zwillman had a very public romance with Jean Harlow, and several big-time mobsters owned popular nightclubs. The New York thug Owney Madden (whose romance with Mae West led her to describe him as "sweet, but oh so vicious") opened the

Cotton Club in a nightspot he had taken over while serving a manslaughter sentence in Sing Sing.

Capone was especially mindful of his public image. Thanks to newspapermen who were either amused or seduced by his accessibility, Chicagoans knew that Capone extended charity to the poor and shared his house on South Prairie Avenue with his siblings and his widowed mother. When Chicago got too hot for him and he sought repose in Miami Beach, Capone announced that he intended to join the Rotary Club. Some might have disputed his description of himself as a "public benefactor," but few could have disagreed when he said, "I give the public what the public wants. I never had to send out high pressure salesmen. Why, I could never meet the demand." He had a point: if you separated the customer service aspect of the bootlegging business from the other pastimes that engaged the mobsters, they could seem about as criminal as a group of jaywalkers. The bootleggers, wrote historian Mark H. Haller, "had customers, not victims." Whoremongers brutalized the women who worked for them, and numbers racketeers and gambling house operators took an extortionate cut off the top, but except when they were pouring colored industrial alcohol into Haig & Haig bottles, the bootleggers gave their customers exactly what they wanted, at a price no one was forced to pay.

The money to be made by violating the Eighteenth Amendment's proscriptions against the sale, manufacture, and transport of intoxicating liquors was spectacular. Emory Buckner believed annual sales of bootleg liquor had reached $3.6 billion nationally by 1926. By way of comparison, that was almost precisely the same as the entire federal budget that year—army, navy, and every other government function included. In 1925 the Bureau of Printing and Engraving printed nearly $300 million more in large-denomination bills than it had in 1920. "What honest businessman deals in $10,000 bills?" Fiorello La Guardia asked the Reed Committee. "Surely these bills were not used to pay the salaries of ministers." Instead, the abundant cash bought armor-plated automobiles (Capone's cost the 2009 equivalent of $350,000), solid silver toilet seats (that was the prize possession of Chicago bootlegger Terry Druggan), and, by the truckload, cops and politicians and judges.

Political corruption had been baked into the system almost from the beginning. Early Prohibition directors for New York and Pennsylvania—a judge and a state senator, respectively—were under indictment within a year of assuming their jobs. On the very day that the director for the Ohio region, former congressman Joshua E. Russell, was telling an audience at the Sidney Baptist Church that "we are now engaged in a struggle with the forces of lawlessness in an effort to sustain the majesty of the law," he and his top aide were in the process of diverting 22,416 gallons of alcohol from a distillery in Troy, Ohio.

Russell served two years in prison for his crimes. So did John W. Langley, a bone-dry congressman of expansive girth and melodious diction who was known in his eastern Kentucky district as either "Promissory John" or "Pork Barrel John," for the vows he made to his constituents and for his ability to fulfill them. On a congressman's annual salary of $7,500, Langley managed to deposit $115,000 in his bank account over a three-year period in exchange for arranging the release of a million gallons of "medicinal" liquor to New York–based bootleggers. He was reelected despite his conviction; then, after losing his appeal and entering prison, his wife was twice elected in his place.

Yet even if the stench of corruption did not linger around some of the politicians who extracted profit from Prohibition—a man who delivered jobs, projects, and pork to his district could be forgiven much—their coconspirators came from a shadowland filled with nightmares for dry and wet alike. The cash that went into the bank account of a popular politician was easily ignored by complacent voters, but the liquor money cascading through the bootlegging industry and into the hands of mobsters—all of it untaxed, of course—also underwrote the expansion of associated rackets like gambling and loan-sharking; created opportunities for new ones, like money laundering; and funded escalating arms races whenever treaties crafted by criminals (you take the north side, I'll take the south) broke down and gave way to intramural gang wars.

Unable to turn to civil authorities to settle disputes, the mobsters had to find other means of conflict resolution. Seattle bootleggers sought to forestall discord when they convened in a ballroom at the New Washington Hotel in 1922; operating under Robert's Rules of Order, they fashioned an agreement to set prices and establish other forms of self-regulation (no doubt impressing an out-of-town associate, Sam Bronfman, who had dropped in on the meeting). In Philadelphia, conflicts between rival gangs were arbitrated in a netherworld one of the local papers called "Racketville," a sort of parallel City of Brotherly Hoodlums with its own mob-selected judges, lawyers, and others "rendering decisions which [its] vassals must obey without question."

But in most cities such civilized proceedings were unknown. The warfare that led to 215 mob killings in Chicago in one three-year period was a direct by-product of broken contracts that did not lend themselves to polite resolution. Clarence Darrow, who despised Prohibition (and was known to represent the occasional indicted bootlegger), gave the best explanation of the bootleggers' dilemma. "The business pays very well," Darrow said, "but it is outside the law and they can't go to court, like shoe dealers or real-estate men or grocers when they think an injustice has been done them, or unfair competition has arisen in their territory.

"So," Darrow concluded, "they naturally shoot."

SOME HISTORIANS ARGUE that our sense of epidemic violence in the 1920s is a distortion fostered by Hollywood. In fact, it did increase by quite a bit, from slightly less than twelve murders or assaults per hundred thousand population in 1920 to sixteen in Prohibition's last year, 1933 (and then subsided to fewer than ten by 1940). But if you had been reading the newspapers of the age, you might have felt the rise in violence was even steeper. When Prohibition was inching toward birth in the summer of 1919, an institution that would grow stronger with every bloody manifestation of the liquor wars also came into being: the American tabloid press, born with the launch of the New York *Daily News*. Seeking to build readership on the trail of bodies that Prohibition left in its wake, "the newspapers began talking about [gangsters'] hiring of *torpedoes, trigger men, gorillas,* and *rods,*" wrote lexicographer Stuart Berg Flexner, and "their use of *pineapples* . . . and *Tommy guns.*" Bishop Cannon condemned the press for "the sewage which pours into our homes almost daily from the[ir] columns." But you could move a lot of papers when the front page was painted with gun battles, sordid deaths, and mob funerals like the one that sent off Brooklyn gangster Frankie Yale. Laid out in a $15,000 silver coffin, accompanied by a cortege of more than two hundred limousines (thirty-eight of them packed with flower arrangements), and guarded by a hundred city cops, Yale starred on front pages all the way to California.

Although the papers made celebrities out of the gangsters, they did not fail to suggest the causal relationship of the Prohibition laws and the bloodshed, not least because wet papers realized that linking the Volstead Act to murderous violence could help the wet cause.* This wasn't hard to do: from the assassination of Dion O'Banion in his Chicago flower shop

---

*The very few dry papers in major cities included the *Des Moines Register,* the *Los Angeles Times,* and the *Brooklyn Eagle.* Another, the *Detroit Free Press,* started off dry but in 1925, wishing to "save the youth of the nation from its present position," declared its earlier stance "a fearful error."

in 1924 through the St. Valentine's Day Massacre five years later, the most famous killings of the era were ignited by alcohol. With 3.6 billion untaxed dollars at stake, how could it be otherwise? Owney Madden once said, "I like an investment where you can put your money in this week and pull it out double next week, or the next." To secure a cash flow like that, murder could seem like bookkeeping—just another thing you had to do to keep your business on track.

ON FRONT STREET in New Bedford, Massachusetts, you didn't have to go far to find entertainment in the early 1920s. Out in the harbor most mornings, a small fleet of motorboats buzzed and roared from Pope's Island to Fort Phoenix and back. They may have looked like bees roused from a hive, but on some days they made a sound that suggested some sort of nautical Armageddon. That was because many of the boats were equipped with full-throated Liberty V-12 engines that you could buy from the federal government for one hundred dollars each, delivered in their original crates. A few years earlier, the four-hundred-horsepower Libertys had powered American military aircraft; now, converted to maritime use by the speedboat racer Gar Wood and other entrepreneurs, the Libertys that had been on the assembly lines when the war ended had become the sine qua non of the rum-running fleet.

As the New Bedford rumrunners prepared to put on their daily harbor show, you could walk along the wharves and see them engaged in congenial conversation with Coast Guard officers. One local boy recalled a guardsman bumming a cigarette from a former fisherman. "Thanks, Charlie. See you tonight," the guardsman said. The rumrunner replied affably, "Not if I can help it." This was characteristic of the early days of Rum Row, just as it would have been in western border towns, or on the waterfront in Windsor, Ontario, or in the woods of northern New England. "We knew the officers and they knew us," a Vermont bootlegger told an interviewer. "You know, the same as you know football players on another team, something like that."

But by mid-decade the value of the goods afloat on American coastal waters had brought a vicious element into the rum-running business: nautical auxiliaries of the violent urban gangs. For crewmen on the mother ships, the days when your customers would bring you groceries or carry your mail ashore had given way to fear-filled nights. The sanguinary chill that settled over Rum Row had been signaled by the scuttling, in 1923, of the *John Dwight,* a 107-foot steam trawler hauling a Canadian cargo of Frontenac Export Ale ("Contains all the alcohol needed for long sea travel," the label read) through "Rum Lane," near Martha's Vineyard. The bodies of eight *Dwight* crewmen were later found in the surf off the Vineyard hamlet of Menemsha. Three had had the skin stripped from their faces. Others had had their eyes burned out, their fingerprints scarred beyond recognition by acid. The son of the *Dwight*'s captain was found adrift in a dinghy, his skull fractured, his body wedged beneath a seat. One of the dead men was known to have been carrying $100,000 in cash for an impending purchase.

From the earliest days of Rum Row, there had been the threat of hijackers looking to commandeer a boat and seize its cargo. But a duffle filled with bills was much easier to handle than a hold jammed with beer, so the early breed of seagoing thieves was soon supplanted by men like those who ravaged the *John Dwight*, predators more interested in cash than in cargo. These pirates, known in the trade as "go-through guys," needed to have decent intelligence sources—disloyal crewmen were prime informants—but beyond that they required only a small boat, a few weapons, and murderous intent.

In time these freebooters were themselves put out of business by the big syndicates, which were savvy enough to remove cash from the equation and powerful enough to scare off freelancing pirates. Contracts were consummated when the captain of the cargo ship and the men receiving the goods on shore could match the halves of a dollar bill that had been torn in two by their respective employers. "Rum running has altered almost unbelievably," reported the *New York Times* in late 1924. "The rules are changed. The amateur is no more."

Given the congenital ineffectiveness of the federal enforcement effort, the big-time smugglers could not have been prepared for the government response to the professionalization of Rum Row: for virtually the only time in the fourteen-year Age of Volstead, federal officials rose to the enforcement challenge. The fleet of fifty-five seaworthy vessels the Coast Guard had had at the beginning of Prohibition had grown somewhat, but was as able to cover 5,000 miles of saltwater coastline, plus another 1,450 miles of shoreline along the Great Lakes and the St. Lawrence River, about as effectively as a napkin could cover Nebraska. Calvin Coolidge's unexpected request for additional funds reflected how grave the situation was. Heeding the words of the Coast Guard's founder—the original Guard, Alexander Hamilton had said, was meant to be a "show of force" directed at "the fraudulent few"—Coolidge suppressed his chronic parsimony and asked Congress for a supplemental appropriation of $14 million to expand and modernize the fleet. Heeding the words of Wayne Wheeler (the boats of Rum Row, he wrote, had been conducting "a practical attack on our sovereignty" by "shooting actual holes in our Constitution"), Congress obliged.

Soon four thousand new guardsmen that Wheeler characterized as "incorruptible" were assigned to twenty reconditioned destroyers and three hundred brand-new small craft. Within months the beefed up "Dry Navy" seized three British rum-running boats in international waters in the North Atlantic, and scores of smaller vessels were apprehended and impounded up and down the Atlantic and Pacific coasts, along the Gulf of Mexico, and in the Great Lakes. In May 1925 an operation that became known as the "Great Offensive" dislodged fifty mother ships from the section of Rum Row that ran from Block Island to Brooklyn. And on the West Coast, what might have been the single most successful bootlegging operation in the nation foundered on the shoals of a new law enforcement technique called wiretapping.

But in the end, additional expenditures and focused effort were not enough. Except for wiretapping, each of these developments turned out to be less effective than it had first appeared. (This should not have been a surprise; even the twelve-mile limit extracted from the British through strenuous negotiation had not worked out, for it required the Coast Guard to patrol a vastly increased area.) Most of the ships chased away from Rum Row retreated to Canada, where their suppliers were led to devise new ways of getting their product to the U.S. market—chiefly, in the case of the Bronfman brothers, by the much more efficient shipment of goods by train through Ontario and across the river to Detroit (or, as Sam Bronfman always called it, "the Windsor market"). The seizure of the three British rumrunners provoked a new outbreak of diplomatic friction with the United Kingdom. Most of the impounded inshore boats, sold at government auction after the conclusion of legal proceedings, were simply repurchased by their original owners, who were usually the only bidders, as if by tacit agreement among the rum-running syndicates. In a single year the steamer *Underwriter* was seized four times, auctioned four times, and returned four times to its role as a rumrunner at the eastern end of Long Island Sound.

The four thousand new uniformed seamen in the Coast Guard, who were working for thirty-six dollars a month plus room and board, found it difficult (if not pointless) to remain incorruptible, and the newspapers were awash in reports of misdeeds, court-martial, and convictions. In 1928 the secretary of the Elks Lodge in Niagara Falls, New York, who had no liquor in his possession and no previous record, was fatally shot through the head after he was apprehended by a Coast Guard crew. "I would not have shot him, and probably you would not," said a philosophical Seymour Lowman, the assistant secretary of the Treasury ultimately responsible for Prohibition enforcement, "but you want to recollect that the men engaged as Coast Guardsmen there are not college professors or lawyers."

Even the well-funded development of the Guard's swift new boats miscarried. Required to make its specifications available to any boatyard interested in bidding on the construction contracts, the government was effectively providing blueprints to the rumrunners, who paid the very same boatbuilders to design vessels that could outrun the ones they were building for the Guard. The Freeport Point Boatyard on the south shore of Long Island built fifteen vessels for the Coast Guard and thirty for the rumrunners they were supposed to chase down, including a trio of forty-two-foot boats for the notorious bootlegger Dutch Schultz, each one equipped with three Packard Liberator 500-horsepower air-cooled engines, bulletproof gas tanks, and room for 600 cases of liquor. On a larger scale, by 1930 a 150-foot blockade runner equipped with diesel engines, Maxim silencers, shortwave radio, armor plating, and a capacity of 8,000 cases could be had for $100,000. At a gross profit of $1 per bottle, any self-respecting bootlegger could have made back virtually his entire investment on a single run.

Just as World War I had accelerated the evolution of airplane technology, the battle between the rumrunners and the Coast Guard provoked the rapid development of powerboat design. The motorized version of the nimble Jersey Sea Skiff, with a nearly flat hull that enabled it to run its payload right up on shore, was a Prohibition product. When the New Orleans levees were breached during the Great Mississippi Flood of 1927, the first rescue boats on the scene were the exceptionally speedy craft developed for, and operated by, upriver bootleggers.

Rumrunners also copied the design of a famous boat celebrated for its speed, and according to the *New York Times* they intended to improve it by equipping it with machine guns. In this particular instance, the Coast Guard eventually acquired the legendary speedster by seizing it from hijackers who had been preying on rumrunners operating near Coney Island. Like its original owners, who were interested only in cash or hostages, the Coast Guard was not concerned with cargo capacity; speed was everything, and this vessel was the fastest boat in the water. Once it became government property, it was known as CG-911; before that, it had earned its reputation with a name that would in time signify thousands of boats built to a modernized version of its revolutionary, Prohibition-bred design: Cigarette.

AS THE 1920S rolled forward, accompanied by the roar of hyperthyroid speedboat engines and punctuated by the rat-a-tat of the Thompson sub-machine gun (during World War I it was called the "Trench Broom"; now it became known as the "Chicago Typewriter"), virtually the only good news for the party of enforcement came from an unlikely place: the United States Supreme Court.

Despite Elihu Root's failed effort in 1920 to persuade the Court that a constitutional amendment could be unconstitutional, wets had hung their hopes for judicial sympathy on a Court that seemed genetically sympathetic to their cause. Before his appointment as an associate justice, Louis D. Brandeis had lobbied the Massachusetts legislature in behalf of the state's breweries, and the ASL, in its maiden venture into Supreme Court politics, had actively opposed his confirmation. Justice Harlan Fiske Stone was a connoisseur of fine wines—he had a 1912 Chateau Ausone in his collection, and a 1916 Beychevelle—who had earlier tried (vainly) to move the contents of his cellar from New York to Washington when he was appointed attorney general; late in life, he would contemplate the unkind destiny that had "inflict[ed] public office and prohibition on me at one and the same time." The court's senior member, Oliver Wendell Holmes, was known to appreciate his whiskey (in 1927 he registered his gratitude for an illegal gift bottle with a characteristically Holmesian aphorism: "I have not forgotten the prayer 'Lead us into temptation'"). And a bloc of archconservative justices led by the reactionary James C. McReynolds was instinctively aligned with James Montgomery Beck and other legal theorists who so loathed the authority of the federal government they would have strangled it had they had the chance.*

But wets hoping for a Supreme Court hostile toward Prohibition

---

*McReynolds, who had been appointed by Woodrow Wilson, hated Prohibition—but hatred was his defining characteristic. Unembarrassed by his virulent anti-Semitism, he not only refused to speak to Justice Brandeis (and, later, Justice Benjamin Cardozo), but he turned his back to them when they spoke during oral arguments. He displayed his consuming misogyny by doing the same to Mabel Willebrandt and other female attorneys who appeared before the Court.

enforcement had placed most of their optimism in the capacious lap of the chief justice, former president William Howard Taft. The Anti-Saloon League loathed him (an ASL publication once referred to him as "the huge, beer-swilled Taft"). Adolphus Busch, whose personal lawyer, Charles Nagel, served in Taft's cabinet, considered him a friend and ally (and offered Taft $50,000 a year to assume the presidency of a St. Louis bank after he left the White House). In his last month as president, Taft had vetoed the Webb-Kenyon Act and its restrictions on the interstate shipment of liquor. Congress overrode his veto, but until the Eighteenth Amendment was ratified, Taft did not moderate his views on constitutional efforts to limit alcohol consumption. Not only did he once declare Prohibition "unenforceable," he also believed it "would put on the shoulders of the Government the duty of sweeping the doorsteps of every home in the land. If national prohibition legislation is passed, local government would be destroyed."

Coming from a professor at Yale Law School—Taft's home between his presidency and his appointment to the Court—this seemed a clear statement of belief, suggesting emphatic support for strong proscriptions against unreasonable search and seizure, and for the prerogatives of local authority. But Taft also believed that the citizen who obeys only laws that he endorses "is willing to govern, but not be governed"—willing, in other words, to destroy the rule of law. Consequently, Taft led a fairly stable bloc of justices who rendered a series of decisions expanding the power of the federal government, over the generally consistent objections of McReynolds and his conservative allies. Two key decisions weakened the Fifth Amendment. In 1922 the Court brushed aside the amendment's proscription against double jeopardy, declaring that the Eighteenth Amendment's "concurrent power to enforce" clause allowed Prohibition violators to be prosecuted in both state and federal courts for the same violation unless Congress enacted legislation barring the practice. Five years later the justices found that requiring a bootlegger to file a tax return on his illegal earnings did not infringe on the Fifth Amendment's protection against self-incrimination.*

But it was the Fourth Amendment's bar against unreasonable search

---

*This case, *United States v. Manly S. Sullivan*, became the foundation of the government's eventual conviction of Al Capone for income tax evasion. It also provoked from Justice Holmes a bemused consideration of the defendant's argument that requiring the filing of a return for illegal income would logically entitle the filer to deduct illegal expenses, such as bribery. Wrote Holmes, "This by no means follows, but it will be time to consider the question when a taxpayer has the temerity to raise it."

and seizure that captured the Court's attention most firmly, and led it, in twenty separate cases between 1920 and 1933, to a broad-strokes rewriting of a century's worth of Supreme Court jurisprudence. The theory behind the Fourth Amendment, which dated back to the colonial era, was embedded in the primacy of the rights of the individual vis-à-vis the powers of the government, and particularly protected the sanctity of the home. During the latter part of the nineteenth century and into the twentieth, it had been judicially extended to foster the freedoms of a laissez-faire economy, shielding businessmen from raids on their premises. But once Prohibition was in place, judges realized that tight limits on searches crippled the government's ability to enforce the Volstead Act. Long-honored restraints on police authority soon gave way. In a *New York World* cartoon by Rollin Kirby, a figure representing the Eighteenth Amendment was shown lynching a representation of the Fourth, with a delighted member of the ASL looking on. Defendants played an active role in this explosion of Fourth Amendment jurisprudence as well: big-time bootleggers could afford expensive lawyers who could chase a case up the judicial ladder to the Supreme Court. The *Cyclopedia of Law and Practice*, published in 1910, gave 15 pages to discussion of searches and seizures; its 1932 successor required 114. Eventually, half of the training classes given to new Prohibition agents were devoted strictly to search-warrant requirements and procedures. In an era when possession seemed ten-tenths of the law, cellars and suitcases and speakeasies and cars no longer appeared to be quite as sacrosanct as they once had seemed.

Especially cars. In some cities they were mobile taverns, their proprietors parking outside factory gates, peddling shots of liquor for twenty cents apiece and speeding off at the first scent of an honest Prohibition agent. As early as 1915 William Jennings Bryan had made the case that the danger of an automobile driven by an inebriated person negated the "personal liberty" argument against Prohibition—when a drunk could take to the streets behind the wheel of a powerful machine, Bryan argued, the health and safety of the driest teetotaler was placed at risk, rendering the driver's rights irrelevant. Drunk driving in fact skyrocketed during the 1920s (in Chicago it multiplied nearly fivefold). This was accurately attributed to the steep increase in the number of cars on the road, but writing it off strictly to that was like blaming the size of an influenza epidemic on population growth. And no one disputed the role of cars in the gangster-dominated bootlegging business and the protection their operators were afforded under the Fourth Amendment. Writing to his brother Horace in 1925, Chief Justice Taft insisted that "the automobile is the greatest instrument for promoting immunity of crimes of violence . . . in the history of civilization."

His letter to Horace was a preview of the decision the Chief Justice, speaking for the Court, would issue the next day. In *Carroll v. United States*, Taft dismantled a constitutional roadblock in favor of a literal one, declaring that Prohibition agents no longer needed a warrant to stop and search a car they believed to be carrying contraband liquor. One justification for this "reasonable" search: the Oldsmobile roadster in *Carroll* was proceeding westward from Detroit, wrote Taft, "one of the most active centers for introducing illegally into this country spirituous liquors for distribution into the interior."

THE RUM ROW that developed along the Pacific Coast never quite grew to the size of the fleet stationed along the Atlantic seaboard and the Gulf of Mexico, nor did the traffic ever become quite as deadly. The West was much less populated than the East, of course (in 1930 there were over a million more people in New York City than in all of California), and robust domestic production in northern California kept the Coast's thirstiest city, San Francisco, stocked with wine. But the Pacific states did have their own version of Detroit in the far Northwest, where spirituous liquors stored near the docks in Vancouver and Victoria could be shipped across the Strait of Juan de Fuca, saturate Seattle, and flow all the way down the coast to Los Angeles. The unlikely figure dominating this trade was Roy Olmstead, who became known locally as "the good bootlegger" and nationally as the appellant in what was arguably the most important and farthest-reaching Supreme Court decision that emerged from the fourteen years of Prohibition.

Olmstead had entered public life as a promising member of the Seattle Police Department, praised by the department's very dry chief as "quick and responsive . . . bright and competent." But Olmstead's competence extended beyond ordinary police work, and while still a member of the department—he had been named a lieutenant when he was only thirty—he began running liquor from Canada. Roy Olmstead was handsome, personable, intelligent, and remarkably ethical. He never diluted his imports or blended them with industrial alcohol as so many other bootleggers did, and he dealt in such volume that he was able to undersell every other bootlegger in the Pacific Northwest. Historian Norman H. Clark wrote that Olmstead "avoided the sordid behavior of others in the same business—no murder, no narcotics, no rings of prostitution or gambling"—and, as a result, "many people could not regard him as an authentic criminal." The *Seattle Post-Intelligencer* explained his popularity: he "served a social purpose."

In time, Olmstead moved out of the retail business, effectively becoming wholesaler to most of the bootleggers in Greater Seattle. He established the city's first radio station, and although Olmstead later denied it, Mabel Willebrandt believed the bedtime stories Olmstead's wife read over the air "constituted code signals to the boats at sea, advising them when the coast was clear and where the Coast Guard boats were likely to be." He bought a grand house in the Mount Baker section of town and socialized with the city's leading figures, who considered him good company. Even more, they considered him useful. In the frescoed dining room of the Arctic Club, Olmstead's services were all but invaluable.

But the Seattle office of the Prohibition Bureau was the personal property of Senator Wesley L. Jones, the very dry Senate majority whip. Determined to arrest and prosecute Olmstead, dry agents in Seattle brought in a gentleman named Richard Fryant to help build their case. Olmstead considered federal agents "too slow to catch cold," but they were nimble enough to realize that Fryant had a practical, and novel, skill: he knew how to tap telephones. Soon the bureau had a collection of transcripts that may have read like a bad film script ("I have seen Doc and all is OK"), but nonetheless helped smother Olmstead and his associates under ninety-one separate indictments.

When he was attorney general, Harlan Fiske Stone had declared that Justice Department personnel (including members of J. Edgar Hoover's brand-new Bureau of Investigation) were forbidden to use wiretaps, which he considered unethical. But Stone had no authority over Treasury Department personnel, including Prohibition agents, nor was his proscription enforced by his successor at justice, John G. Sargent. Still, Mabel Willebrandt, who would normally have represented the government before the Court, declared that she "thoroughly disapproved" of wiretapping tactics, and could not in good conscience argue the case. The solicitor general brought in outside counsel, and Chief Justice Taft led a 5–4 majority that found private telephone communication between two individuals no different from casual conversations overheard in a public place.

"Can it be that the Constitution affords no protection against such invasions of individual security?" asked Brandeis. For the first time, the Court said it did not.

◆　　◆　　◆

THE LAW MADE in *Olmstead v. United States* stayed on the books until it was overturned in 1967, when the only dissenting vote was cast by the old Prohibition prosecutor, Justice Hugo Black. Law yet more enduring was made by Brandeis's *Olmstead* dissent, in which he articulated a constitutional "right to be let alone"—words invoked by the majority nearly half a century later in *Roe v. Wade.*

At the time, though, the most striking response to *Olmstead* came from the Anti-Saloon League. Extracting the gist of comments made by S. E. Nicholson, the ASL's New York superintendent, the *Times* summarized the league position: "It is feared by the dry forces that Prohibition will fall into 'disrepute' and suffer 'irreparable harm' if the American public concludes that 'universal snooping' is favored for enforcing the Eighteenth Amendment." Said Nicholson, "We do not favor the decision unless it is to be interpreted as applying to all criminal cases of every kind." It was an impossible position. On the one hand, the league was acknowledging the unpopularity of this particular expansion of federal authority. But, in an attempt to dodge responsibility for *Olmstead* and the other unpopular snips and slices that were increasingly perforating the Bill of Rights, the league wanted to suggest that these alterations were meant to address crime in general and were not specifically about Prohibition at all.

The ASL leaders were wise to be worried. The only thing that seemed to be multiplying faster than federal power was criminal violence. No sooner had the flow of liquor from Rum Row in the Northeast been stanched than it began to gush in unprecedented quantities through the sluiceway that was Detroit, where an overmatched prosecutor said, "The greatest obstacle to the attainment of Prohibition is the Constitution of the United States, the instrument that decreed its birth." Corruption and incompetence had metastasized throughout the Prohibition bureau to such a degree that Wayne Wheeler had been forced to capitulate and allow bureau agents to be placed under the protection of the Civil Service, even at the cost of ceding the ASL's rich garden of patronage. On the Supreme Court, William Howard Taft, who had once feared the destructive power of Prohibition but had since become its most influential defender, sensed the looming breakup of his coalition as Justices Holmes, Brandeis, and Stone increasingly abandoned pro-enforcement positions.

The tightrope that Wheeler and the ASL walked—the one suspended between its hunger for stiff enforcement and its wish not to offend public sensibilities with federal overreaching—had first threatened to snap in early 1927. Several New Yorkers died and hundreds had been rendered gravely ill during the 1926 holiday season; all had consumed industrial products that had been denatured with poisonous wood alcohol. Wheeler's response was chilling. "The government is under no obligation to furnish the people with alcohol that is drinkable, when the Constitution prohibits it," he told the press. "The person who drinks this alcohol is a deliberate suicide."

Reaction was swift, and enraged. Senator Edward I. Edwards of New Jersey said Wheeler was condoning "legalized murder." Andrew Mellon declared his opposition to the use of toxic denaturants, a practice he considered "inexcusable." Morris Sheppard, trying to bail Wheeler out, argued that overindulgence in alcohol was the real killer. But wets who'd endured years of lectures about the dangers of alcohol easily punctured this argument. "If the Senator's theory is that alcohol is so poisonous," asked wet Senator Edwin S. Broussard of Louisiana, "then why put poison in it?"

Such was the prelude to Wheeler's appearance on the stage of Carnegie Hall three months later, his most widely noticed public appearance since the disastrous Reed hearings. Now he was stepping into the den of a lion who was every bit Jim Reed's equal. Wheeler had agreed to debate Clarence Darrow in front of a sure-to-be-hostile New York audience, despite his own increasingly ill health and Darrow's certain invocation of the still-simmering poison controversy. Darrow did not disappoint, ripping into Wheeler and other drys who, he said, believed that "any man who takes a drink of alcohol today may be poisoned without a trial by a jury, without anything, just be poisoned because he dared take it!" For this one time Darrow was on the prosecution's side, and the prisoner in the dock was Prohibition itself. Vigorous and theatrical, alternating between corrosive sarcasm and heaven-shaking grandiloquence, the seventy-year-old Darrow deployed all his courtroom skills. It was as if he were addressing a jury, but in this case a jury composed of twenty-five hundred New Yorkers, the overwhelming majority of whom had come to Carnegie intent on delivering a conviction. So intent, in fact, that those in the first-tier seats had paid $11 apiece—the 2009 equivalent of $135—for the privilege.

Wheeler's arguments were sharper than Darrow's, and his command of the facts he had invoked so many times over the preceding quarter century was firmer. But he didn't stand a chance. He was steamrollered by his opponent's rhetorical power, overwhelmed by the audience's hunger for blood, and disabled by his physical condition. Wearing his finest uniform—full evening dress, complete with white tie—Wheeler nonetheless looked pale, withered, somehow empty. He didn't even present his opening remarks himself; instead, his colleague Scott McBride read from a prepared text while the audience booed and hissed and jeered. Even the ferociously anti-Wheeler *New York World* expressed sympathy. He was, the paper said, "engaged in a one-handed fight against 2,000 booing, hooting, caterwauling New Yorkers, who tried all at once to tell him where to get off."

But, the paper continued, "the small, spunky, bespectacled, baldish man in the clawhammer coat didn't get off at all." Freeing McBride from his ventriloquist duties during the rebuttal, speaking in a voice that could barely be heard beyond the first few rows, Wheeler presented a logical, acute, and shapely response that took into account every familiar argument for Prohibition and a few others besides ("Did you ever hear of a man eating so much pie or cake or anything of that kind that he'd go home and shoot up the family?").

Near the end of his talk Wheeler landed, like Chief Justice Taft, in Prohibition's best-defended fortress: the rule of law, as established by the will of the people. He declared that the people had placed the Eighteenth Amendment in the Constitution, and only the people could remove it, and everyone in the hall knew that to accomplish that, anti-Prohibition forces would have to muster the support of two-thirds of a dry Congress and three-quarters of a collection of states that were very dissimilar to New York. This was something the night's only other speaker, Mayor Jimmy Walker, had acknowledged. Arriving midway through the event, Walker addressed the audience in his characteristically jovial fashion. To this crowd of knowing New Yorkers, most of whom might have come to Carnegie Hall either on the way to or from a speakeasy, the mayor proclaimed that although he was a confirmed wet, "Prohibition might be a good thing—but I don't know who is going to arrange it."

Yet even Walker knew when it was time to stop with the wisecracks and address the real issue. "Those of us who don't like Prohibition," he concluded, "ought to stop complaining and organize and get rid of it, or shut up."

Chapter 18

The Phony Referendum

DESPITE POLITICAL DIFFERENCES that might have divided less compatible people, Pauline Sabin had no trouble supporting James Wadsworth Jr., the senior senator from New York, when he ran for reelection in 1926. Wadsworth was as wet as they came, and Sabin had not yet abandoned the dry cause. Wadsworth had made his political reputation attacking woman suffrage, and it was the suffrage movement that had propelled Sabin into politics. But a commonality of background prevailed over any divergence in philosophy. Like Sabin, her friend Jimmy was an aristocrat of vast wealth: Skull and Bones at Yale, devoted foxhunter, fourth-generation owner of a fifty-five-square-mile chunk of the fertile Genesee Valley in upstate New York. Also like Sabin, he was Republican down to his genes. His grandfather had been one of the party's founders, and his father had served nine terms as a Republican member of Congress. Wadsworth himself had tightened the bond by marrying the daughter of John Hay, who began his own political career as Abraham Lincoln's private secretary and concluded it as Theodore Roosevelt's secretary of state.

In 1926, though, New York Republicans were an unhappy family. The Democratic nominee for the Senate seat, Judge Robert F. Wagner, was no less wet than Wadsworth. Left without a candidate it could support, the Anti-Saloon League chose to punish Wadsworth (and simultaneously issue a warning to other wet Republicans) by putting forward its own candidate, a former state senator named Franklin W. Cristman, on a third-party line. The party regulars lined up behind Wadsworth, the drys fled to Cristman (his key platform plank: the Volstead Act wasn't strict enough), and Wagner squeezed through the gap between them. During the campaign Pauline Sabin had advised Wadsworth to move a scheduled rally from Madison Square Garden to Carnegie Hall. Her reasons reflected

289

both her political instincts and her upbringing. Carnegie would be easier to fill, she told the senator. And, she added, more dignified.

Sabin had first become active in Republican politics in 1919, when she was thirty-two. The following year the *Southampton Press* reported that she had been host to a buffet lunch for four hundred New York Republicans, "one of the largest and most enjoyable events of the kind ever held in the county." It was a rainy day, but the guests fit comfortably inside the reception hall of Bayberry Land, Sabin's twenty-eight-room manor house in the Shinnecock Hills of Long Island's South Fork. In kinder weather, her summer parties were usually held outdoors on the enormous terrace, where guests might enjoy the view of Peconic Bay, the four formal gardens,* the eight outbuildings, and the nine distinctive pot chimneys on the imported slate roof. Designed in the style of an English country manor, the house was barely a year old when she welcomed her fellow Republicans, but the society architects Cross & Cross had made the roof sag here and there, to lend a feeling of age.

As intelligent as she was beautiful, as energetic as she was elegant, Sabin engaged the Republican Party with the same vitality she brought to her luminous social life. She founded the Women's National Republican Club in 1921, when she was thirty-four, and two years later became the first female member of the Republican National Committee. Her husband, Charles, a J. P. Morgan partner who sat on sixteen corporate boards, was a lifelong Democrat and a committed wet. The friends who gathered at Bayberry Land and at the Sabins' Manhattan residence on Sutton Place were urbane, sophisticated people, and like many of them Pauline Sabin enjoyed a nightly martini before dinner (in this household dinner was always a black-tie event, even in the country, even when the family dined alone). Some of the bottles in the Sabin wine collection were stored in a room hidden behind a movable wall of fake books at Bayberry Land. In the world the couple occupied, among the wealthy and well connected, good liquor and fine wines were plentiful, summoned to hand by a nod to the butler or delivered on request by the chauffeur. At one point, in fact, the Sabins' chauffeur, unknown to his employers, ran a bootlegging business of his own out of their Manhattan garage.

The fact that the rich could consider themselves immune to meaning-

---

*The creation of these gardens was emblematic of the spare-no-expense construction of the Sabin dream house. Convinced that Bayberry Land did not have sufficient topsoil for the elaborate plantings she envisioned, landscape designer Marian Coffin purchased an entire nearby farm, harvested its fertile soil, and hired a convoy of trucks to transport it to Bayberry Land.

ful enforcement (by virtue of well-placed connections, good lawyers, and other convenient assets) enraged Prohibition supporters. "The fashionable rich demand their rum as an inalienable class privilege," the loyally dry *Ladies' Home Journal* said in 1923. After former Yale president Arthur Hadley openly called on Americans to nullify the dry laws by ignoring them—a strategy he attempted to dignify by comparing it to Northern resistance to the Fugitive Slave Act seventy-five years earlier—an angered Chief Justice Taft attacked Hadley's position as characteristic of "the luxury-loving rich." When General Motors founder William C. Durant (who was as dry as Henry Ford) offered prize money for "the best and most practical plan to make the 18th amendment effective," the theme came up again and again. "Punishment is asked 'for the rich and the white as well as the poor and the black,'" Durant wrote in his summary of the entries. "There is demand for action and publicity of action against 'Mr. and Mrs. Prominent Citizen.'" In his own entry, Los Angeles police chief James E. Davis said the rich had "no conception of their own support of an outlaw 'industry.' Their money gives it power, their known sympathy and patronage gives it prestige in places where it should be shown no quarter."

In some instances the attitudes of the well-off were shaped by their sheer sense of entitlement, which was intensified by their loyalty to ruthlessly clear class distinctions. Connecticut silk manufacturer Charles Cheney, who was chairman of the influential National Industrial Conference Board, supported Prohibition publicly, enjoyed liquor privately, and saw no contradiction; Prohibition was apparently designed for lesser beings. This view was not confined to the very rich, as Sinclair Lewis demonstrated so vividly in *Babbitt*. During the "canonical rite" (Lewis's term) of cocktail hour at George Babbitt's house, one of the solid burghers of Zenith insists that requiring drinkers to be licensed was a much better idea than Prohibition: "Then we could have taken care of the shiftless workman—kept him from drinking—and yet not've interfered with the rights . . . of fellows like ourselves." Another says, "You don't want to forget prohibition is a mighty good thing for the working-classes. Keeps 'em from wasting their money and lowering their productiveness." Some drys saw it this way as well. Henry Ford's ghostwriter said, "If only the people of larger incomes are drinking bootleg stuff, it is of course unfortunate in a way, but if someone must drink, it is best for the country that those who can afford it rather than those who cannot afford it should do the drinking."

The difference between the very rich and the Babbitts of the world wasn't just that the former had more money. They also had the freedom to be—take your pick—either more arrogant or less hypocritical. When airplane manufacturer William E. Boeing showed up in court to testify against Roy Olmstead, he had no problem admitting that he had been one of the Seattle bootlegger's customers. But the greater, and more potent, distinction between the small-time businessmen of Zenith and the nation's industrial and financial noblemen lay in the acuity of their political perceptions. Unlike George Babbitt's friends, the men who gathered in December 1927 at James W. Wadsworth's mansion in Washington, D.C., knew that the anger of the workingman could be exploited. What was odd, if you weren't looking closely, was how these wealthy men, who had been sailing through Prohibition as if it had never really happened, would soon be willing to put so much time and treasure into bringing about its end.

THE WAYNE B. WHEELER who limped home to Washington after the Darrow debate in April 1927 was greatly diminished physically, but he did not let this dilute his unholy devotion to his holy cause. He had spent the months following the poison controversy pressuring the Civil Service Commission to require new agents to be "in sympathy with the law," while maintaining his picket duty on Congress, the Treasury Department, and the White House. He had even persuaded Andrew Mellon not to order the removal of fatal denaturants from industrial alcohol until a substance more noxious but less toxic could be developed. Now he turned his attention to the following year's election. Confident of its ability to bring presidential candidates of both parties to heel, the ASL had always concentrated its energies and its financial resources on congressional races. But Al Smith had emerged from the Democratic wreckage of 1924 as the party's leading figure. Fearing that Smith would become the Democratic nominee for the first time and make Prohibition an overtly partisan issue in a presidential campaign, Wheeler obtained from the ASL a special appropriation of $600,000 to combat the efforts of "certain prospective candidates."

But even so grave a threat as a wet at the head of one of the major party tickets did not distract Wheeler from his other efforts. "He literally worked all the time," said ASL national superintendent Scott McBride, his closest colleague. "On a Pullman or parlor car, he would at once take papers from his portfolio and plunge into drafting of a brief for the Supreme Court, a message for a congregation, a reply to an attack on him by wets, an article for a magazine. In the hotel dining room he would meet with committees while he ate. His [own] room was a beehive, the telephone ringing constantly [and] dry leaders clustering around him." Critics described his actions a little differently. According to the *San Francisco Examiner*, "the paid superlobbyist" busied himself "wheedling, threatening, cajoling, bull-dozing, promising and browbeating." What was certain was Wheeler's mindfulness of something he had said a few years earlier: a minority that has lost something will register its protest, he warned his fellow drys, but "the majority who have won the fight turn to other tasks." Wheeler truly believed that the dry cause was the majority cause. But he seemed also to believe that only his relentless efforts could make certain there would be no turning away. He told Lord Astor, one of Britain's leading prohibition-ists (and husband of American émigré Nancy Langhorne Astor), "We are having a rather strenuous fight here these days, but are holding the fort as usual."

In the summer of 1927 Wheeler returned to Battle Creek. At one point he took a break from the Kellogg rest cure to tell reporters that a Smith candidacy could be fatal for the Democrats. "Leaders of the party who are looking ahead," he explained, "do not want to tie up their political future to a corpse." He praised Coolidge's appointment of a new Prohibi-tion boss, a Republican hack from New York named Seymour Lowman ("a well-recognized dry advocate," Wheeler said), insisted that drinking on college campuses was not as prevalent as some people indicated, and criti-cized Nicholas Murray Butler, the wet president of Columbia University, for his "unwarranted attacks" on the Eighteenth Amendment.*

From Battle Creek, Wheeler traveled to the pious summer resort of Little Point Sable in western Michigan, where several dry leaders kept summer cottages (from its advertising: "Homes for Christian families. Happy Childhood, Clean Youth. Strong Young Manhood"). There, with his wife, Ella, and her parents, he took several weeks away from his dry labors to rusticate on the Lake Michigan shore. His well-off father-in-law, Robert Candy, had made it possible for Wheeler to work for a salary that never exceeded eight thousand dollars a year; according to one of the Wheeler grandchildren, Ella "kept the family organized so [Wayne] could go off and save the world with Prohibition." At Little Point Sable, Wheeler stepped away from the pressing business of the Anti-Saloon League for the

---

*Wheeler was somewhat milder here than he had been a few months earlier, when he claimed that Butler supported a program "soaked in avarice, lust, and rum," and that he belonged "with the boot-leggers, rum-runners, owners of speak-easy property, wet newspa-pers, underworld denizens, alcoholic slaves and personal liberty fanatics in his fight to bring back booze." Informed of Wheeler's comments, Butler replied, "It sounds as if something had happened to trouble him."

first time since he'd joined the temperance movement at Oberlin thirty-four years earlier. "He kept in touch with the trend of prohibition affairs throughout the nation," wrote Justin Steuart, Wheeler's research secretary, "but instead of the steady stream of letters and telegrams issuing from his cottage, there was now only a bare trickle."

Wheeler was to some degree becalmed by his weakened constitution and possibly by a genuine wish to cast off the burdens of three decades. But on August 14 he was wrenched from his reverie by unspeakable horror. This is how the Associated Press described the catastrophe: "A large drum of gasoline near which Mrs. Wheeler was working exploded, igniting her clothing. Mrs. Wheeler ran screaming into the living room, where her father, who recently suffered a severe heart attack, was reclining on a couch. At the sight of his daughter, her clothing aflame, [her father] arose, clutched at his heart, and toppled over dead."

The following morning Ella Wheeler died as well. Less than a week later her husband, who had extinguished the flames, departed for a meeting of the World Congress Against Alcoholism in Winona Lake, Indiana. "Wheeler's calmness under the shock of this tragedy amazed even his most intimate friends, who knew the strength of his will and courage," Justin Steuart wrote. "To all expressions of sympathy, [he] returned a simple assurance that this loss would merely mean an increased devotion on his part to the cause in which he was enlisted."

His assurances could not be fulfilled. Two weeks later Wayne B. Wheeler, crippled by a chronically enlarged heart and a lately diminished spirit, was himself dead. He was fifty-seven.

TO THE ANTI-SALOON LEAGUE, no victory in the 1926 congressional elections had been as gratifying as the defeat of James Wadsworth in the New York Senate race ("the greatest loss the wets could suffer," said the league's newspaper). But to Wadsworth, nothing could have been more liberating. He might miss the campaign trail, particularly the amusement devised by the newspapermen who had traveled with him: at every stop, no matter how tiny the town or how brief the stay, the reporters raced to see if they could get a drink. (Not once did they fail, even though some stops were as short as half an hour.) But it wasn't likely that Wadsworth would miss the Senate and its smothering cloud of duplicity. In his final speech he excoriated those senators who either drank or kept company with drinkers yet continued to support the Volstead Act. "Is hypocrisy to be established as the national trait?" he asked. He provided his own reply: only one thing could save the nation from its epidemic of cant and falseness—Repeal of the Eighteenth Amendment.

No wet as prominent as Wadsworth had made so bold a declaration. But Wadsworth enjoyed the freedom of a condemned man. Having been denied reelection, he had nothing to lose. Emancipated by defeat, he spent 1927 traveling the country, from Boston all the way to Honolulu, making the case not for the legalization of wine and beer, or for a redefinition of "intoxicating," but for outright Repeal. Yet Wadsworth's impact on the status of the Eighteenth Amendment registered most firmly within the walls of his home in Washington. There, on December 12, 1927, in his mansion on the rim of Rock Creek Park, two dozen men gathered to address issues that were, said the letter of invitation, nothing less than "vital to the very existence of our government."

The author of that trembling phrase was William H. Stayton, the admiralty lawyer who in 1918 had sent out invitations to six hundred men he knew by first name, asking them to join his new Association Against the Prohibition Amendment (probably a better name than another he had considered, the Association Against Fanatical Minorities). Failing to stop or even to slow the amendment's march, Stayton stayed true to his cause even after ratification, largely financing the AAPA out of his own pocket. He began his days at 4 a.m. and worked ceaselessly, sending out letters, trying to raise additional money (he made a point of eschewing donations from people who had made their money in brewing or distilling), and recruiting prominent supporters. He did not allow himself to be distracted by irrelevancies: when he needed clothing, Stayton would buy half a dozen identical suits (all of them custom-made) and a dozen identical ties so he didn't have to waste a single instant of his day deciding what to wear.

But energy did not translate into effectiveness. In the beginning, Stayton's perception of upper-class manners, coupled with an innate timidity, led him to keep the names of his supporters private. This accomplished little besides suggesting that there was something disreputable about the whole endeavor. In 1922 Stayton did manage to fill Carnegie Hall with an anti-Prohibition rally that drew "some of the best known men and women in the city," but in Manhattan a wet crowd was about as remarkable as a sidewalk. In 1924 his fumbling effort to help wet candidates crashed when the AAPA endorsed seven congressional candidates in Pennsylvania, including three incumbents—and all seven, regarding public support from the AAPA as if it were a social disease, repudiated the endorsements.

By late 1927, though, the list of men Stayton invited to the meeting at James Wadsworth's house suggested that the status of the AAPA had changed. It included three sitting U.S. senators (Blaine of Wisconsin, Broussard of Louisiana, and Bruce of Maryland); one recently deposed one (Wadsworth); the Standard Oil heir Edward S. Harkness, whose philanthropy had inscribed the family name on buildings at Harvard, Yale, Columbia, and Brown; private banker Grayson Mallet-Prevost Murphy, who sat on the boards of Anaconda Copper, Bethlehem Steel, Goodyear Rubber, and five other equally blue-chip companies; and a number of others whose names appeared often in the nation's news pages, regularly on the society pages, and almost daily on the business pages (including Pauline Sabin's husband). "In 1917 the chief spokesman of the [wets] was the president of the United States Brewers' Association," wrote Charles Merz. "In 1927 the leadership of the opposition had passed to the president of the Pennsylvania Railroad or to the chairman of the board of the General Motors Corporation."

General W. W. Atterbury, president of the Pennsy, was an active soldier in the AAPA. But it was the chairman of GM, Pierre S. du Pont, who had become the association's indisputable commander in chief by the time the conferees emerged from two days of meetings at Wadsworth's house. Du Pont was also chairman of the Du Pont Company, unchallenged head of his old and distinguished family, and lord of Longwood, a private paradise of gardens and greenhouses and fountains arrayed across a thousand acres surrounding his thirty-room mansion, twelve miles northwest of Wilmington. His reign over the AAPA was comparably dominant. In the year following the meeting at Wadsworth's house he became the organization's largest single contributor; ranking second, fourth, and sixth were his brothers Irénée and Lammot, and his closest professional colleague, John J. Raskob. Two years after du Pont took control of the AAPA, an associate said his interest in the organization and its mission was "greater than it is in anything else in the United States."

Pierre du Pont was exceptionally wealthy, his net income in a single year at times topping $50 million. He was also exceptionally capable. At first with two cousins, then increasingly on his own, he had built the family's gunpowder business into an industrial colossus. Assisted by the financially astute Raskob, he took effective control of General Motors (the du Pont family owned 36 percent of its stock) in 1920. Ideas developed by the two men concerning capital allocation, accounting methods, and the development of differentiated business units operating within a single corporate structure became the standard for American industry.

Du Pont's aptitude for leadership had emerged at an early age, after his father was killed in an industrial accident. Although he was only fourteen, as the eldest son among ten children Pierre became not just the nominal head of the family but the actual one. His siblings—even his sister Louisa, older by two years—marked his role by calling him "Dad" and its variants, a familial habit that would survive the passing decades. It's both jarring and somehow touching to encounter, in Pierre's vast correspondence, a letter from his brother Irénée addressed "Dear Daddy. " At the time—1920— Pierre was fifty; Irénée, president of the world's largest manufacturer of explosives and other chemicals, was forty-four.

Pierre had handed the job to his younger brother the year before, not long after the conclusion of the war that had transformed the family business. In 1913 Du Pont had produced 8.4 million tons of smokeless powder. By the time the United States entered World War I four years later, annual production capacity had surpassed 450 million tons. Profits were enormous. But along the way, as the Wilson administration prepared for war, it financed the buildup through the Revenue Act of 1916, which took three swings at the du Pont family's wealth: doubling the income tax rates on those in the highest brackets, creating the nation's first peacetime inheritance tax, and assessing a 12.5 percent levy on the profits of munitions manufacturers (no small amount, considering that du Pont stock dividends would increase sixteen-fold between 1914 and 1918).

Pierre du Pont was incensed. He increased his donations to the presidential campaign of Woodrow Wilson's Republican opponent, Charles Evans Hughes, to a staggering $92,500, more than Hughes received from any other individual (2009 equivalent: more than $1.8 million). Du Pont believed that taxation stifled initiative and trespassed on personal freedom. He detested the Sherman Anti-Trust Act, public relief programs, and highway speed limits. When Delaware penal authorities developed a plan to put prisoners to work repairing autos, du Pont bristled: he considered it unfair competition for private repair shops. His faith in the wisdom of democratically elected governments approximated his faith in dancing pixies.

None of this should suggest, however, that Pierre du Pont was without public spirit—only that he believed that decisions about the public welfare belonged in private hands. When du Pont was president of Delaware's board of education in the early 1920s (he later served as state tax commissioner as well), state law forbade taxing white citizens for the education of blacks. Appalled by the dreadful conditions in the state's segregated schools for black children, du Pont didn't call for a new tax, but instead reached into his own pocket for $4 million to build eighty-six new school buildings. He was happy to donate his own money for the public weal if it could be deployed as he saw fit. Yet when he believed that his money was being confiscated by the government and reallocated by the ill-qualified representatives of the ill informed, he seethed.

The Association Against the Prohibition Amendment was made to order for a man who dreamed of a world in which "there would be some chance for intellectually capable people to operate governmental affairs the same way they are permitted to operate corporate affairs." Du Pont had felt somewhat warmly toward Prohibition at its inception, hopeful that it might make America's workers more productive. But by the middle of the decade, troubled by increasingly invasive enforcement laws and reports from his factory managers of declining productivity, he had begun to moderate his position. He asked Stayton to send him some books on the subject (seeking balance, he apparently made the same request of Wayne Wheeler). His brothers had already lined up with the AAPA (Irénée, who told their cousin Coleman du Pont that Prohibition was "the opening wedge to tyranny," believed that the populace had not risen in revolt "only because the average man is rather stupid and rapidly becomes used to his surroundings"). By December 1927, when he arrived in Washington for the meeting at James Wadsworth's house, Pierre had committed himself to the radical idea his host had put forth in his Senate valedictory: Repeal.

Such was the strength of Pierre du Pont's rapidly hardening conviction—not to mention the force of his personality and the availability of his millions—that within weeks of the meeting at 2800 Woodland Drive, he had not simply taken control of the AAPA; for all practical purposes, he owned it. He nudged Stayton into an honorary position and brought in an energetic New Yorker named Henry H. Curran, who declared himself dedicated to "cutting this Prohibition cancer out of the nation's vitals." Along with his brother Lammot, John Raskob, and two others, du Pont underwrote salaries for Stayton and Curran out of a special fund he controlled. He made it clear to staff and colleagues that he was not interested in the reform of existing Prohibition laws, but in "getting back to first principles"—getting back to a Constitution that did not abide, much less require, government intrusion into the lives of citizens.

By the summer of 1928, when he resigned as chairman of General Motors, du Pont had thrown himself into the wet movement nearly full time. Following the principles of private stewardship he had established when he underwrote the construction of black schools, du Pont even conducted his own version of an election, personally soliciting a pro- or anti-Prohibition ballot from every voter in Delaware; the final tally showed wet opinion drowning dry sentiment by a margin of eight to one. (Nearly half the state's voters sent in ballots—presumably a self-selected group over-whelmingly composed of people sympathetic to du Pont's well-known position.) Closer to home du Pont sought the opinions of the three hundred caretakers, gardeners, household servants, and other members of his personal staff, soliciting them with a printed inquiry addressed "To Those Living at Longwood and Interested in Its Welfare." They didn't like Prohibition, either.

During that same season of Pierre du Pont's waxing commitment to the wet cause, he helped his man Curran assemble an entirely honorary "board of directors" for the AAPA—men of stature who were willing to take a public position against Prohibition. While Stayton had kept members' names secret out of a misplaced sense of propriety, du Pont and Curran saw that names—names edged in gilt and redolent of authority—would lend respectability to the AAPA's efforts and perhaps induce a little awe as well. The chemical du Ponts and the oil Harknesses were soon joined by financial Harrimans, automotive Fishers, rubber Goodriches. Within two years an AAPA official could assert that the association's ever-lengthening roster, now numbering in the hundreds, was composed of men who "direct the management of $40,000,000,000 and the employment and occupation of 3,000,000 employees."

In the promising spring of 1928, though, when the Repeal effort was just beginning, it was victory enough to attract sixty-nine of America's most eminent business and financial leaders willing to pledge their names to Pierre du Pont's suddenly vital organization. For decades after, it became a matter of dispute between wets, drys, and historians sympathetic to one side or the other whether the AAPA's outstanding recruitment campaign could be attributed to the deployment of one simple argument. On March 19, 1928, in a letter to William P. Smith, one of the very few non-family members he addressed by first name, du Pont explained that "the object of the Association is not merely the return of the use of alcoholic beverages in the United States." He elaborated: "Another important factor is the tremendous loss of revenue to our Government through the Prohibition laws"—the revenue once collected through robust taxes on liquor and beer. With Repeal, du Pont told his friend Bill, "The revenue of the Government would be increased sufficiently to warrant the abolition of the income tax and corporation tax."

"On the whole," he concluded, "there is much to strive for."

♦   ♦   ♦

THERE HAD BEEN three salient reactions to Wayne Wheeler's death. His enemies attempted to mutilate his legacy: "He made great men his puppets and they danced to his inexorable commands," observed the *Cincinnati Enquirer*. His supporters venerated him, rendering him variously as an immortal crusader ("Although he is gone, his method, like John Brown's soul, will go marching on," sang the *Omaha World-Herald*) or as a warrior hero (according to a cartoon in the *Ohio State Journal*, he was Leonidas, the king of Sparta who held off tens of thousands of Persians with an army of three hundred—an odd image for a man who'd always claimed to represent a majority). But his direct heirs, the leaders of the ASL, immediately went after one another like wildcats before the body of the alpha male was cold.

It was an escalation of an internal battle over the direction of the ASL that had been joined in 1924, when Illinois superintendent F. Scott McBride, Wheeler's candidate, was installed as national superintendent to succeed Purley A. Baker. Like Wheeler, McBride believed that Prohibition's success lay in punitive enforcement. Unlike Wheeler, who had the will and the wit to engage his enemies as effectively as he inspired his allies, McBride was a dour, ponderous sort who seemed to have no greater responsibility than allowing the legislative superintendent—Wheeler's title was never any grander than that—to do whatever he wished. When he read the ailing Wheeler's opening statement at the Darrow debate in Carnegie Hall, McBride was playing a role that suited him well: ventriloquist's dummy.

The other faction inside the ASL, led by publications director Ernest H. Cherrington, believed that law alone could not solve the drinking problem and continued to argue that proselytizing through education, publicity, and other means of persuasion was essential to long-term success. The Wheeler-McBride triumph over the Cherrington forces in 1924 was not without consequences. In 1926 John D. Rockefeller Jr., whose family had supported the league since its very beginning, shut off the financial tap. Rockefeller was particularly offended by the ASL's support for a measure that would have required mandatory prison sentences for Volstead violators. The only donor whose contributions to the ASL over the years exceeded the Rockefellers', merchant S. S. Kresge, also supported the Cherrington strategy. Kresge alone underwrote the expenses of the league's department of education, which was under Cherrington's control. But the party of punishment within the ASL was unimpressed by his generosity, unbowed by Rockefeller's flight, and determined to pursue its retributive policy. Bishop James Cannon, who lined up with McBride, called for legislation that would make drink itself illegal and force buyers to testify against sellers, a proposal even Wheeler had not been able to support. By the summer of 1927, as Wheeler's health deteriorated, internal friction ignited into open flame. The ASL felt compelled to issue a statement. "As in the case of most movements," it said, "the League has had its own inside family problems with which to deal."

Although Wheeler had lined up against the Cherrington faction, his accomplishments were so manifest and his magnetic field was so powerful that he had been able to effect a simmering truce between the warring blocs. With his death, the Cherringtonians made a last effort to seize control of the organization. Their cause had not been helped when detectives employed by Kresge's wife found him in an apartment he maintained under an assumed name on East Forty-eighth Street in Manhattan, in the company of one Gladys Ardelle Fish, identified in the newspapers as a "stenographer." This revelation received even more press coverage than the reckless-driving charge that Kresge had been hit with a few months earlier. Wet congressmen delighted in discussing the generous contributions of "the Kresge of many matrimonial difficulties," a man "who has been adjudged a home wrecker in the New York Supreme Court."

None of this helped the stature of the education-and-enlightenment faction, which saw its chance to steer the ASL away from the hard line slipping away; in fact, with Rockefeller gone and Kresge publicly disgraced, the hard-liners had little reason to accommodate the Cherringtonian point of view. Although Cherrington was the most reasonable, the most lacking in vainglory, and the most temperate—in the generic sense of the word—of the ASL's leaders, the ascension of Cannon and McBride led him into an elaborate (and futile) conspiracy to tarnish Wheeler and his followers. Justin Steuart, who had been Wheeler's research secretary, published a biography of his former boss casting him, as Steuart privately promised Cherrington, "in an uncomplimentary light." It managed to praise his effectiveness while attacking his methods, and concluded with the pointed assertion that there was no successor remotely as capable as Wheeler anywhere in the organization.

Taking part in the assault on Wheeler's reputation could not have been a comfortable undertaking for the otherwise judicious Cherrington. But no one in the directorate running the Anti-Saloon League in late 1927 and early 1928 was especially prudent in his behavior or showed himself to be particularly capable of leadership. "The Anti-Saloon League has lately shown marked signs of weakness," a prominent wet lawyer named Julian Codman told Pierre du Pont, largely because "the Prohibition forces have been disorganized by the death of Wayne B. Wheeler." H. L. Mencken, looking back, would see a deeper problem. Mencken may have loathed everything the ASL believed in, but he knew talent. "In fifty years the United States has seen no more adept a political manipulator" than Wayne Wheeler, Mencken wrote. "His successors, compared to him, were as pee-wees to the Matterhorn."

THE PRESIDENTIAL ELECTION of 1928 has long been considered an unfortunate, or at least awkward, episode in American history. Because of anti-Catholic prejudice, Al Smith, the Democratic candidate, lost states that had never gone Republican. Herbert Hoover, his opponent, was elected on a seemingly unstoppable wave of Republican prosperity just months before the economy came crashing down in a rubble of pipe dreams, false riches, and market manipulation. In its own moment, the 1928 election was seen as a huge victory for Prohibition, the openly wet Smith crushed in an antiliquor surge that turned Congress drier than it had ever been. Eventually, though, the 1928 election would have to be seen as catastrophic for the drys, proving that political complications sometimes generate a fog that reduces visibility to zero.

Consider, for instance, the two constituencies that had the greatest stake in the Eighteenth Amendment and were thus implicit allies. No one had a stronger moral interest in Prohibition than the Baptist and Methodist clergymen who were its tribunes, but no one had a greater financial stake than the criminals who daily sought to undermine it. It's not easy to prove that the big-time mobsters, on-the-take cops, corrupt judges, speakeasy operators, and all the other economic beneficiaries of the Eighteenth Amendment and the Volstead Act gave their financial support to dry politicians. Researchers are unlikely to discover a canceled check made out to a political campaign and signed "Alphonse Capone."

But however the dollars found their way from a mobster's hoard of cash to a pol's campaign treasury, the connection was inevitable, the logic unimpeachable. Partisans as disparate as Senator James W. Wadsworth (wet), Izzy Einstein (dry), the *New York World* (very wet), and Senator George Norris (very dry) all insisted this was the case. Said Jane Addams, "Doubtless all bootleggers would oppose a change in the law," and doubtless Addams was right. In a 1922 Massachusetts referendum, the only counties voting to retain a state enforcement law were Barnstable (Cape Cod), Dukes (Martha's Vineyard), and Nantucket—one jurisdiction surrounded on three sides by water, the others on all four, and each of them direct beneficiaries of the economic activity generated by the mother ships of Rum Row.* One of Roy Olmstead's lieutenants gave $6,000 to the 1926 reelection campaign of the U.S. Senate's most effective dry, Wesley L. Jones, and made at least one financial contribution to the WCTU as well. The bootleggers' agents in government also collaborated with the drys. Big Bill Thompson, the utterly saturated mayor of Chicago ("I'm wetter than the middle of the Atlantic Ocean," he bragged), threw his organization behind dry Senate candidate Frank L. Smith in 1926, and Thompson's collection of pet congressmen included M. Alfred Michaelson, an outspoken House dry.

This was the same Bill Thompson whose portrait hung on the wall behind Al Capone's desk; who was said to have collected more than a quarter of a million dollars from the Capone organization for his 1927 mayoral campaign; and who, having concluded his mayoral tenure with an annual salary of $18,000, left behind nearly $2 million in cash and cash equivalents at his death. Mob support of a wet like Thompson, and Thompson's support of congressional drys like Smith and Michaelson, should not suggest a logical disconnect. Bootleggers required dry laws to keep legitimate businessmen out of the booze industry, and they needed wet administrations to keep the cops and other enforcement officials off their backs. The perfect combination: a dry Congress and state legislatures to pass the laws, and wet mayors and governors to not enforce them—in other words, something very close to the lineup in America's most populous cities and states as the election of 1928 approached.

IN 1926 Rabbi Morris Lazaron polled fellow members of the Central Conference of American Rabbis to gauge their attitudes regarding Prohibition and to learn something about sentiment in their communities. There was a wide range of personal opinion among the 122 who responded, wrote historian Marni Davis, but "nearly every rabbi, from every region, asserted that only two groups seemed to favor Prohibition: evangelical Christians and bootleggers."

The bootleggers may have sent unmarked bundles of cash to candidates for local and legislative offices every election cycle, but presidential politics was of little concern to them. The evangelicals, on the other

---

*Some might argue that less self-interested reasons—religion, ethnicity, political attitudes—explained this phenomenon. But inland counties similarly composed of English and Scots-Irish Protestant stock, and also equally Republican in politics, voted against the enforcement law.

hand, were neither disinterested nor shy. In the 1928 presidential race they became directly involved in electoral politics as never before.

It was not the Republican candidate who excited their interest. Secretary of Commerce Herbert Hoover, who had become rich as a mining engineer in Australia and China, and famous as U.S. food administrator during World War I, was suspiciously worldly, and his record on dry issues was spotty. He once said he did not think 2.75 percent beer was an intoxicant, and during World War I he had opposed interim Prohibition measures. Had the Baptists and other fundamentalists in the dry vanguard known about the excellent wine cellar Hoover had acquired from the estate of Senator Leland Stanford, they might not have been mollified even by the knowledge that Hoover's wife had given it away in 1919. They certainly would not have been pleased to know that on his way home from the Commerce Department, Hoover would stop to have his evening cocktails at the Belgian embassy, a daily ritual he would describe after Prohibition's end as "the pause between the errors and trials of the day and the hopes of the night."

Al Smith's sweeping first-ballot nomination by the Democrats in 1928—he received nearly twelve times as many votes as the top dry candidate, Cordell Hull of Tennessee—appeared to extinguish the flames that had nearly consumed the party during the 103 bloody ballots of 1924.* At its Houston convention the party came together around the wet New Yorker at the top of the ticket; Senator Joseph Robinson, an Arkansas dry, as vice presidential candidate; and a platform that put the Democrats unequivocally behind an equivocal statement in support of "an honest effort to enforce the eighteenth amendment."

But neither the facsimile of party unity nor the platform's illusion of fealty to the law could make dry fundamentalists support the Democrats. Though Hoover was a semisecret drinker, Smith enjoyed his liquor openly (even if not to the degree asserted by the pro-Smith editor of the *Nation*, who said the governor enjoyed four to eight cocktails or highballs daily). Though Hoover, as Walter Lippmann wrote, "regards both wets and drys as substantially insane," Smith made it plain whose side he was on. Though Hoover had the eager public support of Republican wets who were despised by the ultradrys—among them Lammot du Pont, James Wadsworth, and Pauline Sabin—he sent up the right semaphores (for "enforce-

---

*Another potential wet candidate who stepped aside for Smith was Jim Reed of Missouri. Reed had probably not helped his chances when he accepted a $100,000 retainer, plus $1,000 a day, to defend the superdry Henry Ford in a libel suit.

ment," against "nullification," and so on) while Smith offered the wrong ones (demanding "local self-government," attacking "official corruption"). And though Hoover was a Quaker, which gave him little theological common ground with the fundamentalists, at least there was a history of temperance sentiment in American Quakerism. Smith, on the other hand, was a Catholic, and to the fundamentalists of the 1920s no affiliation, religious or otherwise, could have been more poisonous.

Al Smith's candidacy gave bigots and xenophobes a perfect demon. In 1928 the crude impulses that had earlier ignited the rapid growth of the Ku Klux Klan now exploded among those "pure Americans" who saw themselves losing their nation to the Irish and the Italians and all the other foreigners crowding the big cities. Rev. Bob Jones made frequent use of a startling call to arms that year: "I would rather see a saloon on every corner than a Catholic in the White House." If this didn't make his feelings sufficiently clear, Jones's alternative option certainly did: he declared that he would prefer "a nigger president" to the Catholic Smith.

The boiling hatred directed against Smith was intensified by the identity of his most prominent supporter, John J. Raskob, whom Smith installed as chairman of the Democratic National Committee. Some of the more rabid fundamentalists could almost believe it was the other way around—that it was Raskob, who had voted for Coolidge in 1924 and was still listed in *Who's Who* as a Republican, who had picked Smith as a stalking horse for a diabolical papist plot. First they would take over the Democratic Party, and then put the U.S. government into the hands of the Knights of Columbus, in behalf of the pope of Rome. It was the sort of speculation that could make a Catholic-hater quiver with the joy that can be induced only by the thrill of loathing.

Raskob may have been the wealthiest Catholic in the nation. In the minds of dry fundamentalists, this made him the most dangerous. Born poor, the son of a cigar maker in Lockport, New York, his career and his wealth progressed rapidly after Pierre du Pont hired him as a bookkeeper-stenographer at twenty dollars a week when Raskob was twenty-one. Over the next two decades he made tens of millions executing the reorganization of General Motors in Pierre du Pont's behalf; then, once installed as chairman of the GM board's all-powerful finance committee, he devised the company's lending arm, the phenomenally profitable General Motors Acceptance Corporation. Raskob donated a well-publicized million dollars to the Diocese of Washington in February 1928 and gave investment advice to the Society for the Propagation of the Faith, the Loretto Foundation, the North American College of Cardinals, and a capable young

ısignor from Boston named Francis Spellman. The magazine *Com-
ıweal*, founded in 1924 to combat populist anti-Catholicism, was to a
large degree bankrolled by Raskob. Pope Pius XI memorialized Raskob's
contributions to the church's welfare by naming him an honorary chamberlain in the Papal Household.

Bob Jones may have been the most quotable of those spewing their bile
toward Smith, Raskob, and Catholicism during that 1928 campaign, but
the chorus was substantial. Cotton Tom Heflin, sinking to lows even he had
not achieved before, ranted on the Senate floor about Catholic priests who
killed their babies, Catholic control of the Alabama press, and Al Smith's
plans to annex Mexico, presumably to establish a permanent Catholic
majority in the United States. Some anti-Catholics resuscitated the "Rum,
Romanism, and Rebellion" slogan that had languished unused since the
1884 presidential election, when Republicans cited this unholy trinity to
damn the increasing Irish influence in the Democratic Party. After Raskob
arranged to have Smith campaign headquarters moved into the General
Motors Building in New York, just an elevator ride from his own office, the
haters had evidence of their fancied Catholic conspiracy. (It was probably
good for their nervous systems that they didn't know about the $100,000
worth of RCA stock Raskob had given Smith.) A Klan-connected hate
sheet called *Fellowship Forum*, which gave the lie to its anodyne name in
every issue, reached a perverse apogee early in October, when it asserted
that a Smith-led America would be "a vassal state of the Vatican and stink-
slide of booze and corruption."

Bingo! This was the magic formula: the conflation of the perfidious
disloyalty of the Catholics and the shameless iniquity of the wets. Agents
of religious and ethnic prejudice more artful than *Fellowship Forum* didn't
have to spell out the connection. Even so resolute a Catholic-hater as
Bishop Cannon—the man who had famously called the Catholic Church
"the mother of ignorance, superstition, intolerance, and sin"—preferred
to describe Smith with a stand-in vocabulary. "Wet," "New York politician," "Tammany"—these became code for the one word never uttered by
Smith's presumably respectable opponents: "Catholic."

Following ratification of the Eighteenth Amendment, not one of the six
men who ran for president on a major party ticket—Warren G. Harding,
James M. Cox, Calvin Coolidge, John W. Davis, Herbert Hoover, and Al
Smith—had been an unconflicted advocate of Prohibition. Smith, however, was the first who dared to run an openly wet campaign. Funded by an
apparently unprecedented personal contribution of $690,000 in campaign
funds and loan guarantees from Raskob, he attracted wets, particularly in

the Northeast, who had never before voted Democratic. But a candidacy based in part on revocation of the Volstead Act allowed his enemies to gild their ugly religious prejudice with the relatively civilized language of the Prohibition debate. Smith recognized the perils built into the connection when exploitation of anti-Catholic prejudice reached its apogee in the fall, after the Republican National Committee sent Mabel Willebrandt into the fray. Until that point Willebrandt, seven years into her tenure as the most visible face of Prohibition enforcement, had not been terribly active in Hoover's behalf. Most of what she did for the Republican ticket was subtler than open campaigning: for instance, while the Democratic convention was meeting in Houston, she had personally orchestrated a spectacular series of nightclub raids in New York on June 28, the very day Smith won the nomination. If the Democrat was embarrassed by this coup de theatre staged in his hometown, he did not say so. More likely he didn't care.

But when the RNC decided to use the high-profile Willebrandt as an offensive weapon, it scored a direct hit. Her charge: address the Ohio convention of the Methodist Church. Her argument: "Tammany . . . underworld connections . . . New York . . . center of lawlessness . . ." Her plea: "There are 2,000 pastors here. You have in your churches more than 600,000 members of the Methodist churches in Ohio alone. That is enough to swing the election. The 600,000 have friends in other states. Write to them."

There's no evidence that the ever-zealous Willebrandt was herself anti-Catholic, or that she was conscious that her peroration, which never mentioned Smith's religion, would be perceived as anti-Catholic; in fact, she would point out that "the speech to the Methodists," as it became known, had been cleared in advance by the RNC's general counsel, James F. Burke, who was himself Catholic. But the nature of the audience, and the string of code words, and the attempt to mobilize the gathered Methodists and turn them into an active-duty army for Hoover provoked from Smith a response that placed the religious issue at center stage, no doubt satisfying the drys' most cynical operatives. Smith made his stand in Oklahoma City, where an ominous greeting had been provided by burning crosses in the nearby countryside, and was then spelled out when the pastor of the First Baptist Church declared that a vote for Smith was a vote against Jesus Christ. In his speech Smith assailed the Ku Klux Klan, the Republican Party, a renegade Democratic senator, and Mabel Willebrandt for turning his faith into a political issue. Their conduct, said Smith, was "a treasonable attack upon the very foundations of American liberty."

Reports on the speech appeared on front pages across the country. Republicans responded by blaming Smith for introducing religion into the campaign. Willebrandt, addressing another group of Methodists two days after his Oklahoma City speech, said the Democrat was "afraid to come out and face the record that he has made as a champion of the liquor traffic." This election, she and other dry Republicans insisted, was a referendum on Prohibition.

Except it wasn't. "Available evidence suggests that opposition to Smith's Prohibition policy served as a cloak for opposition to his Catholicism," wrote Allan J. Lichtman in *Prejudice and the Old Politics*, his exceptionally careful statistical reading of the Hoover-Smith race. But after the polls closed in 1928, the raw numbers made the exultant drys declare the election their greatest victory since the Eighteenth Amendment itself. Hoover, candidate of the drys—he had declared in his acceptance speech at the Republican convention that Prohibition was "a great social and economic experiment, noble in motive and far-reaching in purpose"—amassed a landslide margin in the Electoral College of 444–87, the largest majority in more than sixty years. Bishop Cannon's ad hoc Conference of Anti-Smith Democrats was strong enough in the South to peel five eternally Democratic states from their shared history and hand them to Hoover. An exultant Scott McBride of the ASL—which had, for the first time in its history, endorsed a presidential candidate—said that the rout of Al Smith guaranteed that the Democrats would never again nominate a wet. Even more gratifying to the ASL and its allies, Americans had elected the driest Congress ever, with top-heavy margins of 80–16 in the Senate and 329–106 in the House. Of the forty-eight governors, forty-three were drys.

Yet these numbers were impressive only insofar as they threw up a smokescreen; in Lichtman's phrase, it was a "phony referendum." Not only had anti-Catholic prejudice been a much more potent issue than Prohibition, but neither mattered as much as the eight years of Republican prosperity that would have ensured a Hoover victory over *any* Democrat. Buried beneath the landslide was a stack of data suggesting that the drys had counted the wrong ballots. In states where the issue could be separated from such complications as party, personality, or the pope—when it was simply a matter of voters choosing whether to live under the protection of the dry law or break free of the hobbles it imposed on their lives—the news for the drys was not good. While only 40 percent of Montanans voted for Smith, 54 percent voted against a statewide Prohibition enforcement law. In Massachusetts, where Smith won barely 50 percent of the vote, a state enforcement repeal measure passed by nearly two to one. Nor was this countertrend confined to the first Tuesday in November. Five months before the presidential election, statewide repeal had captured 48 percent of the vote in North Dakota—*North Dakota!*—where Prohibition had been embedded in the state constitution for four decades. Six months after Hoover beat Smith by nine points in Wisconsin, a 63 percent majority tossed out that state's enforcement law. Americans may have voted against Al Smith in 1928, but that didn't mean they were voting for Prohibition.

The most meaningful consequences of Smith's campaign lay just beyond the vision of the drys who celebrated his defeat. Soon they would realize that, if anything, his devotion to the disembowelment of the Volstead Act had initiated what would become a major realignment of the parties. Catholics flocked to Smith, of course, but so had other wets who finally had a candidate willing to fly their banner. In an era when Republican machines controlled Chicago, Philadelphia, and other urban centers, the Democrats for the first time ever carried the nation's ten largest cities. A candidate appealing to new citizens and other hyphenates drew nearly twice as many votes as had either James Cox in 1920 or John Davis in 1924—two Democrats who hadn't dared embrace the wet cause.

Historian Daniel Boorstin once wrote, in another context, that there is a difference between a political machine and a political party. He could have been writing about the Democrats of 1928. A machine, wrote Boorstin, "exists for its own sake; its primary, and in a sense its only, purpose is survival." A party, on the other hand, "is organized for a purpose larger than its own survival"—by way of example, for a cause. There were several reasons why the ideological coloration of the national Democrats began to change so rapidly starting in 1928, but a critical one was rooted in the campaign of Al Smith. By openly waving the wet flag, a man who had emerged from the nation's most notorious machine had initiated the radical reinvention of his soon-to-be-dominant party.

PART IV

THE BEGINNING
OF THE END,
THE END,
AND AFTER

———·•·———

"As was said before upon a memorable occasion when the very incarnation of morality was about to be sacrificed, 'What thou doest, do quickly.'"

—Malcolm C. Tarver, a Georgia dry, in the House
of Representatives, December 5, 1932

Chapter 19

Outrageous Excess

O N DECEMBER 12, 1928, just five weeks after he learned that his investment in Al Smith's campaign had not enabled him to purchase a president, John J. Raskob made a simpler acquisition: 14 cases of gin, 7¼ cases of Scotch, and 3 cases of rum. The $1,651 price tag was pocket change for Raskob, but still impressive. In 2009 dollars it worked out to about $70 a bottle, which was presumably enough to provide his bootlegger a reasonable profit after the cost of manufacture, bottling, shipping, transfer from a mother ship to an inshore boat, more shipping, probably another transfer or two, and several bribes, protection payments, and related gratuities along the way. Unless Raskob was a connoisseur with discerning taste buds, it might have covered the cost of counterfeit labels and bottles as well.

"I am not a drinking man. Drinking means nothing to me," Raskob told the readers of *Collier's* a few years later. He was still chairman of the Democratic Party at the time, and still trying to impress upon the voting public that a position against Prohibition was not necessarily a position in favor of liquor. He was equally disingenuous in his attempt to suggest that his vast wealth did not make him any different from anyone else. "Ours are simple pleasures," he continued, strumming homespun chords. "Sports out of doors, family talks and games indoors, no smoking, drinking or running around at all hours of the night." Such, apparently, were the earnest days and hearthside evenings Raskob spent at Archmere, his twentieth-century version of a fifteenth-century Italian palazzo on the banks of the Delaware River; at Pioneer Point Farms, his summer estate on Maryland's Eastern Shore (whose manor house he liked to call "Mostly Halls"); at his winter retreat in Palm Beach; or at the Ritz-Carlton in New York, where an entire floor was reserved for his and Pierre du Pont's use.

But Raskob was in fact a drinking man—he favored dry martinis—and he liked to have his drink close at hand. In Palm Beach "liquor is being sold as openly as ever," he told a friend in 1924. He sometimes wished he were abroad, he wrote on another occasion, so he could "forget between drinks that there is such a thing as the Volstead Act." A few years later, he was sharing bootleg connections with his friends and stocking his various yachts with enough cocktail shakers, highball glasses, champagne glasses, cases of tonic water, and containers of cashews to suggest, said a scholar who cataloged Raskob's voluminous papers, that his boats were "floating speakeasies."

And why not? Despite a few spasms like the raids Mabel Willebrandt had supervised on the night of Smith's nomination, by 1929 drinking among the privileged in New York and other major cities was no longer conducted in the closet. (At least not among the publicly wet; Raskob liked to tease his publicly dry pals, auto executives Walter P. Chrysler and Alfred P. Sloan, about the "vintage champagnes, rare old wines and selected brands of old whiskeys" they stored in their club lockers.) A Park Avenue company that rented out bars—"set up right in your home, completely installed for dashing gay usage, gleaming chromium foot rail and all"—advertised unabashedly in *The New Yorker*. So did speakeasies that had once required passwords, membership cards, and a careful eyeballing through a peephole in the door. Out-of-state visitors to "21" who didn't trust their providers back home needed only to ask to have the speakeasy's operators ship their fine goods to them directly. The relatively furtive imbibing at private men's clubs gradually grew more open, too, and if it ended in the sort of embarrassment that befell the members of the Pendennis Club in Louisville, when a raid on their neo-Georgian mansion turned up enough illegal liquor to fill six Prohibition Bureau vehicles, so be it: although much of the booze had been stashed in members' private lockers, the only people arrested by the agents were four employees, including the hapless fellow who ran the club's cigar stand.

At least it could be said of the men of the AAPA that they were not, for the most part, hypocrites. It was true that James Wadsworth, while still a senator, publicly refused to take advantage of his power to name Prohibition agents, yet privately complained that too many of the jobs were going to Democrats. It was also true that the mise-en-scène implicit in Raskob's self-portrait—a cozy fireplace after some brisk tobogganing, cups of cocoa, maybe a round of Chinese checkers for the whole gosh-darn family—was rather at odds with his adventures aboard the *Flying Fox* (monthly cost of provisions: $1,000) or his inveterate Broadway theater hopping. Still, Raskob, Wadsworth, and their colleagues were willing to venture their reputations when they decided to oppose Prohibition actively and in public. Contrarily, Andrew Mellon, who loathed the Eighteenth Amendment and the Volstead Act, was actually in a position to do something about Prohibition enforcement—he was, it was said, "the only Treasury Secretary under whom three presidents served"—but he evidently valued his influence too highly to imperil it. When his son Paul brought some Yale friends home to Pittsburgh one winter, Mellon didn't stop them from having a blowout drinking party; he just asked them not to throw their empties out the window. After the snow melted, he explained, the neighbors might notice.

PAULINE SABIN HAD been among those wet and wealthy Republicans who had stayed loyal to Hoover during the 1928 race. Many of them either had not yet placed Prohibition ahead of other issues at play in the campaign or had chosen to believe that a man as worldly and as educated as Hoover couldn't possibly be a genuine dry. In June 1928 Sabin had announced her leap to the wet side in a magazine article headlined "I Change My Mind on Prohibition." Sabin explained the reasoning behind her switch, and went on to criticize dry women blinded by their devotion to this one cause. She could not understand how they could support a dry candidate for, say, the Senate "without taking enough interest to question his stand on other matters of vital importance to our country." Her loyalty to Hoover throughout the campaign demonstrated that she was not guilty of the same transgression. His favorable words about Prohibition at the Republican convention in August ("noble in motive and far-reaching in purpose") did not loosen her faith. She put together a group of "wives of financiers" to raise money for the campaign, and at a rally of Republican women she hosted at Bayberry Land early in September, she fell into a virtual swoon, calling Hoover "the greatest humanitarian of this age." Following his victory she continued to believe this humanitarian spirit would manifest itself in an enlightened approach to the Volstead Act and the Eighteenth Amendment.

Then, on March 4, 1929, Hoover shredded her hopes. Standing on the East Portico of the Capitol, his face spattered by a constant rain, the new president opened his inaugural address with the usual formal niceties. Then, in the clipped diction that made his public remarks seem even sterner than he likely meant them to be, Hoover leapt into the Prohibition wars by declaring that "disregard and disobedience of law" was the "most malign" of any danger facing America. This was followed by a rapid series of rhetorical blows that would have caused even the most moderate wet to yelp in pain. Hoover assailed states that did not take their responsibility for concurrent enforcement seriously; he castigated otherwise law-abiding citizens for patronizing criminals; and he effectively declared that anyone who looked the other way when Prohibition laws were being violated was personally responsible for the breakdown in law enforcement. "The worst evil of disregard for some law," the new president proclaimed, "is that it destroys respect for all law." And then he revealed his plan to address this vexing problem: he was going to appoint a commission to look into it.

Pauline Sabin, unable to discern in the president's speech even a suggestion that there might be something wrong with the law itself, was stunned. The next day she resigned from the Republican National Committee. A few days after that, she gathered with eleven other socially prominent women, none of them any more accustomed to political agitation than they were to mopping floors. "We had no name for our organization," Sabin wrote years later. "We had no definite platform. All that we had was youth, strength, and conviction." And, she might have added, money, stature, brains, and a determination not to reform Prohibition but to abolish it.

JAMES CANNON JR. was immeasurably gratified by the thoroughness of the Republican victory in 1928. "The enemies of the Eighteenth Amendment have been ignominiously routed," the bishop declared in triumphant glee. The Smith-Raskob attempt "to place the national government in the hands of the wet sidewalks of our cities" had failed. So, of course, had Cannon's ungainly syntax, but that didn't slow him down. He kept his Conference of Anti-Smith Democrats alive well into 1929, another regiment of reinforcements for the crusade he was about to commence.

Cannon and his allies read the election of 1928 as a signal to assault wet resistance and stir dry complacency. Emboldened by what they insisted was a great dry victory, they pursued an agenda more extreme than anything Wayne Wheeler had ever attempted. Where Wheeler had avoided committing the Anti-Saloon League to openly xenophobic positions, Cannon campaigned for a constitutional amendment that would have removed noncitizens from the tallies that determined the size of congressional districts. He called as well for a radical increase in the Prohibition Bureau budget, "even if it should require $100,000,000." Wheeler, of course, had always avoided this red-hot wire, aware that many congressional Republicans would sooner tolerate the bad joke that was Prohibition enforcement than they would abide the expenditure of another federal nickel.

Neither the apportionment amendment nor the budget increase got very far. But Cannon soon alit upon a single instrument that would make use of the huge dry majorities in Congress, demonstrate the wrathful intent of the dry vanguard, whip the federal judicial system into line, and not cost any meaningful money. The legislation Cannon devised became known as the Jones Law, after its nominal sponsor, Wesley L. Jones of Washington, who had spent much of the decade carrying the ASL's water on the Senate floor. It was a vehicle built for punishment, and so severe it seemed powered by vengeance. The Jones Law turned most Volstead violations, which had been misdemeanors, into felonies. First offenders were subject to five years' imprisonment plus a fine of ten thousand dollars. For the first time, purchasers—even witnesses to the sale or transport of liquor—could be considered violators, since failure to report a felony was now itself a felony and could send the bystander to prison for three years. Any citizen unable to pay a Jones Law fine could work it off at a rate of a dollar per additional day spent in prison, while aliens were subject to deportation. The Jones Law passed the Senate by a vote of 65–18 and carried the House 284–90.

It may have been the biggest mistake the ASL ever made. Cannon and his associates had been blinded by fog. Reading the 1928 election results as definitive when they were in fact deceptive, they perceived a national mandate that didn't exist. Although the Jones Law did allow judges some discretion in sentencing—they were allowed to make the distinction between "casual" violators and participants in a "commercial" enterprise—what stuck in the public mind was the idea that the bartender at the local speakeasy, or the widow who ran the mining-camp rooming house, or the farmer who made a few extra dollars peddling hard cider could conceivably be sentenced to five years in federal prison for a single infraction. The original maximum for a first offense had been six months and a thousand dollars. Under the Jones Law, not only had both penalties increased tenfold, but if you couldn't come up with the cash and instead wanted to work off a ten-thousand-dollar fine at a dollar a day, you could theoretically spend another twenty-seven *years* behind bars.

The ASL's rising thirst for retribution provoked the public's plunging tolerance for it, abetted by the most influential man in American journalism. Motivated either by a genuine conversion—he had begun the decade as a dry—or by a newspaper peddler's feel for the tilt of public opinion, William Randolph Hearst called the Jones Law "the most menacing piece of repressive legislation that has stained the statute books of this republic since the Alien and Sedition laws" of 1798. Around the same time he launched his version of William C. Durant's essay-writing competition. In the Hearst contest, however, the object was not to make Prohibition work, but to address the troubles it had provoked. It generated more than seventy thousand entries, including one from a New York lawyer who lamented the change in social habits wrought by Prohibition. Before, he wrote, young women wouldn't dance with young men who had liquor on their breath; now, though, "they follow the breath to the flask." The winning entry called for the immediate legalization of beer and wine through revision to the Volstead Act.

During the weeks before and after enactment of the Jones Law, and against the backdrop of the campaign Hearst conducted on the front pages of his twenty-eight daily newspapers, excessive or misguided enforcement efforts also won the attention of an increasingly disapproving public. The *Chicago Tribune* was particularly aggressive in its coverage of dry malfeasance. Customs agents, said the *Tribune*, employed "terroristic enforcement methods," including the boarding, in New York harbor, of a private yacht belonging to the family of railroad tycoon Stuyvesant Fish. The paper terrified (or titillated) its readers with a report on a twelve-year-old girl, accompanied in court by neither a lawyer nor any friend or family member, who was nevertheless sentenced to thirty days' imprisonment for carrying a quart of liquor across a street in Greenville, South Carolina.

An incident that took place just forty miles west of Chicago provoked the *Tribune*'s editors to indulge in an orgy of coverage that in its frequency, its prominence, and its amplitude suggested that Armageddon was at hand. In the town of Aurora, local officers handed the *Tribune* (and the dozens of papers nationwide that glommed on to the episode) a story it rode for months. In "the peaceful green valley of the Fox River," the *Tribune* sighed, Mrs. Lillian DeKing "lay bleeding to death in the kitchen of her home." She had been shot "over a few bottles of liquor in the DeKing basement," the paper added. If her husband was indeed a small-time bootlegger, his were hardly the sort of crimes that should bring to the family doorstep "six officers of the law, armed with sawed off shotguns, pistols, machine guns, bulletproof vests, and tear bombs."

A *Tribune* editorial headlined "The Massacre in Aurora" fretted that "we have become accustomed to outrageous excesses" in enforcement, but "the cold-blooded cruelty described in this case" was beyond comprehension. Another story claimed that Mrs. DeKing had been shot "while she was telephoning a lawyer to protest against the raiders' invasion of her home." The paper capped its coverage with the creation of that tried and true guarantor of public sympathy, a fund for the education of twelve-year-old Gerald DeKing. Not only had little Gerald witnessed the tragic events, he had heroically grabbed his father's revolver and returned fire, hitting a deputy sheriff in the leg. Concerned Chicagoans responded to the *Tribune's* organ music, and the paper saluted them by publishing their names and the sums they had donated ("V. E. Healy and friends, $200 . . . W. P. Cooney, $10 . . . 'Disgusted Citizen,' $2").

But the case that drew the most intense response, in Chicago and elsewhere, unspooled in Lansing, Michigan, just miles from the state capitol building, where dry legislators had outdone Congress with a law mandating a life sentence for a fourth violation of the liquor laws. A couple of men had already been imprisoned under this draconian statute, but the arrest, conviction, and sentencing of Mrs. Etta Mae Miller—all of which occurred while Wesley Jones was carrying Bishop Cannon's pet bill through Congress—became the apotheosis of enforcement excess. Mrs. Miller was forty-eight. She had ten children. Her husband was already serving time on a Volstead conviction. But her fourth violation was her fourth violation, and the state law requiring a life term was indifferent to the fact that Etta Mae Miller's crime was the sale of two pints of liquor to an undercover cop.

Three comments—two made directly in response to the Miller case, one uttered around the same time in reference to the general state of the Prohibition laws—embodied the general reaction. *Time* magazine said, "In the same court on the same day" that Miller was sentenced to prison for the rest of her natural life, "a bellboy had pleaded guilty to manslaughter [and] had been fined $400 and freed." Dr. Clarence True Wilson of the Methodist Board of Temperance, Prohibition, and Public Morals said, "Our only regret is that the woman was not sentenced to life imprisonment before her ten children were born." And the new president, just one month into his term, told a group of editors that if a law is appropriate, "its enforcement is the quickest method of compelling respect for it." But Herbert Hoover also said, "If a law is wrong, its rigid enforcement is the surest guarantee of its repeal."

IN MOST RESPECTS the Jones Law and the other harsh statutes failed. Designed either to intimidate large-scale bootleggers or to lock them away for meaningful prison terms, the laws had the opposite effect. A sentence like the one imposed on Etta Mae Miller was more likely to scare away amateurs than to disrupt the transnational commerce of the criminal syndicates, which had large complements of lawyers, cops, judges, federal

Prohibition officials, and other useful associates on their payrolls. In some jurisdictions prosecutors didn't even bother to bring cases under the law, and in others they saw juries shrink from convicting when they considered the severe penalties that would result. "In attempting to strengthen enforcement," wrote historian Norman Clark, "the ASL had turned it into an absurdity."

Herbert Hoover was only barely more effective than the Jones Law. In his inaugural address he had identified "a dangerous expansion in the criminal elements" who were threatening the public welfare, and he acknowledged that the menace was rooted in the liquor trade. The St. Valentine's Day Massacre in Chicago, which left seven gangsters dead on the floor of a Chicago garage just three weeks before Inauguration Day, was vivid evidence of an escalation in violence. Three months later the Atlantic City "peace conference" of mobsters from five cities signified the new level of sophistication that criminals had attained.

Unlike Harding, some of whose highest officials actively abetted the bootlegging industry, and unlike Coolidge, whose lack of interest in enforcement was commensurate with his lack of interest in government activity of any kind, Hoover tried to do something about it. Because he was an engineer, he believed that all problems had solutions; because he was a progressive, he considered an efficient, systematized approach to government reform an article of faith. The earnestness of these convictions, which had won him the derisive nickname "Wonder Boy," inspired Hoover to appoint the investigative commission whose creation pushed Pauline Sabin into the wet camp. Chaired by former attorney general George W. Wickersham, it came to conclusions so mushy and indistinct that neither wet nor dry knew whether the commission's final report was a victory or a defeat for their respective positions. Still, Hoover's belief in rational government did lead to some positive initiatives, including placing enforcement responsibility in the hands of professional managers free of the contaminating influence of the Anti-Saloon League. He also made an effort to remove U.S. attorneys who were not fully committed to Prohibition enforcement. But in one moment of despair, when he concluded that the unchecked lawlessness in Detroit indicated "a complete breakdown in Government," Hoover briefly considered sending in the army or the marine corps.

He could have chosen an easier target. Gun violence had turned the Detroit River into a combat zone. "Indiscriminate shooting on the river" caused a group of local yachtsmen to make a formal protest to Congress. At any given hour, as many as fifteen hundred boats were dashing one way or another along its eighteen miles, either laden with illegal cargo or return-ing to the Canadian side for more. During one of the periodic crackdowns that the government bestirred itself to conduct, customs officials somehow managed to seize 366 rum-running boats; 365 of them were subsequently stolen from the government storage facility. The notorious goons of the Purple Gang moved into new enterprises, including a protection racket that erupted into an epidemic of bombings and murders. A breakaway fac-tion that came to be known as the Little Jewish Navy moved in on the Purples' smuggling business. The violence escalated. Had Hoover gone ahead with his plan to send in troops, it would have demonstrated the utter failure of the law; his decision not to do so suggested the utter helplessness of government itself.

An article in *Outlook* was headlined "War on the River." The *New York Times* elaborated: "Rum War Forces Amass on the Detroit Front." None of this was helpful to the drys. The depredations of the big-city mobsters became so well known that any doubt about Prohibition's impact on the spread of violent crime had melted away. This was especially true once the Chicago newspapers, overwhelmingly wet, latched on to the perfect protagonist for the cops-and-bootleggers saga that had gripped urban America. "Alphonse Capone is, without a doubt, the best advertised and most talked of gangster in the United States," a federal agent would write, and no one deserved more credit for that than Capone himself.

Referring to the way his organization provided "the light pleasures" to the people of Chicago, Capone once said, "Public service is my motto." He might as readily have said "public relations." He made himself end-lessly available to the newspapers, feeding them quotable material. When he didn't have anything particularly interesting to say, he seemed willing to let the newspapermen be his ghostwriters. "When I sell liquor, it's boot-legging," either Capone or one of his amanuenses said. "When my patrons serve it on a silver tray on Lake Shore Drive, it's hospitality." It was a recur-rent theme, this shrugging disavowal of evil intent: "Ninety percent of the people of Cook County drink and gamble," he said at another time, "and my offense has been to furnish them with those amusements."

To the tabloid press Capone was known as "Scarface." Inside the mob community he was "the Big Fellow." To his friends, he was known by the substantially less imposing nickname "Snorky," a slang term roughly equivalent to "spiffy." Press photographers couldn't resist the silk robes and pajamas Capone bought by the dozen from Sulka, the camel-hair coats, the popsicle-colored suits, and all the other lush plumage he favored. Through his avid cultivation of the press, and through the press's equally avid exploitation of his avidity, wrote Alva Johnston, "Al Capone was a world figure at an age when Napoleon was still a wretched shavetail."

There should be no doubt: Al Capone was a very bad man. He had a violent streak of terrifying intensity, and he helped establish the ethos of an industry that countenanced murder as a way to end a negotiation (or, in some instances, to begin one). In the brief period he ran Chicago, gunfights and bombings were almost as dependable as sunrises. His racketeers nurtured scores of illegitimate businesses and crippled or devoured legitimate ones. They corrupted labor unions by the dozen and politicians and police officials by the hundreds. The beer the Capone trucks delivered to Chicago speakeasies every Tuesday and Saturday morning wasn't any good— "lousy was the word" for Capone's stuff, a competitor said. Capone's men just happened to excel at a certain kind of violent salesmanship.

In fact, though, the gorillas and gunsels of the Purple Gang were probably more murderous than Al Capone's thugs. Boo Boo Hoff's Philadelphia-based industrial liquor empire covered more territory than Capone's operation. And the Lansky-Luciano combine in New York certainly outdid the Chicago mob in its sophistication and, it would turn out, its longevity. But Capone topped them all in his desire for publicity and his knack for getting it. All those fawning stories, all those bloody headlines, all those wire-service photos of the thick-lipped, jowly, 235-pound Snorky dolled up in outfits that made him look, as a New York reporter once wrote, "like an overstuffed capon"—all of this was very bad for the drys.

"Due to free advertising in the newspapers," an IRS agent wrote during the government's investigation of Capone for income tax evasion in 1931, "he became the 'Big Shot', Capone the immune, Capone the idol of the hoodlum element." And, he might have added, "Capone the creature of Prohibition." Without the one, more and more Americans had come to believe, you couldn't have had the other.

IN SO MANY WAYS, 1929 turned out to be a rotten year for the drys. Overconfidence had led to legislative overreaching and, at the same time, had provoked the smug complacency that accrues to the self-satisfied. Henry Ford, for instance, imperiously declared he would close his factories if drink ever came back. The more the drys preened, the more material they provided to a growing circle of influential cynics and satirists. It was one thing for *The New Yorker* to dispose of Ford's arrogance with mockery ("It would be a great pity to have Detroit's two leading industries destroyed at one blow"). But when the women of the WCTU, confident of their final victory over alcohol, declared war on Coca-Cola, derision came from the formerly friendly. Wrote the ex-dry William Allen White, "At the spectacle of men returning home, sodden with Coca-Cola, to beat their wives, [or] the sight of little children tugging at their fathers as they stand at the Coca-Cola bars long after midnight . . . we remain unmoved."

The high-riding drys of 1929 may have been immune to sarcasm; they may not even have recognized it. But the increasingly wet daily press was influential and vigilant, igniting fireworks that illuminated a sustained streak of corruption and dry transgressions. A fairly large rocket had gone up in August and September of 1928, during the presidential campaign, when a Philadelphia grand jury, supported by a dry mayor, revealed a police conspiracy so vast it had engulfed the entire force and so lush it caught the attention of newspapers across the country. Upon taking office earlier in the year, Mayor Harry A. Mackey had sought to separate the corrupt members of the police department from their accustomed rackets by scrambling their assignments; in one stroke 3,800 of the city's 4,500 cops were transferred from one part of town to another or moved from headquarters duty to the streets, or vice versa. Ensuing investigations turned up some ranking captains and inspectors who, on annual salaries ranging from $2,500 to $4,000, had amassed bank accounts approaching $200,000. Asked to explain his wealth, one cop said he was lucky at craps and poker. Another said he got rich raising "thoroughbred dogs," another by "building bird cages for the retail trade." The most audacious explanation came from the officer who said he had lent money to grateful saloonkeepers who had then died, leaving generous bequests in their wills. One mob operation had become so blasé about bribes that its bookkeepers didn't bother to disguise a payable they recorded in their ledger book: "Cops, $29,400."

As detailed as it was, the Philadelphia story was really just a somewhat richer account of the official venality that had been Prohibition's symbiotic relative since its inception. But 1929 was different, bringing a fistful of stories exposing the hypocrisy of dry politicians sipping—or guzzling—cocktails while voting to slam the pathetic likes of Etta Mae Miller into prison cells. A broad account of this phenomenon appeared in *Collier's* in February, under the headline "Bartender's Guide to Washington." This romp through a city "so wet that it squishes" chronicled a liquor trade so pervasive, so widely accepted, and so essential to the lives of politicians and federal bureaucrats that the author felt it necessary to assure his readers that "there are, of course, Washingtonians and legislators who do not drink." Not many, apparently; one senator noted that a Scotch importer had provided the capital's embassies, which were not subject to American law, with thirteen thousand quarts of "diplomatic whisky" in a single three-month period—the equivalent of twenty quarts for every diplomat, diplomat's relative, or embassy staff member in town. A prominent Washington bootlegger said that "when Congress recessed and the members returned home, the bottom fell out" of the local market.

One of those who claimed to be a lifetime abstainer made Washington's first post–Jones Law splash in late March. Congressman William M. Morgan of Ohio represented a district drier than burnt toast. He stuck by his position even after he was apprehended by customs officers in the port of New York on returning from the Canal Zone with his wife and several other couples. The officers said they'd found two bottles of whiskey and two bottles of champagne in Morgan's bags. They also testified that he had tried to intimidate them, before trying to cajole them, before finally admitting he was bringing the goods back (under the "freedom of the port" granted to members of Congress) as a gift for his father-in-law, a Civil War veteran. When an enterprising reporter reached the old man in Logans Ferry, Pennsylvania, he was of little help to Morgan. "If there was any liquor brought for me," said eighty-seven-year-old Hugh Logan, "I haven't seen any of it around here."

Morgan continued to deny the customs officers' assertions. But while his story was still unreeling in the papers, another dry Republican, M. Alfred Michaelson of Illinois, earned headlines with similar adventures in the importing business. On a railway platform in Jacksonville, Florida, two trunks Michaelson had brought back from a different trip to the Canal Zone sprang leaks. These bags, like Morgan's, had also enjoyed freedom of the port; as *Time* explained it, "many a Congressman during recesses of Congress goes to Panama (wet) for a vacation, pretending to make an official study of the Canal Zone, and thus becomes eligible for 'free entry' on return." According to the indictment, one of Michaelson's trunks contained six quarts of whiskey, two of crème de menthe, one each of several other liqueurs, and a whole keg of something the indictment identified as "plum barbacourt," which was almost certainly Rhum Barbancourt, from Haiti. Like Morgan, Michaelson employed the in-law defense. Upon the guilty plea of his brother-in-law, a Chicago coal dealer who had taken part in this important fact-finding trip to inspect the bolts on the Panama Canal, or maybe the water temperature, the presiding judge addressed the man's lawyer: "I have no desire to punish him for the faults of the escaped congressman—one of those who votes dry and drinks wet," the judge said. The brother-in-law got off with a one-thousand-dollar fine; the congressman declared himself vindicated.

Michaelson's was not the last of the leaking luggage cases, or even the one that provided the wet press with the most piquant opportunity to indulge its appetite for exposing dry deceit. That honor went to the case of Representative Edward E. Denison of Illinois, who had demonstrated his aptitude for dry constituent services back in 1924, when he persuaded Roy Haynes of the Prohibition Bureau to deputize the Klan-affiliated vigilantes who had been terrorizing the Italian-American mineworkers of Williamson County. Denison's imports from Panama—eighteen bottles of Scotch, six of gin—made it all the way to his office in the Capitol Building. According to the *New York Times*, "he explained [to Prohibition agents] it was not liquor but a set of dishes from Panama that was in the trunk. The agents were skeptical." It was liquor, all right, and only the adroit maneuvering of Denison's lawyer kept him, like Morgan and Michaelson, from conviction under the Jones Law—which all three had voted for.*

Each time a prominent dry was dragged dripping into court, the wet press reveled in it. Each time the accused dodged the law's bullet, the wet press vented. When George L. Cassiday, a bootlegger known as "the man in the green hat," was arrested inside the Senate Office Building, reporters suggested that the ensuing prosecution would reveal a lengthy list of drys among his Capitol Hill customers, and they were crushed when it didn't. But the case of dry errancy that most excited the wets, most thoroughly discombobulated the retreating drys, and most rewarded the scandal-hungry press, didn't involve liquor at all. This was the furor that brought down the Anti-Saloon League's most potent operative, James Cannon Jr. In the summer of 1929 the *Lynchburg News* in Virginia, which was owned by Senator Carter Glass, charged that while Bishop Cannon was principal of the Blackstone Female Institute during World War I, he had been guilty of . . . hoarding flour.

On its own, the charge didn't make for the most exciting reading. According to the paper, Blackstone had secured an allotment of 425 barrels of flour for its 385 students, while nearby Randolph-Macon Women's College had needed only 175 barrels for 806 students. Similar figures from five other women's schools established that each young lady at Blackstone had enjoyed 309 loaves of bread per year, while the average at the other colleges was a mere 48. The Blackstone women did not look overfed, so

---

*Denison's testimony about swapped luggage, misplaced keys, inept shipping clerks, and the malevolent intent of investigators could have provided a plotline for a stage farce. "You've got a fairy story in this case," the frustrated young prosecutor shouted during closing arguments. "It's the fairy story of those dishes!" The prosecutor was Mabel Willebrandt's friend, the future federal judge John J. Sirica.

the flour under Cannon's control must have ended up elsewhere—presumably converted to cash and deposited in Cannon's pocket.

Carter Glass was every bit as dry as Cannon, but for twenty years he had been the bishop's sworn rival for control of the Democratic Party in the Commonwealth, and in 1928 he had remained loyal to Smith and the national Democrats. Glass had been husbanding the flour-hoarding information for a decade when Cannon's pious image was defaced in June 1929 by the *New York World*. The paper revealed that the bishop was a hard-core stock speculator. Stolen documents that the *World* had purchased for $4,000 established that over the course of two years, Cannon had traded nearly $500,000 worth of securities through a fraud-riddled brokerage firm whose principals were on their way to jail.* To the devout among Cannon's followers, market speculation was gambling and therefore sinful. The flour-hoarding accusation confirmed the taint of greed that was settling around Cannon, and, worse yet, it allowed his enemies to label him unpatriotic.

Finally, followers of this unfolding catalog of sins arrived at the clincher: lust. Cannon and his second wife had conducted an illicit affair in New York's Union Square Hotel before his first wife's death. A sort of clubhouse for actors, producers, and other figures in the Yiddish theater, the Union Square was the perfect venue for Cannon's trysts, a friend believed, for there were few places in New York where the bishop and his paramour were less likely to be recognized.

The revelation of sexual errancy was juicier than flour hoarding. William Randolph Hearst waved the bloody flag in his newspapers. A group of Methodist clergymen, including the chaplain of the U.S. Senate, accused Cannon of "gross moral turpitude and disregard for the first principles of Christian ethics." The College of Methodist Bishops convened a formal tribunal to investigate the charges. Newspapers in two Georgia cities compared Cannon to Al Capone. In the end, even though neither civil nor ecclesiastic authority convicted Cannon of anything, the public humiliation of the nation's most prominent Prohibitionist was complete. Discredited by the wets and disowned by the drys, James Cannon was through. The man H. L. Mencken had once called "the most powerful ecclesiastic ever heard of in America" had become, wrote historian Michael S. Patterson, "a non-entity both to his church and to the general public."

---

*One of them, Harry Goldhurst, né Herschel Goldhirsch, emerged from his five years' imprisonment for mail fraud under yet another name. More than twenty years later, as Harry Golden, he published the huge bestseller *Only in America*, a collection of columns from his weekly paper, *The Carolina Israelite*.

✦ ✦ ✦

THREE OTHER CRACKS threatened the once-sturdy walls of the dry fortress in 1929. The first, which passed by with surprisingly little notice, showed up early in the year, when Congress finally got around to addressing the nagging little matter of reapportionment. More than eight years had passed since the last census, eight years during which rural (i.e., largely dry) representation had remained inflated out of proportion to rural population. The Senate sponsor of the successful reapportionment bill, Arthur Vandenberg of Michigan (his state would pick up four seats), noted that not only were twenty-three seats in the House misallocated, but in the next presidential election this would place twenty-three electoral votes in undeserving hands as well. Failure to reapportion, said Vandenberg, would not only "taint the validity of Congress, it taints the validity of the Presidency itself."

Cotton Tom Heflin did not miss his cue, invoking the "refuse of foreign countries" who would take over Congress if the reapportionists had their way. His Alabama colleague Hugo L. Black, infinitely more civilized but no less protective of his state (and, by extension, of the dry laws both men supported), called reapportionment "unjust and unrighteous," for favoring the cities over the countryside. But by this point it was no longer tenable to resist the arguments for its passage, including an especially provocative one offered by retired admiral William W. Kimball in a letter to the *Washington Post*. Taking Vandenberg's argument one unsettling step further, Kimball maintained that any action taken by a constitutionally malapportioned Congress was itself, by definition, unconstitutional. Regarding the similarly deformed Electoral College, Kimball wrote that Herbert Hoover "has been formally elected . . . as the de facto president of something, perhaps of the de facto nation with a de facto government occupying the territory of what was the United States."

At the same time the apportionment bill was up for debate, a tremor shot through the executive branch: Herbert Hoover fired Mabel Willebrandt. Newspaper reports indicated that "the professional drys" had been lobbying to get Willebrandt appointed "Prohibition generalissimo," with authority over not only the Justice Department prosecutors but over the Prohibition Bureau agents (and possibly the customs officials, coast guardsmen, and other enforcement troops) who remained under the nominal control of the loathed Andrew Mellon. To drys who had misread the 1928 election results, Willebrandt's dismissal should have been evidence that the president did not feel he owed his election to the Anti-Saloon League.

Reapportionment wouldn't by itself turn Congress around. The departure of a dry partisan from a position as critical as Willebrandt's should not have weakened enforcement, at least not in the administration of a man who had based his presidency on "respect for all law." It was only the last of the batterings that Prohibition endured in 1929 that truly signaled its impending collapse. The devastating stock market crash in October may not have caused the Great Depression, but it certainly sounded the alarm that terrible economic times were around the corner. (The alarm didn't awaken everybody; Andrew Mellon's diary entry for Black Thursday read, "Stock market crash in New York. Dinner Belgian Embassy.") When the Depression did arrive, bringing with it massive unemployment, diminishing respect for the federal government, a dizzying collapse in federal tax collections, and wide distaste for the Republican Party, Prohibition was on the ropes. No constitutional amendment had ever been repealed, but the Eighteenth—already threatened by the excesses of its supporters, the resources of its opponents, and the disillusion of virtually everyone else— was beginning to look like a candidate.

Chapter 20

The Hummingbird That
Went to Mars

T HE FOUR-YEAR MARCH from the stock market crash to Repeal
would turn out to be steady and irresistible, but that wasn't
what most wets expected. As late as January 1932 many wet
leaders and sympathetic journalists were still unconvinced that it was possible to secure a Twenty-first Amendment to unravel the Eighteenth. For
one thing, in more than 140 years of constitutional history, not a single
amendment had ever been repealed. Beyond that, as Charles Merz of the
New York Times's editorial board wrote, the imposing math faced by advocates provided "a devastating argument against the possibility of repeal."
On top of the two-thirds vote needed in each house of Congress (which
could be stopped by just thirty-three dry senators), the requisite concurrence of three-quarters of the states was beyond daunting. Ratification
would require the positive action of both houses in each of thirty-six state
legislatures. Thirteen of those seventy-two separate entities "could block
repeal forever," Merz wrote in March 1931. "These thirteen bodies, rightly
apportioned, could exist in states containing approximately 5 per cent of
the country's population."

That same winter, the eloquent James Montgomery Beck, who had
come to refer to Prohibition as "this ghastly farce," asserted that "the
Eighteenth Amendment cannot be repealed within a decade and possibly not within a generation." Clarence Darrow pointed out in November
1931 that thirty-four U.S. senators represented states that were "hopelessly dry," and another twenty came from the "likely" dry, including such
unpromising states as Alabama, Texas, Indiana, and Georgia.

Darrow and Beck both believed that the "ghastly farce" could be ended
only through revocation of the Volstead Act. That would require simple

majorities in Congress and a presidential signature, which were daunting prospects in themselves. The possibility of achieving the much higher thresholds required by a Repeal amendment was a delusion. This grim reality, said Darrow, "should convince the most stupid and optimistic Wet that if he can never buy a drink without repealing the 18th amendment, he had better start right in learning to make his own." Someone who saw Repeal as the only solution is "not against Prohibition," he concluded. "He's in favor of liquor, but against getting it."

Drys were no less convinced of the impossibility of Repeal. Gifford Pinchot, William G. McAdoo, and Jane Addams loaned their names to a new organization so certain of the continued popularity of Prohibition that members confidently called for a national referendum on the subject. (Just in case, a few drys tried, with some success, to persuade African-American voters that repealing the Eighteenth Amendment could open a path to revoking the Thirteenth, Fourteenth, and Fifteenth.) In September 1930 Morris Sheppard, author of the Eighteenth Amendment, said, "There is as much chance of repealing the Eighteenth Amendment as there is for a hummingbird to fly to the planet Mars with the Washington Monument tied to its tail." Few argued.

It was one of those moments when all the experts are wrong and wisdom arises from unlikely sources. Like, for example, from the members of the Union League Club in Manhattan, who were building a new clubhouse on Park Avenue and Thirty-seventh Street and had placed a bet on the future by including a "large, sumptuous bar" in their plans. "We hope and expect to see Prohibition end very soon," a member of the club's house committee said in February 1931. "Prohibition cannot die any too soon for us."

THE SEERS CONTEMPLATING Prohibition's future were not the only people making predictions as the dry era entered its late stage. In October 1929 Irving Fisher, the Yale economist who had remained Prohibition's leading intellectual defender, offered a comment that would earn him a place in American memory far more enduring than would his groundbreaking work on interest rates or even his loopy statistical analyses of beer's effect on the ability to memorize poetry. "Stock prices have reached what looks like a permanently high plateau," said Fisher on October 15, nine days before the earth gave way on Black Thursday. At least he truly believed it: his considerable fortune, invested in the market, followed the Dow Jones Industrial Average into a death spiral.

This was a grave setback for the credibility of the dry movement's favorite scholar, but the effect of the Crash and the Depression on dry goals extended beyond personal humiliation. As businesses came apart, as banks folded, as massive unemployment and homelessness scoured the cities and much of the countryside, any remaining ability to enforce Prohibition evaporated. President Hoover, trying to balance the budget while a hurricane rattled the scales, slashed funding for the already overburdened federal court system. The Prohibition Bureau cut agents' per diem from six dollars to five, and live training sessions were replaced with correspondence courses. The new Prohibition commissioner, a chemist named James M. Doran, had begun his tenure insisting he needed $300 million to enforce the law. But with no more than $12 million made available to him, Doran defaulted to the reflexive optimism pioneered by his predecessor, Roy Haynes. Here's the good news, said Doran: in Prohibition's first nine years, the government had spent some $141 million on all forms of enforcement while collecting more than $460 million in fines, penalties, and taxes—a profit, he boasted, of precisely $319,323,307.76.*

With an argument like that, it's a wonder Doran didn't get his $300 million. A government running on fumes could have made good use of a humming, for-profit business on the side. It had not taken long for the Depression to corrode the inflow of federal tax collections. Revenue based on 1930 incomes was down 15%; the following year saw a 37% drop, and the year after that another 26%—compounded, it was a vertiginous 60% plunge in just three years. Capital gains taxes that had brought $1.5 billion into the treasury between 1926 and 1929 dove into negative territory over the next five years as the allowance for capital losses piled up. At the same time demand for government spending—for relief, for reconstruction projects, for anything to restart the comatose economy—was soaring. Al Capone poked his finger in the eyes of both the drys and the feds when he opened a soup kitchen on South State Street, serving five thousand meals to hungry Chicagoans on Thanksgiving. He apparently had more resources, and more heart, than the people who ran the country.

BESIDES CAPONE AND his fellow mobsters, one other cadre of Americans saw a way to turn the economic catastrophe to their advantage. For

---

*The unnaturally cheerful Doran was adept at finding positive signs in the crumbling edifice of Prohibition. In 1928 he had told a convention of the National Beauty and Barber Supply Dealers Association that the Eighteenth Amendment had done wonders for male grooming: "Under Prohibition the average man has more money to spend," Doran said, "and since he cannot spend it legally for liquor he spends it for shaves, facials, haircuts and manicures."

decades historians of Prohibition have debated the motivations of Pierre du Pont, John Raskob, and their colleagues in the Association Against the Prohibition Amendment. The argument that they backed Repeal to slash their own tax liabilities was first offered by embittered drys and was consequently dismissed as desperate partisanship. It is also undeniably true that du Pont, Raskob, et al., had other reasons to despise Prohibition, specifically its intrusion on individual liberties and its evisceration of states' rights. These were, in fact, the same arguments many of them employed in their across-the-board opposition to woman suffrage, direct election of senators, the income tax amendment itself, and a pending amendment that would give Congress the power to prohibit child labor. As far as John Raskob was concerned, every one of those measures was "a mistake," and collectively explained why "strong men" didn't get involved in politics.

Still, the record clearly establishes that the strong men who ran the AAPA—"almost a Du Pont subsidiary," said Senator Arthur Robinson of Indiana—clearly intended to maim, or possibly even murder, the income tax, and the Depression handed them a weapon as potent as World War I had been for the drys. Or, to invoke another historical analogy: the organized drys had supported the income tax back in 1913 in order to breathe life into Prohibition. Now, this group of powerful and well-funded wets sought to kill Prohibition so that the income tax might die as well.

The idea did not emerge from the AAPA itself. As early as 1923 *Wall Street Journal* publisher Clarence W. Barron, in one of the homespun "Wall Street Seminars" he periodically published in his newspaper, said giving up on Prohibition would enable the government to "collect $2,000,000,000 per annum from drink [and] abolish the income tax." (Barron also insisted that throughout human history only "regulation and taxation" had been successful in the fight against intemperance.)

By 1925 the pre–du Pont AAPA had tentatively picked up a sliver of the idea for its recruitment letter. The pitch was direct: "You will save in reduced taxes, after the Volstead Law is modified, whatever sum you contribute now." The next year Irénée du Pont told William Stayton that General Motors would save $10 million in taxes each year with the return of the alcohol levies. Stayton determined that if Americans consumed the same amount of alcohol they had in 1914, and if it were taxed at the same rate used in Great Britain, net revenue to the government would reach $1.32 billion.

The AAPA's embrace of the tax issue was to some extent the inevitable outgrowth of the group's composition, largely plutocrats, aristocrats, and the politicians who served their interests. (Drafts of AAPA form letters that turned up in a Senate investigation were addressed "Dear Mr. Multi-Millionaire.") James Wadsworth, for one, argued against a broad membership campaign; that would increase "the danger," he said, that "we might get some undesirables." In the lexicon of the AAPA, "undesirables" was a rather loose term. William Stayton told colleagues, "I simply went sick" upon learning that the membership department "had recommended that we go after licensed automobile owners." He wasn't speaking about those who owned automobiles and hired others to drive them around. "You may have ridden some Saturday or Sunday from Annapolis to Baltimore," Stayton explained, the italics apparent in his voice if not on the page, "*and have seen a parade of the auto owner in his shirt sleeves.*" An organization with this sort of worldview wasn't likely to tailor its appeal to the broad electorate. Replacing a graduated income tax with an excise tax, as Irénée du Pont proposed—specifically, a three-cent tax on every glass of beer—would be of substantial value only to the wealthy. The working poor and the unemployed would finance tax relief for the rich.

The AAPA's publicity campaign was centered on pamphlets with such titles as *What Price Prohibition?* (answer: with the return of legal alcohol, "the necessity of levying income taxes would be eliminated"), *Does Prohibition Pay?* and *The Cost of Prohibition and Your Income Tax.* The last, which was the organization's most widely distributed piece of literature, was perfect for its year of publication, 1929. By 1932, as the Depression plunged toward its devastating nadir, it was superseded by an AAPA handout that spoke more urgently to the historical moment: *The Need of a New Source of Government Revenue.* The authors didn't have to look far to identify one, as Pierre du Pont made clear in a radio address that summer: "The income tax would not be necessary in the future," he said, "and half the revenue required for the budget . . . would be furnished by the tax on liquor alone."

That was for public consumption; privately he was even more direct. "The Repeal of the XVIIIth Amendment would permit Federal taxation in the amount of two billion dollars," Pierre du Pont wrote to his brother Lammot in April 1932. After four years of active engagement in the Repeal cause, he didn't mention states' rights, individual rights, or any similarly lofty notions. "Such taxation would almost eliminate the income taxes of corporations and individuals," he concluded. "I feel sure that you will agree that this is of great importance."

IN LATE 1928 E. B. White wrote an essay that touched on the amount New York City was spending "to enforce prohibition, which does not exist." A few months later the *New York Telegram* posed the question "Where on Manhattan Island can you buy liquor?" The paper's answer: "In open saloons, restaurants, night clubs, bars behind a peephole, dancing academies, drugstores, delicatessens, cigar stores, confectioneries . . ." It went on with thirty-one other suggestions, including paint stores, malt shops, and moving-van companies. "Times certainly are different," a housewife in lower Manhattan told an interviewer. "In the old days you never would have thought of buying your wine at the fish store."

New York was distinctive, but by 1930 it was not nearly as distinctive as it had been. The Wickersham Commission reported, "As things are at present, there is virtual local option" throughout the country. The editor of the *Hutchinson News* in Kansas, a longtime dry, acknowledged the tenth anniversary of Prohibition by admitting that "there is ten times as much drinking in Kansas today as there was ten years ago . . . and consumption is increasing rather than diminishing." The following year, when the *Saturday Evening Post* declared that the bohemian Greenwich Village of the 1920s was dead, Malcolm Cowley knew why. "It was dying," he wrote, "because women smoked cigarettes on the streets of the Bronx, drank gin cocktails in Omaha, and had perfectly swell parties in Seattle and Middletown." The Greenwich Village way of life—the pleasurable mingling of both sexes, usually accompanied by music, always accompanied by alcohol—had been taken up, Cowley said, "by salesmen from Kokomo and the younger country-club set in Kansas City." He almost sounded disappointed.

In places where anything but neutral grain alcohol was hard to come by, grocery stores offered a flavoring substance called Peeko, available for seventy-five cents in rye, gin, rum, cognac, crème de menthe, and several other varieties. Just add these "perfect, true flavors" to your grain alcohol, the advertisements said, and drink up. On a far greater scale, the moonshine industry made some legitimate businesses vastly successful. Production of corn sugar, as essential to moonshine as grapes were to wine, soared from 152 million pounds in 1921 to 960 million pounds eight years later. In one four-year period Standard Brands Inc. sold 64,000 packages of Fleischmann's Yeast in Richmond, Virginia, population 189,000. But in Franklin County, in the foothills of the Blue Ridge, where the population was only 24,000 (and, the Wickersham Commission reported, ninety-nine out of a hundred residents were involved in the moonshine business), Fleischmann's moved 2.25 *million* packages in the same four years. It was not just a southern phenomenon. A single wholesale grocer in Rockford, Illinois, took delivery of two to three railroad carloads of corn sugar every week. Prohibition officials announced that they had seized 35,200 illegal stills and distilleries in 1929, plus 26 million gallons of mash, but judging from the amount of liquor washing over the country by that point, it was as if they had plucked a few blades of grass from a golf course.

Another source of liquid refreshment popped up around this time—the Vino Sano Grape Brick, a solid, dehydrated block of grape juice concentrate mixed with stems, skins, and pulp. The size of a pound of butter, it came in a printed wrapper instructing the purchaser to add water to make grape juice, but to be sure *not* to add yeast or sugar, or leave it in a dark place, or let it sit too long before drinking it because "it might ferment and become wine." For those a little slow on the uptake, newspaper ads indicated the choice of flavors: port, sherry, Tokay, burgundy, and so on. The gangster Jack "Legs" Diamond told the *New York Times*, "It sounds like a good racket to me."

The big-time California grape producers thought so, too. After the makers of Vino Sano survived a court challenge—what they sold contained no alcohol, and home manufacture for personal use remained legal—they were joined in the market by Vine-Glo. Produced and marketed by Fruit Industries Limited, a consortium of five of the largest pre-Prohibition wineries, Vine-Glo was a much more sophisticated product. A Fruit Industries agent would deliver a varietal grape juice (the accustomed Tokay, burgundy, "claret," and so on) to the buyer's home in five-, ten-, twenty-five- or fifty-gallon cans, add yeast and citric acid, and insert a tube to vent off gases. Every few weeks the agent would stop by to monitor progress; after sixty days he would arrive with bottles, foil capsules, corks, and labels, even tissue to wrap the bottles in.

As refined as Vine-Glo's service was, its advertisements were no more subtle than Vino Sano's: "Barreled in charred kegs . . . from the presses of the wineries in California . . . What will you have?" A trade ad said, "Vine-Glo has delivered a new message to the American public. A message it has been awaiting for ten years." It even had its own celebrity endorser. Arthur Brisbane, the Hearst editor who had bought the *Washington Times* with brewery money during World War I, provided a blurb for a Fruit Industries handout: "The Grape Growers are not held responsible for the laws of nature, which seem to have no sympathy with Prohibition, and turn innocent Grape Juice into Wine."

Outside the home, especially in the big cities, public drinking places became more civilized. "Speakeasies have run away with the cream of the dinner trade," according to *Harper's*. Restaurants that stayed dry were doomed not just because of public tastes, but also by labor economics: because tips in speakeasies were so much larger, so was the earning power of their waiters and chefs; this attracted the best in the business. Hotel traffic was up a bit, as a lawyer for the American Hotel Association told a Senate committee, because of customers who "sought refuge from this law behind the guest's door." But hoteliers found that "our furniture and rooms were being damaged and destroyed." The solution to one form of furniture abuse was an invention born of Prohibition necessity: the "combination corkscrew–bottle opener, which may be fastened to a door jamb in the bathroom or otherwise."

Another child of late Prohibition was the "cruise to nowhere," aka the "booze cruise," aka the "weekend whoopee cruise." Whatever its name, it was the precursor of the luxury cruise business. These out-and-back trips, their destination a spot in the sea just beyond U.S. territorial waters, were among the first offerings of the United States Lines after American ships were privatized in 1929. The *Leviathan*, which ran cruises of four days' duration when it wasn't on a transatlantic crossing, had its own shipboard brewery. So did the *George Washington*, a fact that became slightly embarrassing after the U.S. delegation to the 1930 Arms Conference in London (secretary of state, secretary of the navy, three ambassadors, two senators) booked passage on it. Both the Grace Lines and the International Mercantile Marine Company built large liners accommodating as many as 750 revelers strictly for what was euphemistically called "the intercoastal trade."

What once was hidden had burst into the open. The term of art for what was happening across the nation was "social nullification." Coverage in the increasingly wet press flaunted evidence of the changing ethos. The *St. Louis Post-Dispatch*, for example, waxed enthusiastic about the Mounds Country Club across the river in Illinois. The Mounds was described by its promoters as "a high-class night club to take care of a long-felt want." The crowd was "strangely inclusive," running from ex-cons and professional gunmen to "Social Register folk" and "the newly rich." Winking broadly to its readers, the paper reported that "wealthy St. Louisans on occasion smuggle champagne into the bone-dry interior of the club, and, miraculously keeping it a secret from the waiters, pop corks against the ceiling, and toast the cock-eyed world."

The new openness spread beyond the news and editorial columns. Ads for Vine-Glo and Vino Sano ran in tiny type in papers as small as the Havre, Montana, *Daily News Promoter* and with bold headlines on full pages in papers as substantial as the *Washington Star* (where Fruit Industries said it wanted to take "a product that has always been available on the farm and place it within the reach of the city dweller"). In 1930 *Vanity Fair* ran a cigarette ad featuring a stylish woman with marcelled hair accepting hors d'oeuvres from a waiter while holding a martini—you can see the olive—in her other hand. Books of cocktail recipes came from respectable publishers, including one who offered former senator Jim Reed's own formula for "pumpkin gin." (Cut a hole in pumpkin, remove seeds, pack with sugar, seal top back in place with paraffin. In thirty days, the sugar and the meat of the pumpkin would be "transformed into a high-powered gin.") One of these books named its various concoctions for their impact—for instance, the Bridge Table (gin, brandy, apricot brandy, and lime juice), which was "so named because after a few of these your legs will fold up."

BACK IN 1927, when Major Maurice Campbell was named federal Prohibition administrator for the New York district, he made it clear that he believed in the Eighteenth Amendment, that he was a teetotaler, and that he intended to conduct a "dignified and just" enforcement effort. He did not approach the open drinking culture of Manhattan timorously. In the ensuing three years Campbell led raids on nightclubs belonging to Texas Guinan and the torch singer Helen Morgan; on the Ritz-Carlton and Manger hotels; and on Mayor Jimmy Walker's favorite playpen, the Central Park Casino, in each instance either arresting waiters and bartenders or shutting the place down. In April 1930 Campbell appeared to cap off his career when he and his men swept through the Hollywood, a stylish nightclub at Broadway and Forty-eighth Street, and arrested twenty-seven people—sixteen employees and eleven patrons, all of them in evening dress, who happened to have liquor in their possession. Campbell said the "Hip Flask Raid," as it would become known, "is the first instance in which persons in possession of intoxicating liquor in public places have been arrested. But if the practice is not discontinued in New York," he warned, "it will not be the last."

The raid turned out not to be the biggest moment in Campbell's public life after all. That came five months later, after he had either resigned because of lack of support from the Justice Department or had been fired for what was characterized as "nonfeasance" (the evidence supported the former interpretation). Campbell soon became the first high-ranking Prohibition official to make a public airing of the corruption, hypocrisy, and political sleaze permeating the federal enforcement program.

In a series of articles commissioned by the *New York World* and syndicated in several other papers, Campbell revealed that Assistant Treasury Secretary Seymour Lowman had asked him to resume the distribution of more than two million gallons of "sacramental" wine as part of a Republican effort "to obtain the Jewish vote in New York City." Lowman had also told him, Campbell said, that New York had become "too dry" in 1928, that it was a presidential election year and "we mustn't do anything to antagonize the voters." Campbell even fingered Vice President Charles Curtis for trying to aid an industrial alcohol scheme cooked up by Curtis's 1928 campaign manager; a month later the man—a former saloon owner, as it happened—was indicted for trying to import "sheep dip" from the Netherlands that turned out to be 95 percent alcohol. Lowman and Curtis made the customary denials and countercharges, but Campbell had copies of memos that confirmed many of his accusations. Summarizing his own situation, Campbell said, "I am out of it all, and it is like coming out of a cesspool and breathing fresh air." He then became the editor of a magazine called *Repeal*.

The Campbell series, appearing just weeks before the 1930 congressional elections, didn't help the dry cause. Neither did a second newspaper blockbuster by bootlegger George Cassiday (aka the Man in the Green Hat), who maintained that he had regularly sold liquor to "a majority of both Houses [of Congress]" and that his typical congressional customer "had a capacity of two or three quarts a week." The risible reelection candidacies of the Leaky Luggage caucus—Representatives Morgan, Michaelson, and Denison—didn't help either; all three were defeated. But much of the huge wet gain that November (in the House alone the wet roster jumped overnight from 76 to 146) could be attributed to the Depression. The Republicans were held responsible for the economic catastrophe; the Democrats were the beneficiaries of the public's anger; and, outside the South, the Democratic Party (John J. Raskob, chairman) was now demonstrably wet. Traditionally Republican states like Ohio and Illinois sent wet Democrats to the Senate in 1930. Even Kansas—*Kansas!*—replaced a dry Republican with a wet Democrat.

At the same time, a wet rebellion had been bubbling on the Republican side. Most of the men of the AAPA were Republicans, and the party organizations in some of the eastern states where they had the greatest influence (New York, New Jersey, Connecticut) endorsed Repeal in 1930. So did the Republicans of Wisconsin. When the Washington state party declared itself wet, it was a repudiation of the state's leading Republican, Senator Wesley Jones, sponsor of the notorious Jones Law. Republican drys were routed in Michigan, where the former head of the state ASL was denied a fifth term in the House by a wet primary challenger. And just six days before the general election, members of the Women's National Republican Club, founded by Pauline Sabin in 1921, had voted 1,391–197 for Repeal. After the wet victories a week later, Sabin said, "I do think our little organization did something to perfect this wet landslide."

Her "little organization," however, was not the WNRC; it was the Women's Organization for National Prohibition Reform, the child of Sabin's meeting with eleven friends in the days after Herbert Hoover's disappointing inaugural address. Her departure from the Republican Party had been big news. The *New York Times* ran it above the fold on the front page, and it appeared in the *Chicago Tribune*, the *Atlanta Constitution*, and the *Washington Post*. Even the *Los Angeles Times*, faithfully dry, gave Sabin's defection page-one display. The people she soon pulled into the WONPR guaranteed that the group would not stay out of the papers very long— socially prominent women whose names defined them better than any adjectives could: Mrs. Archibald B. Roosevelt and Mrs. Courtlandt Nicoll, Mrs. E. Roland Harriman and Mrs. Cornelius M. Bliss, Mrs. Cummins Speakman and Mrs. Coffin Van Rensselaer.

At first it appeared that the women's pedigrees would subject them to ridicule, and in some respects their customs and habits did work against them. At the initial national organizational meeting, in the Drake Hotel in Chicago, the minutes suggested something out of a Helen Hokinson cartoon in *The New Yorker*: "Mrs. Stuyvesant Pierrepont gave a most interesting and satisfactory report of her progress in the State of New Jersey." Volunteers who signed up in the District of Columbia were described in the press as "the inner circle of exclusive Washington society." Sabin was discussed in terms that likely had never before been used to describe the leader of an American political movement. A profile in *McCall's* reported that she was "fond of sports suits, wears purple and blue well, and usually affects pearl lobe earrings." It said her "color sense is unfaltering," as evidenced by her office walls of "pale green, harmonizing with salmon pink curtains." The *Atlanta Constitution* informed its readers that "she plays golf and dances, but swimming is her favorite recreation, indulging to her heart's content in this latter exercise at The Oaks, her plantation near Charleston." *Vogue* ran a piece headlined "Anti-Prohibitionette."

Sabin knew that this was exactly the sort of thing that would help her movement succeed. In the early days every speech, every interview, every piece of congressional testimony was publicized in a way that gave her words extra weight simply because of the unlikely identity of the speaker. When the *Chicago Tribune* quoted one particular Sabin attack on Prohibition, it explained: "These vehement words were spoken, you must remember, not by the old fashioned type of platform termagant, but by a lady sitting in her beautifully appointed drawing room—rare books, good pictures and rich tapestries all around her. They were spoken by . . . a 'society woman' who . . . might with clear conscience be playing around at Miami Beach or on the Riviera, instead of directing 15 secretaries, planning nation-wide campaigns, answering bundles of letters and speaking twice a week at public meetings."

In other words, Pauline Sabin was making it respectable to say things few women felt comfortable saying in public. When she assailed the "scandalous intrusion of the church into matters of legislation," the fact that it was Pauline Sabin—elegant, refined, fabulously wealthy Pauline Sabin—doing the saying enabled other women to find their voices. A leader of the Missouri chapter of the WONPR described the phenomenon well. Not so long ago, said Mrs. Clifford W. Gaylord, being a dry "seemed to have such an overwhelming blanket of responsibility and being a Wet seemed to have quite the opposite. You know, there are a lot of women who may be morally courageous and socially without courage. In other words," she concluded, with a knowing sense of the crowd she had joined, "if Mrs. Perdoodle who stood for certain social standards will take a definite stand out in the open, all the Mrs. Dusenwackers will follow."

With every Sabin appearance or press interview, the aura surrounding the WONPR grew brighter. In one twelve-month span Sabin proselytized in thirty-one states—no picnic for a woman who, on an earlier cross-country trip, had called Kansas "very uninteresting," declared the wealthy town of Aiken, South Carolina, a bore, and pronounced San Francisco's social elite "provincial." But while *Vanity Fair* celebrated "the Sabine women," whom it considered "beautiful, cultured, and practical to their finger-tips," the drys had other descriptions for them. D. Leigh Colvin of the Prohibition Party picked up *Vanity Fair*'s mythological theme and called them "Bacchantian maidens parching for wine" who "would take the pennies off the eyes of the dead for the sake of legalizing booze." The *American Independent*, a dry publication in Kentucky, eschewed classical references. The women of WONPR were "no more than the scum of the earth, parading around in skirts, and possibly late at night flirting with other women's husbands at drunken and fashionable resorts."

Obviously, something was working; the drys wouldn't waste ammunition like this on an unworthy target. An early demonstration of the group's clout emerged in the District of Columbia in 1930. A severe enforcement bill was pending before the Senate committee that governed the district

45

Al Smith, said one dry leader, "is just the kind of man wanted by those who want that kind of man." His presidential candidacy in 1928 was a critical turning point in the Prohibition saga. He may have been defeated by the anti-Catholic propaganda unleashed by the drys (46), but his public advocacy of the wet cause changed the terms of the political debate.

Cabinet Meeting - If Al Were President

46

47

Aeromarine Airways, departing from Miami, was one of several exploiters of "liquor tourism." Havana's rise as a vacation spot for Americans was a product of Prohibition (the sign at Sloppy Joe's Bar read WHERE THE WET BEGINS), as was the entire cruise-ship industry.

48

The clothing industry developed a new specialty because of Prohibition, with garments designed both for smuggling and for partying. The vial embedded in this high-heel shoe could accommodate a full shot of whiskey.

49

Los Angeles bootleggers managed to hide seventy cases of scotch behind the camouflaged access door of this lumber truck. In Detroit, rum-running traffic across the frozen Detroit River was so lucrative that some overly enthusiastic smugglers kept at it a little too late in the season.

Al Capone's intuitive feel for publicity enabled him to see the value in building a photo opportunity around a meeting with Chicago police captain John Stege, a famously honest cop. "Public service is my motto," Capone said; he could as easily have said "public relations."

By the late '20s, New York's attention to Prohibition was so halfhearted that few bothered to be terribly secretive about their drinking. This glittering event at the Puncheon Club on West Forty-ninth Street was a precursor of yet more glamorous nights at "21," presided over by cofounder Jack Kriendler (second from right).

54   55

After the wealthy, elegant, and extremely able Pauline Morton Sabin (54) became
the public face of Repeal, well-born American women (and those who aspired to the
same social status) flocked to her cause. Her opposite number at the WCTU,
Ella Boole, was opposite in countless ways.

56

Pierre S. du Pont (left) bankrolled the Repeal movement; his associate John J. Raskob
was among its key strategists. They had many reasons to oppose Prohibition, but
reinstating the excise tax on legal liquor (thereby enabling a reduction in the income
tax) was foremost among them. At the time this picture was taken, three years after
Repeal, both men had become principals in the right-wing, antitax, anti-Roosevelt
organization known as the Liberty League.

57

In 1931, as the citadel of Prohibition began to crumble, forty thousand people jammed Military Park in downtown Newark, demanding legal beer. Pauline Sabin was among those who addressed the crowd.

58

Beer's return was hurried along by the Depression. The nation's desperate need for both jobs and tax revenue prompted this labor-sponsored parade in Detroit.

H. L. Mencken and friends celebrated the legalization of beer at the bar of the Rennert Hotel in Baltimore. After draining the first legal glass, Mencken declared it "pretty good—not bad at all." Izzy Einstein and Moe Smith (60), the nation's best-known Prohibition agents, celebrated Repeal by openly doing what they had long done under cover: having a drink.

61

Upon Repeal's arrival in New York, a large crowd mobbed the liquor department at Macy's. A substantially larger one, seeking newly available liquor licenses, lined up outside the city's Board of Health.

62

when the women of WONPR came calling. "No more unusual gathering was ever seen at a Capitol hearing," the *Washington Post* reported in its lead story on page one. "Women whose names stand out prominently in the social register . . . outnumbered the men in the room four to one. These were grandmothers, matrons and debutantes, all pledged to a war on prohibition." When their testimony concluded, the paper said, "there was every evidence that the bill was dead."

And so it went around the country. Unlike their counterparts in the AAPA—many of them their husbands—the Sabine women did not restrict membership. By 1933 the WONPR claimed more than 1.3 million members. In Evanston, Illinois, where the WCTU was headquartered near Frances Willard's hallowed Rest Cottage, a special WONPR campaign signed up 1,500 new members in a single week. The WCTU, which continued to maintain that the woman suffrage amendment guaranteed the permanence of Prohibition ("As long as the Nineteenth Amendment stands, the eighteenth will stand also!"), instead watched the political empowerment of women become Prohibition's undoing. "The real strength of the Sabin organization," said *Time*, "lies in the desire of the small-town matron to ally herself, no matter how remotely, with a congregation of bona fide, rotogravure society figures."

When a member of the Lynbrook Women's Republican Club on Long Island denounced Pauline Sabin as "a traitor to her country" and demanded withdrawal of a speaking invitation that had been extended to her, the club's president would have none of it. "I would rather resign my office than withdraw the invitation," wrote Mrs. John T. Gibbons, "for that would reflect on our breeding." She directed this harrumph to Herbert Hoover himself. "I have always been in the ranks of the Drys," she told the president, "but sentiment is changing."

THE SAM BRONFMAN who rose to address the stockholders of Distillers Corporation-Seagrams Limited at their annual meeting in 1930 was not much different from the Sam Bronfman who had traveled by dogsled across western Ontario fourteen years earlier. At forty-one, his hairline had receded some more, and there's no question that he had acquired a little more polish. But Bronfman had always spoken with more eloquence than most high school dropouts, just as he had always been more combative than most prizefighters and cockier than most roosters.

Those qualities had brought him to a place almost unimaginable for an ill-educated Russian-Jewish immigrant who'd been raised on the prairies

of Saskatchewan and Manitoba. His family controlled the largest distilling firm in North America, and Sam controlled his family. The two-year
renovation of the brick mansion he had purchased on Belvedere Road in
Montreal's Westmount section had just been completed. The staff attending to Sam, Saidye, and their children included a butler (Saidye called him
"the Prince of Belvedere Road"), a cook, three maids, a laundress, a gar-
dener, a chauffeur, a nanny, and a "mademoiselle." Furnishings, menus,
and manners were modeled on the look of the houses and the social rituals
of the women Saidye encountered on European trips. Imitation went several steps further in the company headquarters Sam built on Peel Street in
downtown Montreal. An unlikely pile of limestone topped with crenella-
tions and turrets, its thick walls punctuated by stained glass, carved figures,
and stone coats-of-arms, it was Sam's idea of a Scottish baronial castle.
The entrance featured a spiked portcullis; the interior, a portrait of Robert
Burns.

Nicholas Faith, in his history of the Bronfman family, called the Peel
Street building "a ludicrous tribute to Mr. Sam's beloved Scots." This was
a love so great that when Bronfman talked about "the old country," he had
Scotland in mind, not his native Russia. It was a trope he used often. At
the 1930 annual meeting, he referred to the Scotch lords of the Distillers Company as "our old country friends." That was before he got to the
main item on his agenda—in Sam's precise phrasing, "certain legislation
enacted by the late government which adversely affected the whole distilling industry by closing one of its most profitable markets."

What he was referring to was the Export Act of 1930. For nearly nine
years the American government had been pressuring the Canadians to
cut off the southward movement of liquor. During that period whiskey
exports to the United States that were legal under Canadian law—that
is, exports on which duties were paid on leaving the country—ballooned
from 8,335 gallons a year to more than 1.1 million gallons. This was a
very small portion of the illegal liquor available in the States, but to the
Justice and Treasury departments it was embarrassing evidence of their
ineffectuality. From the Canadian perspective, it was a very big deal: the
liquor export taxes accounted for some 20 percent of all Canadian revenue
collections, both federal and provincial, and were essentially being paid by
American consumers. Pierre du Pont would likely have been pleased to
learn that in 1929, Canada's alcohol export tax brought in twice as much as
its income tax. And this fine civic contribution was provided without any
assistance at all from the bootleggers who were running the stuff across

rivers and lakes and land borders without stopping at the customs office to pay the duty.

With their own government a prime beneficiary of the liquor industry, Canadians saw no reason to support the U.S. government's enforcement of a law far stricter than Canada's own Prohibition codes, almost all of which had in any case expired. A few years earlier, when a Coast Guard cutter in hot pursuit of a Lake Erie rumrunner ran aground near Port Colborne, Ontario, it was looted and ransacked by a crowd of locals, its wiring cut, its cylinders filled with sand. If anything, the Canadian public had since grown even less sympathetic to U.S. Prohibition. Were Canada to help the United States enforce its Prohibition laws, a Toronto newspaper suggested, it "would show itself to be the simpleton in the family of nations." A headline in the *Ottawa Journal* declared "U.S. Enforcement, Like Charity, Should Begin at Home." One of the few demurring opinions came from Sir Henry Thornton, president of the government-owned Canadian National Railways. Said Thornton, "I think our policy should be to assist the Government of the United States in every way to make that country bone dry." But Thornton's interest lay in fostering the booming liquor tourism business, which brought more than three hundred million American dollars to Canada in 1929, or nearly quadruple the 1920 figure. "The dryer [the U.S.] is," Thornton concluded, "the better it will be for us."

Eventually the Canadians surrendered and passed the Export Act, making it illegal for Canadians to ship alcoholic beverages to countries that banned their sale. Thornton was no doubt delighted—but so, it turned out, was Sam Bronfman, who told Seagram shareholders, "Your Company's earnings are 50 percent greater than those of last year," before passage of the Export Act. Even though profit margins were down, he added, "the actual volume of business has been considerably increased." He did not say this, but the fulcrum of Seagram's unexpected success had been relocated fifteen miles off the coast of Newfoundland, in the accommodating harbor of St. Pierre. Legal goods could no longer be cleared to depart Canada for the United States, but St. Pierre was part of France. As a result, wrote Canadian journalists James Dubro and Robin Rowland, "the island was used to launder Canadian liquor."

For the Bronfmans and the other distillers who took advantage of the St. Pierre laundry facilities, the island eventually proved doubly advantageous. Goods could leave Canada, make a pit stop on the island, then head for a revitalized Rum Row. But the bootleggers could also smuggle their goods back *into* Canada from St. Pierre, avoiding the nine-dollar-a-gallon domestic excise tax.*

For American drinkers and American bootleggers, the Canadian Export Act turned out to be a tiny bump in the road. St. Pierre serviced the East Coast perfectly well. Liquor was also still coming over the land border in the eastern and western states by automobile (in Maine, an American official maintained, bootleggers were even pumping booze into their tires, "alcohol in this manner replacing air"). The booze fleets on Lakes Ontario and Erie expanded. Liquor prices did jump briefly in Detroit, and the U.S. government made one of its periodic announcements that the smuggling traffic had disappeared from the nearby river. But Detroit soon emitted one of its periodic giggles, and was once again drenched in booze as gigantic quantities arrived by train in Windsor and moved onward through the rail tunnel. In December 1930 the American consul general in Halifax informed the State Department that these trainloads were disguised as shipments of lumber, pulpwood, fish, even live lobsters. Customs agents presumably could stop them—but, the consul wrote, sighing the discontented sigh that for more than a decade had been emitted by nearly every government official who had tried to enforce this impossible law, "many of these agents are not as scrupulous as they might be in regard to liquor smuggling."

THE HOLES IN the dike grew larger, and more numerous as well. Each time the president, the Prohibition Bureau, or any other agency announced a new effort, brought in new resources, or negotiated a new understanding with other governments, the flood of illegal alcohol found a new (and often more efficient) conduit.

Even the biggest, most publicized victories were essentially useless—for instance, Herbert Hoover's successful effort to put Al Capone in jail. Hoover had received a delegation of Chicago civic leaders two weeks after taking office and was shocked by their description of life in their city. He determined, he later wrote, "that Chicago was in the hands of gangsters,

---

*In one of the surpassing (and at times tragic) ironies of Prohibition, the tax-dodging Canadian distillers had some competition: American liquor shipped north to Canada, similarly out of reach of the Dominion tax collectors. It was vastly inferior to the Canadian goods, in fact almost corrosively raw, but the cutting plants that created it (there were an estimated 150 in the cutting racket in Detroit alone) made few claims in its behalf beyond its sheer potency. This was not a new business; back in 1926 a batch of northbound wood alcohol originating in Buffalo left forty-one people dead on the other side of the Niagara River.

that the police and magistrates were completely under their control, that the governor of the state was futile, that the federal government was the only force by which the city's ability to govern itself could be restored. At once I directed that all the Federal agencies concentrate on Mr. Capone and his allies." Hoover authorized the Treasury and the Justice departments to spend whatever was necessary to put Capone in jail. Another Hoover—the young J. Edgar—was urged to join the Capone posse by his friend and sponsor Mabel Willebrandt "as a personal matter of great importance to me."

Eliot Ness and his Untouchables did manage to disrupt the Capone organization's beer trade for a while, chiefly by using a ten-ton truck equipped with a steel ram to smash through the walls of illicit breweries, Ness directing the operation from the passenger seat, wrote one biographer, with a football helmet on his head. Capone was finally imprisoned in 1931, after the IRS won his conviction for income tax evasion (no thanks to Ness, whose involvement in the case was limited to putting Scarface/Snorky on the train to the Atlanta Penitentiary, or to J. Edgar Hoover). But the only palpable result was a rush of delinquent returns suddenly filed by nervous mobsters, hustlers, and other Chicago bad guys—according to the IRS, "more than double the amount collected from that source in the preceding year." To the extent that the Capone operation was at all weakened, rival mobs soon satisfied Chicago's thirst. Certainly no diminution of scale occurred: among the establishments serviced by gangster Roger Touhy's fleet of trucks were two enormous roadhouses that each served more than six hundred barrels of beer every week.

Worse, the strain imposed by increased federal police activity led to the next development in the organization of organized crime. Two years after John Torrio's 1929 peace conference in Atlantic City, at virtually the same time that the warden in Atlanta was preparing for the arrival of his famous new inmate, mob bosses from twenty criminal families gathered in Chicago to formalize a national conglomerate under the authority of a permanent ruling body called the Commission. "Prohibition had been the catalyst for transforming the neighborhood gangs of the 1920s into smoothly run regional and national criminal corporations," wrote Selwyn Raab in *The Five Families*. Men who had started out "as smalltime hoodlums . . . graduated as underworld Leviathans. Bootlegging gave them on-the-job executive training." It had also given them a structure that would dominate criminal activity in the United States for nearly half a century.

◆　◆　◆

WHILE THE AAPA spent hundreds of thousands of dollars pressing its anti-tax case (and, it should be acknowledged, its arguments in behalf of states' rights, individual rights, the sanctity of the Constitution, and respect for the law); while Pauline Sabin and the WONPR made the Repeal cause respectable, even fashionable; while the government's enforcement efforts remained pointless and its diplomatic efforts turned futile; while there was more drinking, and talking about drinking, writing about drinking, winking about drinking, more everything about drinking (except, perhaps, for more discretion about drinking)—as all this moved the possibility of Repeal from the realm of the unimaginable toward the province of the conceivable, one last roadblock began to crumble. The ASL and the other components of the dry coalition, already strapped for leadership since Wheeler's death and Cannon's disgrace, began to run out of influence, money, and will.

Even Mabel Willebrandt could not be counted on any longer. After leaving the Hoover administration, she picked up a few substantial clients (including Metro-Goldwyn-Mayer and the precursor of American Airlines) and wrote a lengthy series of articles, later turned into a book, reflecting on her years in office. She didn't waver in her support for Prohibition but did offer despairing words about New York that she might have applied to much of the country: "It cannot truthfully be said that prohibition enforcement has failed in New York. It has not yet been *attempted*."

Then she lost control of her own story. The news that Willebrandt had met with the king of the rumrunners, Bill McCoy, while still in office, was marginally embarrassing. (The embarrassment was in fact less Willebrandt's than McCoy's. To combat rumors suggesting he had informed on others during their meeting, she agreed to send him a letter asserting that he had not done so, and authorizing him "to use this statement as you see fit.") It was a more substantive revelation that brought Willebrandt low: the news that one of her clients was Fruit Industries Limited, the California grape conglomerate that made and marketed Vine-Glo.

Mabel Willebrandt was "straight as a string," said an Alabama official who had gotten to know her during the Mobile prosecutions. But in the fashion of so many former Washington officials, she had turned her intimacy with the levers of government into a lucrative law practice. When she signed on with Fruit Industries, they were marketing grape jellies, grape juice, grape candy, grape syrup, anything that could be made from the mountainous crops that accumulated each fall as a result of the overplanting of mid-decade. Her greatest coup was helping Fruit Industries secure a twenty-million-dollar loan from the Federal Farm Board—a loan, it turned out, that would help them launch their home winemaking business.

Oh, did this thrill the wets! Al Smith congratulated Fruit Industries for "hiring so competent a person as Mabel," and saluted her for "collect[ing] a beautiful fee for making the Volstead Act look like 30 cents." Father Charles Coughlin, the demagogic radio priest, referred to Willebrandt as Fruit Industries' "legal guardian." A cocktail recipe book called *Noble Experiments* described "The Mabel Fruit Punch," a concoction made from rum, applejack, and "California pure concentrated Grape juice."

At first drys came to her defense. Ruth Strawbridge of Philadelphia, a wealthy dry crusader whom Willebrandt once said had "made dry parties stylish," sent a comforting letter. Learning about the Vine-Glo connection, wrote Strawbridge, "led me to say to myself: 'Well, no matter what it is, it is right, because she did it.'" In meetings with Ella Boole of the WCTU, Scott McBride of the ASL, and other dry leaders, Willebrandt insisted that she remained committed to the cause. But in November 1930 a top Fruit Industries official sent out a press release announcing Vine-Glo's introduction into the Chicago market: "Upon my arrival in Chicago this noon," wrote Donald Conn, "I was informed that bootleggers and racketeers had served notice upon us that the marketing of Vine-Glo would be resisted."

Conn could not have found a more newsworthy way to indicate that his product was aimed at those looking for an intoxicating kick from their grape juice. He underscored the point by apparently telling some newspapermen he had hired bodyguards to protect him from Capone gunmen. "Here was an announcement from the California housetops for all the country to hear," wrote Carlisle Bargeron for the front page of the *Washington Post*. "There must be something in that California grape juice if it could compete with Al Capone's beer and alky." An apoplectic Willebrandt shot off a telegram to Conn: EFFECT OF THIS DISTORTION IS TO CREATE IMPRESSION THAT FRUIT INDUSTRIES . . . IS STOOPING TO COMPETE WITH BOOTLEGGERS SUCH INFERENCES BY WET PRESS UNFAIR AND DAMAGING.

Unfair, perhaps; damaging, definitely. A California pharmacist began advertising his stock of Vino Sano as "Mabel's Grape Bricks." Three weeks later angry members of the National Temperance Council, a coalition of the leaders of the major dry organizations, attempted to bar Willebrandt from even addressing them. At a time when the dry forces could have used someone with Willebrandt's grasp of the issues and her command of the podium, she effectively disappeared from the public debate. Drys instead found themselves lining up behind hysterics and haters. At that same meeting of the Temperance Council, the group's president, longtime ASL stump speaker Rev. Ira Landrith, exceeded even Bishop Cannon's frothing rhetoric. The wet movement, he thundered, was "a greater danger than open rebellion." Metropolitan newspapers, overwhelmingly wet, were promoting "heresy." Members of the AAPA were "traitors."

The more extreme the ASL's stance, the greater the flight of its supporters. Even Richmond Hobson, whose perorations against the "Great Destroyer" had started the Eighteenth Amendment on its way back in 1914, quit the dry movement altogether. "When people are ripe for reform, the laws will take care of themselves," he told a reporter. "Until then, they are useless." Other allies were hounded out of the dry camp: although Senator George Norris of Nebraska had been loyally pro-Prohibition for more than a decade, drys opposed his reelection in 1930 because Norris, believing other issues more crucial to his state, had backed Al Smith two years earlier. Worried that association with the league was hurting his business in major cities, S. S. Kresge finally withdrew his support.

With the large checks disappearing, the ASL became more dependent on small ones. But these had disappeared into the same canyon that had devoured the economy. While the deepening Depression had made the Repeal argument stronger—it would bring not just more tax revenue but, in reborn breweries and distilleries, more jobs as well—it brought the ASL to the edge of collapse. In the summer of 1931 the Washington office had to cancel its newspaper subscriptions because it was unable to pay the bill. Management and staff took salary cuts or forwent payment altogether. National superintendent Scott McBride, "greatly embarrassed in my account at the bank," pleaded with the accounting office for a half-month advance on his salary. Ernest Cherrington told McBride in August that payment obligations were "almost staggering." By November, rent on the Washington office was four months overdue and the landlord was threatening eviction. By January, at its headquarters in Ohio, the ASL's last lifeline was severed when the Bank of Westerville, long the league's source of short-term credit, became insolvent and locked its doors.

Back in 1920, with Prohibition firmly situated in the Constitution and the Volstead Act already embedded in the law, the Anti-Saloon League spent $2.5 million in support of its cause. In 1933, as both that cause and the ASL faced a desperate emergency, it brought in a total of $122,000 to fund its activities, a brutal 95 percent decline. The most powerful pressure group the nation had ever known had been reduced to looking for nickels under the couch cushions.

✦   ✦   ✦

THERE WAS NO specific signal to indicate that the accumulated frustrations, enmities, and fears that had gathered around the Prohibition debate were finally about to send Morris Sheppard's hummingbird zooming off to Mars with the Washington Monument as its payload. One could have pointed to the plunge in Coca-Cola's stock price and the company's hamhanded effort to convince the capital markets that the return of beer and liquor would not affect its business. Perhaps the rolling chant of "We want beer!" that interrupted Herbert Hoover's address on the economic crisis at the American Legion convention in 1931 was the turning point, or maybe it was Michigan's quiet effort to try to solve its fiscal predicament by placing a tax on malt syrup and other home brewing supplies (well they might: tax receipts soon indicated that Detroiters were producing twenty-eight million gallons of homebrew annually). In Washington the Supreme Court that had expanded federal power in the 1920s began to veer the other way, even declaring the warrantless search of a garage constitutionally unacceptable. In the South it could have been the widely publicized discovery by a Kentucky member of the WONPR that Jefferson Davis had written a letter in 1887 declaring his steadfast opposition to the idea of Prohibition. Davis had called it "a wooden horse" harboring "a disguised enemy to state sovereignty."

But at a time when the nation was mired in the deepening ruts of the Depression, those paying attention to the economy would have recognized the impending shift when the National Distillers Corporation declared its "whiskey dividend" in September 1932. The company, which controlled the rights to more than twenty-five well-known brands, promised shareholders a case of pre-Prohibition whiskey for every five shares owned—deliverable, it said, in the fall of 1934, or earlier if legally possible. The company's confidence that it could expand beyond the medicinal market arose from the widely shared conviction that Franklin D. Roosevelt, carrying the twin flags of Repeal and relief, was well on his way to election.* A reductionist version of the Democrats' argument was offered by Representative John C. Linthicum of Maryland, a leading House wet: with Repeal, said Linthicum, the Depression "will fade away like the mists before the noonday sun." And at the same time, he promised, "The immo-

---

*Roosevelt had waffled on the issue for years, but once he embraced the wet cause he was unstinting in his support for it. On the other hand, his wife was a committed dry who had been outspoken in her advocacy of the Eighteenth Amendment for years. The daughter of an alcoholic, Eleanor Roosevelt did not allow wine to be served at her dinner parties, disapproved of her husband's indulgence in cocktails, and in 1927 wanted the state police to raid the Hudson Valley farm of an uncle who was overly free with his liquor.

rality of the country, racketeering, and bootlegging will be a thing of the past." Even southern Democrats moved toward the wet column, including such previously hard-line drys as Alben Barkley of Kentucky and Hugo Black of Alabama.

More astonishingly, many of the Republican aristocrats who had initiated the Repeal movement came out in support of the Democratic candidate. Roosevelt's open declaration that the legalization of beer would "increase the Federal revenue by several hundred million dollars a year" certainly pleased Pierre du Pont. Sabin required no persuading. "It has been said that the Democratic candidate is a very recent convert to the cause of Repeal because of political expediency," Sabin declared. "It cannot be said that up to this date, the Republican candidate is a convert to Repeal for any reason."

For Sabin 1932 had first been marked by a triumphal tour of the South, where she and some of the other social notables of the WONPR (including Pierre du Pont's wife, Alice) had dazzled the clubwomen of Charleston and Atlanta. "Mrs. Simons V. H. Waring Gives Tea For Dry Reform Delegates," read the headline on the society page of the *Charleston News and Courier*. In Atlanta the *Constitution* ran stories anticipating Sabin's visit and then reporting on it. "A woman of fine intelligence and breeding is Mrs. Charles H. Sabin," the paper said in the first story; unsurprisingly, said the second, *le tout* Atlanta "packed the ballroom of the Biltmore" for the event.

By summer Sabin and her organization (including new recruit Emily Post) had made the permanent leap from the society pages to the front lines of the presidential campaign. In June, Sabin was honored at the Democratic convention when it passed the Repeal platform; in July she persuaded the WONPR to endorse Roosevelt. *Time* put her on the cover, elegant pearls around her delicate neck. When a splinter group of steadfast WONPR Republicans issued a statement protesting the Roosevelt endorsement, Sabin said, "I can find no comfort in this petition. But perhaps the Woman's Christian Temperance Union, the Anti-Saloon League, the Methodist Board of Temperance, Prohibition and Public Morals, and Bishop Cannon will."

Soon dry Republicans fed up with the futility of enforcement, Hoover's temporizing, and a nearly unintelligible platform plank that Walter Lippmann called "a smoke screen of dry slogans" also began to list toward the wet side. The party's new recruits to the cause of Repeal ranged from the teetotaling John D. Rockefeller Jr., whose June 6, 1932, abandonment of the drys was one of the year's biggest news stories, to former representative M. Alfred Michaelson, who had apparently reformed his politics to match his tastes in the years since officials in Florida had apprehended his soggy luggage. Word of Rockefeller's conversion—motivated, he said, by the "colossal scale" of criminal activity—elicited dry reactions ranging from thrashing anger to excruciating bathos (former representative W. D. "Earnest Willie" Upshaw begged him not to help "DuPont and Raskob destroy the eighteenth amendment that was wrapped in your good mother's prayers"). But Rockefeller was followed into the Repeal camp by Alfred P. Sloan of General Motors and tire manufacturer Harvey Firestone. By the end of the campaign, Republicans desperate for anything that might secure their election in the face of the coming Democratic tide clambered to the side of Repeal, among them the senator whose name was attached to the most vengeful of Prohibition laws, Wesley Jones of Washington.

Except that very few mainstream Republicans, and quite a few Democrats as well, actually said they were supporting Repeal. Continuing the chronic chorus of euphemism that had so long afflicted the debate, they said they supported "submission" of a Repeal amendment to the states. It was the same dodge, employing exactly the same weasel word, that drys had used when the Eighteenth Amendment was pending: they weren't imposing their will, just giving the people, through their state legislatures, the chance to decide. Back then it was the way a politician could be dry without being dry; now it was the way some of the same politicians, and many others, could be wet without being wet.

Eight days before Roosevelt's inevitable landslide victory and the expected repopulation of Congress with clear wet majorities, the board of management of the Century Association (including George W. Wickersham of the noncommittal Wickersham Commission) met in their Stanford White–designed clubhouse on West Forty-third Street in Manhattan and voted to appropriate five thousand dollars to the house committee for the purchase of wine. On Election Day an exultant Louis M. Martini tied down the cord to the steam whistle at his Napa Valley winery for fifteen loud and joyous minutes. And on December 28, 1932, the board of directors of Anheuser-Busch authorized fifteen thousand dollars for the purchase of a team of Clydesdales "for advertising purposes."

THE TWENTY-FIRST AMENDMENT to the Constitution of the United States, which came up for debate in Congress in February 1933, was even more concise than the Eighteenth. The key words were the fifteen that opened it: "The eighteenth article of amendment to the Constitution of the United States is hereby repealed." The remaining two clauses outlawed the transportation of intoxicating liquors into states that chose to forbid it and stipulated a ratification process requiring approval not by state legislatures but by state conventions called for this specific purpose. The latter idea was the contribution of a group of wets, led by New York attorney Joseph H. Choate Jr., who were mindful of the complications of legislative schedules and the continued domination of state legislatures by rural minorities.

On February 14 Morris Sheppard rose on the floor of the Senate and began a one-man filibuster. After eight and a half hours he gave up; senators waiting to vote had resolved to outlast him. The final tally was 63–23 in favor of the Repeal resolution. Of the twenty-two members who had voted for the Eighteenth Amendment sixteen years earlier and were still senators, seventeen voted to undo their earlier work. Two days later the House dispatched the measure after just forty minutes of debate, by a vote of 289–121.

On March 4, the day the new president took the oath of office and declared that the only thing America had to fear was fear itself, the Anti-Saloon League rented out one of the rooms in its hotel suite to out-of-towners who had come to Washington to celebrate the inauguration. The ASL thereby enriched its diminished treasury by two dollars.

On March 16, at Franklin Roosevelt's request, the new Congress revisited the linguistic debates of 1919 and came up with a reformulated definition of "intoxicating." The legislation was formally captioned "a bill to provide revenue by the taxation of certain nonintoxicating liquors," but you couldn't have the revenue without the redefinition. Effective April 7, except in those states that expressly forbade it, beer that was no more than 3.2 percent alcohol by weight would be legal. Breweries and bottlemakers, coopers and hop farmers, trucking firms and ice plants and dozens of other businesses immediately began to recruit thousands from the ranks of the unemployed. Coca-Cola, fearing competition, actually considered producing "Coca-Cola Beer," in both light and dark varieties. When April 7 arrived, the Budweiser Clydesdales made their debut, delivering a case to Al Smith in New York. Another Budweiser team pulled up to the White House only to discover that other breweries had gotten there first. The CBS radio network broadcast beer celebrations across the country. In Milwaukee a blanket license was issued to 4,207 taverns precisely at midnight. In Baltimore, H. L. Mencken lifted a stein to his lips, drained its legal contents, and pronounced it "pretty good—not bad at all."

Despite all the beer and liquor that had been floating Manhattan for

several years, only in the spring of 1933 did "Satan's seat," as Bishop ⌐
non called it, truly return to its pre-Prohibition ways. This happened, said
newspaperman Stanley Walker, when "the proprietors of nightclubs and
speakeasies began to suggest to the agents who had been their guests over
the years that it was about time they began paying for what they ate and
drank."

THE FIRST STATE convention to ratify the Twenty-first Amendment acted
on April 10, in Michigan; one of the delegates was Martin S. McDonough
of Iron River, the former prosecutor who had stood up to Alfred V. Dalrymple and his armed agents during the "Rum Rebellion" of 1920. For
his part, Dalrymple had just been named the last head of the Prohibition
Bureau, a position Roosevelt would abolish four months later. In his final
days on the job, Dalrymple would tell reporters that had the ASL been willing to accept legalization of light wines and beer, "the eighteenth amendment would have remained in the Constitution for 100 years." J. Edgar
Hoover refused to bring soon-to-be-unemployed Prohibition agents onto
his own force; they just weren't up to FBI standards.

By midsummer, fourteen more states had ratified. At the New York
convention, broadcast live by NBC and CBS, Governor Herbert Lehman
saluted Pauline Sabin "and her devoted army of women who have so val-
iantly fought towards our common goal." Al Smith presided over the
convention, his nomination seconded by the state Republican chairman,
who lauded the "distinguished Democrat and statesman." Elihu Root,
now eighty-eight, "enjoyed the Repeal Convention very much," he told a
friend. "Nobody seemed to remember that it was his duty to hate anybody
else, and that made the occasion both novel and refreshing."

There were a few hitches. Mississippi balked, some of its anti-Repealists
summoning familiar tropes from the turn of the century. Because of Prohibition, said Judge William M. Cox at a Jackson rally, "many a white
woman has been saved from the polluting touch of lustful vengeance, and
many a Negro man has been saved from the gallows or the flames." But the
South was not solid, and when Arkansas, Alabama, and Tennessee all ratified during the first two weeks of August, any lingering uncertainty ceased
to linger.

Businesses both licit and not took note. National Distillers, whose stock
had traded as low as $17 a share in 1932, saw its price leap to $115 in July
1933. Grain prices on the Chicago Board of Trade soared. On St. Pierre
the Bronfmans had already told their local *négociant* they would no lon-

ger lease warehouses for any period greater than ninety days; in July the island was drained of 973,000 cases of liquor by the last of the rumrunners, racing toward their final payday. In October a Napa County newspaper reported that not a single railcar had departed the valley for the East. The entire harvest was being turned into wine.

On December 5, at 3:31 p.m. local time, Utah became the thirty-sixth state to ratify the Repeal amendment. At the age of thirteen years, ten months, and nineteen days, national Prohibition was dead. (The Mormon Church wasn't happy, but it was accepting; when the president of the church addressed the convention, said the *Salt Lake Tribune*, he resembled "Marc Antony at the burial of Caesar.") The official bootlegger in the Maryland State House was formally dismissed the same day. Pierre du Pont and the men of the AAPA celebrated in the Jade Room of the Waldorf in New York, where du Pont presented his fellow Repealists with commemorative highball glasses filled with "cocktail material," as his instructions had specified, ladled from a sterling silver bowl.

Pauline Sabin and the women of the WONPR marked the occasion with a dinner at the Mayflower Hotel in Washington. No alcohol was served, but that didn't mean that attitudes toward alcohol were retreating toward the furtive tippling of the pre-Prohibition decades. There could have been no clearer demonstration of the domestication of drink than the appearance of brewery advertisements in the *Delineator*, a popular women's magazine mostly known for bringing the famous Butterick sewing patterns into hundreds of thousands of American homes. One ad showed a curly-headed little girl serving a foaming Pabst to a man who is evidently her grandfather. Fifteen years earlier a similar pair might have been portrayed in a rather different scene: the grandfather at the bar of a saloon, slumped over in a stupor; the little girl in tears, begging him to come home.

Chapter 21

Afterlives,
and the Missing Man

O N WAYNE B. WHEELER'S DEATH in 1927, the *Washington Post* didn't hold back: "No other private citizen of the United States has left such an impress upon national history." Six years later, after Prohibition crashed to earth in the storm of Repeal, his impress vanished with his creation. Wheeler's name popped up in the *New York Times* a few times in the wake of the ASL's final defeat, in references to "Wayne Wheeler tactics" and the like, and then, from 1935 until 1975, it appeared in the paper exactly twelve times. Four of those appearances were in obituaries of various dry associates, three others in reviews of books recalling Prohibition. Then, after 1975, nothing at all. American history texts tell the story of Prohibition, but they leave out the name of its author. Wheeler's legacy may have been present in nearly every single-issue political movement that arose in the eight decades after his death, but the person was not. The very fact of Wayne Wheeler's existence disappeared from the national memory.

In the years immediately after Prohibition, Wheeler's allies and heirs followed a variety of paths. On the morning of December 6, 1933, James M. Doran, who had spent the previous six years as director of the Prohibition Bureau and then commissioner of Industrial Alcohol, leapt over the wall that divided the regulators from the regulated, becoming the top official of the liquor manufacturers' trade organization. Seven years after he had lost his job, Izzy Einstein was still publicly defending Prohibition when he dedicated his 1932 autobiography "To the 4,932 persons I arrested, hoping they bear me no grudge for having done my duty." But in 1935, celebrating his son's wedding with 93-proof rye, California sauterne, and a claret-based punch, Einstein said, "If you want my opinion, the quality you get these days is not so hot. The bootleggers sold better stuff in Prohibition days than you can get now." Mabel Willebrandt failed in her effort to obtain a federal judgeship, instead becoming one of the leading lawyers in the entertainment industry. Her client list ran from Clark Gable and Jean Harlow to Frank Capra, who said his "first meaningful action" as president of the Screen Directors Guild was "acquiring the wisdom, experience, and brilliant legal talents of that great lady of the law, Mabel Walker Willebrandt." In 1954, sponsored by her old friend John Sirica, the woman Al Smith had blamed for bringing religion into the 1928 presidential campaign converted to Catholicism.

One who didn't change much at all was Andrew J. Volstead. Three years after losing his reelection bid in 1922, the author of the era's signature law went to work as a staff attorney in the Prohibition Bureau's Northwest Region office in Minneapolis. After returning to his private practice in a small second-floor office in Granite Falls, Volstead spoke to a journalist just four weeks before Repeal. "Mr. Volstead said he wishes people would learn that Prohibition and all its developments are all in the past for Andrew Volstead, private citizen," the reporter wrote. Volstead himself added, "Anything I might say could do nobody any good. All it would do would be just to bring ridicule upon me." Late in life he expressed regret that he was remembered for the National Prohibition Act. He'd rather be known, he said, as coauthor of the Capper-Volstead Act, which exempted certain farmers from antitrust regulation so they could organize voluntary cooperatives. He did not get his wish.

Unlike the sponsor of the Volstead Act, the author of the Eighteenth Amendment was hardly remembered at all. Morris Sheppard of Texas, the courtly, Shakespeare-quoting progressive who may have been Prohibition's most sincere political advocate, did not give up the fight after his failed filibuster of early 1933. That summer, as his state prepared to vote up or down on ratification, Sheppard got into a small Ford truck, loaded a speaker's platform and sound equipment into the back, and traveled more than five thousand miles of Texas roads, speaking against Repeal in fifty cities and towns. But after a late August referendum, when a majority of Texans voted to ratify the Twenty-first Amendment, *Time* invoked Sheppard's infamous prediction of just three years earlier. "Last week," the editors wrote, "humming bird and Washington Monument were well on the way to Mars." For the remaining eight years of his life Sheppard continued to address the evils of alcohol in his annual January 16 speech on the Senate floor. By 1935 he was calling for the repeal of Repeal. On his death in

1941 a Senate eulogist said the end of Prohibition had been "the one great disappointment and abiding sorrow" of his life.

Sheppard's never-say-die dedication to the cause wasn't shared by all of his fellow drys. Less than twenty-four hours after Utah's ratification made Repeal official, waitresses at the Dearborn Inn outside Detroit were serving beer in the dining room. Since the hotel was one of Henry Ford's pet projects, the new addition to the menu, said the *New York Times,* "caused many of those present to speculate on what Mr. Ford's future policy would be." It was a reasonable question, given that Ford had vowed only four years earlier to shut down his factories if drink ever came back. A definitive answer arrived less than three months later, when he began an advertising campaign touting the suitability of Ford trucks for the booming brewery business.

But reformist passions less influenced by commercial exigency did not abate. Instead, time altered them. By 1933 the WCTU had diminished to such an extent that its national convention had to concern itself with pennies, voting to allocate all of $300 to fighting Repeal in Missouri, $150 for an antibeer campaign in Oklahoma. Ella Boole, who in 1947 would step down as president in her ninetieth year, turned the WCTU's attention to international activities and brought Frances Willard's "Do Everything" doctrine (without, of course, Willard's effectiveness) to such issues as disarmament and the status of women. In later years the organization veered right. In 1998, for instance, the Maryland chapter "continued our work against abortion [and] homosexuality . . . and praised women who are home raising their children." In one respect the WCTU did not change: that same year, the organization "celebrated the 100th Anniversary of Frances Willard's Heavenly Birthday"—that is, her death. It also maintained Willard's Carpenter Gothic–style Rest Cottage in downtown Evanston as a memorial and a museum, but had the resources to keep it open only six hours a month.

The ASL fared no better. Within a year of Repeal the Michigan chapter, for one, went into receivership. Scott McBride blamed "repeal drinking" for riots, disorder, industrial strikes, and an increase in the number of deaths by sunstroke. Bishop Cannon "continued to write and speak," a biographer wrote, "but found few interested in the message." Part of Cannon's message was his abiding anti-Catholicism; in 1939 he criticized Congress for adjourning in acknowledgment of the death of Pope Pius XI. One of his last public statements of any sort was a letter to the *Richmond Times-Dispatch* protesting the disappearance of Prince Valiant and the Phantom from the paper's comics pages.

Eventually the ASL tried an identity change, reemerging first as the Temperance League and then as the American Temperance League. That didn't stick, either, and in 1964 it was finally reincarnated as the American Council on Alcohol Problems, promoting "a philosophy of abstinence." From its two-person headquarters in Birmingham, Alabama, the ACAP (né ASL) continued to publish the *American Issue*. At its peak the ASL newspaper had been the mainstay of the league's around-the-clock Westerville printing plant, a robust weekly published in a national edition and several different state editions. In 2008 it was a four-page newsletter, published quarterly.

NOT EVERYONE ON the other side fared better than the drys, but the people who made their living selling alcoholic beverages certainly did. For the big brewing families—the Pabsts and the Busches, the Millers and the Coorses—Prohibition cleared the field. Of the 1,345 American brewers who had been operating in 1915, a bare 31 were able to turn on their taps within three months of the return of legal beer—primarily the big companies that had kept their doors open producing ice cream or cheese or malt syrup during the dry era. Several hundred firms returned to the business in the ensuing years, but the head start seized by the big breweries triggered a consolidation of the market that would never end. (By 1935 five companies controlled 14 percent of the market; by 1958 their share had reached 31 percent; by 2009 the three survivors owned 80 percent.) The brewers didn't just get richer; they also grew smarter. When war arrived in 1941, the men who controlled the dominant brewing families—still almost exclusively German-American—did not make the mistake their fathers and grandfathers had. Anheuser-Busch redrew its logo, putting an American bald eagle where a German version had earlier stretched its wings, and the family purchased the maximum legally authorized quantity of war bonds. Their loyalty was rewarded when the federal government authorized draft boards to grant deferments to brewery workers. Ten years earlier beer had been illegal; now the men who made it were considered essential to the war effort.

The wine industry reconstituted itself more haltingly. Beer could be made quickly, but the gestation time of even halfway decent wines meant that salable inventories were virtually nonexistent when Repeal arrived. In the Napa Valley, endless rows of now-worthless alicante grapes, planted during the homemade wine boom of the early 1920s, choked the valley for years. (As late as 1951 wine writer Frank Schoonmaker could say, "The

sooner this variety is eliminated from superior California vineyards, the better.") Worse yet, the fourteen-year cloud that had hovered over most of the California wine industry had erased winemaking knowledge accumulated in the pre-Prohibition years. It did not help that the University of California at Davis, the Oxford and Cambridge of American oenological science, had shut down all its wine work during the 1920s.

Consequently, recalled vintner Ernest A. Wente, one man was "right in the driver's seat when Repeal came": Georges de Latour. Thanks to his arrangement with the Catholic Church, de Latour and his Beaulieu Vineyards had floated through Prohibition on a river of sanctified wine. While potential competitors labored to build up their inventories in 1933, de Latour was sitting on a million gallons in barrels, which he began bottling in the months leading up to Repeal. "Mr. de Latour has expended a fortune this fall," reported the *St. Helena Star.* "He has furnished many men with work, paid good wages and contributed to the well-being of many families in the valley." Even more valuable was Beaulieu's winemaking skill. While other wineries were trying to relearn their craft, the experienced vintners of Beaulieu were sweeping up the prizes at American wine competitions. When de Latour died in 1940, the means of his ascent did not go unnoticed: four archbishops presided at his funeral.

To some there was also a religious aspect to the post-Repeal distilling business. *Fortune* intimated the Jewish dominance of the liquor industry with a notable lack of grace. In November 1933 the magazine captioned a collection of head shots of industry leaders "Four Gentlemen of the Faith," and eleven months later it elaborated: "For better or for worse, the industry today has hardly the ruling caste that a Hitler would be happy about." The men who dominated the post-Repeal business either arose from the medicinal liquor racket, like Lewis Rosenstiel of Schenley, or they invaded from the north. Among the latter, Sam Bronfman was preeminent.

Repeal had not yet arrived when the Bronfmans purchased the Rossville Union Distillery in Lawrenceburg, Indiana, in 1933. Unlike the Greenbrier Distillery they had acquired in 1922, this one was not dismantled and moved to Montreal. On December 5, as dockworkers and cartage men on distant St. Pierre marked the last day of Prohibition with a funeral cortege led by French and American flags at half mast, Sam Bronfman was already sitting on the four hundred thousand gallons of whiskey in the Rossville warehouse that had been part of the deal. Working closely with his brother Allan, he bought out his Scottish partners, acquired the Calvert Distillery in Maryland, devised the slogan that Seagram's would wear like a badge of civic responsibility ("Drink Moderately"), and introduced Five Crown

and Seven Crown, the brands that would make his legal American fortune. Seagram's sold a million cases of the Crown brands in 1935, their first full calendar year in the U.S. market.

But neither good citizenship nor good business could purge the Bronfman brothers of the reputation that had attached itself to them during the bootlegging years. Late in 1934 the Canadian government investigated several years of dubious commerce and brought a mammoth conspiracy suit against the four Bronfmans and fifty-seven others. They were charged with smuggling liquor out of Canada in violation of the Export Act and smuggling liquor back into Canada, via St. Pierre, without paying appropriate duties. Regarding the outbound smuggling, the Bronfman lawyers made the sensible argument that the Canadian government had been a virtual party to it. Regarding the inbound smuggling, they were more audacious: although Bronfman liquor had gone to St. Pierre and Bronfman liquor had returned from St. Pierre, and more than $3 million had been transferred from Bronfman accounts in St. Pierre to Bronfman accounts in Montreal, they persuaded the court that there was insufficient evidence establishing that the Bronfmans had in fact been responsible for the cross-border shuffle.

Still, American officials were not prepared to welcome Sam Bronfman with open arms. The consul general in Montreal tried to persuade U.S. authorities to bring smuggling charges against the Bronfmans, arguing that a conviction "would constitute a moral and psychological triumph, similar to the capture of Capone." It would also, he suggested, "remove from active 'hostilities' the fertile brain and evil genius of Sam and Allan Bronfman."

But instead of bringing a prosecution, the Treasury Department negotiated a settlement with the Canadian government, providing for payment of U.S. excise taxes on all the Canadian whiskey that had flowed across the border during the Prohibition years. After diplomatic exigencies led the Americans to settle for only $3 million of the $60 million they considered due, the Canadians collected from the various distillers their proportionate share of the back taxes. The Bronfmans, unashamed of their dominant role in the "export business," agreed to pay a full 50 percent of it.

When Treasury Department officials came calling at the Seagram's castle on Peel Street in Montreal, however, Bronfman maintained that the payment was going in the wrong direction. According to a witness, Bronfman told them that "the United States Government should be grateful to him for having smuggled rye and bourbon whiskies into the United States and having thus kept alive an appetite there for these types of whiskies."

Had he not, Bronfman pointed out, the United States would have become a nation of Scotch drinkers, and the American whiskey industry would have never gotten back on its feet.

For Charlie Berns and Jack Kriendler of "21," the only thing they needed in order to become legitimate was the turn of the calendar on the night of Friday, December 5, 1933. The loyal and profitable clientele that the proprietors had built made Saturday's business the same as Friday's business, except that it was taxable. Good connections developed in the 1920s paid off in other ways. In 1941 Franklin D. Roosevelt pardoned Berns for his one Volstead conviction so the former speakeasy operator could get a gun license. The "21" Club of the speakeasy era, with its elaborately engineered system for destroying incriminating evidence in the depths of its subcellar, was best memorialized by a rumor originating in the 1950s, when the land directly behind 21 West Fifty-second Street was excavated for construction of a branch of the New York Public Library on Fifty-third Street. Workers laboring a couple of dozen feet below street level, it was said, were taken aback by the odor of alcohol that permeated the soil.

WITHOUT THE FEDERAL GOVERNMENT'S desperate need for new tax revenue, said Representative John J. O'Connor of New York early in 1934, "we would not have had Repeal for at least ten years." Congress's avid interest in the new liquor taxes suggests that he may have been right. It wasn't just the mandarins of the AAPA who had seen the promise of government revenue in a bottle of booze or beer; a liquor tax bill passed the House in the first week of January, by a vote of 388–5.

Not that the economic conservatives who had pushed so hard for Repeal weren't especially delighted. Ratification had already triggered a clause in the National Industrial Recovery Act, which had become law the previous June: Section 217 provided for the immediate revocation of emergency taxes on dividends and excess profits, effective upon the ratification of Repeal or the passage of a balanced budget, whichever arrived first. This was comparable to setting up a race between a rocket and a rock. In the very first post-Repeal year, even though many states remained dry or severely limited the sale of alcohol, the government collected $258,911,332 in alcohol taxes—instantly, nearly 9 percent of total federal revenue.

All this new money did facilitate a cut in income tax rates. The levy paid by workers earning $2,000 to $3,000 annually dropped by a full 20 percent in the years immediately following Repeal. But it didn't go down for the wealthy. Much of the liquor revenue was treated as additive, and helped to pay for the new government initiatives that began to proliferate in the second half of Franklin Roosevelt's first term. To the economic conservatives who had sponsored Repeal, the combination of high taxes and new programs defined a perfect hell. They had defeated the drys, but in their own view they had ended up similarly vanquished. In the summer of 1934 a small group convened in Washington to discuss their displeasure. Among them were John J. Raskob, Irénée du Pont, James W. Wadsworth Jr., and Al Smith.* Out of this and subsequent discussions emerged the American Liberty League, whose meetings might as well have been AAPA reunions. As they had with the AAPA, the du Pont family took on financial responsibility for the largest chunk of the league's operating costs. Smith and Wadsworth were among the group's first five board members. Pierre du Pont soon joined them.

It did not take long for the Liberty League to become notorious in a nation that was growing increasingly loyal to Franklin Roosevelt. The members' names drew attention, but not necessarily of the complimentary sort: J. Howard Pew of the Sun Oil Company. General Motors chairman Alfred P. Sloan Jr. Steel magnate Ernest T. Weir. And, of course, archmandarin James Montgomery Beck, who referred to New Dealers as "Washington Stalins." Roosevelt could not have wished for a better foil than this alliance of multimillionaires profoundly out of touch with the agonies the Depression had imposed on most Americans. To Roosevelt—and through Roosevelt, to much of the nation—the Liberty Leaguers were "unscrupulous money changers" seeking to manipulate "political puppets" for their own benefit. He was proud, the president said, to have earned "the hatred of entrenched greed."

In 1936 the Liberty League tried to summon the same political and financial power it had brought to defeating Prohibition, this time in an effort to deny Roosevelt a second term. It turned out to be a dreadful year for them. The first debacle was a gathering of two thousand members and supporters, described by a reporter as "jammed elbow to elbow, tailcoat to tailcoat, fluttery bouffant to sleek black velvet dress" as they listened to

---

*Smith was not as unlikely a member of the group as it might appear to those who knew him as the liberal, social-welfare-promoting governor of New York. As Raskob's close friend, he had already embarked on a rightward move during the 1928 presidential campaign, when he became the first Democrat ever to run on a high-tariff platform. The association with Raskob further aligned him with the anti–New Deal right. A more unlikely member of the Liberty League was none other than Richmond Hobson, a dry afloat in a sea of wets.

Al Smith deliver a viciously anti-Roosevelt address "under the gilt plaster ornaments and glittering crystal chandeliers" of the Mayflower Hotel in Washington. At the time, 20 percent of the U.S. workforce was unemployed. National sympathy for the Liberty League sank even lower as the year unfolded. After throwing their full emotional and financial support behind Republican Alfred M. Landon, the league helped him achieve the most mortifying defeat in American presidential election history, losing the electoral vote 523 to 8.

Along the way Pierre du Pont, whose personal tax bill in some years was higher than any other American's, had a revelation: his support for the AAPA, he suddenly concluded, had been misguided. "I acknowledge my mistake," he wrote. "The effort should have been directed against the XVIth Amendment"—the income tax amendment—"which I believe could have been repealed with the expenditure of less time and trouble than was required for the abolition of its little brother," the Eighteenth. Prohibition had been dead for three years, but the damnable taxes du Pont had expected to die with it lived on.

"THERE CAN ONLY be one capital, Washington or Moscow," Al Smith had said at the Liberty League's banquet at the Mayflower. "There can be only one atmosphere of government, the clear, pure, fresh air of free America, or the foul air of communistic Russia." The audience ate it up. "The noise rose in waves," said the *Post.* "Applause shook the ballroom." At the speakers' table, "in an evening jacket of solid white sequins over a black crepe gown," sat one of the program's other stars, a member of the six-member administrative committee that did most of the league's work: Pauline Morton Sabin.

In *Women and Repeal,* an authorized history of the Women's Organization for National Prohibition Reform, author Grace Root attempted to define Pauline Sabin's influence on American politics. Root (who was Elihu Root's daughter-in-law) stated that the founder of WONPR had provoked America's husbands to ask, "What have you done to my wife, Mrs. Sabin? She now insists upon reading the editorial page before she will pour my breakfast coffee!" A similar, if less cringe-inducing, way of putting it was offered decades later by one of Sabin's granddaughters: she had taken at least one phylum of American women "out of their living rooms, away from their canasta packs," Pauline Sabin Willis said, and into active and independent engagement in the nation's political life. Women had won the vote in 1919, but by opposing the dominant position of the

WCTU and its allies, Sabin and the WONPR proved that women were not a monolithic political bloc.

Sabin's early affinity for the American Liberty League suggested that the women who had broken with the WCTU were moved by the same ideas that motivated so many of their husbands. Widowed in 1933, Sabin in 1936 married Dwight F. Davis, a former secretary of war (and the donor of tennis's Davis Cup) who also embraced the Liberty League agenda. Clearly, though, Sabin was also impelled by what she later told a reporter was her favorite activity: "organizing." The Liberty League was there at hand, and Sabin embraced it and helped pull it together.

But when the league crumbled, she did not travel with those fellow league members who migrated to the isolationist America First movement. During World War II Sabin was the extremely effective director of volunteer services for the American Red Cross, coordinating aid that reached some four million families. After the war she actively engaged in political life, chiefly with the Democratic Party, while simultaneously serving, according to columnist Joseph Alsop, as "the most admired hostess" in Washington. (Sabin sold Bayberry Land to the International Brotherhood of Electrical Workers in 1949.) In 1953, two years before her death at sixty-eight, she publicly condemned the "sickness of fear, of mutual suspicion, of unhealthy credulity" engendered by the McCarthyite Red hunts. But Sabin's most telling post-Repeal political act—the one that demonstrated just how far she had traveled—occurred a few years earlier, when she urged her friend Harry Truman to veto a bill that had just passed Congress. Its central provision, which had provoked her to action, was a tax cut.

AT HARVARD UNIVERSITY, where the evidence of money is carved into the facade of nearly every building, the Minda de Gunzburg Center for European Studies, named for Sam Bronfman's eldest child, resides within Adolphus Busch Hall. Neither the illegal foundation of the Bronfman riches nor the saloon culture that launched the Busch fortune (not to mention the political manipulations that protected it for so long) disqualified either family from a proper memorial. Alcohol-derived wealth acquired before Prohibition had long been suspect, but after Prohibition the possessors of the old wealth were rehabilitated, and even those who made their money by breaking the law could buy a free pass to respectability.

To a degree this curiously benign aura came to surround the reputations of the era's homicidal gangsters, truly evil men who managed nonetheless to acquire a romantic glow over the decades. Foremost among these, of course, was Al Capone, who became the beneficiary not only of his own deft use of the press, but of decades of Hollywood mythmaking. Over the years Capone has been played by Rod Steiger, F. Murray Abraham, William Devane, Eric Roberts (*Eric Roberts!*), Robert De Niro, Ben Gazzara, and Jason Robards Jr. (not to mention Paul Muni as Tony Camonte, a fictionalized version of Capone, in the original *Scarface*, and Al Pacino in its remake). If Capone hasn't exactly been portrayed as a hero, all that celluloid has enabled him to maintain a reputation that would delight any narcissistic mobster. More than sixty years after Capone's death, a browser on eBay could make bids in a single day for Al Capone wristwatches, trading cards, bobblehead dolls, toy machine guns, wall clocks, "framed art prints," cigarette lighters, belt buckles, and T-shirts. Other items included a two-sided Al Capone Dog Tag Necklace; a "tiny piece of hat owned and worn by Al Capone, with Certificate of Authenticity"; a photocopy of Capone's death certificate; from the Franklin Mint, an Al Capone Collectors' Knife; and a Hugo Boss "Al Capone–style" suit, available in 40, 42, or 42 long. Literary offerings included several biographies, as well as *Black Hats: A Novel of Wyatt Earp and Al Capone*; the *Travel Guide to Al Capone's Chicago*; *Al Capone Was a Golfer: Hundreds of Fascinating Facts from the World of Golf*; and a much-honored children's book entitled *Al Capone Does My Shirts*—also available in Spanish as *Al Capone Me Lava La Ropa*.

The rapper 50 Cent has said that Capone is his style icon. The Al Capone Memorial Jazz Band issued a CD in 1999. On St. Pierre, where economic life reverted to the hardship-ridden fishing industry in 1933, a small, sad museum in the Hotel Robert displays a straw hat said to have been left behind by Capone—even though there's no reason to think Capone ever heard of St. Pierre, much less ever visited it. Even more bizarrely, the city of Moose Jaw, Saskatchewan, is home to Big Al's Café, a motel called Capone's Hideaway, and stores full of Capone schlock—coffee mugs, refrigerator magnets, and so on. The town boosters who claim that Capone visited Moose Jaw, ran its prostitution and gambling dens, and had his tonsils removed by a local doctor are probably not aware of Capone's colloquy with a Toronto reporter who was in Chicago to cover the mobster's tax evasion trial in 1931. When the reporter asked him about his Canadian connections, Capone replied, "I don't even know what street Canada is on."

Although Capone's immortality seems to reside in a fantasyland of wishes, error, and kitsch, the wider criminal world's bequest to post-Prohibition America was palpable—primarily, of course, the transnational scourge of organized crime. The syndicate built and maintained by Lucky

Luciano, Frank Costello, Meyer Lansky, and others was deeply rooted in Prohibition, when each of these men rose to prominence on a tide of illegal liquor. Once booze became legal, they developed a business that eventually produced profits even greater than those from bootlegging. It was an effort, wrote historian Mark H. Haller in 1976, that "involved the investment of tens of millions of dollars by ex-bootleggers from Boston, New York, New Jersey, Philadelphia, Florida, Cleveland, Chicago, and Minneapolis." Haller was writing under the auspices of a federal commission that had spent three years taking testimony from hundreds of people in law enforcement and other fields. The bootleggers had devised a money machine that proved to be "the culmination of their efforts," Haller concluded—namely, Las Vegas.

Some, though, did decide to invest in the legal liquor industry, even if they did have to pay those damnable new taxes. Longy Zwillman and his old boss, Joseph Reinfeld, operated a distribution business under the name Browne Vintners. A few years after they sold it to Sam Bronfman in 1940, Reinfeld took his share of the payout and, with a new partner, bought the eminently respectable Somerset Importers from Joseph P. Kennedy. This was the same Joseph P. Kennedy who had at the onset of Prohibition taken physical control of much of the stock from his father's legal liquor business; who in 1922 had provided the booze for his tenth Harvard reunion; who had later taken control of the RKO film studio; who was one of the most successful stock market speculators of the 1920s; and who, more than seven decades after the end of Prohibition, was the single individual, except perhaps for Capone, most identified in the public mind with the bootlegging industry. If you tell people you're writing a history of Prohibition, virtually everyone asks the same question: "Do you have any good stuff on Joe Kennedy?"

Now, *there's* a story . . .

ON SEPTEMBER 26, 1933, the same day Colorado became the twenty-fourth state to ratify the Repeal amendment, forty-five-year-old Joe Kennedy was aboard the S.S. *Europa*, bound for Europe with a younger friend and their wives. Their destination was England, where the seeds of Prohibition's most enduring legend were about to be planted.

The younger man was an insurance agent named James Roosevelt. As he was also the eldest son of the new president, he was, said the *Saturday Evening Post*, "something like an American Prince of Wales." Kennedy's fondness for his twenty-five-year-old shipboard companion was such that he sometimes referred to himself as Roosevelt's "foster father." During their stay in London one or the other of them met with Prime Minister Ramsay MacDonald and two of his eventual successors, Neville Chamberlain and Winston Churchill. Together they had lunch with the managing director of the Distillers Company conglomerate. If Joe Kennedy wanted to open political doors or commercial ones, he could have done worse than travel with the son of a president.

By the time he returned from the UK—his wife had continued on to Cannes and then to Rome with the Roosevelts for an audience with the pope—Kennedy had concluded all-but-final agreements to become the sole American importer of Dewar's, Haig & Haig, and Gordon's Gin. These contracts were the crucial third leg of an enterprise that was also balanced on medicinal liquor permits Kennedy had obtained in Washington and the bonded warehouse space he had lined up. Shipments began arriving in November. Having heeded the advice of the president of Kentucky-based National Distillers, who had urged him to "get your skeleton organization in position" before sailing for Britain, Kennedy could anticipate December 6, 1933, as Opening Day for the next expansion of his already substantial fortune. On that morning, before the national hangover from the previous night's revels had entirely subsided, Kennedy, wrote journalist Alva Johnston, "was on the market with one huge shipment of Haig & Haig medicine and another huge shipment of John Dewar medicine." His Somerset Importers was in business, founded on an investment of $118,000. It apparently took its name from the Boston men's club that barred its doors to Kennedy and other Irish Catholics, and it owed its creation to Kennedy's friendship with Franklin Roosevelt's son. Somerset emitted the scent that hovered around most marriages of politics and commerce, but it was in every respect perfectly legal.

That last part—"perfectly legal"—was something Walter Trohan, the longtime Washington bureau chief of the *Chicago Tribune*, failed to include in an article published some twenty years later, when Kennedy's son John was serving his first term as U.S. senator from Massachusetts. In that 1954 article on James Roosevelt's impending divorce, Trohan also related the story of Joseph Kennedy's Roosevelt-assisted entry into the liquor business. After a brief description of Kennedy's deal with the British, Trohan added, "At the time prohibition had not been repealed." This was true as far as it went, but it did not acknowledge that the pre-Repeal liquor Kennedy imported in November 1933 entered the country under legal medicinal permits, and was at first stored in legally bonded warehouse space. From such acorns, nourished by a lifetime's accumulation of rumors, enemies, and vast sums of money, arose the widely accepted story of Joseph P. Kennedy, bootlegger.

Except there's really no reason to believe that he was one. The most familiar legacy of Prohibition might be its own mythology, a body of lore and gossip and Hollywood-induced imagery that comes close enough to the truth to be believable but not close enough to be . . . well, true. The Kennedy myth is an outstanding example. The facts of Kennedy's life (that he was rich, that he was in the liquor business, that he was deeply unpopular and widely distrusted) were rich loam for a rumor that did not begin to blossom until nearly thirty years after Repeal. Three times during the 1930s, Kennedy was appointed to federal positions requiring Senate confirmation (chairman of the Securities and Exchange Commission, chairman of the U.S. Maritime Commission, ambassador to Great Britain). At a time when the memory of Prohibition was vivid and the passions it inflamed still smoldered, no one seemed to think Joe Kennedy had been a bootlegger—not the Republicans, not the anti-Roosevelt Democrats, not remnant Klansmen or anti-Irish Boston Brahmins or cynical newsmen or resentful dry leaders still seething from their humiliation. Nothing in the Senate record suggests that anyone brought up the bootlegging charge; there's nothing about it in the press coverage that appeared in the *New York Times,* the *Washington Post,* the *Wall Street Journal,* or the *Boston Globe.* There was nothing asserting, suggesting, or hinting at bootlegging in the Roosevelt-hating *Chicago Tribune* or in the long-dry *Los Angeles Times.* Around the time of his three Senate confirmations, the last of them concluding barely four years after Prohibition's Repeal, there was some murmuring about Kennedy's involvement in possible stock manipulation schemes and a possible conflict of interest. But about involvement in the illegal liquor trade, there was nothing at all. With Prohibition fresh in the national mind, when a hint of illegal behavior would have been dearly prized by the president's enemies or Kennedy's own, there wasn't even a whisper.

In the 1950s another presidential appointment provoked another investigation of Kennedy's past. This time Dwight Eisenhower intended to name him to the President's Board of Consultants on Foreign Intelligence Activities, an advisory group meant to provide oversight of the Central Intelligence Agency. The office of Sherman Adams, the White House chief of staff, asked the FBI to comb through Kennedy's past associations and activities. The fat file that resulted touched on nearly every aspect of his life, including his business relations with James Roosevelt. Nowhere in the file is there any indication of bootlegging in the Kennedy past or even a suggestion of it from Kennedy's detractors.

And so the record remained, apparently, until his son's presidential campaign. That's when the word "bootlegger" first attached itself to Kennedy's name in prominent places—for instance, in a *St. Louis Post-Dispatch* article dated October 15, 1960, in which Edward R. Woods wrote, "In certain ultra-dry sections of the country Joe Kennedy is now referred to as 'a rich bootlegger' by his candidate-son's detractors." A quiet period followed, and then the inference started showing up again after the 1964 publication of the Warren Commission report. Supporters of the theory that John F. Kennedy was murdered by the Mafia suggested that the assassination had something to do with the aged resentments of mobster Sam Giancana.

Then the mob stories began to pop up like spring blossoms. Meyer Lansky, who'd had plenty of chances to talk about it before, suddenly claimed a pre-Repeal Kennedy connection. In 1973 Frank Costello told a journalist (with whom he was collaborating on a book) that he had done business with Kennedy during Prohibition; the inconsiderate Costello proceeded to die a week and a half later. Another mobster, Joe Bonanno, repeated Costello's assertion on *60 Minutes* ten years after that—while promoting a book of his own. By 1991 a drama critic for the *New York Times* could refer to Kennedy in a theater review as a bootlegger without any elaboration. The same year a potential juror in the rape trial of one of Kennedy's grandsons could assert without challenge, during voir dire testimony, that the family fortune had been founded on bootlegging. By then it had become nearly impossible to ask a reasonably informed individual to name a bootlegger without getting "Joe Kennedy" as a reply.

Some of the less reputable Joe-as-Bootlegger assertions are based on "evidence" as flimsy as one man's recollection that he'd seen Kennedy on the docks near Gloucester, gazing out to sea, waiting for his next shipment to come in. Never mind that during the 1920s, when he was an extremely successful stock market trader and the hands-on owner of a major motion picture studio, Kennedy might have had more productive ways to pass his time. One writer, citing an interview with Al Capone's ninety-three-year-old piano tuner, actually has Kennedy coming to Capone's house for spaghetti dinner to discuss trading a shipment of his Irish whiskey for a load of Capone's Canadian.

Looking backward, many find convincing evidence in the booze Kennedy provided for his Harvard tenth reunion—something any thirty-three-year-old sport could have done in 1922, especially one whose father had legitimately been in the liquor business before Prohibition and retained the right to own his remaining stock.

Others have chosen to leave shards of evidence insufficiently examined—for instance, the biographer who found a 1938 letter from Kennedy to Secretary of State Cordell Hull, in which the new ambassador mentions his twenty years of doing business with Great Britain. The investment industry and the movie industry could have provided Kennedy with plenty of opportunity for transatlantic commerce in those years. Additionally, had the biographer realized that Hull was a lifelong and active dry, he might have been less eager to conclude that Kennedy could have been referring to nothing but the bootlegging business. Others have uncovered the name of a Joseph Kennedy in the transcripts of hearings conducted by the Canadian Royal Commission on Customs in 1927, but do not mention that the "Joseph Kennedy Export House" was based in Vancouver; that its eponym was identified at the time as fictitious; and that the operation in fact belonged to Henry Reifel, a powerful British Columbia distiller who, according to Bronfman biographer Terence Robertson, had simply appropriated the name of a waiter in a Vancouver bar.

Even the most reputable investigators have been unconvincing. Trying to nail down Kennedy's putative bootlegging career, one of the finest reporters of the last forty years tried assiduously to overcome what he called "the remarkable lack of documentation in government files." In hundreds of pages of FBI reports, he found "no mention of any link" between "Kennedy, organized crime, and the boot-legging industry." He then proceeded to retail a batch of second- and third-hand stories from people who had been suspiciously silent for generations. A noted scholar of the Scotch whiskey industry based his case for Kennedy's illegal activity on the memory of a Scotsman he interviewed more than three decades after Repeal—a man who not only might have been remembering the liquor-importing Joe Kennedy of 1934, but who also, as it happened, asked his interviewer not to reveal his name, even after his death.

One can exonerate the old Scot of malicious intent. The Kennedy family's rise to prominence, compounded by the increasing appearance of stray rumors in the 1960s, '70s, and '80s, surely made dimly recalled encounters from the distant past suddenly seem more meaningful (or, as the aspiring litterateurs Costello and Bonanno may have hoped, more profitable). It's harder to forgive writers who stretch logic and research standards as if they were Silly Putty—for instance, the author of a Kennedy family biography who, unable to find substantive evidence of bootlegging, reaches a conclusion that can only be described as mind-boggling: "The sheer magnitude of the recollections," he writes, "is more important than the veracity of the individual stories."

One cannot prove a negative. Perhaps there's a document somewhere, or even a credible memory, that establishes a connection between Joseph P. Kennedy and the illegal liquor trade. But all we know for certain is that Joe Kennedy brought liquor into the country legally before the end of Prohibition and sold a great deal of it after. Along the way the "legally" somehow fell off the page, as it had in Walter Trohan's 1954 article. Given nearly eight decades of journalism, history, and biography, three trips through the Senate confirmation process, and the ongoing efforts of legions of Kennedy haters and Kennedy doubters (and even Kennedy lovers who venerated the sons but despised the father), one would think that some sliver of evidence that he was indeed a bootlegger would have turned up by now.

But Joe Kennedy didn't have to be a bootlegger. After all, nearly everyone else was.

Epilogue

IN ALMOST EVERY RESPECT IMAGINABLE, Prohibition was a failure. It encouraged criminality and institutionalized hypocrisy. It deprived the government of revenue, stripped the gears of the political system, and imposed profound limitations on individual rights. It fostered a culture of bribery, blackmail, and official corruption. It also maimed and murdered, its excesses apparent in deaths by poison, by the brutality of ill-trained, improperly supervised enforcement officers, and by unfortunate proximity to mob gun battles. One could rightfully replace our prevailing images of Prohibition—flappers kicking up their heels in nightclubs, say, or lawmen swinging axes at barrels of impounded beer—with different visions: maybe the bloated bodies of the hijacked rumrunners washing up on the beach at Martha's Vineyard, their eyes gouged out and their hands and faces scoured by acid. Or perhaps the crippled men of Wichita, their lives devastated by the nerve-destroying chemicals suspended in a thirty-five-cent bottle of Jake.

But in one critical respect Prohibition was an unquestioned success: as a direct result of its fourteen-year reign, Americans drank less. In fact, they continued to drink less for decades afterward. Back in the first years of the twentieth century, before most state laws limiting access to alcohol were enacted, average consumption of pure alcohol ran to 2.6 gallons per adult per year—the rough equivalent of 32 fifths of 80-proof liquor, or 520 twelve-ounce bottles of beer. Judging by the most carefully assembled evidence, that quantity was slashed by more than 70 percent during the first few years of national Prohibition. It started to climb as American thirsts adjusted to the new regime, but even Repeal did not open the spigots: the pre-Prohibition per capita peak of 2.6 gallons was not again attained until 1973. (It stayed that high only until the mid-1980s, when it began to drop again, to current levels of roughly 2.2 gallons per person per year.) In *The Thin Man*, released in the summer of 1934, William Powell and Myrna Loy have thirty-three drinks between them, or more than one every three minutes (including a few tossed off at breakfast). In real life, as Morris Markey explained in *The New Yorker*, it was rather different. "I went over to the Ambassador Hotel one afternoon for cocktails," Markey wrote just two weeks after Repeal. "We were four men, all told. We sat there for three hours, and drank three cocktails each—one an hour. And all of us remarked how impossible such temperance would be in any speakeasy we have ever known. In the speakeasies there was always a tension, a pressure to drink and keep on drinking, even after appetite had faded completely."

In the surprisingly slow growth of post-Prohibition drinking lay the central irony of Repeal: across most of the country, *the Twenty-first Amendment made it harder, not easier, to get a drink.* During the latter stages of Prohibition, especially in the big cities or near the coasts or adjacent to the Canadian border, little effort was required to obtain a drink, a bottle, or in some places even a shipment of liquid contraband, few questions asked. What was formally illegal was necessarily unregulated, as if it didn't exist. "Remember the old days before Prohibition," a comic asked, "when you couldn't buy a drink on Sunday?"

But Repeal changed that, replacing the almost-anything-goes ethos with a series of state-by-state codes, regulations, and enforcement procedures. Now there were closing hours and age limits and Sunday blue laws, as well as a collection of geographic proscriptions that kept bars or package stores distant from schools, churches, or hospitals. State licensing requirements forced legal sellers to live by the code, and in many instances statutes created penalties for buyers as well. Just as Prohibition did not prohibit, making drink legal did not make drink entirely available.

IN ENACTING THEIR OWN dry laws some states encouraged a hybrid drinking culture incorporating Prohibition's pieties, Repeal's realities, and a bizarre set of signifiers specifically their own. The Jack Daniel's distillery operation that had fled Tennessee for St. Louis returned home in 1938— to a dry county; they could make the stuff in Lynchburg, but no one could buy it there. Mississippi remained legally dry until 1966, providing the outstanding example of official self-delusion. Liquor sales were outlawed, but for years a 10 percent tax on illegal sales remained in place, which encouraged the state to encourage lawbreaking. In 1950 William Faulkner \ded the prevailing rules, urging his fellow Mississippians not to dis- the long and happy marriage between dry voters and illicit sellers, ch our fair state supplies one of the last sanctuaries and strong- Willie Morris, in his memoir *North Toward Home*, recalled a Yazoo

City bootlegger's campaign slogan when liquor law revision made the ballot: "For the sake of my family, vote dry!"

But even if states didn't want to stop the flow of booze, the second clause of the Twenty-first Amendment allowed them to employ the liquor laws for unrelated purposes.* In some states officials kept nude acts out of nightclubs and bars, not because they had authority over public nudity but because the clause, as interpreted by the courts, established that they had authority over what went on in places that served alcohol. In New York officials used similar powers to keep Billie Holiday from performing in the city's cabarets after her conviction on drug charges.

REPEAL PRODUCED WINNERS and losers in many crannies of American life distant from the alcohol industry. Already pummeled by the Depression, Harlem nightclubs catering to a downtown clientele lost their illicit appeal, and the stylish crowds stopped traveling uptown in ermine and pearls. Intercoastal "booze cruises" disappeared altogether by 1938. On the other hand, the "cruise to nowhere" begat every passenger liner that departs a U.S. port for, say, a luxurious journey to the Caribbean and back. Country boys who had made their living racing souped-up cars ahead of revenue agents on the back roads of the South soon found people were willing to pay to watch them race—hence the birth of NASCAR. Then there were losers who realized that some new ideas and new energy could make them winners again. After his friend Franklin Roosevelt assured him that Prohibition was about to end, the governor general of the Bahamas issued a new challenge to his executive council: "Well, gentlemen, it amounts to this— if we can't take the liquor to the Americans, we must bring the Americans to the liquor." Thus, the Bahamian tourism industry—helped along by the Royal Bank of Canada, which had used the rum trade, a Bahamian commentator wrote, to establish a foothold in the Caribbean that stretched "all the way from Montreal to Belize."

The fate of individuals or businesses or national economies aside, Prohibition's most enduring legacy is probably its robust versatility as an example or a remonstration. The wholesale enactment of national criminal laws during Prohibition gave rise to post-Repeal federal statutes addressing kidnapping and bank robbery; on the other hand, the manifest failures

*The clause reads, "The transportation or importation into any State, Territory, or possession of the United States for delivery or use therein of intoxicating liquors, in violation of the laws thereof, is hereby prohibited."

of federal Prohibition enforcement enabled the states to hold on to most of their authority over the enforcement and administration of criminal law. Because Prohibition proved the nation could not legislate personal morality, advocates for the legalization of drugs have been able to draw a direct parallel to their own argument. And in the 1950s southern politicians who only belatedly discovered that Prohibition was a pretty bad idea made cynical use of a similar line of reasoning. Because the failures of the Volstead Act had established that the moral code of one region could not be imposed on another, they argued, school integration was at least folly and likely catastrophic.

In the end, though, the single indisputable lesson of Prohibition might have been the one offered by Sam Bronfman on a fine summer day in 1966. He was talking with two magazine journalists visiting Belvedere, his estate in Tarrytown, New York. Preparing an article about Bronfman's dominance of the American liquor industry, the journalists wanted to know about his activities during the dry years. For decades Bronfman had deployed a ready stock of autopilot evasions. It wasn't illegal in Canada (which, if one took into account customs and tax laws, wasn't true). Seagram's never sold directly to bootleggers (this was, in fact, true: Seagram's sold to agencies wholly owned by the Bronfman family that sold directly to bootleggers). He had never seen any proof that the goods his family had shipped actually ended up in the United States (not necessarily false, but entirely specious).

But on this July day, surrounded by his leather-bound books and the fine art on his walls, in the comfort of his terraced garden with its expansive view over the Hudson, fresh and relaxed in shorts and a sport shirt after a swim in the pool, seventy-seven-year-old Sam Bronfman was, in his late-life eminence, calm and confident enough to indulge in a bout of candor. There was really only one explanation for what happened during Prohibition, he said: "You people were thirsty."

Acknowledgments

WORK ON THIS BOOK formally began in the winter of 2002–2003, before it was interrupted by an eighteen-month detour through the editorial offices of the *New York Times*. Two specific encounters stirred my initial labors.

The first was a lunch with my old friends Wendy Wolf, Rick Kot, and Liz Darhansoff. Wendy and Rick, who used to be my publishers, convinced me that Prohibition should be my next subject; Liz, who was, is, and always will be my agent, began to design a strategy to make it possible.

Several months later, I ran into Ken Burns while strolling across the Brooklyn Bridge. For years Ken had been saying, "Let's make a film together." Knowing about as much about filmmaking as I do about molecular physics, I had chronically met his cheerful encouragement with an exaggerated rolling of the eyes. This time, though, when I told him I was working on a history of Prohibition, Ken skipped the imperative and moved directly to the declarative: "That's it," he said, extending his hand to clinch the deal. "That's our film."

As it turned out—as it *should* have turned out—Ken and his associate (and my dear friend) Lynn Novick made their own film, and I wrote my own book. But along the way, the exchange of ideas, research, and sources enhanced both projects to such a degree that they can be considered first cousins. My book is better for the input and reactions of Ken, Lynn, Geoffrey Ward, and Sarah Botstein; I hope they'll be able to say as much about whatever I've been able to contribute to their forthcoming film.

As a serial exploiter of research assistants, over the course of this project I was sequentially dependent on several. Foremost among these were Jonathan Lichtenstein, the incredible Patrick McCreesh, Ariel Ratner, Michael Spies, and Dan White. At various times Zane Curtis-Olsen, Amy Ettinger, and Lily Rothman provided additional assistance. Lydia Okrent deserves a category of her own and a form of gratitude (and pride) that only a father can offer.

A project such as this one requires travel to distant archives. My research took me to Cambridge, Washington, Wilmington, Toronto, Detroit, Ann Arbor, Chicago, and San Francisco, and also required me to endure two weeks of extreme hardship in the Napa Valley. Some very capable surrogates plumbed collections I was unable to visit, among them Aaron Akins in St. Louis, Matt Becker in St. Paul, Amy Huprich Cook in Cincinnati, Annie Linskey in Baltimore, and Clifford Scott in Ottawa. Phoebe Nobles followed up on a number of forays I had begun at the Bentley Historical Library in Ann Arbor.

Among the scores of librarians and archivists who extended hospitality, assistance, and experience, I would like to single out four truly exceptional individuals. David Smith of the New York Public Library considers it his mission to help writers with their research, and I am proud to count myself among the hundreds of devoted Smithians who have been blessed with his assistance. Marge McNinch, who presides over the papers of both the du Pont family and the Bronfman family at the Hagley Museum and Library in Wilmington, generously accommodated my presence for one extended stay and my repeated inquiries for three additional years. Jeff Flannery of the Manuscript Division of the Library of Congress knows more about the division's vast holdings than any mortal should; his ability to unearth exactly the right document exactly when I most needed it provoked my constant admiration and gratitude. Elaine McElroy manages an institution at the opposite end of the library spectrum, the Wellfleet Public Library in Wellfleet, Massachusetts. There wasn't a book or a roll of microfilm that Elaine and her staff couldn't hunt down for me, and their courtesy and hospitality on many long summer afternoons made indoor work on outdoor days much less onerous than it otherwise might have been.

Other librarians and archivists who offered assistance above and beyond the call include: Richard James at the Hagley, Brian McLaughlin in the office of the U.S. Senate historian, Brigid Shields at the Minnesota Historical Society, Bo Simons at the Sonoma County Wine Library, Steve Sass at the Jewish Historical Society in Los Angeles, Jacqui Seargeant at John Dewar & Sons Limited, Lisa Tuite at the *Boston Globe*, Tom Vajdik at the Windsor (Ontario) Public Library, Suzanne Wones at the John F. Kennedy School of Government, and for making the impossible possible on a summer morning when everything was closed and I had only four hours to spare before an unmissable flight, Daryl Morrison of the University of California at Davis. Tim Rives of the National Archives, Central Plains Region, unearthed the court records of the Lee Levy case, which yielded the horrifying brand name that Levy had put on his gin.

Although few people alive today have vivid (or reliable) recollections of Prohibition, many have memories or information about family members who figure in my narrative. Conversations with the following—some conducted by me, some by my research assistants—enriched the portraits of the people mentioned in parentheses: Erica and Walter Fuller (Georges de Latour), Pat Levinson and Anthony M. Schulte (David Schulte), Susan Berns Rothchild (Charlie Berns and Jack Kriendler), Julian Stein (Emory Buckner), Christopher W. Wheeler and Robin Wheeler (Wayne B. Wheeler), and Pauline Sabin Willis and Sheila Morton Cochran (Pauline Sabin). Erica and Walter Fuller, Julian Stein, and Robin Wheeler also gave me access to private papers never before examined by scholars or journalists. Additional interviews conducted by Lynn Novick and her colleagues at Florentine Films further enhanced my understanding of the Prohibition era.

A number of scholars kindly answered specific questions, directed me to specific resources, and provided general insight into subjects they have studied far more intimately than I could ever hope to. For the history of tax policy, I turned to Donald J. Boudreaux and Joseph J. Thorndike; for the development of Prohibition-related jurisprudence, Jason Mazzone, Robert Post, and William Stuntz; for Joseph P. Kennedy, David Nasaw; for Al Capone, Jonathan Eig; for the Jewish sacramental wine industry, Marni Davis; for Sam Bronfman, James Dubro; for the British liquor industry, St. Pierre, and Rum Row, Lawrence Spinelli, J. P. Andrieux, and Ronald B. Weir. Ranjit S. Dighe and John F. Fox generously allowed me to read their unpublished papers on Pierre S. du Pont and federal law enforcement, respectively. Michael A. Lerner read my entire manuscript and offered valuable insight and suggestions. My treasured friend Robert Sklar, who first engaged me in the study of history and then waited four decades for me to do something about it, also read the finished manuscript. Like all the others mentioned here, he should be absolved of any responsibility for errors of fact or interpretation.

Friends who assisted me as the book took shape—and whose comments, in some cases, provoked additional work with the chisel—include John U. Bacon, Suzie Bolotin, Taylor Branch, Bobbie Bristol, Lizabeth Cohen, Nicholas Delbanco, Melissa Ciano Ellis, Ray Elman, Leon Friedman, Jim Gaines, Peter Gethers, Joel Gora, Lisa Grunwald, Carol Hofmann, John Huey, Michael Janeway, Joe Kahn, Steve Lipsitz, Bruce McCall, Bill Powers, Geoffrey Precourt, John Rothman, Martha Sherrill, Jack Snyder, Ben Sonnenberg, Susan Tifft, Glen Waggoner, Wendy Wolf, and the breathtakingly loyal Rafael Yglesias.

Another group of friends and colleagues deserves special gratitude. In 2006 Alex Jones and Nancy Palmer of the Joan Shorenstein Center on the Press, Politics, and Public Policy at Harvard's John F. Kennedy School of Government offered me temporary lodging at what has become a second professional home to me, as well as access to Harvard's astonishing libraries. Along with Edie Holway, Tom Patterson, and many others at the Shorenstein Center, these part-time colleagues and wise advisers have become enduring friends.

For more than four years, I have relied on (and been rewarded by) the encouragement and support of Colin Harrison and Susan Moldow of Scribner, and the assistance of their colleagues Jessica Manners and Katie Rizzo.

For a quarter of a century, the incomparable Chris Jerome has prevented me from committing sentences that no self-respecting reader should have to abide (if it appears that she missed a few this time, blame it entirely on my stubbornness). For even longer, Liz Darhansoff has held my hand, endured my complaints, suffered my sulks, and otherwise performed prodigies of tolerance that suggest the inadequacy of the term "literary agent." For always, my beloved Becky, John, and Lydia have convinced me that Lou Gehrig didn't know the half of it. No one has ever been luckier than I am.

D.O.
Wellfleet, Massachusetts
August 2009

Appendix

THE CONSTITUTION OF
THE UNITED STATES OF AMERICA

WE THE PEOPLE of the United States, in Order to form a more perfect Union, establish Justice, insure domestic Tranquility, provide for the common defence, promote the general Welfare, and secure the Blessings of Liberty to ourselves and our Posterity, do ordain and establish this Constitution for the United States of America.

Article 1.

Section 1

All legislative Powers herein granted shall be vested in a Congress of the United States, which shall consist of a Senate and House of Representatives.

Section 2

The House of Representatives shall be composed of Members chosen every second Year by the People of the several States, and the Electors in each State shall have the Qualifications requisite for Electors of the most numerous Branch of the State Legislature.

No Person shall be a Representative who shall not have attained to the Age of twenty five Years, and been seven Years a Citizen of the United States, and who shall not, when elected, be an Inhabitant of that State in which he shall be chosen.

Representatives and direct Taxes shall be apportioned among the several States which may be included within this Union, according to their respective Numbers, which shall be determined by adding to the whole Number of free Persons, including those bound to Service for a Term of Years, and excluding Indians not taxed, three fifths of all other Persons.

The actual Enumeration shall be made within three Years after the first Meeting of the Congress of the United States, and within every subsequent Term of ten Years, in such Manner as they shall by Law direct. The Number of Representatives shall not exceed one for every thirty Thousand, but each

State shall have at Least one Representative; and until such enumeration shall be made, the State of New Hampshire shall be entitled to choose three, Massachusetts eight, Rhode Island and Providence Plantations one, Connecticut five, New York six, New Jersey four, Pennsylvania eight, Delaware one, Maryland six, Virginia ten, North Carolina five, South Carolina five and Georgia three.

When vacancies happen in the Representation from any State, the Executive Authority thereof shall issue Writs of Election to fill such Vacancies.

The House of Representatives shall choose their Speaker and other Officers; and shall have the sole Power of Impeachment.

Section 3

The Senate of the United States shall be composed of two Senators from each State, chosen by the Legislature thereof, for six Years; and each Senator shall have one Vote.

Immediately after they shall be assembled in Consequence of the first Election, they shall be divided as equally as may be into three Classes. The Seats of the Senators of the first Class shall be vacated at the Expiration of the second Year, of the second Class at the Expiration of the fourth Year, and of the third Class at the Expiration of the sixth Year, so that one-third may be chosen every second Year; and if Vacancies happen by Resignation, or otherwise, during the Recess of the Legislature of any State, the Executive thereof may make temporary Appointments until the next Meeting of the Legislature, which shall then fill such Vacancies.

No person shall be a Senator who shall not have attained to the Age of thirty Years, and been nine Years a Citizen of the United States, and who shall not, when elected, be an Inhabitant of that State for which he shall be chosen.

The Vice President of the United States shall be President of the Senate, but shall have no Vote, unless they be equally divided.

The Senate shall choose their other Officers, and also a President pro tempore, in the absence of the Vice President, or when he shall exercise the Office of President of the United States.

The Senate shall have the sole Power to try all Impeachments. When sitting for that Purpose, they shall be on Oath or Affirmation. When the President of the United States is tried, the Chief Justice shall preside: And no Person shall be convicted without the Concurrence of two-thirds of the Members present.

Judgment in Cases of Impeachment shall not extend further than to removal from Office, and disqualification to hold and enjoy any Office of honor, Trust or Profit under the United States: but the Party convicted shall nevertheless be liable and subject to Indictment, Trial, Judgment and Punishment, according to Law.

Section 4

The Times, Places and Manner of holding Elections for Senators and Representatives, shall be prescribed in each State by the Legislature thereof; but the Congress may at any time by Law make or alter such Regulations, except as to the Place of Choosing Senators.

The Congress shall assemble at least once in every Year, and such Meeting shall be on the first Monday in December, unless they shall by Law appoint a different Day.

Section 5

Each House shall be the Judge of the Elections, Returns and Qualifications of its own Members, and a Majority of each shall constitute a Quorum to do Business; but a smaller number may adjourn from day to day, and may be authorized to compel the Attendance of absent Members, in such Manner, and under such Penalties as each House may provide.

Each House may determine the Rules of its Proceedings, punish its Members for disorderly Behavior, and, with the Concurrence of two-thirds, expel a Member.

Each House shall keep a Journal of its Proceedings, and from time to time publish the same, excepting such Parts as may in their Judgment require Secrecy; and the Yeas and Nays of the Members of either House on any question shall, at the Desire of one fifth of those Present, be entered on the Journal.

Neither House, during the Session of Congress, shall, without the Consent of the other, adjourn for more than three days, nor to any other Place than that in which the two Houses shall be sitting.

Section 6

The Senators and Representatives shall receive a Compensation for their Services, to be ascertained by Law, and paid out of the Treasury of the United States. They shall in all Cases, except Treason, Felony and Breach of the Peace, be privileged from Arrest during their Attendance at the Session of their respective Houses, and in going to and returning from the same; and for any Speech or Debate in either House, they shall not be questioned in any other Place.

No Senator or Representative shall, during the Time for which he was elected, be appointed to any civil Office under the Authority of the United States which shall have been created, or the Emoluments whereof shall have been increased during such time; and no Person holding any Office under the United States, shall be a Member of either House during his Continuance in Office.

Section 7

All bills for raising Revenue shall originate in the House of Representatives; but the Senate may propose or concur with Amendments as on other Bills.

Every Bill which shall have passed the House of Representatives and the Senate, shall, before it become a Law, be presented to the President of the United States; If he approve he shall sign it, but if not he shall return it, with his Objections to that House in which it shall have originated, who shall enter the Objections at large on their Journal, and proceed to reconsider it. If after such Reconsideration two-thirds of that House shall agree to pass the Bill, it shall be sent, together with the Objections, to the other House, by which it shall likewise be reconsidered, and if approved by two-thirds of that House, it shall become a Law. But in all such Cases the Votes of both Houses shall be determined by Yeas and Nays, and the Names of the Persons voting for and against the Bill shall be entered on the Journal of each House respectively. If any Bill shall not be returned by the President within ten Days (Sundays excepted) after it shall have been presented to him, the Same shall be a Law, in like Manner as if he had signed it, unless the Congress by their Adjournment prevent its Return, in which Case it shall not be a Law.

Every Order, Resolution, or Vote to which the Concurrence of the Senate and House of Representatives may be necessary (except on a question of Adjournment) shall be presented to the President of the United States; and before the Same shall take Effect, shall be approved by him, or being disapproved by him, shall be repassed by two-thirds of the Senate and House of Representatives, according to the Rules and Limitations prescribed in the Case of a Bill.

Section 8

The Congress shall have Power To lay and collect Taxes, Duties, Imposts and Excises, to pay the Debts and provide for the common Defence and general Welfare of the United States; but all Duties, Imposts and Excises shall be uniform throughout the United States;

To borrow money on the credit of the United States;

To regulate Commerce with foreign Nations, and among the several States, and with the Indian Tribes;

To establish an uniform Rule of Naturalization, and uniform Laws on the subject of Bankruptcies throughout the United States;

To coin Money, regulate the Value thereof, and of foreign Coin, and fix the Standard of Weights and Measures;

To provide for the Punishment of counterfeiting the Securities and current Coin of the United States;

To establish Post Offices and Post Roads;

To promote the Progress of Science and useful Arts, by securing for limited Times to Authors and Inventors the exclusive Right to their respective Writings and Discoveries;

To constitute Tribunals inferior to the supreme Court;

To define and punish Piracies and Felonies committed on the high Seas, and Offenses against the Law of Nations;

To declare War, grant Letters of Marque and Reprisal, and make Rules concerning Captures on Land and Water;

To raise and support Armies, but no Appropriation of Money to that Use shall be for a longer Term than two Years;

To provide and maintain a Navy;

To make Rules for the Government and Regulation of the land and naval Forces;

To provide for calling forth the Militia to execute the Laws of the Union, suppress Insurrections and repel Invasions;

To provide for organizing, arming, and disciplining the Militia, and for governing such Part of them as may be employed in the Service of the United States, reserving to the States respectively, the Appointment of the Officers, and the Authority of training the Militia according to the discipline prescribed by Congress;

To exercise exclusive Legislation in all Cases whatsoever, over such District (not exceeding ten Miles square) as may, by Cession of particular States, and the acceptance of Congress, become the Seat of the Government of the United States, and to exercise like Authority over all Places purchased by the Consent of the Legislature of the State in which the Same shall be, for the Erection of Forts, Magazines, Arsenals, dock-Yards, and other needful Buildings; And

To make all Laws which shall be necessary and proper for carrying into Execution the foregoing Powers, and all other Powers vested by this Constitution in the Government of the United States, or in any Department or Officer thereof.

Section 9

The Migration or Importation of such Persons as any of the States now existing shall think proper to admit, shall not be prohibited by the Congress prior to the Year one thousand eight hundred and eight, but a tax or duty may be imposed on such Importation, not exceeding ten dollars for each Person.

The privilege of the Writ of Habeas Corpus shall not be suspended, unless when in Cases of Rebellion or Invasion the public Safety may require it.

No Bill of Attainder or ex post facto Law shall be passed.

No capitation, or other direct, Tax shall be laid, unless in Proportion to the Census or Enumeration herein before directed to be taken.

No Tax or Duty shall be laid on Articles exported from any State.

No Preference shall be given by any Regulation of Commerce or Revenue to the Ports of one State over those of another: nor shall Vessels bound to, or from, one State, be obliged to enter, clear, or pay Duties in another.

No Money shall be drawn from the Treasury, but in Consequence of Appropriations made by Law; and a regular Statement and Account of the Receipts and Expenditures of all public Money shall be published from time to time.

No Title of Nobility shall be granted by the United States: And no Person holding any Office of Profit or Trust under them, shall, without the Consent of the Congress, accept of any present, Emolument, Office, or Title, of any kind whatever, from any King, Prince or foreign State.

Section 10

No State shall enter into any Treaty, Alliance, or Confederation; grant Letters of Marque and Reprisal; coin Money; emit Bills of Credit; make any Thing but gold and silver Coin a Tender in Payment of Debts; pass any Bill of Attainder, ex post facto Law, or Law impairing the Obligation of Contracts, or grant any Title of Nobility.

No State shall, without the Consent of the Congress, lay any Imposts or Duties on Imports or Exports, except what may be absolutely necessary for executing its inspection Laws: and the net Produce of all Duties and Imposts, laid by any State on Imports or Exports, shall be for the Use of the Treasury of the United States; and all such Laws shall be subject to the Revision and Control of the Congress.

No State shall, without the Consent of Congress, lay any duty of Tonnage, keep Troops, or Ships of War in time of Peace, enter into any Agreement or Compact with another State, or with a foreign Power, or engage in War, unless actually invaded, or in such imminent Danger as will not admit of delay.

Article 2.

Section 1

The executive Power shall be vested in a President of the United States of America. He shall hold his Office during the Term of four Years, and, together with the Vice President chosen for the same Term, be elected, as follows:

Each State shall appoint, in such Manner as the Legislature thereof may direct, a Number of Electors, equal to the whole Number of Senators and Representatives to which the State may be entitled in the Congress: but no Senator or Representative, or Person holding an Office of Trust or Profit under the United States, shall be appointed an Elector.

The Electors shall meet in their respective States, and vote by Ballot for two persons, of whom one at least shall not be an Inhabitant of the same State with themselves. And they shall make a List of all the Persons voted for, and of the Number of Votes for each; which List they shall sign and certify, and transmit sealed to the Seat of the Government of the United States, directed to the President of the Senate. The President of the Senate shall, in the Presence of the Senate and House of Representatives, open all the Certificates, and the Votes shall then be counted. The Person having the greatest Number of Votes shall be the President, if such Number be a Majority of the whole Number of Electors appointed; and if there be more than one who have such Majority, and have an equal Number of Votes, then the House of Representatives shall immediately choose by Ballot one of them for President; and if no Person have a Majority, then from the five highest on the List the said House shall in like Manner choose the President. But in choosing the President, the Votes shall be taken by States, the Representation from each State having one Vote; a quorum for this Purpose shall consist of a Member or Members from two-thirds of the States, and a Majority of all the States shall be necessary to a Choice. In every Case, after the Choice of the President, the Person having the greatest Number of Votes of the Electors shall be the Vice President. But if there should remain two or more who have equal Votes, the Senate shall choose from them by Ballot the Vice President.

The Congress may determine the Time of choosing the Electors, and the Day on which they shall give their Votes; which Day shall be the same throughout the United States.

No person except a natural born Citizen, or a Citizen of the United States, at the time of the Adoption of this Constitution, shall be eligible to the Office of President; neither shall any Person be eligible to that Office who shall not have attained to the Age of thirty-five Years, and been fourteen Years a Resident within the United States.

In Case of the Removal of the President from Office, or of his Death, Resignation, or Inability to discharge the Powers and Duties of the said Office, the same shall devolve on the Vice President, and the Congress may by Law provide for the Case of Removal, Death, Resignation or Inability, both of the President and Vice President, declaring what Officer shall then act as President, and such Officer shall act accordingly, until the Disability be removed, or a President shall be elected.

The President shall, at stated Times, receive for his Services, a Compensation, which shall neither be increased nor diminished during the Period for which he shall have been elected, and he shall not receive within that Period any other Emolument from the United States, or any of them.

Before he enter on the Execution of his Office, he shall take the following Oath or Affirmation:

"I do solemnly swear (or affirm) that I will faithfully execute the Office of President of the United States, and will to the best of my Ability, preserve, protect and defend the Constitution of the United States."

Section 2

The President shall be Commander in Chief of the Army and Navy of the United States, and of the Militia of the several States, when called into the actual Service of the United States; he may require the Opinion, in writing, of the principal Officer in each of the executive Departments, upon any subject relating to the Duties of their respective Offices, and he shall have Power to Grant Reprieves and Pardons for Offenses against the United States, except in Cases of Impeachment.

He shall have Power, by and with the Advice and Consent of the Senate, to make Treaties, provided two-thirds of the Senators present concur; and he shall nominate, and by and with the Advice and Consent of the Senate, shall appoint Ambassadors, other public Ministers and Consuls, Judges of the supreme Court, and all other Officers of the United States, whose Appointments are not herein otherwise provided for, and which shall be established by Law: but the Congress may by Law vest the Appointment of such inferior Officers, as they think proper, in the President alone, in the Courts of Law, or in the Heads of Departments.

The President shall have Power to fill up all Vacancies that may happen during the Recess of the Senate, by granting Commissions which shall expire at the End of their next Session.

Section 3

He shall from time to time give to the Congress Information of the State of the Union, and recommend to their Consideration such Measures as he shall judge necessary and expedient; he may, on extraordinary Occasions, convene both Houses, or either of them, and in Case of Disagreement between them, with Respect to the Time of Adjournment, he may adjourn them to such Time as he shall think proper; he shall receive Ambassadors and other public Ministers; he shall take Care that the Laws be faithfully executed, and shall Commission all the Officers of the United States.

Section 4

The President, Vice President and all civil Officers of the United States, shall be removed from Office on Impeachment for, and Conviction of, Treason, Bribery, or other high Crimes and Misdemeanors.

Article 3.

Section 1

The judicial Power of the United States, shall be vested in one supreme Court, and in such inferior Courts as the Congress may from time to time ordain and establish. The Judges, both of the supreme and inferior Courts, shall hold their Offices during good Behavior, and shall, at stated Times, receive for their Services a Compensation which shall not be diminished during their Continuance in Office.

Section 2

The judicial Power shall extend to all Cases, in Law and Equity, arising under this Constitution, the Laws of the United States, and Treaties made, or which shall be made, under their Authority; to all Cases affecting Ambassadors, other public Ministers and Consuls; to all Cases of admiralty and maritime Jurisdiction; to Controversies to which the United States shall be a Party; to Controversies between two or more States; between a State and Citizens of another State; between Citizens of different States; between Citizens of the same State claiming Lands under Grants of different States, and between a State, or the Citizens thereof, and foreign States, Citizens or Subjects.

In all Cases affecting Ambassadors, other public Ministers and Consuls, and those in which a State shall be Party, the supreme Court shall have original Jurisdiction. In all the other Cases before mentioned, the supreme Court shall have appellate Jurisdiction, both as to Law and Fact, with such Exceptions, and under such Regulations as the Congress shall make.

The Trial of all Crimes, except in Cases of Impeachment, shall be by Jury; and such Trial shall be held in the State where the said Crimes shall have been committed; but when not committed within any State, the Trial shall be at such Place or Places as the Congress may by Law have directed.

Section 3

Treason against the United States, shall consist only in levying War against them, or in adhering to their Enemies, giving them Aid and Comfort. No Person shall be convicted of Treason unless on the Testimony of two Witnesses to the same overt Act, or on Confession in open Court.

The Congress shall have power to declare the Punishment of Treason, but no Attainder of Treason shall work Corruption of Blood, or Forfeiture except during the Life of the Person attainted.

Article 4.

Section 1

Full Faith and Credit shall be given in each State to the public Acts, Records, and judicial Proceedings of every other State. And the Congress may by general Laws prescribe the Manner in which such Acts, Records and Proceedings shall be proved, and the Effect thereof.

Section 2

The Citizens of each State shall be entitled to all Privileges and Immunities of Citizens in the several States.

A Person charged in any State with Treason, Felony, or other Crime, who shall flee from Justice, and be found in another State, shall on demand of the executive Authority of the State from which he fled, be delivered up, to be removed to the State having Jurisdiction of the Crime.

No Person held to Service or Labour in one State, under the Laws thereof, escaping into another, shall, in Consequence of any Law or Regulation therein, be discharged from such Service or Labour, But shall be delivered up on Claim of the Party to whom such Service or Labour may be due.

Section 3

New States may be admitted by the Congress into this Union; but no new States shall be formed or erected within the Jurisdiction of any other State; nor any State be formed by the Junction of two or more States, or parts of States, without the Consent of the Legislatures of the States concerned as well as of the Congress.

The Congress shall have Power to dispose of and make all needful Rules and Regulations respecting the Territory or other Property belonging to the United States; and nothing in this Constitution shall be so construed as to Prejudice any Claims of the United States, or of any particular State.

Section 4

The United States shall guarantee to every State in this Union a Republican Form of Government, and shall protect each of them against Invasion; and on Application of the Legislature, or of the Executive (when the Legislature cannot be convened) against domestic Violence.

Article 5.

The Congress, whenever two-thirds of both Houses shall deem it necessary, shall propose Amendments to this Constitution, or, on the Application of the Legislatures of two-thirds of the several States, shall call a Convention for proposing Amendments, which, in either Case, shall be valid to all Intents and Purposes, as part of this Constitution, when ratified by the Legislatures of three-fourths of the several States, or by Conventions in three-fourths thereof, as the one or the other Mode of Ratification may be proposed by the Congress; Provided that no Amendment which may be made prior to the Year One thousand eight hundred and eight shall in any Manner affect the first and fourth Clauses in the Ninth Section of the first Article; and that no State, without its Consent, shall be deprived of its equal Suffrage in the Senate.

Article 6.

All Debts contracted and Engagements entered into, before the Adoption of this Constitution, shall be as valid against the United States under this Constitution, as under the Confederation.

This Constitution, and the Laws of the United States which shall be made in Pursuance thereof; and all Treaties made, or which shall be made, under the Authority of the United States, shall be the supreme Law of the Land; and the Judges in every State shall be bound thereby, any Thing in the Constitution or Laws of any State to the Contrary notwithstanding.

The Senators and Representatives before mentioned, and the Members of the several State Legislatures, and all executive and judicial Officers, both of the United States and of the several States, shall be bound by Oath or Affirmation, to support this Constitution; but no religious Test shall ever be required as a Qualification to any Office or public Trust under the United States.

Article 7.

The Ratification of the Conventions of nine States, shall be sufficient for the Establishment of this Constitution between the States so ratifying the Same.

Done in Convention by the Unanimous Consent of the States present the Seventeenth Day of September in the Year of our Lord one thousand seven hundred and Eighty seven and of the Independence of the United States of America the Twelfth. In Witness whereof We have hereunto subscribed our Names.

Amendments to the Constitution of the United States

Amendment 1 (1791)

Congress shall make no law respecting an establishment of religion, or prohibiting the free exercise thereof; or abridging the freedom of speech, or of the press; or the right of the people peaceably to assemble, and to petition the Government for a redress of grievances.

Amendment 2 (1791)

A well regulated Militia, being necessary to the security of a free State, the right of the people to keep and bear Arms, shall not be infringed.

Amendment 3 (1791)

No Soldier shall, in time of peace be quartered in any house, without the consent of the Owner, nor in time of war, but in a manner to be prescribed by law.

Amendment 4 (1791)

The right of the people to be secure in their persons, houses, papers, and effects, against unreasonable searches and seizures, shall not be violated, and no Warrants shall issue, but upon probable cause, supported by Oath or affirmation, and particularly describing the place to be searched, and the persons or things to be seized.

Amendment 5 (1791)

No person shall be held to answer for a capital, or otherwise infamous crime, unless on a presentment or indictment of a Grand Jury, except in cases arising in the land or naval forces, or in the Militia, when in actual service in time of War or public danger; nor shall any person be subject for the same offense to be twice put in jeopardy of life or limb; nor shall be compelled in any criminal case to be a witness against himself, nor be deprived of life, liberty, or property, without due process of law; nor shall private property be taken for public use, without just compensation.

Amendment 6 (1791)

In all criminal prosecutions, the accused shall enjoy the right to a speedy and public trial, by an impartial jury of the State and district wherein the crime shall have been committed, which district shall have been previously ascertained by law, and to be informed of the nature and cause of the accusation; to be confronted with the witnesses against him; to have compulsory process for obtaining witnesses in his favor, and to have the Assistance of Counsel for his defence.

Amendment 7 (1791)

In Suits at common law, where the value in controversy shall exceed twenty dollars, the right of trial by jury shall be preserved, and no fact tried by a jury, shall be otherwise re-examined in any Court of the United States, than according to the rules of the common law.

Amendment 8 (1791)

Excessive bail shall not be required, nor excessive fines imposed, nor cruel and unusual punishments inflicted.

Amendment 9 (1791)

The enumeration in the Constitution, of certain rights, shall not be construed to deny or disparage others retained by the people.

Amendment 10 (1791)

The powers not delegated to the United States by the Constitution, nor prohibited by it to the States, are reserved to the States respectively, or to the people.

Amendment 11 (1798)

The Judicial power of the United States shall not be construed to extend to any suit in law or equity, commenced or prosecuted against one of the United States by Citizens of another State, or by Citizens or Subjects of any Foreign State.

Amendment 12 (1804)

The Electors shall meet in their respective states, and vote by ballot for President and Vice President, one of whom, at least, shall not be an inhabitant of the same state with themselves; they shall name in their ballots the person voted for as President, and in distinct ballots the person voted for as Vice President, and they shall make distinct lists of all persons voted for as President, and of all persons voted for as Vice President and of the number of votes for each, which lists they shall sign and certify, and transmit sealed to the seat of the government of the United States, directed to the President of the Senate;

The President of the Senate shall, in the presence of the Senate and House of Representatives, open all the certificates and the votes shall then be counted;

The person having the greatest Number of votes for President, shall be the President, if such number be a majority of the whole number of Electors appointed; and if no person have such majority, then from the persons having the highest numbers not exceeding three on the list of those voted for as President, the House of Representatives shall choose immediately, by ballot, the President. But in choosing the President, the votes shall be taken by states, the representation from each state having one vote; a quorum for this purpose shall consist of a member or members from two-thirds of the states, and a majority of all the states shall be necessary to a choice. And if the House of Representatives shall not choose a President whenever the right of choice shall devolve upon them, before the fourth day of March next following, then the Vice President shall act as President, as in the case of the death or other constitutional disability of the President.

The person having the greatest number of votes as Vice President, shall be the Vice President, if such number be a majority of the whole number of Electors appointed, and if no person have a majority, then from the two highest numbers on the list, the Senate shall choose the Vice President; a quorum for the purpose shall consist of two-thirds of the whole number of Senators, and a majority of the whole number shall be necessary to a choice. But no person constitutionally ineligible to the office of President shall be eligible to that of Vice President of the United States.

Amendment 13 (1865)

1. Neither slavery nor involuntary servitude, except as a punishment for crime whereof the party shall have been duly convicted, shall exist within the United States, or any place subject to their jurisdiction.

2. Congress shall have power to enforce this article by appropriate legislation.

Amendment 14 (1868)

1. All persons born or naturalized in the United States, and subject to the jurisdiction thereof, are citizens of the United States and of the State wherein they reside. No State shall make or enforce any law which shall abridge the privileges or immunities of citizens of the United States; nor shall any State deprive any person of life, liberty, or property, without due process of law; nor deny to any person within its jurisdiction the equal protection of the laws.

2. Representatives shall be apportioned among the several States according to their respective numbers, counting the whole number of persons in each State, excluding Indians not taxed. But when the right to vote at any election for the choice of electors for President and Vice President of the United States, Representatives in Congress, the Executive and Judicial officers of a State, or the members of the Legislature thereof, is denied to any of the male inhabitants of such State, being twenty-one years of age, and citizens of the United States, or in any way abridged, except for participation in rebellion, or other crime, the basis of representation therein shall be reduced in the proportion which the number of such male citizens shall bear to the whole number of male citizens twenty-one years of age in such State.

3. No person shall be a Senator or Representative in Congress, or elector of President and Vice President, or hold any office, civil or military, under the United States, or under any State, who, having previously taken an oath, as a member of Congress, or as an officer of the United States, or as a member of any State legislature, or as an executive or judicial officer of any State, to support the Constitution of the United States, shall have engaged in insurrection or rebellion against the same, or given aid or comfort to the enemies thereof. But Congress may by a vote of two-thirds of each House, remove such disability.

4. The validity of the public debt of the United States, authorized by law, including debts incurred for payment of pensions and bounties for services in suppressing insurrection or rebellion, shall not be questioned. But neither the United States nor any State shall assume or pay any debt or obligation incurred in aid of insurrection or rebellion against the United States, or any claim for the loss or emancipation of any slave; but all such debts, obligations and claims shall be held illegal and void.

5. The Congress shall have power to enforce, by appropriate legislation, the provisions of this article.

Amendment 15 (1870)

1. The right of citizens of the United States to vote shall not be denied or abridged by the United States or by any State on account of race, color, or previous condition of servitude.

2. The Congress shall have power to enforce this article by appropriate legislation.

Amendment 16 (1913)

The Congress shall have power to lay and collect taxes on incomes, from whatever source derived, without apportionment among the several States, and without regard to any census or enumeration.

Amendment 17 (1913)

The Senate of the United States shall be composed of two Senators from each State, elected by the people thereof, for six years; and each Senator shall have one vote. The electors in each State shall have the qualifications requisite for electors of the most numerous branch of the State legislatures.

When vacancies happen in the representation of any State in the Senate, the executive authority of such State shall issue writs of election to fill such vacancies: Provided, That the legislature of any State may empower the executive thereof to make temporary appointments until the people fill the vacancies by election as the legislature may direct.

This amendment shall not be so construed as to affect the election or term of any Senator chosen before it becomes valid as part of the Constitution.

Amendment 18 (1919)

1. After one year from the ratification of this article the manufacture, sale, or transportation of intoxicating liquors within, the importation thereof into, or the exportation thereof from the United States and all territory subject to the jurisdiction thereof for beverage purposes is hereby prohibited.

2. The Congress and the several States shall have concurrent power to enforce this article by appropriate legislation.

3. This article shall be inoperative unless it shall have been ratified as an amendment to the Constitution by the legislatures of the several States, as provided in the Constitution, within seven years from the date of the submission hereof to the States by the Congress.

Amendment 19 (1920)

The right of citizens of the United States to vote shall not be denied or abridged by the United States or by any State on account of sex. Congress shall have power to enforce this article by appropriate legislation.

Amendment 20 (1933)

1. The terms of the President and Vice President shall end at noon on the 20th day of January, and the terms of Senators and Representatives at noon on the 3d day of January, of the years in which such terms would have ended if this article had not been ratified; and the terms of their successors shall then begin.

2. The Congress shall assemble at least once in every year, and such meeting shall begin at noon on the 3d day of January, unless they shall by law appoint a different day.

3. If, at the time fixed for the beginning of the term of the President, the President elect shall have died, the Vice President elect shall become President. If a President shall not have been chosen before the time fixed for the beginning of his term, or if the President elect shall have failed to qualify, then the Vice President elect shall act as President until a President shall have qualified; and the Congress may by law provide for the case wherein neither a President elect nor a Vice President elect shall have qualified, declaring who shall then act as President, or the manner in which one who is to act shall be selected, and such person shall act accordingly until a President or Vice President shall have qualified.

4. The Congress may by law provide for the case of the death of any of the persons from whom the House of Representatives may choose a President whenever the right of choice shall have devolved upon them, and for the case of the death of any of the persons from whom the Senate may choose a Vice President whenever the right of choice shall have devolved upon them.

5. Sections 1 and 2 shall take effect on the 15th day of October following the ratification of this article.

6. This article shall be inoperative unless it shall have been ratified as an amendment to the Constitution by the legislatures of three-fourths of the several States within seven years from the date of its submission.

Amendment 21 (1933)

1. The eighteenth article of amendment to the Constitution of the United States is hereby repealed.

2. The transportation or importation into any State, Territory, or possession of the United States for delivery or use therein of intoxicating liquors, in violation of the laws thereof, is hereby prohibited.

3. The article shall be inoperative unless it shall have been ratified as an amendment to the Constitution by conventions in the several States, as provided in the Constitution, within seven years from the date of the submission hereof to the States by the Congress.

Amendment 22 (1951)

1. No person shall be elected to the office of the President more than twice, and no person who has held the office of President, or acted as President, for more than two years of a term to which some other person was elected President shall be elected to the office of the President more than once. But this Article shall not apply to any person holding the office of President, when this Article was proposed by the Congress, and shall not prevent any person who may be holding the office of President, or acting as President, during the term within which this Article becomes operative from holding the office of President or acting as President during the remainder of such term.

2. This article shall be inoperative unless it shall have been ratified as an amendment to the Constitution by the legislatures of three-fourths of the several States within seven years from the date of its submission to the States by the Congress.

Amendment 23 (1961)

1. The District constituting the seat of Government of the United States shall appoint in such manner as the Congress may direct: A number of electors of President and Vice President equal to the whole number of Senators and Representatives in Congress to which the District would be entitled if it were a State, but in no event more than the least populous State; they shall be in addition to those appointed by the States, but they shall be considered, for the purposes of the election of President and Vice President, to be electors appointed by a State; and they shall meet in the District and perform such duties as provided by the twelfth article of amendment.

2. The Congress shall have power to enforce this article by appropriate legislation.

Amendment 24 (1964)

1. The right of citizens of the United States to vote in any primary or other election for President or Vice President, for electors for President or Vice President, or for Senator or Representative in Congress, shall not be denied or abridged by the United States or any State by reason of failure to pay any poll tax or other tax.

2. The Congress shall have power to enforce this article by appropriate legislation.

Amendment 25 (1967)

1. In case of the removal of the President from office or of his death or resignation, the Vice President shall become President.

2. Whenever there is a vacancy in the office of the Vice President, the President shall nominate a Vice President who shall take office upon confirmation by a majority vote of both Houses of Congress.

3. Whenever the President transmits to the President pro tempore of the Senate and the Speaker of the House of Representatives his written declaration that he is unable to discharge the powers and duties of his office, and until he transmits to them a written declaration to the contrary, such powers and duties shall be discharged by the Vice President as Acting President.

4. Whenever the Vice President and a majority of either the principal officers of the executive departments or of such other body as Congress may by law provide, transmit to the President pro tempore of the Senate and the Speaker of the House of Representatives their written declaration that the President is unable to discharge the powers and duties of his office, the Vice President shall immediately assume the powers and duties of the office as Acting President.

Thereafter, when the President transmits to the President pro tempore of the Senate and the Speaker of the House of Representatives his written declaration that no inability exists, he shall resume the powers and duties of his office unless the Vice President and a majority of either the principal officers of the executive department or of such other body as Congress may by law provide, transmit within four days to the President pro tempore of the Senate and the Speaker of the House of Representatives their written declaration that the President is unable to discharge the powers and duties of his office. Thereupon Congress shall decide the issue, assembling within forty-eight hours for that purpose if not in session. If the Congress, within twenty-one days after receipt of the latter written declaration, or, if Congress is not in session, within twenty-one days after Congress is required to assemble, determines by two-thirds vote of both Houses that the President is unable to discharge the powers and duties of his office, the Vice President shall continue to discharge the same as Acting President; otherwise, the President shall resume the powers and duties of his office.

Amendment 26 (1971)

1. The right of citizens of the United States, who are eighteen years of age or older, to vote shall not be denied or abridged by the United States or by any State on account of age.

2. The Congress shall have power to enforce this article by appropriate legislation.

Amendment 27 (1992)

No law, varying the compensation for the services of the Senators and Representatives, shall take effect, until an election of Representatives shall have intervened.

Notes

Abbreviations

AC	*Atlanta Constitution*
AJTP	Arthur J. Tuttle Papers
AJVP	Andrew J. Volstead Papers
ANB*	*American National Biography*
BATF	Bureau of Alcohol, Tobacco and Firearms
CGG	*California Grape Grower*
COHP	Columbia Oral History Project
CR	*Congressional Record*
CT	*Chicago Tribune*
CWH	California Wine History
DAB*	*Dictionary of American Biography*
DFP	De Latour Family Papers
DN	*Detroit News*
JJRP	John J. Raskob Papers
JPKP	Joseph P. Kennedy Papers
JWWP	James W. Wadsworth Jr. Papers
LAT	*Los Angeles Times*
LD	*Literary Digest*
LFA	Leo Franklin Archive
MWWP	Mabel Walker Willebrandt Papers
NYT	*New York Times*
OrH	Oral history
PSDP	Pauline Sabin Davis Papers
PSdPP	Pierre S. du Pont Papers
RAC	Rockefeller Archive Center

*When no page number accompanies these citations, reference is to the entry on the named individual.

RCCE   Royal Commission on Customs and Excise
RPHP   Richmond P. Hobson Papers
SEAP*   *Standard Encyclopedia of the Alcohol Problem*
SFC   *San Francisco Chronicle*
SLP-D   *St. Louis Post-Dispatch*
SMC   Seagram's Museum Collection
TPP   Temperance and Prohibition Papers (subsections of these papers are denoted with the name of the subsection following TPP. For example, TPP/Cherrington, R4, refers to the Ernest H. Cherrington papers within the TPP, Reel 4)
WGHP   Warren G. Harding Papers
WJBP   William Jennings Bryan Papers
WP   *Washington Post*
WSJ   *Wall Street Journal*

page   Prologue: January 16, 1920

1   **San Francisco:** *SFC,* 1/17/20; Asbury, 145.
1   **Deemed the impossible:** *St. Helena Star,* 1/16/20. **Lilly:** *Daily Palo Alto,* 1/16/20; *SFC,* 1/17/20, 5; Migdol, 55.
2   **Every bottle:** Golden, 125. **Masterson:** Stanley Walker, 5–12. **Chiclet:** unidentified clipping, eBay.
2   **Detroit stills:** *CT,* 1/18/20, 5. **New Brunswick:** *Fredericton Daily Mail,* 1/14/20, 1, cited in Grant, 17. **Roosevelt:** Ward, 476n.
2   **Sunday:** Asbury, 144.
3   **A new nation:** ASL press release, 1/15/20, cited in Nelli, 148. **Cease to exist:** *New York World,* 1/16/20. **Lane:** "The Letters of Franklin Lane," at http://www.gutenberg.org.

Chapter One: Thunderous Drums and Protestant Nuns

7   **Marryat:** Marryat, 124.
7   **Winthrop ship:** Lender and Martin, 2–3. **Franklin:** Mencken, *American,* 266. **Distilleries:** William Grimes, 21–22. **Tea:** Rorabaugh, 99.
8   **Americans drank:** Rorabaugh, 20–21. **Johnny Appleseed:** Pollan, 9, 21–22. **Washington:** Mark A. Vargas, "The Progressive Agent of Mischief: The Whiskey Ration and Temperance in the United States Army," *The Historian,* Summer 2005, 204.
8   **Clinton:** Rorabaugh, 48. **Washington:** Carr, 11–13. **Adams:** William Grimes, 20. **Jefferson:** Bear and Stanton, 519. **Madison:** Clark, *Deliver,* 21.
8   **Fourteen thousand:** Fuller, 75. **Seven gallons:** Rose, *American,* 12.
9   **Devastator:** Lincoln speech at Springfield, Illinois, 2/22/1842.
9   **Rush:** Asbury, 27; Furnas, 189.
9   **Ticknor:** Rorabaugh, 6. **Garrison:** *ANB;* Lender, *Dictionary,* 186–87. **Foul water:** Rorabaugh, 97.
9   **Lincoln on Washingtonians:** Donald, 82.
10 **Gough:** *ANB; Journal of Commerce,* 9/22/1845.
10 **Barnum:** Barnum, 225, 362; *ANB.*

11 **Manilow (fn):** The show ran for forty-eight performances at the 13th Street Theater in New York in 1970.

11 **Neal Dow opened our eyes:** Barnum, 362. **Burlesque occasions:** Dow, 102.

11 **Hate-Evil:** Dow, 16.

12 **Maine Law:** Furnas, 175. **Horace Mann:** Kobler, 87.

13 **Dio Lewis:** *ANB*; Asbury, 69; Kobler, 115–16; Seldes, 261–62.

13 **Our Girls:** Eastman, 160.

13 **Thompson:** Eastman, 154–65; http://www.wctu.org/crusades.html; Bordin, "Baptism," 402.

14 **Spread of Crusade:** http://www.wctu.org/crusades.html. **Tax collections:** Asbury, 85. **Closed establishments:** Blocker, "Separate," 462.

14 **Sherwood Anderson:** Sinclair, 15.

14 **Bloomer and Stone:** *ANB*.

15 **All-debasing wine:** *DAB*.

15 **Listen and learn:** Catt and Shuler, 22. **Unclean Thing:** Furnas, 219.

15 **Intellectual cranks:** Seldes, 279–80.

15 **Sexual abstinence:** Tyrrell, "Women," 141.

16 **Syphilis of the innocent:** Burnham, "Progressive," 885.

16 **Universal ear:** Willard speech in Chicago, 1893, quoted at http://memory.loc .gov/learn/features/timeline/progress/prohib/policy.html.

16 **250,000:** http://www.wctu.org/frances_willard.html, quoting Susan B. Anthony. **Frank:** Willard, *Wheel*, 65; Furnas, 277. **Beveridge:** *Our Day*, 9/1898, 442.

16 **Willard, generally:** *ANB, DAB*. **A pledge:** Cherrington, *Standard*, 2849. **Methodist heaven:** Kobler, 134. **Sanctified learning:** http://www.northwestern.edu/ about/history/vision.

17 **Unwashed:** Willard, *Glimpses*, 341.

17 **In 1876:** Rose, *American*, 21. **Unseat:** Mezvinsky, 213. **Lucy:** in TPP/WCTU, R4, 103.

17 **I have cared, stenographer:** *Our Day*, 3/1898, 107–16. **Travel:** Cherrington, *Standard*, 2849. **Tolstoy:** Tatiana Tolstoy to Willard, 2/28/90, in TPP/WCTU, R17. **As nearly:** Willard, *Wheel*, 74. **Hibbie:** Furnas, 287.

18 **Protestant nuns:** *Union Signal*, 6/6/95, 2–3. **Christian socialist:** John A. Mayer, "Social Reform After the Civil War to the Great Depression," in Lippy and Williams, 1441; *Our Day*, 3/1898, 107–16. **Clothing:** Gusfield, 90. **White Life:** Murdock, 21.

19 **Douglass:** Williamson, 80–81. **Phillips:** Lender, *Dictionary*, 393–94.

19 *Washington's Farewell:* Lebeau, 22; Freeman, 467.

20 **Great hunger:** Cherrington, *Standard*, 1268. **Did more:** Bryan, *In His*, 171.

20 **State of siege:** *ANB*. **Our duty:** Zimmerman, 1.

21 **Aiming higher, state campaigns:** Ibid.

21 **Dropsy, down the throat:** David F. Musto, "Alcohol in History" *SA*, 4/96, 81. **Stimulant:** Silver, Burdett to Hunt, 3/8/1892, in TPP/STF, R4. **50 percent:** Lamme, 107.

22 **Hunt's home:** Zimmerman, *ANB*. **Stowell negotiations:** Hunt to Stowell, 8/24/1889, in TPP/STF, R4. **Unscientific:** Zimmerman, 29. **Narcotic poison:** Stowell, *Essentials*, 43. **Drew the line:** Silver, Burdett to Hunt, 3/8/92, in TPP/ STF, R4.

22 **I have studied:** Billings, 34. **Utter impossibility:** Hunt to Silver, Burdett, 8/22/1891, in TPP/STF, R4.

22 **Hunt's final conflict with Silver, Burdett:** O. S. Cook to Hunt, 1/25/1892, and Silver, Burdett to Hunt, 1/26/1892, in TPP/STF, R4.

23 **Unjust charges, rumor:** Minutes, advisory board of WCTU Dept. of Scientific Instruction, 1/21/1897, in TPP/STF, R4.

23 **Clearinghouse:** Lamme, 107. **In whole or in part:** Memorandum enclosed in Marie C. Brehm to Cora F. Stoddard, 6/28/06, in TPP/STF, R4.

23 **The day:** Cherrington, *Standard*, 1269.

Chapter Two: The Rising of Liquid Bread

24   **My constant:** Nation, 63. **Bulldog, whey-faced:** Kobler, 146–47; 153. **The public:** Nation, 90.
24   **I ran behind, Mr. Cook:** Grace, 89–90.
25   **They need:** Nation, 179. **Yale:** photograph, collection of Bobbie Bristol. **Harvard:** Nation, 139.
25   **Not radically:** Rorabaugh, 8.
25   **In 1850:** Clark, *Deliver,* 55.
26   **Domestic misery, liquid bread:** Burnham, *Bad,* 56.
26   **Beecher (fn):** Cherrington, *Standard,* 296.
26   **Competing for Europeans:** Higham, 17–18. **Busch:** *ANB.*
26   **Infidel population:** Rose, *American,* 26. **Minnesota:** Rumbarger, 138. **New colony:** *McClure's,* 7/07, 576–79. **Census:** *McClure's,* 9/09, 532.
27   **Erickson's:** *Third Age News,* 10/93. **Metal trough (and fn):** Powers, 30–31. Also e-mail from Madelon Powers, 5/28/2008. **Lucy Adams:** Ransom, 130–32. **Brings his growler:** Riis, *How,* 213–14.
27   **Number of saloons:** Rose, *American,* 17. **Leadville:** West, 121–22. **San Francisco:** Rose, *American,* 17. **I would have dropped:** *Cincinnati Post,* 12/9/98.
28   **Colossal shadow, congregations larger:** Riis, *How,* 210.
28   **Poor creatures:** Bourgeois, 111. **Rudkus:** Sinclair, *Jungle,* chapter 14. **Life was different:** London, 24.
29   **Free lunch:** Kingsdale, 477. **Silent partners:** Ade, 46.
29   **All Nations:** author's collection.
29   **Brewer subsidies:** Duis, 25–26.
29   **License fee:** Timberlake, 150.
29   **No man:** *McClure's,* 7/07, 576. **Half the population:** Powers, 18. **By 1909:** Timberlake, 104; Kingsdale, 474.
30   **Convention in German:** Furnas, 210. **Tax reduced:** Asbury, 64. **Fully one-quarter:** Hu, v. **Bribe:** Purley A. Baker, in Anti-Saloon League, *Proceedings,* 11/10/13, 63–64.
30   **Fanatical, whatever party:** Baron, 220.
31   **Paying editors:** Asbury, 108. **Pabst and DuBois:** Cochran, 312.
31   **Busch, generally:** *ANB, DAB,* Plavchan.
31   **Large city:** *Union Signal,* 12/4/19. **$30,000:** *Time,* "Benton v. Adams," 3/4/46.
32   **Fired a cannon:** Hernon and Ganey, 45. **Promoting:** Odegard, 249. **It may cost:** quoted in *House Ways and Means 1932,* 629. **Poll taxes:** Clark, *Deliver,* 116–17. **We have sent:** *Senate Judiciary 1919,* 1088. **Best not written:** Odegard, 255.
32   **Besides losing:** *House Ways and Means 1932,* 629. **Cirrhosis:** *DAB.*
33   **Selling in prohibited:** *Senate Judiciary 1919,* 1065.
33   **Decidedly inimical:** Baron, 223. **Eighty-one companies:** Arthur Capper in Walnut, 157. **Worst and cheapest:** Charles Nagel Papers, Busch to Charles Nagel, 12/8/09.
34   **Westheimer speech:** 12/19/14, quoted in *Senate Judiciary 1919,* 1058.
34   **Almighty God:** Odegard, 6.

Chapter Three: The Most Remarkable Movement

35   **Plant a colony:** John J. Shipherd, quoted in Fletcher, 180. **Dietary restrictions:** Rorabaugh, 120.
35   **Prayerful influence:** *SEAP;* **Front row:** Chalfant, 296.
36   **Not in politics:** Purley A. Baker in *Cincinnati Enquirer,* 2/23/08, quoted in Westheimer, 131–39.
36   **Political retribution:** Lamme, 63. **Gould's credo:** Timberlake, 140. **Is he right:** Henry M. Chalfant, in Walnut, 282.
37   **Minimum of 75 percent:** *Senate Judiciary 1930,* 4281. **Real secret:** *Baltimore*

Sun, ca. 1922, in TPP/ASL Legal, R12. **I can dictate:** S. E. Nicholson, quoted in Odegard, 21.

37 **Pilgrimage:** http://www.franceswillardhouse.org/franceslife/.

37 **Lamented leader:** RPHP, Margaret Dye Ellis to Hobson, 9/28/14.

38 **In no instance:** *Cincinnati Enquirer*, 2/23/08, quoted in Westheimer, 131–39.

38 **Generalship:** *New York Herald Tribune*, 10/23/27. **Conquest:** Reprinted in *Columbus Dispatch*, 9/11/27. **Dispassionate men:** *Baltimore Evening Sun*, 9/6/27, editorial page.

38 **A good boy:** *Cincinnati Enquirer*, reprinted in *American Issue*, 9/17/27. **Wheeler, generally:** *ANB*; *SEAP*; *NYT*, 6/26/27, XX, 6; Kobler, 181–82; Steuart. **Great men his puppets:** Reprinted in *Columbus Dispatch*, 9/11/27.

38 **Loving, spirited; praying:** "A Hasty Sketch Appreciative of Wayne B. Wheeler," in TPP/Russell, R4. **Altruism:** Steuart, 38–39. **Locomotive:** Steuart, 24.

39 **Bicycle:** Furnas, 307. **Petitions:** Odegard, 115. **Not enough Wheeler:** Hamm, 145.

39 **Rockefeller match:** RAC, B44, F475. **High crimes:** Russell speech in 1897, quoted in Lamme, 63. **Targeted, defeated:** Odegard, 97.

40 **Herrick and Wheeler:** http://www.ohiohistory.org; Kerr, 109–10; Odegard, 89–90, 114–15; Randall and Ryan, 452.

40 **Murder mills:** *Columbus Dispatch*, 10/16/05.

40 **Rockefeller reduces:** Frederick T. Gates to Rockefeller, 2/11/05; Rockefeller to Gates, 2/17/05, both in RAC, B44, F475. **Never again:** Kobler, 196. **Controlled six Congresses:** Steuart, 11.

41 **Reckon with:** Fox to USBA members, 1/6/09, from *Senate Judiciary 1919*, 806.

41 **Remarkable, autocratic:** Gilmore speech, 1908, quoted in Odegard, 22–23. **Salvation:** Feigenspan speech, 12/29/14, from *Senate Judiciary 1919*, 1058. **Reducing licenses:** Sunstein speech, 12/29/14, from *Senate Judiciary 1919*, 1058. **Suppression:** Carlson, 225–26.

42 **South slow to enlist:** Coker, 83 *et seq.* **Negro problem, terrible condition:** Corrigan, 9/07, 328–34. **Dark faced mobs:** Ida B. Wells-Barnett, *A Red Record* (Salem, NH: 1895), 83, quoted in Morone, 299.

42 **Under slavery:** Pickett et al., 291–93. **Moral responsibility:** *Collier's*, 5/31/13, 32. **Tillman:** *CR*, 12/17/17, 449–51.

43 **Eyes bloodshot:** Dixon, *Leopard*, 125. **Half child:** Dixon, *Clansman*, 292–93. **Off the sidewalks:** Cronon, 485.

43 **Third wave:** Woodward, 389. **Hoke Smith:** Walton and Taylor.

44 **Stronghold:** Sellers, 101.

44 **Busch agents in Texas:** O. Paget to G. H. Luedde, 12/7/10, in Anti-Saloon League, *Brewers*, vol. 2, 1481.

44 **Foreign enterprise:** *CR*, 12/17/17, 449. **Jewish type:** *McClure's*, 9/09, 528–43.

44 **Gentleman of St. Louis:** *Collier's*, 5/16/08, 10.

45 **Coleman:** Pfeifer, 142–43. **If I should:** *Collier's*, 5/16/08, 10. **Wholly unfit, Black Cock:** *U.S. v. Lee Levy and Adolph S. Asher*, Eastern District of Missouri, 1908, Grand Jury indictment and sentence rendered. **Mostly nude:** Isaac, 148.

45 **Nameless crime:** *Collier's*, 8/15/08. **Nigger gin:** *Collier's*, 5/16/08. **Wholesale price:** *U.S. v. Levy and Asher.* **Brief wave (fn):** *Collier's*, 5/2/25. **Fairly docile:** *Tennessean*, 6/17/08, quoted in Isaac, 148. **This gin:** *Tennessean*, 6/14/08, quoted in Isaac, 148. **Insult:** *Memphis Commercial Appeal*, 6/20/08.

46 **Atlanta to Los Angeles:** *AC*, 1/5/09; *LAT*, 10/22/08. **Improper:** *SLP-D*, 10/21/08. **Expelled:** *Collier's*, 8/15/08. **Opening a place:** *U.S. v. Levy and Asher.*

46 **Stupid, sodden:** Edmund Morris, 162. **Low, venal:** Morison and Blum, vol. 1, 1470. **String three, unutterably:** Edmund Morris, 162–63.

47 **Kick you:** Edmund Morris, 166. **Twelve of twenty-four:** Odegard, 248. **Saloon Slate:** Kingsdale, 484. **Affiliation:** Albert Kennedy, quoted in Duis, 114.

47 **144 gallons:** Rorabaugh, 213.

48 **Patrick and Sambo:** Stanton speech from 1868, "Manhood Suffrage," reprinted in Ann D. Gordon, 196.
48 **Most of them:** Jordan to Prescott F. Hall, 2/28/10, Immigration Restriction League Papers, B2, F560, Folder 1. **Lifted up:** Rumbarger, 114. **Killing off (fn):** Timberlake, 62.
48 **The fact:** Link, 847. **Laboring man:** Engelmann, 30. **Decent kennel:** W. A. White, 389–90.
49 **Gross evils:** Addams, *The Second*, 221–62. **Home Salon:** Melendy, 459–61.
50 **Eliot forswore:** Timberlake, 55.
50 **Born middle-aged:** Leuchtenberg, *Perils*, 149.
50 **Eagle-faced:** ms. of James W. Wadsworth memoir in JWWP, B15.
50 **More than two thousand:** Furnas, 258–59. **Raines sandwich:** Riis, *Battle*, 224.
51 **Committee of Fourteen:** Gilfoyle, 419.
51 **The passage:** Fox to USBA members, 2/27/15, *Senate Judiciary 1919*, 259–62.
51 **Use of liquor:** quoted in report from Fox to Percy Andreae, 1914, *Senate Judiciary 1919*, 283.
52 **This one thing:** *Current History*, 2/24, 848.

Chapter Four: "Open Fire on the Enemy"

53 **There appears:** "Spirits, Foreign and Domestic," 3/5/1792, in Hamilton, *Works*, 316.
53 **Congress could:** *CR*, 12/22/14, 602. **Indirection:** Hamm, 172.
54 **Medium of exchange, delivery:** Brenda Yelvington, "Excise Taxes in Historical Perspective," in Shughart, 34. **Lender and Martin**, 31.
54 **We now see:** Washington to Hamilton, 9/17/1792, quoted in Chernow, *Hamilton*, 468–69.
54 **Federal revenue:** Hamm, 95–96. **War's cost:** Baron, 293. **Assist:** United States Brewers' Association, 1909, 14.
54 **By 1910:** Rose, *American*, 56; Hamm, 95–96.
55 **Clad:** "Cross of Gold" speech, 1896 Democratic National Convention. **Breakfast:** Sloane Gordon, cited in *CGG*, 9/1/25, 3.
55 **Fundamentalist Pope, Morondom:** Kazin, 261, 284.
55 **Rock of Ages:** *DAB*.
56 **Gaseous:** Weisman, 210.
56 **Dred Scott:** Buenker, *Income*, 21. **Galahad:** Hinton, 137.
57 **Equable:** *Union Signal*, 2/15/1883. **Pledge on the part:** *The Voice*, 3/7/1895. **Alleged loss:** Finley E. Hendrickson to A. E. Shoemaker, 4/4/08, in TPP/ASL of DC.
57 **Hull:** Hinton, 180; Hull, 140–45.
58 **Roosevelt and ASL:** Friedel, *Apprenticeship*, 127–28.
58 **Chief cry:** "The Next and Final Step," 4/22/13, in TPP/Cherrington, R82.
59 **Union shop:** Steuart, 34. **New cadre:** Hogan, 144.
59 **Goggle-eyed:** Hogan, 173. **Bully:** Kobler, 274.
59 **Wheeler and Steffens:** Steffens, 860.
60 **Wielded no power:** Blocker, *Retreat*, 215.
60 **Rather die:** Cochran, 315–17.
61 **Irresistible:** *Time*, 9/25/39. **Our customers:** Odegard, 57. **Create the appetite:** Ibid., 41.
61 **Fair Cohorts:** *WP*, 11/30/13, 1. **Description of ASL march and demonstration:** *WP*, 12/11/13, 1; *NYT*, 12/11/13; *Outlook and Independent*, "The Dry Decade," 10/30. **Open fire:** *NYT*, 3/29/26, 21.
62 **Bryan's first campaign:** Coletta, 82.
62 **Lived to twenty-one:** *ANB*. **Acquired taste:** London, 2. **Alcohol made:** Mencken to Sinclair, 12/10/24, quoted in Johns, 43.
62 **Ombibulous, every known:** Johns, 5. **Bulk cocktails:** William Grimes, 64.

63 **London voting:** London, 1. **The moment women:** London, 204.
63 **Anthony to Duniway:** Murdock, 31.
64 **Commander-in-chief:** Mezvinsky, 192.
64 **Anthony to Erwin:** 12/27/99, in TPP/Russell, R1.
64 **When woman has:** Murdock, 28–29. **Gentlemen, we need:** Mezvinsky, 220.
64 **Oregon's saloonkeepers:** Alan P. Grimes, *Puritan,* 114; Drescher, 241. **Observations made:** *SLP-D,* 5/9/09. **Annuity:** Couzins to William Howard Taft, 9/25/10, in Herbert S. Hadley Papers. **If ever should:** Busch to Henry Nicolaus, 12/25/05, quoted in Hernon and Ganey, 72.
65 **Brewers in Texas:** *New Republic,* 8/21/15, 62–64.
65 **The antidote:** Odegard, 85. **Faker:** Kerr, 109–10.
66 **Fanatical:** Hernon and Ganey, 69. **Macomb:** *Collier's,* 4/12/13. **Exigency:** OrH, Montana Women, Montana Historical Society: Belle Winestine, Rankin aide.
66 **Illegal:** Gould, 245.

Chapter Five: Triumphant Failure

67 **Contumely:** ms. by Grizelda Hull Hobson, in RPHP, B12, F4.
67 **Coventry:** Pittman, *Navalist,* 8. **Got along:** *Nation,* 3/11/15, 286.
67 **Most terrible:** Hobson, *Buck,* 326.
68 **Waltzes:** Rosenfeld, 62. **Smouldering:** *DAB.* **Women lined up, when the kissing:** Shaw, 54–60.
68 **Time speeches:** Pittman, dissertation, 134. **Another round:** *ANB.*
69 **Japan prediction:** Finding Aid to RPHP, Library of Congress Manuscript Division. **Sex (fn):** Pittman, *Navalist,* 8–9; 134.
69 **Illegal in DC:** Shaw, 54–60. **Open Annapolis:** Sheldon, dissertation, 218–19. **Despite warnings:** Sheldon in *Alabama Review,* 259. **I saw black:** quoted in *The Nation,* 2/11/15, 286.
70 **Cannibals,** *CR,* 12/11/13, 736 *et seq.* **Only Southerner:** Sheldon in *Alabama Review,* 260. **Negroes, negritos:** Quoted in Sheldon, dissertation, 219.
70 **Ten mortal:** *CR,* 12/22/14, 495. **Galleries:** *WP,* 12/23/14, 1.
71 **Clark drunk:** *CT,* 12/3/14, 1; *NYT,* 12/3/14, 1. **Omit all:** Hobson to Eugene Chafin et al., in RPHP, B35, F6.
71 **Rucker, Mann:** *NYT,* 12/23/14, 1. **Morrison:** *CR,* 12/22/14, 586.
72 **Stacks:** *CT,* 12/23/14. **Postcards:** Pittman, *Navalist,* 145. **Sandwich:** ms. by Grizelda Hull Hobson, in RPHP, B12, F4.
72 **Hobson speech:** *CR,* 12/22/14, 602 *et seq.*
73 **Knight errant, lunatic:** *NYT,* 12/3/14, 1.
73 **Judgment day:** *CT,* 12/22/14. **Progressive Party:** Timberlake, 172.
74 **Not for results:** *Nation,* 2/11/15, 286. **Ecstasy:** Quoted in Epstein, 24.
74 **Last speech:** *CR,* 1/12/15. **Hobson in Atlantic City:** Odegard, 157–58.
74 **1915 convention speakers:** *NYT,* 7/9/15, 20. **Fighting Germans:** Odegard, 157.
75 **Onslaught, le delirium, drinking licenses:** *Atlantic Monthly,* 12/15, 739–50. **Trade regulations and sumptuary laws:** Spinelli, xiv. **German industrial, Norway, Finland:** Weir, *History,* 254. **Iceland:** Jimerson et al., 214–16. **Canada:** Marrus, 63–64.
75 **Russia:** Cherrington, *ASL Yearbook 1920,* 250–52. **Tens of thousands:** *Atlantic Monthly,* 12/15, 739–50. **Tacoma:** Clark, *Dry,* 145. **Lenin, 1923:** Barnes, 227–33.
75 **Randolph:** Lerner, *Dry,* 35. **IWW enemy:** Clark, *Dry,* 145. **Leaflets:** Samuel S. White, letter to the editor, *New Republic,* 7/25/23.
76 **I here announce:** *CR,* 12/23/14, 602 *et seq.*; *WP,* 12/24/14, 6.
76 **Tumulty:** *NYT,* 3/28/26, E1. **Mackerel:** William Allen White, quoted in Lord, 290–91.
77 **Wilson's Scotch:** Tribble, xvii. **No open opposition:** *NYT,* 3/28/26, E1.
77 **Wine mess, Sir Josephus:** Hanson Baldwin, 16005.

77 **Futile distraction:** Levine, 107–8. **Grape juice:** Bryan, *Memoirs*, 187, 351; *NYT*, 4/25/13, 1.
77 **Russian ambassador:** Bryan, *Memoirs*, 351. **Grape juice diplomacy:** *DAB*. **Shaw:** Kazin, 250.
78 **Sporty:** Volstead to Forrester, 12/23/21, in AJVP, B2. **So-called:** Murdock, 6. **Water flowed:** Anthony, *First*, 229.
78 **Ten tons:** Kerr, 151. **Newspapers:** Dotson, 15. **Captains:** Timberlake, 142. **Expenditures:** *Nation*, 7/7/26. Modern equivalents for this and other sums cited throughout were determined with the Bureau of Labor Statistics CPI Calculator, http://www.bls.gov/data/inflation_calculator.htm. **Russell activities:** Rumbarger, 179. **Water wagon:** Jimerson et al., 336.
79 **Trained lecturers:** Kobler, 201–2, puts the figure at 50,000, but other sources indicate it was quite a bit lower. See Hogan, 152. **By policy:** Odegard, 191. **Landrith, Taber:** "Campaign Speakers," 1918, in TPP/Ohio ASL. **Do not beg:** "Suggestions to Speakers," 1914, in TPP/Cherrington, R82.
79 **Ten speeches:** Levine, 111. **Ann Arbor, Philadelphia:** Coletta, 66. **A little easy:** *New Republic*, 3/20/15, 165.
79 **A great deal:** Coletta, 70–71. **Bryan, Hobson fees:** Odegard, 203–4. **Two million copies:** Rosenfeld, 185–86. **His strength:** Grizelda Hull Hobson to J. A. White, 10/16/15, in RPHP, B36, F1.
80 **Lack the funds:** Anna Gordon to Hobson, 1/18/15, in RPHP, B35, F7.
80 **If both:** *CR*, 12/11/13, 736. **ASL officer:** Odegard, 205.
81 **We must:** Hobson to Cherrington, 3/18/15, in RPHP, B35, F7.
81 **Great cities:** Carter, *Decline*, 35. **Possible to re-district:** Cherrington to Cannon, 3/26/15, in TPP/Cherrington, R77.
81 **Terrified members:** *WP*, 5/6/14. **Make it safe:** *NYT*, 3/28/26, E1.
82 **We knew:** *NYT*, 3/30/26, 27. **Barrage:** Merz, 17. **Twenty-three states, would be submitted:** *NYT*, 3/30/26, 27.

Chapter Six: Dry-Drys, Wet-Drys, and Hyphens

83 **Candler:** *NYT*, 3/14/29. **Shubert:** Lerner, *Dry*, 36.
83 **Too busy:** Batterberry, 197.
84 **Lager's amber:** advertisement reproduced in Philip P. Mason, 26. **Anti-Profanity:** Dabney, 123. **Start with hell:** *NYT*, 5/25/96, obituary of Joseph Mitchell.
84 **Blacklist, drunken darkies:** *Senate Judiciary 1919*, 119, 144–50; *NYT*, 11/12/18.
85 **Purchased newspapers:** Lardner, 58; Drescher, 181; *NYT*, 9/20/18, 11/20/18; *Senate Judiciary 1919*, 70–71. **We looked:** Steuart, 126.
85 **Busch family:** Hernon and Ganey, 89–91.
85 **Infidel foreign:** Rose, *American*, 26. **Staunchest friends:** Andreae speech 10/3/13, reprinted in *Senate Judiciary 1919*, 349–59. **Salary:** Memorandum, 6/9/13, reprinted in *Senate Judiciary 1919*, 1127. **Spokesman:** USBA Minutes, 10/15/15, reprinted in *Senate Judiciary 1919*, 1073. **Editorials:** *Senate Judiciary 1919*, 472, 841. **Bankrolled:** Andreae to Charles J. Hexamer, 12/31/13, quoted in *Senate Judiciary 1919*, 900.
86 **Oppose enactment:** Drescher, 60–61. **Arrests for speeding:** *Slanders Against Prohibition Refuted*, 12.
86 **99 percent:** Woodward, 389. **Never been told:** Wolfe, 229. **Bourbon-swilling:** McGill, 131. **Wife was daughter:** Marni Davis, 189.
87 **No quarrel:** Wilson message to Congress, Senate document 5, Serial No. 7264, 65th Congress, 1st session. **Watson (fn):** MacLean, 120. **Born under other:** Kennedy, *Over*, 24.
87 **Out-of-state shipper:** Suitts, 185.
87 **Cannon, generally:** *ANB*, *DAB*. **Beard, best brain:** Virginius Dabney in *NYT Book Review*, 10/23/55. **Merest wink:** Dabney, 306.
88 **I do not remember:** *Richmond Times-Dispatch*, 11/6/28, quoted in Dabney, 100.

88   **No young ladies:** Dabney, 16. **In 1914:** *DAB.*
88   **Interdenominational:** ASL of Ohio stationery, in RAC, B44, F476. **Democrat with Democrats:** H. L. Mencken, "The Bishop Loquitir," *Baltimore Evening Sun,* 10/12/31.
89   **Back of a gnat:** Florence Dickinson Stearns, quoted in Dabney, 333. **Humorless:** Golden, 124–25. **Violent:** Asbury, 322. **Mother of ignorance:** *Baltimore and Richmond Christian Advocate,* 12/17/06 and other dates, cited by Dabney, 181.
89   **Gambling:** Kobler, 186. **Many were drunk:** John Garland Pollard, quoted in Dabney, 183. **Dry-drys:** Mencken, *American,* 305. **One of only three:** *NYT,* 1/25/27.
89   **Fondness for moonshine:** Simon, 77; *CT,* 1/17/30, 1. **Rest of his life:** *American Brewer,* 3/18, 93. **As they pray:** *NYT,* 6/26/27, XX, 6.
90   **Vestal virgins:** *CR,* 12/22/14, 581. **Not a square foot:** Hamm, 230. **Mother's Day:** http://www.senate.gov/artandhistory/. **Carnality, every county:** *CR,* 12/17/17, 457–458.
91   **No hearings:** Hamm, 240. **Single afternoon:** Kyvig, *Explicit,* 222–23. **No sumptuary action:** *CR,* 12/22/14, 602 *et seq.* **Choice of battleground:** Hobson, "Brief on the Proposed Changes in the Wording of the National Prohibition Amendment Prepared for the Special Committee of Nineteen," 8/20/15, in RPHP, B33, F8.
92   **Coauthors:** Odegard, 152. **Telegram:** Cherrington to Cannon, 3/27/17, in TPP/Cherrington, R77.
92   **Maintain the balance:** Odegard, 157–58.
92   **Thirteen million gallons:** Sexton, 114. **Invested capital:** U.S. Census Report, 1914, cited in Asbury, 111. **Fifth largest:** *World's Work,* 7/17, 295–96. **Bolsheviki:** *New Republic,* 1/25/19, 359.
93   **Sinned away:** Pickett et al., 98. **Garrett speech:** *CR,* 12/22/14, 526.
93   **Not a moral issue:** quoted in Murray, *Harding,* 16. **Scotch and soda:** Anthony, *Florence,* 291–93. **Owned stock:** Mellon, 104. **No mistaking:** Downes, 280.
93   **Harding-Wheeler negotiation:** Russell, 299; Odegard, 172. **Insult to private:** Carter, *Another,* 102.
94   **Alcoholic/intoxicating:** B. E. Prugh to R. P. Hobson, 1/21/15, in RPHP, B35, F7; Wayne Wheeler to Louis Cramton, 3/23/27, Louis C. Cramton Papers, B1.
94   **We are not willing:** Wheeler to Baker, 2/28/18, in Steuart, 118–19.

Chapter Seven: From Magna Carta to Volstead

96   **Sunday, generally:** *ANB.* **Wages:** *ANB.* **American Association, Sportsman's:** Nemec, 16, 22, 25. **Recreation Park:** Flamm, 61–63.
96   **Across the street:** Lindsay Denison, "Billy Sunday and His War on the Devil," *American Magazine,* 9/07. **Sentences, Gospel gun:** Henry F. May, 126. **Dibbly-dibbly:** Hofstadter, *Anti-Intellectualism,* 116.
97   **Flings:** Francis Hackett, "Billy Sunday," *New Republic,* 3/20/15. **Worst enemy:** Kobler, 12. **I will fight:** Philip P. Mason, 15.
97   **Liquor interests hate:** *American Issue,* quoted in *SEAP.* **Tied with Carnegie, does not smite:** Hofstadter, *Anti-Intellectualism,* 115, 119.
98   **Officially denounced:** Jimerson et al., 69. **Passion for dollars:** Levine, 118–20. **Steadiness of nerve:** Kerr, 201.
98   **Fisher group:** "The Memorial for National Prohibition," in Ernest Gordon, *Wrecking,* 265–67. **Eleven million loaves:** Kerr, 199–200. **Wildly inflated:** Fisher, in "The Case for War-Time Prohibition," pamphlet, in Annenberg Rare Book and Manuscript Library, University of Pennsylvania. **Five million:** *NYT,* 11/3/18, 28. **How can we:** Levine, 118–20. **Flap-jacks:** Allsop, 29.
99   **Grain production:** Scott, 6697. **Heatless days:** Wheeler to Wilson, 4/1/18, quoted in Steuart, 106–7. **Full-page ad:** *NYT,* 11/3/18, 28.
99   **At this point:** Burner, *Hoover,* 218. **Extremists:** Morison and Blum, vol. 6, 1131.

Particularly annoying: Morison and Blum, vol. 5, 699. When we must: Morison and Blum, vol. 8, 1259.

100 Seize railways: Merz, 25.
100 German enemies: *Milwaukee Journal*, 2/13/18, quoted in Cochran, 320.
100 Recruited, bankrolled: Wheeler to Purley A. Baker, 2/28/18, quoted in Steuart, 119. Mostly by slogans: Zeitz, 198. Important element: Barry, *The Great*, 127.
101 Ground glass: Leuchtenberg, *Perils*, 43–44. There are men: *NYT*, 8/16/17, 1. Speaking German: Kennedy, *Over*, 67–68. Beethoven: Drowne, 17. Execute the Huns: Michie and Ryhlick, 149.
101 Robert Prager: Kennedy, *Over*, 68.
102 Our German women: Alan P. Grimes, *Puritan*, 116. Membership two million: Plavchan, 139. Leaders urge: *NYT*, 11/9/17, 9.
102 Prophets: Ohlinger, "The Germans," in Davis and Schwartz, 125. 250 years: *Senate Judiciary 1919*, 8. Before he had: Wheeler to Baker, 2/28/18, quoted in Steuart, 119. Gluttons: Sinclair, 117.
102 United States Brewers' Association had funded: *Senate Judicary 1919*, 932. Implicitly supported: *NYT*, 12/4/18. Cabled cash, not mitigated: Hernon and Ganey, 91. Blacklist leaked: *NYT*, 11/21/18.
103 Removing German names: Plavchan, 135. Australia, Canada, flag: Hernon and Ganey, 91. Portraits removed: Wittke, 184–86. More substantively: Baron, 305.
103 Hypnotized: *Senate Judiciary 1919*, 63.
103 Does anyone: Rose, *American*, 165.
104 Fifteen minutes: *NYT*, 1/9/18.
104 Hobson had asserted: "Brief on the Proposed Changes in the Wording of the National Prohibition Amendment Prepared for the Special Committee of Nineteen," 8/20/15, in RPHP, B33, F8.
104 Sailing-ship: F. L. Allen, *Only*, 18. Most important: Powe, 200.
104 New York statistics: Merz, 43. New Jersey statistics: U.S. census. Maryland statistics: Hacker, 23–24; U.S. census.
105 Missouri vote: Krebs, 139; Odegard, 175. Ohio: Odegard, 175; Kyvig, *Repealing*, 14.
105 Once ratified: "Brief . . . ," 8/20/15, in RPHP, B33, F8. Catholic percentages: Odegard, 31. More than 80 percent: Dabney, 132.
106 Studebaker, invested: Johns, 9. Bryan passed: WJBP, B32. Truman: Truman to Wallace, 1/21/19, http://www.archives.gov/education/lessons/volstead-act/images/truman-letter-1.gif.
106 Spokane: Clark, *Dry*, 130.
107 Avenue de Booze: Engelmann, *Intemperance*, 34. Detroit details: *DN*, 2/20/19–2/22/19. Billingsleys (fn): Blumenthal, 77–78. Boesky arrested (fn): *DN*, 2/21/19.
108 Resolution legalizing: *CR*, 12/22/14, 499. Quasi criminal: Taft to Allen B. Lincoln, 9/2/18, quoted in Post, 85.
108 Volstead, generally: *ANB*.
108 Few inferiors: Henry F. Pringle, "Obscure Mr. Volstead," *World's Work*, 7/29. Tobacco, chokecherry, tie: Carol L. James, 16, 30, 1. I have gazed: Senate speech, 8/18/21, quoted in United States Brewers' Association, *Year Book 1920–21*, 48–50.
109 Never delivered, joined, vast movement: *CR*, 7/1/19, 2296. Twice put up: *ANB*.
110 Wheeler did, too loosely: Volstead to William F. Shea, 2/10/34, in AJVP, B3. Nearly as much: *House Appropriations, 1922*, 482. Only in part: *DN*, 7/3/26.
110 No user would: George Norris, cited by Hamm, 243. Hoover: Burner, *Hoover*, 218.
111 Amendment would have died: Wheeler to George Norris, 3/17/27, in George Norris Papers, B2, F7. No one who: House of Representatives Report 91, 66th Congress, 1st Session, 5. Sponge: *CR*, 7/19/19, 2869.

111 **Surprising willingness:** Wheeler in *Current History*, 2/24, 848. **Much to the dismay:** Rabbi Samuel M. Gup to Rabbi Leo M. Franklin, 12/13/21, in LFA; Central Conference, 116–18. **Many hard-line:** Dobyns, 289.
112 **Jury to determine:** *NYT*, 10/19/19, XX1. **Corn juice:** Sinclair, 169.
112 **Conserve fruits:** *Senate Judiciary 1926*, 855.
112 **Filled with Wets:** Volstead to Mrs. Joseph M. Gazzam, 2/2/22, AJVP, B2, F1. **Muskrat pelts:** *NYT*, 5/25/20.
113 **As much deliberation:** Frankfurter, "A National Policy for Enforcement of Prohibition," in Walnut, 193. **Pressure groups:** Seeking to identify the origin of the term, William Safire, in the revised edition of *Safire's Political Dictionary* (New York: Oxford University Press, 2008), cites the *Oxford English Dictionary*, which traces it to the *Nebraska State Journal*, 1/16/24. However, Wheeler delivered a speech entitled "Pressure Groups" at Columbia University on 10/16/23, quoted in Steuart, 209. **Lineal descendants:** Wheeler Columbia speech, quoted in Steuart, 209.
113 **Dumb stupor:** *LD*, 3/8/19. **Did not employ:** Kyvig, *Repealing*, 10. **Twenty cases:** Cannadine, 275. **Stepped up, cut sales:** Plavchan, 230. **Wet list:** Ward, 420n.
113 **Bronfman activity:** Gray, *Booze*, 131–32; Prince, 24–26.
114 **All laws:** Kerr, 222–23.

Chapter Eight: Starting Line

117 **First Congregational Church rally, generally:** *Commoner*, 2/20. **Luminaries:** *Union Signal*, 1/22/20, 3; Coletta, 78. **Equal Pay:** *Union Signal*, 1/22/20, 7.
117 **No man living:** Kobler, 14. **Obliterated:** Bagby, 111. **Delivering speeches:** *Commoner*, 2/20, 12.
118 **Broad vowels:** Recordings of Bryan speeches in Vincent Voice Library at Michigan State University. **Doxology, They are dead:** Coletta, 78.
118 **Stolen:** *CT*, 1/18/20, 5.
118 **Deaths, drunkenness:** Slosson, 119. **Muncie:** Lynd and Lynd, 227. **Holland House:** Asbury, 191; William Grimes, 80–81.
119 **Welch's:** Lender and Martin, 146. Grand Rapids: *Survey*, 11/6/20, 193. **Chicago jail:** Cherrington, *ASL Year Book*, 21. **Elated:** Addams, *Forty*, 220. **I Never Knew:** author's collection.
119 **All Liquor Stains:** *American Issue*, 1/17/20, 1. **Consumption:** Miron and Zwiebel, 242.
119 **We learned:** Sann, 92.
119 **Morrow:** Leon Adams, OrH, CWH.
120 **Goldwater:** Barry Goldwater, in film *Barry Goldwater: American Life* (1991), cited in *New Times* (Phoenix, AZ), 10/19/2006. **Kennedy sold:** Amanda Smith, 8. **Cellared:** Goodwin, 441–42.
120 **Union Club:** *NYT*, 1/14/20, 17. **Walter Parker:** Parker to Pierre S. du Pont, 12/21/33, in PSdPP, F1023–48, B1537. **Hennessy:** Beauchamp, 95.
121 **Chief pleasure:** Jessup, 477–78. **Financed Root's:** Kyvig, *Repealing*, 17.
121 **Butler's description:** Jessup, 479–80.
121 **Half to his house:** *NYT*, 9/26/20.
122 **Portable stills:** Asbury, 157. **Enough smuggled:** quoted in Grant, 17–18. **Infinitesimal:** George W. Ashworth, quoted in Merz, 57.
122 **Iron River episode, generally, including all quotations not otherwise identified:** *CT*, 2/23/20–2/26/20; *NYT*, 2/23/20–2/27/20. **Armed Invasion:** *St. Louis Globe-Democrat*, 2/25/20.
122 **Dago red, open revolt:** Engelmann, *Intemperance*, 178–79.
123 **Necktie, high school kids:** eyewitness account in *The Rum Rebellion*, published by Iron County Museum, 2/20/70, 4, 18.
124 **Father-in-law:** Ashlee, 194.

124 **900,000 cases:** Engelmann, *Intemperance*, 72. **Consumption** math based on 1921 Canadian census figures. **Ten bottles a day:** Philip P. Mason, 38.
124 **Honest inspector:** *NYT*, 6/27/20, 27; *CT*, 6/7/20.
125 **Suspicious gurgles:** *Boston Evening Transcript*, 6/7/20, 2.
125 **He was pleased:** Steuart, 161. **Fearing that:** Ibid., 157.
126 **Unanimously repealed:** Elizabeth Anne Brown, 34. **Necessary as coffee:** *SFC*, 1/1/20, 13.
126 **In communion:** *NYT*, 7/5/20. **Bourbon, small committees:** Mencken, *Heathen*, 179. **Samaritans:** *NYT*, 6/9/20.
127 **Plank modifying:** Tumulty, 421. **Private reasoning:** Cannon, 297. **Shrank from:** *NYT*, 7/3/20.
127 **Beerless:** Kazin, 270. **Several hundred:** *NYT*, 6/9/20, 5. **I put an old coat:** *NYT*, 3/26/26, 1.
127 **Overwhelmed:** *NYT*, 7/3/20. **My heart:** Cannon, 298. **How Dry:** Coletta, 124.

Chapter Nine: A Fabulous Sweepstakes

128 **Better than no:** In a ten-minute Internet search, one can find this aphorism attributed variously to Will Rogers, Ring Lardner, or the Indiana newspaper humorist Kin Hubbard (although his name is usually rendered, erroneously, as "Ken"). Less well-known candidates include "a farmer in Wisconsin," "a man down in Florida," "a dry Mississippian," and "an economist." **Gennas:** Nelli, 159–61.
128 **Rotting flesh:** Roy Haynes in *NYT*, 7/20/23, 15. **Various stills:** Carr, 182–99. **Absolutely impossible:** Bingay, 323.
129 **Chevy Chase Club:** Anthony, *Florence*, 293. **Seized liquor:** Russell, 521. **Slightest intention, gin, Balfour:** Longworth, 314.
129 **Harding never:** William Stayton, in Walnut, 33. **Brass rail:** Quoted in Dean, 24.
129 **Liquor transferred, Ochs:** Julius Ochs Adler memorandum, 11/17/21, Adolph S. Ochs Papers, New York Times Archives, courtesy of Susan Tifft. **Other direction:** Andrew J. Volstead to W. A. Goslen, 6/15/21, AJVP. **Refilling:** Anthony, *Florence*, xix. **Guests:** Samuel Hopkins Adams, in Leighton, 90; for Mellon, David Cannadine, author interview. **No rumor:** Longworth, 324.
130 **Timely death:** Leighton, 89. **Open gates:** F. L. Allen, *Only*, 108. **Harding and blacks:** Murray, *103rd*, 28–29. **Birmingham:** Dean, 125. **Debs:** Sann, 63; Dean, 128.
130 **I listen:** Leuchtenberg, *Perils*, 89. **Stuff contents:** Starling, 170. **Moral qualities:** quoted in Dean, 67.
131 **Wheeler and Harding:** For instance, Wheeler to Harding, 9/17/21, and Harding to Wheeler, 9/17/21, in WGHP, F35. **Shields:** Isaac, 259. **I need not:** Harding to Wheeler, 9/17/21. **Somehow:** Murray, *Harding*, 404.
131 **Lacked influence:** Steuart, 13. **Unacceptable:** *Senate Lobby 1930*, 4359.
131 **Upshaw:** Dabney, 68–69; unidentified clipping, 7/17/32, in TPP/ASL, R14. **Very dry:** Odegard, 205. **Ranting:** Press release, New York chapter of ASL, 5/3/28, in TPP/ASL, R14. **KKK and suffrage:** McLean, 116. **Move about (fn):** unidentified clipping of 7/17/32, as above. **Scottish Chiefs:** Merz, 165.
132 **Editor in Hillsboro:** *NYT*, 10/21/40. **Special pet:** OrH, COHP, William Anderson, 126–28.
132 **Church membership:** *NYT*, 8/10/23, 13.
132 **Sworn off, vaudeville:** Murray, *Harding*, 404. **Drinks with death:** *NYT*, 7/26/23, 17. **Mellon, generally:** *ANB*. **Expected to talk:** Cannadine, 297. **Pass a law:** *NYT*, 6/4/11; Cannadine, 205 *et seq.*
133 **Ice-water smile:** Quoted in Beebe, 287–88. **Mellon drank:** Gunther, 139.
134 **Old Overholt:** Cannadine, 275; Downard, *Dictionary*, 137. **Alarmed notice:** Anderson to Purley A. Baker, 2/17/21, in TPP/Cherrington, R76. **A thief:** Koskoff, *Mellons*, 241.

134 **Civil service:** Wayne Wheeler, in *Current History*, 2/24, 848.
135 **Norris position:** Norris to Mrs. H. R. H. Williams, 6/21/30, in George Norris Papers, B2, F7. **Volstead himself:** Volstead to J. H. Hoffman, 1/6/22, in AJVP, B2. **Hindrance:** Van Riper, 287. **Chaos:** Van Riper, 290.
135 **Harreld:** Lowitt, 322. **Pie counter:** Lowitt, 325. **Drys charged:** *WP*, 9/18/30, 1. **New Jersey, Maryland:** *DN*, 7/30/26. **Plain fact:** Asbury, 174.
136 **George Eliot:** Heimel, 20. **Semidrunk:** Bergreen, 613; Tucker, 20–21.
136 **Thespian:** *NYT*, 2/26/22. **Sewer:** *NYT*, 3/15/22. **Faints:** *NYT*, 7/17/22.
136 **Gonzaulles, Hervey:** *Mobile Register*, 11/14/23, 1. **Kurtzman:** Lerner dissertation, 227. **Wolff:** Heimel, 12. **Simpson:** *CGG*, 4/1/26, 13; *NYT*, 3/22/26.
136 **McMullin:** *NYT*, 10/14/20; Lerner, *Dry*, 66–71. **Young:** Angle, 157. **Norfolk:** interoffice memoranda from agents Layton Blood, 3/9/26, 3/17/26, and D. D. Mayne, 7/5/26, reprinted in Senate Doc. 198, 69th Congress, 2nd Session, "Prohibition Enforcement: Letter from the Secretary of the Treasury," 1/25/27.
137 **Men clamor:** *Senate Judiciary 1926*, 196. **Never extortionate:** Stanley Walker, 76.
137 **Nation-wide scandal:** Harding message to Congress, 12/8/22.
137 **Bath:** Frances Parkinson Keyes, "Homes of Outstanding American Women," *Better Homes and Gardens*, 3/28, 101. **Bodily contact:** Willebrandt letter to her parents, quoted in Dorothy M. Brown, 33. **Reindeer:** Dorothy M. Brown, 211, 221. **Tent, darlings:** Dorothy M. Brown, 128.
138 **Keenest:** *NYT*, 6/12/28, 4. **Studied, courses:** Dorothy M. Brown, 28.
138 **I have asked:** Keyes, *Better Homes and Gardens*, 3/28, 12.
139 **Neither paints:** *AC*, 6/23/25.
139 **Girly:** *LD*, 3/31/23, 42. **Wide, earnest:** *NYT*, 6/12/28, 4. **Invariable:** Keyes, *Better Homes and Gardens*, 3/28, 100.
139 **Laura, Cochran, Mayer:** Dorothy M. Brown, 211, 219, 229. **Brandeis parties:** Willebrandt, "Smart Washington After Six O'Clock," *Ladies' Home Journal*, 7/29, 10. **Sirica:** Dorothy M. Brown, 219. **Hoover:** Alpheus Mason, *Stone*, 150.
140 **Social drinker:** Willebrandt, 78. **Prostitutes:** Dorothy M. Brown, 36. **Told Stone (fn):** Willebrandt to Stone, 1/31/51, quoted in Alpheus Mason, *Stone*, 150. **Johnson sponsored:** Dorothy M. Brown, 47.
140 **Sheep's clothing, regime:** Ibid., 53. **Can't catch:** *NYT*, 1/25/25.
141 **I refuse:** Willebrandt, 121.
141 **Insobriety in Vermont, flasks in Indiana:** Dabney, 174. **Indiana vested:** Leonard Moore, 150. **Mississippi:** Wickersham, vol. 4, 636. **Sterno:** Merz, 202.
141 **Dear Jerry:** Leonard Moore, 148. **60 percent:** Clark, *Deliver*, 165.
141 **Sleeping sickness:** Dorothy M. Brown, 56. **Only eighteen:** Rose, *American*, 47. **Any state:** Cherrington, *ASL Yearbook 1920*, 5514.
142 **Rather dictate:** *ANB*.
142 **Pinchot pledged:** Lender, *Dictionary*, 398. **Honest-to-God:** *NYT*, 3/9/23. **Gave credence:** Burton Hersh, 228.
143 **McConnell scandal:** *NYT*, 10/19/21, 40; 3/25/22, 18; 5/1/23, 12; Asbury, 178. **Politics first, expected:** *NYT*, 10/15/23.
143 **Features so fine:** O'Toole, 81–82. **Raids in eighteen, reminding:** *NYT*, 3/4/23. **Unbought:** *NYT*, 3/28/23.
143 **Five million dollars sufficient:** Wheeler to Sheppard, 4/3/20, reprinted in *CR*, 4/14/20, 5655. **Columbia payroll:** *NYT*, 5/9/20. **Haynes boasting:** Merz, 123–24.
143 **Initial staff:** Lerner, dissertation, 139–40. **Entire fleet:** Canney.
144 **Pep talks:** See Willebrandt to Tuttle, 6/20/22, in AJTP, B24, Topical Office Files, 1921–1925, Prohibition Department. **Threatened:** *NYT*, 10/23/24, 1. **Tax, tariff:** *NYT*, 8/14/24, 1. **Puny, toothless:** Dorothy M. Brown, 56.
144 **Pinchot turned:** *Time*, 7/4/26; Frazier, 16. **Thanked Mrs. George:** McGeary, 304–5.

Chapter Ten: Leaks in the Dotted Line

146 **Sam paid:** OrH, Saidye Bronfman: SMC, Series 1A, Box 10. **Venison:** Marrus, 66–67.

147 **Hoped to find:** Ibid. **Purchased in Montreal:** Peter C. Newman, 81. **I could:** Marrus, 66–67.

147 **Coarseness:** Faith, 15. **A horse:** Bronfman interview, Philip Siekman and Ann Tyler, 7/6/66, notes in SMC, B1.

147 **Bronfman family history, generally:** Faith, Marrus, Robertson. Terence Robertson's book, commissioned by the Bronfman family, was based largely on lengthy interviews the Canadian journalist conducted with Sam Bronfman in the late 1960s. Displeased with the resulting work, the family decided not to publish it. Robertson, who later committed suicide, accused the Bronfman family of suppressing the book because, he told friends, "I found out things they don't want me to write about." (See *Toronto Star,* 11/22/77, B2.) The absence of particularly shocking material suggests that Robertson's charges were unfounded, but the accuracy of what he wrote, based on Sam Bronfman's own recollections, has never been successfully challenged. Copies of the manuscript in the Hagley Museum and at the University of Western Ontario remain the primary source material for most biographical work on Bronfman's early career.

147 **Prescriptions:** Robertson, 48. **Shifts:** Gray, *Booze,* 132.

148 **Skirts:** Robertson, 25.

148 **Jews in Canadian business:** Gray, *Roar,* 234–42.

148 **Manitoba police, Manitoba cleric:** Gray, *Roar,* 248. **Rights enjoyed:** Peter C. Newman, 133.

149 **Sipping near beer:** *Ontario,* 26.

149 **Bronfmans imported:** Gray, *Booze,* 164. **Mixed it:** *Winnipeg Tribune,* 10/27/22. **Caramel:** Peter C. Newman, 90. **Prune, creosote:** *NYT,* 7/26/23. **Before the end:** Saskatchewan Liquor Commission, R. J. Keyes to R. E. A. Leach, 11/30/20, Saskatchewan Archives, R1064, FA41.

149 **Labels:** RCCE, Bronfman testimony, 23,040–58. **Glen Levitt:** Gray, *Booze,* 136. **Well, children (fn):** Bellow, 160.

150 **Sam and Harry agreed:** RCCE, Bronfman testimony, 23,061–23,182. **Controlled by me:** *Winnipeg Tribune,* Harry Bronfman interview conducted 10/15/22, quoted in Gray, *Booze,* 141. **Family's profits:** *Winnipeg Tribune,* 10/27/22.

150 **Boozoriums adorned:** Peter C. Newman, 95–96. **Vehicles:** Ibid., 94; Robertson, 70. **Thick chains:** Gray, *Booze,* 157. **Used receipts:** Fahey, 49.

150 **Only in Dominion:** Edgar Bronfman, "Name Your Brand—Anywhere in the World," *Columbia Journal of World Business,* 11–12/69. **Never clear:** Edgar Bronfman, *Good,* 25.

151 **Matoff killed:** Marrus, 103. **North Dakota police:** Prince, 33. **Representatives:** Robertson, 77–80. **Advertising:** Peter C. Newman, 92–93. **Lansky:** Lacey, 461.

151 **Tuttle, generally:** Veselenak; AJTP. **Jumped threefold:** Fine, 59. **Second August:** *Hiram A. Walker & Sons v. Richard I. Lawson and John A. Grogan,* AJTP, B18, Opinions, 1921–1923. **Grand gesture:** James C. Young in *NYT,* 5/22/27, XX, 5. **Cuba:** Marrus, 134.

152 **Gundy:** *New York Herald,* 8/15/21, 1.

152 **Heavily laden:** *New York Herald,* 8/15/21, 15. **Not a single boat:** *DN,* 8/12/21, 1.

153 **Carnduff:** *Winnipeg Tribune,* 10/11/22. **A tidy bit:** Peter C. Newman, 93.

153 **Dotted line:** *NYT,* 7/29/23, XX, 1. **In the West:** *NYT,* 8/3/23, 17. **Me work?:** OrH, Federal Writers' Project, Library of Congress: subject identified only as "Callano."

154 **Chauffeur:** Saidye Bronfman, 3. **Cadillac:** Robertson, 124. **You were somebody:** quoted in Marrus, 165. **Interest:** Bronfman interview, Philip Siekman and Ann Tyler, 7/25/66, notes in SMC, B10.

154 **Later acknowledge:** Marrus, 132. **Vats:** Gray, *Booze*, 134.
154 **Saidye on Sam:** Saidye Bronfman, 1–31.
155 **Greenbrier:** Marrus, 749. Marrus and other sources spell it "Greenbriar." There were distilleries in Kentucky with both spellings, but the one spelled with an *e* was connected to the Wathen family, with whom Bronfman had a lengthy professional relationship beginning in the 1920s.
155 **Hour of devotion:** Robertson, 214–33. **Since 1920:** Peter C. Newman, 117–18. **Highland:** Edgar Bronfman, 25.
155 **DCL:** Daiches, 114–115; Weir, "Alcohol," 1294. **Schedule:** Weir, *History*, 274.
156 **Savoy:** Robertson, 313–28. **No special:** Allan Bronfman interview, Philip Siekman and Ann Tyler, 8/4/66, notes in SMC, B10.
156 **El Greco, No man:** Lockhart, 135–37.
156 **Report:** Ross/Herd memorandum of 11/10/26, Distillers Corporation Papers.
157 **Market dropped:** Weir, "Alcohol," 1295. **Dividend:** *Fortune*, 11/33, 45.
157 **Goyim (fn):** Edgar Bronfman, 25–26. **Prime minister, queen:** Saidye Bronfman, 114–15. **One man:** Bronfman interview, Philip Siekman and Ann Tyler, 7/27/66, notes in SMC, B10.
158 **Abe:** Robertson, 224–31. **Agent in Havana:** RCCE, Barney Aaron testimony, 22,036–72. **Prevent their name:** quoted in Dubro and Rowland, 211–12.
158 **Burnt them:** RCCE, Abe Bronfman testimony, 23,101–5. **Lima:** RCCE, Barney Aaron testimony, 22,03 6–72.
158 **No proof:** Bronfman interview, Philip Siekman and Ann Tyler, 7/27/66, notes in SMC, B10.

Chapter Eleven: The Great Whiskey Way

159 **Ellerslie:** *SFC*, 1/17/20, 6; http://www.shipbuildinghistory.com.
159 **Parade:** Asbury, 248. **Waterfront:** *Times* (London), 3/3/20; *New York Herald*, 8/22/21, 1, 5; photographs in Lythgoe (Flat Hammock edition).
160 **Hill & Hill, trade:** Van de Water, 37, 2. **Soared:** Ross Wilson, 298–99. **Peak:** Canney, 4. **Spreading:** *NYT,* 8/26/21.
160 **Loaded after:** *New York Herald*, 8/22/21, 1, 5. **Supervening:** Lythgoe, Flat Hammock edition, 37. **Generator, wharf, harbor, statues:** Craton and Saunders, 240, 237.
160 **Lucerne:** Lythgoe, 52, 62, 86; Andrews, 123; *WP,* 8/24/21.
161 **Never sailed:** Hugh Bell, quoted in Craton and Saunders, 238. **Bankers ready:** Bell, 189; *NYT,* 7/23/23, 15; *New York Herald*, 8/22/21, 1, 5. **Symonette earned:** Craton and Saunders, 240.
161 **Chief smuggler:** Latham to Secretary of State, 8/26/22, State Department Archives, F811.114. **Real McCoy:** According to the *Dictionary of American Regional English*, the term goes back as far as 1890; lexicographer Eric Partridge traces it to Scotland in the 1880s. **Estimates:** Kobler, 256–57.
162 **Slit-eyed:** Van de Water, 89–91. **Orgy:** Craton and Saunders, 241. **Bootleggers' Ball:** *WP,* 8/24/21, 9.
162 **Gertrude Lythgoe:** Most sources from the 1920s, including the *WSJ*, referred to her as Grace Lythgoe; her own book, however, bears the name Gertrude. **Not responsible:** *WSJ*, 9/18/23.
162 **Obtain British:** *NYT,* 7/23/23, 15; Spinelli, 3.
162 **Arethusa, Tomoka:** Willoughby, 18; *Southern Boating*, 2/98, 81–82, 99. **Each time:** Van de Water, 91.
163 **Dispensing refreshment:** quoted in Everett S. Allen, 30. **Near Miami:** Andrews, 122.
163 **Rendezvous:** Moray, 25. **Timber trade, comparison shopping:** Moray, 1, 214. **Supermarket:** Everett S. Allen, 43. **Johnson:** Keller, 208–9.
164 **$1 tariff, all partook:** Moray, 95, 242.
164 **Taken for a ride:** Stanley Walker, 261. **Free State:** Maryland state archives web-

site, http://www.mdarchives.state.md.us/. **Scofflaw:** *Oxford English Dictionary;* *Boston Herald,* 10/27/2002; *American Issue,* 2/30.
165 **Rum variants:** *Dictionary of American Regional English.*
165 **Anything with:** Van de Water, 193–94.
165 **Get bearings:** Willoughby, 105–6. **Distress call:** Canney, 10.
165 **Dark patch, you knew:** Everett S. Allen, 72, 137. **Repair vessels:** Dorothy M. Brown, 63. **Sardines:** *St. John Telegraph-Journal,* 6/25/25, 3, quoted in Grant, 12.
166 **Halfway, Gun:** Laster, 12/80. **Shuttered houses, salt dissolved:** Everett S. Allen, 151. **Hams:** *Southern Boating,* 2/98, 99.
166 **Hundreds of such:** *NYT,* 12/14/24, XX, I. **Unprecedented:** Canney, 6. **Loaded deep:** *NYT,* 12/14/24, XX, I. **Gulf Coast:** Asbury, 241. **A city:** Everett S. Allen, 43.
167 **McCoy claim:** Kobler, 256–57. **Runyon:** "The Lily of St. Pierre," 49–67.
167 **St. Pierre history:** Andrieux, *Prohibition,* 16–17. **Wildlife:** Hansen, 1–10.
167 **Bahamian government raised:** Spinelli, 62–63. **July 8:** Andrieux, *Prohibition,* 21–25. **Pungent smell:** Peter C. Newman, 126. **Vessels, stockrooms, customs income:** Andrieux, *Prohibition,* 21–25, 109. **Six million:** Marrus, 139–40.
168 **Le temps de:** Marrus, 139–40. **Hotel Robert, Villa Cutty:** LeFrancois, 42 *et seq.*
168 **Norwegian:** LeFrancois, 37. **Isle of:** Sann, 94.
169 **Get legal stamps:** Andrieux, *Prohibition,* 38–39. **Northern Export:** LeFrancois, 42 *et seq.* **Bronfman inventory:** Marrus, 141. *Mazel Tov:* Robinson, iii.
169 **Steam straight, verbal codes, lead-covered:** Andrieux, *Prohibition,* 33–39. **Numerical code:** LeFrancois, 42 *et seq.* **Bronfman radio:** Marrus, 141.
169 **His duties:** Andrieux, *Prohibition,* 55.
170 **Doomed:** *NYT,* 7/24/23, 23. **Parade of ships:** Spinelli, 63–64.
170 **Conflated brands:** Ross Wilson, 302. **Lansky:** Lacey, 54. **Squeezing:** Eisenberg et al., 107–8.
170 **Pinching domestic:** Lockhart, 131–32. **Doubling taxes:** Spinelli, xiv.
170 **Dewarisms:** confirmed to author by Jacqui Seargeant, Global Archive Manager, John Dewar & Son Ltd. **Virus:** Weir, "Alcohol." **Cleverly contrived:** Spinelli, 4.
171 **Force of arms:** *Evening Standard,* 12/29/19, 4.
171 **Inflicted hardship:** British National Archives, FO 371/A4379/4588. **Bryan threatened:** *NYT,* 4/25/21; Spinelli, 4. **Widely reported:** Spinelli, 4; for instance, *The Times* (London), 4/26/21.
172 **Doing our best:** *Nassau Tribune,* 11/4/22, enclosed in Lorin A. Lathrop to Secretary of State, 11/9/22, in State Department Archives, F811.BWI/117.
172 **Accusing State:** Willebrandt to Harry Daugherty, 10/3/22, quoted in Spinelli, 19.
172 **Puritanism:** Spinelli, 46.
172 **Flatly refused:** R. Sperling to governor of Bahamas, 6/28/21, British National Archives, FO 371/A5728; H. J. Read to Under Secretary of State, 8/10/21, British National Archives, FO 371/A5891; Spinelli, 5. **Affront:** Churchill in *Collier's,* 8/13/32, 21.
173 **We would not:** Weir, *History,* 274.

Chapter Twelve: Blessed Be the Fruit of the Vine

174 **Stoll:** Introduction by F. T. Bioletti, in Stoll; Pinney, 328; *Wines & Vines,* 11/47, 13.
174 **Vineyard gone:** Charles L. Sullivan, *Companion,* 349. **How Prohibition:** Although the brochure is unsigned, it would have been Stoll's responsibility to produce it, and the prose is unmistakably his. Bo Simons, director of the Sonoma County Wine Library, concurs in this judgment.
175 **Ninety thousand:** Heintz, *Alicante,* 45. **Seventy-five million dollars:** *St. Helena Star,* 8/29/19.
175 **Sebastiani:** *Sonoma Index-Tribune,* 2/2/18.
175 **No preparations:** *CGG,* 12/1/19.

176 **Large sums:** E. Clemens Horst, in *Outlook*, 3/12/30, 407–8. **Unexpected demand:** *CGG*, 12/1/19.
176 **Price $105:** *St. Helena Star*, 9/23/21. **Shocking $375:** Heintz, *Alicante*, 18–19. **Grape imports:** Hugh F. Fox, "The Consumption of Alcoholic Beverages," in Walnut, 140.
176 **On pleasant days:** Alfred J. Hill, "Kansas and Its Prohibition Enforcement," in Walnut, 138.
177 **Grapes so valuable:** quoted in Heintz, *California's*, 249. **More than $500:** Carl Wente, "A Look Backward at the Dark Days," in *Wines & Vines*, 12/1/62, 17–18. **Pledge next year's:** OrH, CWH: Carl Wente, "Economics of Grape Growing in California, 1918–1942." **Viano:** Richard Paul Hinkle, "Shed No Tears for Prohibition," *Wine Country*, 2/82, 10.
177 **Gallo rooster:** Hawkes, 51. **Uprooted grapes:** OrH, CWH: Wente, "Economics." **Vineyardists grafted:** OrH, CWH: Maynard A. Amerine. **Gooseberry:** quoted in Heintz, *Alicante*, 45.
177 **Alicante characteristics:** Heintz, *Alicante*, 14–15. **Italian is willing:** *CGG*, 9/1/21, 12. **Color scale:** *The California Grower*, 11/29, 26.
178 **Parsnips:** *Senate Judiciary 1926*, testimony of William J. McSorley, 222. **Add sugar:** OrH, CWH: Maynard A. Amerine. **Bearcreek:** OrH, Montana Historical Society: Vera Naglich.
178 **Sour fumes:** *Sunset*, 4/28. **Trucks:** *Wines & Vines*, 4/1/74. **While You Wait:** Angelo Papagni, "The Long Memory," *Wine West*, 3–4/83, 22. **Iron miners (fn):** Mondavi, 35–39. **What happens:** *Sunset*, 4/28. **One would select:** OrH, CWH: Leon Adams.
179 **Sold and resold:** Carl Wente, "A Look Backward," *Wines & Vines*, 12/1/62, 17–18. **Carloads to New York:** *California Grower*, 1/32. **Another 40,000:** *Sunset*, 4/28. **Would have taken:** *St. Helena Star*, 4/6/23. **Vivid way:** *Fresno Republican*, 11/22/25, quoted in *CGG*, 1/1/26, 15. **Stand aside:** "Jolly Grapes Roll Eastward to Market," *Business Week*, 9/7/29.
179 **Jersey City:** *Business Week*, 9/7/21. **Army of pushcart:** *CGG*, 12/1/26, 1. **Block buyers:** John Parducci, quoted in *Wines & Vines*, 5/1/89, 54. **Twilight zone:** Walton Green, "The Twilight Zone of Prohibition," *Saturday Evening Post*, 5/8/26, 42. **Pomace or waste:** *CGG*, 4/1/29, 6.
180 **150 million:** Wickersham, vol. 1, 136.
180 **Half grapes die:** OrH, CWH: Carl Wente. **Fix prices:** *St. Helena Star*, 6/3/27. **Argued against:** *CGG*, 5/1/26, 10; 4/1/27, 11. **Silk shirts:** OrH, CWH: Carl Wente.
180 **Canning:** Richard Paul Hinkle, "Shed No Tears for Prohibition," *Wine Country*, 2/82, 10. **Fleet of wineries:** *San Francisco Examiner*, 1/10/19, 1. **Grape butter:** *CGG*, 3/1/26, 10.
181 **Wente clone:** Vintners' Hall of Fame, http://www.ciaprochef.com. **Sell entire:** OrH, CWH: Ernest A. Wente, 21. **I will tell:** Ernest A. Wente, quoted in Heintz, *Beaulieu*, 78.
181 **de Latour generally:** *ANB*; Rod Smith, *Private*. **Best known families:** *San Francisco Examiner*, 11/16/24, quoted in Heintz, *Beaulieu*. **Dressed for dinner:** OrH, CWH: Andre Tchelistcheff.
182 **Pyle:** Rod Smith, 37–40. **Elegant, patrician:** OrH, CWH: Louis M. Martini.
182 **This letter will:** Riordan, 3/8/12, archives of Archdiocese of Northern California.
183 **First board:** Rod Smith, 40–43. **Crowley:** Archbishop Edward J. Hanna to de Latour, 3/25/20, BATF Papers, Collection D-140, B47.
183 **Beringers, Concannons:** OrH, CWH: Tchelistcheff. **Martinis:** *Wines & Vines*, 1/94, 21–22.
183 **Full fourteen years:** OrH, CWH: Ernest A. Wente, 21. **Fay:** Lapsley, 77; Hennings, 267. **Congratulated:** Archbishop Edward J. Hanna to de Latour, 3/25/20, BATF Papers, Collection D-140, B47. **Distributors:** various, DFP. **Storing:**

Beaulieu Vineyards application for renewal of A-1 permit, 12/14/25, BATF Papers, Collection D-140, B47. **Acre, rail spur:** *St. Helena Star*, 9/17/26, 9.

184 **Go missing:** Agents Louis F. Cole and James E. Verrall to H. L. [Duncan?], divisional chief, 2/19/32, BATF Papers, Collection D-140, Box 47. **Illegal channels:** quoted in Heintz, *Beaulieu*, 74. **Not uncommon:** "Applications to Procure Wine for Sacramental Purposes," from Fathers Prim, O'Donnell, and Rodriguez, DFP. **Mundelein:** Unsigned to Messrs. D. Recher & Co., 12/12/32, DFP. **I advise:** de Latour to Yellowley, 8/15/22, BATF Papers, Collection D-140, Box 47. **Close friend:** Yellowley to de Latour, 11/22/32, DFP. **When friars (fn):** Napa Valley, interview with Brother Basil of the Christian Brothers.

184 **Move a lot:** Rod Smith, 66–71. **Many favorable, sheltered, offering:** Brochure, 2/15/22, archives of Archdiocese of Northern California. **Had added:** See order forms in DFP; e.g., "Permit to Purchase," 10/16/31. **Medicinal exception (fn):** Contract between Beaulieu and Joseph Callan and I. Domnitz, 2/20/27, DFP.

185 **Celebrities:** Heintz, *Beaulieu*, 104. **de Latour home:** "California Rural: Mrs. Georges de Latour's 'Beaulieu,'" *Vogue*, 11/47, 172–73. **Pool:** Charles L. Sullivan, *Napa*, 196. **Invited to join:** de Latour guestbook, *passim*, DFP.

185 **We started out:** Randolph Churchill, 84–85. **Comic:** *Daily Telegraph* (London), 12/2/29. **Ganymede:** Churchill to Clementine Churchill, 9/18/29, Baroness Spencer-Churchill Papers.

186 **Moment's halt:** de Latour guestbook, 9/9/29, DFP. **Goodly sight:** Martin S. Gilbert, 93. **Christ has come:** Randolph Churchill, 84–85.

186 **Jewish rabbis:** Memorandum of agreement between Beaulieu and A. Z. Halperin and Harry Schutz, 3/22/23 (top sheet of agreement is marked in pencil "1925"). **Imprimatur:** de Latour to Rabbi B. Robinson, 2/25/27, DFP. **Palatable:** Louis P. Martini, quoted in *Napa Valley Register*, 12/5/93.

186 **Ecclesiastic tyrants:** Quoted in Drescher, 326–27.

187 **Beneath dignity:** *NYT*, 7/7/14, 5. **Lobbied Volstead:** Rabbi Samuel Gup to Rabbi Leo M. Franklin, 12/13/21, LFA.

187 **The temptation:** Sprecher, 153. **More wine:** *LAT*, 3/13/21; Kobler, 250–51. **Trustee charged:** *LAT*, 3/13/21.

188 **Third appearance:** *LAT*, 2/17/23, 1. **Into jeans:** *LAT*, 8/31/22, II 7. **Disposed:** *LAT*, 6/14/21, II 1.

188 **San Leandro:** Coffee, 366–67. **Alameda:** Rabbi Rudolph I. Coffee, "Stamping Out the Wine Congregations," *Survey*, 12/15/22, 366–67. **Promiscuously:** *LAT*, 6/30/24, A2.

188 **Free-for-all:** Sprecher, 153. **Tiny rooms:** Einstein, 134–35. **Sell to anyone:** Gup to Franklin, 12/13/21, LFA. **Public scandal:** Krauskopf to Franklin, 12/12/21, LFA.

189 **Took commissions:** *Providence Journal*, 12/23/21, 2. **Wine stores:** *Collier's*, 10/21/27, 9. **Signing up:** Underwood & Underwood photograph; *NYT*, 7/30/23, 15. **Schapiro's:** Marni Davis, 210. **Champagne:** Einstein, 134–135. **Not the content:** *WP*, 4/6/22, 3. **100-proof:** *New York Herald*, 4/5/22, quoted in *CGG*, 5/1/22, 13.

189 **Any man:** Asbury, 239. **Houlihan and Maguire:** *NYT*, 1/14/22, 4. **Harlem Negroes:** *Collier's*, 10/1/27, 8.

190 **Hillul:** Central, 116–18.

190 **Jewish luck:** "The Jewish Element in Bootlegging Evil," *Dearborn Independent*, 12/31/21.

190 **Direct quotation:** Franklin address to Central Conference of American Rabbis, 4/21, quoted in "The Jewish Element in Bootlegging Evil," *Dearborn Independent*, 12/31/21.

191 **Maintained cordial:** Neil Baldwin, 127. **Petition Congress:** Franklin to Rabbi Edward N. Calisch, 12/15/21, LFA.

191 **Case of necessity:** Central, 108–18. **Insinuate:** Behr, 46. **Dr. Welch's:** Barr, 362.

191 **Sentiments:** Joselit, 91. **Threatening letters:** Sprecher, 157. **Ask Jews:** *NYT,* 1/25/23, 10.
191 **Rabbis Reap:** quoted in Central, vol. 32, 107. **Revoking:** Sprecher, 165. **Slicing, plummeted:** *Collier's,* 10/1/27, 9, 37.
192 **Deutsch:** *LAT,* 7/7/14, 15. **Wolsey:** Joselit, 86.

Chapter Thirteen: The Alcohol That Got Away

193 **Drug-stores, grain alcohol:** Fitzgerald, *Gatsby,* 87, 106.
193 **Frankfort brochure:** author's collection.
193 **Fifteen thousand:** Asbury, 218–19. **Purchase, have it filled:** Sexton, 115–116. **Veterinarians:** *NYT,* 7/28/23, 4.
194 **Pinkham, generally:** *ANB.* **Sewing kits, text-book:** eBay.com. **20.6:** The label on the package said Pinkham's contained 15 percent alcohol, but testing by the Massachusetts Board of Health indicated the correct proportion was 20.6 percent. Edward Bok, *Ladies' Home Journal,* 5/04.
194 **Temperance worker:** Murdock, 53.
194 **Mrs. Jones:** Wikipedia.com.
195 **Testing:** Edward Bok, *Ladies' Home Journal,* 5/04.
195 **No scientific value:** Timberlake, 47. **Referendum:** "The Referendum on Alcohol," *Journal of the American Medical Association,* 1/21/22, 194. **Serious interference:** "The St. Louis Session," *Journal of the American Medical Association,* 6/3/1922, 1709.
196 **Taylor, Gutierrez:** certificates in author's collection. **Take three:** Engelmann, *Intemperance,* 33.
196 **Too jealous:** *NYT,* 1/11/20. **Unexcelled:** author's collection. **Bought in bulk:** *Senate Judiciary 1926,* 119–21. **Burned their tongues:** Leonard Grossman to Francis X. Busch, William E. Dever Papers, B3, F24.
196 **Iceman:** Sheaffer, 490. **Continued to operate:** Sheaffer, 44; Wetzsteon, 147.
197 **Seriously injure:** *Senate Campaign Expenditures 1926,* 70. **Billingsley opened:** Blumenthal, 91.
197 **Hoping to block:** Ambrose Hunsberger, "The Practice of Pharmacy Under the Volstead Act," Walnut, 185.
197 **Doubtful that milk:** John U. Bacon, author of authorized history of Walgreen's. **Fire department:** Bacon, 63.
198 **Saw a chance:** quoted in Kobler, 316–17. **Pharmacist:** Ibid., 316. **Teetotaler:** *SLP-D,* 1/3/26. **Remus deposited:** Furnas, 220.
198 **Within three hundred:** Kobler, 316–17. **Buy counterfeits:** Sexton, 118.
198 **Jack Daniel's:** *Tennessee Encyclopedia of History and Culture,* online at http://www.tennesseeencyclopedia.net. **Purchased pharmacy, began withdrawing, hijacked:** Sexton, 120.
199 **Business so large, draining the contents:** Kobler, 315–17. **Hundreds of:** Mee, 146–47. **Booze-scented, Millionaires' Row (fn):** Willebrandt, 98–99. **Tried to corner:** *SLP D,* 1/3/26. **Peaceful hush (fn):** Werner, *Privileged,* 273–77. **No prison (fn):** Kobler, 320.
199 **Twenty-nine million:** Sexton, 115. **Fifty-eight additional:** Downard, *Dictionary,* 128. **Old Forester:** 115–16.
200 **Heavy demand:** *Louisville Herald-Post,* 11/24/26. **Purchasing Early Times:** Brown-Forman website.
200 **Strawberries:** interview, Patricia Levinson (Schulte's granddaughter). **Clerk, cigar, grocery:** *Time,* 10/21/49. **Bought Overholt, sold:** *Fortune,* 11/33, 35, 113. **Hard-earned:** *Time,* 10/21/29.
200 **Pierce price list:** author's collection. **Should have permitted:** *Time,* 6/6/27.
201 **Hundreds of uses:** *NYT,* 7/27/23, 15. **Tripled:** Merz, 116. **Doubled:** Nelli, 153. **60 million, exported to Canada:** *Senate Judiciary 1926,* Emory Buckner testimony, 112. **How to keep:** Quoted in *LD,* 9/24/27, 13.

201   Denaturants: *NYT,* 7/26/23, 17. **Sreben, other firms:** *CT,* 2/4/31; *NYT,* 2/11/30.
201   **Beyond jurisdiction:** Asbury, 225.
202   **Perfect carnival:** Mayer, 196.
202   **Almost a million:** *Collier's,* 10/15/27, 8. **Sewer lining:** *Washington Times,* 2/20/24.
       Quaker, etc.: Temple University Library website, http://www.exhibitions
       .library.temple.edu/prohibition/booboo.jsp. **Hoff produced:** Haller, "Philadel-
       phia," 218. **Forty loaded:** Frazier, 84.
203   **Butler, generally:** *ANB, DAB.* **Day has passed:** Merz, 141. **Torn apart:** *NYT,*
       12/17/23.
203   **Buy off:** Frazier, 171, 88. **Estimated:** Haller, "Philadelphia," 223. **Privilege of**
       assignment: *Time,* 9/17/28. **Golder:** Haller, "Philadelphia," 219.
203   **Shipping agreement, Union National:** Frazier, 90–92. **Spider:** *Time,* 9/17/28.
204   **Complicity:** Weigley, 581. **Wall Street:** Frazier, 89. **Butler returned:** *DAB.*
       Trying to enforce: Asbury, 186. **Sherman:** Haller, "Philadelphia," 215.
204   **Refused to allow:** *NYT,* 12/28/25, 1.

Chapter Fourteen: The Way We Drank

205   **The Hero:** Drowne, 1, citing *WSJ,* 4/15/19.
205   **Prigs:** *Time,* 9/28/31. **Gloria:** quoted in Drowne, 82. **Gowan Stevens:** Faulkner,
       33. **Half the pages:** Burnham, *Bad,* 36. **Does not exist:** quoted in Jeffrey A.
       Schwarz.
205   **Devastating:** quoted in Johns, 11. **Waiting:** quoted in Engelmann, *Intemperance,*
       9. **Well, folks:** Lewis, 127. **Hemingway's expatriate (fn):** Hemingway, 128.
206   **Fierce protracted:** Edmund Wilson, 89–91.
206   **Hazlitt:** This is maxim number 40 from *Characteristics.*
207   **Glittering tray:** Cather, *Lost,* 43–44. **Powell:** Wetzsteon, 509–10. **World broke:**
       Cather, *Not,* unnumbered prefatory page. **Nobody stays:** *NYT Book Review,*
       12/21/24.
207   **The party:** Cowley, 65. **Social hook:** *Vanity Fair,* 1/21.
207   **Mencken traced:** Drowne, 96. **Ulysses (fn):** Google Books edition, 745. **Gus:**
       New York Evening Sun, 3/12/30, 28.
208   **Hooch, buffet, all-white:** Drowne, 156. **Beer flats:** *NYT,* 5/3/28. **Southern**
       Italian: Baughman; Flamm, 50. **Bucket:** "My Friend," in Josephine F. Gomon
       Papers, B10. **Curley:** Beatty, 272–73. **Sheboygan:** *CT,* 3/30/29, 2.
208   **Thirty-two thousand:** Kobler, 224. **Kriendler and Berns:** interview, Susan
       Berns Rothchild. **Confuse tax, only arrests:** Kobler, 229–30. **Stop paying:** *New*
       Yorker, 4/7/34. **Tumbling down:** Kobler, 231; *New Yorker,* 4/7/34. **Not admis-**
       sible: Louis Sobol, "Speakeasy," *Cosmopolitan,* 4/34, 54.
209   **Bath Club, O'Leary's:** Hirschfeld and Kahn, 20–22.
209   **Brothers convicted:** Rosenthal, 327–28. **Hartwell:** *Time,* 3/24/24; *NYT,*
       12/31/25. **Chianti market:** *New Yorker,* 1/16/26, 7.
210   **Created Cutty:** Spinelli, 2. **Haig:** Weir, "Alcohol," 1289. **Squirrel:** *Dundee* (Scot-
       land) *Evening Telegraph,* 10/16/13, courtesy of Jacqui Seargeant, John Dewar &
       Sons.
210   **Soaked in sea:** *New Yorker,* 3/6/26, 25. **Perfectly:** Kennedy to Matthew Brush,
       6/26/22, in Amanda Smith, 33. **Dollar-a-drink:** *Collier's,* 10/15/27, 8. **Brand X:**
       Mercer Ellington, cited in Batterberry, 213.
211   **Blind pig (fn):** Drowne, 96. **Pretty girl:** Terkel, 177. **More than close:** Mur-
       dock, 69.
211   **Peculiarly attractive:** Scott, 123.
211   **Arrests spiked:** Lerner, dissertation, 258. **Portals:** Louis Sobol, "Speakeasy,"
       Cosmopolitan, 4/34. **Sex barriers, light laughter:** *Vanity Fair,* 10/28. **Schoolgirls:**
       O'Connor, 72.
212   **Harlem clubs:** Wintz and Finkleman, 910, 1121. **Detroit:** Sunnie Wilson. **Most**
       democratic: Drowne, 128. **More to improve:** Lerner, *Dry,* 215.

212 **Many had welcomed:** Lynd, 265; Lerner (book), 36. **Frenzied filming:** Jowitt, 238–39.
213 **Clean films:** Rose, *American*, 64. **Devil and Jews:** Couvares, 589. **Scholarly survey:** Dale, 168. **Hundred million:** Leuchtenberg, *Perils*, 195.
213 **Clarence Brown:** Burnham, *Bad*, 37.
213 **Chic and charming:** *DN*, 1/3/24, 4. **Shut down:** *DN*, 1/2/24, 1.
213 **Kresge:** *DN*, 1/4/24, 1–2. **Hepburn:** *Columbus Dispatch*, 7/25/27. **Heflin:** *AC*, 4/9/29, 13. **Bounder:** *DN*, 1/3/24, 4.
214 **Children's:** Fitzgerald, *Crack-Up*, 15. **Faunce:** *LD*, 7/10/26, 45. **Babylonian:** *DN*, 1/2/24, 1. **Almost a Yale:** Mellon, 107–14. **Casey:** Murphy, 188. **Idiotic:** Coulter to J. A. Bursley, 12/13/23, Vice President of Student Affairs Papers, University of Michigan, B1.
214 **Bowdoin labs:** Laster. **Gin is aged:** quoted in William Grimes, 93.
214 **Consolation:** Cather, *Lost*, 43. **Went into:** *Fortune*, 11/33, 29. **Cassatt:** *Time*, 10/8/28. **Varnish:** Haller, "Philadelphia," 222.
215 **Beverage known:** Asbury, 229. **Garbo:** William Grimes, 92.
215 **Trust:** *CGG*, 8/21, 3. **Caffo, Buschtee, Kicko:** Hernon and Ganey, 108. **Sales triple:** Kyvig, *Daily*, 24. **Drink That Cheers:** Tchudi, 77.
216 **So good under:** *NYT*, 1/21/27, 1.
216 **Considerable part:** *Montreal Gazette*, 1/29/25, quoted in testimony of Hudson Maxim, *Senate Judiciary 1926*. **Taxi ride:** Brault, 85,105. **Never touched:** Scott Wheeler, 33–36.
216 **Their appearance:** *Daily Colonist*, 6/30/25, 14, quoted in Stephen T. Moore. **A great many:** Willebrandt to C. C. Boynton, 8/6/28, in MWWP, B4. **Windsor warehouse:** *NYT*, 3/21/27, 7.
217 **Bimini Rod:** *New York Tribune*, 5/16/20, magazine section, 3. **Human stomach:** *Collier's*, 7/16/21, 22. **Learned about:** *NYT*, 2/23/27, 3.
217 **Uppercu, Aeromarine:** William M. Leary, 180–193. **Limousines:** www.time tableimages.com/ttimages/aeromwet.htm. **Donovan:** Curtis, 165. **Bathe in Bacardi:** Gjelten, 111. **Inviting, never so good:** *New Yorker*, 2/9/29, 14.
218 **Bible classes:** Kazin, 262. **Lecture:** Leuchtenberg, *Perils*, 183.
218 **View from lawn:** Coletta, 161. **Conspiring:** Bryan to Oldfield, 4/3/22, WJBP, B35.
218 **Dear little:** French Line brochure, quoted in Maxtone-Graham, 170. **Where the Wet:** Curtis, 165.
218 *Mauretania: Daily Express* (London), 2/16/20. **Sounded their horns:** White to Scott Elledge, 6/16/82, in E. B. White, 654. **Stereotype:** Maxtone-Graham, 170.
219 **It hurt:** *New York Tribune*, 11/26/22, VI, 1.
219 **Relaxed:** Spinelli, 38–39. **Excellent Cuisine, menus:** *Current History*, 6/22, 377–85.
219 **Incomparably the biggest:** Plavchan, 202. Busch sent his letter to his son, Adolphus Busch III, and asked him to forward it to Harding.
220 **Waving a series:** Wheeler to A. J. Volstead, 6/22/22, AJVP, B3. **Simultaneously announced:** *NYT*, 10/7/22, 1.
220 **If the measure:** *NYT*, 10/10/22, 1. **Parliament considered, pause to dump:** Spinelli, 46–47. **Renders ridiculous:** Royden to Ashley Sparks, 7/4 [or 5?]/23, Cunard Archive, D42/S3/17. **Such asses:** Wadsworth to James R. Sheffield, 5/9/23, JWWP, B19.
220 **Driving ranges, movies, caviar:** Gunther, 131.
220 **Foil:** F. L. Allen, *Secret*, 172–73.
221 **Sterno:** Kobler, 314. **Rust improved:** Asbury, 281. **Like a milkman:** Inquest testimony, 8/10/26, in Archives of Ontario, RG 4–32, F 1926 #1828 (1). **Jake, neurotoxin:** Kobler, 301–2; "Jake Leg Blues," liner notes, by John P. Morgan, M.D. **Lyrics:** Dan Baum, "Jake Leg," *New Yorker*, 50.
222 **Opera star:** Room, 11–18. **Arrests soared:** Joseph R. Gusfield, "Prohibition: The Impact of Political Utopianism," in Braeman, 274. **Cirrhosis, psychosis:**

Adam Gifford Jr., "Whiskey, Margarine, and Newspapers: A Tale of Three Taxes," in Shughart, 66. **Rate of consumption:** Jellinek, 10.
222 **Over-indulgence:** *LD*, 7/10/26, 47. **Men swallow:** Igglesden, 164. **People expect, advice:** Cannadine, 310. **Anodyne:** *Vanity Fair*, 3/31, 60. The piece was published under a pseudonym Brokaw often used, "Julian Jerome."
222 **Girls simply won't, almost everybody:** Lusk, 46. **For a girl:** Jean Hamilton to parents of Pauline Izor, 4/8/26, Clarence Cook Little Papers, B2, F20.
223 **Izor, generally:** Hamilton correspondence; *Michiganensian 1964* (University of Michigan yearbook), 296; interview with Izor's son LaMott F. Bates.
223 **Meads:** *NYT*, 6/17/20, 1; *CT*, 9/16/20. **Vomitings:** O'Hara, *Appointment*, 86.
224 **A world without:** Sabin, "I Change My Mind About Prohibition," in *Outlook*, 6/13/28.
224 **Girls did not drink, Why American:** Fulton, 35.
224 **Attempt to enthrone:** *NYT*, 4/4/29, 1.

Chapter Fifteen: Open Wounds

227 **Strong appeal:** *NYT*, 6/26/23. **Stop drinking:** Anthony, *Florence*, 427; Murray, *Harding*, 407. **Same suite, simple way:** Diary, 8/10/23, PSDP, F1. **Slob, front parlor:** Longworth, 324–25.
227 **Should go out of:** Kennedy, *Freedom*, 30. **Indolent:** Lippmann, 12–13.
228 **Whacked:** *CGG*, 1/26, 13. **Not a stranger:** Miller, 132. **I must remember:** McCoy, 397. **Toasted:** *NYT*, 1/17/28, 2. **The rest would:** Merz, 285.
228 **Brother-in-law:** Willard obituary, *Springfield Republican*, 12/23/31. All details of investigation from Harlan Fiske Stone Papers, B24, F. **Amherst College bootlegging, particularly:** Stone to Willard, 6/20/24 (telegram), 6/26/24; Willard to Stone, 6/21/24; Stone to Waddell (student), 6/28/24; J. Edgar Hoover to Stone, 8/11/24, 8/25/24.
229 **Pinchot flirted:** Sobel, 255.
229 **Enemy of, shot:** Steuart, 303–4. **Anarchist:** Nethers, 178. **Sackett:** Sexton, 94–95. Although some sources spell Sackett's first name with a concluding *k*, his official congressional biography spells it without.
230 **Dispatched:** Steuart, 226. **Was not voted:** *NYT*, 6/26/27, XX6. **Frowning Nero:** *New Yorker*, 1/30/26. **Generalissimo:** *CR*, 4/5/22, 5073.
230 **Pleased to support:** Thomas to Wheeler, 3/4/24, in TPP/ASL Legis and Legal, R1. **Ruin field hand, pap sucker, etc.:** Simon, 1252.
231 **Jones:** *ANB*. **Felder:** *NYT*, 4/21/22, 12, and 5/9/22, 4. **Representing McCoy:** William Hayward to Attorney General, 10/9/22, F 23–3962–5, Department of Justice archives. **Clarence Wilson:** *DAB*. **McGee:** *Time*, 2/23/25; http://www.mnd.uscourts.gov. **Baruch:** Baruch, 180. **Ford:** *Ladies' Home Journal*, 4/30, 25. **Willebrandt:** Gentry, 125–26.
231 **Thrown acid:** Pepper, 146. **Half-drunk, furies:** Reed, "The Pestilence of Fanaticism," *American Mercury*, 5/25. **Black men:** Meriwether, 85. **Supreme artist:** Reed, *Rape*, dust jacket copy.
232 **In business to protect:** *New York World*, 4/6/22. **Lives by headlines:** *Time*, 11/24/24. **Get arrested, hundred-million:** Kessner, 112. **150,000:** McLaughlin, 184. **250,000:** *Senate Judiciary 1926*, 651.
232 **Frivolity:** *ANB*. **Dark and sombre:** Beck to H. L. Mencken, 12/15/24, James M. Beck Papers, B5, F24. **Cascading quotations:** Keller, 154–55.
233 **Resigned as solicitor:** *ANB*. **Handed him:** Keller, 196.
233 **Cornelia Pinchot found out:** Lender, *Dictionary*, 398. **Movement as a whole:** Murdock, 31.
233 **Announced birth:** November 12, 1918, per Kyvig, *Repealing*, 43. **Solicitation letter:** *Life* (original), 7/24/31, 15. **Fish et al.:** Names from early AAPA letterhead, circa 1922, author's collection. **Yacht Club:** Kyvig, *Repealing*, 46–47.

234 **Freighted with warning:** Heckman, 280. **Ran the other way:** Ibid., 281; Kyvig, *Repealing*, 48.
234 **Refuse to contribute:** du Pont to Arthur W. Little, 1/7/27, PSdPP, Series A, F765. **Futile for people, must learn:** du Pont to Charles N. Fowler, 1/28/27, PSdPP, Series A, F765.
234 **Thirteen dry, vacation on Mars:** Kobler, 341.
234 **Naturally made:** Carol L. James [page unclear]. **Unyielding:** *CR*, 1/18/22, 1338. **Convicted of murder:** Unsigned to Mrs. Andrew J. Volstead, 4/29/20, AJVP, B1. **Made a Bolshevik:** unsigned to Volstead, 10/29/19, AJVP, B1. **Cootie's:** "Democritus" to Volstead, 10/20/21, AJVP, B2.
235 **Dryer than Volstead:** *St. Paul Pioneer-Press*, 11/9/22, 1. **Sunday morning:** Carol L. James, 10–11. **Wets eager:** *St. Paul Pioneer-Press*, 11/9/22, 10.
236 **Streams of undersized, lowest layer:** Kenneth Roberts, "Ports of Embarkation," *Saturday Evening Post*, 5/7/21, 12. **Most backward:** Kenneth Roberts, "The Goal of Central Europeans," *Saturday Evening Post*, 11/6/20, 12. **Nordics, the cross (fn):** Madison Grant, *Passing*, 228, 18. **Half the bootleggers (fn):** Haller, "Philadelphia," 217.
236 **80 percent to aliens:** *NYT*, 1/12/23, 3. **Ought to know:** Imogen Oakley, "The Prohibition Law and the Political Machine," in Walnut, 171. **General information:** *House Immigration 1922*, 544.
237 **Dazzling opportunities:** Higham, 267–68.
237 **Scum:** Rose, *American*, 26. **Because, they declare:** *NYT*, 12/21/20. **In many places:** Merz, 89–91.
237 **Gives aliens:** Rosenbaum, 422. **Semicivilized:** Eagles, *Democracy*, 38. **Gnawing:** *CR*, 5/28/29, 2054–2056. **Not fair:** *NYT*, 1/15/31, 48.
238 **Wets argued:** Anderson, 152–53. **This eliminated:** Kennedy, *Freedom*, 14. **Pug dog:** Kenneth Roberts, "The Goal of Central Europeans," *Saturday Evening Post*, 11/6/20, 61.
239 **Preserve racial:** *NYT*, 4/27/24, XX, 3. **Klan more concerned:** Jackson, 26. **Inferior, riff-raff:** MacLean, 91. **SYMWA:** Jackson, 133. **Motivated by anti-Semitism:** Link, 847.
240 **Communications private:** Cherrington to Hobson, 3/30/15, in RPHP, B35, F7. **Win it now:** "Proceedings of the 1917 Convention of the Anti-Saloon League of America," 75.
240 **Less than nine:** Eagles, *Democracy*, 51. **On guard:** *Current Opinion*, 1/21, 35–38. **Forty-two separate:** Schmeckebier, 120–21.
240 **Men from the farms, many do not speak, silent consent:** Eagles, *Democracy*, 39, 61, 45–46. **Silly:** *WP*, 3/13/27, 1.
241 **497,000 each:** *WP*, 8/11/26, 9. **Ten separate in Missouri, city versus:** Eagles, *Democracy*, 72, 66.
241 **Not be violated:** *WP*, 2/6/29, 6.
241 **Al Smith, generally:** *ANB*, Handlin. **In a bank:** Handlin, 28.
242 **Brown derby:** *New York Sun*, 12/28/32.
242 **Jack up:** Handlin, 109.
242 **Jurymen would have:** *Collier's*, 7/16/21, 23. **Rightfully belongs:** Lerner, *Dry*, 94. **Leon and Eddie's:** Louis Sobol, "Speakeasy, *Cosmopolitan*, 4/34, 54.
242 **Massachusetts:** Walnut, 54. **Maryland:** Clark, *Deliver*, 167–68. **Very stupid:** Stanley Walker, 17.
243 **Bier, grave:** Murray, *103rd*, 144.
243 **Hopeful idiots:** Roosevelt to Bryan, 6/20/23, quoted in Friedel, *Ordeal*, 162.
243 **Einstein and Wheeler:** Einstein, 41. **Appetitive, humidity:** Palmer Canfield in *NYT*, 6/21/24, 3.
243 **Reception committees, my best men:** OrH, COHP: Claude Bowers, 52. **Five thousand speakeasies:** Lerner, dissertation, 203. **Good rye:** *Variety*, 3/6/24.
244 **Neither willing to risk:** Murray, *103rd*, 143–144. **Avert disaster, old wounds:** Stanley Frost, *Outlook*, 6/18/24, 265–68.

244 **Expelled:** "Monteval," 13. **Bourbon, Birth:** McGill,132. **Klan of the 1920s:** Coben, 136. **Over half a million:** Jackson, 90. **Oregon:** Leuchtenberg, *Perils*, 209. **Colorado, Kansas:** McVeigh, 2–3. **Avalanche:** Jackson, 138.

245 **Wheeler and Catholics:** Timberlake, 31–32. **Jews:** Marni Davis, 235. **Cherrington:** Cherrington to Justin Steuart, telegram, 7/12/28, in TPP/Cherrington, R66.

245 **Denison:** Angle, 140–41. **Grip of bootleggers:** Higham, 295; Angle, 284; *NYT,* 9/14/24. **Glaring disgrace:** Angle, 157. **Hauling:** *NYT,* 9/14/24. **Stickney:** Angle, 140–41. **Submachine gun:** Angle, 141. **Twenty dead:** Higham, 295.

245 **Wets supporting Underwood:** Murray, *103rd*, 155. **Drys backing McAdoo:** McVeigh, 7. **Heavily guarded:** Murray, *103rd*, 108. **They were afraid:** Leuchtenberg, *Perils*, 133.

246 **Worst-hated:** *NYT,* 6/23/24, 8. **Fixed fact:** Davis to Wheeler, 2/14/23, John W. Davis Papers, B22, F136.

246 **A mob:** Beck to Harlan Fiske Stone, 7/11/24, Harlan Fiske Stone Papers, B6. **The kind of man:** William H. Anderson to "members of the 68th Congress," 3/15/23, in TPP/Cherrington, R76.

Chapter Sixteen: "Escaped on Payment of Money"

247 **Vogt:** Fisher, *Prohibition*, 126. **Odyssey:** Gordon, *Anti-Alcohol*, 123. **Two to four, will add:** Eugene B. Benge, "Effects of Prohibition from the Viewpoint of an Employment Manager," in Walnut, 111.

248 **Bananas (fn):** I. N. Fisher, *My Father*, xi. **Abolition:** quoted in Justin Fox, 21. **Dropped 20:** Fisher, *Prohibition*, 99. **Billion of GNP, Feldman:** Thornton, 16.

248 **Pronouncements:** *NYT,* 8/10/23, 13. **Bowling, gambling spike:** *Survey*, 11/16/20, 198.

248 **Savings lower, virility:** Monahan, 222. **Chastity:** *NYT,* 8/10/23, 13.

249 **Bellevue:** Kellogg to Barron, 5/7/23, in John H. Kellogg Papers, B1, Correspondence.

249 **Gibbs:** *New Yorker,* 4/4/31, 26. **Fell sharply:** Miron and Zwiebel, 242–47.

249 **Tastes like:** Dabney, 174. **Just for Bevo:** Hernon and Ganey, 105.

250 **Pre-war taste, Pablo, etc.:** author's collection.

250 **Almost negligible:** Plavchan, 161–62. **Hobart, Feigenspan's:** George S. Hobart, "The Volstead Act," in Walnut, 96.

250 **Twenty gallons:** Warburton, in *Annals of American Academy of Political and Social Science*, 9/32, 91–92.

251 **Product that will:** Plavchan, 179.

251 **Apple butter, etc.:** Brochure, Department of Agriculture, Bureau of Chemistry, File 470.2 (464), to A. Lonnquest, 7/10/18, Frankenmuth (MI) Historical Society; Hernon and Ganey, 134. **Pabst:** Cochran, 334. **Anheuser:** Hernon and Ganey, 132. **Trade associations:** Kobler, 238. **Magazine:** *NYT,* 4/4/26. **Time is ripe:** Wheeler to Louis C. Cramton, 10/12/25, in Louis C. Cramton Papers, B1. **Smack (fn):** Hernon and Ganey, 134.

251 **Final gasp:** Merz, 123–24. **Six million:** Plavchan, 179. **Biggest bootlegging:** Hernon and Ganey, 132.

252 **Simms:** William Hayward to Attorney General, 10/9/22, F 23–3962–5, Department of Justice archives. **Small pint, as honest as:** MacLean, 100–101. **Public demand:** Boorstin, 84.

252 **Not by next:** Jimerson et al., 241–42.

253 **First four thousand:** *Collier's*, 7/6/21, 23. **Does not fit:** Willebrandt, 251. **15 percent:** *NYT,* 12/28/25, 3.

253 **Buckner, generally:** *ANB, DAB*, Mayer.

254 **Licked:** Stein Family Papers, Buckner to Elihu Root Jr. et al., 3/17/25.

254 **Swore off:** Stanley Walker, 60. **Brandy:** Stein Family Papers, Buckner to "Dear Four," 1/20/32. **Subcellar, six judges:** Mayer, 186–87. **Fifty thousand:** *Senate Judiciary 1926*, 96–97. **Easy to amend:** *NYT,* 1/3/26, VIII, 9.

254 **Seething:** *Senate Judiciary 1926*, 96–97. **Perjury, ten thousand, grotesque, escaped:** Mayer, 186–87. **Pay $100 fine (fn):** *Nation*, 4/28/26, 472.
255 **Staff consisted:** Dorothy M. Brown, 50.
255 **Staggering 90:** Asbury, 170. **Please the Drys:** Quoted in A. Mason, *Stone*, 156.
255 **Rewarded with bounty:** *NYT*, 3/2/20. **Bannick:** Clark, *Dry*, 157–58. **Liquor courts:** See *Dugan v. Ohio*, 277 U.S. 63 (1928); *Tumey v. Ohio*, 273 U.S. 521–522 (1927); and *Journal-News* (Hamilton, Ohio), 2/12/2003.
256 **Less than 15:** Merz, 277. **Old local-option:** *Collier's*, 7/16/21, 23–24.
256 **Connecticut:** Everett Allen, 105. **Detroit Board:** *NYT*, 5/3/28. **Graft trust:** Asbury, 184.
257 **Reopen places:** Lindberg, 184–85. **Cleanest, soberest:** Sayler to Collins, 10/8/23, William E. Dever Papers, B3, F24.
257 **Reduced the quality:** Reeves, vii.
257 **Semiofficial:** *NYT*, 12/6/33. **Fund for disabled:** Ernest Gordon, *Wrecking*, 169. **Knee-deep:** quoted in Johns, 35. **Be introduced:** *Baltimore Evening Sun*, 10/12/31.
258 **Indicted for diversion:** Willebrandt, 118. **Mistaken idea:** Overton, 53. **Double duty:** Elizabeth Anne Brown, 29. **Demijohns:** OrH, CWH: Antonio Pirelli-Minetti, 16–17. **Orgy:** Hans Schmidt, 169.
258 **General disregard:** Bruere, 90. **35 seconds:** Kobler, 295–98. **Lucrative Louisiana:** Order forms from Louisiana (Father Prim, etc.) in DFP. **Mereaux:** Barry, *Rising*, 236. **From appearances:** Crane to Tuttle, 3/1/27, in AJTP, B65, Correspondence.
259 **On a Still:** Lender and Martin, 142. **Half a million cases:** *NYT*, 6/23/29, XX, 4. **Sealed:** RCCE, Barney Aaron testimony, 22,036–72; Harry Low testimony, 16,522. **Three boats:** *NYT*, 5/22/27, XX, 5. **Pipeline, cable:** *DN*, 1/24/31. **In less than:** Bingay, 325.
259 **On to Chicago:** Nelli, 158. **7,000, three times:** *DN*, 1/11/14; *NYT*, 5/3/28. **Single block:** Engelmann, "Separate," 51–73. **Carnival:** *DN*, 1/1/24. **Union efforts:** Engelmann, *Intemperance*, 136.
260 **Poor place:** *DN*, 7/12/23. **Darrow:** Diary entry, 11/26/25, Josephine F. Gomon Papers, B6.
260 **Left alone, tragic joke, Lodge practical:** Engelmann, "Separate." **Notables:** advertisement, *Detroit Saturday Night*, 11/15/27, reprinted in Engelmann, "Separate."
261 **Wracked:** Tuttle to Harry M. Daugherty, 4/21/22, AJTP, B24, Topical Office Files, Prohibition Dept. (1). **Expecting Uncle Sam:** Tuttle to Mrs. F. P. Anderson, 11/9/23, AJTP, B24, Topical Office Files, Prohibition (2). **Crowding:** Tuttle to Merlin Wiley, 7/5/22, B24, Topical Office Files, Prohibition (1).
261 **McGee:** *NYT*, 2/6/25, 1.
261 **Leaving to the states:** *New Republic*, 1/15/22, 305–6.
262 **Spectacular but ineffectual:** *McClure's*, 9/09, 539. **Wrong cannot:** Suitts, 457.
262 **Maximum sentences, first few:** Suitts, 133–34, 452–53.
262 **Izzy believes, Einstein told:** *Mobile Register*, 11/14/23, 1. **Sad news:** Kobler, 295–98.
263 **Bank president et al.:** *Mobile Register*, 12/20/23, 1; also "Teflon Tycoon," in *Register*, 12/19/2001. **O'Shaughnessy:** *Mobile Register*, 12/19/23, 1. **Wanted a drink:** Webb.
263 **Broyles arrested:** *Mobile Register*, 12/19/23, 1. **Stone's effort:** Webb. **I ate it:** Roger K. Newman, 64. **Klansmen:** Klan leader James Esdale, quoted in Roger K. Newman, 65.
264 **I really should:** Mayer, 204–5. **$150 a week:** *New Yorker*, 10/16/26, 36. **Common pool:** Kobler, 229. **It is clear:** Willebrandt, 171–72.
264 **Could process:** Mayer, 192–93; Mazzone to author, 7/3/2009.
264 **Harlan, collect evidence, Buckner obligingly:** Mayer, 187–188. **Necklace:** Stanley Walker, 94–96.

265 **Conjunction:** Quoted in Lerner, dissertation, 228.
265 **Seems an impossible:** Buckner to Elihu Root Jr., et al., 3/17/25, Stein Family Papers.
265 **Man who buys:** *New Yorker,* 11/14/25, 7.
265 **Two days after, could not countenance, gloated:** *NYT,* 11/17/25, 2; 11/21/25, 1. **Regard slight:** Buckner to Ruth Buckner, 3/7/26, Stein Family Papers. **Stampede, Liquor Market:** *New Yorker,* 11/25/27, 7.

Chapter Seventeen: Crime Pays

267 **Very presence:** *CR,* 6/22/22, 9186. **Wet list:** *House Appropriations 1922,* 491.
268 **Censure:** *WP,* 8/24/21, 2. **Spinsters:** *New Republic,* 12/15/6, 102. **Better hater:** Villard, 89.
268 **Truculent:** *New Republic,* 6/8/26, 86. **War of words:** *NYT,* 4/18/26, XX, 1. **Bellowing:** *Philadelphia Inquirer,* 6/27/26.
268 **Dry reception:** *Time,* 6/27/26. **Blight:** Asbury, 147. **Pockets:** *Senate Campaign Expenditures 1926,* 19.
269 **Forced to admit:** *Senate Judiciary 1926,* 843. **Asbestos:** *Senate Judiciary 1926,* 1108.
269 **Colored people:** *Senate Judiciary 1926,* 689. **Fanatics and fools:** *NYT,* 4/23/26, 1.
269 **All-absorbing:** *NYT,* 4/18/26, XX, 1. **Long years:** Wheeler to McBride, 5/22/26, TPP/McBride, R15. **Corpse:** Steuart, 269.
270 **Spectacular war:** *NYT,* 4/22/26, 1. **The very fact, Reed had not:** *NYT,* 4/25/26, 1.
270 **Smiling exterior, three-week:** Steuart, 21, 274. **Enemas:** Kellogg to Wheeler, 6/13/26, Robin Wheeler Papers. **Overdraw:** Wheeler to McBride, 5/22/26, TPP/McBride, R15.
271 **Not settled:** Ernest Gordon, *Wrecking,* 120.
271 **Agents spending:** *NYT,* 6/28/26.
271 **Shoots from ambush:** *NYT,* 9/9/23, XX, 3.
272 **Like modern business:** Bergreen, 86.
272 **Lansky launched:** Lacey, 51. **Forwarding services:** Engelmann, *Intemperance,* 143. **Using planes:** Nelli, 172. **Jewish lake:** Meyer Lansky, quoted in Eisenberg et al., 79. **Overland corridor:** *American Mercury,* 4/28, 393–99.
273 **Control entire, fixed prices, rewarded:** Nelli, 174.
273 **Eventually sell:** Mark H. Haller, "Bootleggers as Businessmen: From City Slums to City Builders," in Kyvig, *Law,* 145. **Birth certificates:** No two sources—including FBI records and Zwillman's own biographer—seem to agree on a date of birth.
273 **Anti-KKK:** David Goldberg, 136. **Sweet but, while serving:** "Encyclopedia of Arkansas History and Culture," http://www.encyclopediaofarkansas.net, entry for Madden.
274 **Rotary Club:** Bergreen, 269. **Give the public:** *CT,* 12/6/27. **Customers, not victims:** Haller, "Urban," 619.
274 **Buckner believed:** *Senate Lobby 1930,* 4166. **What honest:** *Senate Judiciary 1926,* 649–52. **Automobiles:** Joseph Epstein, "Browsing in Gangland," *Commentary,* 1/72, 46–55.
275 **Now engaged:** *Memorial Records,* 275–76. **Diverting:** *Cincinnati Enquirer,* 2/28/25.
275 **Promissory:** Langley, 237. **Pork barrel, managed to deposit, release of a million:** Sexton, 110; Dorothy M. Brown, 68.
275 **Seattle bootleggers:** Clark, *Deliver,* 162; Marrus, 98. **Racketville:** *Philadelphia Record,* 10/21/28, 1. **Rendering:** *NYT,* 9/3/28, 10.
276 **Business pays:** Bergreen, 128.
276 **It did increase:** Gary M. Anderson, "Bureaucratic Incentives and the Transition from Taxes to Prohibition," in Shughart, 154. **Newspapers began:** Flexner, 73. **Sewage:** Sinclair, 313. **Yale funeral:** *NYT,* 7/6/28.

277 **Pull it out double:** Stanley Walker, 106–9. **Few dry papers (fn):** Heckman, 87, 95–96.
277 **One hundred dollars each:** Everett Allen, 176. **Gar Wood:** Fostle, 154.
277 **Thanks, Charlie:** Everett Allen, x–xi. **Knew the officers:** OrH, Federal Writers' Project, Library of Congress: subject identified only as "Callano."
277 *John Dwight* episode: *Boston Globe*, 4/7, 4/9, 4/17, 4/24, and 5/23/23, all p. 1; also David Arnold, "Bodies Told Tale of Torture at Sea," *Boston Globe*, 7/31/96.
278 **Go-through, match halves:** Willoughby, 35–36, 58–59. **Altered unbelievably:** *NYT*, 12/14/24, XX, 1.
278 **Fleet of fifty-five, show of force:** Canney, 3. **Practical attack:** Wheeler, "Liquor in International Trade," Walnut, 151. **Four thousand new:** Wheeler to Louis C. Cramton, 10/12/25, Louis C. Cramton Papers, B1. According to Canney, there were four thousand Guardsmen when Prohibition began; Wheeler mentions eight thousand, following the expansion of the force. **Incorruptible:** Wayne B. Wheeler, "The Romance of Rum Row," *The Forum*, 1/25. **Seized three:** Spinelli, 96. **Great Offensive:** Canney, 8.
279 **Through Ontario:** RCCE, Harry Low testimony, 16,522; Marrus, 132. **Windsor market:** Sam Bronfman to Harry Hatch, 11/16/32, SMC. **Only bidders:** Moray, 243. *Underwriter:* Willoughby: 57.
279 **Thirty-six dollars, I would not have shot:** Calder, 107–12. **Elks Lodge:** *Time*, 5/21/28.
280 **Dutch Schultz:** Newsletter, Unqua Corinthian Yacht Club, 8/93, noted as "reprinted from *Antique Wooden Boat* magazine," collection of Fred Scopinich Jr. **Larger scale:** Van de Water, 300.
280 **Levees breached:** Barry, *Rising*, 276.
280 **Machine guns:** *NYT*, 6/2/25, 3. **Seizing from hijackers, cigarette:** Aronow, 85–86. **CG-911:** *Southern Boating*, 2/98, 99–100.
281 **ASL opposed:** *NYT*, 5/17/16, 12. **Stone's wines:** wine labels in Harlan Fiske Stone Papers, B87. **Inflicted:** Alpheus Mason, *Stone*, 733. **Holmes's prayer:** Holmes to Lady Leslie Scott, 12/24/27, in Oliver Wendell Holmes Papers, cited by Post. **McReynolds (fn):** Harriet Ford Griswold, "Justices of the Supreme Court I Have Known," *Quarterly Newsletter of the Supreme Court Historical Society*, 1987, Issue 4.
282: **Beer-swilled:** *American Issue*, 4/24/04. **Busch friend, offered:** Hernon and Ganey, 81. **Unenforceable:** Henry B. Joy quoting Taft speech circa 1919, *House Judiciary 1930*, 151.
282 **Willing to govern:** *Ladies' Home Journal*, 5/19, 78. **Brushed aside:** Kyvig, *Explicit*, 275–76. **Manly S. Sullivan (fn):** *NYT*, 5/17/27, 31.
283 **Twenty separate, Cyclopedia:** Murchison, 48, 83–84. **Kirby cartoon:** *New York World*, 8/31/21, reprinted in United States Brewers' Association, *Year Book*, 1921. **Training classes:** Clyde McElmore to Harry M. Dengler, Clyde McElmore Papers, 1/23/31.
283 **When a drunk:** Coletta, 62. **In Chicago:** Miller, 302. **Writing to Horace:** William Howard Taft to Horace Taft, 3/1/25, quoted in Post, 120.
284 **Most active centers:** *Carroll v. United States*, 267 U.S. 160 (1925).
284 **Good bootlegger:** *Seattle Post-Intelligencer*, 5/16/31.
284 **Quick, avoided sordid:** Clark, *Dry*, 161, 166. **Social purpose:** *Seattle Post-Intelligencer*, 5/16/31.
285 **Constituted code:** Willlebrandt, 232, 234. **Arctic Club, personal property:** Clark, *Dry*, 207, 184.
285 **Catch cold, seen Doc:** Metcalfe, 48, 45.
285 **Considered unethical:** Post, 134–35. **Thoroughly disapproved, outside counsel:** Willebrandt, 232.
285 **Can it be:** *Olmstead v. United States*, 277 U.S. 438 at 474 (1928).
286 **Only dissenting:** *Katz v. United States*, 389 U.S. 347 (1967). **Let alone:** *Roe v. Wade*, 410 U.S. 113, concurring opinion by Justice Potter Stewart.

286 **Feared by the dry, we do not:** *NYT,* 6/4/28, N3.
287 **Greatest obstacle:** Robert Toms, quoted in Engelmann, *Intemperance,* 130. **No obligation, legalized murder:** *NYT,* 12/30/26, 1. **Inexcusable:** *NYT,* 12/31/26, 1. **Why put poison:** *NYT,* 1/4/27, 1.
287 **Any man who takes:** *NYT,* 4/24/27, 1. **$11 apiece:** ticket stub, Robin Wheeler Papers.
288 **Caterwauling, spunky:** *New York World,* 4/24/27, 1. **Pie or cake, might be a good thing, stop complaining:** *NYT,* 4/24/27, 1.

Chapter Eighteen: The Phony Referendum

289 **Fifty-five-square-mile:** Burk, 42.
289 **Key platform:** *NYT,* 10/17/26, 4. **Easier, more dignified:** Sabin to Wadsworth, 8/26/26, JWWP, B19.
290 **First active:** *ANB.* **One of the largest:** *Southampton Press,* 7/22/20. **Description of Bayberry Land:** Mary Cummings, "Southampton Village: The Premier Resort," http://www.hamptonsview.com; also "Bayberry Land: Rest and Refuge in Southampton," "special gallery" on Town of Southampton website. **Fellow Republicans:** While other sources place this event in 1916, the generally reliable *Southampton Press* dates it to 1919.
290 **Sixteen boards:** Wolfskill, 37–39. **Sabin home life:** Interviews with Sabin's granddaughters, Pauline Sabin Willis and Sheila Cochran.
291 **Fashionable rich:** *Ladies' Home Journal,* 3/23, quoted in Carter, *Another,* 88. **Luxury-loving:** Taft to Charles H. Strong, quoted in Post, 90–91. **Best and most, punishment is asked, no conception:** Durant, title page, 34.
291 **Cheney:** Irénée du Pont to William H. Stayton, 3/20/29, in Irénée du Pont Papers, Series J, F122. **Shiftless workman, mighty good:** Lewis, 115–16. **If only:** Samuel Crowther, "Where Prohibition Is a Success," *Ladies' Home Journal,* 2/30, 9. Although this article appeared under Crowther's own name, he had early ghosted Ford's autobiography and worked with him on several other occasions.
292 **Boeing:** Clark, *Dry,* 172.
292 **In sympathy:** Wheeler to ASL state superintendents, 3/15/27, reprinted in *New York American,* 7/15/27, 1. **Persuaded Mellon:** *NYT,* 1/1/27, 1. **Fearing:** *NYT,* 7/25/27; also Wheeler to Louis C. Cramton, 6/4/27, in Louis C. Cramton Papers. **Certain prospective:** *NYT,* 6/26/27, XX, 6.
292 **On a Pullman:** *Columbus Dispatch,* date unclear, report on Wheeler funeral. **Wheedling:** *San Francisco Examiner,* 2/1/27. **Majority who:** *CGG,* 11/1/26, 13. **Rather strenuous:** Wheeler to Viscount Astor, 5/23/27, Robin Wheeler Papers.
293 **Leaders of the party, well-recognized, unwarranted:** *NYT,* 6/25/27, 15. **Somewhat milder, trouble him (fn):** *NYT,* 2/13/27, 21.
293 **Homes for Christian:** http://www.littlepointsable.org/id66.htm. **Salary:** Odegard, 207; Steuart, 292. **Kept the family:** interview, Christopher W. Wheeler. **Steady stream:** Steuart, 292.
294 **Large drum:** *NYT,* 8/15/27, 19.
294 **Calmness:** Steuart, 293.
294 **Enlarged heart:** Lloyd D. Verity, MD, to Henry Hyde Russell, 9/6/27, TPP/ Russell.
294 **Greatest loss:** *American Issue,* 10/30/26. **Reporters raced, spent 1927:** OrH, COHP: Wadsworth, 345, 358–59. **Is hypocrisy:** *NYT,* 1/25/27, 1. **Vital:** William H. Stayton to Pierre S. du Pont et al., 11/1/27, PSdPP, F1023, B1417.
295 **Fanatical:** Heckman, 7. **Eschewing, recruiting, names private:** Stayton to John J. Raskob, 10/2/19 and 12/5/19, JJRP, F2168. **Suits, ties:** Kyvig, *Repealing,* 42.
295 **Some of the best:** *NYT,* 4/7/22, 1. **Fumbling effort:** Heckman, 281.
295 **Men invited:** William H. Stayton to Pierre S. du Pont et al., 11/1/27, PSdPP, F1023, B1417. **Leadership had passed:** Merz, 215.

296 **Largest single, ranking:** Dobyns, 9. **Greater than it is:** *Senate Lobby 1930*, William H. Stayton testimony, 4245.
296 **Exceptionally wealthy:** IRS Form 1040 for 1922, in PSdPP, File 670, B1115, F1925. **Du Pont generally:** *ANB, DAB.*
297 **Dad:** Chandler and Salsbury, 16. **Daddy:** Irénée du Pont to Pierre S. du Pont, 2/25/20, Irénée du Pont Papers, F240, B63.
297 **Annual production:** *ANB.* **Increase sixteen-fold:** Kennedy, *Over,* 139.
297 **Increased donations:** Craig, 252–53. **Detested:** See correspondence between du Pont and Fred S. Smith, 1/19/24, quoted in Dighe. **Unfair competition:** Burk, 79.
297 **Into his own pocket:** Burk, 27. **Eighty-six new:** *Time,* 1/31/27, 22.
298 **Some chance, somewhat positive:** du Pont to Arthur Little, 1/7/27, quoted in Craig, 258; Craig, 252–53. **Reports from managers:** Burk, 26. **Same request:** Stayton made this assertion in an interview in *Life* [original version], 7/24/31, 15. **Opening wedge:** letter of 10/16/26, quoted in Craig, 250.
298 **This cancer:** Curran, 320. **Special fund:** Burk, 45. **Getting back:** du Pont to Julian Codman, 1/3/28, PSdPP, B1023, F1417.
299 **Half the state's:** AAPA Minutes, meeting of 8/2/28, in PSdPP, B1486, F1023–1031. **To Those Living:** du Pont to staff, 2/10/28, in Irénée du Pont Papers, Series J, F122.
299 **Men who direct:** William H. Stayton to Noel B. Martin, 2/10/30, quoted in *Senate Lobby 1930,* 4241.
299 **Letter to Smith:** du Pont to Smith, 3/19/28, in PSdPP, B1417. F1023.
300 **His puppets, Brown's soul:** quoted in *Columbus Dispatch,* 9/11/27. **Leonidas:** reprinted in *American Issue,* 9/27/27, 8.
300 **Financial tap shut:** Raymond Fosdick to Howard Hyde Russell, 11/18/25, RAC, B43, F473. **Offended:** Fosdick to Rockefeller, 3/19/25, RAC, B43, F473. **Kresge:** Jimerson et al., 254–56. **Called for legislation:** Dabney, 296. **Family problems:** *NYT,* 7/5/27, 5.
301 **Kresge scandal:** *NYT,* 8/25/27, 3; 12/17/27. **Matrimonial difficulties:** Sen. John J. Blaine, *Senate Lobby 1930,* 4375. **Home wrecker:** *NYT,* 12/24/28, 36.
301 **Uncomplimentary light:** Steuart to Cherrington, 5/11/28, in TPP/Cherrington, R66.
301 **Signs of weakness:** Codman to du Pont, 12/27/27, PSdPP, F1023, B1417. **Pee-wees:** *American Mercury,* 12/32, 385.
302 **Wadsworth:** Wadsworth to G. C. Hinckley, 3/2/27, JWWP, B19. **Einstein:** Einstein, 258. **World:** 12/3/26. **Norris:** Lowitt, 324. **Doubtless:** Addams, *Second Twenty,* 255. **Olmstead's:** Clark, *Dry,* 214–15. **Wetter than:** Allsop, 129. **Smith:** Douglas Bukowski, "Big Bill Thompson: The 'Model' Politician," in Green and Holl, 71. **Michaelson:** Bukowski, *Big Bill,* 231.
303 **Portrait, left behind, salary:** Allsop, 360–61, 374–75; Bukowski, *Big Bill,* 254. **Collected from Capone:** Frank J. Loesch of Chicago Crime Commission, cited in Lindberg, 143.
303 **Nearly every rabbi:** Marni Davis, 240–41.
304 **Hoover:** Burner, *Hoover,* 218–19.
304 **Honest effort:** Democratic platform, 1928.
304 **Four to eight daily:** *Nation,* 11/30/27. **Insane:** Burner, *Hoover,* 218.
305 **I would rather see:** Murray, *103rd,* 278. **Nigger president:** Myers, 270.
305 **Voted for Coolidge:** *NYT,* 7/15/28, XX, 5. **Papist plot:** See Williams, generally, 242 *et seq.*
305 **Raskob, generally; investment advice; chamberlain:** Biographical Note, Hagley Library, http://www.hagleyorg/raskob/. **Donated one million:** *NYT,* 7/15/28, XX, 5.
306 **Annex Mexico:** *NYT,* 1/24/28, 1. **Headquarters, RCA stock:** Burk, 51–53. **Vassal state:** Lichtman, 58–59.
306 **$690,000:** Burk, 53. **Spectacular raids:** Though Willebrandt downplayed her role in these raids, the testimony of Maurice Campbell, the federal Prohibition

administrator for New York, persuasively suggests otherwise. See especially *WP*, 9/24/30, 1.
307 **Willebrandt Ohio speech:** *LD*, 9/29/18, 14.
307 **Cleared by Burke:** Willebrandt, 11–12. **Burning crosses:** Dorothy M. Brown, 161. **Vote against Jesus:** Burner, *Politics*, 203–4. **Treasonable:** *NYT*, 9/21/28.
308 **Afraid to come out:** Brown, 163.
308 **Great experiment:** *NYT*, 8/12/28. Hoover's statement was immediately truncated by commentators into the straight declaration that Prohibition was "a noble experiment"; it has been similarly abbreviated ever since. **Exultant McBride:** *LD*, 11/24/28, 14–15. **Driest Congress, forty-three governors:** Dobyns, 39.
308 **Phony referendum:** Lichtman, 92. **Montana, Massachusetts, other results:** Kyvig, *Repealing*, 116–17; Burk, 56.
309 **Ten largest:** Slosson, 121–22.
309 **Political machine, party:** Boorstin, 255.

Chapter Nineteen: Outrageous Excess

313 **Simpler acquisition:** Invoice, 12?/12/28, JJRP, F1917.
313 **I am not, simple pleasures:** *Collier's*, 3/5/32. **Mostly Halls:** *Philadelphia Bulletin*, 9/24/28, 40. **Entire floor:** OrH, COHP, Eddie Dowling, p. 104.
314 **Dry martinis:** Order form aboard SS *Europa*, 5/3/31, JJRP, F2795. **Sold openly:** Raskob to Walter Butler, 2/27/24, JJRP, F2295. **Forget between:** Raskob to Butler, 2/27/25, F317. **Sharing:** Raskob correspondence with Herbert Witherspoon, autumn 1926, in JJRP, F2501. **Floating speakeasies:** Richard James, archivist, Hagley Library.
314 **Stored in lockers:** Raskob to Chrysler, 9/27/28, JJRP. **Gleaming foot rail:** Advertisement reproduced in Lerner, dissertation, 213. **Ship their goods:** Charles Berns, in Kobler, 229. **Pendennis raid:** *Louisville Courier-Journal*, 8/10/30, 1; 8/11/30, 1; 8/12/30, 2.
314 **Wadsworth complained:** Wadsworth to Lincoln Andrews, 7/24/25, JWWP, B19. **Monthly cost:** e-mail from Richard James, Hagley Library. **Under three presidents:** Leuchtenberg, *Perils*, 98. **Neighbors might:** Beebe, 288.
315 **I Change:** *Outlook*, 6/13/28, 254. Some histories, apparently drawing on an article that appeared in *Time* in 1932, say that Sabin was motivated to come out as a public dry in response to a statement made by Ella Boole, head of the WCTU, at a congressional hearing. According to this version, Boole declared, "I represent the women of America!" which led Sabin to say to herself, "Well, lady, here's one woman you don't represent." But Boole never said those words at a congressional hearing, and there's no evidence that Sabin ever attended a hearing at which Boole testified. Sabin did once tell a congressional panel, "I am here to refute the contention made by dry organizations, that all the women of America favor national prohibition," but that was in 1930, two years after she went public with her opposition to Prohibition. See *House Judiciary 1930*, 41. **Other vital matters:** *NYT*, 6/8/28, 35. **Wives of financiers:** Press release, 9/12/28, in Herbert Hoover Papers, F: Campaign and Transition/Campaign Literature/Subject— Mrs. Charles H. Sabin. **Humanitarian:** *NYT*, 9/6/28, 5.
316 **No name, platform:** Sabin letter to the editor, *NYT*, 1/12/44.
316 **Ignominiously:** Clark, *Deliver*, 192. **Wet sidewalks:** Dabney, 187–88.
316 **Even if it:** Cannon, "Spend Whatever Is Needed," in Durant, 111.
317 **Legislation Cannon devised:** Clark, *Deliver*, 194–95.
317 **Casual, commercial:** *NYT*, 3/3/29, 1.
317 **Most menacing:** Clark, *Deliver*, 196. **Follow the breath:** *New York Journal*, 4/3/29.
318 **Terroristic, Fish:** *CT*, 4/3/29, 3. **Greenville:** *CT*, 3/30/29, 2. **Dozens of papers:** Ernest Gordon, *Wrecking*, 124. **DeKing case:** *CT*, 3/29/29, 1; 3/30/29, 2; 10/27/29, B1.

319 **Etta Mae Miller, bellboy, Wilson:** *Time*, 1/14/29. **If law is wrong:** Calder, 106.
320 **Some jurisdictions:** Willebrandt, 170. **In attempting:** Clark, *Deliver*, 195.
320 **Professional managers, remove:** Calder, 2–3; 225–26. **Breakdown, army:** Hoover to Attorney General William D. Mitchell, 6/5/29, quoted in Calder, 86.
320 **Indiscriminate:** Detroit Yachting Association, quoted in Philip Mason, 147. **Fifteen hundred boats:** *Nation*, 9/4/29, 242. **365 stolen, Jewish Navy:** Engelmann, *Intemperance*, 114, 144.
321 **War:** *Outlook*, 7/4/29, 507. **Forces amass:** *NYT*, 6/23/29, XX, 4. **Best advertised:** Internal Revenue Service memorandum, agent W. C. Hodgins et al. to agent-in-charge of Chicago office, 7/8/31, http://www.irs.gov/pub/irs-utl/file-1-letter-dated-07081931-in-re-alphonse-capone.pdf.
321 **Public service:** *CT*, 12/6/27. **When I sell:** Boorstin, 84. **My offense:** Heimel, 57.
321 **Snorky:** Miller, 303. **Sulka:** Kobler, 14. **Shavetail:** Alva Johnston, "The Future of Racketeering," *Vanity Fair*, 4/31, 50.
322 **Tuesday and Saturday:** Wickersham, vol. 4, 327. **Lousy:** Gus Schaffer to Ron Martinelli, 9/10/75, Gus Schaffer [also Schaefer] Papers, Chicago Historical Society.
322 **Capon:** Joseph Driscoll, "Men of Action," in Moquin and Van Doren, 123.
322 **Capone the immune:** IRS memo of 7/8/31, as above.
322 **Close factories:** *Pictorial Review*, 9/29. **Great pity:** Quoted in Sinclair, 316. **War on Coca-Cola:** Hays, 86. **Unmoved:** Pendergrast, 162.
323 **Scrambling assignments:** *NYT*, 9/9/28. **Bank accounts:** Tydings, 73. **Craps, dogs, bequests:** Report of the Special August Grand Jury, quoted in Haller, "Philadelphia," 225. **Ledger book:** *NYT*, 9/9/28.
323 **Squishes:** *Collier's*, 2/16/29, 8. **Equivalent of twenty:** Pearson, *More*, 306–7. **Bottom fell:** George Cassiday, in *WP*, 10/24/30, 1.
324 **Morgan:** *NYT*, 3/30/29, 1; 4/4/29, 1; 4/5/29, 1.
324 **Michaelson:** *CT*, 3/30/29, 2. **Many a Congressman, trunks contained:** *Time*, 4/8/29; *WP*, 3/30/29, 1. **No desire:** *CT*, 10/23/29, 16. **Vindicated:** *CT*, 5/9/29, 1.
325 **Denison:** *NYT*, 11/20/29, 1. **Fairy story (fn):** *CT*, 3/14/31.
325 **Cassiday arrested:** 12/18/29, 2. Most early stories about him spelled his name "Cassidy," but when the *Washington Post* ran an as-told-to series under his byline in 1930, this was persuasively established that "Cassiday" was correct. **Cannon flour hoarding:** Dabney, 201.
326 **Stock speculator:** Golden, 137–45.
326 **Union Square:** Dabney, 296. **Less likely:** Golden, 124–25.
326 **Cannon's fall:** Dabney, 190, 269, 272. **Non-entity:** Patterson, 493.
327 **Twenty-three electoral:** Sweeting, 442–44. **Vandenberg:** *WP*, 1/26/29, 6.
327 **Refuse, unjust:** Eagles, *Democracy*, 77, 75. **Kimball letter:** *WP*, 1/9/29, 6.
327 **Generalissimo:** *NYT*, 6/3/29, 12.
328 **Dinner Belgian:** Cannadine, 391.

Chapter Twenty: The Hummingbird That Went to Mars

329 **Devastating argument, block repeal:** Merz, 297, ix.
329 **Beck:** *NYT*, 1/18/31, 125. **Darrow:** *Vanity Fair*, 11/31, 62.
330 **New organization:** Engelmann, *Intemperance*, 215. **African American:** Root, 147; *Amsterdam News*, 9/7/32, 1. **Hummingbird:** *WP*, 9/25/30, 5.
330 **Union League:** *NYT*, 2/24/31, 1.
330 **High plateau:** *NYT*, 10/16/29, 8.
331 **Slashed:** Calder, 120. **Per diem, training:** Prohibition Dept. order no. 2219, 9/21/31; Harry M. Dengler to McElmore, 5/6/32, both in Clyde McElmore Papers. **Doran:** Sinclair, 356–57; Kobler, 338. **Profit:** Asbury, 319. **Unnaturally cheerful (fn):** Associated Press dispatch, 10/3/28, in TPP/ASL, R8.
331 **Revenue based:** Boudreaux and Pritchard. **Piled up:** Seltzer et al., 203. **Soup kitchen:** *CT*, 12/5/30.
332 **A mistake:** Raskob to Pierre du Pont, 8/31/48, quoted in Lopata, 257.

332 **Subsidiary:** *Senate Lobby 1930*, 3858–59.
332 **Barron:** *WSJ*, 2/14/23.
332 **You will save:** G. C. Hinckley to John J. Raskob, 7/2/25, JJRP, B1, F102. **Irénée told:** Irénée du Pont to H. L. Blanchard, 10/27/30, citing earlier conversation with Stayton, Irénée du Pont Papers, Ser J, F122. **Stayton determined:** Heckman, 186.
333 **Dear Mr.:** *Senate Lobby 1930*, 3999. **The danger:** Wadsworth to Henry H. Curran, 10/7/29, quoted in Fulton, 5762. **Shirt sleeves:** *Senate Lobby 1930*, 4170.
333 **Necessity of levying:** "What Price Prohibition," 1927. **Most widely:** Craig, 356. **The Need:** Kyvig, *Repealing*, 13. **Liquor alone:** Burnham, *Bad*, 46.
333 **Two billion:** Pierre du Pont to Lammot du Pont, 4/28/32, PSdPP, F1023, B1423.
333 **White:** *New Yorker*, 12/29/28, 9. Although unsigned, the piece is credited to White in the *New Yorker* archives. **Where on Manhattan:** Asbury, 211. **Fish store:** Ware, 57.
334 **Virtual local:** *Senate Judiciary 1932*, 27. **Kansas:** *Commonweal*, 2/25/30. **It was dying:** Cowley, 65.
334 **Flavors:** Murdock, 92. **Soared:** Merz, 260. **Fleischmann's in Virginia:** Carr, 114–15. **Ninety-nine out of a hundred, Rockford:** Wickersham, vol. IV, 1075, 261. **Stills and mash:** Merz, 258–60.
335 **Printed wrapper:** *Time*, 8/17/31; *NYT*, 8/6/31, 1. **Ads:** *Sheboygan* (WI) *Press*, 9/25/31, 9. **Diamond:** *NYT*, 8/17/31, 19.
335 **Fruit Industries agent:** Heintz, *California's*, 272–73; OrH, CWH: Philo Biane, 7–8.
335 **Charred kegs:** California Vineyards Co., advertising card, author's collection. **Trade ad:** *California Grower*, 1/31, 2. **Brisbane:** General Fruit Packaging Distributors handout, in Sonoma Wine Library, Healdsburg, CA.
336 **Run away:** quoted in Barr, 105. **Tips:** Engelmann, *Intemperance*, 131–32. **Door, furniture, corkscrew:** Lusk, 46–52.
336 *Leviathan: Baltimore Sun*, 7/29/31. **George Washington:** unidentified clip, 1/8/30, in TPP/ASL, R13. **Delegation:** Herbert Hoover, statement on the London Naval Conference, 1/7/30. **Intercoastal:** de la Pedraja, 110, 227.
336 **Mounds Club:** *SLP-D*, 4/7/29, 3/18/30.
337 **City dweller:** *Washington Star*, 3/11/31. **Cigarette ad:** reprinted in Burnham, *Bad*, photo section. **Pumpkin gin:** Sinclair, 439. **Bridge Table:** Judge Jr., 29.
337 **Dignified:** *NYT*, 7/2/27, 19. **Raids:** *NYT*, 4/26/30, 1; 10/17/42, 15.
337 **Nonfeasance:** *NYT*, 7/1/30, 1.
338 **Jewish vote:** *WP*, 9/16/30, 1. **Lowman also:** *WP*, 9/9/30, 1. **Sheep dip, Curtis:** *NYT*, 11/13/30, 2; *Time*, 9/22/30; *WP*, 11/10/28, 1. **Memos:** *WP*, 9/13/30, 1. **Cesspool:** *WP*, 9/8/30, 1. **Magazine:** *NYT*, 10/17/42, 15.
338 **Majority, capacity:** *WP*, 10/24/30, 1; 10/28/30, 1. **Wet roster:** Burk, 74.
338 **Endorsed Repeal:** Kyvig, *Repealing*, 142. **Just six days:** *NYT*, 10/31/30, 48. **I do think:** Lerner, *Dry*, 287.
339 **Women's names:** Root, appendix.
339 **Pierrepont:** Minutes, organizing meeting of WONPR, 6/1/29, PSdPP, B1568. **Inner circle:** *NYT*, 8/1/29, 12. *McCall's* **profile:** Dorothy Ducas, "In Miniature: Mrs. Charles H. Sabin," *McCall's*, 9/30. **Plays golf:** AC, 3/3/32, 15. **Anti:** *Vogue*, 9/1/30, 80.
340 **Vehement words:** *CT*, 3/9/30, 1.
340 **Scandalous:** *CT*, 4/25/30, 2. **Gaylord:** Dorothy M. Brown, 247.
340 **Thirty-one states:** *New Yorker*, 10/22/32, 20. **Earlier trip:** diary entries, 2/4, 2/12, w 3/27/23, in PSDP, F1. **Sabine women:** *Vanity Fair*, 8/31, 42. **Bacchantian:** *NYT*, 5/24/32, 8. Other contemporary sources rendered "parching" as "parched." **Scum:** quoted in Murdock, 150.
341 **Women whose names:** *WP*, 4/26/30, 1.
341 **Evanston:** Neumann, 4. **As long as:** *Union Signal*, 5/17/30, cover. **Real strength:** *Time*, 7/18/32.

341 **Rather resign:** Gibbons to Hoover, 4/22/31, Herbert Hoover Papers, Presidential Secretary's File, LymanR-Lynb.

342 **Prince of Belvedere:** Saidye Bronfman interview, Philip Siekman and Ann Tyler, 8/12/66, notes in SMC, B10. **Staff:** Edgar Bronfman, 23–24. **Saidye encountered:** Marrus, 167–68. **Burns, ludicrous:** Faith, 77.

342 **Annual meeting:** Transcript of speech, 10/30/30, in SMC.

342 **Ballooned:** Kobler, 254. **20 percent:** Engelmann, *Intemperance*, 78. **Twice as much:** Robertson, 409.

343 **Port Colborne:** *Port Colborne Citizen*, 10/28/26, in Archives of Ontario, RG 4–32, F1926, #1560. **Show itself:** Kottman, 112. **Charity:** Marrus, 133. **Assist the government:** Thornton to Minister of Railways and Canals, 1/7/29, quoted in Stephen T. Moore. **Quadruple:** Dispatch, 11/9/32, State Department Archives, 811.114 Canada 4642.

343 **Actual volume:** Transcript of annual meeting speech, 11/30/31, in SMC. **Launder:** Dubro and Rowland, 208.

343 **Smuggle back:** Dispatch, 1/9/31, State Department Archives, 811.114 Canada 4400. **Cutting racket (fn):** *DN*, cited in Asbury, 269. **Buffalo batch (fn):** James Dubro and Robin Rowland, "Prohibition: Saint John's Connection," *Atlantic Insight*, 3/88, 32.

344 **Replacing air:** Dispatch, 10/30/30, State Department Archives, 811.114 Canada 4362. **Periodic announcements:** Engelmann, *Intemperance*, 119–21. **Halifax:** Dispatch, 12/12/30, State Department Archives, 811.114 Canada 4380.

344 **Hands of gangsters:** Hoover, 276–77. **Whatever necessary:** Calder, 17–19. **Personal matter:** Willebrandt to Hoover, 3/22/29, quoted in Bergreen, 323.

345 **Football helmet:** Heimel, 98. **More than double:** "75 Years of Criminal Investigation," IRS document 7233, 1999. **Six hundred barrels:** Gus Schaffer to Ron Martinelli, 8/27/75, Gus Schaffer [also Schaefer] Papers, Chicago Historical Society.

345 **The Commission:** Raab, 32–36.

346 **Not been attempted:** Willebrandt, 170.

346 **Use this statement:** Willebrandt to McCoy, 1/14/30, reproduced in Van de Water, 263.

346 **String:** Attorney General Harwell Davis, quoted in Roger K. Newman, 63. **Secure loan, beautiful fee:** Dabney, 304. **Guardian:** Coughlin sermon, CBS Radio, 3/8/31, transcript in MWWP, B4, F: Fruit Industries. **Fruit Punch:** Judge Jr., 48.

347 **Stylish:** Willebrandt, 277. **Because she did it:** Strawbridge to Willebrandt, enclosed in Willebrandt to Donald Conn, 11/29/30, MWWP, B4, F: Fruit Industries. **Meetings:** "Grape Juice Hubbub," *WP*, 11/21/30; Dorothy M. Brown, 184. **Upon my arrival:** press release, 11/13/30, MWWP, B4, F: Fruit Industries.

347 **Bodyguards:** OrH, CWH: Leon Adams, 32. **Compete with Capone's:** "Grape Juice Hubbub," *WP*, 11/21/30. **Effect of this:** Willebrandt to Conn, 11/19/30, MWWP, B4, F: Fruit Industries.

347 **Mabel's Bricks:** United Press dispatch, 11/19/31, in *Oshkosh* (WI) *Daily Northwestern*, 11. **Attempted to bar, Landrith:** *NYT*, 12/9/32, 19; 12/10/32.

348 **Ripe:** *NYT*, 2/13/30. **Drys opposed Norris:** Norris to Mabel Willebrandt, George Norris Papers, 7/17/30. **Kresge withdrew:** Kerr, 265.

348 **Cancel subscriptions:** Justin Steuart to E. H. Cherrington, 7/8/31, in TPP/Cherrington, R68. **Salary, rent:** Scott McBride to Cherrington, 11/30/31, in TPP/Cherrington, R90. **Embarrassed:** McBride to Cherrington, 7/14/31, R90. **Bank:** Kerr, 272–73.

348 **1920, 1933:** Rose, *American*, 60.

349 **Convince markets:** F. L. Allen, *Secret*, 202. **We want:** *NYT*, 9/25/31, 1. **Tax on syrup, twenty-eight million:** Engelmann, *Intemperance*, 200, 138. **Warrantless:** *Taylor v. U.S.*, 1932. **Widely publicized:** Root, 33–34. **Wooden horse:** Davis to Frank R. Lubbock, 7/20/1887, PSdPP, F1023, B1417.

349 **Whiskey dividend, twenty-five brands:** *Fortune,* 11/33, 35–36. **Daughter of alcoholic, disapproved (fn):** Clark, *Deliver,* 203–4; Beasley, 421–24. **Raid (fn):** Cook, 554. **Fade away:** Sinclair, 396. **Barkley:** Scott, 37. **Black:** Roger K. Newman, 125.

350 **Increase Federal:** *NYT,* 10/22/32, 1. **Has been said:** Rose, *American,* 120.

350 **Mrs. Simons:** *Charleston News and Courier,* 3/2/32, 5. **Fine, packed:** *AC,* 3/3/32, 15; 3/4/32, 1.

350 **Post:** Fulton, 50–51. **Pearls:** *Time,* 7/18/32. **No comfort:** Root, 90 *et seq.*

350 **Smoke screen:** Burk, 97. **Colossal scale:** *NYT,* 6/7/32, 1. **Mother's prayers:** Telegram, Upshaw to Rockefeller, 6/8/32, RAC, B41, F442. **Sloan, Firestone:** Ernest Gordon, *Wrecking,* 194. **Jones:** *Baltimore Sun,* 10/30/32, 1.

351 **Century Association:** Minutes, Board of Management, 10/31/32, Century Association Archives. **Whistle:** Louis P. Martini (son of Louis M.), quoted in *Napa Valley Register,* 12/5/93, 1. **Clydesdales:** Plavchan, 217.

352 **Filibuster:** *NYT,* 2/15/33; *Union Signal,* 2/25/33. **Of the twenty-two:** Alan P. Grimes, *Democracy,* 112.

352 **Rented out:** Justin Steuart to E. H. Cherrington, 2/8/33, in TPP/Cherrington, R68.

352 **Coca-Cola Beer:** F. L. Allen, *Secret,* 204–5. **Blanket license:** *Time,* 4/17/33. **Pretty good:** Fecher, 213.

353 **Satan's Seat:** *NYT,* 6/9/32. **Proprietors:** Stanley Walker, 71–72.

353 **McDonough:** *The Rum Rebellion,* published by Iron County Museum, 2/20/70. **Would have remained:** *NYT,* 7/27/38, 17. **Weren't up:** Hoover to Homer Cummings, FBI File 66–11–38–88, cited in John F. Fox.

353 **Devoted army, distinguished:** Everett S. Brown, 298. **Nobody seemed:** Jessup, 476.

353 **Many a white:** Hines, 25.

353 **Grain prices:** *CT,* 7/12/33, 25. **Bronfmans told:** LeFrancois, 59. **973,000:** Andrieux, *Prohibition,* 71. **Not a single:** *St. Helena Star,* 10/13/33.

354 **Marc Antony:** *Salt Lake Tribune,* 12/6/33, 1. **Bootlegger dismissed:** *NYT,* 12/6/33, 1. **Cocktail material:** du Pont to Jouett Shouse, 11/29/33, PSdPP, F1023–1048, B1557.

354 **No alcohol:** Rose, *American,* 132. **Curly-headed:** Burnham, *Bad,* photo section.

Chapter Twenty-one: Afterlives, and the Missing Man

355 **No other:** *SEAP,* 2835. **Tactics:** *NYT,* 11/24/35.

355 **Doran leapt:** *Christian Science Monitor,* 12/5/33. **Dedicated:** Einstein, frontmatter. **If you want:** *NYT,* 6/17/35, 20. **Failed:** Willebrandt to Franklin D. Roosevelt, 3/21/39, Franklin Delano Roosevelt Library, Hyde Park, NY; also see Dorothy M. Brown, 249. **Clients, meaningful, converted:** Dorothy M. Brown, 231, 233, 253.

356 **Mr. Volstead said, anything:** *NYT,* 11/8/33, 17. **Rather be:** Carol L. James, 12.

356 **Traveled more:** Sheppard, xvii. **Last week:** *Time,* 9/4/33. **Repeal of Repeal:** *Liberty* magazine, 12/15/34, 21–25. **Abiding sorrow:** Sen. Theodore G. Bilbo, *CR,* 4/25/41.

356 **Caused many:** *NYT,* 12/7/33, 19. **Ford trucks:** Pierre S. du Pont to William H. Stayton, 2/28/34, PSdPP, F1023–48, B1556.

357 **Diminished:** 1932 WCTU convention proceedings, in TPP/WCTU, R10, 52. **Turned WCTU's:** *DAB, ANB.* **Continued our work:** WCTU of Maryland website, http://www.wctumd.org. **Six hours:** http://www.wctu.org.

357 **Receivership:** Engelmann, *Intemperance,* 223–24. **Riots:** *Liberty,* 12/15/34, 12–15. **Continued to write:** Michael R. McCoy in *DAB.* **Criticized:** Introductory note to James Cannon Papers, Duke University. **Prince Valiant:** Dabney, 333–34.

358 **American Council:** http://www.alcoholproblemswi.org; *American Issue,* April–June 2008.

358 **Number of brewers:** Martin Stack, "A Concise History of America's Brewing Industry," 7/5/03, in Whaples; Baron, 322–23. **A-B logo, eagle, bonds:** McGahan, 261–62. **Deferments:** Burnham, *Bad*, 71.
359 **Sooner eliminated:** Heintz, *Alicante*, 45. **UC–Davis:** OrH, CWH: Harold Olmo, 125.
359 **Driver's seat:** OrH, CWH: Ernest A. Wente, 21. **Million gallons:** *SFC*, 12/6/33, 4W. **Expended:** *St. Helena Star*, 11/24/33. **Prizes:** OrH, CWH: André Tchelistcheff. **Archbishops:** Leon Adams, 309–10.
359 **Four gentlemen, better or worse:** *Fortune*, 11/33, 38; 10/34, 104.
359 **Cortege:** Andrieux, *Prohibition*, 125. **Rossville, slogan, sales:** Marrus, 180, 190, 192.
360 **Conspiracy suit:** Dubro and Rowland, 215. **Sensible argument:** Wesley Frost to Secretary of State, 4/23/35, State Department Archives, 811.114 Canada/4923. **Inbound smuggling:** *Montreal Star*, 110/35; Andrieux, *Prohibition*, 139; Marrus, 206–11.
360 **Fertile brain:** Memorandum, enclosed in "Liability of Bronfman Brothers for United States Income Taxes and Customs Duties," Wesley Frost to Secretary of State, 3/21/35, State Department Archives, 811.114 Canada.
360 **Settlement:** Hull, 206–7; Marrus, 231.
361 **Grateful, nation of Scotch:** Wesley Frost memorandum, as above.
361 **Gun license:** copy of pardon in possession of Berns's daughter, Susan B. Rothchild.
361 **O'Connor:** Leff, 31–32.
361 **9 percent:** Hu, 160–61.
361 **Levy dropped:** Boudreaux, "Thoughts." **Small group, du Pont family:** Wolfskill, 25, 63. **Hobson (fn):** Wolfskill, 58–59.
362 **Members:** Wolfskill, 60, 25. **Stalins:** Beck to H. L. Mencken, 8/7/33, James Montgomery Beck Papers, B5, F24. **Entrenched:** Wolfskill, 146.
362 **Jammed:** *WP*, 1/26/36, M1.
363 **Personal tax bill:** Burk, 67. **Little brother:** Burk, 214; du Pont to L. E. Staplin, 1/16/36, Ser A, F765.
363 **One capital:** *NYT*, 1/26/36. **Noise, evening jacket:** *WP*, 1/26/36, 1.
363 **What have you:** Root, 123. **Canasta:** interview, Pauline Sabin Willis.
364 **Organizing:** Hoopes and Brinkley, 219.
364 **Red Cross:** *ANB*. **Most admired:** Alsop, 267. **Sickness of fear:** *WP*, 5/29/53, 12. **Urged Truman:** *WP*, 6/10/47, 10.
365 **Style icon:** http://www.straight.com. **Straw hat:** *NYT*, 7/15/2003. **Moose Jaw:** *NYT*, 11/16/2004. **What street:** Donaldson and Lampert, 52–57.
366 **Culmination:** Haller, *Bootleggers*, 135.
366 **Bought Somerset:** Beauchamp, 338.
366 *Europa:* Amanda Smith, 108.
366 **Prince:** *Saturday Evening Post*, 7/2/38, 60. **Foster father:** Kennedy to James Roosevelt, 1/8/37, JPKP, B71, F: James Roosevelt. **Met prime ministers, Distillers Company:** *NYT*, 10/12/33, 27; Koskoff, *Kennedy*, 52.
367 **Audience:** *NYT*, 10/24/33, 23. **Agreements:** Amanda Smith, 108. **Permits:** Beauchamp, 332; *NYT*, 6/30/38, 18. **November:** Peter Dewar to Kennedy, 8/7/36, JPKP, B1938, F: Correspondence 1934–1936. In indicating his wish to end his contract with Kennedy, Dewar noted when the shipments had begun. **Haig medicine:** *Saturday Evening Post*, 7/2/38, 60. **$118,000:** *NYT*, 11/19/69, 50.
367 **Trohan article:** *CT*, 1/31/54.
368 **No reason:** My quest for mentions of any Kennedy connections to the bootlegging industry included online searches of digital databases containing the complete text of the following papers: *Atlanta Constitution, Chicago Defender, Chicago Tribune, Los Angeles Times, New York Times, Wall Street Journal,* and *Washington Post*; Elizabeth Tuite, of the *Boston Globe*, conducted a detailed search of that paper's files. I also examined the official records relating to Kennedy's three Sen-

ate confirmations, as well as coverage of the appointments in a varied group of other newspapers.

368   **FBI file:** interview and correspondence, David Nasaw.

369   **Lansky:** Eisenberg, Dan, and Landau, 107–8. **Costello:** John H. Davis, 48–49. **Bonanno:** *WP,* 4/29/83; *60 Minutes,* CBS, 5/1/83. **Drama critic:** David Richards, "'Nick and Nora' By Way of 'Rashomon,'" *NYT,* 12/15/91, H2. **Juror:** *NYT,* 11/1/91, A14.

369   **Gloucester docks:** Goodwin, 442–43. Goodwin does not endorse the veracity of this anecdote; she offers it as an example of unsubstantiated reports about Kennedy's activities. **Spaghetti:** Leamer, 38–40.

370   **Hull letter:** Kessler, 38. **Royal Commission:** Leamer, 38–40. **Eponym:** *NYT,* 5/22/27, XX, 5. **Reifel:** Douglas L. Hamilton, passim. **Waiter:** Robertson, 303.

370   **Remarkable lack, no mention:** Seymour M. Hersh, 47. **Noted scholar:** Ronald B. Weir, correspondence with author; also Weir, *History,* 280.

371   **Sheer magnitude:** Leamer, 41.

Epilogue

373   **2.6 gallons:** Clark Warburton, "Prohibition," in Sills, vol. 12, 507. **1973:** National Institute on Alcohol Abuse and Alcoholism, http://www.niaaa.nih.gov. **Ambassador Hotel:** *New Yorker,* 12/23/33, 41.

374   **Remember the old:** Judge Jr., 27.

374   **Mississippi tax:** *WP,* 1/26/53, B1. **Happy marriage:** Drowne, 48, quoting letter in *Oxford Eagle,* 9/14/50. **Vote dry:** Willie Morris, 54–55.

375   **Booze cruises:** de la Pedraja, 227. **NASCAR:** Hemphill, 84–86. **Bring the Americans:** Craton and Saunders, 263–64. **Montreal to Belize:** Bell, 189.

376   **Bronfman in Tarrytown:** Bronfman interview, Philip Siekman and Ann Tyler, 7/6/66, notes in SMC, B10.

Sources

Manuscript Collections and Other Archival Materials

American Life Histories: Manuscripts from the Federal Writers' Project, 1936–1940, Library of Congress, Washington, DC.

Archdiocese of Northern California Archives, San Francisco.

William Jennings Bryan Papers, Manuscript Division, Library of Congress, Washington, DC.

Emory Buckner Papers, private collection, Baltimore, MD.

Bureau of Alcohol, Tobacco and Firearms Papers, Special Collections, General Library, University of California, Davis.

California Wine History, Bancroft Library, University of California, Berkeley.

Century Association Archives, New York, NY.

Colonial Office Archives, (British) National Archives, Surrey, UK.

Central Registry, Criminal and Civil Files, Archives of Ontario, Toronto.

Louis C. Cramton Papers, Bentley Historical Library, University of Michigan, Ann Arbor.

Cunard Archive, Special Collections and Archives, University of Liverpool Library, Liverpool, UK.

John W. Davis Papers, Yale University Library, New Haven, CT.

Pauline Sabin Davis Papers, Arthur and Elizabeth Schlesinger Library, Harvard University, Cambridge, MA.

De Latour Family Papers, private collection, Rutherford, CA.

William E. Dever Papers, Chicago Historical Society.

John Dewar & Sons Ltd. Archives, Glasgow, UK.

Distillers Corporation Archives, Diageo PLC, London, UK.

Irénée du Pont Papers, Hagley Museum, Wilmington, DE.

Pierre S. du Pont Papers, Hagley Museum, Wilmington, DE.

Foreign Office Archives, (British) National Archives, Surrey, UK.

Fortune editorial files, Time Inc. Archives, New York, NY.

Frankenmuth (MI) Historical Society.

Leo Franklin Archive, Temple Beth El, Detroit, MI.

Josephine F. Gomon Papers, Bentley Historical Library, University of Michigan, Ann Arbor.

Herbert S. Hadley Papers, Western Historical Manuscript Collection, Ellis Library, University of Missouri, Columbia.

Warren G. Harding Papers, Ohio Historical Society, Columbus.

Richmond P. Hobson Papers, Manuscript Division, Library of Congress, Washington, DC.

Herbert Hoover Library, West Branch, IA.

Hyde Family Papers, Carl A. Kroch Library, Cornell University, Ithaca, NY.

Immigration Restriction League, Houghton Library, Harvard University, Cambridge, MA.

Justice Department Archives, National Archives, Washington, DC.
Joseph P. Kennedy Papers, John F. Kennedy Library, Boston, MA.
Henry King Papers, Oberlin College Library, Oberlin, OH.
Clarence Cook Little Papers, Bentley Historical Library, University of Michigan, Ann Arbor.
Clyde McElmore Papers, Montana Historical Society, Helena.
Charles Nagel Papers, Yale University Library, New Haven, CT.
George Norris Papers, Library of Congress, Manuscript Division, Washington, DC.
John J. Raskob Papers, Hagley Museum, Wilmington, DE.
Office of the Messrs. Rockefeller (Welfare Interests—General), Rockefeller Archive Center, Pocantico Hills, NY.
Franklin D. Roosevelt Library, Hyde Park, NY.
Royal Commission on Customs and Excise, Interim Reports 1–10 and Final Report, Library and Archives Canada, Ottawa.
Saskatchewan Archives, Regina and Saskatoon.
Gus Schaffer [Schaefer] Papers, Chicago Historical Society.
Seagram Museum Collection, Hagley Library, Wilmington, DE.
Baroness Spencer-Churchill Papers, Churchill Archives Centre, Cambridge, UK.
State Department Archives, National Archives, Washington, DC.
Harlan Fiske Stone Papers, Jones Library, Amherst, MA.
Temperance and Prohibition Papers, Ohio Historical Society (microfilm).
Arthur J. Tuttle Papers, Bentley Historical Library, University of Michigan, Ann Arbor.
U.S. District Court for the Eastern District of Missouri, National Archives (Central Plains Division), Kansas City, MO.
Vice President of Student Affairs Papers, Bentley Historical Library, University of Michigan, Ann Arbor.
Andrew J. Volstead Papers, Minnesota Historical Society, St. Paul.
James W. Wadsworth Jr. Papers, Manuscript Division, Library of Congress, Washington, DC.
Robin Wheeler Papers, private collection, Bechtelsville, PA.
Mabel Walker Willebrandt Papers, Library of Congress, Manuscript Division, Washington, DC.

Bibliography

Newspapers, magazines, oral histories, websites, and interviews conducted by the author or his associates are cited in the notes. Books, scholarly journal articles, dissertations, and unpublished papers listed here are identified in the notes by author's name.

Adams, Leon. *The Wines of America.* New York: McGraw-Hill, 1985.
Adams, Samuel Hopkins. *Incredible Era: The Life and Times of Warren Gamaliel Harding.* Boston: Houghton Mifflin, 1939.
Addams, Jane. *Forty Years at Hull-House: Being "Twenty Years at Hull-House" and "The Second Twenty Years at Hull-House."* New York: Macmillan, 1935.
———. *The Second Twenty Years at Hull-House: September 1909 to September 1929.* New York: Macmillan, 1930.
Ade, George. *The Old-Time Saloon.* New York: Long & Smith, 1931.
Albini, Joseph. *The American Mafia: Genesis of a Legend.* New York: Appleton Century Crofts, 1971.
Allen, Everett S. *The Black Ships.* Boston: Little, Brown, 1979.
Allen, Frederick Lewis. *Only Yesterday: An Informal History of the 1920's.* New York: Harper & Row, 1931.
———. *Secret Formula: How Brilliant Marketing and Relentless Salesmanship Made Coca-Cola the Best-Known Product in the World.* New York: HarperCollins, 1994.
———. *Since Yesterday: The Nineteen-Thirties in America.* New York: Harper, 1940.

Allsop, Kenneth. *The Bootleggers and Their Era.* Garden City, NY: Doubleday, 1961.
Alsop, Joseph W., with Adam Platt. *I've Seen the Best of It: Memoirs.* New York: Norton, 1992.
Anderson, Margo J. *The American Census: A Social History.* New Haven, CT: Yale University Press, 1988.
Andrews, Allen. *The Whisky Barons.* London: Jupiter Books, 1977.
Andrieux, J. P. *Over the Side.* Lincoln, ON: W. F. Rannie, 1984.
———. *Prohibition and St. Pierre.* Lincoln, ON: W.F. Rannie, 1983.
Angle, Paul. *Bloody Williamson.* New York: Knopf, 1952.
Anthony, Carl Sferrazza. *First Ladies: The Saga of the Presidents' Wives and Their Power, 1789–1961.* New York: HarperPerennial, 1992.
———. *Florence Harding: The First Lady, the Jazz Age, and the Death of America's Most Scandalous President.* New York: Morrow, 1998.
Anti-Saloon League. *The Brewers and Texas Politics.* Vols. 1 and 2. San Antonio: Passing Show Printing, 1916.
———. *Proceedings of the Fifteenth Annual Convention of the Anti-Saloon League of America.* Westerville, OH: 1913.
Aronow, Michael. *Don Aronow: The King of Thunderboat Row.* Fort Lauderdale: Write Stuff Syndicate, 1994.
Asbury, Herbert. *The Great Illusion: An Informal History of Prohibition.* Garden City, NY: Doubleday, 1950.
Ashlee, Laura R. *Traveling Through Time: A Guide to Michigan's Historical Markers.* Ann Arbor: University of Michigan Press, 2005.
Bacon, John U. *America's Corner Store: Walgreens' Prescription for Success.* Hoboken: Wiley, 2004.
Bagby, Wesley. *The Road to Normalcy: The Presidential Campaign of 1920.* Baltimore: Johns Hopkins University Press, 1962.
Baldwin, Hanson. "The End of the Wine Mess." *U.S. Naval Institute Proceedings,* August 1958.
Baldwin, Neil. *Henry Ford and the Jews: The Mass Production of Hate.* New York: PublicAffairs, 2001.
Barnes, Joseph. "Liquor Regulation in Russia." *Annals of American Academy of Political and Social Science,* September 1932.
Barnum, P. T. *The Life of P. T. Barnum.* London: Sampson Low, 1855.
Baron, Stanley. *Brewed in America: A History of Beer and Ale in the United States.* Boston: Little, Brown, 1962.
Barr, Andrew. *Drink: A Social History of America.* New York: Carroll & Graf, 1999.
Barry, John M. *The Great Influenza: The Epic Story of the Deadliest Plague in History.* New York: Viking, 2004.
———. *Rising Tide: The Great Mississippi Flood of 1927 and How It Changed America.* New York: Simon & Schuster, 1997.
Baruch, Bernard M. *Baruch: The Public Years.* New York: Holt, Rinehart and Winston, 1960.
Batterberry, Michael and Ariane. *On the Town in New York: A History of Eating, Drinking and Entertainments from 1776 to the Present.* New York: Scribner, 1973.
Baughman, Ilona. "Italian Food in America or How Prohibition Gave Us the Olive Garden." Paper delivered at Northeast Popular Culture Association meeting, Nashua, NH, Autumn 2006.
Baum, Dan. *Citizen Coors: An American Dynasty.* New York: William Morrow, 2000.
Bear, James A. Jr., and Lucia C. Stanton, eds. *Jefferson's Memorandum Books: Accounts, with Legal Records and Miscellany, 1767–1826.* Princeton, NJ: Princeton University Press, 1997.
Beasley, Maureen, ed. *The Eleanor Roosevelt Encyclopedia.* Westport, CT: Greenwood Press, 2001.
Beatty, Jack. *The Rascal King: The Life and Times of James Michael Curley.* Reading, MA: Addison-Wesley, 1992.

Beauchamp, Cari. *Joseph P. Kennedy Presents: His Hollywood Years.* New York: Knopf, 2009.
Beebe, Lucius. *The Big Spenders.* New York: Doubleday, 1966.
Behr, Edward. *Prohibition: Thirteen Years That Changed America.* New York: Arcade, 1996.
Bell, H. MacLachlan. *Bahamas: Isles of June.* New York: Robert M. McBride, 1934.
Bellow, Saul. *Herzog.* New York: Penguin, 2003.
Bergreen, Laurence. *Capone: The Man and the Era.* New York: Simon & Schuster, 1994.
Billings, John S. *Physiological Aspects of the Liquor Problem.* Boston: Houghton Mifflin, 1903.
Bingay, Malcolm. *Detroit Is My Home Town.* Indianapolis: Bobbs-Merrill, 1946.
Birkenhead, Frederick Edwin Smith, Earl of. *America Revisited.* London: Cassell, 1924.
Blocker, Jack S., Jr. *American Temperance Movements: Cycles of Reform.* Boston: Twayne, 1982.
———. *Retreat from Reform: The Prohibition Movement in the United States, 1890–1913.* Westport, CT: Greenwood, 1976.
———. "Separate Paths: Suffragists and the Women's Temperance Crusade." *Signs: Journal of Women in Culture and Society,* Spring 1985.
Blum, John Morton, ed. *From the Morgenthau Diaries: Years of Crisis, 1928–1938.* Cambridge, MA: The Riverside Press, 1959.
Blumenthal, Ralph. *Stork Club.* New York: Little, Brown, 2000.
Boorstin, Daniel. *The Americans: The Democratic Experience.* New York: Vintage, 1974.
Bordin, Ruth. "'A Baptism of Power and Liberty': The Women's Crusade of 1873–1874." *Ohio History,* Autumn 1978.
———. *Women and Temperance: The Quest for Power and Liberty, 1873–1900.* Philadelphia: Temple University Press, 1981.
Boudreaux, Donald J. "Thoughts on Freedom: Alcohol, Prohibition, and the Revenuers." *The Freeman,* January 2008.
Boudreaux, Donald J., and A. C. Pritchard. "The Price of Prohibition," *Arizona Law Review,* Spring 1994.
Bourgeois, Michael. *All Things Human: Henry Codman Potter and the Social Gospel in the Episcopal Church.* Urbana: University of Illinois Press, 2004.
Braeman, John, Robert H. Bremner, and David Brody, eds. *Change and Continuity in Twentieth-Century America: The 1920's.* Columbus: Ohio State University Press, 1968.
Brault, Jean-Remi. *History of Abercorn, 1929–2004.* Montreal: Editions du Septentrion, 2004.
Bray, James Morgan. "The Impact of Prohibition on Napa Valley Viticulture, 1919–1933." MA thesis, California State University, San Jose, 1974.
Bronfman, Edgar. *Good Spirits: The Making of a Businessman.* New York: Putnam, 1998.
Bronfman, Saidye Rosner. *My Sam: A Memoir by His Wife.* Privately published, 1982.
Brown, Dorothy M. *Mabel Walker Willebrandt: A Study of Power, Loyalty and Law.* Knoxville: University of Tennessee Press, 1984.
Brown, Elizabeth Anne. "The Enforcement of Prohibition in San Francisco, California." MA thesis, University of California, Berkeley, 1948.
Brown, Everett Somerville. *Ratification of the Twenty-first Amendment to the Constitution of the United States.* Ann Arbor: University of Michigan Press, 1938.
Bruere, Martha Bensley. *Does Prohibition Work?* New York: Harper, 1927.
Bryan, William Jennings. *In His Image.* New York: Fleming H. Revell, 1922.
Bryan, William Jennings, and Mary Baird Bryan. *The Memoirs of William Jennings Bryan.* Chicago: John C. Winston, 1925.
Buenker, John D. *The Income Tax and the Progressive Era.* New York: Garland, 1985.
Buenker, John D., John C. Burnham, and Robert M. Crunden. *Progressivism.* Cambridge, MA: Schenkman, 1986.
Bukowski, Douglas. *Big Bill Thompson, Chicago, and the Politics of Image.* Urbana: University of Illinois Press, 1998.
Burk, Robert F. *The Corporate State and the Broker State.* Cambridge, MA: Harvard University Press, 1990.

Burner, David. *Herbert Hoover: A Public Life*. New York: Knopf, 1979.

———. *The Politics of Provincialism: The Democratic Party in Transition, 1928–1932*. New York: Knopf, 1970.

Burnham, John C. *Bad Habits: Drinking, Smoking, Taking Drugs, Gambling, Sexual Misbehavior, and Swearing in American History*. New York: New York University Press, 1993.

———. "The Progressive Era Revolution in American Attitudes Toward Sex," *Journal of American History*, March 1973.

Burns, Eric. *The Spirits of America: A Social History of Alcohol*. Philadelphia: Temple University Press, 2004.

Butler, Smedley Darlington. *The Letters of a Leatherneck, 1898–1931*. Ed. Anne Cipriano Venzon. New York: Praeger, 1992.

Calder, James D. *The Origins and Development of Federal Crime Control Policy*. Westport, CT: Praeger, 1993.

Cannadine, David. *Mellon: An American Life*. New York: Knopf, 2006.

Canney, Donald L. "Rum War: The U.S. Coast Guard and Prohibition." http://www.uscg.mil/History/articles/RumWar.pdf.

Cannon, James, Jr. *Bishop Cannon's Own Story*. Ed. Richard L. Watson Jr. Durham, NC: Duke University Press, 1955.

Carlson, Oliver. *Brisbane: A Candid Biography*. New York: Stackpole, 1937.

Caron, Paul L., ed. *Tax Stories: An In-Depth Look at Ten Leading Federal Income Tax Cases*. New York: Foundation Press, 2003.

Carr, Jess. *The Second Oldest Profession: An Informal History of Moonshining in America*. Radford, VA: Commonwealth Press, 1972.

Carter, Paul A. *Another Part of the Twenties*. New York: Columbia University Press, 1977.

———. *The Decline and Revival of the Social Gospel: Social and Political Liberalism in American Protestant Churches, 1920–1940*. Ithaca, NY: Cornell University Press, 1954.

Cartwright, Gary. *Galveston: A History of the Island*. Fort Worth: Texas Christian University Press, 1998.

Cash, W. J. *The Mind of the South*. New York: Knopf, 1941.

Cather, Willa. *A Lost Lady*. Lincoln: University of Nebraska Press, 2003.

———. *Not Under Forty*. Lincoln: University of Nebraska Press, 1988.

Catt, Carrie Chapman, and Nettie Rogers Shuler. *Woman Suffrage and Politics: The Inner Story of the Suffrage Movement*. New York: Scribner, 1926.

Central Conference of American Rabbis. *Year Book*. Vol. 31. Richmond: CCAR, 1922.

Chalfant, Harry Malcolm. *These Agitators and Their Idea*. Nashville: Cokesbury Press, 1931.

Chandler, Alfred D. Jr., and Stephen Salsbury. *Pierre S. du Pont and the Making of the Modern Corporation*. New York: Harper & Row, 1971.

Chernow, Ron. *Alexander Hamilton*. New York: Penguin Press, 2004.

———. *Titan: The Life of John D. Rockefeller Sr.* New York: Random House, 1998.

Cherrington, Ernest Hurst, ed. *The Anti-Saloon League Year Book 1920: An Encyclopedia of Facts and Figures Dealing with the Liquor Traffic and the Temperance Reform*. Westerville, OH: American Issue, 1921.

———. *Standard Encyclopedia of the Alcohol Problem*. Westerville, OH: American Issue, 1929.

Churchill, Randolph. *Twenty-One Years*. Boston: Houghton Mifflin, 1965.

Clark, Norman H. *Deliver Us from Evil: An Interpretation of American Prohibition*. New York: Norton, 1976.

———. *The Dry Years: Prohibition and Social Change in Washington*. Seattle: University of Washington Press, 1965.

Coben, Stanley. *Rebellion Against Victorianism: The Impetus for Cultural Change in 1920s America*. New York: Oxford University Press, 1991.

Cochran, Thomas C. *The Pabst Brewing Company: The History of an American Business*. New York: New York University Press, 1948.

Coker, Joe L. *Liquor in the Land of the Lost Cause: Southern White Evangelicals and the Prohibition Movement*. Lexington: University Press of Kentucky, 2007.

Coletta, Paolo E. *William Jennings Bryan*. Vol. 3. *Political Puritan*. Lincoln: University of Nebraska Press, 1969.

Conaway, James. *Napa*. Boston: Houghton Mifflin, 1990.

Cook, Blanche Wiesen. *Eleanor Roosevelt: Volume 1, 1884–1933*. New York: Viking, 1992.

Corrigan, John F. "The Prohibition Wave in the South." *American Review of Reviews*, September 1907.

Couvares, Francis G. "Hollywood, Main Street, and the Church: Trying to Censor the Movies Before the Production Code." *American Quarterly*, December 1992.

Cowley, Malcolm. *Exile's Return*. New York: Penguin, 1994.

Craig, Douglas B. *After Wilson: The Struggle for the Democratic Party, 1920–1934*. Chapel Hill: University of North Carolina Press, 1992.

Craton, Michael, and Gail Saunders. *Islanders in the Stream: A History of the Bahamian People*. Vol. 2. Athens: University of Georgia Press, 2000.

Creamer, Robert. *Babe: The Legend Comes to Life*. New York: Simon & Schuster, 1974.

Cronon, E. David, ed. *The Cabinet Diaries of Josephus Daniels: 1913–1921*. Lincoln: University of Nebraska Press, 1963.

Curran, Henry H. *Pillar to Post*. New York: Scribner, 1941.

Curtis, Wayne. *And a Bottle of Rum: A History of the New World in Ten Cocktails*. New York: Crown, 2006.

Dabney, Virginius. *Dry Messiah: The Life of Bishop Cannon*. New York: Knopf, 1949.

Daiches, David. *Scotch Whisky: Its Past and Present*. London: Macmillan, 1969.

Dale, Edgar. *The Content of Motion Pictures*. New York: Macmillan, 1935.

Daniels, Josephus. *The Navy and the Nation: War-Time Addresses*. New York: George H. Doran, 1919.

Darrow, Clarence. *The Story of My Life*. New York: Scribner, 1960.

Davis, John H. *The Kennedys: Dynasty and Disaster, 1848–1983*. New York: McGraw-Hill, 1984.

Davis, Marni. "On the Side of Liquor: American Jews and the Politics of Alcohol, 1870–1936." PhD diss., Emory University, 2006.

Davis, Philip, and Bertha Schwartz, eds. *Immigration and Americanization: Selected Readings*. New York: Ginn, 1920.

Dean, John W. *Warren G. Harding*. New York: Times Books/Henry Holt, 2004.

de la Pedraja, Rene. *A Historical Dictionary of the U.S. Merchant Marine and Shipping Industry: Since the Introduction of Steam*. Westport, CT: Greenwood Press, 1994.

Dictionary of American Biography. New York: Scribner, various editions.

Dictionary of National Biography. Oxford: Oxford University Press, various editions.

Dighe, Ranjit S. "Pierre S. du Pont and the Making of an Anti-Prohibition Activist." Unpublished paper provided by author, State University of New York at Oswego, 2007.

Dixon, Thomas, Jr. *The Clansman*. New York: Doubleday Page, 1905.

———. *The Leopard's Spots*. New York: Doubleday Page, 1902.

Dobyns, Fletcher. *The Amazing Story of Repeal: An Exposé of the Power of Propaganda*. Evanston, IL: Signal Press, 1974.

Donald, David Herbert. *Lincoln*. New York: Simon & Schuster, 1995.

Donaldson, Gerald, and Gerald Lampert. *The Great Canadian Beer Book*. Toronto: McClelland and Stewart, 1975.

Dotson, Jo Ann. "News Coverage by Selected Publications of Prohibition from 16 January 1919 to 16 January 1920." MA thesis, Pennsylvania State University Graduate School of Journalism, 1964.

Douglas, Marjory Stoneman. *The Wide Brim*. Ed. Jack E. Davis. Gainesville: University Press of Florida, 2002.

Dow, Neal. *Reminiscences of Neal Dow*. Portland, ME: Evening Express Publishing Company, 1898.

Downard, William L. *Dictionary of the History of the American Brewing and Distilling Industries*. Westport, CT: Greenwood, 1980.

————. *The Cincinnati Brewing Industry: A Social and Economic History*. Athens: Ohio University Press, 1973.

Downes, Randolph C. *The Rise of Warren Gamaliel Harding, 1865–1920*. Columbus: Ohio State University Press, 1970.

Drescher, Nuala McGann. "The Opposition to Prohibition, 1900–1919: A Social and Institutional Study." PhD diss., University of Delaware, 1964.

Drowne, Kathleen. *Spirits of Defiance: National Prohibition and Jazz Age Literature, 1920–1933*. Columbus: Ohio State University Press, 2005.

Dubro, James, and Robin Rowland. *Undercover: Cases of the RCMP's Most Secret Operative*. Toronto: McClelland and Stewart, 1972.

Duis, Perry R. *The Saloon: Public Drinking in Chicago and Boston, 1880–1920*. Urbana: University of Illinois Press, 1983.

Durant, William Crapo, ed. *Law Observance: Shall the People of the United States Uphold the Constitution?* New York: Durant Award Office, 1929.

Eagles, Charles W. *Democracy Delayed: Congressional Reapportionment and Urban-Rural Conflict in the 1920s*. Athens: University of Georgia Press, 1990.

————. "Urban-Rural Conflict in the 1920s: A Historiographical Assessment," *Historian*, November 1986.

Eastman, Mary F. *The Biography of Dio Lewis*. New York: Fowler & Wells, 1891.

Einstein, Izzy. *Prohibition Agent No. 1*. New York: Frederick A. Stokes, 1932.

Eisenberg, Dennis, Uri Dan, and Eli Landau. *Meyer Lansky: Mogul of the Mob*. New York: Paddington Press, 1979.

Ellis, Edward Robb. *The Epic of New York City*. New York: Coward-McCann, 1966.

Engelmann, Larry. *Intemperance: The Lost War Against Liquor*. New York: Free Press, 1979.

————. "A Separate Peace: The Politics of Prohibition Enforcement in Detroit, 1920–1930." *Detroit in Perspective*, Autumn 1972.

Epstein, Edward Jay. *Agency of Fear*. New York: Verso, 1990.

Fahey, Edmund. *Rum Road to Spokane*. Missoula: University of Montana Publications in History, 1972.

Faith, Nicholas. *The Bronfmans: The Rise and Fall of the House of Seagram*. New York: St. Martin's, 2007.

Fass, Paula S. *The Damned and the Beautiful: American Youth in the 1920's*. New York: Oxford University Press, 1977.

Faulkner, William. *Sanctuary*. New York: Vintage, 1993.

Fausold, Martin L. *James W. Wadsworth, Jr.: The Gentleman from New York*. Syracuse, NY: Syracuse University Press, 1975.

Fecher, Charles A. *Mencken: A Study of His Thought*. New York: Knopf, 1978.

Feightner, Harold C. *150 Years of Brewing in Indiana: The Story of Politics, Prohibition and Patronage*. Indianapolis: N.p., n.d.

Fine, Sidney. *Frank Murphy: The Detroit Years*. Ann Arbor: University of Michigan Press, 1975.

Fisher, Irving. *Prohibition at Its Worst*. New York: Macmillan, 1926.

Fisher, Irving Norton. *My Father Irving Fisher*. New York: Comet Press, 1955.

Fitzgerald, F. Scott. *The Crack-Up*. New York: New Directions, 1993.

————. *The Great Gatsby*. New York: Oxford University Press, 2008.

Flamm, Jerry. *Good Life in Hard Times: San Francisco in the '20s & '30s*. San Francisco: Chronicle, 1999.

Fletcher, Robert S. "The Government of the Oberlin Colony." *Mississippi Valley Historical Review*, September 1933.

Fostle, D. W. *Speedboat*. Mystic, CT: Mystic Seaport Museum, 1988.

Fowler, Gene. *Beau James: The Life and Times of Jimmy Walker*. New York: Viking, 1949.

Fox, John F. "From Watches and Juries to Agents: How Traditional Law Enforcement Boundaries Gave Way to Federal Ones." Unpublished paper, presented at annual meeting of Organization of American Historians, Seattle, 2009.

Frazier, Paul. "Prohibition Philadelphia: Bootleg Liquor and the Failure of Enforcement." PhD diss., State University of New York at Albany, 2001.

Freeman, Douglas Southall. *George Washington: A Biography.* Vol. 5. New York: Scribner, 1952.

Friedel, Frank. *Franklin Delano Roosevelt: The Apprenticeship.* Boston: Little, Brown, 1952.

———. *Franklin Delano Roosevelt: The Ordeal.* Boston: Little, Brown, 1954.

Fuller, Robert C. *Religion and Wine.* Knoxville: University of Tennessee Press, 1996.

Fulton, Crystal S. A. "The Women's Organization for National Prohibition Reform, 1929–1933." MA thesis, University of Western Ontario, 1990.

Furnas, J. C. *The Life and Times of the Late Demon Rum.* New York: Capricorn, 1965.

Garraty, John, and Mark C. Carnes, eds. *American National Biography.* New York: Oxford University Press, online edition.

Gentry, Curt. *J. Edgar Hoover: The Man and the Secrets.* New York: Norton, 2001.

Gilbert, Charles. *American Financing of World War I.* Westport, CT: Greenwood, 1970.

Gilbert, Martin S., ed. *Winston S. Churchill.* Companion Volume 5. Boston: Houghton Mifflin, 1981.

Gilfoyle, Timothy J. *City of Eros: New York City, Prostitution, and the Commercialization of Sex, 1790–1920.* New York: Norton, 1992.

Gjelten, Tom. *Bacardi and the Long Fight for Cuba: The Biography of a Cause.* New York: Viking, 2008.

Goldberg, David J. *Discontented America: The United States in the 1920s.* Baltimore: Johns Hopkins University Press, 1999.

Goldberg, Robert Alan. *Hooded Empire: The Ku Klux Klan in Colorado.* Urbana: University of Illinois Press, 1981.

Golden, Harry. *The Right Time.* New York: Putnam, 1969.

Goodwin, Doris Kearns. *The Fitzgeralds and the Kennedys: An American Saga.* New York: Simon & Schuster, 1986.

Gordon, Ann D., ed. *The Selected Papers of Elizabeth Cady Stanton and Susan B. Anthony: Against an Aristocracy of Sex, 1866–1873.* New Brunswick, NJ: Rutgers University Press, 2000.

Gordon, Ernest. *The Anti-Alcohol Movement in Europe.* New York: Fleming H. Revell, 1913.

———. *The Wrecking of the Eighteenth Amendment.* Francestown, NH: Alcohol Information Press, 1943.

Gould, Lewis L. *Progressives and Prohibitionists: Texas Democrats in the Wilson Era.* Austin: Texas State Historical Association, 1992.

Grace, Fran. *Carry A. Nation: Retelling the Life.* Bloomington: Indiana University Press, 2001.

Grant, B. J. *When Rum Was King.* Fredericton, NB: Gooselane, 1984.

Gray, James H. *Booze: When Whisky Ruled the West.* Toronto: Macmillan, 1972.

———. *The Roar of the Twenties.* Toronto: Macmillan, 1975.

Green, Paul M., and Melvin G. Holl, eds. *The Mayors: The Chicago Political Tradition.* Carbondale: Southern Illinois University Press, 2005.

Grimes, Alan P. *Democracy and the Amendments to the Constitution.* Lexington, MA: Lexington Books, 1978.

———. *The Puritan Ethic and Woman Suffrage.* New York: Oxford University Press, 1967.

Grimes, William. *Straight Up or On the Rocks.* New York: North Point, 2001.

Guetat, Gerald, with Eric Ledru. *Classic Speedboats, 1916–1939.* Trans. James Taylor. Osceola, WI: Motorbooks International, 1997.

Gunther, John. *Taken at the Flood: The Story of Albert D. Lasker.* New York: Harper, 1960.

Gusfield, Joseph R. *Symbolic Crusade: Status Politics and the Temperance Movement.* Chicago and Urbana: University of Illinois Press, 1986.

Hacker, Andrew. *Congressional Districting: The Issue of Equal Representation.* Washington, DC: The Brookings Institution, 1963.

Haller, Mark H. *Bootleggers and American Gambling 1920–1950. Report on the Review of the National Policy Toward Gambling.* Washington, DC: Government Printing Office, 1976.

———. "Philadelphia Bootlegging and the Report of the Special August Grand Jury." *Pennsylvania Magazine of History and Biography*, April 1985.

———. "Urban Crime and Criminal Justice: The Chicago Case." *Journal of American History*, December 1970.

Hamilton, Alexander. *The Works of Alexander Hamilton*. New York: Francis, 1851.

Hamilton, Douglas L. *Sobering Dilemma: A History of Prohibition in British Columbia*. Vancouver: Ronsdale, 2004.

Hamm, Richard F. *Shaping the Eighteenth Amendment: Temperance Reform, Legal Culture, and the Polity, 1880–1920*. Chapel Hill: University of North Carolina Press, 1995.

Handlin, Oscar. *Al Smith and His America*. Boston: Atlantic/Little, Brown, 1958.

Hansen, Ben. *St. Pierre and Miquelon*. Halifax, NS: Nimbus, 1994.

Harvard College. *Class of Ninety-seven Fiftieth Anniversary Report*. Cambridge, MA: Class of 1897, 1947.

———. *Class of 1912 Twenty-fifth Anniversary Report*. Cambridge, MA: Class of 1912, 1937.

———. *Class of 1921 Twenty-fifth Anniversary Report*. Cambridge MA: Class of 1921, 1946.

Hawkes, Ellen. *Blood & Wine: The Unauthorized Story of the Gallo Wine Empire*. New York: Simon & Schuster, 1993.

Hays, Constance L. *The Real Thing: Truth and Power at the Coca-Cola Company*. New York: Random House, 2004.

Heckman, Dayton E. "Prohibition Passes: The Story of the Association Against the Prohibition Amendment." PhD diss., Ohio State University, 1939.

Heimel, Paul W. *Eliot Ness: The Real Story*. Nashville: Cumberland House, 2000.

Heintz, William F. *The Alicante Bouschet Grape and the Alicante Bouschet Wine in California and the United States, 1883–1975*. St. Helena, CA: Napa Valley Wine Library Archives, 1976.

———. *The Beaulieu Winery, Rutherford, California: A Brief Historical Study, 1890–1950*. St. Helena, CA: Napa Valley Wine Library Archives, 1974.

———. *California's Napa Valley: One Hundred Sixty Years of Wine Making*. San Francisco: Scottwall, 1999.

———. *The Simi Winery: A Narrative History*. St. Helena, CA: Napa Valley Wine Library Archives, 1972.

Hemingway, Ernest. *The Sun Also Rises*. New York: Scribner, 2006.

Hemphill, Paul. *Wheels: A Season on NASCAR's Winston Cup Circuit*. New York: Simon & Schuster, 1976.

Hennings, Robert E. "California Politics in the Period of Republican Ascendancy." *Pacific Historical Review*, August 1962.

Hernon, Peter, and Terry Ganey. *Under the Influence: The Unauthorized Story of the Busch Dynasty*. New York: Avon, 1992.

Hersh, Burton. *The Mellon Family: A Fortune in History*. New York: Morrow, 1978.

Hersh, Seymour M. *The Dark Side of Camelot*. Boston: Back Bay Books, 1998.

Hicks, Brian. *When the Dancing Stopped: The Real Story of the Morro Castle Disaster and Its Deadly Wake*. New York: Free Press, 2006.

Higham, John. *Strangers in the Land: Patterns of American Nativism 1860–1925*. New York: Atheneum, 1970.

Hillje, John Wylie. "The Progressive Movement and the Graduated Income Tax, 1913–1919." PhD diss., University of Texas, 1966.

Hines, Tom S., Jr. "Mississippi and the Repeal of Prohibition." *Journal of Mississippi History*, January 1962.

Hinton, Harold B. *Cordell Hull: A Biography*. Garden City, NY: Doubleday Doran, 1942.

Hirschfeld, Al, and Gordon Kahn. *The Speakeasies of 1932*. Milwaukee: Glenn Young, 2003.

Hobson, Richmond Pearson. *Alcohol and the Human Race*. New York: Fleming H. Revell, 1919.

————. *Buck Jones at Annapolis*. New York: Appleton, 1907.

Hofstadter, Richard. *The Age of Reform: From Bryan to F.D.R.* New York: Vintage, 1955.

————. *Anti-Intellectualism in American Life*. New York: Vintage, 1963.

Hogan, Charles Marshall. "Wayne B. Wheeler: Single Issue Exponent." PhD diss., University of Cincinnati, 1986.

Hoopes, Townsend, and Douglas Brinkley. *Driven Patriot: The Life and Times of James Forrestal*. New York: Knopf, 1992.

Hoover, Herbert. *The Memoirs of Herbert Hoover: The Cabinet and the Presidency, 1920–1933*. New York: Macmillan, 1952.

Hu, T. Y. *The Liquor Tax in the United States, 1791–1947: A History of the Internal Revenue Taxes Imposed on Distilled Spirits by the Federal Government*. New York: Columbia Graduate School of Business, 1950.

Hull, Cordell. *The Memoirs of Cordell Hull*. New York: Macmillan, 1948.

Igglesden, Sir Charles. *A Mere Englishman in America*. Ashford, UK: Kentish Express Office, 1930.

Irey, Elmer. "A Narrative Briefly Descriptive of the Period 1919 to 1936, for the IRS Commissioner, Bureau of Internal Revenue, Guy T. Helvering." Internal Revenue Service, http://www.irs.gov/pub/irs-utl.

————. *The Tax Dodgers: The Inside Story of the T-Men's War with America's Political and Underworld Hoodlums*. New York: Greenberg, 1948.

Isaac, Paul E. *Prohibition and Politics: Turbulent Decades in Tennessee, 1885–1920*. Knoxville: University of Tennessee Press, 1965.

Jackson, Kenneth T. *The Ku Klux Klan in the City, 1915–1930*. New York: Oxford University Press, 1967.

James, Carol L. "Andrew J. Volstead: A Summary of Research." Unpublished paper, 1978, in Andrew J. Volstead Papers, Minnesota Historical Society.

James, Edward T., Janet Wilson James, and Paul Boyer, eds. *Notable American Women, 1607–1950: A Biographical Dictionary*. Cambridge, MA: Belknap/Harvard University Press, 2004.

Jellinek, E. M. *Recent Trends in Alcoholism and in Alcohol Consumption*. New Haven, CT: Hillhouse Press, 1947.

Jessup, Philip C. *Elihu Root*. Vol. 2. New York: Dodd Mead, 1938.

Jimerson, Randall C., Francis X. Blouin, and Charles A. Isetts. *Guide to the Microfilm Edition of Temperance and Prohibition Papers*. Ann Arbor: University of Michigan, 1977.

Johns, Bud. *The Ombibulous Mr. Mencken*. San Francisco: Synergistic Press, 1968.

Johnson, R. K. *Builder of Bridges: The Biography of Bob Jones, Sr.* Murfreesboro, TN: Sword of the Lord, 1969.

Johnson, William E. "Pussyfoot." *Ten Years of Prohibition in Oklahoma*. Westerville, OH: American Issue, 1918.

Jones, Bartlett Campbell. "The Debate Over National Prohibition, 1920–1933." PhD diss., Emory University, 1962.

Joselit, Jenna Weissman. *Our Gang: Jewish Crime and the New York Jewish Community, 1920–1940*. Bloomington: Indiana University Press, 1983.

Jowitt, Garth. *Film: The Democratic Art*. Boston: Little, Brown, 1976.

"Judge Jr." *Noble Experiments*. New York: John Day, 1930.

Kaytor, Marilyn. *"21": The Life and Times of New York's Favorite Club*. New York: Viking, 1975.

Kazin, Michael. *A Godly Hero: The Life of William Jennings Bryan*. New York: Knopf, 2006.

Keller, Morton. *In Defense of Yesterday: James M. Beck and the Politics of Conservatism*. New York: Coward-McCann, 1958.

Kennedy, David M. *Freedom from Fear: The American People in Depression and War, 1929–1945*. New York: Oxford University Press, 1999.

————. *Over Here: The First World War and American Society*. Oxford: Oxford University Press, 1980.

————, ed. *Progressivism: The Critical Issues*. Boston: Little Brown, 1971.

Kerr, K. Austin. *Organized for Prohibition: A New History of the Anti-Saloon League*. New Haven, CT: Yale University Press, 1985.

Kessler, Ronald. *The Sins of the Father: Joseph P. Kennedy and the Dynasty He Founded*. New York: Warner, 1996.

Kessner, Thomas. *Fiorello H. La Guardia and the Making of Modern New York*. New York: McGraw-Hill, 1989.

Kingsdale, Jon M. "The 'Poor Man's Club': Social Functions of the Urban Working-Class Saloon." *American Quarterly*, October 1973.

Kobler, John. *Ardent Spirits: The Rise and Fall of Prohibition*. New York: Da Capo, 1973.

Koskoff, David E. *Joseph P. Kennedy: A Life and Times*. Englewood Cliffs, NJ: Prentice-Hall, 1974.

————. *The Mellons*. New York: Crowell, 1978.

Kottman, Richard N. "Volstead Violated: Prohibition as a Factor in Canadian-American Relations." *Canadian Historical Review*, June 1962.

Krebs, Roland. *Making Friends Is Our Business: 100 Years of Anheuser-Busch*. St. Louis: Anheuser-Busch, 1953.

Kyvig, David E. *Daily Life in the United States, 1920–1940*. Chicago: Ivan R. Dee, 2004.

————. *Explicit and Authentic Acts, 1776–1995*. Lawrence: University Press of Kansas, 1996.

————. *Repealing National Prohibition*. Kent, OH: Kent State University Press, 1979.

————, ed. *Law, Alcohol, and Order: Perspectives on National Prohibition*. Westport, CT: Greenwood, 1985.

Lacey, Robert. *Little Man: Meyer Lansky and the Gangster Life*. Boston: Little, Brown, 1991.

Lamme, Margot Opdycke. "The Campaign Against the Second Edition of Hell: An Examination of the Messages and Methods of the Anti-Saloon League." PhD diss., University of Alabama, 2002.

Langley, John W. *They Tried to Crucify Me, or: The Smoke-Screen of the Cumberlands*. Pikeville, KY: John W. Langley, 1929.

Lapsley, James T. *Bottled Poetry: Napa Winemaking from Prohibition to the Modern Era*. Berkeley: University of California Press, 1996.

Lardner, Ring, Jr. *The Lardners*. New York: Harper & Row, 1976.

Laster, Judy. "An Oral History of Brunswick During Prohibition," student paper, Bowdoin College, December 1980.

Leamer, Laurence. *The Kennedy Men: 1901–1963, The Laws of the Father*. New York: Morrow, 2001.

Leary, David T. "Winston S. Churchill in California." *California History*, Winter 2001.

Leary, William M., Jr. "At the Dawn of Commercial Aviation: Inglis M. Uppercu and Aeromarine Airways." *Business History Review*, Summer 1979.

LeBeau, Bryan F. "Art in the Parlor: Consumer Culture and Currier and Ives." *The Journal of American Culture*, March 2007

Leff, Mark H. *The Limits of Symbolic Reform: The New Deal and Taxation, 1933–1939*. Cambridge: Cambridge University Press, 1934.

LeFrancois, Thierry. *La Prohibition et St.-Pierre et Miquelon*. La Rochelle, France: Musée du Nouveau Monde, 1991.

Leighton, Isabel, ed. *The Aspirin Age: 1919–1941*. New York: Simon & Schuster, 1949.

Lender, Mark E. *Dictionary of American Temperance Biography*. Westport, CT: Greenwood, 1984.

Lender, Mark Edward, and James Kirby Martin. *Drinking in America: A History*. New York: Free Press, 1987.

Lerner, Michael. *Dry Manhattan*. Cambridge, MA: Harvard University Press, 2007.

————. "Dry Manhattan: Class, Culture, and Politics in Prohibition-Era New York City, 1919–1933." PhD diss., New York University, 1999.

Leuchtenberg, William E. *Franklin D. Roosevelt and the New Deal*. New York: Harper & Row, 1963.

————. *The Perils of Prosperity.* Chicago: University of Chicago Press, 1993.

Levine, Lawrence W. *Defender of the Faith: William Jennings Bryan: The Last Decade, 1915–1925.* New York: Oxford University Press, 1965.

Lewis, Sinclair. *Babbitt.* New York: Harcourt Brace, 1922.

Lichtman, Allan J. *Prejudice and the Old Politics: The Presidential Election of 1928.* Chapel Hill: University of North Carolina Press, 1979.

Liebling, A. J. *Between Meals.* New York: Modern Library, 1995.

Lindberg, Richard C. *To Serve and Collect: Chicago Politics from the Lager Beer Riot to the Summerdale Scandal.* New York: Praeger, 1991.

Link, Arthur S. "What Happened to the Progressive Movement in the 1920's?" *American Historical Review,* July 1959.

Lippmann, Walter. *Men of Destiny.* New York: Macmillan, 1927.

Lippy, Charles H., and Peter Williams, eds. *Encyclopedia of the American Religious Experience.* New York: Scribner, 1988.

Lockhart, Sir Robert Bruce. *Scotch: The Whisky of Scotland in Fact and Story.* London: Putnam, 1970.

London, Jack. *John Barleycorn.* New York: Oxford University Press, 1998.

Longworth, Alice Roosevelt. *Crowded Hours.* New York: Arno, 1980.

Lopata, Roy H. "John J. Raskob: A Conservative Businessman in the Age of Roosevelt." PhD diss., University of Delaware, 1975.

Lord, Walter. *The Good Years: From 1900 to the First World War.* New York: Harper, 1960.

Lowitt, Richard. *George W. Norris: The Persistence of a Progressive, 1913–1933.* Urbana: University of Illinois Press, 1971.

Lusk, Rufus S. "The Drinking Habit." *Annals of the American Academy of Political Science,* September 1932.

Lynd, Robert S., and Helen Merrell Lynd. *Middletown.* New York: Harcourt Brace, 1957.

Lythgoe, Gertrude C. *The Bahama Queen.* New York: Exposition Press, 1964.

MacLean, Nancy. *Behind the Mask of Chivalry: The Making of the Second Ku Klux Klan.* New York: Oxford University Press, 1994.

Marrus, Michael R. *Samuel Bronfman: The Life and Times of Seagram's Mr. Sam.* Hanover, NH: Brandeis University Press/University Press of New England, 1991.

Marryat, Frederick. *A Diary in America.* Second pt., vol. 1. London: Longman, 1839, at Google Books.

Mason, Alpheus T. *Harlan Fiske Stone: Pillar of the Law.* New York: Viking, 1956.

————. *William Howard Taft: Chief Justice.* New York: Simon & Schuster, 1975.

Mason, Philip P. *Rumrunning and the Roaring Twenties.* Detroit: Wayne State University Press, 1995.

Maxtone-Graham, John. *The Only Way to Cross.* New York: Macmillan, 1972.

May, Henry F. *The End of American Innocence: The First Years of Our Own Time, 1912–1917.* New York: Knopf, 1969.

May, Lary. *Screening Out the Past: The Birth of Mass Culture and the American Motion Picture Industry.* New York: Oxford University Press, 1980.

Mayer, Martin. *Emory Buckner.* New York: Harper & Row, 1968.

McAdoo, William G. *Crowded Years.* Boston: Houghton Mifflin, 1931.

McCoy, Donald R. *Calvin Coolidge: The Quiet President.* New York: Macmillan, 1967.

McDonough, Eileen L., and H. Douglas Price. "Woman Suffrage in the Progressive Era: Patterns of Opposition and Support in Referenda Voting, 1910–1918." *American Political Science Review,* June 1985.

McGahan, A. M. "The Emergence of the National Brewing Oligopoly: Competition in the American Market, 1933–1958." *Business History Review,* Summer 1991.

McGeary, M. Nelson. *Gifford Pinchot: Forester, Politician.* Princeton, NJ: Princeton University Press, 1960.

McGill, Ralph. *The South and the Southerner.* Boston: Little, Brown, 1959.

McLaughlin, Andrew Cyrus. "Satire as a Weapon Against Prohibition, 1920–1928: Expression of a Cultural Conflict." PhD diss., Stanford University, 1969.

McVeigh, Rory. "Power Devaluation, the Ku Klux Klan, and the Democratic National Convention of 1924." *Sociological Forum*, March 2001.

Mee, Charles L. *The Ohio Gang: The World of Warren G. Harding*. New York: M. Evans, 1981.

Mehrotra, Ajay K. "Creating the Modern Fiscal State: The Political Economy of U.S. Tax Policy 1880–1930." PhD diss., University of Chicago, 2003.

Melendy, Royal L. "The Saloon in Chicago, II." *American Journal of Sociology*, January 1901.

Mellon, Paul. *Reflections in a Silver Spoon*. New York: Morrow, 1992.

Mencken, H. L. *The American Language*. Supplement 1. New York: Knopf, 1945.

———. *Heathen Days*. New York: Knopf, 1943.

———. *My Life as Author and Editor*. New York: Knopf, 1993.

Meriwether, Lee. *Jim Reed, Senatorial Immortal*. Webster Groves, MO: International Mark Twain Society, 1948.

Merz, Charles. *The Dry Decade*. Garden City, NY: Doubleday Doran, 1931.

Metcalfe, Philip. *Whispering Wires: The Tragic Tale of an American Bootlegger*. Portland, OR: Inkwater Press, 2007.

Mezvinsky, Norton. "The White Ribbon Reform: 1870–1920." PhD diss., University of Wisconsin, 1971.

Michie, Allan A., and Frank Ryhlick. *Dixie Demagogues*. New York: Vanguard, 1969.

Migdol, Gary. *Stanford: Home of Champions*. Champaign, IL: Sports Publishing, 1997.

Miller, Nathan. *New World Coming: The 1920s and the Making of Modern America*. Cambridge, MA: Da Capo, 2003.

Miron, Jeffrey A., and Jeffrey Zwiebel. "Alcohol Consumption During Prohibition." *American Economic Review*, May 1991.

Mitchell, Franklin D. *Embattled Democracy: Missouri Democratic Politics, 1919–1932*. Columbia: University of Missouri Press, 1968.

Monahan, M., ed. *A Text-Book of True Temperance*. New York: United States Brewers' Association, 1911.

Monteval, Marion [Edgar Fuller]. *The Klan Inside Out*. Westport, CT: Negro Universities Press, 1970.

Moore, Leonard Joseph. "White Protestant Nationalism in the 1920's." PhD diss., UCLA, 1985.

Moore, Stephen T. "Defining the 'Undefended': Canadians, Americans and the Multiple Meanings of Border During Prohibition." *American Review of Canadian Studies*, Spring 2004.

Moquin, Wayne, with Charles Van Doren, eds. *The American Way of Crime: A Documentary History*. New York: Praeger, 1976.

Moray, Alastair. *The Diary of a Rum-Runner*. London: Philip Allan, 1929.

Morison, Elting Elmore, and John Morton Blum, eds. *The Letters of Theodore Roosevelt*. Vols. 1–8. Cambridge, MA: Harvard University Press, 1951.

Morone, James A. *Hellfire Nation: The Politics of Sin in American History*. New Haven, CT: Yale University Press, 2003.

Morris, Edmund B. *The Rise of Theodore Roosevelt*. New York: Ballantine, 1979.

Morris, Willie. *North Toward Home*. New York: Macmillan, 1968.

Murchison, Kenneth M. *Federal Criminal Law Doctrines: The Forgotten Influence of National Prohibition*. Durham: Duke University Press, 1994.

Murdock, Catherine Gilbert. *Domesticating Drink: Women, Men, and Alcohol in America, 1870–1940*. Baltimore: Johns Hopkins University Press, 1998.

Murphy, Mary. "Bootlegging Mothers and Drinking Daughters: Gender and Prohibition in Butte, Montana." *American Quarterly*, June 1994.

Murray, Robert K. *The Harding Era: Warren G. Harding and His Administration*. Minneapolis: University of Minnesota Press, 1969.

———. *The 103rd Ballot*. New York: Harper & Row, 1976.

Myers, Gustavus. *History of Bigotry in the United States*. New York: Capricorn, 1960.

Napa Valley Wine Library. *History of Napa Valley: Interviews and Reminiscences of Long-Time Residents*. St. Helena, CA: n.d.

Nation, Carry A. *The Uses and Need of the Life of Carry A. Nation*. Topeka: F. M. Steves, 1905.

Nelli, Humbert. *The Business of Crime*. New York: Oxford University Press, 1976.

Nemec, David. *The Beer & Whiskey League*. Guilford, CT: Lyons, 2004.

Neumann, Caryn E. "The End of Gender Solidarity: The History of the Women's Organization for National Prohibition Reform in the United States, 1929–1933." *Journal of Women's History*, Summer 1997.

Newman, Peter C. *Bronfman Dynasty*. Toronto: McClelland and Stewart/Bantam, 1978.

Newman, Roger K. *Hugo Black: A Biography*. New York: Pantheon, 1994.

Nicolson, Harold. *Curzon: The Last Phase*. London: Constable, 1934.

Norris, George W. *Fighting Liberal: The Autobiography of George W. Norris*. New York: Macmillan, 1945.

O'Connor, Richard. *Heywood Broun*. New York: Putnam, 1975.

Odegard, Peter H. *Pressure Politics: The Story of the Anti-Saloon League*. New York: Columbia University Press, 1928.

O'Hara, John. *Appointment in Samarra*. New York: Bantam, 1966.

———. *Sermons and Soda-Water*. New York: Random House, 1960.

Oney, Steve. *And the Dead Shall Rise: The Murder of Mary Phagan and the Lynching of Leo Frank*. New York: Pantheon, 2003.

Ontario: Six Years Dry. Toronto: The Dominion Alliance, 1922.

O'Toole, Patricia. *When Trumpets Call: Theodore Roosevelt After the White House*. New York: Simon & Schuster, 2005.

Overton, Grant, ed. *Mirrors of the Year: 1926–1927*. New York: Frederick A. Stokes, 1927.

Patterson, Michael S. "The Fall of a Bishop: James Cannon, Jr., Versus Carter Glass, 1909–1934." *Journal of Southern History*, November 1973.

Pearson, Drew ["Anonymous"]. *More Merry-Go-Round*. New York: Liveright, 1932 .

———. *Washington Merry-Go-Round*. New York: Blue Ribbon, 1931.

Pegram, Thomas R. *Battling Demon Rum: The Struggle for a Dry America, 1800–1933*. Chicago: Ivan R. Dee, 1998.

Pendergrast, Mark. *For God, Country and Coca-Cola: The Unauthorized History of the Great American Soft Drink and the Company That Makes It*. New York: Collier, 1993.

Pepper, George Wharton. *Philadelphia Lawyer*. Philadelphia: Lippincott, 1944.

Pfeifer, Michael James. *Rough Justice: Lynching and American Society, 1874–1947*. Urbana: University of Illinois Press, 2004.

Pickett, Deets, Clarence True Wilson, and Ernest Dailey Smith. *Cyclopedia of Temperance, Prohibition and Public Morals*. New York: Methodist Book Concern, 1917.

Pinney, Thomas. *A History of Wine in America*. Vol. 2. *From Prohibition to the Present*. Berkeley: University of California Press, 2007.

Pittman, Walter E., Jr. *Navalist and Progressive: The Life of Richmond P. Hobson*. Manhattan, KS: MA/AH Publishing, 1981.

———. "Richmond P. Hobson, Crusader." PhD diss., University of Georgia, 1967.

Plavchan, Ronald Jan. *A History of Anheuser-Busch, 1852–1933*. New York: Arno, 1976.

Pollan, Michael. *The Botany of Desire: A Plant's-Eye View of the World*. New York: Random House, 2001.

Post, Robert. "Federalism, Positive Law, and the Emergence of the American Administrative State: The Case of Prohibition in the Taft Court Era." Draft chapter provided by author, Yale University Law School.

Potter, Ryan A. "Enforcing National Prohibition Along the Detroit River, 1920–1933." MA thesis, Eastern Michigan University, 2000.

Powe, Lucas A., Jr. *The Warren Court and American Politics*. Cambridge, MA: Harvard University Press, 2000.

Powers, Madelon. *Faces Along the Bar: Lore and Order in the Workingman's Saloon, 1870–1920*. Chicago: University of Chicago Press, 1998.

Pratt, Julius W. *Cordell Hull: 1933–44*. Vol. 1. New York: Cooper Square Publishers, 1964.

Prince, Therese Lefebvre. *The Whiskey Man: The Balmoral Hotel–Bronfman Saga*. Yorkton, SK: Yorkton Municipal Heritage Sub-Commission, 2003.

Raab, Selwyn. *Five Families*. New York: St. Martin's, 2005.

Randall, Emilius Oviatt, and Daniel Joseph Ryan. *History of Ohio: The Rise and Progress of an American State*. Vol. 4. New York: Century, 1912.

Ransom, Jay Ellis. "Country Schoolma'am." *Oregon Historical Quarterly*, Summer 1985.

Reddig, William M. *Tom's Town: Kansas City and the Pendergast Legend*. Philadelphia: Lippincott, 1947.

Reed, James A. *The Rape of Temperance*. New York: Cosmopolitan Book, 1931.

Reeves, Ira L. *Ol' Rum River*. Chicago: Rockwell, 1931.

Riis, Jacob A. *The Battle with the Slum*. New York: Macmillan, 1902.

———. *How the Other Half Lives: Studies Among the Tenements of New York*. New York: Scribner, 1890.

Robertson, Terence. "Bronfman: The Life and Times of Samuel Bronfman, Esq." Unpublished ms., 1969, in Seagram Museum Collection.

Robinson, Geoff, and Dorothy Robinson. *It Came by the Boatload: Essays on Rum-Running*. N.p.: Self-published, 1972.

Rockaway, Robert A. *But He Was Good to His Mother: The Lives and Crimes of Jewish Gangsters*. Jerusalem: Gefen, 2000.

Room, Robin. "The Movies and the Wettening of America: The Media as Amplifiers of Social Change." *British Journal of Addiction*, January 1988.

Root, Grace C. *Women and Repeal: The Story of the Women's Organization for National Prohibition Reform*. New York: Harper, 1934.

Rorabaugh, W. J. *The Alcoholic Republic: An American Tradition*. New York: Oxford University Press, 1979.

Rose, Kenneth D. *American Women and the Repeal of Prohibition*. New York: New York University Press, 1996.

———. "'Dry' Los Angeles and Its Liquor Problems in 1924." *Southern California Quarterly*, Spring 1987.

Rosenbaum, Betty B. "The Urban-Rural Conflict as Evidenced in the Reapportionment Situation." *Social Forces*, March 1934.

Rosenfeld, Harvey. *Richmond Pearson Hobson: Naval Hero of Magnolia Grove*. Las Cruces, NM: Yucca Tree Press, 2001.

Rosenthal, Michael. *Nicholas Miraculous: The Amazing Career of the Redoubtable Nicholas Murray Butler*. New York: Farrar, Straus, and Giroux, 2006.

Roueche, Berton. *The Neutral Spirit: A Portrait of Alcohol*. Boston: Little, Brown, 1960.

Rumbarger, John J. *Profits, Power, and Prohibition: Alcohol Reform and the Industrializing of America, 1800–1930*. Albany: State University of New York Press, 1989.

Runyon, Damon. *Guys and Dolls*. New York: Frederick A. Stokes, 1931.

Russell, Francis. *The Shadow of Blooming Grove: Warren G. Harding in His Times*. New York: McGraw-Hill, 1968.

Salvatore, Nick. *Eugene V. Debs: Citizen and Socialist*. Urbana: University of Illinois Press, 1982.

Sanders, Matthew J. "An Introduction to Phoebe Wilson Couzins." Unpublished final paper for "Women in the Legal Profession," Stanford University, 2000.

Sann, Paul. *The Lawless Decade: A Pictorial History of a Great American Transition: From the World War I Armistice and Prohibition to Repeal and the New Deal*. New York: Crown, 1957.

Schlesinger, Arthur M. *The American as Reformer*. Cambridge, MA: Harvard University Press, 1968.

Schmeckebier, Laurence F. *Congressional Apportionment*. Washington, DC: Brookings Institution, 1941.

Schmidt, Hans. *Maverick Marine: General Smedley D. Butler and the Contradictions of American Military History*. Lexington: University Press of Kentucky, 1998.

Schmidt, John R. *The Mayor Who Cleaned Up Chicago: A Political Biography of William E. Dever*. DeKalb: Northern Illinois University Press, 1989.

Schwarz, Jeffrey A. "'The Saloon Must Go, and I Will Take It with Me': American Prohibition, Nationalism, and Expatriation in *The Sun Also Rises*." *Studies in the Novel*, Summer 2001.

Schwarz, Jordan A. *Interregnum of Despair*. Urbana: University of Illinois Press, 1970.

Scott, William Rufus. *Revolt on Mount Sinai: The Puritan Retreat from Prohibition*. Pasadena: Self-published, 1944.

Seldes, Gilbert. *The Stammering Century*. Gloucester, MA: Peter Smith, 1971.

Sellers, James B. *The Prohibition Movement in Alabama, 1702–1943*. Chapel Hill: University of North Carolina Press, 1943.

Seltzer, Lawrence Howard, Selma F. Goldsmith, and M. Slade Kendrick. *The Nature and Treatment of Capital Gains and Losses*. National Bureau of Economic Research, 1951, available at http://www.nber.org/chapters/c4485.

Sexton, Robert Fenimore. "Kentucky Politics and Society: 1919–1932." PhD diss., University of Washington, 1970.

Shaw, Barton C. "The Hobson Craze," *U.S. Naval Institute Proceedings*, February 1976.

Sheaffer, Louis. *O'Neill: Son and Artist*. Boston: Little, Brown, 1973.

Sheldon, Richard N. "Richmond Pearson Hobson as a Progressive Reformer." *Alabama Review*, October 1972.

———. "Richmond P. Hobson: The Military Hero as Reformer During the Progressive Era." PhD diss., University of Arizona, 1970.

Sheppard, Morris. *What Shakespeare Says About It: More Than Four Thousand Comments of Shakespeare on Subjects of General Interest*. N.p.: Privately published, 1935.

Shindler, Colin. *Hollywood in Crisis: Cinema and American Society, 1929–1939*. London: Routledge, 1996.

Shughart, William F. II. *Taxing Choice: The Predatory Politics of Fiscal Discrimination*. New Brunswick, NJ: Transaction, 1997.

Sills, David, ed. *International Encyclopedia of Social Sciences*. New York: Free Press, 1968.

Silverman, Joan L. "The Birth of a Nation: Prohibition Propaganda." *Southern Quarterly*, Spring/Summer 1987.

Simon, Bryant. "The Appeal of Cole Blease of South Carolina: Race, Class and Sex in the New South," *Journal of Southern History*, February 1996.

Sinclair, Andrew. *Era of Excess: A Social History of the Prohibition Movement*. New York: Harper Colophon, 1964.

Sinclair, Upton. *The Jungle*. http://www.online-literature.com.

Slanders Against Prohibition Refuted. Baltimore: Manufacturers Record, 1925.

Slosson, Preston William. *The Great Crusade and After, 1914–1928*. New York: Macmillan, 1931.

Smith, Amanda, ed. *Hostage to Fortune: The Letters of Joseph P. Kennedy*. New York: Viking, 2001.

Smith, Rod. *Private Reserve: Beaulieu Vineyard and the Rise of Napa Valley*. Stamford, CT: Daglan Press, 2000.

Spinelli, Lawrence. *Dry Diplomacy: The United States, Great Britain and Prohibition*. Wilmington, DE: SR Books, 1989.

Sprecher, Hannah. "'Let Them Drink and Forget Our Poverty': Orthodox Rabbis React to Prohibition." *American Jewish Archives*, Fall/Winter 1991.

Starling, Edmund W. *Starling of the White House*. New York: Simon & Schuster, 1946.

Steffens, Lincoln. *Autobiography*. New York: Harcourt Brace, 1931.

Steuart, Justin. *Wayne Wheeler, Dry Boss*. Westport, CT: Greenwood, 1971.

Stoll, Horatio F. *Wine-Wise: A Popular Handbook on How to Correctly Judge, Keep, and Store Wines*. San Francisco: H. S. Crocker, 1933.

Stowell, Charles H. *The Essentials of Health*. Boston: Silver Burdett, 1892.

Stuntz, William J. "Self-Defeating Crimes." *Virginia Law Review*, November 2000.

Suitts, Steve. *Hugo Black of Alabama: How His Roots and Early Career Shaped the Great Champion of the Constitution*. Montgomery, AL: New South, 2005.

Sullivan, Charles L. *A Companion to California Wine*. Berkeley: University of California Press, 1998.

———. *Napa Wine: A History from Mission Days to Present*. San Francisco: Wine Appreciation Guild, 1994.

Susman, Warren. *Culture as History: The Transformation of American Society in the Twentieth Century*. New York: Pantheon, 1984.

Sweeting, Orville J. "John Q. Tilson and the Reapportionment Act of 1929," *Western Political Quarterly*, June 1956.

Tapson, Alfred J. "The Sutler and the Soldier." *Military Affairs*, Winter 1957.

Tchudi, Stephen N. *Soda Poppery: The History of Soft Drink in America*. New York: Scribner, 1986.

Terkel, Studs. *Hard Times*. New York: Pantheon, 1970.

Thompson, William Norman. *Gambling in America: An Encyclopedia of History, Issues, and Society*. Santa Barbara, CA: ABC-CLIO, 2001.

Thornton, Mark. *The Economics of Prohibition*. Salt Lake City: University of Utah Press, 1991.

Timberlake, James H. *Prohibition and the Progressive Movement, 1900–1920*. New York: Atheneum, 1970.

Tribble, Edwin, ed. *A President in Love: The Courtship Letters of Woodrow Wilson and Edith Bolling Galt*. Boston: Houghton Mifflin, 1981.

Tucker, Kenneth. *Eliot Ness and the Untouchables: The Historical Reality and the Film and Television Depictions*. Jefferson, NC: McFarland, 2000.

Tumulty, Joseph P. *Woodrow Wilson as I Knew Him*. Garden City, NY: Garden City Publishing Company, 1925.

Turner, John. "State Purchase of the Liquor Trade in the First World War." *The Historical Journal*, September 1980.

Tydings, Millard E. *Before and After Prohibition*. New York: Macmillan, 1930.

Tyrrell, Ian R. *Sobering Up: From Temperance to Prohibition in Antebellum America, 1830–1860*. Westport, CT: Greenwood, 1979.

———. "Women and Temperance in Antebellum America, 1830–1860." *Civil War History*, June 1982.

United States Brewers' Association. *Year Book, 1909*. New York: USBA, 1910.

———. *Year Book, 1920–21*. New York: USBA, 1922.

Van de Water, Frederic F. *The Real McCoy*. Garden City, NY: Doubleday Doran, 1931.

Van Riper, Paul V. *History of the United States Civil Service*. Evanston, IL: Row, Peterson, 1958.

Veselenak, Aaron J. "Arthur J. Tuttle, Dean of the Federal Bench." *The Court Legacy*, Historical Society for the United States Court for the Eastern District of Michigan, April 1999.

Villard, Oswald Garrison. *Prophets True and False*. New York: Knopf, 1928.

Walker, Clifford James. *One Eye Closed, the Other Red: The California Bootlegging Years*. Barstow, CA: Back Door Publishing, 1999.

Walker, Stanley. *The Night Club Era*. Baltimore: Johns Hopkins University Press, 1999.

Walnut, T. Henry, ed. *Prohibition and Its Enforcement*. Philadelphia: American Academy of Political and Social Science, 1923.

Waltman, Jerold L. *Political Origins of the U.S. Income Tax*. Jackson: University Press of Mississippi, 1985.

Walton Hanes, Jr., and James E. Taylor. "Blacks and the Southern Prohibition Movement." *Phylon*, Summer 1971.

Ward, Geoffrey. *A First-Class Temperament*. New York: Harper & Row, 1989.

Ware, Caroline F. *Greenwich Village, 1920–1930: A Comment on American Civilization in the Post-War Years*. Boston: Houghton Mifflin, 1935.

Warren, Harris Gaylord. *Herbert Hoover and the Great Depression*. New York: Oxford University Press, 1959.

Weigley, Russell F., et al., eds. *Philadelphia: A 300-Year History*. New York: Norton, 1982.

Weir, Ronald B. *The History of the Distillers Company, 1877–1939*. Oxford, UK: Clarendon Press, 1995.

———. "Obsessed with Moderation: The Drink Trades and the Drink Question." *British Journal of Addiction*, March 1984.

Weisband, Edward, and Thomas M. Franck. *Resignation in Protest*. New York: Penguin, 1976.

Weisman, Steven R. *The Great Tax Wars*. New York: Simon & Schuster, 2002.

Wentworth, Harold, and Stuart Berg Flexner, eds. *Dictionary of American Slang*. New York: Crowell, 1960.

Werner, M. R. *Bryan*. New York: Harcourt Brace, 1929.

———. *Privileged Characters*. New York: Robert McBride, 1935.

West, Elliott. *The Saloon on the Rocky Mountain Mining Frontier*. Lincoln: University of Nebraska Press, 1979.

Westheimer, Morris F. "Present American Business Conditions in the Distilling Industry." *Annals of the American Academy of Political Science*, November 1909.

Wetzsteon, Ross. *Republic of Dreams: Greenwich Village, The American Bohemia 1910–1960*. New York: Simon & Schuster, 2002.

Whalen, Richard J. *The Founding Father: The Story of Joseph P. Kennedy*. New York: New American Library, 1964.

Whaples, Robert, ed. *Encyclopedia of Business and Economic History*. http://www.eh.net/encyclopedia.

Wheeler, Scott. *Rumrunners & Revenuers: Prohibition in Vermont*. Shelburne, VT: New England Press, 2002.

White, E. B. *Letters of E.B. White*. Rev. ed. New York: HarperPerennial, 2007.

White, William Allen. *The Autobiography of William Allen White*. New York: Macmillan, 1946.

[Wickersham, George, et al.]. *Official Records of the National Commission on Law Observance and Enforcement*. Washington, DC: Government Printing Office, 1931.

Wilkinson, Alec. *Moonshine: A Life in Pursuit of White Liquor*. New York: Knopf, 1985.

Willard, Frances E. *Glimpses of Fifty Years: The Autobiography of an American Woman*. Chicago: H. J. Smith, 1889.

———. *A Wheel within a Wheel: How I Learned to Ride the Bicycle*. London: Hutchinson, 1895.

Willebrandt, Mabel Walker. *The Inside of Prohibition*. Indianapolis: Bobbs-Merrill, 1929.

Williams, Michael. *The Shadow of the Pope*. New York: Whittlesey House, 1932.

Williamson, Scott C. *The Narrative Life: The Moral and Religious Thought of Frederick Douglass*. Macon, GA: Mercer University Press, 2002.

Willoughby, Malcolm F. *Rum War at Sea*. Washington, DC: Government Printing Office, 1964.

Wilson, Edmund. *The American Earthquake*. New York: Da Capo, 1996.

Wilson, Ross. *Scotch: The Formative Years*. London: Constable, 1970.

Wilson, Sunnie, and John Cohassey. *Toast of the Town: The Life and Times of Sunnie Wilson*. Detroit: Wayne State University Press, 1998.

Wintz, Cary D., and Paul Finkleman. *Encyclopedia of the Harlem Renaissance*. New York: Routledge, 2004.

Wittke, Carl. *German Americans and the World War*. Columbus: Ohio State Archaeological and Historical Society, 1936.

Wolfe, Thomas. *Look Homeward, Angel*. New York: Scribner, 2006.

Wolfskill, George. *The Revolt of the Conservatives: A History of the American Liberty League*. Boston: Houghton Mifflin, 1962.

Woodward, C. Vann. *Origins of the New South: 1877–1913*. Baton Rouge: Louisiana State University Press, 1951.

Yandle, Bruce. "Bootleggers and Baptists: The Education of a Regulatory Economist." *Regulation*, May–June 1983.

Zehnder, Rev. Herman F. *Teach My People the Truth: The Story of Frankenmuth, Michigan.* Bay City, MI: Privately published, 1970.
Zeitz, Joshua. *Flapper: A Madcap Story of Sex, Style, Celebrity, and the Women Who Made America Modern.* New York: Crown, 2006.
Jonathan Zimmerman. "The Queen of the Lobby: Mary Hunt, Scientific Temperance, and the Dilemma of Democratic Education in America, 1879–1906." *History of Education Quarterly*, Spring 1992.

Congressional Documents

Senate and House documents are cited in the notes. For citations from the following hearings, *House Appropriations 1922*, 315, represents page 315 in the transcript of the first of the hearings listed here, and similar abbreviation is used for the others (listed here chronologically by chamber).

House of Representatives, Appropriations Committee. "Department of Justice," 1922.
House of Representatives, Immigration and Naturalization Committee, "Deportation of Aliens," 1922.
House of Representatives, Judiciary Committee, "The Prohibition Amendment," 1930.
House of Representatives, Ways and Means Committee, "Modification of the Volstead Act," 1932.
Senate, Judiciary Committee, "Brewing and Liquor Interests and German and Bolshevik Propaganda," 1919.
Senate, Judiciary Subcommittee, "National Prohibition Act," 1926.
Senate, Special Committee on Campaign Expenditures, 1926.
Senate, Judiciary Subcommittee, "Lobby Investigation," 1930.
Senate, Judiciary Committee, "Modification or Repeal of National Prohibition," 1932.
Senate, Finance Committee, "Modification of the Volstead Act," 1933.

Index